Excel 2002:
The Complete Reference

About the Authors

Kathy Ivens has been a computer consultant since 1984, and has written or co-authored more than 40 computer books. She is a contributing editor to *Windows 2000 Magazine* and *Windows NT Magazine.*

Conrad Carlberg is a many-time Microsoft MVP for Excel, and the president of NCS, Inc., a provider of statistical control and analysis software for the health care industry. He has authored numerous books on Microsoft Office applications.

Excel 2002:
The Complete Reference

Kathy Ivens
Conrad Carlberg

Osborne/**McGraw-Hill**

New York   Chicago   San Francisco
Lisbon   London   Madrid   Mexico City
Milan   New Delhi   San Juan
Seoul   Singapore   Sydney   Toronto

Osborne/**McGraw-Hill**
2600 Tenth Street
Berkeley, California 94710
U.S.A.

To arrange bulk purchase discounts for sales promotions, premiums, or fund-raisers, please contact Osborne/**McGraw-Hill** at the above address. For information on translations or book distributors outside the U.S.A., please see the International Contact Information page immediately following the index of this book.

Excel 2002: The Complete Reference

234567890 CUS CUS 01987654321

ISBN 0-07-213245-0

Publisher
   Brandon A. Nordin

Vice President & Associate Publisher
   Scott Rogers

Acquisitions Editors
   Megg Bonar and Gretchen Ganser

Project Editor
   Jennifer Malnick

Acquisitions Coordinator
   Alissa Larson

Technical Editor
   Bruce Hamilton

Copy Editor
   Sally Engelfried

Proofreader
   Marian Selig

Indexer
   Claire Splan

Computer Designers
   Roberta Steele
   Kelly Stanton-Scott
   Carie Malnekoff

Illustrator
   Lyssa Sieben-Wald

Series Design
   Peter F. Hancik

This book was composed with Corel VENTURA™ Publisher.

For Sarah and Amy Lewites,
just for being perfectly wonderful.
—Kathy Ivens

For Ray and Robin and Sue and True.
My parents thank you. And so do I.
—Conrad Carlberg

Contents at a Glance

Contents

Part I

Getting Started

Part II

Analyzing Data

Part III

The Outside World

Part IV

Extending Excel's Reach with VBA

Part V

Appendixes

Acknowledgments

The authors owe kudos and gratitude to the people at Osborne/McGraw-Hill who worked so hard on this book. Megg Bonar, an Acquisitions Editor with insight and intelligence, has a permanent place on our short list of "editors we really like to hear from." Working with Jenny Malnick and Alissa Larson is a joy; their efficiency and professionalism made our lives easier than we had any right to expect. Thanks also to Sally Engelfried for contributing such a high degree of skill and talent to this work.

Solid technical edits aren't really rare, but there are plenty of books on the shelves that lack them and get published anyway. To go beyond a solid technical edit and produce one that makes a book not just more accurate but stronger *is* rare. To do so with wit and flair, and to gently point the way for two authors with diverse styles and cranky dispositions, is a tour de force. Ladies and gentlemen, we give you Bruce Hamilton of Agilent Technologies.

Introduction

The book you hold in your hand is written to help you on your way to Excel stardom. We wrote it to provide the information and tips you need to become so comfortable using Excel that you can use the software to do most anything you want. We think you'll also be able to help other Excel users who are just starting to find their footing. Believe it: that *will* make you a hero at work.

When you feel secure about performing all the functions and features we cover in this book, you should be able to gain certification as a Microsoft Office User Specialist. This really makes you stand out as an Excel user, and you'll join the ranks of people who have proven their proficiency with this certification—it's a great advantage in job hunting or promotions (and you get a nifty certificate to hang on your wall).

What's in This Book?

This book offers information about Excel in a variety of methods and styles. You'll find straightforward descriptions of Excel features and functions (what they do, how they work, what they look like), along with specific explanations about using those tools (step-by-step instructions). You'll also find suggestions about when to use specific functions and features, along with plenty of examples from real life (both the authors' experiences in running our own businesses, and creative approaches we developed while solving problems for our clients).

We structured the information in a way that's called "task-oriented," which means that chapters are organized around specific subjects. This should make it easy for you to leap right to the subject you need to investigate. However, if you want to start right here and read the rest of the book straight through, you'll learn tons about using Excel. In addition, we'll be flattered, even though we didn't write this tome with the thought that you'd read it like a novel. It's okay if you don't—we're content with the fact that we've written an information-filled, helpful book.

There are illustrations throughout the book to help you understand and use what you see on your computer monitor. Some of the illustrations are annotated to help you understand dialog boxes and windows that might be complicated, confusing, or filled with too many choices.

Is This Book for You?

When we were planning and writing this book, we imagined who you are, and we wrote this book for you. It seems fair to explain who we think you are so you know if you should purchase this book (after all, if we wrote it for your cousin, he's the one who should buy it).

You aren't new to computers, so we don't have to explain to you how to turn on your computer. You've worked with Microsoft Windows, and the notion of a graphical user interface (GUI, pronounced *goo-ey*) isn't something new and shocking.

You know how to open the basic Windows elements, like Windows Explorer, or the Start menu. You know how to use a mouse; you know what it means to click, double-click, or right-click an object in Explorer or in a dialog box (and you know, at least roughly, what we mean when we use the terms "dialog box" and "object").

You already know that a spreadsheet program like Excel is used for tasks that require calculations of some kind—even if you've never used spreadsheet software, you know that much about it.

You understand the basic tasks of computing, such as the concept of a data file (and the fact that a data file isn't the same thing as a software program file), and the need to save a file and name it in order to create a permanent object on your system.

In essence, you're not a beginner in computing. You're comfortable enough with computers and Microsoft Windows to want to move to a higher level of achievement. This book is designed and written to do just that—at least when it comes to Excel. We want to move you up the ladder of knowledge. With your help, we think we can do that.

How to Use This Book

You can read this book from beginning to end, use it for bedtime reading, take it to the beach or on picnics, or take it to boring parties so you have something to do to relieve your boredom. But you probably won't because you've already recognized that there's no plot, no interesting characters, and it's not a novel.

Use the Table of Contents to jump to the chapter that covers a subject of interest to you. Use the Index to rush to the page that provides specific information about a task.

When you get there (to the chapter or the page), you'll find we've included some conventions that will help you figure out how to use our book as you use Excel.

Choices and messages that appear in dialog boxes are described and displayed with a special typesetting convention: Each Important Word in the Sentence is Capitalized. That convention is not usually found on the dialog box itself (where usually only the first word is capitalized): we're using it to point out the fact that we're talking about dialog box text.

User input is displayed in bold type. That means you'll see sentences like: Enter **explode this myth** in the UserOptionsForFun dialog box. Just follow our instructions; it'll work fine.

Definitions are in italic type. If we use a term that we also define, you'll see sentences like: "You supply the arguments to the function. An *argument* is just a value that the function works with."

Note
> *Tips, Notes, and Cautions are special text that add to the information in the regular paragraphs. They're set apart from the regular text. The contents provide extra information, or important information. Don't skip them—they're significant. We didn't set them apart from the text so you'd think they're unimportant; we set them apart so you wouldn't miss them.*

Sidebars, on the other hand, can be skipped if you are absolutely devoid of curiosity about the background or technical significance of a feature or function. Both authors suffer from terminal curiosity (we're both cats), so we know a lot of this stuff. When we find something we think is especially useful or interesting, we tell you about it. We set it apart in a boxed sidebar to indicate that you don't need this information to perform your work in Excel, but if you read it you'll learn something that other Excel users may not know. This can help you establish your credentials, or least provide interesting one-liners you can toss out when you want to impress people.

And Now, a Word from Our Sponsor—Excel

Excel 2002 is the latest incarnation of the world's most popular spreadsheet program. It has more features, functions, bells and whistles than the last version of Excel, which is why it has a new version number in its name.

There are lots of things you can do in Excel 2002—its power is awe inspiring. The capacity you get from it has a direct relationship to the knowledge you have about its power. We wrote this book so you can master and use the power of the software.

Excel is far more than a simple calculation program that lets you add lists of numbers. You can use robust and intricate formulas to work with data, use functions to perform complicated manipulations, sort and select data as you need it, and even let Excel tell you what data you need to enter to get to a predetermined goal.

You can rearrange the way data is presented, import information from other programs, export information to other programs, send documents to your Web site, and get data from others' Web sites.

Excel automates a lot of work you'd find boring, time-consuming, or difficult. When you make changes to your data, Excel recalculates the results automatically. Calculation totals in one part of a worksheet can be used in another part of a worksheet, and changes made in one place are automatically accounted for during recalculation.

You can work with multiple worksheets, keeping their contents separate or linking them to get the data from one worksheet into another. You can have more than one workbook open at a time and move between them with a click of the mouse. You can customize Excel so it looks and behaves to suit your personal preferences. You can write programs in Visual Basic to extend the power of what came in the shrink-wrap.

The more you learn about Excel, the more you can learn about Excel, which means that each discovery leads you into a deeper understanding of even more complex and powerful features.

The Complete Reference

Excel
2002

Part I

Getting Started

Chapter 1

Excel Basics

3

ay Hello to Excel 2002. This chapter introduces you to the basic entities of Excel—
the window, the menu system, the toolbars, and the configuration options you have
at your disposal.

If you worked with, or just dabbled in, previous versions of Excel, you'll notice that
one of the biggest changes is the user interface. Some of the elements in the Excel window
interact with you in a different manner than previous versions.

The Excel Window

When you first launch Excel, the software window opens displaying two panes (see
Figure 1-1). On the left (and occupying most of your screen) is a blank workbook. On
the right is the task pane. The window is crowded with lots of other elements, but it's
easy to sort it all out.

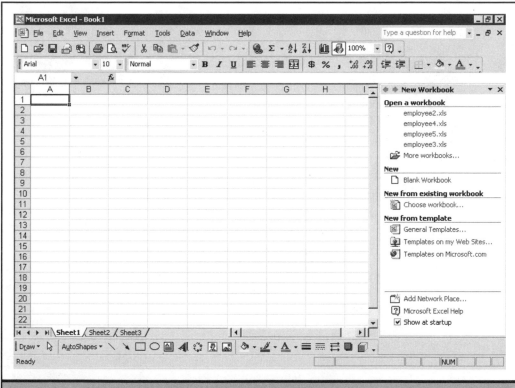

Figure 1-1.   *The opening window for Excel may seem a bit overwhelming, but it's
easy to get used to the elements (and get rid of the things you don't
want on the screen)*

The Task Pane

By default, when you open Excel the New Workbook task pane displays (additional task panes are available by clicking the arrow next to the close button: the Office Clipboard task pane and the Search task pane).

The Open A Workbook section displays the last four files you worked on, and you can click one to open it again. This is the same list that appears at the bottom of the File menu. To see all your Excel files, click More Workbooks to open the My Documents folder (which is the same as clicking the Open icon on the Standard toolbar). The options for creating a new workbook are the same as those available from File | New Command. Three commands are available at the bottom of the task pane:

- Add Web Folder, which opens a wizard to walk you through the process of creating a link to a network folder.

- Microsoft Excel Help, which opens the Help system.

- Show At Startup, which you can deselect if you want to open Excel without the task pane.

You can close the task pane by clicking the X in its upper right corner, and you can open the task pane by selecting View | Task Pane.

To change the number of existing files that are displayed in the task pane or the File menu, choose Tools | Options and go to the General tab. Change the number of files specified for the Recently Used File List (or eliminate the feature by deselecting it).

The Worksheet

The centerpiece of the window is a worksheet, an array of cells waiting for you to enter data (you learn how to do that in Chapter 2). The bottom of the worksheet area has worksheet tabs (usually called *sheet tabs*). By default, there are three worksheets in a workbook.

A worksheet is a grid of rows and columns into which you enter data. A workbook is an Excel document, or file. It can contain as many worksheets or chartsheets (worksheets that hold charts) as you wish.

Navigating the Window

To move between cells on a worksheet, click on the cell or use the arrow keys. When you move to a cell, it becomes the *active cell*. To scroll through a worksheet, use these navigation movements:

- To scroll one row at a time, click the arrow in the vertical scroll bar once for each row.

- To scroll one column at a time, click the arrow in the horizontal scroll bar once for each column.
- To scroll up or down one window at a time, click above or below the scroll box in the vertical scroll bar.
- To scroll left or right one window at a time, click to the left or right of the scroll box in the horizontal scroll bar.
- To move quickly over a large worksheet, drag the scroll box.

Sizing and Closing Worksheet Windows

There are Minimize, Maximize, Restore, and Close buttons for each worksheet, and you can size the worksheet independently of the current size of the Excel software window. For example, you can use Excel maximized and use the Restore button on the worksheet(s) to create a small window.

Sometimes, if you are running Excel in a window instead of maximized, clicking the Restore button on a worksheet causes the right side of the worksheet to run off the edge of the software window. Maximize the worksheet—its maximum size is the same size as the software window (the worksheet won't become a full-screen document that's larger than the software window). If you can't reach the Maximize button easily (it's disappeared off to the right), double-click the worksheet title bar.

To close a worksheet, click the Close button. If you've made changes since the last time you saved, Excel will prompt you to save the worksheet before closing it.

The Toolbars

By default, Excel displays two toolbars: the Standard toolbar and the Formatting toolbar. Hold your mouse pointer over any tool to see a screen tip explaining the tool.

Adding and Removing Toolbars from Your Window

Excel has an extraordinary number of toolbars, although many of them are used for very specific tasks. To place a toolbar in the window, right-click anywhere on an existing toolbar to display the list of toolbars. Then select the toolbar you want to add. A check mark appears to the left of the toolbar name. To remove a toolbar from your window, click its listing to remove the check mark (it's a toggle).

Positioning Toolbars in Your Window

You can move any toolbar to any position in your window by dragging it. There are two types of toolbar positions: docked and floating.

Docked toolbars have the following characteristics:

■ The toolbar occupies a horizontal position above or beneath the worksheet area. You can also dock a toolbar along either side of the worksheet area, in which case it will be displayed vertically.

■ To move the toolbar, use the dragging handle on the left edge of the toolbar (it's a vertical line). When you position your mouse pointer over that edge, the pointer turns into a four-headed arrow.

■ If you drag a docked toolbar into the worksheet area of the window, it becomes a floating toolbar.

■ To remove the toolbar from your window, right-click anywhere on a toolbar and deselect the toolbar from the list.

Floating toolbars have these characteristics:

■ The toolbar is positioned on the worksheet area (covering cells).

■ To move the toolbar, drag the title bar.

■ To remove the toolbar from your window, click the Close button in the upper-right corner.

■ If you drag a floating toolbar outside of the worksheet (where the docked toolbars are), it becomes a docked toolbar.

The decision you make about positioning toolbars is an exercise in striking the right balance. If you have a lot of toolbars open and you make them all docked toolbars, each occupying its own row, the worksheet area shrinks to accommodate the space needed by the toolbars. On the other hand, floating toolbars cover cells and you'll spend time repositioning them in order to use those cells.

The Menu Bar

Like all Windows software, Excel displays a menu bar at the top of the window. The menus you see when you select any item on the menu bar contain the commands for that menu item.

Personalized Menus

Office XP uses the *personalized menu* feature, which means the software watches you as you work and determines which commands you commonly use. Then it adjusts the display of menu items to make your favorite commands more accessible.

The effect of this design is that menu lists are shortened when you access them, and only some of the commands display when you initially choose a menu item. For example, if you click the View command, you may see something like this:

Notice the chevron (it's a double down-arrow, but it looks like a chevron to me) at the bottom of the menu list, which indicates there's more to see. You can see the rest of the list by employing one of these methods:

- Click the chevron.
- Wait (about four seconds).

Regardless of the method you use, the menu changes to reveal the entire list of commands.

Notice that the menu items that were present in the short display are not in the same order; the previously hidden commands are not together at the bottom of the command list. Each menu list operates similarly; to wit, the order of the items in the full list does not necessarily match the order of the shortened list.

When you use a command, it appears the next time you see the menu list. As you work, the commands you haven't used recently, or haven't used very much, are taken off the short menu and repositioned below the chevron.

This means that the display of commands on the menu lists frequently changes to reflect your work habits. There are two common reactions to this:

■ Great! The commands I use most can always be found on the short listing, and the order in which they appear changes so my favorite commands are near the top of the display. I love it!

■ Arrgh! I can't memorize the location of commands and automatically click one, I have to search the list each time I need a command because the order keeps changing. I hate it!

Changing the Menu Behavior

If you want the old-fashioned interaction with your menu system, and you're willing to give up being a cutting-edge kind of person, you can change the way the menus behave. Here's how:

1. Choose Tools | Customize from the menu bar (the Customize command is on the short menu).

2. In the Customize dialog box, click the Options tab.

3. Click the check box for the option named Always Show Full Menus.

4. Click Close.

Hereafter, you'll see full menu lists, and none of the commands will budge from their assigned positions.

If you're keeping the personalized interaction feature, you may want to make use of the two other menu-connected choices on the Options tab of the Customize dialog box:

■ Select the check box next to the option named Show Full Menus After A Short Delay to deselect the check mark. This means the only way to display the entire menu is to click the chevron, which gives you total control over that feature (instead of an automatic display after a few seconds).

■ Click the Reset My Usage Data button to tell Excel to forget about your history and display menus as if you had never used any commands (as if you're just beginning to use Excel).

If you're starved for entertainment while you work at your computer, examine the Menu Animation options at the bottom of the dialog box. You can change the animation that occurs when the display of commands appears:

- **System Default** The command list just appears.
- **Random** The way the command list appears changes from time to time, using the other options randomly.
- **Unfold** The command list unfolds from the upper-left corner.
- **Slide** The command list slides down from the menu bar.
- **Fade** The command list fades up from gray to black.

Caution *The changes you make in the menu system are for all Office applications, not just Excel.*

The Help System

By default, the help system is based on using the Assistant, that animated creature that was introduced in an earlier version of Office. (If you don't find the little rascal charming enough to keep around, I'll discuss how to get help without the Assistant later in this chapter.)

To display the assistant, use one of these methods:

- Click the Help button on the Standard toolbar (the question mark).
- Press F1.
- Choose Help | Microsoft Excel Help from the menu bar.

The Assistant appears with a balloon into which you can enter a query.

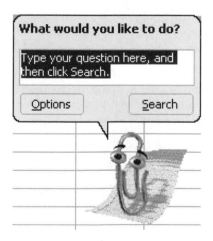

Enter your question, using a word, a couple of words, or a phrase. For example, if you want help on printing headers, you could enter *headers*, *print headers*, or *how do I print headers*—or any other combination of words you think describes the topic for which you need help. Then click Search.

The assistant pops up a list of help topics related to your query.

Click the See More entry to display more topics, and then click the button next to the topic that most directly responds to your need for information.

    The last choice on the second page of topics is always an option to look for help on the Web. Clicking that option opens your Internet connection (if you're not already connected) and then opens your browser to travel to Microsoft's Web help.

Using the Help Pages

The help page for a topic appears after you select the topic from the Assistant's list, as shown in Figure 1-2.

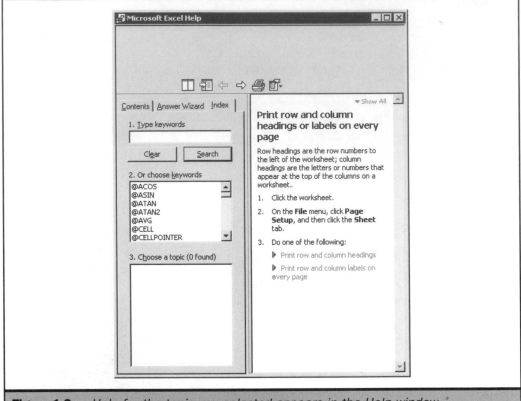

Figure 1-2. *Help for the topic you selected appears in the Help window*

The help page occupies about half your window and the following icons appear at the top of the help page (reading from left to right):

- **AutoTile** Click to tile the windows, which means your worksheet window shrinks to accommodate the Help window (see Figure 1-3). The icon changes its name to Untile.

- **Hide** Click to hide the left pane of the help page (the button changes its name to Show so you can reverse the action).

■ **Back**   Go back one page (not active until you've moved to another page).

■ **Forward**   Go forward one page (not active until you've used the Back button).

■ **Print**   Print the contents of the current page.

■ **Options**   Other options available for the help page.

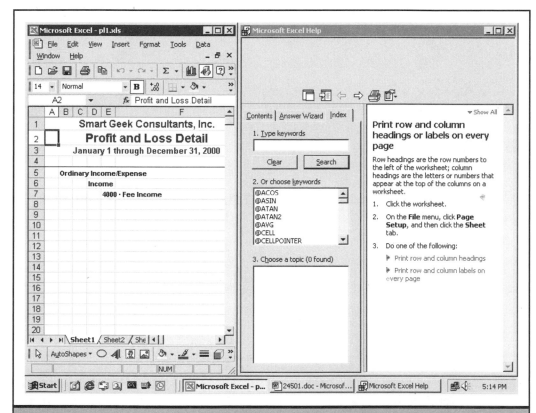

Figure 1-3.   *When you tile the windows, the worksheet scrollbars, the minimize button, and the close button are all available*

Help pages frequently have hyperlinks to other help pages on the same, or a similar, topic. You can also click another topic on the Assistant's list to move to another help page.

Using the Help Tabs

If the left pane of the Help window is displayed, you can use the tabs. (If the left pane isn't showing, click the Show icon.)

Click the Contents tab to see the help system organized by subject. Expand a topic by double-clicking the book icon.

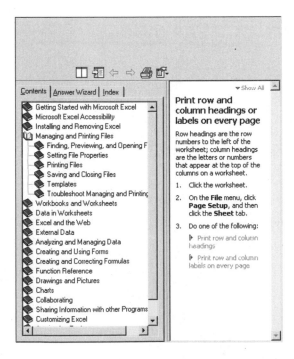

The Answer Wizard tab lets you enter a query, using your own words and phrasing.

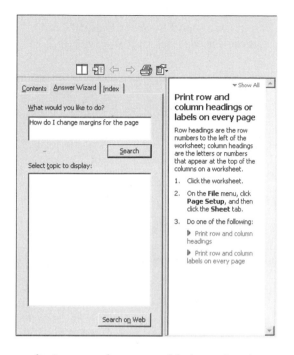

Usually, a query results in several suggested help topics. As you select each topic, the attendant help page appears in the right pane.

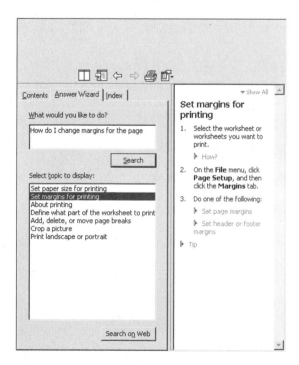

Hyperlinks in the help page expand to provide additional information, or to send you to additional help pages (use the Back button to return).

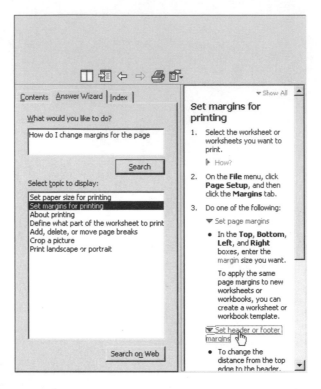

The Index tab works like the traditional Windows Help Index feature—enter a term to move to that section of the index, and then click the Search button to find all the related help pages.

When you close the Help window, your worksheet returns to its previous size.

Manipulating the Assistant

You can hide the Assistant or get rid of it entirely. You can also change the persona.

Hiding the Assistant

When the Assistant appears in response to your request for help, you can get rid of the balloon by clicking on the Assistant. But the Assistant sticks around after the balloon disappears. To hide the Assistant, right-click on it and choose Hide.

Getting Rid of the Assistant

If you want to bid goodbye to the Assistant, click on Options on the Assistant icon to open the Options tab of the Office Assistant dialog box.

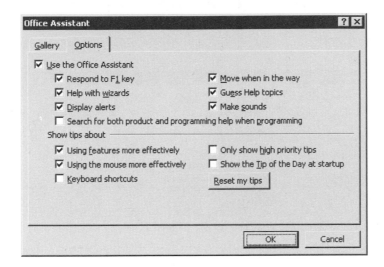

Click the check box named Use The Office Assistant to deselect it. You can also use this dialog box to configure the Assistant instead of turning it off.

If you change your mind and want the Assistant back in your life, choose Help | Show Office Assistant from the menu bar. When the Assistant shows up, it automatically puts the check mark back in the Use The Office Assistant option.

Changing the Assistant's Persona

To audition a new Assistant, click Options on the Office Assistant and move to the Gallery tab of the Office Assistant dialog box. Then click the Next button to move through all the available Assistants. When you find one you like, choose OK.

Getting Help Without the Assistant

If you get rid of the Assistant, use the same methods to get help as described earlier in this chapter. Opening the help system results in the display of the full screen, two-pane window (if the left pane is missing for some reason, click the Show button).

Getting Help from the Web

To reach the Microsoft Office Internet support site, choose Help | Office on the Web. Your browser opens, and you travel to the Microsoft Office support page.

If you didn't configure your browser to open your Dial-Up Networking or RAS connection automatically, you must open the connection before using this command.

Detecting and Repairing Problems

If things go awry with your Excel installation, choose Help | Detect and Repair to try to mend the problem.

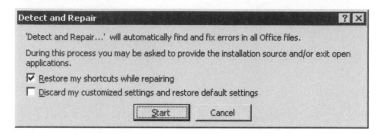

You'll need your original installation CD because the process looks at all the software files and replaces any that are missing or seem to be corrupt.

Customizing Toolbars and Menus

It's always faster to click an icon than open a menu item and find the right command. You can put your favorite (well, oft-used) commands on a toolbar. You can even invent your own toolbars.

Adding a Button to a Toolbar

You can add buttons to an existing toolbar so they're easy to get to. I usually use the Standard toolbar for my additional tools because it has more room than the Formatting toolbar. Here's how to add your own new icon:

1. Right-click on any toolbar and choose Customize from the menu.
2. In the Customize dialog box, move to the Commands tab.
3. Select the Category and Command you want to turn into a toolbar button.

4. Drag the Command icon to a toolbar.

Removing a Button from a Toolbar

To get rid of a toolbar button you don't need, look for the down-arrow on the extreme right edge of the toolbar that holds the extraneous (to you) button. Choose Add Or Remove Buttons, and then pick the toolbar name. Click the check box next to the button, to remove it from the toolbar.

Creating Your Own Toolbar

It's very easy to create a toolbar for yourself, and it's commonly done to hold all those new toolbar buttons you've created in an effort to stay away from the menu system.

Another good reason to create a new toolbar is to put all the tools you need for a special project on one toolbar. In fact, you should include all the "normal" buttons— include the buttons on the Standard and Formatting toolbars you use most often. Then everything you need is in one place. After the project is over, you can get rid of the toolbar.

The process is as easy as this:

1. Right-click on any toolbar and choose Customize from the menu.

2. Move to the Toolbars tab.

3. Click New.

4. In the New Toolbar dialog box, enter a name for the toolbar and click OK.

5. The toolbar is added to the list in the dialog box, and it floats in your Excel window (drag it to the top, bottom, or side to anchor it).

6. Move to the Commands tab of the Customize dialog box and choose the Category and Command for the first button you want to place on the new toolbar.

7. Drag the Command to the new toolbar.

8. Continue until you have put all the commands you need on this toolbar.

9. Close the Customize dialog box.

Customizing Toolbar Buttons

Some of the commands you place on a toolbar don't have icons; instead, they have names. Then again, some of the icons aren't terribly elucidating when you glance at them, and a name would be easier to work with. You can change the appearance of any button on any toolbar with these steps.

1. Right-click on any toolbar and choose Customize from the menu. You won't work in the Customize dialog box, but it must be open in order to customize buttons.

2. Right-click on the button you want to change to see its shortcut menu.

3. Use the commands on the shortcut menu to make the changes you need.

4. Close the Customize dialog box.

Changes to buttons aren't global. If you've placed buttons on a toolbar you created that also exist on Excel toolbars, you can change the appearance of a button on your toolbar without changing the appearance of that same button on other toolbars.

Nifty Configuration Changes

There are a couple of configuration changes that are really handy, and you may want to consider them. All of these changes are made in the Options dialog box, which you open with the Tools | Options command.

- **Calculation tab** Here, select Manual calculation if you find there's a delay every time you enter data in a cell that is referenced in a formula. This speeds up working in Excel, but you can't forget to press F9 to recalculate when you need to see totals.

- **Edit tab** Here, if you usually enter data across columns instead of down rows, go to the Move Selection After Enter option and change the Direction to Right (the default is Down).

- **General tab** Here, change the default number in the Sheets In New Workbook to match the way you use Excel. If you usually confine your work to one worksheet, make that the default, and if you usually need more than one sheet per workbook, make a larger number the default.

Go through all the configuration options in the Options dialog box to see what other changes you want to make.

The
Complete
Reference

Excel
2002

Chapter 2

Entering Information

The basic data entry container for Excel is a cell. Each cell has an address, which is determined by its location on the worksheet grid. The column letter and row number determine the address.

In addition to entering data into cells, you can put charts, drawings, maps, pictures, and other items into your worksheet. These graphical elements aren't entered into cells; instead, they reside on the worksheet's draw layer, which is a transparent layer that sits on top of the worksheet. Those topics are covered in other chapters in this book.

Entering Data

In order to put data into a cell, you must first select the cell by clicking within it. As you type, the data you're entering is also automatically entered in the formula bar, shown here.

You can put a variety of data types into cells, including text, numbers, dates, and formulas. Just so you can keep up with the jargon, I'll mention that sometimes text entries are called *labels* (because you frequently use text to label a column or row of figures). Data entries that are used for calculations (numbers, percentages, dates, and so on) are called *values*.

Entering Text

Most worksheets have text entries, and they're frequently used to name columns or rows, or both. It's difficult to understand a worksheet if it contains nothing but numbers; some explanation of those numbers is needed.

Text entries can include numbers as part of the character set; for example, your address or telephone number, an inventory part number, or any other number that isn't involved in a calculation is text.

Most people begin building a worksheet by naming the columns and rows they're going to use. For example, if you want to track your expenses for each week, you'd probably start by setting up each column as a day of the week.

To enter text into your worksheet, follow these steps:

1. Click the cell you want to use for the text. The cell is highlighted with a black border.

2. Enter the text. You can type as many characters as you wish (we'll go over ways to wrap and format the characters later in this chapter).

3. If you need to separate text into separate lines (for instance, a two-line address), use ALT-ENTER to enter a carriage return between the lines.

4. When you have finished entering text, use one of these methods to move out of the cell:

- Press ENTER to move to the cell below.
- Press TAB to move to the cell to the right.
- Press the keyboard arrow keys to move in any direction.
- Use your mouse to click on the next cell you want to use.

When you enter text that has more characters than fit across the width of the column, Excel spills the excess text into the column(s) to the right, if it's empty.

	C1	▾ ✕ ✓ _fx_	Wednesday	
	A	B	C	D
1	Monday	Tuesday	Wednesday	
2				

If the adjacent cell isn't empty, Excel displays as many characters as will fit in the column width. Adjusting the width of the column is covered later in this chapter.

 If you need to see all the text in a cell, click the cell to select it, and then look at the formula bar.

Entering Numbers

Numbers are used to keep track of quantities. You can track items or money. In fact, many worksheets are designed to track both items and money. For example, you might want to track all the different types of parasols you have in your warehouse, which means you'd enter the number of green parasols, red parasols, and striped parasols. When you enter the cost of each parasol (different colors have different prices, of course), you can begin analyzing your parasols and your financial investment in parasols.

You don't have to enter commas, dollar signs, or other symbols as you type, because you can tell Excel to add those symbols automatically (covered later in this chapter).

Working with Dates and Times

Dates and times are frequently used as labels, but they can also be values that are used in calculations. For example, you might want to design a way to determine how much longer you have to wait between today and your birthday. Excel has numerous methods for entering and translating date and time entries.

Entering Dates

There are all sorts of ways to enter a date, and Excel recognizes your entry and converts it to the default date formats (which are operating system defaults that you can change). You can use slashes, dashes, text, or a combination of those items to enter a date. For instance, here are some of the choices you have for entering the date November 23, 2001. If you can't find something you want to use in this list, you're far too fussy.

- 11-23-01
- 11-23-2001
- 11/23/01
- 11/23/2001
- 11-23/01
- Nov 23, 2001
- 11/23
- 11-23
- Nov 23
- 23 November, 2001
- 23.11.2001

To enter the current date, press CTRL-; (a semicolon).

 If you don't enter the year, Excel assumes you mean the current one.

Default Display of Dates

The way the date displays in your worksheet depends on the keystrokes you used to enter it.

- If you don't enter a year, the default display in the cell is in the format DD-MMM, where DD is the date and MMM is a three-letter abbreviation for the month. For example, if you enter 11/23, 11-23, or Nov 23, the cell displays 23-Nov.

- If you enter a year, either with two or four digits, the cell displays DD/MM/YY or DD/MM/YYYY, depending on your system default. For Windows 2000, the system default is a four-digit year; for all previous versions of Windows, the system default is a two-digit year. For example, entering 11/23/01 produces 11/23/2001 in Windows 2000; it produces 11/23/01 in Windows NT/9x.

- The formula bar always displays DD/MM/YYYY.

The default appearance is determined by your Windows settings for date entries, specifically the *short date* format, which you can view (and change) with these steps:

1. Choose Start | Settings | Control Panel.

2. Open the Regional Settings icon in Control Panel (called Regional Options in Windows 2000).

3. Move to the Date tab.

4. Click the arrow to the right of the Short Date Style text box to choose a different default format (see Figure 2-1).

5. Enter a new separator if you want to replace the forward slash (for instance, you may prefer a dash).

6. Click OK to save your changes and close the dialog box.

Note   *The changes you make to the Regional Settings dialog box date options are applied to all your Windows software, not just Excel. This isn't dangerous because if you prefer a certain display in Excel, it's probable you prefer the same display everywhere.*

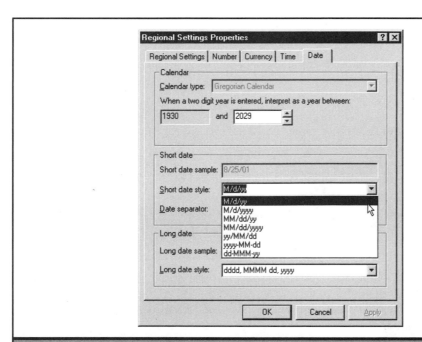

Figure 2-1.   *You can change the appearance of dates for all your Windows software*

Excel is Year 2000–compliant and makes assumptions about the way to interpret a two-digit year based on the cutoff date displayed in the Date tab. You can change the cutoff date for determining whether your two-digit year should be interpreted as 1900 or 2000 if necessary.

If you make a mistake while you're entering the characters for a date—perhaps you use a period or a backward slash instead of a forward slash mark—Excel will use the data in the cell as text instead of a date. There's a quick way to make sure your date is entered correctly—look at the justification of the entry in the cell. Dates are right-justified, and text is left-justified.

Formatting the Date Display

You can change the way dates display on your worksheet by formatting the cells that contain the dates.

1. Select the cells (or column or row) that contain the dates and choose Format | Cells.
2. When the Format Cells dialog box opens, go to the Number tab.
3. Select Date as the category (it's probably preselected for you).
4. Choose a display type from the list of Types in the dialog box (see Figure 2-2).
5. Click OK.

Notice that the display in the formula bar doesn't change; its display matches the system default.

Entering Time

When you want to enter times in your spreadsheet, you use a colon (:) between the hour, minute, and second (if you're using seconds).

When you type the characters for the hour, Excel assumes you mean AM. If you select the cell and look at the formula bar, you see an AM or PM designation for times, but the AM/PM designation doesn't appear by default in the cell display.

This means if you type 6:15, any formula that involves this cell calculates the time as 6:15 AM. Here's how to enter times so there's no mistaking what you mean:

- Use military time—for example, 13:20 for 1:20 PM. The cell displays the military time you enter.
- After you enter the time, leave a space and type an "A" or a "P" (you can use lowercase letters, Excel converts them to capital letters). The designation AM or PM appears in the cell.

 No matter how you format the cell display, the formula bar displays HH:MM:SS AM or PM. If you don't enter the seconds, the formula bar displays 00 for that part of the time.

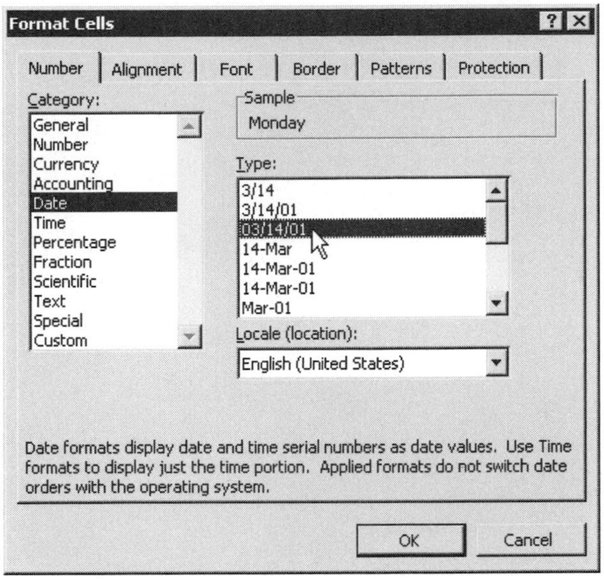

Figure 2-2.   *Select a display type for dates in this worksheet*

Changing the Default Display of Times

To change the default for displaying time, open the Regional Settings dialog box in Control Panel and follow the instructions earlier in this chapter for changing the default appearance of dates. Remember that changes you make in this dialog box are made to any times that you enter in any Windows software.

Changing the Display of Times in Your Worksheet

To change the appearance of time entries in your worksheet, follow these steps:

1. Select the column(s) or row(s) that contains the time entries.

2. Choose Format | Cells from the menu bar to open the Format Cells dialog box.

3. In the Numbers tab, select Time as the Category.

4. Choose the format you want to use for time entries in this worksheet (see Figure 2-3).

Entering Date and Time in the Same Cell

You can combine a date entry and a time entry in the same cell. Just enter the date and then enter a space followed by the time. If the cell is too narrow to display all the data,

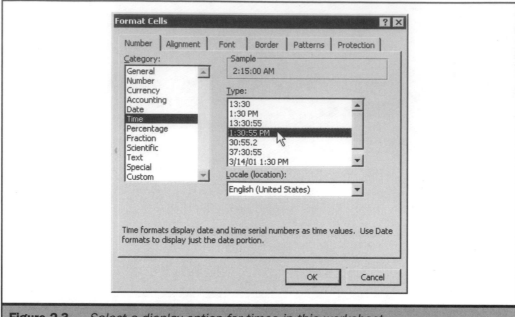

Figure 2-3. *Select a display option for times in this worksheet*

the formula bar has everything, so any formulas you build will work. Notice that by default, when you have both the date and time in a cell, the time displays in 24-hour format (military time).

You can specifically format the display of cells that contain both date and time data. Select the column(s) or row(s) in which you've entered both items in the same cell and choose Format | Cells from the menu bar. In the Format Cells dialog box, select either the date or time category and choose a display type that includes both elements.

Editing Data

If you made a mistake when you entered data in a cell, or the data has to be changed, you can edit your work. You can delete the contents of a cell, replace them with totally new data, or make some small change to the data.

Deleting Cell Contents

To remove the contents of a cell, select the cell and press DELETE. To remove the contents of multiple cells, select them using one of these actions and then press DELETE:

- ■ Hold the CTRL key while you select all the cells you want to delete.
- ■ Drag your mouse pointer across or down to include a range of cells.
- ■ Click the column or row heading button to select the entire column or row.

When you use the DELETE button to clear the contents of a cell (or a group of cells), only the data you entered is removed from the cell. Any other attributes of the cell, such as formatting or comments, remain in the cell.

If you want real control over deleting cells, the DELETE button just doesn't do it. Instead, choose Edit | Clear from the menu bar, and then select the action you need from the submenu that appears.

Here's what those submenu items do:

- ■ **All**   Clears everything from the cell—contents, formatting, whatever.
- ■ **Formats**   Clears only formatting, leaving the data you entered in the cell.
- ■ **Contents**   Clears the contents and leaves everything else (same as the DELETE key).
- ■ **Comments**   Clears any comments attached to the cell.

Changing Cell Contents

You can edit anything you entered in a cell, either to replace the total contents or to make some small change to the contents.

Replacing Everything in the Cell

You may need to replace the data you previously put into a cell, and it's quite easy to do this. When you activate a cell by clicking it, the contents of the cell are automatically selected (even though they aren't highlighted the way selected text is highlighted in a word processor). As soon as you begin typing, the original contents of the cell disappear and are replaced by your typing.

Editing the Contents of a Cell

If a cell has a lot of characters or a complicated formula and you just need to make a modification, you can edit the cell. There are a couple of ways to do this:

- Double-click on the cell (or press F2) and edit the contents directly in the cell.

- Click on the cell to activate it, then click in the formula bar and do your editing there.

No matter which method you decide to use, two additional icons appear on the left side of the formula bar while you're editing:

- The red X cancels your edit and puts everything back the way it was. The ESC key does the same thing.

- The green check mark puts the edited contents into the cell and ends the editing process. The ENTER key does the same thing.

When you begin to edit, your cursor turns into a vertical bar and you can move it with the arrow keys. Use normal editing functions such as deleting and adding characters, and make all the changes you require.

If the cell has a formula, you can edit the formula as if it were text, but you must be careful that you don't make changes that prevent the formula from working properly. You can also use the Formula palette, which appears if you click the equal sign icon to the left of the formula bar. See Chapter 8 for more information on using the Formula palette.

Using Comments

A cell comment is a way to annotate the contents of a cell. You can use a comment for yourself (as a reminder) or to provide explanations for a recipient if you send your worksheet to someone else. There are lots of scenarios in which a cell comment can be useful. Sometimes you use a value that might seem arbitrary without an explanation. A text label (for example, initials) benefits from a comment that gives details. If you forget why you entered a long, complicated formula, you'll be grateful for the note you wrote to yourself in a comment.

Comments are also terrific if you share worksheets. Ask another person to check your formula or provide a formula that's better. If you make changes in someone else's worksheet, it's impolite not to explain in a comment.

Entering Comments

You can enter comments as you create the cells in your worksheet, or you can wait until you've completed your data entry (depending on how good your attention to detail and memory are). Here's how to add a comment to a cell:

1. Select the cell.

2. Choose Insert | Comment from the menu bar. A comment box that points to the active cell appears with your name already in it.

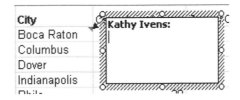

3. Enter the text for the comment. If you have a lot of text, the first lines scroll out of sight, but you can use the sizing handles around the comment box to enlarge the box to display everything you wrote.

4. Click anywhere in the worksheet to hide the comment box. A small red triangle appears in the upper-right corner of the cell to indicate that there is a comment for that cell.

Editing Comments

If you want to change the text in a comment, right-click on its cell and choose Edit Comment from the shortcut menu that appears. The comment box opens and you can delete, add, and change text.

Viewing Comments from Others

Most of the time you use comments to send information to somebody who is using the worksheet you created. You may also receive worksheets that have comments from other users, or the comments in your own worksheet may have additional text added when other users return your worksheet to you.

There are several methods you can use to view comments. Try each of the techniques to see which you prefer. The fact is, you'll probably use different methods at different times, depending on how you need to use the comments.

Viewing All Comments

By default, comments can't be seen when you open a worksheet. If you want to see all the comments in a worksheet, choose View | Comments from the menu bar. This command is a toggle, so if you want to hide all the comments, select it again.

When you opt to view all the comments, the Reviewing toolbar appears.

This toolbar contains tools that make it quick and easy to work with comments, whether they're your own or those of other users. You can add or edit a comment and move forward and backward through all the comments in the worksheet. (This toolbar should be called the Comments toolbar, because it's dedicated to working with comments, but the programmers apparently preferred to call it the Reviewing toolbar.)

You can also open the toolbar without displaying all the comments. Just right-click on any blank spot on a toolbar that's on your Excel window and then select Reviewing from the list of toolbars.

Viewing a Single Comment

You can also view a comment by holding your mouse pointer over the red triangle in the cell (you don't need to click the triangle). To hide the comment again, right-click on the red triangle and choose Hide Comment from the shortcut menu.

 When you view a comment from another user, the user's name appears at the top of the comment box.

Deleting a Comment

To get rid of a comment, right-click on the cell with the red triangle and choose Delete Comment from the shortcut menu.

Validating Data Entry

You can control the type of data a cell accepts using the *data validation* feature . Applying this feature means other users won't be able to add the wrong type of data to a cell that's involved in a formula (thus messing up your formula). In fact, it means you yourself won't be able to mess up your own worksheet.

To use the data validation feature, select the cell you want to control and choose Data | Validation from the menu bar. The Data Validation dialog box, seen in Figure 2-4, appears.

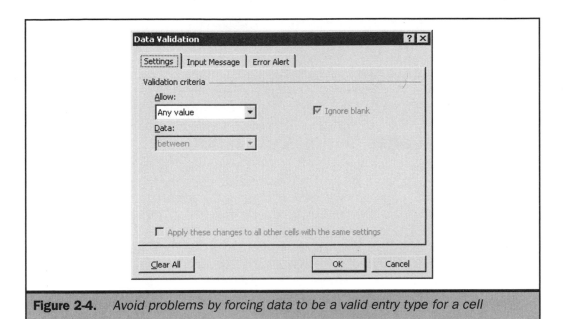

Figure 2-4.   *Avoid problems by forcing data to be a valid entry type for a cell*

Specifying Valid Data Types

Use the Settings tab of the Data Validation dialog box to specify the type of data the selected cell can accept. Start by clicking the arrow to the right of the Allow text box and choosing the criteria for data.

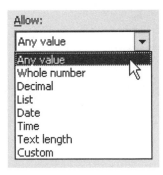

The options on the dialog box change, depending on the data type you select. For most data types, after you select the type, you can select additional criteria to limit the value of any data that's entered. For example, if you choose to allow numbers or dates, you can then specify that they must be within a certain range. You can use values, cell contents, or formulas to set the limits. The Ignore Blank check box indicates whether or not you're willing to accept a blank cell.

Displaying Messages During Data Input

You can display a message when a cell is selected so the user (and that may be you) understands the validation criteria you've established. Click the Input Message tab on the Data Validation dialog box to avail yourself of this feature (see Figure 2-5).

If you enter text in the Title text box, it appears in bold above your message. The title text is optional. The user sees the message as soon as the cell is selected. If the Office Assistant is already on the screen, the message is displayed by the Office Assistant. If the Office Assistant is hidden, the message appears in a plain box.

Displaying Invalid Data Error Messages

If a user enters data that doesn't match the criteria you set for the cell, you can issue an error message and control the user's response. To accomplish this, move to the Error Alert tab of the Data Validation dialog box (see Figure 2-6).

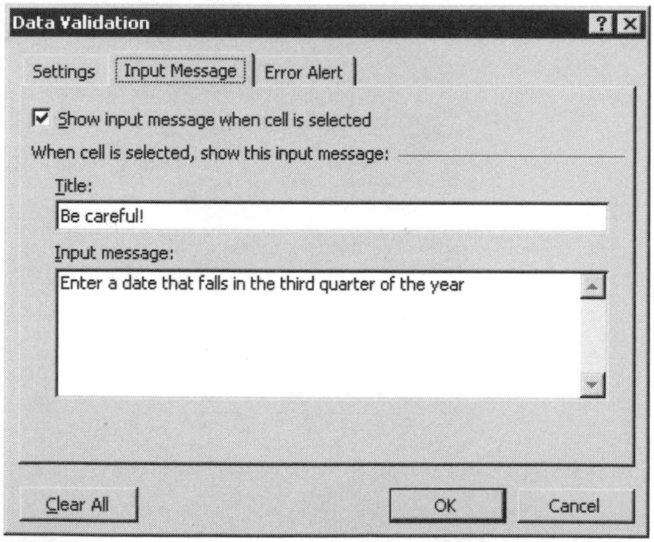

Figure 2-5. *To make sure users understand your criteria, display a message when the cell is selected*

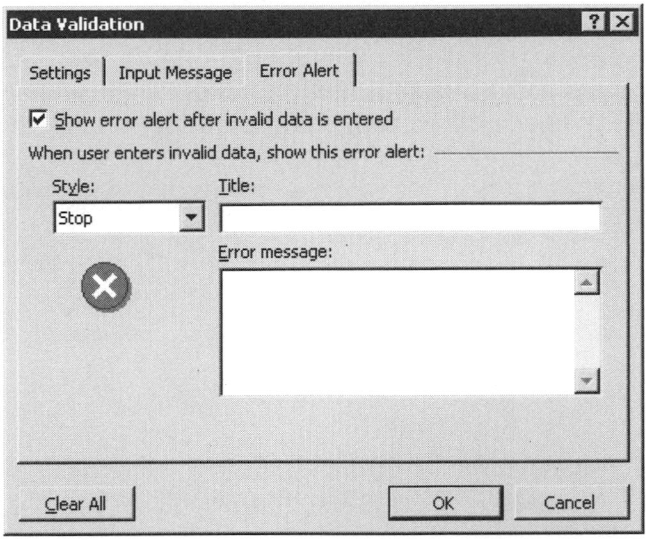

Figure 2-6.   *You can control user activity and issue a message to explain what's going on*

In the Style text box, select an error level, choosing from Stop, Warning, or Information.

Stop presents a dialog box with the error message and two buttons: Retry, which returns the user to the cell, and Cancel, which returns the original data to the cell. If there was no data in the cell, the cell is returned to a blank state. The user cannot enter invalid data.

Warning displays a warning message on a dialog box that also has the text "Continue?" There are buttons for Yes, No, and Cancel, which produce these results:

- **Yes**   Puts the invalid data in the cell.
- **No**   Returns the user to the cell to try again.
- **Cancel**   Returns the original data to the cell.

Information displays a warning message on a dialog box that offers two buttons to the user: OK, which permits the invalid data to be written, and Cancel, which returns the original data to the cell.

After you select the level you want to use for this error message, you can enter your own text for the error message. If you don't enter your own text, Excel provides a message that says "The value you entered is not valid. A user has restricted values that can be entered into this cell."

If you'd prefer your own words, enter them in the Error message box in the dialog box. You can enter text in the Title text box too, and it will appear with bold lettering above the error message.

When a user enters data that falls outside the configuration you established, your error message displays in the Office Assistant (if available) or a dialog box.

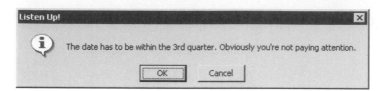

The buttons that display (and therefore the available options) are controlled by the level of error message you configured.

 The data validation feature only works for direct user entry. It does not work if a user pastes data into the cell.

Controlling the Appearance of Data

You have lots of control over the way your data looks, both in its formatting (font properties) and placement in the cell. Additionally, there are special formatting features for numbers.

Formatting Numbers

It's hard to figure out what a number means or what it represents if it looks like a bunch of digits. Money should look like money, percentages should look like percentages, and so on. Fortunately, Excel provides a way to format numbers that makes your presentation clear and easy to interpret.

 Usually, the numbers in a row or column are related. They're all money, percentages, or just plain numbers. The same is true for text, which is usually grouped as a title or data (perhaps names). Selecting the row or column header is a quick way to select all these related cells at once. Otherwise, select an individual cell or a specific group of cells to format.

There are several methods available to you when you want to format numbers. You can use buttons on the toolbar, shortcut keystrokes, or the menu system.

Sometimes Excel automatically formats a number for you. For instance, if you type the characters **3%** *in a cell, Excel automatically assigns the formatting for percentages. If you put a dollar sign in front of a number, Excel automatically formats the cell for currency.*

Formatting Numbers with the Toolbar

The most common formats are preconfigured and appear as toolbar buttons on the Formatting toolbar.

$$\boxed{\$ \quad \% \quad \textbf{,} \quad {}^{+}_{.00}^{.0} \quad {}^{.00}_{+.0}}$$

Select the cell(s) you want to format and use one of the buttons. Table 2-1 explains what the buttons do.

Formatting Numbers with Keyboard Shortcuts

You can also apply formatting to numbers right from the keyboard. Just select the cell(s) and press the appropriate combination of keys. You'll find that the keystrokes for the formatting you use frequently will embed themselves in your brain and your fingertips rather quickly, and you won't have to look at Table 2-2 anymore.

Button	Formatting
Currency Format	Puts a dollar sign on the left; displays two numbers to the right of the decimal point; adds commas to separate thousands.
Percent Format	Displays the number as a percentage with no decimals.
Thousand Separator	Used to separate thousands.
Increase Decimal	Increases the number of characters (numbers) to the right of the decimal point by one each time you click the button.
Decrease Decimal	Decreases the number of characters (numbers) to the right of the decimal point by one each time you click the button.

Table 2-1. *Using the Formatting Toolbar*

Key Combo	Formatting
CTRL-SHIFT—	Plain numbers (no formatting)
CTRL-SHIFT-$	Currency Format
CTRL-SHIFT-%	Percent Format
CTRL-SHIFT-!	Thousand separator; two decimal places
CTRL-SHIFT-#	Date Format

Table 2-2.   *Keyboard Shortcuts for Formatting Numbers*

Formatting Numbers with the Format Cells Command

If the toolbar buttons and keyboard combinations don't offer the formatting you need for numbers, you can use the Format Cells command. This command gives you additional controls over the appearance of numbers.

The Format Cells command opens the Format Cells dialog box (see Figure 2-7), which has multiple tabs. Of course, you need to use the Number tab to format

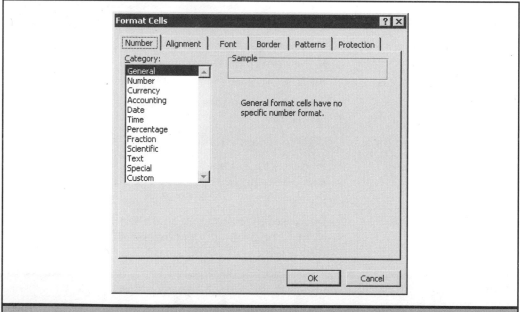

Figure 2-7.   *Use the Number tab of the Format Cells dialog to make sure numbers appear exactly the way you prefer*

numbers. There are several ways to open the Format Cells dialog box. First select the cell(s) you want to work with, and then perform one of these actions:

■ Choose Format | Cells from the menu bar.

■ Right-click on a selected cell and choose Format Cells from the shortcut menu.

■ Press CTRL+1

Notice that the category list contains more number types than the formatting toolbar—dates, times, fractions, and other types are included.

As you select a category, the right side of the dialog box changes to display the choices for that category. For most of the categories, you can make changes to the default appearance. You can, for example, configure the number of decimal places and the appearance of negative numbers (use a minus sign, parentheses, red instead of black, and so on).

Figure 2-8 is a worksheet in which the number 123456 has been formatted with the default settings for the commonly used Number categories. Notice that if you format numbers as text, the cell is left-justified (all other number formatting types are right-justified). The peculiar appearance of the Accounting category stems from the fact that this scheme leaves room for additional numbers on both sides of the decimal point. The important feature of the Accounting format is that all the decimal points and commas line up under each other.

You can also control the standard formatting options for numbers, such as attributes (bold, italic, and so on), font, size, and justification. Those formatting features are discussed in the next section, "Formatting Characters."

	A	B
1	Category	Example
2	General	123456
3	Number	123456.00
4	Currency	$123,456.00
5	Accounting	$ 123,456.00
6	Percentage	12345600.00%
7	Scientific	1.23E+05
8	Text	123456

Figure 2-8.   *The category you select determines the display of numbers*

Number Formats vs. Accurate Display

It's imperative that you realize the formatting changes you make to numbers affect appearance only. Formatting changes don't alter the value of the number, a fact that sometimes causes problems. For example, look at the worksheet in Figure 2-9. Cell A3 is the sum of cells A1:A2.

You don't have to grab your calculator to know there's a problem. This confusion pops up frequently, and it's caused by a mismatch between the formatting (display) and the actual numbers. For example, in this case numbers with three decimal places were entered into cells preformatted for two decimal places.

The real values are displayed in the formula bar when you select the cell. The value of A1 is 123.105, which rounded to 123.11. The value of A2 is 425.109, which rounded to 425.11. The value of A3 is really 548.214, which, as shown, rounded to 548.21.

The best solution is to format cells to match the data—that is, a cell that has numbers up to four decimals should be formatted for four decimals.

There's another solution, which involves telling Excel to change the values to match the formatting. This is called Precision as Displayed, and it's an option you can set by choosing Tools | Options and moving to the Calculations tab of the Options dialog box, where this choice appears. (Excel warns you that underlying numbers will be changed permanently if they don't match the formatting.) Don't try this on any worksheet where the real numbers are important; it's only a workable solution if you're dealing with imprecise data.

Formatting Characters

You can manipulate the appearance of all the characters in your worksheet. This is a feature usually applied to text, but you can perform all the same formatting handiwork on any characters, including numbers.

Remember that any changes you make to formatting are applied to the cells you select: select first, format next.

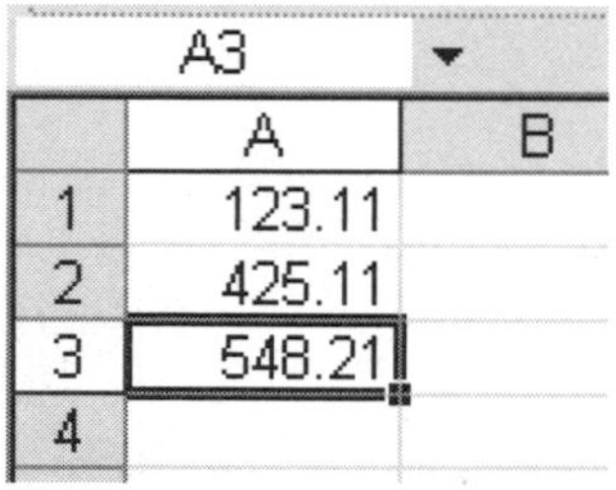

Figure 2-9.   *Oops, something isn't right*

Attributes

You can make data more dramatic or more noticeable by changing the attribute of the characters. This is usually reserved for text, and it's handy for titles and labels. The attribute tools—Bold, Italic, and Underline—are on the Formatting toolbar, and you can apply any or all of the attributes with a click of the mouse. Another click turns off the attribute (it's a toggle). You can tell if an attribute is already applied to the selected cell(s) because the button on the toolbar changes its appearance.

Alignment

Alignment is usually predetermined by the type of data you enter in a cell. Text is left-justified; values (numbers, dates, time, and so on) are right-justified. It's not a good idea to change the alignment of values, but realigning text often helps you make your worksheet easier to read and understand.

Aligning text in a worksheet isn't quite as straightforward as aligning text in a word processor because you're restricted to the size of the cell. Here's how the alignment buttons work in Excel:

- **Align Left** Aligns text to the left edge of the cell. If the text doesn't fit, excess text is placed in the cell to the right if that cell is empty. If the cell to the right isn't empty, the display of the text ends at the right edge of the cell.

- **Center** Aligns the text in the center of the cell. Spillover text appears in the adjoining cells if either or both are empty. Otherwise, the display of the text is truncated.

- **Align Right** Aligns text to the right edge of the cell. Spillover text appears in the cell to the left if it's empty. Otherwise, the display of the text is truncated.

- **Merge and Center** Merges the selected cells and centers the combined text in the resulting single cell.

You can also align the contents of a cell vertically, which means you can position your data along the top, center, or bottom of the cell. To do this:

1. Choose Format | Cells and go to the Alignment tab of the Format Cells dialog box.

2. Click the arrow to the right of the Vertical text box and choose a vertical alignment (see Figure 2-10).

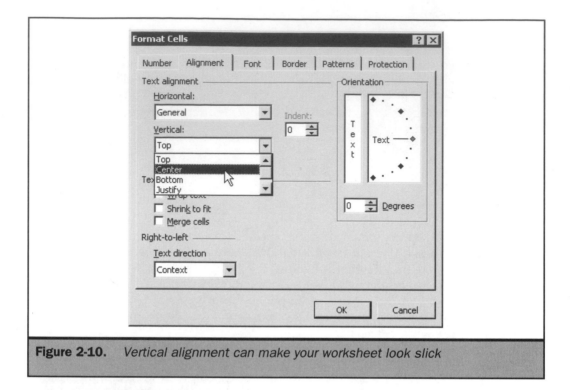

Figure 2-10. *Vertical alignment can make your worksheet look slick*

You can change the size of a column of cells to eliminate truncated text. There are two ways to accomplish this: automatically widen the column to match the longest text, or drag the column to make it the width you prefer.

1. Position your pointer on the column heading, on the line to the right of the column you want to change. Your pointer turns into a double arrow.

2. Double-click to widen the column so the widest cell is accommodated automatically.

3. Drag the line in either direction to widen or narrow the column.

To change the size of rows (which means you make them taller or shorter), drag the line between the rows in the left-most column.

Fonts

Changing fonts and font sizes is one of the best ways to make text stand out. You can perform these tasks from the toolbar or in the Format Cells dialog box.

To use the toolbar, click the arrow to the right of the Font box on the toolbar to select a new font. Do the same to the Font Size tool to change font sizes.

For more controls, choose Format | Cells from the menu bar and move to the Fonts tab in the Format Cells dialog box. As you can see in Figure 2-11, the entire range of font attributes is available.

Colors

You can change the color of the text and the color of the background of the cell. The buttons that perform these tasks are on the Formatting toolbar. Each button shows the last selection you made, so clicking the button applies the color to the newly selected cell(s). An arrow to the right of each button provides a way to change the selected color.

Borders

Technically, borders aren't applied to text, they're applied to cells. But a border can enhance the appearance of text. A border is a line drawn around the cell(s) you select,

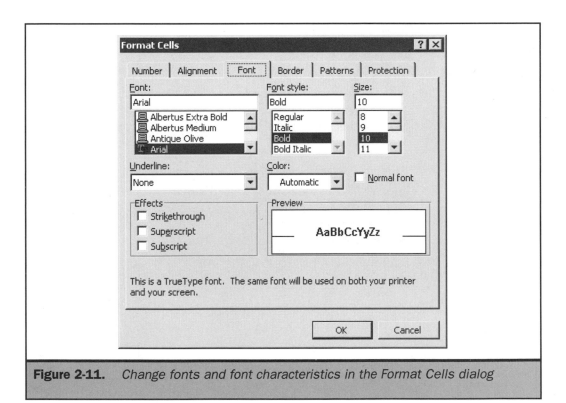

Figure 2-11.   *Change fonts and font characteristics in the Format Cells dialog*

and there are a number of border style choices available. Click the arrow to the right of the Borders tool and make a selection.

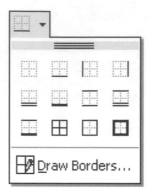

 When you're creating borders in your worksheet, you can drag the Borders tool out of the Formatting toolbar so that it floats in your Excel window. Very handy!

Rotating Text

Rotating text can be an effective way to handle titles and labels in your worksheet. Sometimes displaying text at an angle can help you fit text in a cell without widening a column. The best reason to rotate text, though, is that it's a nifty, slick way to display a row of titles. Here's how to accomplish this:

1. Choose Format | Cells from the menu bar.
2. Move to the Alignment tab of the Format Cells dialog box.
3. Specify the rotation (see Figure 2-12), using one of these methods:

   ■ Click a degree point in the orientation box.
   ■ Drag the degree indicator in the orientation box.
   ■ Specify a number in the Degrees spin box.
   ■ Click the word Text (it's displayed vertically) to make the text absolutely vertical.

 Give the row with rotated text more pizzazz by expanding its height.

You can also select the option Shrink to Fit or Wrap Text to tweak the appearance of your rotated text.

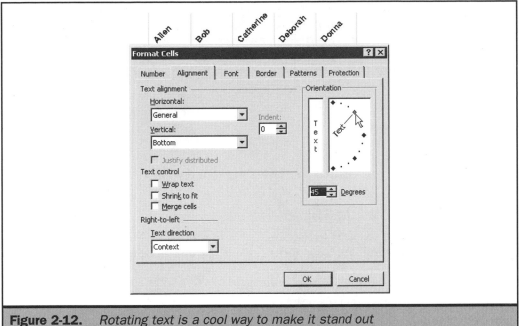

Figure 2-12.   *Rotating text is a cool way to make it stand out*

Indenting Text

Another way to make text stand out, and therefore easier to notice and read, is to indent it. This guarantees there's some space between the text and the contents of the adjacent cell.

You can also increase or decrease the indentation. Just click the appropriate Indent button on the toolbar to increase or decrease the indentation within the cell.

Note	*Indentation only works for left-aligned text.*

Working with Styles

The third or fourth time you find yourself decorating a cell, row, or column in the same manner, stop and think about what you're doing. You're reinventing a wheel you've designed to perfection, and it's time to automate the task. Use a style. The fact that Excel supports styles comes as a surprise to many users (including people who have used Excel for a long time), although the same people enthusiastically embrace the concept when they work in a word processor.

Excel comes with several built-in styles. There's Normal (yawn) and a number of other styles used to control settings for numbers and hyperlinks. When you create your own Excel styles, you can apply settings for as many as six attributes, including:

- Font (including color and size)
- Alignment (both horizontal and vertical)
- Number format
- Pattern
- Border
- Protection settings (hidden and locked)

Defining a Style by Example

The best way to define a style is to use a set of formatting options you've already applied to a cell that you think looks terrific. Here's how to accomplish this:

1. Select the cell you want to use as the basis of your style.

2. Choose Format | Style from the menu bar to open the Style dialog box.

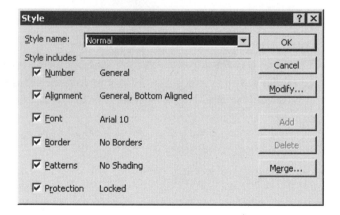

3. In the Style Name box, replace the name of the current style (probably Normal) with the name you want to use. (Excel adds the words *By Example* to the dialog box to note the fact that this style is based on an existing example.)

4. The formatting options for the cell you selected are displayed on the dialog box. Click any check box you don't want to include in this style to deselect that option.

5. Click OK to save the style.

Defining a Style from Scratch

You can also define a style by designing it from the ground up in the Style dialog box. Enter a name for this style in the Style Name box, then click the Modify button to design the formatting. The Format Cells dialog box opens, and you can move through the tabs to select all the settings you want to include in your new style.

 The style you design is applied automatically to the cell that was active when you opened the Style dialog box. You can change the style or override it, as explained in the following sections.

Changing a Style

If you want to modify a style, open the Style dialog box and choose that style from the drop-down list. If the changes you want to make are covered in the settings displayed in the Style dialog box, you can select and deselect the appropriate options. Or, click the Modify button to open the Format Cells dialog box and make your changes there.

Deleting a Style

If you want to remove a style from the assortment of styles available, open the Style dialog box and select the style from the drop-down list. Click Delete. Excel does not ask you to confirm the deletion; the style just disappears and the Normal style is applied to cells formatted with that style..

 You cannot delete the Normal style—the DELETE *button is grayed out and inaccessible when you select it.*

Applying a Style

You probably just moved your mouse pointer to the left side of the toolbar to apply a style (because that's where the Style tool resides when you work in your word processor). But oops, guess what? There's no Style tool on your Formatting toolbar.

Excel does not place the Style tool on the toolbar by default. Microsoft and all Excel trainers are aware that most Excel users don't use (or know about) styles. I think there's a connection between those two statements.

Here's how to put the Style tool on your Formatting toolbar:

1. Right-click on any toolbar and choose Customize from the shortcut menu.

2. Move to the Commands tab.

3. In the Categories List box, select Format.

4. In the Commands box (on the right), click the Style tool (the one with the box next to it).

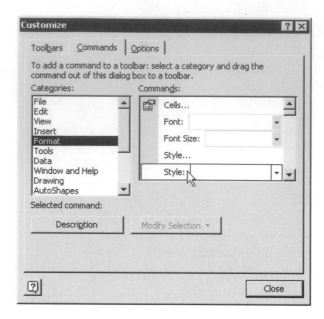

5. Drag the Style tool to your Formatting toolbar and position it where you want it.

6. Close the Customize dialog box.

 You're not restricted to putting the Style tool on the Formatting toolbar, you can choose any toolbar, but the Formatting toolbar makes the most sense.

Now you can apply styles. Select the cell(s) and click the arrow to the right of the Styles tool. Choose a style. Easy, huh?

Overriding a Style

After you apply a style to a cell or group of cells, you can apply any additional formatting to the cell. Use the tools on the Formatting toolbar or use the Format Cells dialog box. The modifications you apply to the cell(s) have no effect on the style.

Checking Your Spelling

When you finish building a clever, complicated worksheet that answers every financial question anyone might have about the current state of affairs at your company, you pass it along to your boss. How embarrassing it would be if there were words misspelled! That kind of sloppiness undermines the professional cast you tried to apply to your efforts. Avoid a red face and the need to mumble an apology by using the Excel spelling tool.

Deciding What to Check

If you select an individual cell before launching the spell check, the entire worksheet is perused for errors. The spell checker looks at cell contents, text in graphics objects, headers, footers, and comments. Even hidden cells are checked. If you select a range of cells, only the cells in that range are checked.

Running a Spell Check

To launch the spell check tool, use one of these methods:

- ■ Press F7.
- ■ Click the Spelling tool on the Standard toolbar.
- ■ Choose Tools | Spelling from the menu bar.

When the spelling tool finds a word that isn't in its dictionary, it displays the Spelling dialog box (see Figure 2-13).

Click one of these buttons to have the spelling tool take the associated action:

- ■ **Ignore** Ignores the word and continues checking.
- ■ **Ignore All** Ignores all instances of the word in the worksheet.
- ■ **Add** Adds the word to the dictionary.

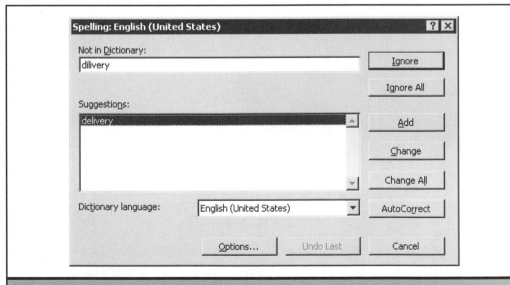

Figure 2-13. *The spelling tool finds mistakes and suggests corrections*

- **Change** Replaces the original text with the selected word in the Suggestions box.

- **Change All** Changes all instances of the original text with the selected word in the Suggestions box.

- **Auto Correct** Adds the mistake and correct word to the AutoCorrect feature's list.

Click Options to open the Options dialog box and configure the way the spelling tool works.

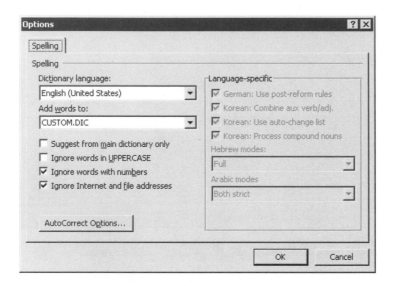

 Select the Ignore Words in UPPERCASE option if you use a lot of uppercase abbreviations.

Don't forget to save your workbook after you've corrected all your spelling errors.

Using AutoCorrect

Excel's AutoCorrect feature automatically makes changes in spelling as you type. It comes preloaded with a long list of common spelling errors, and you can add your own spelling peculiarities to the list by using the AutoCorrect option on the Spelling dialog box or by entering them manually.

Open the AutoCorrect dialog box by choosing Tools | AutoCorrect Options from the menu bar. When the AutoCorrect dialog box opens (see Figure 2-14), you can perform several tasks:

- Deselect any functions you don't want the AutoCorrect feature to impose.
- Select any AutoCorrect entries you don't want to use and delete them.
- Add your own entries to the list.

The personal entries you add to AutoCorrect don't have to be spelling errors—you can use this feature to create shortcuts that automatically expand to full text. For example, I frequently refer to Dial-Up Networking clients, so my AutoCorrect list includes dupn (which I placed in the Replace text box) and Dial-Up Networking (which I placed in the With text box). I thought about using dun, but it's a word that I might need.

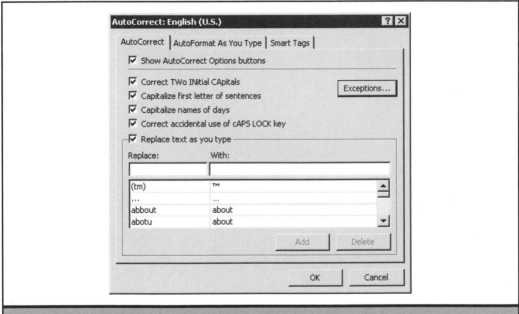

Figure 2-14.   *You can use AutoCorrect to save time when you're entering data*

Certification Skills Covered in This Chapter

If you're preparing for Microsoft Office User Specialist certification, here are the skills you learned in this chapter.

Skill Set	Activity
Working with cells and cell data	Insert, delete, and move cells
Working with cells and cell data	Enter and edit cell data, including text, numbers, and formulas
Working with cells and cell data	Check spelling
Formatting and Printing worksheets	Apply styles
Workgroup collaboration	View and edit comments

The
Complete
Reference

Excel
2002

Chapter 3

Working with Files

It's hard to work with computers without understanding files and how to manage them. Each time you create and save a document in Excel, you've created a file.

Excel workbook files use the format *filename*.xls. When you want to work on a file you've previously saved, that's the file type you open.

Saving Files

While you're working in Excel, you should save your files early and often. Don't wait until you've finished your work. In fact, it's a good idea to save a new workbook after you've entered data in the first cell. Then save again (and again, and again) as you continue your work.

I've lost count of the number of calls I've received from clients who cried, "Something happened and all my work just disappeared from the screen, how do I get it back?" There's usually no way to help; they can't retrieve their work and have to start all over again. After spending four hours working and then losing all their data, those Excel users never forgot my suggestion to save constantly.

Excel gives you four methods to save your workbook:

■ Click the Save button on the Standard toolbar.

■ Press CTRL-S.

■ Choose File | Save from the menu bar.

■ Press SHIFT-F12.

Saving a Workbook for the First Time

The first time you save a workbook, you have to give it a name. When you invoke the Save command (using any of the methods described here), a Save As dialog box opens, which resembles the dialog box shown in Figure 3-1.

Choose a Folder

By default, Excel saves your workbook files to the My Documents folder. That's usually exactly where you want to save the file.

If you have a reason to change folders, the left side of the Save As dialog box displays buttons for other folders, and you can choose one of them to save this file there. You can also click the arrow to the right of the Save In text box at the top of the dialog box to see a hierarchical display of your computer.

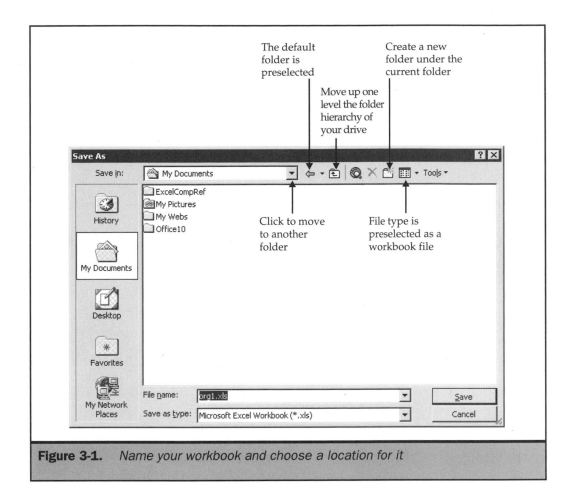

The default folder is preselected

Create a new folder under the current folder

Move up one level the folder hierarchy of your drive

Click to move to another folder

File type is preselected as a workbook file

Figure 3-1.   *Name your workbook and choose a location for it*

The common reason to change folders is to keep related files together. For instance, you may have one folder for budgets, another for projects, and so on.

Choose a folder on a higher level, or choose your hard drive. All the folders are displayed (along with any existing workbook files). Double-click the folder you want to use for this file.

Create a New Folder

You can create a new folder to hold this file by following these steps:

1. In the Save In text box, select the folder or drive in which you want to locate your new folder.
2. Click the Create New Folder button on the toolbar.
3. In the New Folder dialog box, enter a name for the new folder, then click OK.
4. Double-click the new folder to make it the current folder.
5. Click Save to save the file in the new folder.

Name the File

By default, Excel inserts the name of the current blank workbook in the File Name text box. It's highlighted (selected), so as soon as you type a character, the selected text disappears and the characters you type replace the original characters. Enter a filename, using these rules:

- Filenames can be up to 255 characters long, including spaces.
- The following characters may not be used: / ? : * " < > |.
- You can use upper- or lowercase characters or a combination of both.

You don't have to enter the file extension (.xls) because Excel will automatically add it to the filename for you.

Configuring File Options

You can take advantage of several features when you save a file for the first time. If you want to use these features after you've already saved a file, you can choose File | Save As to access the options. Click the Tools button on the Save As dialog box toolbar, then choose General Options from the drop-down menu to see this Save Options dialog box.

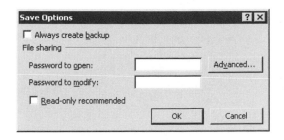

Select the options you want to apply to this file.

Create a Backup Copy When Saving

It's a good idea to select the option to create a backup. This means that every time you save this file, the last saved file is also saved. The backup copy has the filename Backup of *<your filename>*.xlk. There are lots of occasions when the backup file is handy. For example, you may save a file and then perform some complicated sorting routine on the worksheet, followed by a change to a formula or two. You save the file and then realize your changes messed up the worksheet. You don't have to make corrections; you can open the backup copy instead.

Incidentally, if you use Microsoft Word, you probably know you can set an option to create a backup file as part of the basic configuration of the software. That is not true for Excel—you have to configure each file independently for backup copies.

Password-Protecting the File

If you want to prevent other users from opening or changing your file, you can password-protect it. Enter a password for each possibility. It's a good idea to use one password for opening the file and a different password for changing it.

Optionally, you can click the Advanced button to specify the type of encryption applied to the password. The default selection is Office 97/2000–compatible, and that is probably the selection of choice for most Excel users. Check with your network administrator to see if another encryption scheme is being applied across the network.

When you click OK, Excel asks you to confirm the password by reentering it. If you used two passwords, a confirmation dialog box appears for each one. Now, when anyone (including you) tries to open the file, Excel displays the Password dialog box.

The password you create can be up to 255 characters and can include numbers, spaces, and symbols. Passwords are case-sensitive, so entering Xy doesn't work for the password xy.

If an incorrect password is entered, Excel returns an error message and refuses to open the file. If the file is also protected against modifications, a second dialog box appears asking for that password.

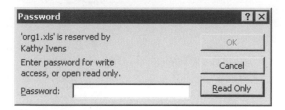

Knowing the password is the key to modifying the file and saving the changes. Any user who doesn't know the password must click the Read Only button to open the file. That user can view the file but can't modify it. (Actually, the user can modify the file like crazy, but those changes won't be saved because the Save command will produce an error message.) However, the Save As command (discussed later in this chapter) does work, although the file is saved with a different name.

To change or eliminate the password, you must have the right to modify the file. This means you have to remember the password you entered. If you forget the password, you can't change it.

Making the File Read-Only

You can prevent anyone from saving a modified version of your file by simply making the file read-only. This doesn't require any passwords; it just means that nobody, including you, can save changes to the document.

Don't invoke this feature while you're continuing to build your worksheet. It's best used when your work is complete.

Saving Summary Information

Every Excel file has information about itself stored in a Properties dialog box. It's not information about the data you've entered but about the file itself—its creation, its size, and other facts that may or may not be useful.

If you share your files with other users, perhaps passing them around for additional data or corrections, the Properties dialog box can provide an information trail about who did what and when they did it.

To see the summary information available in the Properties dialog box, open the file and choose File | Properties from the menu bar.

The Properties dialog box has five tabs:

- **General**   Shows general information about the file, such as the file type, its location, dates (creation, last modification, and so on), and other information the system keeps. You can't make changes to the information on this tab.

- **Summary**   This is the tab you see when you choose to save summary information (see Figure 3-2). You can fill in whatever level of information you want to. The information you put in the Summary tab is used when you want to search for files based on criteria found here.

- **Statistics**   Shows the basic information about the file (like the General tab) along with some additional details about work performed on the file.

- **Contents**   Displays information about the worksheets in the file.

- **Custom**   Displays information you choose to keep about the file. You can create your own definitions of the type of information you want to track.

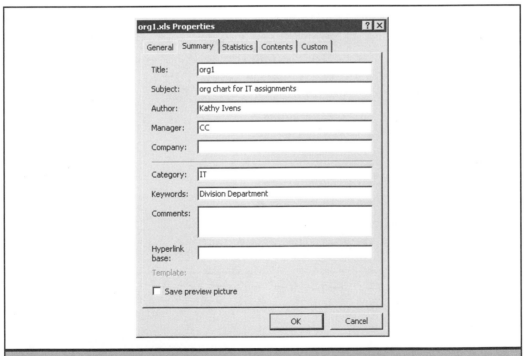

Figure 3-2.   *Summary information is handy when you want to find all the worksheets that relate to a particular topic*

You can tell Excel to bring up the Summary tab of the Properties dialog box automatically when you save a file for the first time. This is handy if you really use the information; otherwise, you'll find it a pain. To order a summary for every file, follow these steps:

1. Choose Tools | Options from the menu bar.
2. Move to the General tab (see Figure 3-3).
3. Select Prompt for Workbook Properties.
4. Click OK.

Hereafter, the Summary tab of the Properties dialog box will appear in your Excel window after you save a new file.

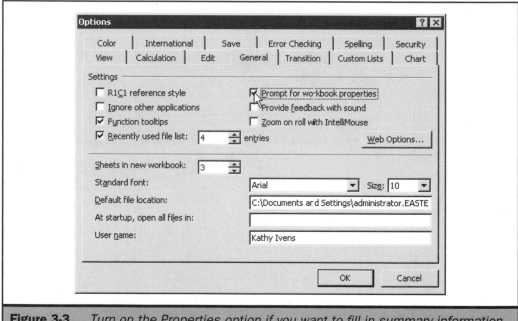

Figure 3-3.   *Turn on the Properties option if you want to fill in summary information for every new file*

Excluding Personal Information from Workbooks

Excel has a new feature that lets you exclude personal information from the workbooks you create. You can exclude your name from the Workbook Properties and from any comments you enter. To enable the feature, choose Tools | Options and move to the Security tab. Under Privacy Options, select Remove Personal Information from This File on Save. When you save the file, any references to your name are removed.

Saving the File Again

After you've saved a workbook for the first time, you should—excuse me, you *must*—continue to save it as you work. Use any of the keystrokes or mouse clicks mentioned earlier to save the file again, using the same name. No dialog box opens, but the file is saved, replacing the last version you saved.

Do this frequently; there's no such thing as saving too often. Trust me, the day will come that you'll either thank me or curse yourself for ignoring this advice.

Using the AutoSave Feature

Excel provides a feature called AutoSave that saves your work automatically. If you get so caught up in entering numbers, designing formulas, and admiring your work that you forget to save, this feature compensates for your neglect if your computer freezes, hangs, loses power, or suffers any other emergency. If you save your changes and close Excel normally, the automatically saved copies are deleted.

At long last, Excel 2002 lets you turn on AutoSave from the Options dialog box. (In previous versions of Excel, the AutoSave feature was an add-on application, and you had to go through a separate installation process to be able to use this feature). To configure AutoSave, choose Tools | Options and move to the Save tab.

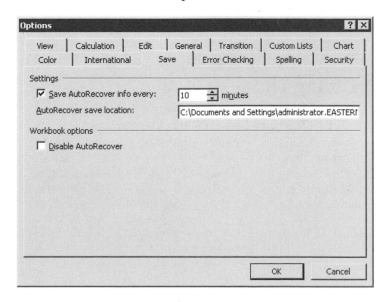

Configure the AutoSave feature with the following guidelines:

- **Save AutoRecover Info Every**   This is where you specify the number of minutes that should elapse between each automatic save action. You can choose any interval (in minutes) between 1 and 120.

 When the AutoSave feature does its job, it uses resources and memory. You may notice a slow-down in your own work. Therefore, autosaving too often can be annoying. On the other hand, if you live in an area where sudden electric failures occur frequently, you don't want to wait too long between automatic saves. Another consideration is the speed with which you work. If you work quickly, ten minutes of work could produce a great deal of data.

- **AutoRecover Save Location**   Specifies the folder in which the files are saved.

These two options turn the AutoRecover feature on or off. The other option on the dialog box, Disable AutoRecover, is for the currently active workbook. This permits you to stop auto-saving for a particular workbook without changing the default values you've set for Excel.

Tip *AutoSave doesn't bother to save if you haven't made any changes to the file since the last time the file was saved. However, if you make even the tiniest change, the file is saved for you after the specified amount of time.*

Opening Files

You can open any existing Excel file in order to work on it, or you can open a blank worksheet to begin a new file.

Opening an Existing File

Excel offers a host of methods for opening an existing file. If you want to open a file you worked on recently, it may be listed on your File menu or on the Side Pane (if the Side Pane is currently visible). This feature, called the Recently Used File List, displays the names of the last four files you opened, so you can just click the listing of the file you want to use. This is faster than opening a dialog box and selecting a file.

If you find this feature handy, you may also find it useful to list the last six or eight files you used, instead of only four. To change the number of files on the list, follow these steps:

1. Choose Tools | Options from the menu bar.

2. On the General tab, specify the number of files you want to display in your Recently Used File List.

3. Click OK.

If the file you want to use isn't listed, display the Open dialog box and select the file you want to use. There are four ways to get to the Open dialog box:

- Click the Open button on the Standard toolbar (it looks like an open file folder).

- Choose File | Open from the menu bar.

- Press CTRL-O.

- Click More Workbooks from the Side Pane (if you're using the Side Pane).

The Open dialog box, seen in Figure 3-4, appears in your Excel window. If you save files in multiple folders, travel to the folder that has the file you want to open. Select the appropriate file and click Open, or double-click the file listing.

If you're not currently working in Excel, you can open an Excel file from Windows Explorer or My Computer. Excel files have the extension .xls and the Excel logo as the file icon. Double-click on the file listing, and Excel opens automatically with that file loaded in the window. If Excel is already up and running, the file is loaded into a new window.

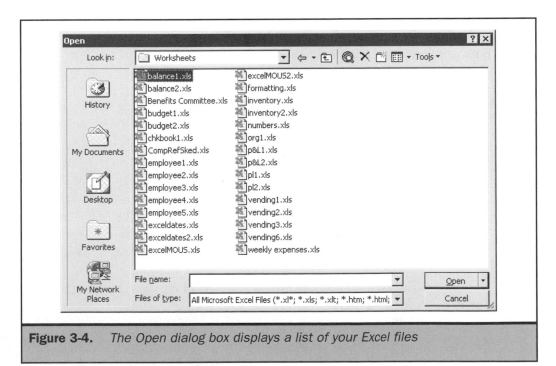

Figure 3-4.   *The Open dialog box displays a list of your Excel files*

Starting a New Workbook

When Excel first starts, it displays a blank workbook in the window. You can begin creating a new file by entering data in this blank workbook. As soon as you save it, it's a file.

If you've been working on a file and want to start a new one, you have to bring up a blank workbook. Excel provides four ways to do this:

- Click the New button on the Standard toolbar (it looks like a piece of paper with the top right corner folded down). A blank workbook appears in the Excel window.

- Press CTRL-N. A blank workbook appears in the Excel window.

- Click Blank Workbook in the Side Pane. A blank workbook appears in the Excel window.

- Choose File | New from the menu bar to open the New Workbook Side Pane, which offers a choice of templates you can use for your new file.

Using Save As

If you're working on a file that has already been saved (it has a filename), you may want to save the file in a different manner, such as:

- With a different name
- As a different file type
- With different options (passwords, backup options)
- In a different folder

Excel provides a way to do any of these chores with the Save As dialog box. Choose File | Save As from the menu bar to open the Save As dialog box, seen in Figure 3-5.

You can make as many changes to the way the file is saved as you wish; in fact, you can change every available option.

- To change the folder, click the arrow to the right of the Save In box and move through the hierarchy of your system to find the folder you need. This is handy if you want to place a copy of the file in an affiliated folder, such as a folder for projects or for specific customers.

- To change the filename, enter the new filename (Excel will add the .xls extension for you).

- To change the file type, click the arrow to the right of the Save As Type box and choose a new type.

- To change the options, click the Tools button and choose General Options from the drop-down menu. Then make the selections you require.

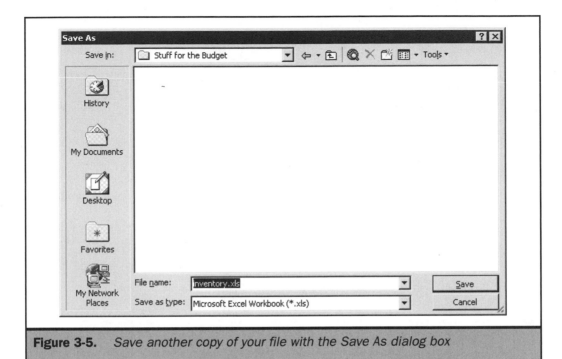

Figure 3-5.   *Save another copy of your file with the Save As dialog box*

Note   *If you opened a worksheet that is configured as read-only, the only way to save the changes you made is to change the filename save the file as a new file with the Save As dialog box.*

Saving as HTML

You can save your Excel worksheet as an HTML file so that any user with a browser can view it (without having to install Excel).

To accomplish this, choose File | Save As. In the Save As dialog box, click the arrow to the right of the Save As Type box and choose Web Page. The file extension automatically changes to .htm, and several additional options appear on the dialog box (see Figure 3-6).

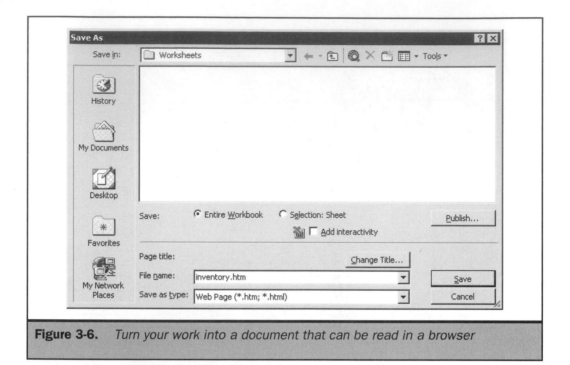

Figure 3-6.   *Turn your work into a document that can be read in a browser*

- You can save the entire workbook or the current worksheet.

- If you select the worksheet, the Add Interactivity option becomes accessible so you can create a link to the worksheet instead of embedding it in the document.

- Click the Change Title button to open a dialog box in which you can enter a title for the Web page (which appears in the title bar of the browser).

If you have access to the company intranet or Internet site, you can use the Publish button to publish this page to the Web. (More information about using Excel on the World Wide Web is in Chapter 18.)

Choose Save to turn your Excel document into a Web-enabled document.

If you want to see what it looks like in a browser, choose File | Web Page Preview from the menu bar to open your browser and see the results.

Note   *After you use the Save As dialog box to save your workbook as a Web document the first time, the Save As Web Page command appears on your File menu. This is a quicker way to save a workbook as a Web document.*

Closing Workbooks

When you've finished with a workbook, you can close it, which frees up some memory. If you've made any changes to the workbook since the last time you saved it, Excel will make sure you have a chance to save again as you close the workbook. Here are all the ways you can close a workbook:

- Click the X in the right corner of the workbook title bar.
- Choose File | Close from the menu bar.
- Press CTRL-F4.
- Press CTRL-W.

If you want to close all the open workbooks, press SHIFT and choose File | Close while you continue to hold the SHIFT key. Excel will ask if you want to save changes for any workbook that has changes.

Mailing and Routing Workbooks

You can send a workbook via e-mail or route it to a group of other users. You don't have to leave Excel to accomplish this; it's all available and automatic. Choose File | Send To and then choose an option from the submenu.

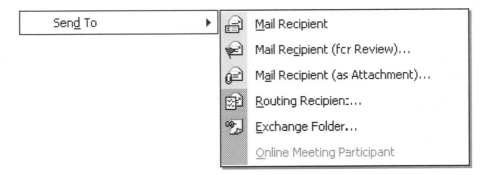

Send To	▶

- Mail Recipient
- Mail Recipient (for Review)...
- Mail Recipient (as Attachment)...
- Routing Recipient...
- Exchange Folder...
- Online Meeting Participant

Note   *You may not have every option, depending on whether or not your company is running Exchange Server.*

All of the commands in the submenu are covered in the following sections.

E-Mailing an Excel Workbook

If you select any of the Mail Recipient commands, your e-mail software opens (unless it already is open). Take any necessary steps to complete its launch (perhaps you must choose a profile, select an account, or start a Dial-Up Networking session). Your worksheet is then shipped to the recipient. Depending on the submenu command you choose, your work is delivered as described in the following sections.

Mail Recipient

Choosing the Mail Recipient command puts the data from the workbook right into the message. If you use Outlook (you probably installed Outlook when you installed Office), the message form is customized to handle this chore (see Figure 3-7).

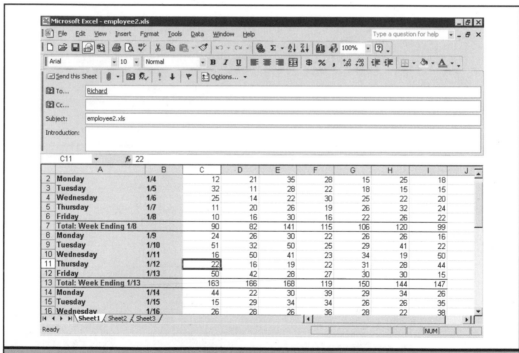

Figure 3-7.   *Outlook turns the currently selected worksheet into an e-mail message—notice the Send button changed its title to Send This Sheet*

If you're not using Outlook, your e-mail client must be MAPI-enabled (such as Eudora).

On the recipient side, opening your message reveals the worksheet without the need to open an attachment or open Excel.

employee2.xls - Message (HTML)					
File Edit View Insert Format Tools Actions Help					
Reply Reply to All Forward					
From: Valerie				Sent: Sat 11/4/00 5:56 AM	
To: Richard					
Cc:					
Subject: employee2.xls					

	Date	Allen	Bob	Catherine	Deborah	Donn
Monday	1/4	12	21	35	28	1
Tuesday	1/5	32	11	28	22	1
Wednesday	1/6	25	14	22	30	2
Thursday	1/7	11	20	26	19	2
Friday	1/8	10	16	30	16	2
Total: Week Ending 1/8		90	82	141	115	10
Monday	1/9	24	26	30	22	2
Tuesday	1/10	51	32	50	25	2
Wednesday	1/11	16	50	41	23	3
Thursday	1/12	22	16	19	22	3
Friday	1/13	50	42	28	27	3
Total: Week Ending 1/13		163	166	168	119	15

If you applied formatting to the data in your worksheet, the recipient won't appreciate the effort unless he or she has an e-mail client capable of displaying formatted text. However, the data is delivered, even if it's converted to plain text, which is the important fact.

Mail Recipient (for Review)

Use this option when you're sending the file in order to have other people check your workbook. Excel performs the following tasks:

■ Reminds you that files need to be marked as "shared" for reviewing and offers to perform the chore.

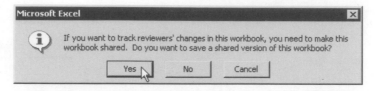

■ Opens the Save As dialog box so you can save the file as a shared document. You can use the same filename or create a new file (I usually opt for the latter choice, adding "-shared" to the filename as a reminder).

■ Opens your e-mail software (if it isn't already open), and attaches the file to the message.

■ Enters text in the message box asking the recipient to review the file.

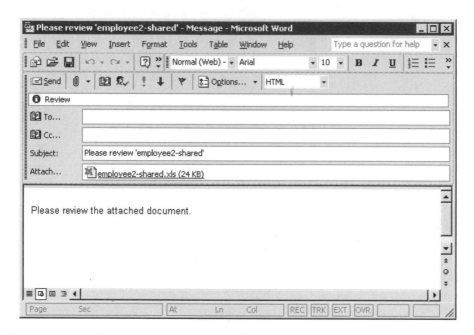

All you need to do is fill in the recipient name(s) in the header. You can, of course, also modify the message text.

If you use Outlook and you're attached to Exchange Server, the message is automatically flagged for follow-up. On the recipient side, the follow-up flag icon appears on the message listing in addition to the attachment icon.

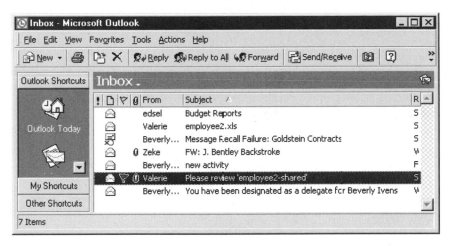

If the recipient is using Outlook 2002 (instead of an older version of Outlook), the reviewing toolbar opens when the recipient opens the message. The Track Changes feature is turned on, and the reviewing toolbar contains the command Reply with Changes. The submenu under File | Send To now contains the command Original Sender.

When you open the returned message from your recipient, and open the workbook, Excel displays a message asking if you'd like to merge the reviewer's changes into the original workbook. The reviewing toolbar appears so you can move through the recipient's changes and accept or reject them.

Mail Recipient (as Attachment)

This command opens a blank message form in your e-mail software and attaches the current file. Fill in the name of the recipient, enter text in the message box, and send the message.

Routing a Workbook

Routing a workbook is similar to sending a workbook via e-mail, except there's a routing slip attached to the message. The purpose of routing is to ask people to make changes and suggestions and then collect their input. For example, this is a great way to put together a budget, with each person on the routing slip adding information.

Your e-mail software and server must be capable of handling this task. Office 2000 includes Outlook as an e-mail client, which supports routing. If you're on a network that uses Exchange Server for e-mail, the routing feature works beautifully. If you're using other server software, check with your system administrator. Luckily, I have both Outlook and Exchange Server on my system, so I can show you how this nifty feature works.

Choose File | Send To and then choose Routing Recipient from the submenu. This opens a routing slip, as seen in Figure 3-8. The subject line contains the name of your workbook.

Add the names of recipients from the system address list and enter any message text you think is necessary. Then select a routing scheme (explained next) and click Route.

Routing a Workbook to One Person at a Time

Choose One After Another on the routing slip to send the workbook to each person on your list in the order in which the names appear. You can select any name on the list and use the up and down arrows to change the routing order.

As the routed file wends its way through the recipient list, Exchange Server takes care of giving instructions to each recipient, making it possible to track the document's travels (see Figure 3-9).

After the first person on the route has made changes to the workbook and saved them, Excel takes care of moving the document to the next person. When a routed file is in the Excel window, the File | Send To submenu changes to include the command Next Routing Recipient.

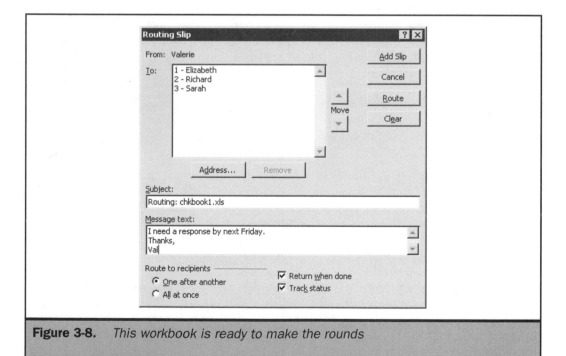

Figure 3-8. *This workbook is ready to make the rounds*

GETTING STARTED

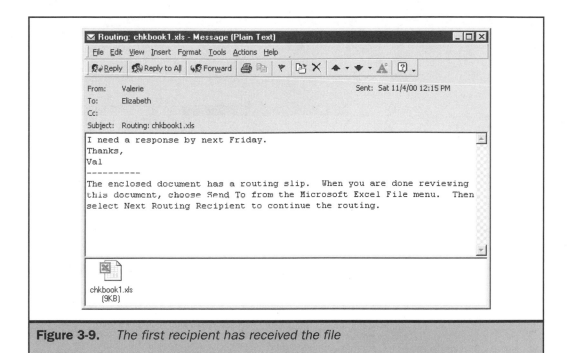

Figure 3-9.   *The first recipient has received the file*

Choosing Next Routing Recipient opens a Routing Slip dialog box that has the name of the next recipient on the routing list. (There's an additional choice to send the document without a routing slip, but that kills the whole point.)

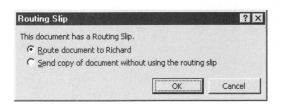

Clicking on OK sends the workbook off to the next person, where the same procedures occur. A status report is sent to the Inbox of the workbook's creator as each person routes the file to the next.

Eventually, the file returns to the person who started the whole thing, along with everyone's changes and comments.

Routing a Workbook to Everyone at Once

If you select All at Once as the routing scheme, each person gets a copy, along with routing instructions. When the recipients choose File | Send To | Next Routing Recipient, the routing message displays the original sender's name as the target recipient.

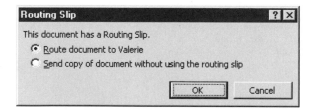

Eventually, the creator gets the files back from each recipient.

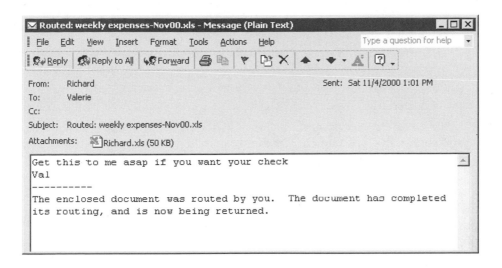

Posting Workbooks to Exchange Folders

If you're working with an Exchange Server system, there may be a public folder to which you should send your workbook. Perhaps a folder exists for budgets or expense account worksheets.

To post your workbook to an Exchange folder, choose File | Send To | Exchange Folder to open the Send To Exchange Folder dialog. Expand the public folders to find the target you need, select it, and click OK.

- You must have permission to post items to the target folder.

- If you have the right to create a public folder, you can click New Folder to create a new folder for this workbook.

Opening Text Files

Excel excels at data analysis, so it's quite common to import information from other software and let Excel "do its thing." Commonly, the data is a report from an accounting program. Letting Excel manipulate the data is a great way to learn what will happen if costs go up, sales prices are reduced, or any other event occurs that affects the bottom line.

When you export information from another software program, the resulting data file is usually text. However, the way the text is separated and positioned differs according to the type of export file you're creating. When you export from a program, be sure to select a file type that is suited for spreadsheet software. Usually, that means the file extension is .csv or .prn, but sometimes you find .txt.

After your exported file is saved, you can import it into Excel by following these steps:

- Click the Open button on the Standard toolbar (or use your favorite method of opening files).

- Click the arrow to the right of the Look In box and go to the folder that has the exported file.

- In the Open dialog box, click the arrow to the right of the Files of Type box and choose the type named Text Files (*.prn; *.txt; *.csv). Alternatively, you could choose All Files as the file type.

- Select the file you want to import into Excel and click Open.

This launches the Text Import Wizard, which walks you through the process of importing the text file into Excel. Figure 3-10 shows the first window the wizard presents.

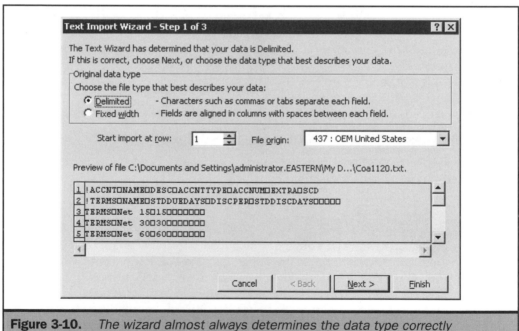

Figure 3-10. *The wizard almost always determines the data type correctly*

You can select a different row as the beginning of the import (some people like to omit the titles on the first row). Click Next to move to the next wizard window.

The second wizard window displays information that's related to the data type selected in the first window. Figure 3-11 is the second window if the data type is delimited.

Although Excel usually gets it right, if the delimiter character or the text qualifier is wrong, information about the proper settings should be available from the exporting program. If everything's okay, click Next.

The third wizard window (see Figure 3-12) is the place to do some preliminary formatting. Click each column and choose the formatting type for its data. Click the Advanced button to configure decimal and thousand separators.

Click Finish to import the file into Excel. If it looks right, congratulations! Choose File | Save As and save the file as an Excel Workbook. Now you can start manipulating the data without harming the data in the original software. If it doesn't look the way it should, close the file (don't save it) and start the import procedure again (using different selections).

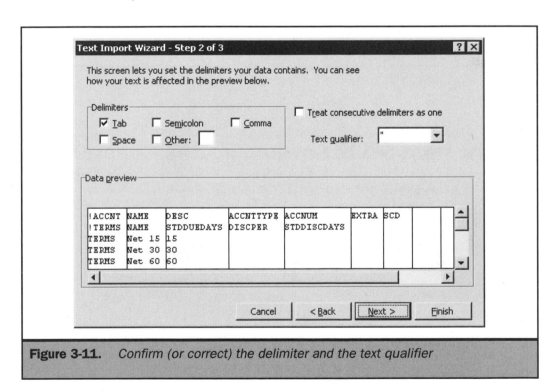

Figure 3-11.   *Confirm (or correct) the delimiter and the text qualifier*

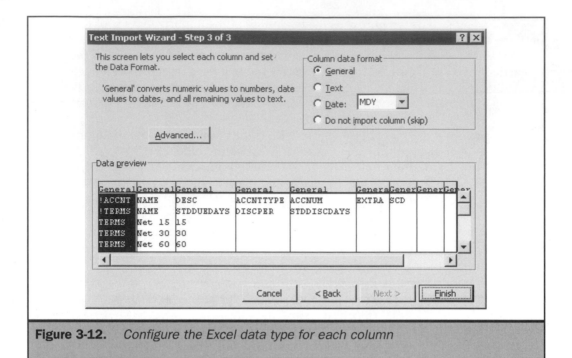

Figure 3-12. *Configure the Excel data type for each column*

Certification Skills Covered in This Chapter

If you're preparing for Microsoft Office User Specialist certification, here are the skills you learned in this chapter.

Skill Set	Activity
Managing workbooks	Manage workbook files and folders
Managing workbooks	Create workbooks using templates
Managing workbooks	Save workbooks using different names and file formats
Workgroup collaboration	Convert worksheets into Web pages

The
Complete
Reference

Excel
2002

Chapter 4

Manipulating Data

Very few workbooks have static data, and part of the reason for using Excel (instead of, for instance, a word processor) is to have the advantage of a dynamic document in which you can see the result of changes. It's a common occurrence to move, remove, and copy data and cells.

Moving and Copying

If cells in one row or column are needed in another row and column, you don't have to enter the data again. Instead, you can move or copy cell contents to another location in your workbook. You can also move and copy characters that are contained in a cell.

Moving removes an item from one location and places it in another location; copying leaves the first instance intact and replicates it in another location. The Windows terminology for these actions is *cut and paste* (for moving data) and *copy and paste* (for copying data).

Moving and Copying Contents

If there is a character or a string of characters in a cell that you want to use in another cell, use these steps to accomplish the task:

1. Double-click the cell that contains the characters.

2. Select the characters you want to manipulate.

3. Click the Cut tool on the Standard toolbar to remove the characters from the cell and place them on the clipboard.

4. Click the Copy tool on the Standard toolbar to copy the characters to the clipboard.

5. Double-click the target cell.

6. Click the Paste tool on the Standard toolbar to copy the contents from the clipboard to the target cell.

 Double-clicking a cell puts the cell in Edit mode. When you move the arrow keys, they stay within the cell instead of moving to an adjacent cell. Press the ENTER key to end Edit mode.

Moving and Copying Cells

You can move one or more cells from one location to another, either on the same worksheet or to another worksheet. There are several ways to accomplish this; the method you choose depends on the proximity of the target cells and whether or not those cells are empty.

GETTING STARTED

Start by selecting the cell(s) you want to move or copy. Then use one of these techniques to complete the action:

■ To move the cells to a blank column or row, drag your selection to the upper-left cell of the target location.

■ To copy the cells to a blank column or row, hold down the CTRL key as you drag them.

To drag cells, move your pointer to a border of the selection so the pointer turns into an arrow.

■ To replace existing cells, drag to the upper-left cell of the range you want to replace.

■ To move cells and insert them in a range of existing cells, press the SHIFT key while you drag.

■ To copy cells and insert them in a range of existing cells, press SHIFT-CTRL while you drag.

■ To move cells to a target location on another sheet or workbook, click the Cut button on the Standard toolbar. Select the upper-left cell of the target location and click the Paste button.

■ To copy cells to a target location on another sheet or workbook, click the Copy button on the Standard toolbar. Select the upper-left cell of the target location and click the Paste button.

You can right-click a selected cell or cells and choose the Cut, Copy, or Paste commands from the shortcut menu.

If you prefer the keyboard to the mouse, Excel offers keyboard combinations to accomplish cut, copy, and paste tasks:

Key Combination	Resulting Action
CTRL-C	Copies the selected cells
CTRL-C, CTRL-C (press twice)	Opens the Office Clipboard
CTRL-X	Cuts the selected cells
CTRL-V	Pastes the cells
DELETE	Clears the contents of the selected cells
CTRL- - (hyphen)	Deletes the selected cells
CTRL-SHIFT-+ (plus sign)	Inserts blank cells

Paste Options

After you paste cells, the animated border remains around the original cells. This means you can continue to paste the cells. This is a nifty way to put a formula or text into multiple locations. Press the ESC key to remove the animated border from the original cells.

When you copy and paste (not cut and paste), the Paste Options button appears next to the target cell. Move your pointer over the button to reveal an arrow, which you can click to display the options for pasting this data.

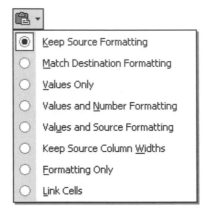

The number of options on the list varies, depending on the type of data you're copying.

Office Clipboard

Office 2002 comes with its own clipboard, and it collects multiple items as you cut and copy data from any application that recognizes and uses the Cut, Copy, and Paste commands.

Opening the Office Clipboard

You can open the Office Clipboard manually by choosing Edit | Office Clipboard. The clipboard appears on the task pane on the right side of your screen, and a clipboard icon appears on the taskbar tray (see Figure 4-1).

 If either the New Workbook or Search pane is open in the task pane, you can switch to the clipboard by clicking the arrow at the top of the task pane and selecting Clipboard.

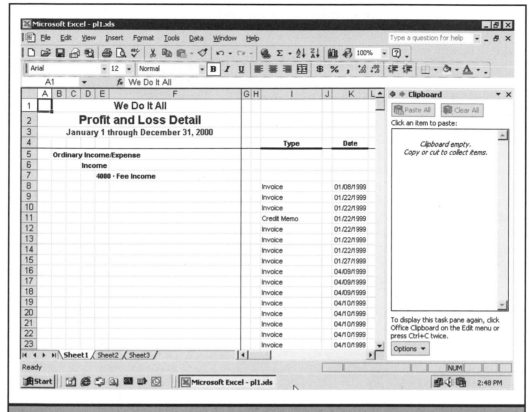

Figure 4-1.   *The clipboard pane appears in the application you're using when you open it; the clipboard icon on the taskbar tray is available to all the open applications*

When you're working in Excel (or another Office application), the clipboard opens automatically as a result of any of the following actions:

- Copying or cutting two different items consecutively in the same program
- Copying one item, pasting it, and then copying another item in the same program
- Copying one item twice in succession

Placing Data in the Office Clipboard

The clipboard collects the items you cut or copy in any application that can use the Cut or Copy commands. As soon as you cut or copy data, it's added to the clipboard collection. Then you can paste it from the clipboard into any document. The items stay on the clipboard until you exit all Office applications. If the clipboard is in the task pane, you can see the items you've collected.

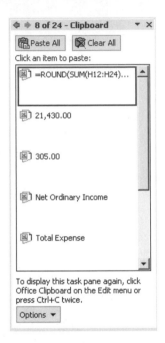

Here are the guidelines for sending items to the clipboard:

■ The clipboard can hold 24 items; when you add a 25th item, the oldest item is removed to make room for the new one.

■ The most recent item is at the top of the list.

- The most recent item is also copied to the Windows clipboard (which holds only one item at a time).
- If you cut or copy a cell that contains a formula, the current contents of the cell are sent to the clipboard, not the formula.
- To copy a formula to the clipboard, click the cell, specifically select the contents of the formula bar, and then choose Cut or Copy.
- Each item in the clipboard has an icon to indicate the source application.

If you switch to another Office application, the clipboard pane stays with the application you were using when you opened it. However, the clipboard icon in the taskbar tray is visible, and when you cut or copy in any Office application the taskbar icon displays information.

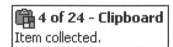

Pasting Data from the Office Clipboard

You can paste a single item by selecting the target cell and then clicking the item in the clipboard window. The Paste Options button appears. If you've been meandering through your spreadsheet, collecting data that you want to gather together in one place, choose Paste All. The items are pasted into consecutive cells in a column in the order in which you sent them to the clipboard.

Note *If only the clipboard icon on the taskbar is visible while you're in Excel, double-click the icon to display the clipboard contents.*

If you want to paste the last item you sent to the clipboard, you don't have to access the clipboard. Because the last item you cut or copied is always on the Windows clipboard, you can use the standard Windows paste functions (press CTRL-V, click the Paste icon on the standard toolbar, or use the Paste command from the Edit menu or the right-click shortcut menu).

Removing Items from the Office Clipboard

You can eliminate an item from the Office Clipboard in either of two ways:

- Right-click the item and choose Delete from the shortcut menu
- Select the item, then click the arrow and choose Delete from the drop-down menu.

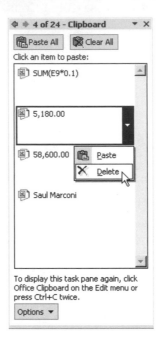

To get rid of all the items, click Clear All. No confirmation dialog appears, but the items are removed immediately.

Configuring the Office Clipboard

You can set options to control the way the clipboard works by clicking the Options button on the bottom of the clipboard pane. (If the clipboard isn't displayed, choose Edit | Office Clipboard or press CTRL-C twice in succession.)

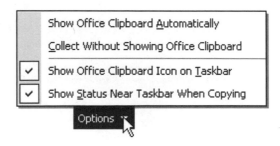

Select the options that make the clipboard useful and convenient for you:

- **Show Office Clipboard Automatically**   This option displays the clipboard automatically as soon as you cut or copy an item.
- **Collect Without Showing Office Clipboard**   This option automatically copies items to the clipboard without displaying the clipboard in the task pane.
- **Show Office Clipboard Icon on Taskbar**   This option puts a clipboard icon on the taskbar whenever the clipboard is active.
- **Show Status Near Taskbar When Copying**   This option turns on the display of messages over the taskbar icon whenever you put an item on the clipboard from any application

Using Undo and Redo

Excel records your actions in an Undo list, and if you change your mind after you've performed an action you can tell Excel to "undo" it. Use the Undo tool on the Standard toolbar to restore your worksheet to its previous state.

- Click the Undo button (or press CTRL-Z) to reverse your last action.
- Click the Redo button (or press CTRL-Y) to undo your Undo action.

Undo does not work if you save your workbook because the process of saving removes the contents of the Undo list.

Note   *You can never undo any action from the File menu.*

You can also take advantage of the Undo list and use Undo to reverse multiple actions. Each time you click the Undo button (or press CTRL-Z), you undo the next action in the list. The list starts with your last action, then moves to your next-to-last action, and keeps going back.

To view the Undo list, click the arrow to the right of the Undo button on the Standard toolbar.

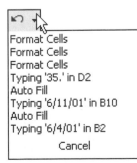

To undo multiple actions in one fell swoop, select the earliest action you want to undo from the Undo list. All the actions you've performed since that action are also selected, and all of them are reversed. You cannot selectively undo an action that's within the list.

As you undo actions, they're placed in the Redo list. You can click the Redo button (or press CTRL-Y) repeatedly to redo the actions you've undone, or click the arrow to the right of the Redo button to select a group of actions

Using Go To

Excel provides a tool named Go To, which has two uses: it can move you quickly to any cell in your worksheet; or it can select cells based on their content. The latter function is a quick way to see an overview of your worksheet design, and it's also a quick way to select cells for moving or copying operations.

To use the Excel Go To feature, press CTRL-G (or choose Edit | Go To from the menu bar) to open the Go To dialog box.

The primary use of the Go To dialog box is to move to a specific cell. When the dialog box opens, your cursor is in the Reference field so you can enter the cell address you wish to move to, and then click OK to move to that cell. This is easier than scrolling through a large worksheet to get to a cell that's not currently visible.

However, if you click Special in the Go To dialog box, the Go To Special dialog box opens, offering a list of criteria you can use to select cells automatically.

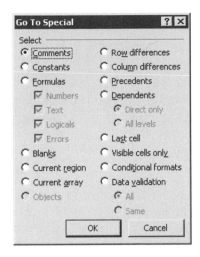

The choices in this dialog box let you select cells by specifying the contents. Using the Go To Special dialog box is certainly easier than going through all the cells in your worksheet to see which cells meet the condition you need.

If you preselect a range before opening the dialog box, only that range is searched. If you select a cell, the entire worksheet is searched. Select the data type to search for by clicking the item, using these guidelines:

- **Comments** Includes all cells with comments.

- **Constants** Includes cells that do not contain a formula or begin with an equal sign.

- **Formulas** Selects cells that contain formulas. Use the Numbers, Text, Logicals, and Errors options to narrow the choices.

- **Blanks** Selects all blank cells up to the last cell that has content.

- **Current Region** Selects a region around the selected cell, using the nearest blank rows and columns as the outside border of the region.

- **Current Array** If the selected cell is part of an array, the entire array is selected.

- **Objects** Selects graphic objects, such as charts or buttons you've placed in cells.

- **Row Differences** Selects all cells that have different content from the comparison cells in a row (which are all the cells in the same column as the selected cell).

- **Column Differences**   Same as Row Differences, applied to columns.

- **Precedents**   Selects all the cells that are referenced by the formula in the selected cell.

- **Dependents**   Selects all the cells that contain formulas that reference the selected cell. You can narrow the choices by opting for direct or indirect references.

- **Last Cell**   Selects the last cell in the worksheet that has content (either data or formatting).

- **Visible Cells Only**   Selects only visible cells. If you make changes to the cells selected with this option, those changes will not affect hidden cells.

- **Conditional Formats**   Selects cells that have had conditional formats applied to them. Use the All and Same buttons to select all such cells or to select only those cells that have the same conditional formats as the selected cell.

- **Data Validation**   Selects cells with validation rules. Use the All and Same buttons to select all cells with rules or to select only those cells that have the same rules as the selected cell.

After you select the criteria, choose OK to return to your worksheet, where the cells that meet your criteria are selected.

- Move or copy the selected cells using the tools described earlier in this chapter.

- Apply formatting or otherwise manipulate the selected cells.

There's another use for selecting cells depending on their content. You can view your worksheet with the cells highlighted to see how the selected cells fit in your worksheet design. For example, you can select all the cells with formulas to make sure there's a formula in every cell in a row or column that you've designated a total row or column.

To get a bird's-eye view, zoom out by choosing View | Zoom from the menu bar to open the Zoom dialog box.

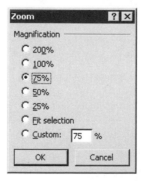

Change the zoom setting to see more of your worksheet (see Figure 4-2).

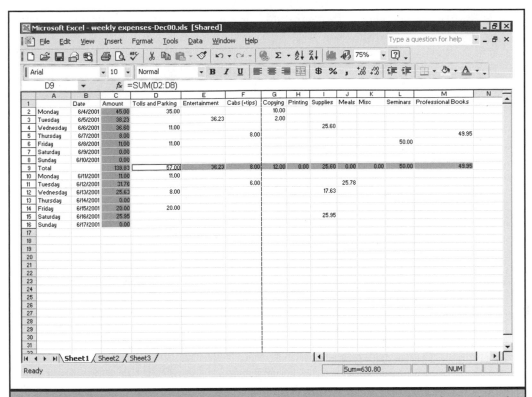

Figure 4-2. *Check to see that your selected cell types are all there and are placed where they should be*

Using Paste Special

Paste Special is the flip side of Go To Special. It enables you to narrow your choice of what to paste after you've performed a copy action (Paste Special doesn't work with Cut). This means that after you select cells and choose Copy, you can decide to paste only the data that meets your specifications. For example, you can opt to paste only formulas.

Here's how to be selective about what you paste:

1. Highlight the cells you want to manipulate.

2. Press CTRL-C.

3. Select the upper-left cell of the target (Paste) location.

4. Right-click and choose Paste Special from the shortcut menu to open the Paste Special dialog box.

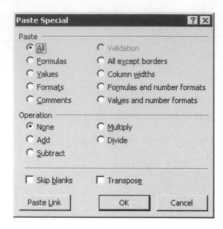

5. Select the appropriate Paste option, using these guidelines:

- **All**   This is identical to clicking the Paste tool or pressing CTRL-V—it pastes everything you just copied.

- **Formulas**   Pastes only formulas as displayed in the formula bar.

- **Values**   Pastes only values, as displayed in the cells. If the cell has a formula, this pastes the formula result as a value.

- **Formats**   Pastes only cell formatting.

- **Comments**   Pastes only comments.

- **Validation**   Pastes data validation rules.

- **All Except Borders**   Pastes contents and formatting, except borders.

- **Column Widths**   Pastes the width of one column to another column. Useful for resizing columns based on the width of a selected column.

- **Formulas and Number Formats**   Pastes only the formulas and the number formatting configuration options.

- **Values and Number Formats**   Pastes only the values and the number formatting configuration options.

If your target location is not a range of blank cells but instead is a range of cells with content, you can use the Operations section of the dialog box to instruct Excel to perform a mathematical operation with the numerical contents of the original and target cells.

- **None**   The paste operation is a straightforward paste, and the copied cells replace the cells in the target location.

■ **Add**   Adds the numerical data you're pasting to the numerical data already in the cell. For example, if you copy three cells whose values are 1, 2, and 3 and paste them over three cells whose values are 4, 5, and 6, the results will be three cells whose values are 5 (4+1), 7 (5+2), and 9 (6+3).

■ **Subtract**   Subtracts the values of the copied cells from the cells into which you're copying the data.

■ **Multiply**   Multiplies the values of the copied cells by the values of the target cells.

■ **Divide**   Divides the values of the target cells by the values in the copied cells.

■ **Skip Blanks**   Selects this to ensure that blank cells you've copied don't overwrite target cells with data.

■ **Transpose**   Selects this to switch copied rows to columns and copied columns to rows.

Working with Multiple Worksheets

Excel workbooks have multiple worksheets (also called *sheets*), among which you can consolidate and link information.

Moving Between Worksheets

To move between worksheets, click the tab for the worksheet (called a *sheet tab*). Worksheet tabs appear just below the worksheet window. By default, the sheets are not named (unless you count Sheet 1, Sheet 2, and so on as a name).

Renaming Worksheets

If you use multiple worksheets, it's a good idea to name them so you can remind yourself of each sheet's contents. Sheet 3 is not a terribly descriptive name if you've used the sheet to store totals from cells in other sheets. Use these steps to rename a worksheet:

1. Double-click the sheet tab to highlight the name (type and background colors are reversed).

2. Enter the new name.

3. Press ENTER.

Inserting and Deleting Worksheets

By default, Excel workbooks have three worksheets. If you need additional sheets, you can add them. You can also delete unused worksheets to save disk space.

To insert a worksheet, follow these steps:

1. Click the sheet tab of the worksheet to the right of the place you want the new sheet (sheets are automatically inserted to the left of the currently selected sheet).

2. Choose Insert | Worksheet from the menu bar.

Don't worry about the placement of the new sheet (you may want it to be the last sheet and there seems to be no way to do that) because you can change it. (This is covered in the next section, "Moving and Copying Worksheets.")

To delete a worksheet, click the sheet tab and choose Edit | Delete Sheet. Excel asks you to confirm the fact that you want to delete the worksheet.

To delete multiple worksheets, hold down the CTRL key as you click on each sheet tab. Then choose Edit | Delete Sheet.

 The deletion of a sheet is not sent to the Undo list, so you can't undo your action.

Moving and Copying Worksheets

You can move worksheets within a workbook or to another workbook. Moving sheets within a workbook is really just changing the position of a worksheet. You can line them up from left to right in any order that makes sense to you. Moving worksheets to another workbook removes the sheet from the first workbook and inserts it in the target workbook.

Moving and Copying Worksheets Within a Workbook

To move or copy a worksheet within the same workbook, right-click on the sheet tab and choose Move or Copy from the shortcut menu. This opens the Move or Copy dialog box.

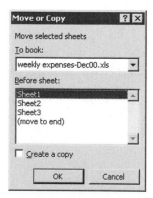

- Select the sheet you want to appear to the right of the sheet you want to move, or choose the (Move to End) option.

■ If you want to copy the sheet, select the Create a Copy option at the bottom of the dialog box.

If you copy a sheet, the new sheet tab displays the same name as the original sheet with (2) appended to the name. You'll probably want to change the name.

Moving and Copying Worksheets to Another Workbook

You can also move or copy a worksheet to another workbook, but in order to accomplish this, both the source and target workbooks must be loaded in Excel. Right-click on the sheet tab and choose Move or Copy from the shortcut menu. Click the arrow to the right of the To Book text box and select the target workbook. If you're copying instead of moving, select the Create a Copy option at the bottom of the dialog box.

You can also move or copy a worksheet and start a new workbook at the same time. Click the arrow to the right of the To Book text box and select the (New Book) option. A new workbook opens with the selected sheet installed.

Linking Worksheets

If you have data in one worksheet that you would like to use in a second worksheet you can, of course, copy from the original worksheet and paste it into the second. However, if the original information is not static and you want any changes in the original to be reflected in the second worksheet, you must create a link. This means that any time the data in the original worksheet is updated, the change appears in the worksheet into which the information was copied.

Here's how you can link information from one worksheet to another:

1. In the original worksheet, select the cells you want to copy.

2. Press CTRL-C to copy the cells.

3. Move to the target worksheet.

4. Move the cursor to the first cell of the target paste area.

5. Right-click and select Paste Special to open the Paste Special dialog box.

6. Select the appropriate Paste and Operation options (see the discussion in the section "Using Paste Special," earlier in this chapter).

7. Click the Paste Link button to paste the data as a link and return to the target worksheet.

You can also use the Paste Link option to copy and link data from one part of the current worksheet to another. The procedure is the same as linking between worksheets, except that you copy and paste within the same worksheet.

Using AutoFill

There are times when you may want to copy the contents of a cell to one or more adjacent cells. You could, of course, follow the earlier steps and use the Copy and Paste functions, or you could save yourself some work and use the AutoFill feature.

The AutoFill feature has two uses: copying and extending. *Copying* is replicating the data in the original cell to a target cell, or multiple target cells. *Extending* is filling the target cells with data that is really a series (such as the days of the week).

Automatically Copying Data

If you want to copy the data in one cell to a group of adjacent cells, select the source cell and place your mouse pointer over the lower-right corner of the cell. Your pointer turns into a fill marker. Then drag over all the adjacent cells into which you want to copy the data. Release the mouse button, and Excel automatically "fills" each selected cell with the contents of the original cell.

Automatically Copying Formulas

If the source cell has a formula, the AutoFill feature adjusts the formula logically. For example, if the source cell address is B15 and the formula is =SUM(B2:B14), dragging across columns C through F produces the formula =SUM(C2:C14) in cell C15, and so on.

AutoFilling a Series

One handy use of the Fill feature is to create incremental series of number or dates. When you select two or more cells that demonstrate the series pattern, Excel does the rest.

For instance, suppose you want to create a sales report and have the columns include weekly sales data. Rather than title each column in the report with the starting date of the individual reporting weeks, you can have Excel do it for you automatically. Here's how:

1. In the title cell of the first column, enter the starting date of the first week.

2. Move to the cell to the right and enter the date of the second week. By entering the second date, you've established the pattern. In this case it will be the first date plus seven days.

3. Select both cells.

4. Drag the fill handle of the second cell to the right and cover as many columns as you have weeks for which to report sales.

5. Release the mouse button, and Excel automatically fills in the dates for you.

Tip *As you drag, Excel displays the data it's entering in each cell as a screen tip.*

The same procedure works with numbers. If you create enough source cells to establish a pattern, Excel will figure it out. For example, type the number **3** in a cell, the number **7** in the next cell, and the number **11** in the third cell. Select the three cells and drag to AutoFill a group of adjacent cells. The AutoFill feature will put 15 in the next cell, 19 in the cell after that, and so on.

AutoFill can even be used with a combination of numbers and text. For example, if you have ten cash registers to track, you could enter **Register1** in the first row, highlight it, and drag the fill handle down 9 cells, and Excel would enter *Register2, Register3,* and so on for each succeeding cell.

Using Built-In AutoFill Series

Excel comes with some built-in series so you don't have to use two cells to establish a pattern. The built-in series are for the days of the week and months of the year. Therefore, if you type **Monday** in the first cell and drag the fill handle over the next three cells, you'll end up with Tuesday, Wednesday, and Thursday in those cells.

Creating an AutoFill Series

You can even create your own custom series that Excel will automatically fill in whenever you need to use the series. This is useful for any list you use frequently in Excel—perhaps a list of branch offices or employee names. To make your own custom series, follow these steps:

1. Select Tools | Options from the menu bar to open the Options dialog box.

2. Click the Custom Lists tab to view the existing Custom Lists.

3. Select New List from the Customs Lists box.

4. Click Add to activate the List entries text box, which puts a blinking cursor in the List Entries text box.

5. Type the first entry, then press ENTER to move to the next line and create the next entry (see Figure 4-3).

6. Continue until all entries have been added.

7. Click Add to save the list in the Custom Lists box.

8. Click OK to close the dialog box.

If the items you want to turn into an AutoFill Custom List are already entered in your worksheet, you don't have to type the entries. Instead, enter the cell range in the Import List From Cells box and click the Import button.

To use the new list, simply type one of the entries from the list into a cell and drag the fill handle across adjacent cells. Excel starts with the entry you typed and fills cells with each subsequent list entry.

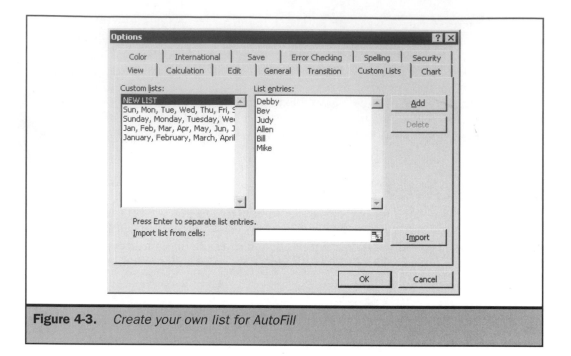

Figure 4-3. *Create your own list for AutoFill*

Overriding AutoFill

For those times when you actually need a group of adjacent cells that repeat the word Monday, or the same date, you certainly don't want to enter the data in each cell—it's far easier to drag. Hold down the CTRL key while you drag, and Excel will fill each cell you pass with the same data as the source cell.

Finding and Replacing Data

If you need to find some particular string of characters in your worksheet, it's much too onerous to look into each cell. Even more oppressive is the need to find a string of characters that must be changed. For instance, perhaps you entered a customer named Smith, Inc., in a zillion cells, and you just learned the company was sold and is now receiving invoices as Jones, Inc. Excel has features to help you find data and also replace it.

Using Find

When you need to find data, press CTRL-F (or choose Edit | Find from the menu bar) to open the Find and Replace dialog box with the Find tab in the foreground.

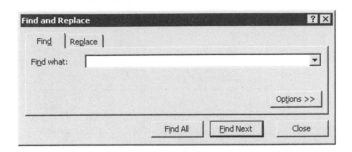

 You can select a range of cells in the worksheet before opening the Find dialog box if you want to limit the search to those selected cells.

Follow these steps to search for data:

1. Enter the word(s) or number(s) you want to locate in the Find What text box.

2. Click Find Next (or press ENTER), and Excel finds the first occurrence of your search criteria and selects it.

3. To search for the next occurrence, press ENTER or click Find Next again. (The Find dialog box remains on the screen so you can continue to press ENTER and search).

4. Press ESC or click Close to stop searching.

To search again after you close the dialog box, press CTRL-F to reopen it. The Find What text box contains the last string you searched for. Click the arrow to the right of the Find What text box to see previous search strings.

Finding All Occurrences of a String

If you know the string you're searching for exists in multiple cells, you don't have to keep pressing ENTER or clicking Find Next to get to a specific location. Instead, after you enter the string, click Find All. The results are returned in a box below the Find and Replace dialog box. Select the appropriate listing and close the dialog box to move to that cell immediately.

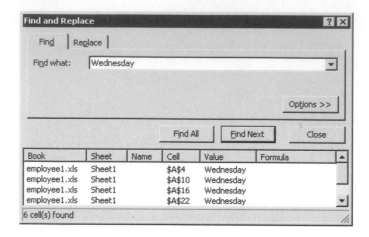

Using Wildcards

You can use wildcards to narrow your search so that you find only information that starts with, ends with, or contains certain characters. For example, suppose you want to find all instances of *northeast* and *southeast*. You could perform a separate Find operation for each, or you could use wildcards in your search and get both in one pass. Here's how you use wildcards when finding and replacing:

- **?**   A question mark is a stand-in for an individual character. If you wanted to find both *Bookman* and *Bookmen*, enter **Bookm?n** in the Find What text box. Entering ???4 matches all numbers that have any three characters before the number 4.

- *****   An asterisk stands in for multiple characters. In the earlier example of *northeast* and *southeast*, you would enter ***east** to find any word ending in east.

- **~**   The tilde enables you to search for wildcard characters, because it negates the character's role as a wildcard. For instance, enter **~?** to search for a question mark.

Setting Additional Criteria for Find

The Find and Replace dialog box offers additional options that let you narrow the search by being more specific. Click the Options button to open additional choices on the dialog box.

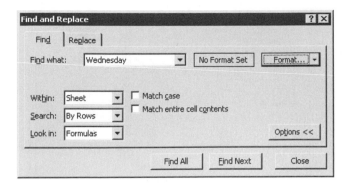

- **Within**   Click the arrow to the right of the text box to select Sheet or Workbook.

- **Search**   Click the arrow to the right of the text box to instruct Excel to search by rows or columns. Usually, searching by columns is faster (unless your worksheet has a hundred columns and ten rows).

- **Look In**   Click the arrow to the right of this box to restrict the search to a particular element. Your choices are Formulas, Values, or Comments.

- **Match Case**   Select this option to tell Excel to find only those occurrences that match the case in the Find What box. If you entered **Smith**, the Find tool won't stop at *smith*.

- **Match Entire Cell Contents**   This option tells Excel to skip cells that have data in addition to the search string. For example, if you're searching for **book**, the Find tool won't stop at cells that contain *bookman* or *bookie*.

- **Match Format**   You can use the format button to instruct the Find tool to check the formatting in order to determine whether a cell that contains your string is really a match:

  - Click the Format button to open the Find Format dialog box shown in Figure 4-4 (which is exactly like the Format Cells dialog box).

  - Click the arrow to the right of the format button and select Choose Format from Cell to return to your worksheet where you can click a cell that has the formatting you're looking for.

Using Replace

If the reason you need to find data is to change it, you don't have to find it, close the dialog box, change the data, open the dialog box to find the next occurrence, change

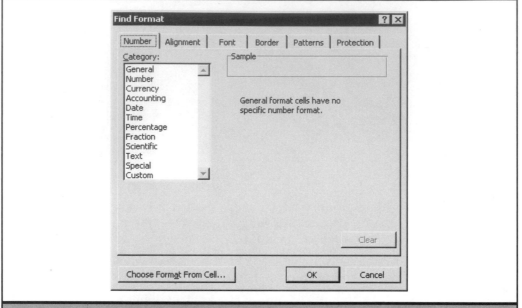

Figure 4-4. *Use the tabs in the Find Format dialog box to specify the formatting you're looking for*

that, and keep performing this task over and over. Instead you can use the Replace tool. Here's how to tell Excel to replace data it finds with other data:

1. Press CTRL-H to open the Find and Replace dialog box with the Replace tab in the foreground.

2. Enter the search string in the Find What box.

3. Enter the replacement text in the Replace With text box.

4. Click the Options button to set any additional criteria (these are the same options available in the Find tab).

To approve each replacement, follow these steps:

1. Click Find Next. Excel moves to the next occurrence of the search data and selects the cell.

2. Click Replace if you want to make the replacement, then click Find Next to move to the next occurrence.

3. If you don't want to approve the replacement, click Find Next to move on.

To replace all the instances of the search data with the replacement data, click Replace All. This can be dangerous, especially if the search data is a common word. For example, if you want to replace *other* with *else*, you could end up with *melse*, *brelse*, *elsewise*, or other strange combinations.

Tip *Save the workbook before performing a Replace All operation. If things don't turn out the way you expected, you can close the workbook without saving it and then open it to start again.*

Certification Skills Covered in This Chapter

If you're preparing for Microsoft Office User Specialist certification, here are the skills you learned in this chapter.

Skill	Activity
Working with cells and cell data	Find and replace cell data and formats
Modifying workbooks	Insert and delete worksheets
Modifyng workbooks	Modify worksheet names and positions

Chapter 5

Structuring Worksheets

The way your worksheet looks on the screen and in print plays a large part in determining its usefulness. It's far easier to read and understand a worksheet that's structured properly. This chapter is focused on all the skills you need to design, arrange, and present data in a worksheet that is professional, slick, and useful.

Adding Columns, Rows, and Cells

It's common to decide you need some additional columns and rows in your worksheet after you've been working on it for a while. Perhaps you need to insert an entire new set of data items in the middle of an existing series of rows, or some new categories require you to put additional columns within existing columns.

Understanding Excel Limits on Columns and Rows

You can't really add columns and rows to your worksheet. Every Excel worksheet has 65,536 rows and 256 columns (the last column is IV). That never changes. If you reach the maximum number of columns and insert a column, you lose a column from the extreme right edge (it just falls off the end of the world). If you already have data in the 256th column, you can't add another column because Excel won't push a column off the edge of the world if it contains any data. This is true even if lots of columns before the 256th column are empty. In this case, you must delete a column in order to add one. The same rule applies to rows.

This knowledge can be useful if you want to impose controls over your worksheet. You can create a deterrent to adding columns or rows for users with whom you share your worksheets. To make it much more difficult for other users to change your lineup of rows and columns, just put data into the 256th column and the 65,536th row. Here's how:

1. Press CTRL-G (or choose Edit | Go To from the menu bar).

2. In the Go To dialog box, enter **iv65536** and click OK to travel to that cell.

3. Enter any character into the cell (just type an *x*).

4. Press CTRL-HOME to return to the top of your worksheet.

If any user tries to add a column or a row, an error message displays.

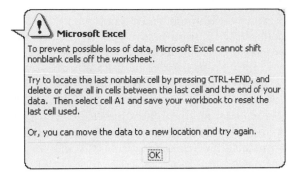

The error message will stop most users because it seems to be a lot of trouble to perform the necessary tasks and also because many users are afraid they'll mess up the worksheet. In fact, many users don't understand the error message because they're not aware of the fixed number of columns and rows. Nor are they aware of the fact that inserting data in the outside edge column and row prevents additions. I call this a psychological deterrent.

Adding Columns

New columns are inserted to the left of your pointer's position. For example, if your pointer is in column F, the new column will be column F and the column in which your pointer was located when you added the column will become column G.

There are a couple of methods you can use to insert a new column:

■ Click any cell in a column, or a column heading, and then choose Insert | Columns from the menu bar.

■ Click the column heading to select an entire column, and then right-click and choose Insert from the shortcut menu.

As soon as the new column is created, an icon for the Format Painter tool appears next to it. Place your pointer on the icon to reveal an arrow, which you can click to display a menu of choices for formatting the new column.

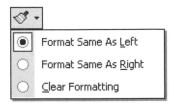

If you want to add multiple columns, you don't have to do so one column at a time. Instead, you can select multiple columns before you invoke the Insert command. Excel adds the same number of new columns as you originally selected.

For instance, select multiple cells that are horizontally adjacent (drag your mouse from cell D3 to cell F3, spanning three columns). Choose Insert | Columns from the menu bar to have Excel insert three new columns to the left of cell D3.

Or drag your mouse across the column headings to select a specific number of columns. Right-click and choose Insert from the shortcut menu. Excel inserts the same number of columns as you originally selected.

Adding Rows

Inserting new rows is similar to inserting new columns. The new rows are inserted above the row in which your pointer is located when you invoke the Insert command. Use either of these methods to insert a single row:

- Position your pointer in a cell and choose Insert | Rows from the menu bar.

- Select an entire row by clicking on the row heading. Then right-click and select Insert from the shortcut menu.

Once again, the Format Painter icon offers an easy way to format the new row without taking extra steps.

To insert multiple rows, use one of these methods:

- Select multiple cells in a column and choose Insert | Rows from the menu bar. The number of new rows added is equal to the number of cells you selected.

- Select multiple rows with the row heading buttons and right-click. Choose Insert from the shortcut menu to insert the same number of rows you selected.

Adding Cells

You can also insert cells, which is a bit more complicated because this procedure usually results in data being moved. There are fewer reasons to perform this maneuver than there are to add columns or rows, but on those rare occasions when it's needed, it's really handy. (Most people never have a reason to use this procedure). The fact is, the only time I've ever inserted cells is when I needed to correct a mistake—I'd placed data in the wrong cells. If I'm off by one cell, this procedure fixes it.

For example, look at Figure 5-1. It's a checkbook worksheet and the person who uses it just realized that starting with check #111, everything is wrong. The amount entered for check #111 should have been entered for check #112, and the real amount

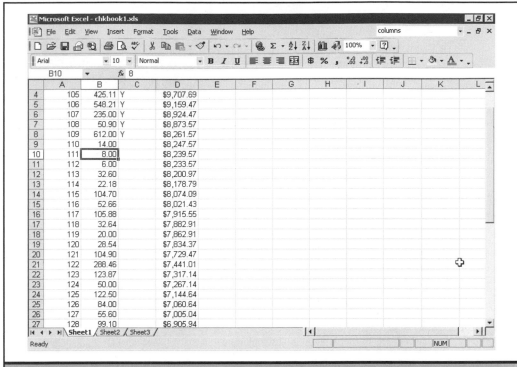

Figure 5-1.   *The prospect of reentering all the numbers is daunting, but luckily inserting a cell fixes everything*

for check #111 ($6.00) must be entered. Of course, every check amount below this point is wrong. The amounts should be attached to the next highest check number.

There's a quick fix for the problem, thanks to the ability to insert a cell:

1. Select the cell that has to be emptied of data.

2. Right-click and choose Insert from the shortcut menu.

3. In the Insert dialog box, select the appropriate movement for the cells (the choices are to the right or down, and in this case the appropriate selection is down).

4. Click OK.

Now look at the checkbook worksheet, shown in Figure 5-2. The empty cell receives the correct amount for the check ($8.00), and the rest of the data is correct.

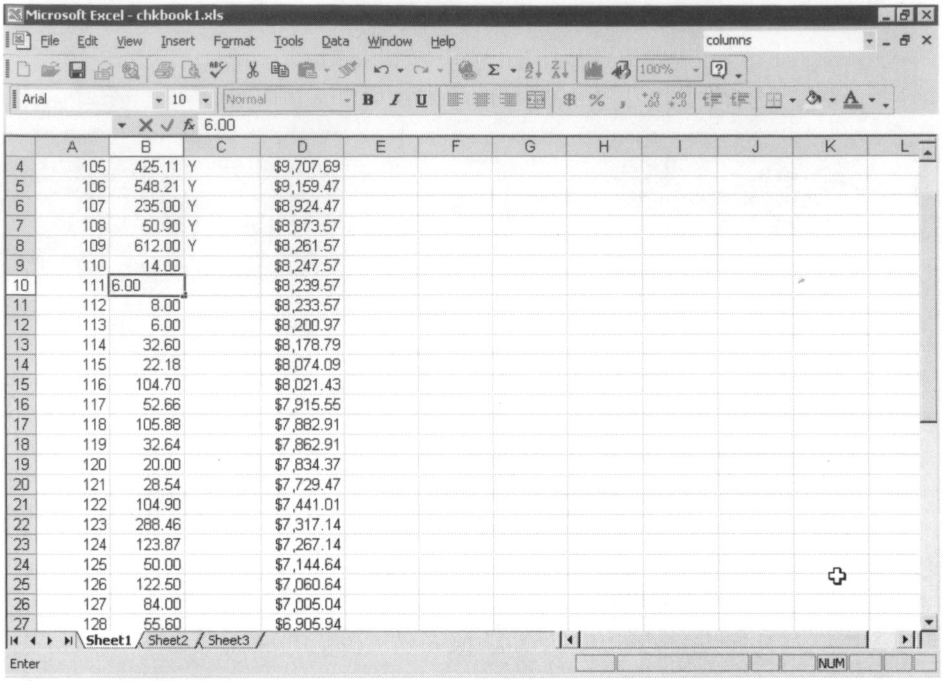

Figure 5-2. *Inserting a cell can save a lot of work*

Deleting Columns, Rows, and Cells

It's occasionally necessary to get rid of a column, row, or cell. I don't mean delete the data, I mean delete the element. Most of the time you need to delete a column or a row because you don't need it; you are never going to put data in it. This usually happens when you predesign your worksheet and overestimate the columns or rows you'll need. For instance, you may design a worksheet that tracks items by the days of the week. You fill in seven columns with weekday names and then realize you don't need the weekends because you're tracking stuff you did at work (and you never work on the weekends).

Select any cell in the column or row and right-click. If you're deleting a cell, select that cell. Then choose Delete from the shortcut menu. (You could also choose Edit | Delete from the menu bar.) The Delete dialog box appears.

- If you want to delete a cell, choose Shift Cells Left or Shift Cells Up, depending on the way you want your data to move.
- Choose Entire Row to delete the row.
- Choose Entire Column to delete the column.

 Remember that there are potentially dangerous results when you delete a cell. All the remaining data moves to other rows or columns.

If you make a mistake, click the Undo button on the Standard toolbar.

Hiding Columns and Rows

There are a couple of reasons to hide columns and rows in your worksheet. The most common (and most obvious) reason is that you don't want users to see those columns or rows. When you print a worksheet, hidden columns and rows don't print.

However, I also use this feature to "neaten up" my worksheets. I hide all the columns and rows that aren't used. This means my data-filled worksheet is the only thing on the screen, and it's not surrounded by a lot of empty columns and rows. Eventually, as I gather data, those columns and rows will fill with data, but now they're just in my way. A nice side effect is that it makes my worksheet look smaller, more compact, and therefore less complicated (making it easier to face the work that has to be done).

You're not really hiding the columns and rows you decide to secrete; you're just reducing their size (width or height) to zero.

Hiding Columns

When you want to hide a column, you begin by clicking its heading button to select it. You can also hide multiple columns by using one of these methods:

- Drag your mouse across contiguous columns.
- Select the first of contiguous columns; then hold down the SHIFT key while you click the last column in the group.
- Hold down the CTRL key while you click the heading button for columns that are not contiguous.

When you've selected the columns you want to hide, right-click and choose Hide from the shortcut menu (or choose Format | Column | Hide from the menu bar). The column disappears.

 You can also drag a column's border (the line to the right of the heading button) to the left until it meets the border of the adjacent column.

Hiding Rows

If you want to hide a row, select it by clicking its heading button. Then right-click and choose Hide from the shortcut menu (or choose Format | Row | Hide from the menu bar).

To hide multiple rows:

- Drag your mouse up or down across contiguous rows.
- Select the first of contiguous rows, then hold down the SHIFT key while you click the last row in the group.
- Hold down the CTRL key while you click the heading button for multiple rows that are not contiguous.

After the rows are selected, right-click and choose Hide. The row disappears.

 You can also hide a row by dragging its border (the line below the heading button) upward until it meets the border of the row above.

Unhiding Columns and Rows

You can deduce which columns or rows are hidden in a worksheet because the letters in the column headings or the numbers in the row headings are missing (see Figure 5-3). Also, if you look very carefully, you have a very good monitor, and you have excellent

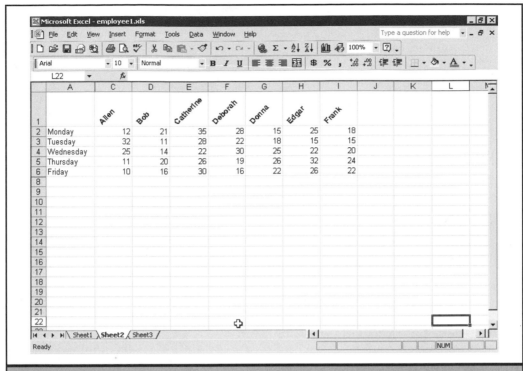

Figure 5-3. *Column B and Row 7 are obviously missing*

eyesight, you can see that the border line where the column is hidden is slightly thicker than the other border lines in the column or row.

There are two ways to unhide a column or row:

- Select both of the columns on either side of the hidden column (or the rows on either side of the hidden row) and right-click. Choose Unhide from the shortcut menu.

- Press F5 to open a Go To dialog box and then enter any cell in the hidden column or row. For example, to unhide column G, enter G1 (or G2 or Ganything). This selects that cell, and you can choose Format | Column | Unhide from the menu bar.

Freezing Panes

Most of your worksheets have headings or titles in the top row or the first column (or both). As the worksheet grows larger and you scroll over and down, you can lose track of the titles (see Figure 5-4).

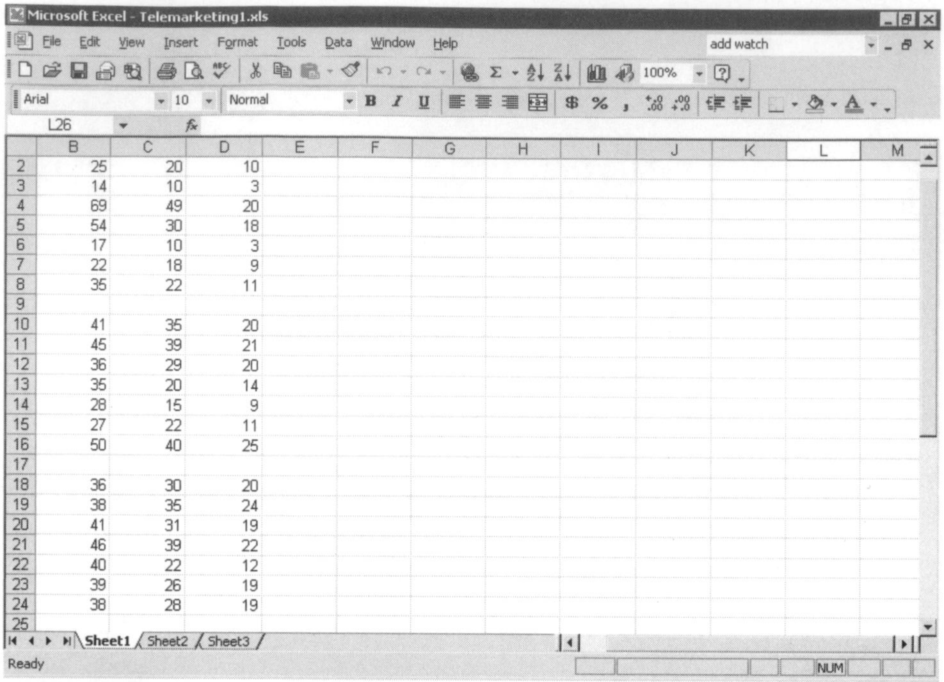

Figure 5-4. *This is a bunch of meaningless numbers*

It would be handy if the title columns and rows were always on the window so you could see the meaning of the data. That feature is called *freezing panes,* and it's easy to accomplish. Move your pointer so it's in the cell that's below the row you want to freeze and to the right of the column you want to freeze. For example, if you want to freeze the first two columns and the top row, select cell C2.

	A	B	C	D
1	Day	Date	Calls	Apptmts
2	Monday	5/7/2001	25	20
3	Tuesday	5/8/2001	14	10
4	Wednesd:	5/9/2001	69	49
5	Thursday	5/10/2001	54	30
6	Friday	5/11/2001	17	10

Choose Window | Freeze Panes from the menu bar. A thin line appears to indicate the pane. More important, as you scroll across and down, the rows and columns in your frozen pane remain in the window.

To unfreeze the panes, choose Window | Unfreeze Panes from the menu bar. It doesn't matter where your pointer is when you're unfreezing panes.

Changing Column Width and Row Height

If you want to change the size of cells, Excel has a couple of methods you can use. You cannot, of course, change the size of one individual cell, you can only change the size of a column or a row.

Changing Column Width

Technically, Excel measures the width of a column in terms of the number of characters you can enter into the cell if you start with 0 (that's a zero) and type 1, 2, and so on. The measurement for the default cell width is 8.43, which means you'll have room left after you type the 8, and you'll overflow into the next cell when you type the 9. That's a silly, meaningless number of course, because if you're using proportional fonts (the default font, Arial, is a proportional font), the 3 is twice the width of the 1, so you couldn't fit 8.43 characters in a cell if all the characters were the number 3. Also, the whole mathematical approach falls apart if you change the size of the font.

Changing the Width of a Single Column

If you only need to change the width of a single column or a couple of individual columns, there are several methods you can use to accomplish this quickly:

- Double-click the right border of the column heading button to widen the column to the size of the widest entry in that column.

- Drag the right column border to the width you need.

- Select the heading button and right-click. Then choose Column Width from the shortcut menu to bring up the Column Width dialog box, where you can specify a new number (using the Excel measurement value system of number of characters).

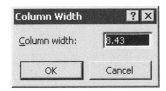

Changing the Width of a Group of Columns

If you need to change the width of an entire section of your worksheet, select all the columns you want to change using one of the following methods:

- Drag your mouse across all the columns.

- Hold down the CTRL key while you click on each column heading button to select additional columns.

- Select the first column; then hold down the SHIFT key and select the last column. All the columns between the first and last are selected.

After you've selected the columns, right-click and choose Column Width from the shortcut menu. Then enter a new number in the Column Width dialog box.

Changing the Width of All Columns

There are two ways to change the width of all the columns in your worksheet.

Click the Select All button (the button in the upper-left corner of your worksheet) to select every column. Then right-click, choose Column Width, and enter a number in the Column Width dialog box.

Without selecting any columns, choose Format | Column | Standard Width to open the Standard Width dialog box. Enter a new number for the width, which becomes the new default width for the worksheet.

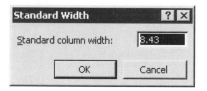

It's important to realize that the new standard width number you enter is the default for those columns that haven't been changed by any of the methods described here. If you change the width of specific columns, you've configured them to ignore the default width. Changing the default width doesn't change the fact that they're configured individually. If you want all the columns in your worksheet to be the same width, don't change individual columns, just change the standard width. Of course, if you make the decision to standardize after you've already customized a column or two, you'll have to go back and change their width measurements to match the new standard.

Changing Row Height

Row height is a measurement based on points (a point is the unit of measurement used in printing to measure the height of a character).

The default height of the rows in an Excel worksheet is set to match the size of the default font size, which is 10 points.

Changing Row Height Automatically

Excel doesn't lop off the top or bottom of characters in a cell the way it truncates characters that don't fit into the width of the cell. Therefore, if you make your characters taller, the height of the row changes to accommodate your new size.

1. Select the cell(s) or the row for which you want to change the size of the font.

2. Click the arrow to the right of the Font Size box on the Formatting toolbar to see the available sizes for the current font.

3. Select a font size.

   ■ If you select a cell or several cells, only the characters in those cells change size, but the entire row changes its height (if you make the font larger).

   ■ If you select a row or multiple rows, all the characters in all the cells on the row change their font size.

Sometimes, changing the size of the font for the whole row doesn't work well because the results are confusing or unattractive. Figure 5-5 shows a worksheet in which the row height has been altered in two ways:

■ Rows 2 through 8 are formatted for a larger font, increasing the height of those rows.

■ Rows 10 through 16 have column A formatted for a larger font, and height of the entire row is increased as a result. However, the remaining columns continue to display the original font size.

Changing Row Height Manually

There are lots of situations in which you may want to change the height of rows without changing the font size. Sometimes, in a worksheet crowded with numbers, it makes the data easier to read. Or you may want to make certain rows taller than others,

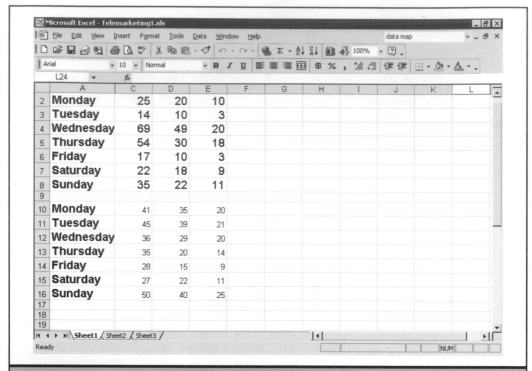

Figure 5-5. *There's a difference in appearance between changing the font size of specific cells and changing the font size of all cells in a row, even though both actions change the height of the row*

perhaps to make it easy to find the rows in which you've entered subtotals. Figure 5-6 shows a worksheet in which the rows that hold totals are higher than the other rows, making it a bit easier to separate the totals from the daily data.

Notice that the size of the characters in the taller rows isn't larger, just the row heights are changed. In fact, on the rows that have changed, the text in the first column is one point smaller than the text in the other rows (but it's bold). This is a better solution than putting empty rows between groups of rows that have totals.

To change the height of the row manually, use one of these methods:

■ Drag the border on the bottom of the row to make the row taller or shorter.

■ Select the row and right-click, then choose Row Height from the shortcut menu. Enter a new value in the Row Height dialog box.

Use the standard Windows multiple selection keys to include multiple rows: SHIFT for selecting contiguous rows, CTRL for selecting multiple individual rows.

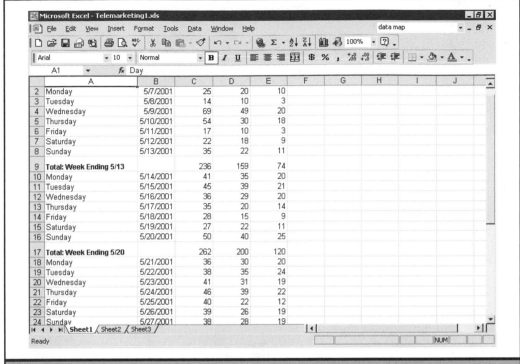

Figure 5-6. *Rows with totals are taller so the worksheet doesn't look like a jumble of numbers, and it's easy to find the important data*

Wrapping Text in a Cell

If the characters in a cell are truncated because the column isn't wide enough, you don't have to widen the column to display all the characters; instead you can wrap the text. This means you have to increase the height of the row, which is sometimes preferable to changing column width.

1. Select the cell (or the row that has cells with truncated displays) and right-click.

2. Choose Format Cells from the shortcut menu.

3. In the Format Cells dialog box, move to the Alignment tab.

4. Select Wrap Text and click OK.

Now change the height of the row so that all the characters are displayed. The easiest way to accomplish this is to put your mouse pointer on the line below the row in the left-most column (the column that contains the row numbers). When your pointer turns into a double-headed arrow, double-click to increase the height of the row automatically to display the contents of every cell in the row.

Autofitting Text to Avoid Resizing Columns or Rows

If you have cells with more data than the cell can display and you don't want to change the column width or the row height, you can tell Excel to change the font size in order to display all the data.

1. Select the cell(s) with the problem and right-click.

2. Choose Format Cells from the shortcut menu.

3. In the Format Cells dialog box, move to the Alignment tab.

4. Select Shrink To Fit and click OK.

Figure 5-7 shows the same entry, repeated on three rows. Cell C3 is the original entry, cell C6 has been formatted for wrapped text, and cell C9 is formatted with Shrink To Fit.

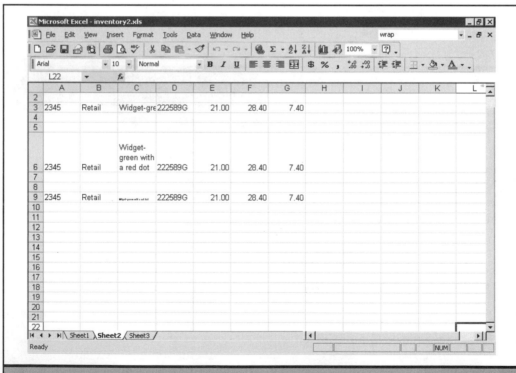

Figure 5-7. *Sometimes sizing options are a matter of taste*

Automatically Formatting Columns and Rows

Most worksheets have sections that present similar data—for example, rows or columns of titles. Perhaps some rows or columns have special data, such as subtotals. You can let Excel help you automatically format rows and columns that have similar data using a feature called AutoFormat.

Applying AutoFormats

To select and apply an AutoFormat, move your pointer to any cell with data (to automatically format the entire worksheet) or select a range of cells (to automatically format that range). Choose Format | AutoFormat from the menu bar to open the AutoFormat dialog box shown in Figure 5-8.

Scroll through all the format choices and click on the design that fits your worksheet (and your taste). Choose OK to have Excel apply the format to your worksheet or range (see Figure 5-9).

Examine your worksheet after you use the AutoFormatting feature because you'll probably find some subtle, intelligent application of formatting attributes.

For example, in Figure 5-9, you can see that Excel changed the rows that contained formulas by placing a line above and below them. This makes the subtotals stand out from the rest of the data. In addition, columns were automatically widened to make sure all the data displays.

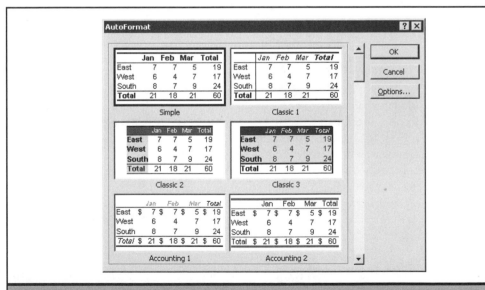

Figure 5-8.   *Scroll through the designs to find one you like*

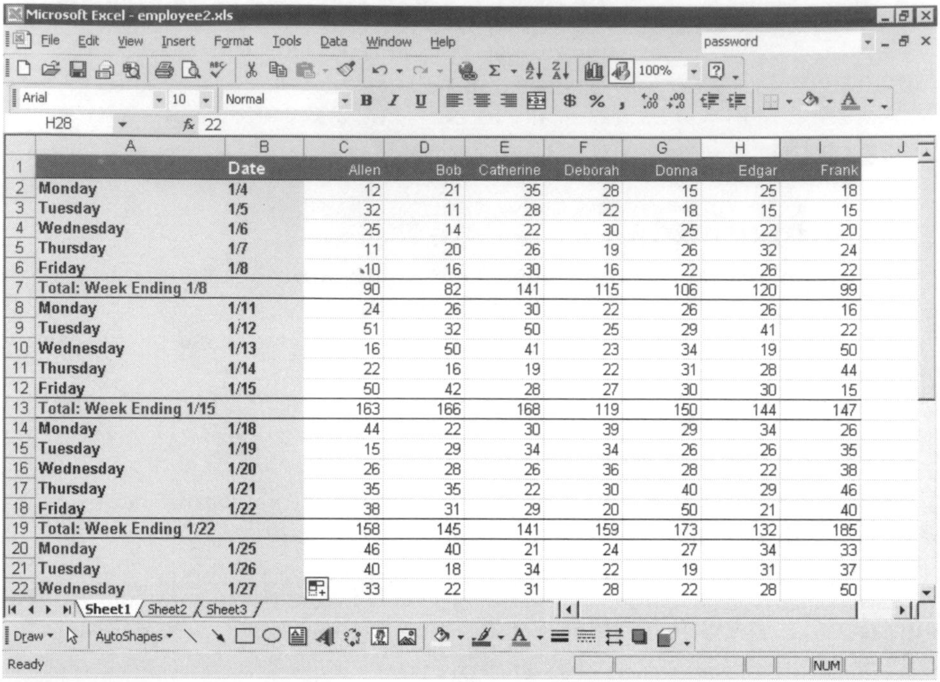

Figure 5-9. *Worksheets certainly look different after AutoFormatting*

Limiting AutoFormat Features

Sometimes AutoFormatting does more than you need—or want. You can't create your own AutoFormat designs (although I can't believe that option won't appear in some future version of Excel—of course, I've said that every time there's a new version). You can, however, limit the types of formatting that Excel applies.

When the AutoFormat dialog box is open, click the Options button. This reveals an additional section of the dialog box in which you can select the formats you want to apply and deselect those you don't care to use (see Figure 5-10).

For example, if you like having all your columns the same width, deselect the Width/Height option because the AutoFormat feature changes each column's width to be exactly the size needed to display the widest cell in that column.

Using Conditional Formatting

It's nifty to have a way to format cells depending on their content. Perhaps you'd like negative numbers to have a bright background, or have numbers exceeding

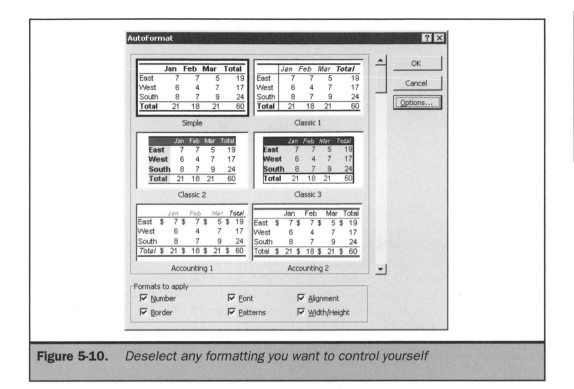

Figure 5-10.   *Deselect any formatting you want to control yourself*

1000 highlighted in some manner. Or you may need something more complicated than those examples. Whatever the degree of intricacy, Excel provides a feature that can perform this task called *conditional formatting*.

Conditional formatting works with selected columns or rows (or a range including both). After you've selected the columns or rows, choose Format | Conditional Formatting from the menu bar to see the Conditional Formatting dialog box.

The condition you establish can be based on the cell's value or on a formula you invent. If you want to create a formula, it must return a Boolean result.

Creating a Condition Based on Cell Value

If you choose Cell Value as the condition, use the controls in the dialog box to specify the condition. Click the arrow next to the first control box (it probably says "between") and choose the first condition.

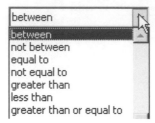

Then use the next control box to set the value you want to use as criteria. For instance, if you chose Greater Than as the condition, set the value that must be exceeded in order to match your criteria. You can use a real value or reference a cell value.

Click Format to bring up the Format Cells dialog box seen in Figure 5-11.

Use the tabs in the dialog box to make changes to the font, create a border, or place a color or pattern in the cell.

You cannot change the font or font size or apply a border to any cell that is formatted with a number format. You can, however, add an attribute (bold, italic), change the font color, or add a background color to the cell.

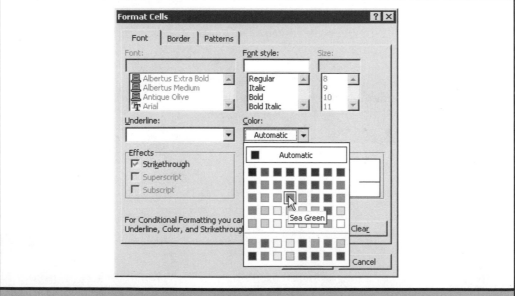

Figure 5-11.   *Format the cells that match the conditions you set*

When you're finished, click OK. You're returned to the Conditional Formatting dialog box, where you can see a preview of your formatting.

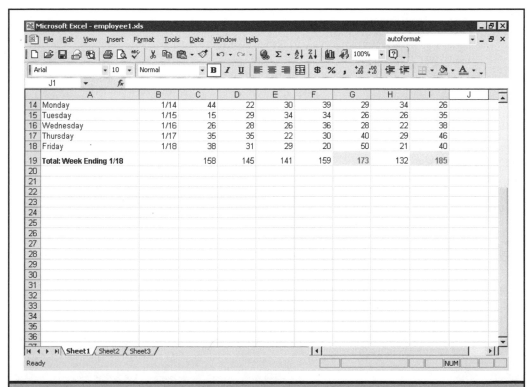

If you want to specify an additional condition, choose Add to expand the dialog box to accept the new condition.

It's probably easier to understand this with a real example. In Figure 5-12, row 19 contains the weekly total numbers of something (sales, trips to the water cooler, whatever) for each employee for a given week. The company awards a special parking space (closer to the door) to any employee who garners some minimum number (in this

Figure 5-12. *The cell or cells that match the criteria are easy to spot*

case any number greater than 160). The person in charge of awarding the parking spaces wants to make the process as easy as possible. So he creates a worksheet with conditional formatting and tells Excel to display green numbers on a light green background in any cell that matches the condition.

Then he just prints the worksheet and hangs it up. Nothing else needs to be done, no notifications, no extra work. Just print a worksheet that may or may not have a green-number cell (he has a color printer). It's up to the employee who has that cell to collect the parking permit.

Creating a Condition Based on a Formula

If you want to use a formula as the condition, select Formula Is in the first control box of the Conditional Formatting dialog box. Then, in the next box, enter the formula, using these guidelines:

- Your formula must return a logical value of True (1) or False (0).

- Enter an equal sign as the first character of the formula.

- If you use worksheet data, the data must be in the active worksheet (although a cell in the active worksheet can reference data in another worksheet).

- You can use values or cell references.

- You can use any Excel function.

- You can use any user-defined function (unless the function you defined produces a dialog box asking for information, because that will cause the formatting feature to crash).

Duplicating Formatting Features with the Format Painter

After you experiment successfully with a formatting scheme, you might want to use it on other columns, rows, or ranges in your workbook. The Format Painter is a handy helper.

Select the section that has the formatting you like and click the Format Painter tool on the Standard toolbar (it looks like a paintbrush). Then select the target range and click to apply the formatting.

Note   *The Format Painter works once if you single-click on it, but you can repeat the copy procedure by double-clicking on the icon after you select the source range. When you're finished copying, click once on the Format Painter icon to clear it. A handy use of the Format Painter is to copy a column width you've tweaked to perfection to another column or to all columns.*

Using Headers and Footers

A header is text that automatically appears at the top of each printed page, and a footer is text that shows up at the bottom of each printed page. More information about printing your worksheets, including printing headers and footers, is in Chapter 6, but you can't print them if you haven't created them. Therefore, this section explains how to create these useful features.

To create a header, a footer, or both, choose File | Page Setup from the menu bar. In the Page Setup dialog box, move to the Header/Footer tab, seen in Figure 5-13.

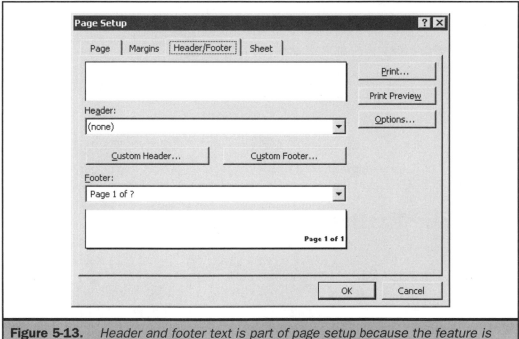

Figure 5-13. *Header and footer text is part of page setup because the feature is used for printing*

Using Predefined Headers and Footers

Click the arrow to the right of the Header or Footer text box to see a list of predefined elements (including one that matches the filename of your worksheet). You can select one if it fits your needs.

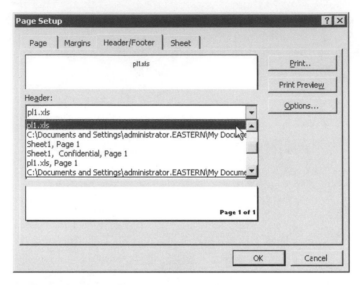

After you've selected a predefined header or footer, you can make changes to it. Click the Custom Header or Custom footer button and add or eliminate text and codes.

Creating Your Own Headers and Footers

You can also create your own header or footer from scratch. Click the Custom Header button (unless you're creating a footer, in which case you should click the Custom Footer button). This displays the Header or Footer dialog box seen in Figure 5-14.

The dialog box is set up to make it easy to divide your header or footer into sections, which is very handy. You could use the left side for a title, the right side for a page number, and the center for explanatory text (or your name). Here are some guidelines for headers and footers.

- Each section applies text justification appropriately.

- If you want to force text to the next line, press ENTER.

- The page code inserts only the page number itself; you must enter the word *Page*, followed by a space, in front of the code if you want the header or footer to say "Page X."

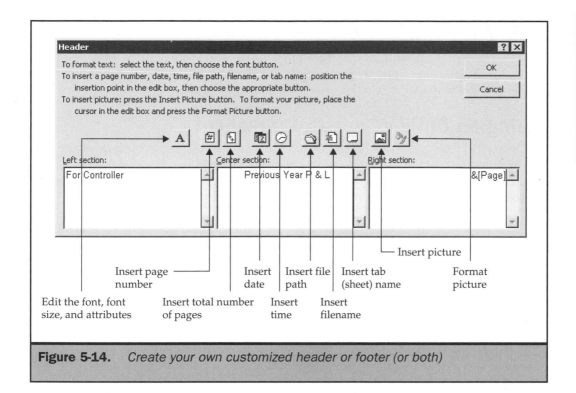

Figure 5-14. *Create your own customized header or footer (or both)*

Fine Tuning Headers and Footers

By default, Excel puts a half-inch margin between the edge of the page and the headers and/or footers you insert. If you want to change the size of the margin, move to the Margins tab of the Page Setup dialog box and adjust the Header and Footer margin values.

Be sure the size of the margin for headers and footers is smaller than the related margin for the workbook. For instance, if you want a larger margin for a header, adjust the margin for the top of the workbook document accordingly. Otherwise, text in the header and the beginning of the workbook may overlap.

You can see what your printed document will look like with your headers and footers by clicking the Print Preview button.

Note *When you create custom headers or footers, they're added to the list of preconfigured elements. You don't have to reinvent the wheel every time you want to use them.*

Using Outlines

If you need to present summary information about a worksheet that has a lot of detail and many subtotals, you should learn to use worksheet outlines. Applying an outline to a worksheet lets you control the level of detail that appears.

Preparing an Outline-Friendly Worksheet

Outlines work best when the information in the worksheet is hierarchical in nature. The broadest part of the hierarchy should be at the top, and the data should cover smaller and smaller parts of the hierarchy as it travels down through the rows. A profit-and-loss statement or a budget usually follows this pattern and works well in outline form.

Successful outlines also require the right type of formulas. You need subtotals that are placed consistently at each level of the hierarchy. The best rule of thumb is to place subtotals at the end of each section of the hierarchy. For example, in Figure 5-15, the total income for each month in the budget is a formula that uses the subtotals of the detail lines.

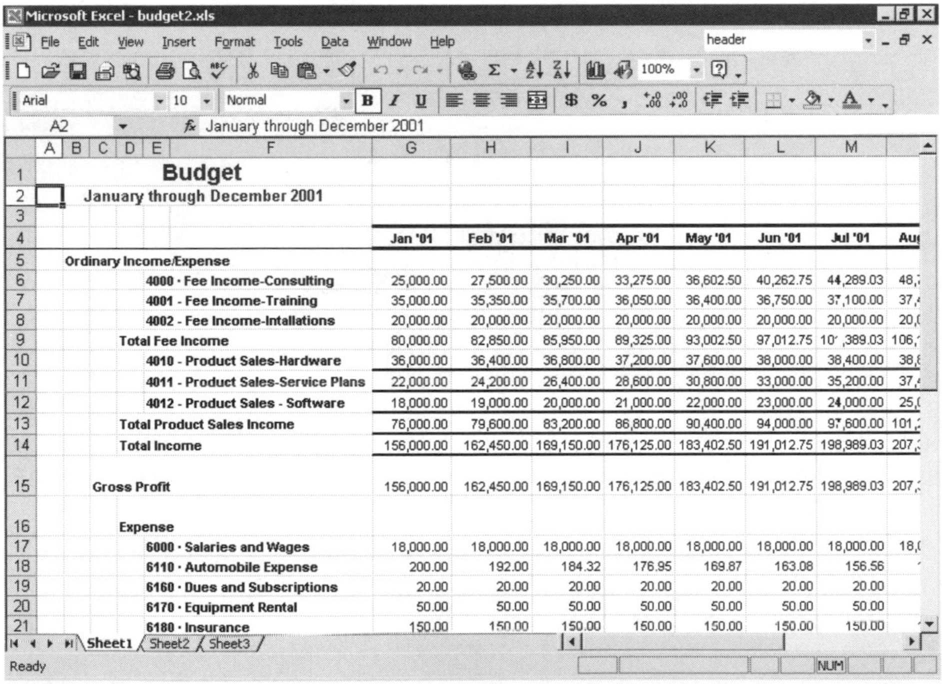

Figure 5-15. *Configure the placement of subtotals and totals with an outline in mind*

Creating an Automatic Outline

If your worksheet is set up properly, Excel can usually create exactly the outline you need automatically. If the automatic outline doesn't work the way you thought it would, you can then create a manual outline (covered next). Here's how to proceed:

1. Select any cell in the range you want to use for your outline.

2. Choose Data | Group And Outline | Auto Outline.

Note *If there is an existing outline for the worksheet, a message appears asking if you want to modify it. Choose Yes to replace the old outline with this outline.*

Excel creates an outline, which may or may not be *the* outline (the one you envisioned). As shown in Figure 5-16, the left side of your screen displays the outline levels.

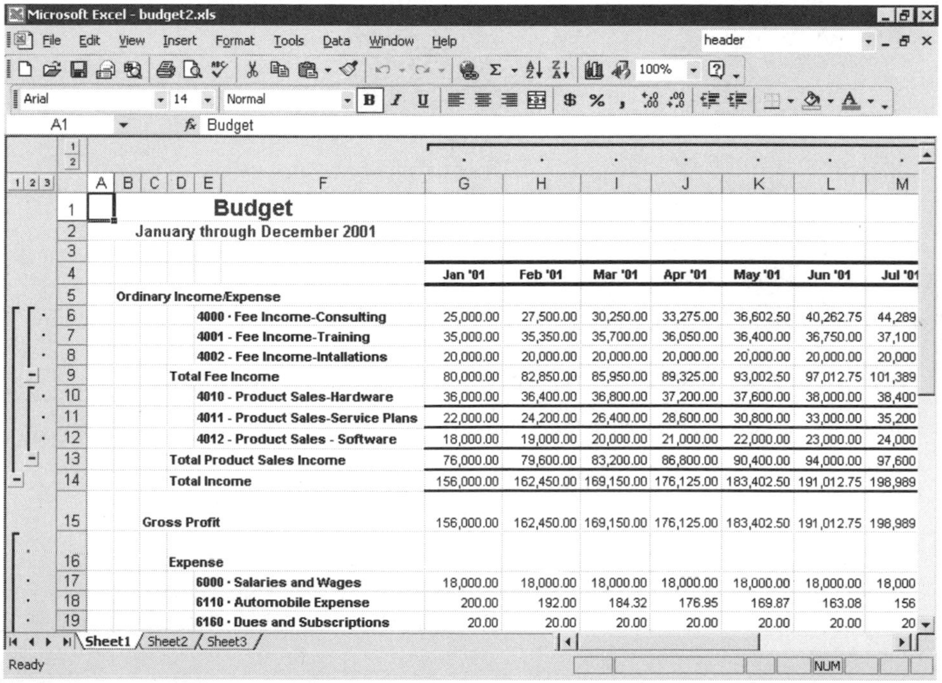

Figure 5-16. *The outline levels are clearly indicated—this section of the worksheet has three levels*

Click the minus signs to collapse the outline, whereupon the minus signs turn into plus signs (click to expand the outline).

If there's a problem with the way your outline arranged the levels, here are some things to check before you go through the work of creating a manual outline.

■ Make sure all subtotals are in rows (or columns) adjacent to the items they reference. (It's aesthetically better to have the subtotals below the detail lines because that's what people expect to see, but technically it works either way.)

■ Make sure your worksheet has formulas—Excel uses formulas to determine outline levels.

If the outline is almost right, make any necessary adjustments and repeat the steps to create an automatic outline (remember to say Yes to the question about replacing the current outline).

Creating a Manual Outline

There are two common reasons to create an outline manually:

■ The automatic outline procedure didn't produce the outline in the form you need.

■ The worksheet has no formulas but has information you want to display in a variety of levels (such as an organization chart, an agenda, or other similar document).

To create an outline, you have to create groups of rows or groups of columns (depending on whether you're creating a row outline or a column outline). Here are some guidelines to help you conceptualize this process:

■ Start with the lowest (most indented) level.

■ Assign each group a level.

Follow these steps to create a manual outline of your worksheet.

1. Check the settings by choosing Data | Group And Outline | Settings to display the Settings dialog box. Select or deselect the options, depending on the way your data is positioned in the worksheet.

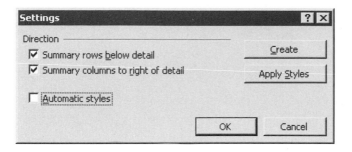

2. Select the rows (or columns) for the first group. Do not select the row (or column) that contains summary information.

3. Choose Data | Group And Outline | Group. The data is grouped and the level indicator appears to the left of the worksheet window.

	A	B	C	D	E	F	G	H	I	J
1		Date	Allen	Bob	Catherine	Deborah	Donna	Edgar	Frank	
2	Monday	1/4	12	21	35	28	15	25	18	
3	Tuesday	1/5	32	11	28	22	18	15	15	
4	Wednesday	1/6	25	14	22	30	25	22	20	
5	Thursday	1/7	11	20	26	19	26	32	24	
6	Friday	1/8	10	16	30	16	22	26	22	
7	Total: Week Ending 1/8		90	82	141	110	106	120	99	7

4. Repeat for the next group.

If you put the wrong row(s) in a group, select the problem row(s) and choose Ungroup instead of Group.

Displaying Outlines

You can use the buttons at the top of the outline graphics on the left side of your window to expand and collapse the worksheet outline quickly. Click the highest-level button (the highest level is level 1) to close up the outline, and click the next-level button to expose all of the next level. Or click the plus sign on any individual section of a level to expose just that section (see Figure 5-17).

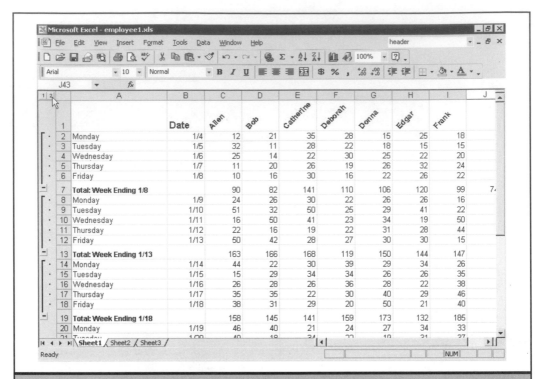

Figure 5-17. *Click the level button to expand or collapse the entire outline; click the minus signs to collapse a particular section of the outline (then you can click the plus signs to expand that section)*

Note *When you print a worksheet that has an outline, the current outline display level is what's sent to the printer.*

Working with Views

Sometimes you want to look at a workbook with a particular aggregation of format settings. There may be another group of settings you use for printing or for publishing the worksheet on the Web. Perhaps you sometimes want to look at a worksheet with certain columns and rows hidden or after you apply a filter. You can create multiple views of a workbook with the Views feature, which means you can look at your workbook in different ways by selecting a view.

Creating a View

To create a view, first establish the formatting of the workbook you want to save as a view. Then choose View | Custom Views from the menu bar to open the Custom Views dialog box. Click the Add button to open the Add View dialog box.

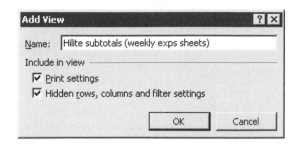

Name the view and select the options you want. Because Excel saves the view as part of the workbook, it's a good idea to indicate the worksheet on which you established this view in the name. Repeat this procedure to create as many views as you need.

Selecting a View

After you create a view or multiple views, when you want to use one, open the Custom Views dialog box and select it.

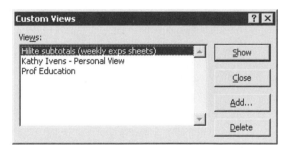

Removing a View

If you no longer need a view you created, you can remove it. Choose View | Custom Views to open the Custom Views dialog box. Select the view that's no longer useful and click the Delete button. Excel asks you to confirm that you want to delete the view. Click Yes to remove the view.

Certification Skills Covered in This Chapter

If you're preparing for Microsoft Office User Specialist certification, here are the skills you learned in this chapter.

Skill Set	Activity
Formatting and printing worksheets	Apply and modify cell formats
Formatting and printing worksheets	Modify row and column formats
Formatting and printing worksheets	Use automated tools to format worksheets
Formatting and printing worksheets	Modify page setup options for worksheets
Formatting and printing worksheets	Preview and print worksheets and workbooks

The
Complete
Reference

Excel
2002

Chapter 6

Printing

T he workbooks you create are designed to provide information, and it's common to share and distribute that information via printed copies. Excel offers a robust selection of printing features and options to assist you.

Before you print, you have an opportunity to set up the page, the printer, and the print options. This means you can establish a group of settings that will do the best job of printing the current workbook. In this chapter, I'll discuss the options you have (except for the Header/Footer options, which are covered in Chapter 5).

Using the Page Setup Dialog Box

You can control the configuration of printed pages with the Page Setup dialog box, which is accessed by choosing File | Page Setup. This is a dialog box with four tabs, giving you a full range of options.

Configuring the Page Options

You can configure the way the printed page appears on the Page tab of the Page Setup dialog box (see Figure 6-1).

The changes you make to the page settings depend on the size and layout of your workbook.

Setting the Orientation

Orientation is the direction in which paper is printed. Portrait pages are vertical, taller than they are wide. Landscape pages are horizontal, wider than they are tall.

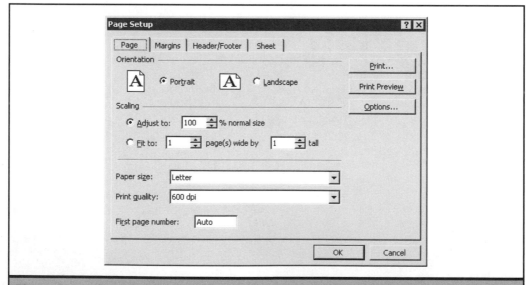

Figure 6-1.   *Start preparing your print job by designing the page layout*

Landscape is useful if your workbook has a great many columns. Your printer uses the same 8.5″ × 11″ paper but prints sideways to create a landscape page.

 You cannot print landscape pages on a dot-matrix printer.

Configuring Scaling

Scaling is a method of reducing or enlarging your workbook in order to make it fit the page better. You can select a percentage of normal size (normal size is 100 percent) that you think will work best, or tell Excel to scale the output automatically in order to make everything fit on a certain number of pages.

Tip *A good way to scale the size of the workbook automatically is to specify one page in the Page(s) Wide By box and leave the Fit To box empty. Excel scales the workbook to fit across one page and then prints as many pages as it takes to complete the print job.*

Choosing the Paper Size

You can select a different paper size by clicking the arrow to the right of the Paper Size box to see the choices. Those choices are determined by the capabilities of your printer, and some printers have more options than others. Of course, you must make sure the paper size you select is in the printer tray.

Configuring Print Quality

You can change the quality of the printing, which is really a change to the printer resolution. Higher resolution may be necessary if your workbook is scaled to the point that the font is quite small. However, higher resolution takes longer to print. The choices of quality depend on the capabilities of your printer.

Setting the First Page Number

Use this option if you've created a header or footer that includes a page number. Normally, you start printing page numbers to match the actual page (usually 1), but if your workbook is part of a large report, and it follows a word processing document that ends at page 23, you can begin the page number printing at 24.

Setting Up Margins

Move to the Margins tab of the dialog box to configure the page margins (see Figure 6-2). The margin, which is the amount of white space between the edge of the paper and the printing, is usually a matter of taste. However, sometimes adjusting margins can save the need to print a final page that holds only a small amount of data.

You can adjust the margin between the paper edge and the data and the margin between the paper edge and the header/footer.

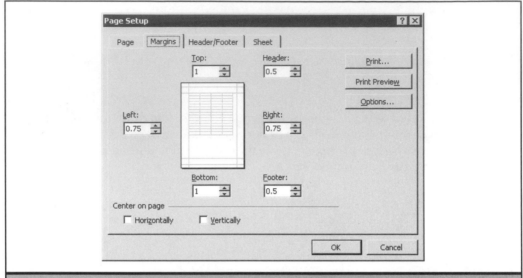

Figure 6-2.   *Move the margins to change the appearance of the printed document or to make room for more data on each page*

You can also center the data on the page. Click the Horizontally check box to center the printing between the left and right margins of the paper. Click the Vertically check box to center the printing between the top and bottom margins.

Setting Up Sheet Options

The Sheet tab, shown in Figure 6-3, is the place to control the options that are connected to your workbook.

Configuring the Print Area

Print area is the range in the current worksheet that's defined as the area to print. If the Print Area box is empty, it means the entire workbook is selected for printing.

You can preselect a print area by dragging your mouse across a range of cells and choosing File | Print Area | Set Print Area from the menu bar. Then when you open the Page Setup dialog box, the print area information is displayed on the Sheet tab.

Alternatively, you can enter a range in the Print Area box after you begin working in the Sheet tab. In the Print Area text box, enter the range, for example A1: J22.

To clear the print area while you're working on the worksheet, choose File | Print Area | Clear Print Area. To clear the print area from the Page Setup dialog box, delete the range.

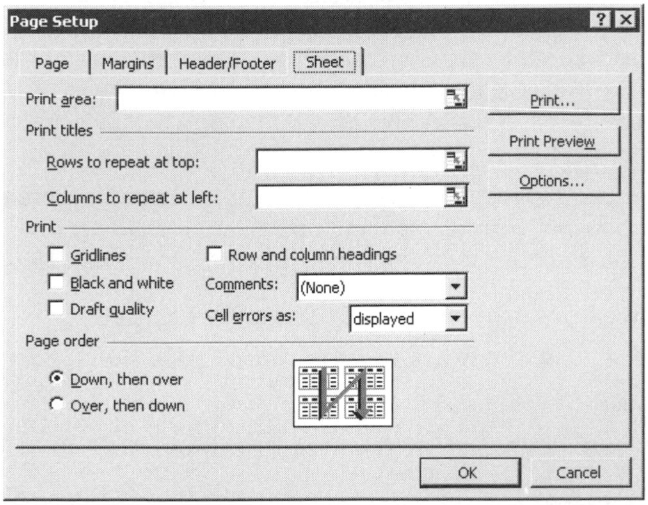

Figure 6-3.   *Use the Sheet tab to fine-tune the print job*

Configuring the Printing of Titles

Use the Print titles section of the dialog box to make sure a multiple-page print job is easy to understand. Since most worksheets have titles across the top row or in the first column, all the pages after the first page will lack the title information. The recipients of your printed document will have to refer back to the first page, which is really annoying.

Use the control boxes in the Print Titles section of the dialog box to name the columns, rows, or both that should print on every page. You can specify different print titles for each worksheet in your workbook.

Selecting the Elements to Print

Use the Print section of the dialog box to specify which elements of the worksheet to print.

■ **Gridlines**   Prints the lines that delineate each cell.

■ **Black And White**   Instructs Excel to ignore any colors in the worksheet, even if you have a color printer.

■ **Draft Quality**   Provides a way to print quickly because gridlines, graphics, and borders aren't printed.

■ **Row And Column Headings**   Prints the letters and numbers that appear on your Excel window. Usually it's not necessary (or desirable) to print this information, but if you're asking people to make corrections or comments, it's a good idea to let them see and use the cell addresses.

- **Comments**   Any comments you've placed in cells can be printed, and you have a choice between two methods (click the arrow to select your choice). You can print the comments in a separate page at the end of the printed document or print the comments just as they are displayed in your worksheet. If you select the latter option, be sure to display all or selected comments on your worksheet before printing.

- **Cell Errors As**   Specifies whether you want to print the contents of cells that have errors (usually problems with formulas). Click the arrow to choose the way you want to print the errors from the drop-down list. The choices are

  - **Displayed**   Matches the display of your worksheet
  - **<blank>**   Nobody who sees your printout sees your errors
  - **--**   Puts the two dashes in the cell
  - **N/A**   Puts the characters "N/A" in the cell

 If you're printing your worksheet in order to gain input from other people, print the errors as displayed. Perhaps someone can offer a suggestion for a solution.

Setting the Page Printing Order

If your worksheet is too wide to fit on one page, you have choices about the way the partial pages print.

- Choose Down, Then Over to print the left side of each page first, and then the right side.

- Chose Over, Then Down to print the right side of a page before printing the left side of the next page.

Your choice depends on the way you want to glue or tape the pages together.

Previewing the Print Job

All the tabs on the Page Setup dialog box have a button for Print Preview, and you can click the button to use this feature while you're configuring the page setup. You can also use the Print Preview feature by choosing File | Print Preview from the menu bar. In fact, here are all the ways to open the Print Preview window:

- Choose File | Print Preview from the menu bar.
- Click the Print Preview button on the Standard toolbar.
- Hold down the SHIFT key while you click the Print button on the Standard toolbar.
- Click on the Print Preview button on any page of the Page Setup dialog box.
- Click the Print Preview button in the Print dialog box.

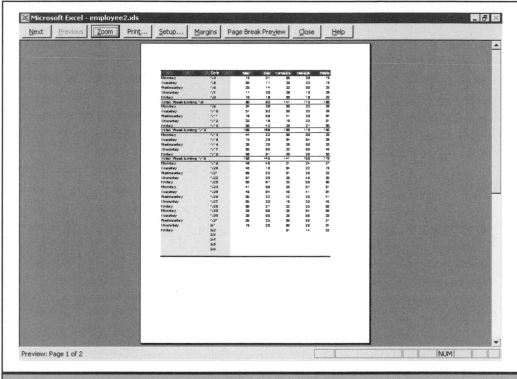

Figure 6-4.   *You can see a printed version of your worksheet before you
actually print*

The Print Preview window is an image of the way the printed output will look (see
Figure 6-4). It's a way to get a sense of the results of your configuration choices, so you
can make changes if you don't like what you see.

The Print Preview window is more than a way to check the way the printed copy
of your workbook will look. It also has some tool buttons along the top:

- **Next** Displays an image of the next page. This is a good way to make a
  decision about the scaling options discussed in the previous section. For
  example, if the next page of your print image looks like the one in Figure 6-5,
  it's probably a good idea to rescale the page so everything fits on the first page.

- **Previous** Moves to the previous page.

- **Zoom** Moves the display forward and back.

- **Print** Opens the Print dialog box so you can send the job to the printer.

- **Setup** Opens the Page Setup dialog box.

- **Margins** Displays the margins in the preview window. Both column and
  margin markers appear (see Figure 6-6). You can drag any marker to make
  changes, which are written back to the worksheet.

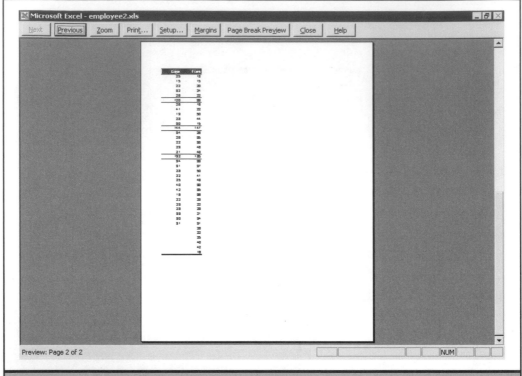

Figure 6-5.   *It's silly to print a page that contains only a couple of columns—instead, change the page layout to fit everything on one page*

- **Page Break Preview**   Shows the worksheet displayed with page breaks inserted. See the next section, "Manipulating Page Breaks," for more information.
- **Close**   Closes the preview window.
- **Help**   Displays the help pages for the Print Preview feature.

Manipulating Page Breaks

When you print a workbook, the location of page breaks makes a big difference. You can clearly define different sections, different topics, and different ranges with totals by printing each on a separate page.

Sometimes the natural (default) page breaks fall in awkward places. Perhaps a page prints with only one or two columns or rows, but a more natural page break occurs in the middle of the columns or rows.

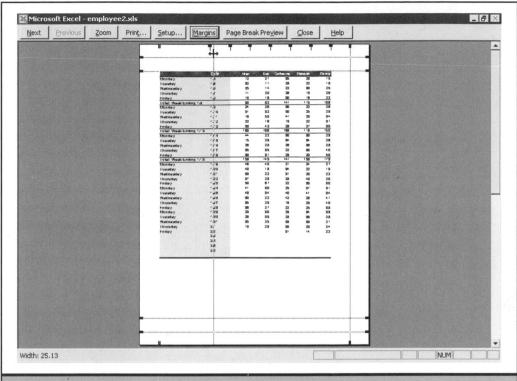

Figure 6-6. *Change column widths or margins by dragging the markers*

The best way to work with page breaks is to do the rest of your print setup configuration first. Set up headers and footers, margins, and select the paper size and orientation. Then use the page break feature to tweak your print job so it looks professional and slick.

> **Tip**
>
> *I find it best to finish the page setup and then return to my workbook to take a last-minute look at the column width, row height, the display of comments, and so on. The new page setup may cause me to tweak some or all of those items.*

After you use Print Preview and return to your worksheet, you see vertical or horizontal (or both) dashed lines on your workbook that indicate the position of page breaks.

Inserting Page Breaks

You can insert either a horizontal or vertical page break at the point you deem most suitable.

- ■ To insert a horizontal page break, select either the heading button for the row you want to appear at the top of the new page, or the cell in column A of that row. Then choose Insert | Page Break from the menu bar.

- ■ To insert a vertical page break, select the heading button for the column you want to appear on the left side of the new page, or the cell in row 1 of that column. Then choose Insert | Page Break from the menu bar.

- ■ If you select anything except the heading button or the first cell, you get two for the price of one: both a vertical page break and a horizontal page break are inserted around the cell.

Any "natural" breaks in the worksheet move or disappear when you insert a manual page break.

Using the Page Break Preview View

Excel provides a view of your worksheet that makes it extremely easy to see the effects of page breaks. Choose View | Page Break Preview to see the results of your work (see Figure 6-7).

Before showing you the preview, Excel displays a message reminding you that you can adjust the page breaks. You can select the option to stop showing this message every time you use the page break preview feature.

When you're working in Page Break Preview view, you can drag the break marks to a new position. Position your pointer over a break line so it turns into a double-headed arrow, and then drag the break line in the appropriate direction. Excel automatically adjusts the scaling so your document prints the way you want it to.

Choose View | Normal to return to the worksheet.

Removing Page Breaks

If you're working in Normal view, you remove a page break in much the same way you inserted it. Select the heading button or first cell in the row/column, and then choose Insert | Remove Page Break from the menu bar.

If you're working in Page Break Preview view, drag the page break line to the left edge of the worksheet (if it's a vertical break) or the top edge of the worksheet (if it's a horizontal break).

When you remove manual page breaks, the "natural" breaks return.

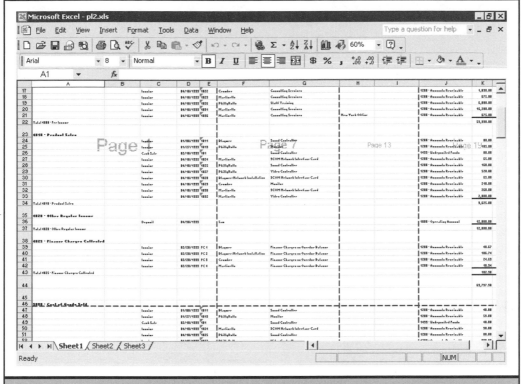

Figure 6-7.   *Check and adjust the page breaks*

Creating Custom Views

Frequently, workbooks are large and cover a lot of ground. Perhaps there's a year's worth of information broken down by months, or perhaps you're an information junkie and use a worksheet to hold a week's worth of information broken down to a minute-by-minute analysis.

You can create custom views for the purpose of printing, and include specific data, display options, or other configuration elements. (You can also use your custom views for onscreen views; they're not limited to printing.)

Each custom view starts with the entire workbook, but displaying only those elements you define when you create the view. Excel memorizes each view you create.

For example, one of my clients uses one method for reimbursing employees when they spend money on professional seminars and technical reference books and another method for casual out-of-pocket expenses such as parking fees, tolls, and meals. This is because the company tracks in-service education and gives merit points in addition to reimbursement. The employees would find it onerous to keep separate workbooks or worksheets for separate expense types, so all of them create two views of their expense files: one for petty cash and one for education.

Creating a Custom View

Make all the configuration and display changes you want to include in your view. This can include any or all of the following elements:

- Window size and position
- Frozen panes
- Hidden rows and columns
- Print settings
- Print range selection
- Selected cells or ranges
- Filter settings

Choose View | Custom Views to bring up the Custom Views dialog box.

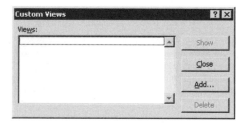

Click Add to open the Add View dialog box, where you must enter a name for the view.

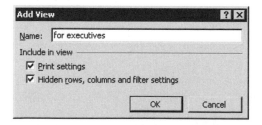

You can eliminate the options to include print settings, hidden rows, columns, and filter settings if they're not important to your custom view.

Removing a Custom View

To remove a custom view, choose View | Custom Views from the menu bar. Select the custom view you no longer need and choose Delete.

Printing Your Document

When you've tweaked the appearance, page breaks, views, and everything else into a state of perfection, you're ready to print. You have two choices for printing: use the Print button on the Standard toolbar or use the Print dialog box.

Using the Print Button

Click the Print button to send your document to the printer. You have no opportunity to view or change any print settings. Here are the default settings for printing with the Print button:

- The active worksheet is printed.
- If additional worksheets are selected, they are printed.
- Embedded charts or other graphic objects (drawings) are printed.
- The print job goes to the default printer or the last printer you selected in this session of Excel.
- The orientation is portrait.
- Wide worksheets that require multiple pages are printed down, and then across.
- The default page margins (1 inch top/bottom, .75 inch left/right) are applied.
- No headers or footers are printed.
- No scaling is applied.
- One copy prints.

Obviously, the Print button is safe to use only when you are printing a small worksheet, or when you've already adjusted font sizes, column sizes, and other configuration options that you've tested by previously printing this workbook.

Using the Print Dialog Box

If you want (or need) controls for printing, you must use the Print dialog box. There are two ways to open it:

- Choose File | Print from the menu bar.
- Press CTRL-P.

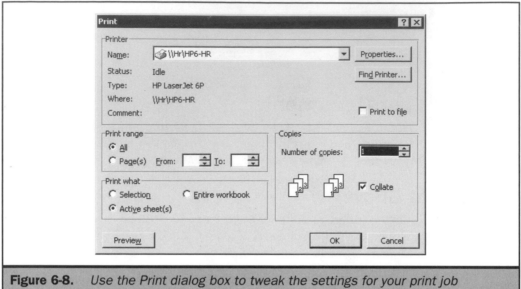

Figure 6-8.   *Use the Print dialog box to tweak the settings for your print job*

When the Print dialog box opens, it looks similar to Figure 6-8.

Select a Printer

If you have more than one printer available, click the arrow to the right of the Name text box to display a list of printers and select the one that's appropriate for this print job.

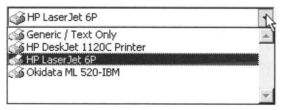

For example, if you're relying on colors to indicate special cells or ranges, a color printer would work better (but a good black-and-white printer probably can handle levels of gray well enough to highlight those cells). If you have a printer that's capable of handling long sheets of paper, select that printer for a wide workbook.

Set the Printer Properties

Click the Properties button to select any special settings for the printer. Each printer's properties differ, of course, so the dialog box for the printer I selected (see Figure 6-9) may not look like yours.

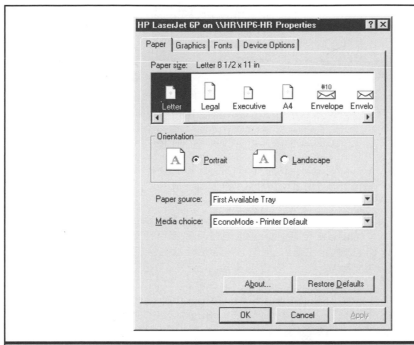

Figure 6-9. *Most printers allow you to select paper, resolutions, and graphics settings*

Select What to Print

In the Print Range section of the dialog box you can choose among these options:

- **All**   Prints everything (the definition of "everything" changes according to the selections in the Print What section).

- **Page(s) From/To**   Lets you specify the first and last page in the From and To spin boxes. If you want to print one specific page, enter that page number in both spin boxes.

In the Print What section of the dialog box, choose one of the following options:

- **Selection**   Prints a selected part of the worksheet (you must select the range before opening the Print dialog box).

- **Entire Workbook**   Prints all the worksheets in the workbook, including chart sheets.

- **Active Sheet(s)**   Prints the currently active worksheet and any additional worksheet you selected. Hold down the CTRL key and click the sheet tabs for all the sheets you want to print. If you select and print multiple sheets, each sheet prints on a new page.

> **Note** *If you've created a header or footer (or both), it prints automatically.*

Select Copy and Collating Options

You can print multiple copies of your workbook by specifying the number of copies in that spin box. If the Collate check box has a check mark, each copy prints the pages in order. If the Collate check box is deselected, multiple copies of page 1 print, followed by multiple copies of page 2, and so on.

Printing to a File

You can opt to send the print job to a file instead of to a printer. To accomplish this, click the Print To File check box. You're asked to supply a filename for the print job.

Do not confuse this with a text file; it isn't the same thing. A print file is saved to disk like a text file, but it contains all the codes needed by your printer. The file can be sent to your printer via the command line, using the command `copy printfile name port /b`. The print file contents are specific to the printer you selected in the Print dialog box.

The only reason to print to a file is that the printer you want to use isn't available. Perhaps you have a powerful color printer in your office and you're working at home. Of course, you must install the drivers for the powerful color printer in your home machine. It's okay to lie to Windows about this; I install all sorts of printers I don't really have (but can gain access to at a different location and then use via a print file). Your Windows operating system has no way to peek through the monitor and say, "Hey, I don't see one of those printers."

Certification Skills Covered in This Chapter

If you're preparing for Microsoft Office User Specialist certification, here are the skills you learned in this chapter.

Skill Set	Activity
Formatting and printing worksheets	Modify page setup options for worksheet
Formatting and printing worksheets	Preview and print worksheets and workbooks

The
Complete
Reference

Part II

Analyzing Data

Chapter 7

Managing Data

The amount of data in a worksheet can get voluminous in a hurry. Sometimes it seems as if there's an overabundance of information—all those details can be overwhelming. Each cell, each detailed entry, is important, but sometimes you want to see only certain data. Perhaps you have to prepare a summary report; perhaps you're looking for specific details and don't want to scroll through all the rollups.

You can manage and manipulate the data in your worksheet to make it easier to find and analyze information, and this chapter is all about those features that allow you to do so.

Understanding Lists

A list is a collection of related information that is organized in a logical manner. It has a row of headers (which you may call titles or descriptions). Below the row of headers are rows of data, which can be of any data type (numbers, text, dates, and so on).

In fact, if you've ever worked with database design, a worksheet that fits this description should remind you of a database table. The columns are fields; the rows that contain data are records (one row has titles). However, in the world of worksheets we call this a *list*.

Figure 7-1 is a worksheet list, with headers in row 1 and six rows of data. The columns have a variety of data types—values, text, and dates. Column F is a formula calculated on column E (it's 10 percent of column E).

Excel has a bunch of features that are designed to work on lists, and we'll cover them in this chapter.

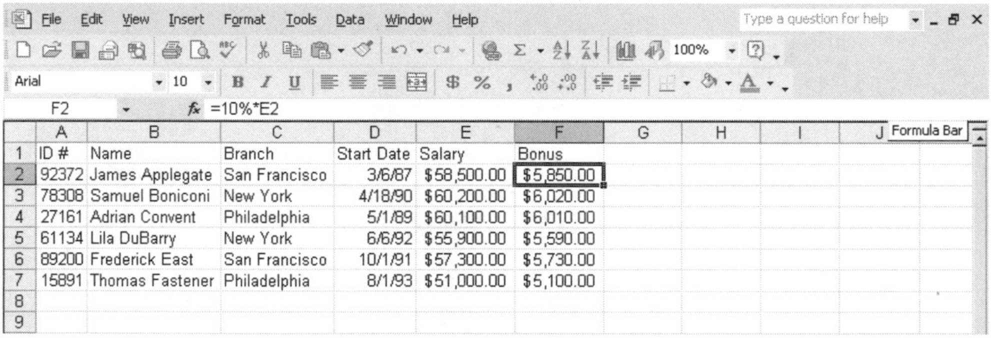

	A	B	C	D	E	F
1	ID #	Name	Branch	Start Date	Salary	Bonus
2	92372	James Applegate	San Francisco	3/6/87	$58,500.00	$5,850.00
3	78308	Samuel Boniconi	New York	4/18/90	$60,200.00	$6,020.00
4	27161	Adrian Convent	Philadelphia	5/1/89	$60,100.00	$6,010.00
5	61134	Lila DuBarry	New York	6/6/92	$55,900.00	$5,590.00
6	89200	Frederick East	San Francisco	10/1/91	$57,300.00	$5,730.00
7	15891	Thomas Fastener	Philadelphia	8/1/93	$51,000.00	$5,100.00

Figure 7-1. *This worksheet is really fields and records, which Excel calls a* ***list***

Designing Lists

When you create a worksheet that qualifies as a list (and can be managed as a list), it takes a bit more planning than a worksheet that is just a collection of data. Here are some guidelines to use for your lists:

■ Don't use empty rows to separate data groups. Excel interprets an empty row as an "end of list" marker. If you have different data groups, perhaps you should distinguish them by adding another column to your list.

■ Columns should be dedicated to a data type, such as dates, currency, or text, instead of being mixed (with the exception of the header cell). If you find that you are mixing data types within a column, perhaps that column doesn't represent a single field—as it should.

■ Formulas should be calculated based on a field in the same record—equivalently, in the same row. If you must use a formula that's based on data outside of the list, use an absolute reference (see Chapter 8). If you sort the list, formulas with relative references often wind up wrong.

■ Worksheets that contain lists shouldn't contain any data besides the records for that list. Things that you do with lists (in particular, filtering them) can cause other data to become hidden and subsequently lost.

Entering Data for Lists

There's really nothing different about basic data entry when you're entering data into a cell that's part of a list. What is special is the fact that some of the data entry features Excel provides work extraordinarily well for lists.

Using Data Entry Shortcuts

It's common for columns to have similar or repetitive data in a worksheet list. For example, if you have a field called Salesman or Branch Office, multiple records probably have the same entry. Salesman Peter Profit probably appears in lots of records, or the New York branch office is referenced in multiple records. Excel has two features that make it much faster to enter data under these circumstances:

■ **Pick Lists**   Lets you pick an entry for a cell based on the fact that it already exists somewhere in the column. Right-click on the cell, choose Pick From List in the shortcut menu, and pick an entry from the list.

- **AutoComplete**   Causes Excel to search the current column to find matching entries as you enter characters. If you type an *N* in a column that already has *New York* in a cell, Excel fills in the cell with New York. If that matches what you were planning to enter, you can press ENTER to complete the cell entry instead of continuing to type.

Note   *If the current column contains both New York and Newark, Excel won't fill in the cell until you reach the fourth character. If you then type a blank space, Excel proposes New York, and if you type an a, Excel proposes Newark.*

Using the Data Form Dialog Box

When you work with an Excel list that's wide, a data form is an efficient way to enter records because you don't have to keep scrolling to reach all the columns in the worksheet. A data form shows all the column labels in your list and provides an area for you to fill in data. Using a data form lets you be as productive as when you use a database record screen. To access the data form, click any cell within the list, and then choose Data | Form from the menu bar. The data form that opens resembles the one in Figure 7-2.

The dialog box displays the first record in the list and also indicates how many records currently exist.

1. Click New to clear all the entries in the dialog box so you can input a new record.

2. Enter the data for each field, using TAB to move through the fields (SHIFT-TAB moves backward).

3. Formula cells are entered automatically.

4. Press ENTER or click New to save the new record (it's appended to the end of the list, so it will occupy the next row on your worksheet).

5. Click Close when you're finished entering new records.

You can also use the buttons on this dialog box to accomplish other tasks:

■ Move through the existing records if you need to make any changes. (You cannot change a formula with this dialog box; you must perform that task on the worksheet.)

■ Delete the currently displayed record.

■ Restore a record to its original data if you've made changes (the Restore button only works before you press ENTER, or click the Close or New button).

■ Use the Find Prev and Find Next buttons to move through the existing records.

You can also view records that meet your specifications. Click the Criteria button to clear the form so you can enter values in one or more fields in order to locate matching records.

■ Enter a specific value in a field.

■ Enter criteria such as **>10000**.

Then use the Find Prev and Find Next buttons to see all the records that match your criteria.

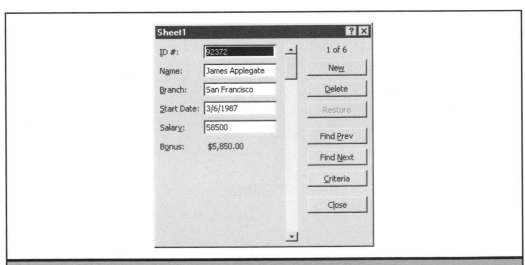

Figure 7-2. *Filling out an easy-to-use form is more convenient than scrolling through a large worksheet*

Filtering Lists

If you need to see only that portion of your spreadsheet that meets some criterion that's important at the moment, you can filter the lists. Filtering hides any rows that don't meet your criteria, making it much easier to view the data that's meaningful. For instance, you may need to see only those rows that are connected to a particular customer, salesperson, or branch office. Excel has two methods you can use for filtering: AutoFilter and Advanced Filter.

Using AutoFiltering

To filter a list automatically, select any cell in your list and choose Data | Filter | AutoFilter from the menu bar. This changes your header row by adding a drop-down arrow to every field name.

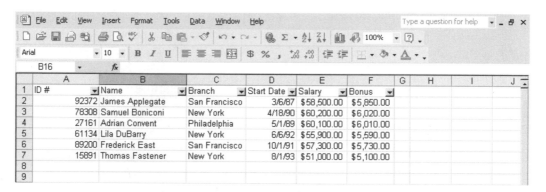

Click the arrow on the column that represents the criteria you're using and select a record that meets your specifications. For example, if you only want to see records connected to your New York office, click the arrow on your office field and choose New York.

After you filter the list, three changes occur on your Excel window:

- Only the rows that meet the criteria display in your worksheet.

- The triangle on the arrow of the column you used changes color (although you may have to peer carefully to notice).

■ The status bar displays the number of records found (they matched your filter), along with the total number of records—for example, "6 of 25 records found."

Note *Formulas that operate on columns do not recalculate for the filtered rows. If a formula produces a sum of all 50 rows and your filtering results in a display of 10 rows, the formula cell continues to display the sum of all 50 rows.*

To display the whole list again, click the arrow on the column you used and select All from the drop-down menu. Alternatively, you can choose Data | Filter | Show All from the menu bar.

To leave AutoFilter mode, choose Data | Filter | AutoFilter to remove the check mark (it's a toggle).

The drop-down list you used has several choices in addition to the items contained in the column:

■ **All**   Displays all the rows (removes the filtering for the column).

■ **Top 10**   Automatically filters for the top 10 items (see the next section).

■ **Custom**   Gives you the capability of filtering by multiple items (see the section "Custom AutoFiltering," later in this chapter).

■ **Blanks**   Filters on blanks (if they exist), resulting in a list that has rows with blank cells in this column.

■ **NonBlanks**   Does the opposite of Blanks.

Using the Blanks and NonBlanks items can be useful when you might have missing data in your list. If you choose Blanks from the drop-down list, you can focus on records that have no values in that column. Perhaps some action remains to be taken with those records, or someone accidentally omitted some information.

If instead you choose NonBlanks, you focus on only the records that have information in that column. This keeps the other records out of the way.

Top 10 AutoFiltering

This option is misnamed because it's not an AutoFilter that produces the top 10 items for any type of data. In fact, you're not limited to filtering down to 10 items. I guess it's a generic name, indicating "popular items" (or perhaps the programmers watch David Letterman's show).

However, the option does provide a way to filter by a ranking criterion you design for yourself. For example, you may want to see a list of a certain number of employees who have been with the company the longest. Or perhaps you need to see the six lowest-paid employees. Whatever your need, keep in mind that Top 10 AutoFiltering requires *numeric* data.

To design your Top 10 criteria, click the down arrow on the column you want to use and choose the Top 10 option. The Top 10 AutoFilter dialog box appears.

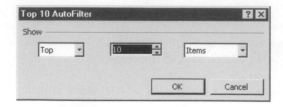

1. In the first control box, choose Top or Bottom (depending on whether you want to filter for the highest or the lowest values).

2. In the second control box, specify the number of filtered items you want to see.

3. In the third control box, specify whether you want to see Items or Percent:

   ■ Choose Items to filter down to the rows that contain the highest (or lowest) values for the selected column.

   ■ Choose Percent to filter down to the rows that have values that make up the highest (or lowest) percentage of the selected column.

AutoFiltering Multiple Columns

You can refine your filtering process by adding a filter on another column after you've filtered the first column. For example, you may want to filter your list to see only the records that refer to your San Francisco office, and then only the records of a particular salesperson.

To accomplish this, perform the first AutoFilter as described in the previous section. Then, when the filtered list displays, click the drop-down arrow on the second column and choose the appropriate data. You can continue to filter additional columns one column at a time.

Custom AutoFiltering

All the AutoFiltering methods I've discussed so far involve the selection of a single value from a column and then using that value as the filter criteria. However, if you choose Custom in the drop-down list, you see the Custom AutoFilter dialog box, which brings you more filtering power.

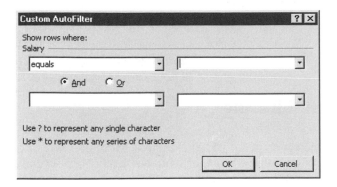

You can establish two sets of criteria and tell Excel to use both of them, or choose either one. For instance, you can filter for both greater than $50,000 and less than $60,000, or you can filter for either New York or San Francisco. Here's how to use the dialog box to establish your filters:

1. Click the arrow next to the first combo box to choose the criteria. (Notice that the combo box displays the name of the column you selected.)

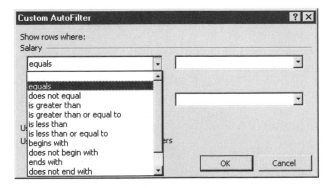

2. Click the arrow to the control box to the right of the first box and choose the data against which you're matching the criteria you set in the first box (the list that displays contains all the data in the column).

3. Select And to combine this criteria with another criteria, or select Or to use either criteria.

4. Fill out the two bottom control boxes (they contain the same choices as the top two control boxes).

If you are setting criteria for a column that contains text entries, you can use the * and ? characters as wildcards. For example, you can enter **Ba*** to search for all entries that begin with those letters, or **B?tter** to find *batter*, *butter*, and *bitter*.

Using Advanced Filtering

Most users find that AutoFiltering takes care of all their filtering needs, but once in a while you need to filter your list in a way that AutoFilter can't handle. Perhaps you need to use very complex criteria, or you need to compute criteria instead of selecting existing data. When that need arises, you can turn to Excel's advanced filtering feature.

Setting the Advanced Filtering Criteria

Advanced filtering requires you to establish the criteria before you do anything else. The criteria occupy a range that you create with these rules:

- There must be at least two rows in the range.
- The first row must have the field names (usually found in the first row of your worksheet).
- Additional rows consist of the criteria.

Furthermore, the criteria range is created outside the worksheet list, which means you can place it above the worksheet contents (add rows to create the space) or below them (see Figure 7-3).

To create the criteria rows, follow these steps:

1. Right-click on a column label from your list for a column that contains the fields you want to use for your filter.

2. Choose Copy from the shortcut menu.

3. Right-click on the first cell in the first blank row of your criteria range and choose Paste.

4. Repeat step 3 for each label you want to use for your criteria.

5. In the rows below the label row of your criteria range, enter the criteria you want to match for your filtering process, using these guidelines:

   - Criteria in the same row act as though they are connected by an AND operator. That is, a record must meet both criteria in order to appear.

   - Criteria in the same column act as though they are connected by an OR operator. That is, a record must meet only one criterion in order to appear.

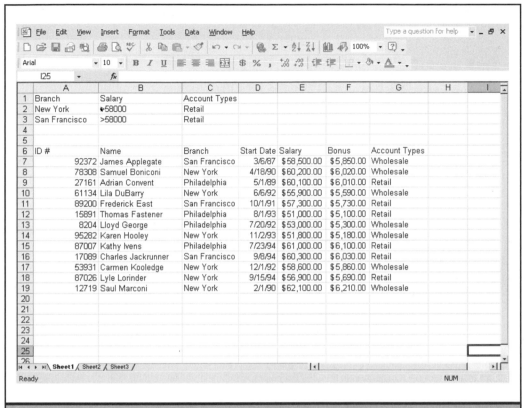

Figure 7-3. *The criteria range is created outside the list*

Performing the Filtering Action

After you've established your criteria range, click anywhere inside the list to activate that part of your worksheet. Then choose Data | Filter | Advanced Filter from the menu bar. The Advanced Filter dialog box appears.

The dialog box has already entered the range for the list you want to filter (that's why you clicked inside the list before opening the dialog box). Now enter the criteria range you created, including the cells that hold the labels.

In the Action section of the dialog box, select one of the placement options:

■ **Filter The List, In-Place**   Performs the filtering on your existing list. Any rows that don't match the criteria you established will disappear (they're automatically hidden).

■ **Copy To Another Location**   Displays a filtered list at another location of your worksheet. Then use the Copy To box to enter the cell address for the upper-left corner of the area you want to use as the location.

Tip   *The disadvantage to filtering the list in place is that you can't continue filtering using additional filters because the hidden rows won't be part of the list examined by the filter. However, if you're not going to keep filtering, it's easier to filter the list in place.*

Caution   *Be careful if you use the Copy To Another Location option. Make certain first that there's no data in the same column that you're copying to. If there is anything in the Copy To column—even if it's all the way down in row 65536—it will be deleted, Excel won't warn you, and there's no Undo available.*

Here are the results of the filtering action used in Figure 7-3.

	A	B	C	D	E	F	G
1	Branch	Salary	Account Types				
2	New York	>58000	Retail				
3	San Francisco	>58000	Retail				
4							
5							
6	ID #	Name	Branch	Start Date	Salary	Bonus	Account Types
16	17089	Charles Jackrunner	San Francisco	9/8/94	$60,300.00	$6,030.00	Retail
20							
21							

You can save the filtered list (use Save As so you can give the worksheet a different filename), print it, or just examine it. If you filtered the list in place, choose Data | Filter | Show All to return the entire list to the worksheet.

Sorting Data

When you work with a list, it's common to add records as the data becomes available, and there's no particular order to the way the data appears. Often, however, you need to see the data in some sort of order, whether you need to arrange your list alphabetically or arrange a column that contains values in ascending order.

Rearranging the order of rows is called *sorting*, and Excel provides a number of ways to perform a change in the sort order.

Tip *If you wind up with a sort order that doesn't work, you can choose Edit | Undo to get back to the original order. If you're sufficiently concerned, save your worksheet before you begin sorting your list. If you end up with something that doesn't work, you can close the file (say No when Excel asks if you want to save your changes) and then open it again.*

Understanding the Sorting Criteria

It's not always clear the way information is sorted. Of course, if you have a column of values, such as currency or numbers, figuring out what an ascending sort does isn't difficult. But some of the other sorting rules may not be clear. Table 7-1 describes Excel's rules for sorting.

Tip *In the text sorting rules, if you use the Sort dialog box and select case-sensitive sorting, lowercase a–z follows uppercase. Additionally, apostrophes are ignored, and hyphens are ignored unless there are two text phrases that are the same except for a hyphen (perhaps one row has the text* first-only *and another row has the text* first only*), in which case the text without the hyphen comes first.*

Using Simple Sorting Schemes

The quickest way to sort data is to use the column that contains the data you want to use as the basis of the sort order. Click the list's header, and then click the Sort Ascending button or the Sort Descending button on the Standard toolbar. The entire list re-sorts based on the column you sorted, so the records stay together.

There are a couple of caveats you need to be aware of when you use this simple sorting technique:

■ Start by clicking some value in the column. If you sort by clicking the Column Heading button only (for example, the *H* at the top of Column H) the column itself is sorted, and the records don't necessarily stay together.

Data Type	Sorting Rule
Numbers	From largest negative to largest positive, assuming an ascending sort
Dates and Times	Actual values, regardless of the formatted appearance (April does not come before February, because alphabetical formatting is ignored)
Text	0–9 space ! " # $ % & ( ) * + , . / : ; < + > ? @ [\ ] ^ _ ' {	} ~ A–Z
Logical values	False before True
Error values	Error values are not sorted
Blank cells	Blank cells are last, whether the sort order is ascending or descending

Table 7-1. *Excel Rules for an Ascending Sort*

■ If a record contains a relative reference formula, the formulas won't be accurate after you sort. Use an absolute cell reference for formulas that contain cell references (see the section "Sorting with Formulas" for more information).

Using Complex Sorting Schemes

If you need to subsort by a second column, the "click on the column" shortcut doesn't work, of course—because the whole list re-sorts using the values in the second column. To sort by more than one field simultaneously, follow these steps:

1. Choose Data | Sort from the menu bar to open the Sort dialog box seen in Figure 7-4.

2. Click the arrow to the right of the Sort By box and choose the field you want to use for the sort.

3. Select Ascending or Descending for this field.

4. Click the arrow to the right of the Then By box, and choose the field you want to use for the subsort.

5. Select Ascending or Descending for the subsort field.

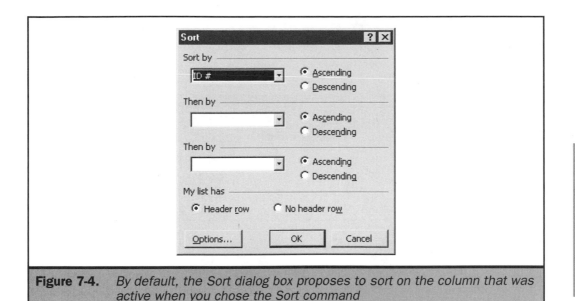

Figure 7-4. *By default, the Sort dialog box proposes to sort on the column that was active when you chose the Sort command*

6. If you need another level of subsorting, repeat the previous two steps, using the next Then By box.

7. If you have labels on the header row, select the Header Row radio button so the contents of those cells won't be involved in the sort. ·

8. Choose OK to sort your worksheet.

If the sort produces an unexpected result (perhaps you subsorted where you should have sorted), you have a couple of options for putting everything back the way it was:

■ Click the Undo button on the Standard toolbar.

■ If you saved before you sorted, close the file without saving changes, and then open it again.

■ Create a column before you begin to sort, and use it to re-sort. I put a column at the last column position and enter the alphabet (or numbers if there are more than 26 rows), one to each cell. Selecting the header row for that column and clicking the Sort Ascending button on the toolbar puts everything back.

Using Advanced Sort Options

You can bring even more flexibility and power to your sorting procedures by clicking the Options button on the Sort dialog box.

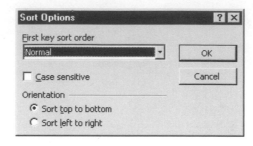

You can use the choices on the Sort Options dialog box to refine the sorting process.

- **First Key Sort Order**   This box offers the normal sort order (as described in Table 7-1) or a custom sort order (discussed in the next section).

- **Case Sensitive**   Checking this lets uppercase text be sorted before lowercase.

- **Orientation**   These choices give you the option to sort columns by using the values in the rows.

Using the Custom Sort Order

A custom sort order is one in which you design your own definition of ascending and descending. If you click the arrow to the right of the First Key Sort Order box of the Sort Options dialog box, you see a good example of a custom sort. These are text strings that have their own unique sorting order, and the alphabet has nothing to do with it.

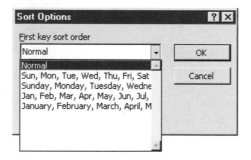

Excel provides these four custom sort options for you because they're commonly used. (Actually, there are just two sort options, but each is presented with both an extended version [*January*] and an abbreviated version [*Jan*].)

Creating Your Own Custom Sort Order

You may have a reason to have a sort order for certain fields that doesn't work with the normal sorting order. You can add it to the four custom codes Excel has already devised. Here's how to accomplish this:

1. Choose Tools | Options from the menu bar to open the Options dialog box.

2. Go to the Custom Lists tab (see Figure 7-5).

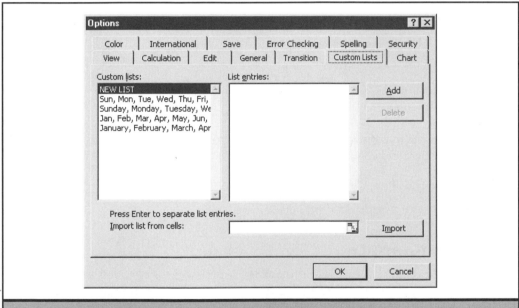

Figure 7-5. *Existing lists are displayed in the left pane of the Custom Lists tab*

3. Select the NEW LIST option to highlight it.

4. Enter the list items in the right pane, pressing the ENTER key between each item.

5. Click Add when you have made all the entries. The list moves to the left pane.

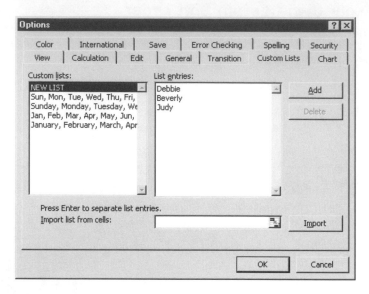

If the list exists in a range of contiguous cells, you can enter the range in the Import list From Cells box and click the Import button to add the list to your system.

    After you've created a list, if you enter the first item in a cell you can use the AutoFill feature to complete the data entry of additional cells.

Sorting with Formulas

An earlier section in this chapter, "Simple Sorting Schemes," suggested that if your sort range contains formulas, you should make them absolute rather than relative.

The reason for this recommendation will become clear when you read about formulas in Chapter 8. Here's an alternative if you don't want to convert formulas in your sort range from relative to absolute.

Suppose that your worksheet looks something like this:

	A	B	C
1			
2			
3			
4			86
5			60
6			45
7			12
8			96
9			36
10			41
11			24
12			66
13			69
14			19
15			58
16			

You want to sort the data in the range C4:C15, but those cells contain relative references. To work around that problem, take these steps:

1. Select the range E4:E15. (You can select any range you like, but it should consist of one column and 12 rows.)

2. Type this formula, but don't press ENTER yet:

   =SMALL(C4:C15,ROW(A1:A12))

3. Hold down the CTRL and SHIFT keys, and press ENTER. This keystroke sequence is termed *array-entering* a formula, and this book has much more to say about array formulas in Chapter 10.

ANALYZING DATA

Your worksheet should now look like this.

	A	B	C	D	E	F
	File Edit View Insert Format Tools Data Window Help					
E4			*fx* {=SMALL(C4:C15,ROW(A1:A12))}			
1						
2						
3						
4			86		12	
5			60		19	
6			45		24	
7			12		36	
8			96		41	
9			36		45	
10			41		58	
11			24		60	
12			66		66	
13			69		69	
14			19		86	
15			58		96	
16						

What you have done is to use the worksheet function SMALL to arrange the data in C4:C15 in ascending order and put the results in E4:E15. The formula also invokes the ROW() function to bring the numbers 1, 2,..., 12 into the formula. That done, the formula calls for the first smallest, then the second smallest, through the twelfth smallest value in the range C4:C15.

Because this method doesn't actually move anything in C4:C15, it can't tamper with any relative references in that range.

You might regard it as a drawback that this "sort" winds up with the sorted data in a different location. On the other hand, it can be an advantage. Suppose the data in the original range changes (and if that range has references in it, you probably expect that to happen). Usually, when sorted values change, you have to re-sort them. Using this approach, you know that no matter the values in C4:C15, they will appear in sorted order in E4:E15.

Finally, note that if you wanted to use a worksheet function to sort in *descending* order, you would replace SMALL with LARGE in the formula just given.

Examining Alternatives with Scenarios

Do you ever start sentences with "If things were different..."? Or ask, "What would life be like if I were rich and gorgeous? What would be different if my boss appreciated my genius?" Those are "what-if" games, and financial professionals play them all the time. What if costs go up? What if corporate taxes rise?

You cannot change the figures in your accounting software reports to see what changes appear in the bottom line as a result of a different scenario, but you can use Excel to design your what-if models. You can design all sorts of scenarios, using combinations of changes for any values.

Creating a Scenario

You can create one or multiple scenarios to answer your what-if questions, and Excel provides a substantial level of automation to assist you. The way it works is you create different values (called *changing cells*) for as many variables as you need and name that set of changes. You can even create multiple sets, so you can look at the differences between them. For example, you may want to create scenarios you call Great Year, Fair Year, and Uh-Oh.

 It's helpful to keep in mind that changing cells are cells whose values you change. They are not cells that change in response to a recalculation.

Choose Tools | Scenarios to open the Scenario Manager dialog box.

To create a scenario, click Add to open the Add Scenario dialog box shown in Figure 7-6.

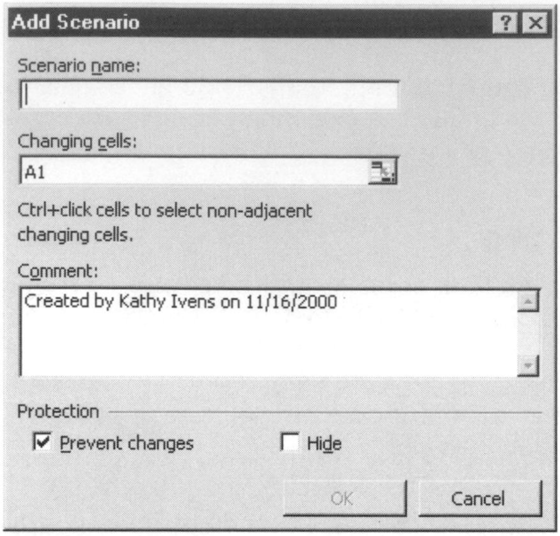

Add Scenario

Scenario name:

Changing cells:

A1

Ctrl+click cells to select non-adjacent changing cells.

Comment:

Created by Kathy Ivens on 11/16/2000

Protection

☑ Prevent changes   ☐ Hide

OK   Cancel

Figure 7-6. *Create the scenario in the Add Scenario dialog box*

Name the scenario, using a phrase that is relevant to the changes you're making. For example, if you're playing "What if the cost of goods rises?" you might want to name the scenario Higher COG.

In the Changing Cells box, enter the cells you want to use for this scenario, using these guidelines:

- You can enter the cell addresses directly or click on cells to select them.

- The cells do not need to be adjacent to each other.

- You can have up to 32 cells.

You can use the same cells for another scenario or for multiple scenarios. This gives you a way to see a number of possible outcomes.

The Comment box contains the name of the creator and the date of creation automatically, but you can eliminate that data, add to it, or skip comments altogether. The Protection options offer these two choices:

- **Prevent Changes**   Bars anyone from making changes to the scenario. For this option to take effect, you must also choose Tools | Protection | Protect Sheet and make sure the Edit Scenarios check box is cleared.

- **Hide**   The scenario doesn't appear in the Scenario Manager dialog box.

After you've entered the information, click OK to see the Scenario Values dialog box.

All the cells you indicated you wanted to change in this scenario are displayed (five cells at a time), along with their current values. Use the TAB key to move through the cells. Click OK when you're finished making changes to return to the Scenario Manager dialog box. The name of your scenario displays, along with the list of changing cells and your comments.

There are several buttons on the dialog box, which work as follows:

■ **Show**   Causes Excel to insert the new values into the changing cells for the selected scenario, which also recalculates the formulas that use those cells.

■ **Close**   Closes the dialog box.

■ **Add**   Opens the Scenario Values dialog box so you can create a new scenario.

■ **Delete**   Removes the selected scenario.

- **Edit**   Opens the Scenario Values dialog box so you can make changes to the selected scenario.

- **Merge**   Combines the selected scenario with any other scenarios for the same worksheet (see the discussion on merging scenarios that follows).

- **Summary**   Produces a summary report (see the discussion on scenario reports that follows).

Does all this seem like overkill? Are you thinking that you could simply enter new values into changing cells and look at the result? If so, good. Your understanding of what Excel is all about is on firm ground. But here's why it isn't overkill:

It's useful to keep a set of values for changing cells together, in one place, with a name for that set of values. It's particularly useful if you have more than one set of values. In that case, you can switch back and forth between the two (or more) sets—between the two or more scenarios, that is—and view their effects on the cells that respond to those values.

In sum, scenarios are a good way to group different sets of inputs together and to go from one group to another conveniently.

Merging Scenarios

If you have a workgroup at your company and a number of people are working on the same project or budget, they might well have developed scenarios using different worksheets, or even using different workbooks. If those scenarios are related to one another, as they probably are, it can be useful to bring them together on a single worksheet. Doing that is called *merging* scenarios.

When you merge two or more scenarios, all you're doing is making them available on the same worksheet. You're not combining them in any arithmetic sense. But when they're available on the same worksheet, the Scenario Manager can get its hands on them all at once. Then they're even easier to compare and analyze.

To merge scenarios, open the appropriate workbook and open the Scenario Manager; then click the Merge button. The Merge Scenarios dialog box opens.

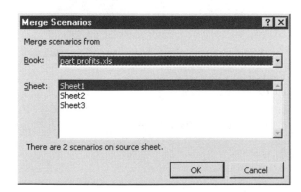

The dialog box tells you which sheets have scenarios and how many scenarios are linked to each sheet. Select the sheet you want to work with and click OK. You return to the Scenario Manager dialog box, which lists the scenarios that were merged. You can then use the action buttons on the merged scenario.

Running Scenario Reports

The important function in the Scenario tool is running the report that lets you see what happens if the values in the scenario are imposed on your workbook. When you select a scenario and click Summary, Excel uses the Scenario Summary dialog box to offer options.

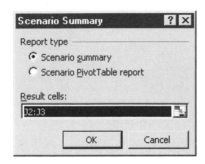

- **Scenario Summary**   Lets you see a report that's similar to an outline, showing the relevant cells. This works for most scenarios because the resulting new numbers are what you want to see.

- **Scenario PivotTable Report**   Shows the report as a pivot table, which gives you more viewing flexibility. This is usually needed only if you have created multiple scenarios that produce results in multiple cells.

- **Result Cells**   Lets you enter the cells in which you want to see the results of your scenario. These are the cells that contain formulas that are affected by the changes you made when you created the scenario. You can enter a single cell, a range, or multiple cells separated by a comma.

Click OK to generate the report. Excel adds a worksheet (named Scenario Summary) to the workbook to hold the summary report. Figure 7-7 shows a scenario summary report.

A few comments about Scenario Summaries are in order.

- The Current Values are the values that are in the scenario's cells at the time the summary is created. These values usually belong to an existing scenario, but not necessarily. The user might have entered new values on the worksheet without establishing them as a scenario, and then created a Scenario Summary.

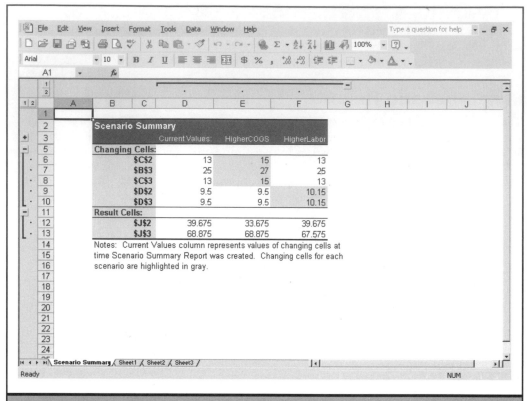

Figure 7-7. *A summary report displays the changed cells and the result cells*

■ Different scenarios might have different changing cells. You can tell a scenario's changing cells from the Scenario Summary: they're highlighted in gray. Because the Current Values don't necessarily belong to an existing scenario, you don't see gray cells in their column.

■ Scenarios that make use of different changing cells, or different result cells, don't coexist well in a Scenario Summary. After all, the purpose of such a summary is to view simultaneously the outcomes—the results—of different changing cell values on the same result cells. If these differ across the scenarios, there's probably little point in summarizing them.

Tip   *If you name the cells used in the scenarios by means of the Name Box or by choosing Insert | Name | Define, the Scenario Summary will display those names instead of the cell references.*

If you select a pivot table to summarize your scenarios, the new worksheet is named Scenario Pivot Table. You can use Excel's pivot table features on this report (see Chapter 13 for information on pivot tables).

Save the workbook to keep the scenario report worksheets.

Using a Business Case with the Scenario Manager

Now that you're familiar with the basic tools for managing scenarios in Excel, take a look at a common sort of business case. A company that manufactures portcullises is considering bringing out a new line. To help management decide whether that's desirable, the marketing and the production departments agree on the structure of the business case and then provide their own values for the scenarios' changing cells.

Figure 7-8 shows Marketing's scenario.

In Marketing's scenario, the break-even point occurs during the second quarter; that is, Marketing assumes that revenues will exceed expenses during that quarter.

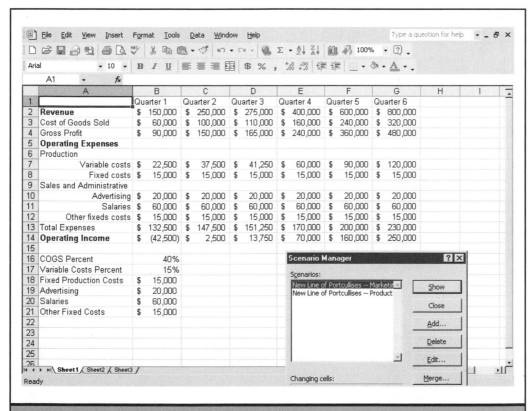

Figure 7-8. *Cost of Goods Sold and Variable Costs are calculated as a percentage of Revenue*

It will take another couple of quarters for the cumulative flow to turn positive—the initial loss of $42,500 during the first quarter will be hard to make up if the portcullis market remains soft—but the firm will be turning a quarterly profit by the second quarter. At least, so says Marketing.

Figure 7-9 shows Product Management's scenario.

The point here is neither Marketing's rosy-glow optimism nor Product Management's grinch-like pessimism. It is that you can easily switch back and forth between the two scenarios by using the Show button on the Scenario Manager. This puts you in a position to decide which set of figures is the more realistic—or that neither scenario represents the most likely outcome.

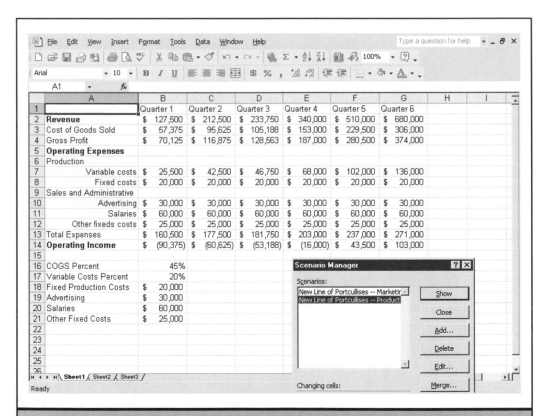

Figure 7-9.   Slower revenue growth and higher costs push the break-even point out to the fifth quarter

In that event, you might decide to change some numbers. If you do, the Scenario Manager can help track such changes in the Comments box, as shown here.

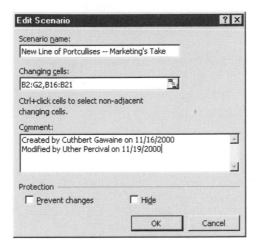

Once the tinkering is complete, you can view the scenario summary:

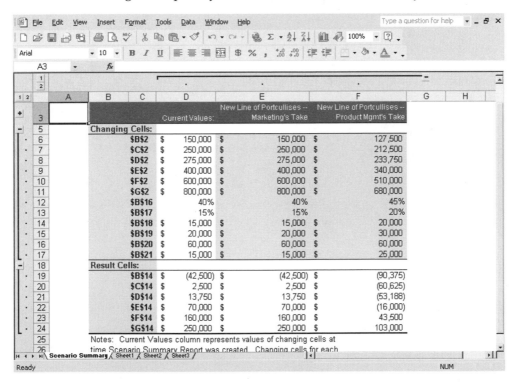

Or, if you prefer to view the summary as a pivot table (Chapter 13 covers the use of pivot tables in Excel) you can choose Scenario PivotTable Report in the Scenario Summary dialog box. The pivot table summary can be a good compromise between the two methods of viewing scenarios discussed. It looks like this:

A	B	C	D	E	F	G	H
1 $B$2:$G$2,$B$16:$B$21 by	(All)						
2							
3	Result Cells						
4 $B$2:$G$2,$B$16:$B$21	Q1	Q2	Q3	Q4	Q5	Q6	
5 New Line of Portcullises -- Marketing's Take	-$42,500	$2,500	$13,750	$70,000	$160,000	$250,000	
6 New Line of Portcullises -- Product Mgmt's Take	-$90,375	-$60,625	-$53,188	-$16,000	$43,500	$103,000	
7							
8							

If you use the Show button on the Scenario Manager to switch back and forth between scenarios, it's harder to compare the effect of individual changing cells on the results. If you use the Scenario Summary, you can make those comparisons, but the summary outline is a fairly rigid framework.

The Scenario PivotTable Report makes it easy to compare the result cells, but it doesn't show you the associated values in the changing cells. If you are already familiar with Excel's pivot tables, you should keep in mind these unique aspects of scenario pivot table summaries:

- You can't refresh its data. If the underlying scenarios change, you must rebuild the pivot table.

- If you select the pivot table and then start the PivotTable Wizard, you have access to Step 3 only.

- The pivot table's row field items correspond to the names of the scenarios.

- The pivot table's page field items correspond to the names of users who have created the underlying scenarios.

The
Complete
Reference

Excel
2002

Chapter 8

Using Formulas

Previous chapters in this book have dealt with the Excel interface: how to navigate in workbooks and worksheets, how to enter and manipulate data, how to sort and filter information, and so on. These are crucial skills, and you can't expect to get anywhere in Excel without them.

But at its core Excel is a giant calculation engine. You arrange to supply the input data, and then you tell Excel what calculations you want it to make. The most basic and essential way to define those calculations is by way of formulas. You certainly won't understand how to enter and modify formulas without the skills presented in Chapters 1 through 7.

Formulas can be as simple as 14 + 82 or 365 / 7. They can also be so complex that it's necessary to break them into their component parts to figure out what's going on inside. But this chapter starts with the fundamentals.

Entering Formulas: Values, Cells, and Operators

Formulas consist of three basic components:

- **Values**   Values include numbers, such as 5, –284, and 15%, and text, such as Q, Fred, and Plan 9 from Outer Space. Excel treats dates and times as numbers and therefore as values.
- **Cell references**   Cells are, of course, the intersection of rows and columns on the worksheet.
- **Operators**   Operators tell Excel what to do with values and cell references; for example, add them together or divide one by another.

Formulas can also include functions such as SUM or MAX. Chapter 9 discusses in some detail how to use functions in formulas. The next section describes how to mix and match values, cells, and operators to create formulas.

Entering and Editing Formulas

Excel provides you with a variety of ways to actually enter formulas into the worksheet. And once the formula has been entered, you have different ways to edit it.

Using the Formula Bar

The most efficient way to enter a formula is with the formula bar. The formula bar and its components are shown in Figure 8-1.

To use the formula bar, begin by selecting the cell where you want to put the formula. Then click in the formula bar and type a formula such as this:

= .07 * 100000

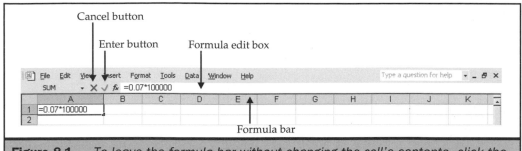

Figure 8-1.   *To leave the formula bar without changing the cell's contents, click the Cancel button*

> **Note**   *The asterisk is an operator. It stands for multiplication, so in words the formula means "point zero seven times one hundred thousand."*

You should begin the formula with an equal sign. This signals Excel that the remainder of what you're typing is a formula, not a static value.

When you've finished typing the formula, press ENTER or click the Enter button.

Excel displays the formula that you typed in the formula bar and shows the result of the formula in the cell that was active when you entered the formula.

Entering Cell Addresses

As you will find through experience, it's only in special circumstances that you will enter a formula that consists entirely of static values such as .07 * 100000. It's typical that you will want your formula to combine the values that are in cells, possibly with static values. Here are two examples:

= .0745 * C5

= .2 * C5

Suppose that cell C5 contains a salary amount in dollars, that the current FICA rate is 7.45 percent, and that the Federal tax rate is 20 percent. The first formula would calculate the amount of the FICA contribution; the second formula would calculate the dollar amount of Federal tax. The virtue of this approach is that you can change the dollar amount in cell C5 and in response, Excel recalculates both formulas to show the new FICA and Federal tax amounts.

You needn't type the cell addresses yourself when you enter the formula (although you can do so if you wish). Instead of actually typing, say, C5, just click on cell C5—Excel enters the address for you. The sequence to create the FICA formula example above is

   1. Click on any blank worksheet cell other than C5.

2. Click the formula bar's edit box. Type an equal sign.

3. Type **.0745***.

4. Click on cell C5.

5. Press ENTER or click the Enter button.

Formulas and Simple Operators

All formulas in Excel share one common trait: they start with an equal sign. For example, select a cell and type in the formula bar's edit box

= 14 + 82

If you don't start it with an equal sign, Excel doesn't treat it as a formula. If you do start it with an equal sign, Excel displays the result, 96, in the cell where you entered the formula.

Note	*To assist new users who are transitioning from 1-2-3, Excel permits the use of the plus sign to initiate a formula. But if you use the plus sign, Excel immediately changes it to an equal sign.*

But if you enter

14 + 82

Excel doesn't find an equal sign and therefore treats it as a static value—in this case, as a string of characters, also termed *text* or a *string*.

Begun with an equal sign, the formula evaluates to the sum of the two numbers because it uses the plus sign, also termed the *addition operator*. That probably sounds pretentious, but the usage helps to enumerate other operators used in Excel. The set of arithmetic operators will be familiar to you. Besides the addition operator, there are these:

- **Subtraction operator, the minus sign**   Subtract the second number from the first. Example: = 96 – 82 returns 14.

- **Negation operator, again the minus sign**   This indicates a negative number such as –14.

- **Multiplication operator, the asterisk**   Multiply the first number times the second. Example: = 14 * 8 returns 112.

- **Division operator, the forward slash**   Divide the first number by the second. Example: = 25 / 6 returns 4.17. (Excel does *not* use an integer division operator, usually the backward slash, on the worksheet.)

- **Exponentiation operator, the caret**   Raise the first number to the power of the second. Example: = 9 ^ 3 returns 729.
- **Percent operator, the percent sign**   Divide the number by 100 and show the percent sign after it. Example: = 20% returns 0.2, but appears in the cell as 20%.

Each of the arithmetic operators produces a numeric result—or, if the formula violates calculation rules, they can produce error values. For example, it's legal to enter the formula

= 9 / 0

but because the result of dividing by zero is undefined, Excel displays the #DIV/0! error value in the cell containing the formula.

Excel has one text operator, the ampersand. It is used to join, or *concatenate*, two text values. For example, this formula:

="William " & "Shakespeare"

returns *William Shakespeare*. The formula combines two text values. Excel interprets the values as text, because each is surrounded by a pair of quote marks.

This chapter has no more to say about text values in formulas, but Chapters 9 and 10 deal with them in some detail. The same is true of the comparison operators such as <, >, <>, and so on.

If formulas were limited to numeric values and arithmetic operators, their usefulness would be limited as well. But formulas can also use cell addresses. For example, the formula

= A15 + B15

entered in, say, cell C15 returns the sum of the values in cells A15 and B15. Suppose that A15 contains 14 and B15 contains 82. Then the formula in cell C15 returns 96, the sum of those two numeric values.

Now suppose that you change the value in A15 from 14 to 20. Here's where formulas start to become truly powerful: in response to the change you make to cell A15, Excel recalculates the result of all the formulas that use A15. The formula in cell C15, instead of returning 96, now returns 20 + 82, or 102.

This recalculation capability is the basis for much of the work that you cause Excel to do. The grand old term "what-if analysis" is actually little more than recalculating formulas based on changing the values of the cells that the formulas refer to. In the above example, which adds the values in the two cells A15 and B15, those values might be the amounts of last month's phone and electricity bills, respectively. To change the value in A15 from 14 to 20 is to ask, "How much must I pay if next month's phone bill is 20 and the electricity bill remains the same?"

Because you can use cell references in formulas, there are some special operators that have to do with cell references. They are most useful when combined with Excel functions, as you will see in Chapter 9. These reference operators are as follows:

- **The range operator, or colon**   Returns a reference to the two cells on either side of the colon and all cells in between. Example: A1:A5 returns a reference to A1, A2, A3, A4, and A5.

- **The union operator, or comma**   Combines multiple references into one reference. Example: A1,B6 returns one reference to those two nonadjacent cells.

- **The intersection operator, the space**   Returns a reference to the cell or cells common to two ranges of cells. Example: C1:D5 A2:E3 returns the reference C2:D3—that is, the four cells that the two ranges have in common.

Relative, Absolute, and Mixed References

An extremely useful aspect of formulas is that you can copy them and then paste them to other locations in the worksheet. For example, suppose that this formula is in C15:

=A15 + B15

If you select cell C15, choose Edit | Copy, then select cell C16, and choose Edit | Paste, you will get this formula in cell C16:

=A16 + B16

In the process of copying the formula one row down, from row 15 to row 16, you automatically arranged for Excel to adjust the references in the formula, again from row 15 to row 16.

This capability makes your life much simpler. It is very often the case that you have values in columns that you want to add (or otherwise combine by subtraction, division, and so on). In that and similar cases, you need create the formula once only, and then you can copy and paste it into other cells. The formula's references adjust to take their new locations into account. See Figure 8-2 for more examples.

Figure 8-2 shows two typical uses of a copied formula. The formula

= B2 – C2

was entered into cell D2. Then, with D2 selected, the user chose Edit | Copy and selected the range D3:D7. Edit | Paste was used to paste the formula into D3:D7. Excel adjusted the original references to B2 and D2, so that they adjusted by one row for each instance of the formula: B3 and D3, B4 and D4, and so on.

It works the same way when you're copying from column to column. In Figure 8-2, the formula in B13 was copied and pasted into C13 and D13. In this case, because the

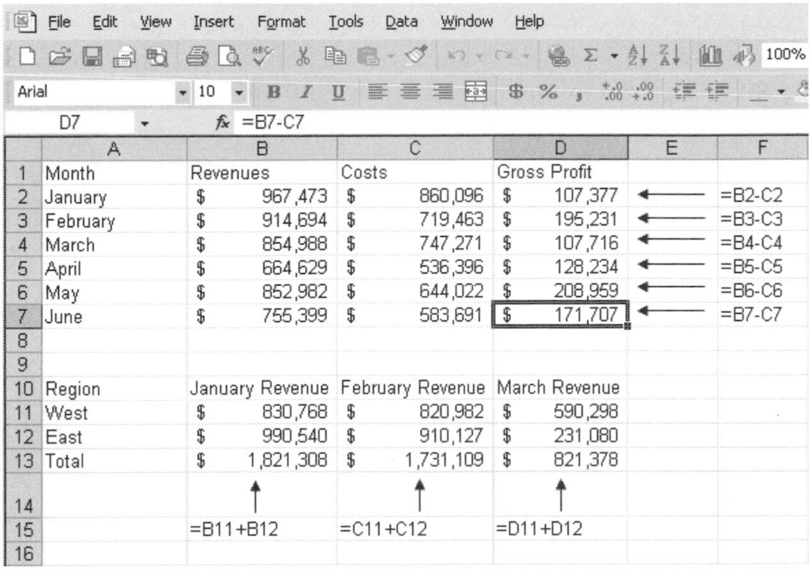

Figure 8-2.   *Copying through rows adjusts row numbers; copying through columns adjusts column numbers*

formula was being copied into new columns, the original column B was adjusted to columns C and D, respectively.

There's a shortcut for this copy-and-paste process that will save you considerable time in the long run. Use the fill handle on the cell that contains the first instance of the formula: in Figure 8-2, that's cell D2 or B13. You could select cell D2 and drag its fill handle down through cell D7. And you could select cell B13 and drag its fill handle right, through cell D13. These are instances of the AutoFill process, which was introduced in Chapter 4. (Using AutoFill, you can drag vertically or horizontally, not diagonally. But you can drag up or down, right or left.)

Why does this capability work? That is, how does Excel know to adjust the cell addresses in a formula when you first copy and then paste that formula to a new location? The answer is in how you specify the addresses. The examples you've seen in this section use *relative references*. For example, the formula in cell B13 of Figure 8-2 is

=B11 + B12

The formula itself is in B13, and the formula adds the value in B11 (two rows up) to the value in B12 (one row up). When the formula is copied into cell C13, it becomes

=C11 + C12

Note that the formula still adds the value found two rows up to the value found one row up. *These references are* relative *to the cell that contains the formula.*

Before you move on to the next section, be sure you see how the concept of relative referencing works with the formula in cell D2 of Figure 8-2, as copied into cells D3:D7.

Absolute Referencing

As you might expect, the opposite of relative referencing is *absolute referencing*. An absolute reference is distinguished from a relative reference by its use of dollar signs. Here's a formula that uses absolute references:

=$C$11 + $C$12

The dollar signs indicate to Excel that it should not adjust the references when the formula is copied and pasted—or, equivalently, when the formula is used as the basis for an autofill.

If that formula is in, say, cell C13, you can copy it to D13, to B13, or IV65536, and it will still return the sum of the values in cells C11 and C12.

One use of absolute references in Excel can occur when you create a report. See Figure 8-3 for an example.

Perhaps you are preparing a monthly profit-and-loss report. As you build the report, you enter the formulas shown in column D in Figure 8-3 to calculate the gross profit for each month.

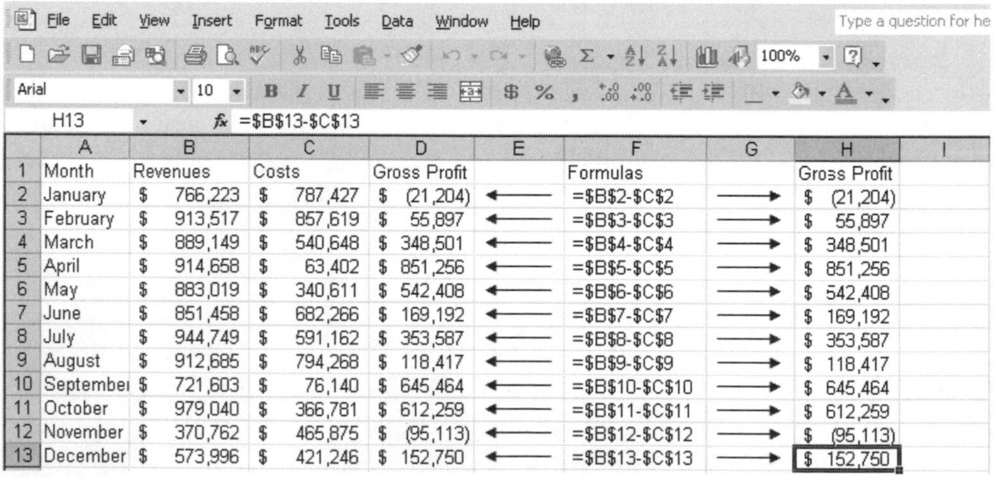

H13 =$B$13-$C$13

	A	B	C	D	E	F	G	H
1	Month	Revenues	Costs	Gross Profit		Formulas		Gross Profit
2	January	$ 766,223	$ 787,427	$ (21,204)	←	=$B$2-$C$2	→	$ (21,204)
3	February	$ 913,517	$ 857,619	$ 55,897	←	=$B$3-$C$3	→	$ 55,897
4	March	$ 889,149	$ 540,648	$ 348,501	←	=$B$4-$C$4	→	$ 348,501
5	April	$ 914,658	$ 63,402	$ 851,256	←	=$B$5-$C$5	→	$ 851,256
6	May	$ 883,019	$ 340,611	$ 542,408	←	=$B$6-$C$6	→	$ 542,408
7	June	$ 851,458	$ 682,266	$ 169,192	←	=$B$7-$C$7	→	$ 169,192
8	July	$ 944,749	$ 591,162	$ 353,587	←	=$B$8-$C$8	→	$ 353,587
9	August	$ 912,685	$ 794,268	$ 118,417	←	=$B$9-$C$9	→	$ 118,417
10	Septembei	$ 721,603	$ 76,140	$ 645,464	←	=$B$10-$C$10	→	$ 645,464
11	October	$ 979,040	$ 366,781	$ 612,259	←	=$B$11-$C$11	→	$ 612,259
12	November	$ 370,762	$ 465,875	$ (95,113)	←	=$B$12-$C$12	→	$ (95,113)
13	December	$ 573,996	$ 421,246	$ 152,750	←	=$B$13-$C$13	→	$ 152,750

Figure 8-3. *D2:D13 could have been copied to H14:H25 with the same result*

But when you get ready to print the report, you aren't interested in showing the monthly revenues and costs, just the gross profit. If the formulas in column D use absolute references, you can copy the range D2:D13 to, say, H2:H13 (well away from the revenue and cost information), and the formulas will return the same results in both ranges—because they use absolute references.

You can use both relative and absolute references in the same formula (see Figure 8-4).

The situation shown in Figure 8-4 calls for part of a formula to adjust and part to remain fixed. The part that adjusts is the reference to a cell in column B: for example, B2. Notice that *B2* uses no dollar signs and therefore is a relative reference. The part that remains fixed is the reference to $E$1. Notice that *$E$1* uses dollar signs and therefore is an absolute reference.

The problem is to determine how an initial investment will grow during each of ten years at a constant rate of growth. The rate of growth is shown in cell E1. The formula in cell B3 is

=B2*(1+$E$1)

In words, add 1 to the growth rate in cell E1 and multiply that amount times the value of the investment in the prior year.

The prior year's value is given as a relative reference: for example, B2. As the formula is copied down through B4:B12, that reference adjusts so that it always points at the cell immediately above.

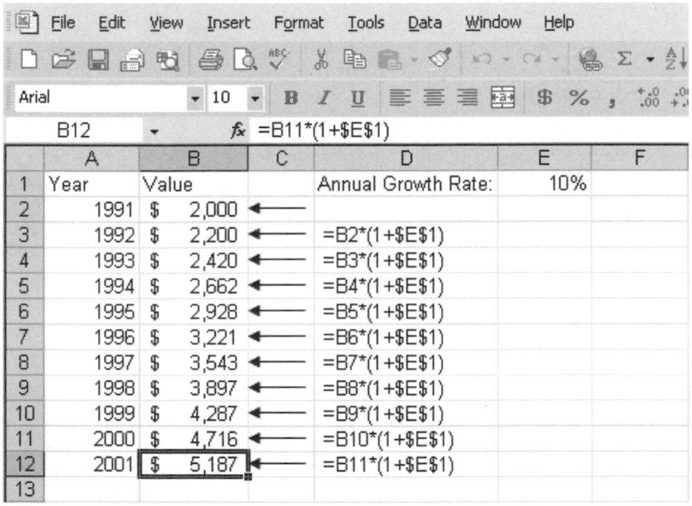

	A	B	C	D	E	F
1	Year	Value		Annual Growth Rate:	10%	
2	1991	$ 2,000	←			
3	1992	$ 2,200	←	=B2*(1+$E$1)		
4	1993	$ 2,420	←	=B3*(1+$E$1)		
5	1994	$ 2,662	←	=B4*(1+$E$1)		
6	1995	$ 2,928	←	=B5*(1+$E$1)		
7	1996	$ 3,221	←	=B6*(1+$E$1)		
8	1997	$ 3,543	←	=B7*(1+$E$1)		
9	1998	$ 3,897	←	=B8*(1+$E$1)		
10	1999	$ 4,287	←	=B9*(1+$E$1)		
11	2000	$ 4,716	←	=B10*(1+$E$1)		
12	2001	$ 5,187	←	=B11*(1+$E$1)		
13						

Figure 8-4. *The formulas shown are useful whenever you apply a constant to a range of cells*

The growth rate is given as an absolute reference: $E$1. As the formula is copied down, it does *not* adjust to $E$2, $E$3, and so on but remains fixed at its original address.

One virtue in this approach is that you can change the value, 10%, in cell E1 and see that one change reflected in all the formulas in column B—because the absolute reference ensures that all the formulas depend on cell $E$1.

Mixed References

You will find that you use mixed references much more frequently than you use purely absolute references. A mixed reference is one that fixes the column but not the row, or that fixes the row but not the column. For example, these two formulas:

=$A3 / 2

=A$3 / 2

both involve a mixed reference. Suppose you copy a formula that uses the reference $A3. No matter where you paste it—into column Q, into row 76—it will still refer to column A. The row portion of the reference will adjust, because it's not immediately preceded by a dollar sign. But the column will remain fixed.

Similarly, if you copy a formula that uses the reference A$3, its column will adjust but its row will remain fixed. See Figure 8-5 for an example.

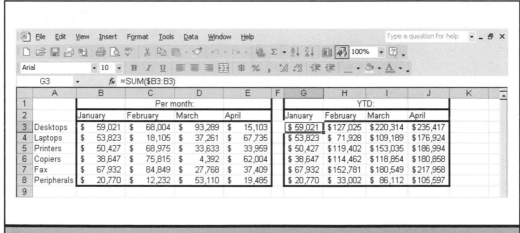

Figure 8-5. *Mixed references are ideal for creating running totals*

The range G3:J8 in Figure 8-5 contains formulas that give the year-to-date total revenues for each of six product lines. That's 24 formulas. But if you manage things right, you need enter one formula only; you can create the others using AutoFill.

Begin by entering this formula in cell G3:

=SUM($B3:B3)

That formula employs the SUM function. It returns the total of the values in the range within the parentheses. Here, that range runs from B3 to B3—that is, the range is the cell B3. The sum of the value in cell B3 is $59,021, and that's what shows up in cell G3.

Next, drag the fill handle on cell G3 one column to the right, into H3. Because the cell on the left of the range operator has a dollar sign before the column identifier, it remains fixed: $B remains $B. The cell on the right of the range operator has no dollar sign before it, so it adjusts: B becomes C. And the rows do not adjust because the formula remains in the same row: you autofill the formula from G3 to H3. Therefore, the formula

=SUM($B3:B3)

in cell G3 becomes the formula

=SUM($B3:C3)

in cell H3. For every additional column you drag the fill handle to the right, the range increments by another column: $B3:C3, $B3:D3, and $B3:E3. That's how you obtain the four year-to-date totals for Desktops in cells G3:J3 of Figure 8-5.

What about the other five product lines? Once you've autofilled from G3 into H3:J3, all four cells are selected. If you haven't yet done so, release the mouse button. Then drag the fill handle in cell J3 down through J4:J8.

Because the formulas do *not* have dollar signs before their row identifiers, they are relative with respect to rows. The formulas increment the row identifiers as you autofill from rows 3 through 7. And the formula in cell J8 turns out to be

=SUM($B8:E8)

Cycling Through Reference Types

It's a little exacting to position your mouse pointer so that the insertion point is in the right place to put a dollar sign. This is especially true if you're using a laptop's pointing device, sitting in a cramped seat on a jet that's flying through turbulence.

Here's a better way. Select a cell that contains a formula with a reference. Use your mouse pointer to drag across that reference in the formula bar, like this:

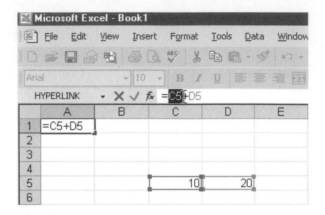

Notice that the selected reference happens to be a relative reference, C5. Now press the F4 key. The relative reference changes to the absolute reference $C$5. Press F4 again to change the absolute reference $C$5 to the mixed reference C$5. Another F4 gets you $C5. And one final F4 returns you to the original relative reference C5.

At whatever point you have reached the reference type that you want, either press ENTER or click the Enter Formula button on the Formula palette. This establishes the reference, as edited with the F4 key, in the formula.

Linking Formulas, External References, and 3-D References

References in formulas are not restricted to cells and ranges on the same sheet. They frequently refer to cells and ranges on other worksheets in the same workbook, as well as in other workbooks. Some formulas use a special kind of reference, termed a 3-D reference, that refers simultaneously to several sheets in the same workbook.

Creating Links

Suppose that a worksheet named Quarterly is active, and that the same workbook contains a worksheet named Monthly (see Figure 8-6).

You would like cell B2 on the Quarterly worksheet to contain the total of the January, February, and March results on the Monthly worksheet. To bring this about, take these steps:

1. Select cell B2 on the Quarterly worksheet and type an equal sign.

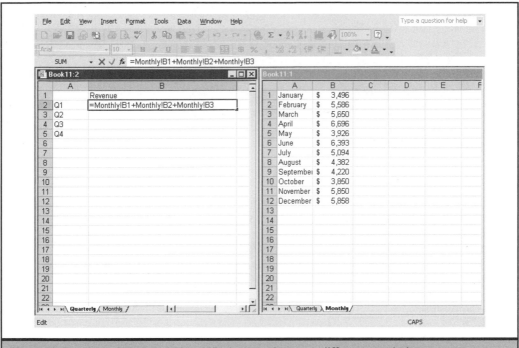

Figure 8-6. *Use Window | New Window to view two different worksheets
simultaneously*

2. Switch to the Monthly worksheet by clicking on it if its window or its
   worksheet tab is visible, or by using the Window menu otherwise.

3. Click on cell B1 on the Monthly worksheet and type a plus sign.

4. Click on cell B2 on the Monthly worksheet and type a plus sign.

5. Click on cell B3 on the Monthly worksheet. Switch to the Quarterly
   worksheet and press ENTER.

The result is this formula in cell B2 of the Quarterly worksheet:

= Monthly!B1 + Monthly!B2 + Monthly!B3

This formula uses 3-D references, so-called because the formula points to different
worksheets (for more information, see the section on 3-D references later in this chapter).
Notice that the cell addresses are preceded by the name of the worksheet where they
are located; an exclamation point separates the name of the worksheet from the address
of the cell. Formulas like this that refer to cells on other worksheets (whether or not the
cells are in the same workbook) are termed *links*.

This process of summarizing data that's found in different locations is sometimes termed data consolidation. Although the consolidation is often managed by means of a 3-D reference, there's nothing magical about the multisheet nature of the reference. It simply happens that many people store information on different worksheets that represent different sources: for example, months or regions or product lines or biotech companies. Subsequently, the user finds it expedient to consolidate the data, and a 3-D reference is used because the source data exists on separate worksheets.

Creating External Links

Suppose that the Monthly and the Quarterly worksheets in Figure 8-6 were in different workbooks. You would go through almost exactly the same sequence of steps to create the formula in cell B2 of the Quarterly worksheet: the only difference would be that instead of switching to the Monthly worksheet in the same workbook, you would switch to a different workbook.

This small difference has a major impact on the formula and its behavior. If the Monthly worksheet were in a workbook named Details, then the formula would now appear in the formula bar like this:

= [Details]Monthly!$B$1 + [Details]Monthly!$B$2 + [Details]Monthly!$B$3

The formula indicates that the worksheet named Monthly is located in a workbook named Details. Also, notice the dollar signs in the cell references in the formula; Excel makes references absolute when they are to cells in other workbooks.

There's yet another difference in the formula if, after creating the formula, you close the workbook named Details. Then Excel adds the path to the filename. For example, if Details.xls were saved in the directory C:\, the formula would appear as

='C:\[Details.xls]Monthly'!$B$1 + 'C:\[Details.xls]Monthly'!$B$2 + 'C:\[Details.xls]Monthly'!$B$3

Note that the text value that consists of the workbook's path, its name, and the name of the worksheet, are enclosed in single quote marks.

Updating Links

It's not just the appearance of the formula that changes when you create an external link such as this. When you open a workbook that contains external references, you may see a message box that informs you, "The workbook you opened contains automatic links to information in another workbook." The message goes on to ask you whether to update those links, in case the data in the other workbook has changed.

Usually, you will choose Yes, in order that the workbook you're opening be current with the data in the external references. On rare occasions—for example, you have so many links that it takes a long time to update them all—you might choose No.

If you want to suppress that message box and update the links automatically without confirming your intent, select Tools | Options and click the Edit tab. Clear the check box that's labeled "Ask to update automatic links."

This option belongs not to the workbook, but to the application. That is, if you change the option, it applies to all workbooks, not just to the one that was active when you changed the option.

| **Caution** | *Use this option with care. If you clear the Ask to Update Automatic Links check box,*
Excel will update your links without informing you that it is doing so. |

Using External Links to Recover Corrupted Files

Sometimes you might be unable to open an Excel workbook because it has somehow become corrupted. An errant bit—to say nothing of cross-linked clusters or bad file allocation table entries—can make it impossible to open the workbook.

If you don't have a backup, you might still be able to retrieve some information from the corrupted file by using external references. Suppose the file you're unable to open is named Corrupt.xls, that it has a worksheet named Sheet1, and that its path is C:\. Open a new workbook and enter this formula in Sheet1, cell A1:

=' C:\[Corrupt.xls]Sheet1'!A1

(If the workbook named Corrupt.xls is password protected, you'll need to enter the correct password before Excel will return the data to the new workbook.) Copy the formula as far to the right and down as necessary to capture the desired columns and rows. When you have finished with a given worksheet, select the range that contains all the external reference formulas. Choose Edit | Copy, and then choose Edit | Paste Special | Values and click OK.

This approach can recover cell values in the corrupted file. It cannot recover formulas, only their results. For example, if cell A5 on Sheet1 in the corrupted file contains the formula

=10 / 2

then this formula in the new workbook

=' C:\[Corrupt.xls]Sheet1'!A5

returns not the formula but its result, 5.

And, of course, this approach cannot recover such items as cell formats, list boxes, drawing objects such as arrows, or cell comments.

ANALYZING DATA

Creating 3-D References

You've already seen a few instances in this chapter of the range operator, the colon. Its use has been to create a range of cells: those cells between and including the cells on either side of the colon. So the reference A1:C1 refers to A1, B1, and C1, while the reference A1:B2 refers to A1, A2, B1, and B2.

You can also use the range operator with worksheet names. The sheet name just replaces the cell address in the reference. For example, the reference Sheet2:Sheet4 refers to Sheet2 and Sheet4 and any worksheets that intervene—usually, but not necessarily, this is Sheet3.

This use of the range operator is the basis for the 3-D reference. The term comes from the notion that a range of cells can have a vertical dimension consisting of rows, a horizontal dimension consisting of columns, *and* a depth dimension consisting of worksheets. For example:

Sheet3:Sheet5!A1:B2

In practice, it's unusual to employ all three of the available dimensions in one formula. More frequently, you are likely to want to apply some function (such as SUM, AVERAGE, MAX, or the like) to a single cell across several worksheets, as here:

Sheet3:Sheet5!A1

Suppose that you are reviewing data on winter snowfall amounts in mountain areas where runoff will supply water to your community during the coming year. You have in one workbook a worksheet for measurements taken during November, during December, and on through March. Each worksheet records, in cell D3, the depth of snowpack measured during that month. As the best estimate of typical snowpack, you use the AVERAGE function on a 3-D reference:

=AVERAGE(November:March!D3)

To build this formula, take these steps:

1. Activate the worksheet that will contain the formula. Select a cell to contain the formula, and type the following:

   =AVERAGE(

2. Click on the sheet tab of the first worksheet in the 3-D range. In this example, you would click on the sheet tab labeled *November*.

3. Hold down the SHIFT key. While continuing to hold it down, click on the sheet tab of the final worksheet in the 3-D range to activate it. Release the SHIFT key. All the included sheet tabs are now selected. The formula bar should now contain

   =AVERAGE('November:March'!

Although you have clicked on the 3-D range's final worksheet tab, the first worksheet in the range (here, the sheet named November) should still be active. Click on cell D3. Type a closing parenthesis, and press enter. The formula should now appear in the formula bar as:

=AVERAGE('November:March'!D3)

and the sheet tabs should appear as shown next.

Notice that you don't need to supply either the range operator or the exclamation point that separates the sheet names from the cell address. Excel supplies them for you when you click the final sheet tab and when you click on the cell to use in the formula.

In the previous example, suppose you enter the formula and then:

- Insert a worksheet named Sheet1 somewhere between the worksheet named November and the worksheet named March. The AVERAGE() function would then incorporate any value it finds in Sheet1!D3.

- Delete the March (or the November) worksheet. The formula adjusts to end with February (or to begin with December).

- Move the March worksheet so that it precedes the November worksheet. The formula adjusts to end with February.

There are some characteristics of references to cells on a single worksheet that don't apply to 3-D references:

- You can't use 3-D references in array formulas (see Chapter 10).

- The intersection operator (the single blank space) doesn't work with 3-D references.

- The implicit intersection (also see Chapter 10) doesn't work with 3-D references.

Auditing Formulas

It's usually pretty easy to tell what references a formula depends on. When you look at the formula

    =B2/A5

you know immediately that it divides the value in B2 by that in A5. And because both cells are on the sheet that contains the formula (otherwise, you'd see a sheet name associated with the cell reference), it's easy to tell what's in B2 and in A5.

But what if you want to know whether B2 is used by a formula in another cell? Just looking at B2 doesn't tell you that cell Z192 uses its value as a numerator, or that some cell on another worksheet uses B2 as a minuend.

Finding Precedents and Dependents

In these and similar cases, Excel's auditing capability is useful (see Figure 8-7).

In Figure 8-7, note the two arrows that point to cell D4. These are termed *tracer arrows*. The cell that they point to is termed the *dependent cell*. The cells that they point from are termed the *precedent cells*.

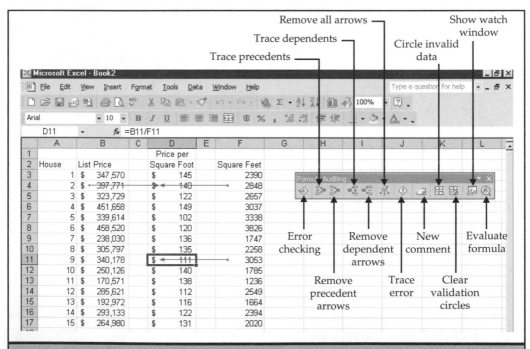

Figure 8-7.   *Tracer arrows are the same color whether they are created with Trace Precedents or with Trace Dependents*

Because cell D4 has two arrows pointing to it, you can tell that it has two precedent cells: cell F4 and cell B4. These arrows were put on the sheet by first selecting cell D4, then choosing Tools | Auditing and clicking Trace Precedents on the submenu.

Figure 8-7 also shows a single arrow pointing from cell F11 to cell D11. F11 has just one dependent cell: D11. The arrow was created by selecting cell F11, choosing Tools | Auditing, and clicking Trace Dependents on the submenu.

Note   *Tracing precedents creates arrows only to cells that are precedent to the active cell. Similarly, tracing dependents creates arrows only to cells that are dependent on the active cell.*

Instead of the Tools menu, you can use the Formula Auditing toolbar, also shown in Figure 8-7. It's a good idea to use this toolbar because it has some command buttons that perform tasks you can't get at via the Excel menus:

- **The Remove Precedent Arrows and the Remove Dependent Arrows buttons**   These enable you to remove one sort of tracer arrow and leave the other sort on the worksheet. The Auditing submenu includes only the Remove All Arrows command.

- **The Circle Invalid Data and the Clear Validation Circles buttons**   These are the only way to show, or suppress, circles that identify the location of cells that contain data that violates any validation rules that you have set up. (Chapter 2 discusses data validation.)

You display the Formula Auditing toolbar in the usual way, via View | Toolbars. You can also choose Tools | Auditing and click Show Formula Auditing Toolbar on the submenu.

Figure 8-8 shows a slightly more complicated situation.

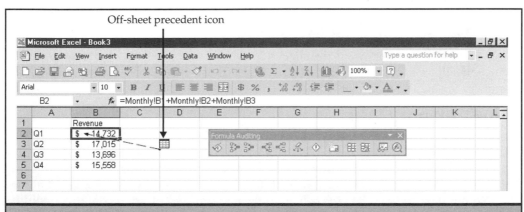

Figure 8-8.   *The sheet names in the Formula Bar confirm that the precedent cell is off-sheet*

There's a new symbol in Figure 8-8, the Off-Sheet Precedent icon. It indicates that one or more references in the audited formula are from another worksheet, or even from another workbook. When you double-click the dashed line that leads to the icon, the Go To dialog box appears:

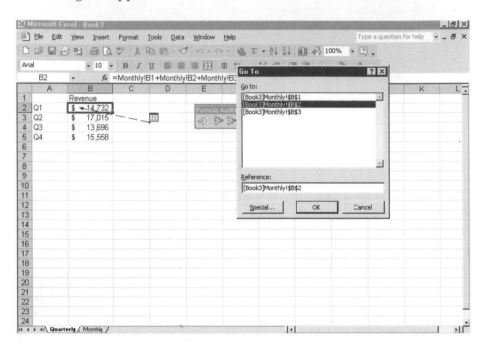

Don't try to click the Off-Sheet Precedent icon itself; nothing will happen. You must click the dashed line leading to the icon, hard as it is to hit. When your mouse pointer has located the dashed line, it will turn from a cross to an arrow.

The off-sheet precedent cells appear in the list box. If you click on one of them and then choose OK, Excel activates the sheet that contains the precedent and selects the precedent cell.

Locating Invalid Data

The validation buttons (Circle Invalid Data and Clear Validation Circles) on the Formula Auditing toolbar are useful if a worksheet contains data that violates validation rules that you have established. However, the error message you choose when you set up the validation must be either Warning or Information—otherwise, Excel will not allow you to enter data directly into the cell. If you want to locate cells that contain invalid data, click the Circle Invalid Data button. The cell or cells in question are then surrounded by red circles—ovals, actually.

Remove the circles by clicking the Clear Validation Circles button.

Dealing with Errors in Formulas

Error values occur when something goes wrong with a formula or with the values and cells that the formula refers to.

The errors in formulas cascade—that is, if A1 contains an error value and A2 depends on A1, then A2 contains the same error value. These errors can be particularly difficult to locate if the cell where the error originates is in another worksheet—or even in another workbook. This section discusses how to trace error values, how to find errors, and how to interpret their meanings.

Suppose that you see the error value #DIV/0! or #NUM! or a similar error on a worksheet. It's quite possible that the cell displaying the error message contains a formula such as:

=A4/A5

where cell A5 has a zero value—the formula is instructed to divide by zero and therefore returns the #DIV/0! error value.

Equally possible, though, is that the formula that returns the #DIV/0! error value is

=A4 + Sheet3!B6

Nothing's being divided in this formula. Nevertheless it will return the #DIV/0! error value if one of its precedents—that is, either cell A4 or cell B6 on Sheet3—results in a division by zero. See Figure 8-9 for another example.

The error tracers in Figure 8-9 were created by selecting the dependent cell (here, cell A1 on Sheet3) that contains an error value and then clicking the Trace Error button on the Formula Auditing toolbar. Excel draws an arrow from cell A4 to cell A1, because A4 is a precedent to A1 and A4 contains an error value.

Excel also puts the Off-Sheet Precedent icon on the worksheet pointing to cell A4, because cell A4's precedents are on another sheet. The formula in cell A4 is

=Sheet1!A1/Sheet1!C1

Because cell C1 on Sheet1 contains zero, the formula results in the #DIV/0! error value.

The Trace Error button creates two different sorts of arrows, and what governs is which cell is selected when you click the button. Assume that

- Cell A1 contains the value 10.
- Cell A2 contains the value 0.
- Cell A3 contains the formula

  = A1 / A2

  and returns the #DIV/0! error value.
- Cell C3 contains the formula

  = A3

  and returns the same error value as appears in cell A3.

If you select cell A3 and click the Trace Error button, Excel places blue precedent tracer arrows from cell A1 to cell A3 and from cell A2 to cell A3. Cell A3 does not itself depend on an error value: it creates the error value.

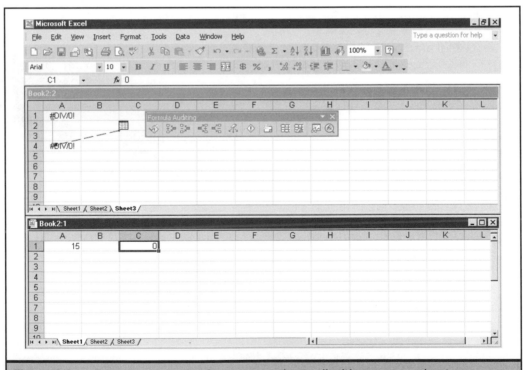

Figure 8-9. *Error tracers point from a precedent cell with an error value to a dependent cell*

If you select cell C3 and click the Trace Error button, Excel places a red error tracer arrow from cell C3 to cell A3. The arrow is red because cell C3 depends on a cell that contains an error value. When the error has been corrected (for example, by changing the value in cell A2 to a nonzero number), the arrow remains in place but appears in blue.

Checking for Errors

Excel 10 offers a new method for dealing with errors on the worksheet. In much the same way as the Spelling tool searches for misspelled words in the worksheet's cells, the Error Checking tool searches for errors in formulas. Figure 8-10 gives an example.

Notice cell C3 in Figure 8-10. It contains the #DIV/0! error value discussed in the previous section. In Figure 8-10, though, cell C3 also contains an error indicator in its upper-left corner. This indicator means that Excel has found one of several possible errors in the cell. If you select a cell with an error indicator, a Warning icon appears.

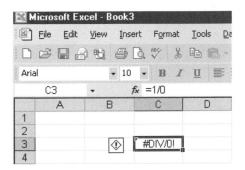

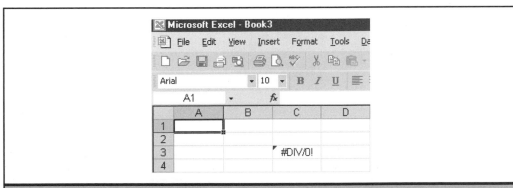

Figure 8-10. *The error value was created with a formula that divides 1 by 0*

And, if you click the Warning icon, the menu shown in Figure 8-11 appears.

The menu shown in Figure 8-11 differs according to the type of error that Excel is reporting. These types of errors are discussed in the following sections. But regardless of the type of error that Excel reports, some items in the Error Checking menu remain the same. You always have these menu options:

- **Help on this error**   Click this menu item to invoke context-sensitive Help.

- **Ignore Error**   Click this menu item to remove the cell's error indicator. Note that choosing to ignore the error means that only this instance of the error is ignored. Other cells with the same error will continue to display the error indicator.

- **Edit in Formula Bar**   Clicking this menu item emulates clicking in the Formula Bar. The Formula Bar is activated and the Enter button and the Cancel button appear.

- **Error Checking Options**   Click this menu item to display the Error Checking dialog box. (See Figure 8.12, later in this chapter.)

- **Show Formula Auditing Toolbar**   Click this menu item to display the toolbar.

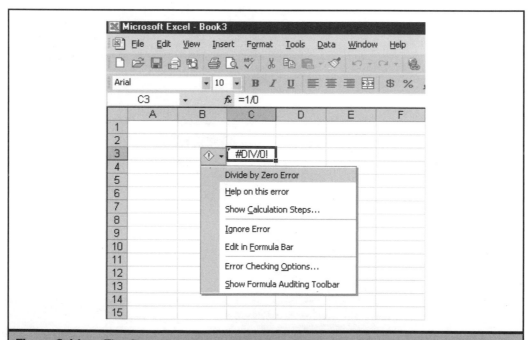

Figure 8-11.   *The first line in the menu always describes the type of possible error*

The following sections discuss the different types of possible errors that Excel can report, and the consequent changes to the Error Checking menu that result.

Checking for Error Values

There are several types of error values that formulas can return. This chapter has already discussed one such error: division by zero and the error value that results, #DIV/0!. The other error values and their typical causes are discussed below.

In each case, the Error Checking menu supplies a Show Calculation Steps item. Selecting that item displays the Evaluate Formula dialog box.

#NUM!   The #NUM! error means that Excel can't calculate a result. It usually occurs when your formula's result is too large or too small for Excel to calculate. An example is =10^1000 (that is, 10 followed by 1000 zeros). Excel can't calculate so large a result. Another possibility is that you have called for the square root of a negative number.

The Error Checking menu that results from the #NUM! error is shown next.

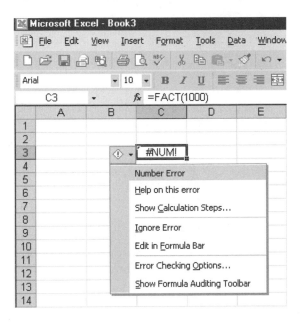

#N/A!   The #N/A! error means that no value is available. It occurs when you use one of the lookup or other reference functions (see Chapter 10) to find a value in an array—and that value doesn't appear in the array.

#NAME?   The #NAME? error means that Excel doesn't recognize the text portion of a formula. It is usually caused by mistyping the name of a function. If you were typing too fast and typed =SM(A4,B6) instead of =SUM(A4,B6), Excel would return the #NAME? error value.

#NULL!   The #NULL! error value belongs to the intersection operator. Recall from early in this chapter that the intersection operator, a blank space, returns the cells where two ranges intersect. If the ranges have no cells in common—as, for example, A1:A5 B1:B5—then Excel returns #NULL!.

#REF!   The #REF! error typically means that a formula refers to a nonexistent cell. For example, in cell D4, enter the formula =**A4**. Then copy and paste the formula from D4 one column to the left, into cell C4. Because A4 is a relative reference, C4 attempts to set itself equal to the contents of whatever cell is to the left of A4—and there isn't one. The error value can also occur when a cell is deleted. In the present example, if you deleted cell A4, then cell D4 would return #REF!.

#VALUE!   The #VALUE! error nearly always occurs when you attempt to combine incompatible values in a formula. For example, you can't sensibly perform a numeric operation on a text value, so the formula ="Fred" + 9 returns the #VALUE! error. Similarly, if A1 contained the value "Fred", the formula =A1 * A2 returns the #VALUE! error no matter what is in A2.

#######   The ####### error value usually doesn't indicate a true error, just that the column isn't wide enough to display the value in that cell. You can fix that easily enough by dragging the column's right border to the right, or by selecting the column and choosing Format | Column. On occasion, you might enter a negative date or time value, or subtract a later date from an earlier date. Negative date or time values display the value ####### across the width of the cell.

> **Note**   *The instance of the ####### error value that is caused by negative date and time values does not occur if you are using the 1904 date system. To do so, choose Tools | Options, click the Calculation tab, and fill the 1904 date system check box. See Chapter 9 for more information on this date system.*

Although Excel's Help documentation terms this an error, a negative date or time value is a perfectly acceptable and logical quantity. Error Checking recognizes this by omitting the error indicator from a cell that contains a negative date or time value.

You can remove the display of the ####### value by setting its cell's format to something other than one of the date and time formats or by using the 1904 date system.

Correcting Text Dates

If you enter a text date with a two-digit year, Excel assumes that you might have made an error. For example, if you enter this text value (the presence of the single quote mark makes it text)

'1/1/99

in a cell, Excel warns you with the error indicator. If you then select the cell and click the Warning icon, you see the menu shown next.

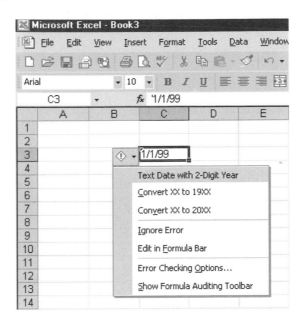

Using the menu items, you can change

'1/1/99

to either

'1/1/1999

or to

'1/1/2000

Correcting Numbers Entered as Text

Suppose that you enter in some cell this value:

'1000

There are good reasons that you might do so, but it's a little unusual. Excel assumes that you might want to be warned: although the value looks like a number, it isn't.

When you click the associated Warning icon after selecting the cell, the menu offers you an option to convert the text value to a number. If you do so, this value

'1000

would be converted to this value

1000

Managing Inconsistent Formulas

Suppose that you enter this formula in cell B1:

=C1

and then autofill the formula in B1 into B2:B5. In that case, each formula in the range B1:B5 is dependent on the value in the cell immediately to its right, C1:C5.

Having done that, you change (either deliberately or inadvertently) the formula in cell B3 from

=C3

to

=A3

Now, four of five cells in the B1:B5 range point one column to the right, and one points one column to the left. Although the worksheet context might mean that this arrangement is correct, it's also plausible that someone made a mistake. Excel assumes that to be the case and warns you with an error indicator in the cell with the inconsistent formula.

If you select the cell with the inconsistent formula and click the Warning icon, the menu offers an item that will copy the formula from the cell above. In this example, the formula in B2 would be copied into B3, changing it from

=A3

to

=C3

If the range discussed here, B1:B5, were instead oriented horizontally (for example, A1:E1) then the Error Checking menu would offer to change the inconsistent cell by copying from the cell to its left.

Correcting Missing Cells

In cell A1, you have entered this formula:

=SUM(J1:J10)

If you aren't yet familiar with worksheet functions such as SUM, don't worry. In this case all it means is that you have asked Excel to add the values in the cells from J1 to J10 and show the result of the addition in the cell that contains the formula.

Perhaps the values in the range J1:J10 are your firm's revenues for January through October. Come December 1, you enter the revenues for November in J11—but you forget to change the formula in A1 from

=SUM(J1:J10)

to

=SUM(J1:J11)

Again, you might not consider this an error. Perhaps you aren't yet ready to add November's revenue to the year-to-date figure. But it's possible that you just forgot to change the formula. Excel can remind you.

Continuing the present example, if your formula's function refers to cells J1:J10 and there is a value in J11, Excel warns you by means of the error indicator in the cell that contains the formula. The Error Checking menu offers to update the formula to include the apparently missing cells; choosing that option would change the formula to include the range J1:J11.

This error check works the same way if your formula refers to cells that occupy the same row. For example, if you have entered this formula:

=SUM(A5:E5)

and there is a value in F5, Excel will notice that and will warn you by means of the error indicator.

Locking Cells That Contain Formulas

It sometimes happens that you want to protect a formula from being changed, whether the change is deliberate or inadvertent. The standard way to do that is to protect the worksheet that contains the formula by choosing Tools | Protection | Protect Sheet.

But this action protects only cells that are locked at the time you choose Protect Sheet. It is possible to change any formula or value that's in an unlocked cell, whether or not the sheet is protected.

ANALYZING DATA

Therefore, Excel warns you if there is a formula in an unlocked cell, again by means of displaying that cell's error indicator. If you display the Error Checking menu, you will see the menu item Lock Cell. Clicking it locks the cell just as though you had chosen Format | Cell, clicked the Protection tab and filled the Locked check box.

If the default status of worksheet cells were Unlocked, then you would often be confronted by a grid full of error indicators, each caused by a formula in an Unlocked cell. But, for several good reasons, the default status of worksheet cells is Locked.

Note   *Protecting a worksheet suppresses the display of error indicators, even in unlocked cells.*

Referring to Empty Cells

You can arrange to be warned if a formula refers to a cell that's empty. For example, you might use this formula:

=C15 + C43 + C72

to return the total of different kinds of taxes on a lengthy income statement. You probably can't see each of those cells without scrolling up and down on the worksheet. If the contents of any one of these three cells were accidentally deleted, your total would be inaccurate.

Excel's error indicator can let you know that your formula refers to an empty cell. The error menu displays the item Trace Empty Cell. Clicking that item results in a tracer arrow that points from the empty cell to the cell with the formula.

Setting Options for Error Checking

Figure 8-12 shows the Error Checking tab on the Tools | Options dialog box.

Several aspects of this tab are of interest:

- You can turn background error checking on and off with the Enable Background Error Checking check box. If you turn it off by clearing the check box, Excel will not display an error indicator every time you enter a formula that violates a rule. You can find errors later, if you want, by choosing Tools | Error Checking, or by clicking the Error Checking button on the Formula Auditing toolbar.

- As noted at the beginning of this section, one of your options on the error menu is Ignore Error. By clicking the Reset Ignored Errors button shown in Figure 8-12, you cause Excel to reevaluate the worksheet's formulas and display error indicators for formulas you previously chose to ignore.

- If you change the error indicator's color, you should avoid setting the indicator color to the color of the cells' background.

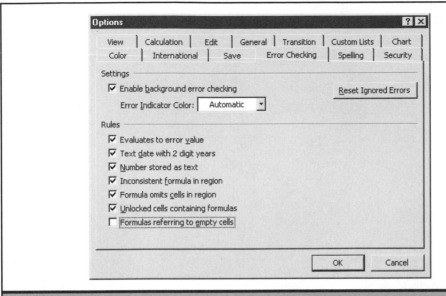

Figure 8-12. *Use the Error Indicator Color drop-down to select another color for the cell's error indicator*

■ The Rules section of the Error Checking tab enables you to decide which rules you want to apply. If you clear a check box, Excel will not insert an error indicator in a cell that appears to violate the associated rule.

A formula can violate more than one rule simultaneously. If it does, you will need to resolve all violations before the error indicator is turned off for that cell.

Keeping Your Eye on Formulas

The Formula Auditing toolbar in Excel 10 offers three new buttons: an Error Checking button, a Cell Watch button, and an Evaluate Formula button. Although the tasks these buttons perform stray from this toolbar's original role of tracing precedent and dependent cells, you'll find them useful in managing your formulas.

Using Error Checking

The Error Checking button initiates a check of the worksheet for errors, as described in the prior section. This button can be useful if you have turned off background error checking. If there is a formula error on the worksheet, clicking the Error Checking button causes Excel to display the dialog box shown in Figure 8-13.

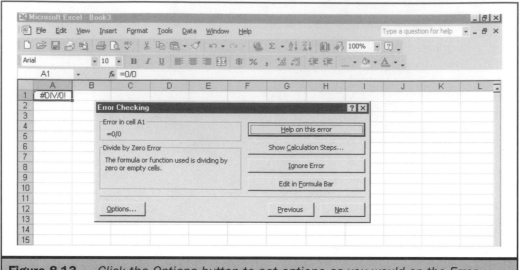

Figure 8-13. *Click the Options button to set options as you would on the Error Checking tab of the Options dialog box*

Note the similarity between the dialog box in Figure 8-13 and the menu that appears when you click a cell's Warning icon.

Using the Cell Watch Window

When you click the Cell Watch button on the Formula Auditing toolbar, the Cell Watch window appears (see Figure 8-14).

The Cell Watch window has two valuable features:

- It gives you a way to view the contents of cells that aren't visible in your current view of the worksheet. These cells might be 50 columns or 100 rows away from the cells visible on your monitor. They might be on a different worksheet, and without the Cell Watch window you could find it necessary to open a new window to see them. If the cells of interest are in a different workbook, you'll need to have that workbook open before you can view their contents in the Cell Watch window.

- It shows you the cells' formulas and values simultaneously. The only other way to see a formula and its value simultaneously is to select a cell and watch its formula in the formula bar and its value in the cell itself.

Suppose that you want to check that a Total Expenses value on a budget summary does not exceed, say, $10,000. You're not working in the budget summary worksheet, so

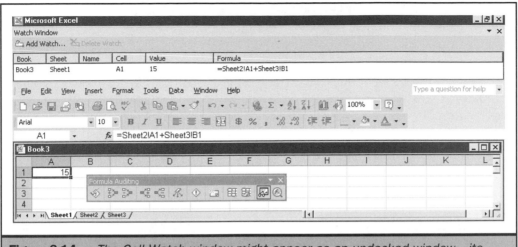

Figure 8-14. *The Cell Watch window might appear as an undocked window—its location depends on where the previous user placed it*

the Total Expenses cell isn't visible. Data Validation isn't the answer, because it responds only to data typed directly into a cell, not to the result of a formula. There are workarounds, of course, but they all have drawbacks: opening up new worksheet windows is not the answer when you have seven or eight distant cells to keep your eye on.

The Cell Watch window is a simple, even elegant solution to this kind of problem. Take these steps:

1. Open the window by clicking the Cell Watch button on the Formula Auditing toolbar, or choose Tools | Formula Auditing | Show Cell Window.

2. Choose Add Watch.

3. Click in the cell (or drag through the worksheet range) that you want to watch.

4. Click the Add button.

Using Formula Evaluation

For those who write complex array formulas, it was once a struggle to determine what was going on inside the formula. You could evaluate expressions nested inside the formula, but you had to drag across them in the Formula Bar and then press F9 to see how Excel interpreted that expression. And it was all too easy to hit ENTER instead of Cancel: in that case, you might well convert that part of your formula to constant values.

Excel 10 provides you with a new tool to ease this process. To anticipate some material from the next chapter, suppose that you have entered the names of the months of the year in cells A1:A12. There are easier ways to determine how many months begin with the letter J, but here's how you could use Excel to do it:

=SUM(IF(LEFT(A1:A12,1)="J",1,0))

You would array-enter this formula into some cell by holding down the CTRL and SHIFT keys as you pressed ENTER. As expected, the formula returns the number 3. How does the formula work?

You can find out by selecting the cell that contains the formula and clicking the Evaluate Formula button on the Formula Auditing toolbar (or choose Tools | Formula Auditing | Evaluate Formula). When you do so, you see the dialog box shown in Figure 8-15.

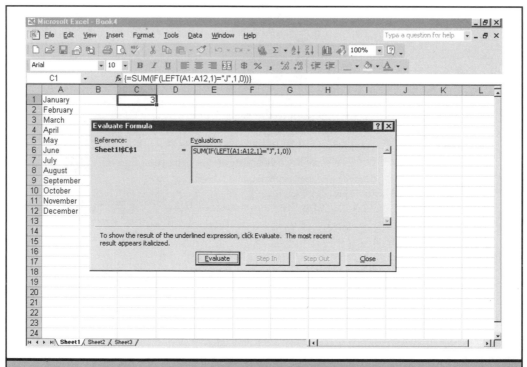

Figure 8-15.   *Formula Evaluation eases the process of debugging complicated formulas*

Notice in Figure 8-15 that the formula fragment

LEFT(A1:A12,1)

is underlined. Excel's formula evaluation works from the inside out, so it starts with the innermost portion of the formula. This fragment uses the LEFT function, which finds the left-most character (or characters) in a text string. Here, there are 12 such text strings to evaluate: the names of the months entered in A1:A12. The numeral 1 following the cell reference indicates the number of leftmost characters to find "J", "F", "M", "A", and so on. If the numeral 2 had been used instead of 1, the function would find "Ja", "Fe", "Ma", "Ap", and so on.

Returning to Figure 8-15, if you now click the Evaluate button, the dialog box shows the result of the first evaluation, as shown next.

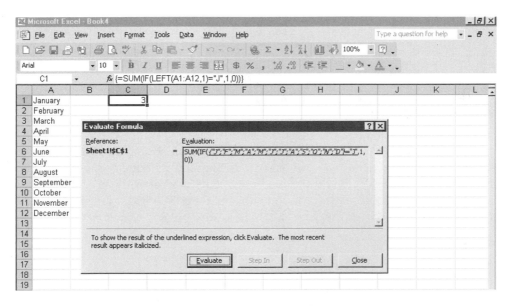

Notice the sequence of letters, within quote marks, each corresponding to the first letter in the name of each month in the range A1:A12. The letters are in italics, in conformance with the note at the bottom of the dialog box that "The most recent result appears italicized."

Also notice that a logical test is underlined. It is the next portion of the formula to be evaluated. The test is whether each element in the 12-character array equals the letter J. Either a letter in the array is a J or it isn't, so the tests will result in an array

of TRUE or FALSE values. When you click Evaluate, the dialog box changes to the
following illustration.

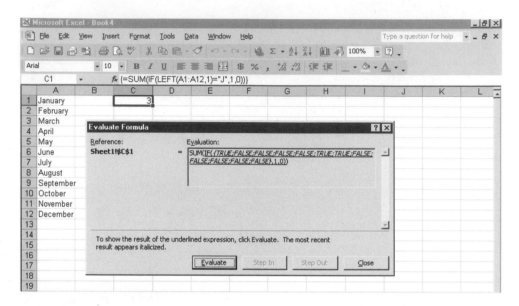

According to the currently underlined portion in the formula, the next portion to
evaluate is the IF statement. In words, as written here the statement says "If TRUE,
then 1; if FALSE, then 0." This should therefore result in an array of 1s and 0s. There
should be three 1s if there are three months that begin with a J, and nine 0s to
correspond to the other months. Click Evaluate to see the next dialog box.

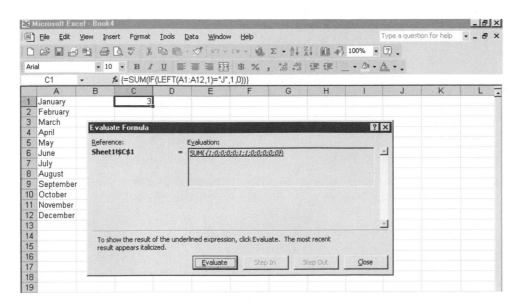

The IF function has simplified to the expected array of 1s and 0s. The SUM function totals the 1s in that array and returns the value 3, the number returned by the original array formula as entered on the worksheet. Note that when the formula evaluation has reached the final value, the Evaluate button changes to Restart.

Stepping In and Out

You probably noticed that there are two additional buttons in the Formula Evaluation dialog box: Step In and Step Out. These buttons are disabled if the formula under evaluation does not refer to another cell. If it does refer to a precedent cell, and if that cell's address is currently underlined in the Evaluation box, then clicking the Step In button displays the contents of the precedent cell.

When you have stepped into a precedent cell, the Step Out button becomes enabled. Click it to return to the dependent cell.

Of course, you can click Close at any time to dismiss the Formula Evaluation dialog box and return to the worksheet.

Certification Skills Covered in This Chapter

If you're preparing for Microsoft Office User Specialist certification, here are the skills you learned in this chapter.

Skill Set	Activity
Modifying workbooks	Use 3-D references
Creating and revising formulas	Create and revise formulas
Creating and revising formulas	Use statistical, date and time, financial, and logical functions in formulas

The
Complete
Reference

Excel
2002

Chapter 9

Worksheet Functions

lthough basic, the types of formulas that Chapter 8 discussed are useful. No matter how sophisticated a user of Excel you are or become, you will always need to do things such as summing the contents of 12 cells, multiplying a couple of numbers, or getting the intersection of two ranges.

But Excel doesn't get beyond the status of an expensive hand calculator until you start using its worksheet functions. Functions turn Excel into a polymath: financial analyst, geometer, statistician, engineer, scheduler, and logician.

Excel offers you the use of over 230 worksheet functions. The use of the term *worksheet* is to distinguish the functions that are automatically and always available to you on the worksheet from those that are included with add-ins such as the Analysis ToolPak and from user-defined functions.

This chapter does not detail the proper use and syntax of each of the available functions—there are just too many of them. The chapter does show you how to use functions, both singly and in combination. Armed with that knowledge, and with occasional reference to Excel's Help documentation, you will be in a position to use any of the available worksheet functions.

Functions and Arguments

In Excel terminology, a *function* is a formula that's already been written for you and that's been given a descriptive name. One of the simplest is the SUM function. As you saw in Chapter 8, if you want to obtain the sum of the values in cells A1:A5, you could enter this formula:

    =A1+A2+A3+A4+A5

in, say, cell A7. But someone has already written that formula for you in the guise of the SUM function. Instead of writing the formula yourself, you can save time by entering:

    =SUM(A1:A5)

Clearly, the time saved increases as the number of values increases. You save just a few seconds by using the SUM function on five values. Using SUM saves you several minutes and probably prevents keystroke errors if you need to find the sum of 100 values.

Excel makes it easy to enter a formula such as this one, which uses a range of cells. For example, with cell A7 active, type **=SUM(** in the formula bar. Then, left-click in cell A1 but don't release the mouse button. Drag the mouse pointer down until it highlights the range A1:A5. Release the mouse button and press ENTER or click the Enter Formula button. (You can type the closing right parenthesis if you want, but Excel supplies it for you if you don't.)

Note   *Excel 2002 brings the Range Finder to bear earlier in the process than did prior versions. The Range Finder outlines the worksheet range that your formula refers to. In Excel 2002, it appears as you enter that range in the Formula Bar. In prior versions, the Range Finder appeared only when you began to edit a formula that you had already entered.*

In addition, Excel provides an AutoSum function. Select the cell at the bottom or right of a group of cells you want to add and click the AutoSum tool on the standard toolbar. Excel automatically inserts the formula =SUM(XX:ZZ) where XX is the first cell in the range and ZZ is the last cell in the range. If you want a subset of that range in your summing cell, just edit the formula.

Function Arguments

There are three components to the function:

- **The equal sign**   Just as with the formulas discussed in Chapter 8, when you enter a function on the worksheet, you must begin with an equal sign.
- **The name of the function, such as SUM or MEDIAN**.
- **The arguments to the function**   These are enclosed in parentheses and, if there is more than one, they are separated by commas.

Arguments is a term that has been used for centuries in mathematical writing. (The *Oxford English Dictionary* notes that the usage derives from its use by astronomers to mean an angle.) It simply means the values on which you want the function to operate. The example

=SUM(A1:A5)

has one argument: the range of cells from A1 through A5. This example returns the same result:

=SUM(A1,A2,A3,A4,A5)

but has five arguments, which are the five individual cells.

Users sometimes encounter, in the Help or in other documentation, the statement that worksheet functions can take a maximum of 30 arguments. Misunderstanding the meaning of this limit, they post indignant protests in various newsgroups and in other forums that Excel is underpowered: it can't even calculate the total of 31 numbers.

It's true that you will get an error message if you enter a function with more than 30 arguments. But keep in mind that this example:

=SUM(A1:A31)

has but one argument—the range of cells from A1 through A31. It totals 31 values, but it has just one argument.

You can mix different kinds of arguments in a function. For example, this is legal usage:

=SUM(A1,42.5,A11:A20,B5:C8,TRUE)

The example returns the total of the value in a single cell, A1, plus the numeric constant 42.5, plus the values in a range of cells that occupy rows 11 through 20 in column A, plus the values in rows 5 through 8 in columns B through C, plus the value TRUE.

Note *Excel interprets the logical value TRUE as 1; it interprets FALSE as 0. This fact has profound implications for the use of array formulas, discussed in Chapter 10.*

You cannot, however, put a text value in the mix. If you do, you'll get the error result #VALUE!. For example

=SUM(1,5,"Q")

is not legal usage because it calls for Excel to add the text value "Q" to the numeric values 1 and 5. Neither you, nor I, nor Excel knows what that totals to.

Because they're prefabricated, many worksheet functions are very particular about how many arguments you supply and in what order you supply them. Other worksheet functions don't much care. For example:

=PRODUCT(5,20)

returns the same result, 100, as does

=PRODUCT(20,5)

But you must be careful to supply the arguments in a particular order for many other functions. For example, the POWER function raises its first argument to the power of its second argument:

=POWER(5,2)

This returns five to the second power, or 25. And

=POWER(2,5)

returns two to the fifth power, or 32. Clearly, you must pay attention to the required order of the arguments—if you don't, you might get a result that looks right but in fact is wrong.

Some functions take no arguments at all. The PI() function is an example: it returns the value of pi to 14 decimal places. If you put an argument within its parentheses, Excel just informs you that you've made an error. Even though there's nothing within the parentheses, you need to supply them in order to inform Excel that you've entered a function.

So, to use a function properly, you need to know whether it takes arguments, and if it does, whether the order of the arguments makes a difference. This knowledge is partly a matter of experience and partly a matter of using the Insert Function button, which is discussed later in this chapter.

Function Categories

Because Excel offers so many different functions, it's useful to group them according to the general area to which they apply. While the categories' names are reasonably descriptive, there are some arbitrary classifications. For example, the MAX function is considered a statistical function; it could just as easily be considered a mathematical function.

Financial Functions

These functions calculate results such as a payment amount given a particular interest rate, loan amount, and term. These variables are closely related to one another. For example, the function that calculates the payment amount is PMT. An example of the PMT function is

=PMT(0.006,360,-300000)

where 0.006 is the interest rate that applies to each payment, 360 is the number of payments, and –300000 is the present value of the series of 360 payments. (In the calculation of payment amounts, present and future values, at least one of the variables is always a negative amount.) Given these arguments, the function returns the value 2036.36.

In contrast, the function that calculates the interest rate is RATE. Its syntax is

=RATE(nper,pmt,pv)

where *nper* is the number of periods, *pmt* is the periodic payment amount, and *pv* is the present value of the series of payments. An example using the same numbers as in the PMT example is

=RATE(360,2036.36,-300000)

This returns 0.006, a value that's consistent with the PMT example, above. But if you hadn't paid attention to the order of the arguments and entered

=RATE(2036.36,360,-300000)

then Excel would have returned the #NUM! error value, because it can't deal with 2036.36 payments of 360 dollars each in the context of deriving the associated loan rate.

Other financial functions include the family of depreciation functions, such as straight-line, declining, double declining, and variable declining balance. For example, suppose you want to know how much depreciation to take on an asset that cost you $20,000, has a useful life of five years, and will be worth $1,000 at the end of its useful life. If you calculate the straight-line depreciation:

=SLN(20000,1000,5)

you find that you depreciate the asset by $3,800 each year. But if you use the declining balance method:

=DB(20000,1000,5,1)

you find that you depreciate the asset by $9,020 for the first year. The declining balance method results in an accelerated depreciation schedule, with different amounts of depreciation each year. Therefore, the DB function requires that you supply an additional argument: the period for which you want to calculate the depreciation amount. In this example, that's 1: the first period.

Excel, smart as it is, isn't smart enough to know whether the taxing authorities will let you use an accelerated depreciation method. You're required to know what to do; Excel is required to know how to do it.

Date and Time Functions

The year 1999 brought with it an interesting cultural spasm called Y2K. As was the case with the swine flu virus a quarter century earlier, more people were damaged by the Y2K hype than by the actual event.

Y2K did not directly affect applications such as Excel because Excel does not have trouble distinguishing between the year 1900 and the year 2000. Excel was born long after the time that it was considered extravagant to store the first two digits of a four-digit year.

With memory storage capacity plentiful, Excel treats dates and times as floating-point numbers. The integer portion of the number identifies the date, and the decimal portion identifies the time. For example, this number:

37266.5834

identifies 2:00 PM on January 10, 2002. That day is the 37,266th day counting from January 1, 1900. 2:00 PM is 14 hours through the 24-hour day, and 14/24 is equal to

.5834. Adding 1 to that number results in 37267.5834, which identifies January 11, 2002, at 2:00 PM—the next day in sequence.

You can prove this to yourself by entering the number 37266.5834 in some worksheet cell. Then use Format | Cells and pick one of the date formats. After clicking OK, you'll find that you see something such as 1/10, or 1/10/02, or January 10, 2002—depending on the format you chose. If, instead, you pick one of the time formats, you will see 14:00 (on a 24-hour clock) or 2:00 PM, or something similar.

When January 1, 2000, came along, Excel had no trouble with it. It was just day number 36,526 counting from January 1, 1900.

> **Note** *By default, Excel counts days from January 1, 1900. Some early versions of Excel for the Macintosh, for technical reasons, counted from January 1, 1904. If you open a workbook and it looks like all the dates are four years earlier than they should be, choose Tools | Options and fill the 1904 date system check box on the Calculation tab.*

Why should you care about how Excel keeps track of dates and times? Because understanding that is central to understanding how Excel's date and time functions work.

For example, the formula

=DAY(37266)

uses the DAY function to return the day of the month on which the date identified by the argument falls. In the example, the argument 37266 identifies January 10, 2002. So the function returns 10 as its result: the tenth day of the month.

Similarly, the formula

=HOUR(.5834)

returns 14. As noted earlier in this section, .5834 corresponds to a time of 14:00, or 2:00 PM. (Excel starts counting hours at 0, which corresponds to 12:00 AM.)

Excel tries very hard to numb the user to sore thumbs like date serial numbers. So even though the Help documentation gives the syntax for date functions such as HOUR as

=HOUR(serial_number)

you are nevertheless allowed to enter a text string that identifies the time. That is, this formula is syntactically correct:

=HOUR("2:00 PM")

In the process of calculating the function's result, Excel converts the string "2:00 PM" to its serial number and then returns the correct result of 14.

If you want to place the current date and time in a cell, use the NOW function. It requires no arguments, it shows the result in the cell, and the formula bar displays =NOW().

The DATE function is based on three arguments—the year, month, and day. It's a useful function if the three arguments are available in three discrete cells (perhaps there are columns for each type of data). Enter

=DATE(A2,B2,C2)

and, regardless of any changes to the function's arguments, the cell with the DATE function displays the appropriate value.

Lookup and Reference Functions

The Lookup functions pertain to finding values in worksheet ranges. The Reference functions pertain to worksheet addresses. The two types are closely related.

Suppose you have a table of sales commissions. Each commission percentage depends in part on the product sold and in part on whether the transaction is an outright purchase or a lease. See Figure 9-1 for an example.

Figure 9-1 shows the table of commissions in the range A1:F3. In that table, the first row contains labels that identify products (B1:F1), and the first column contains labels that identify types of transaction (A2:A3). What is the commission for selling Maintenance? As shown in the figure, the formula

=VLOOKUP("Sale",A1:F3,5,0)

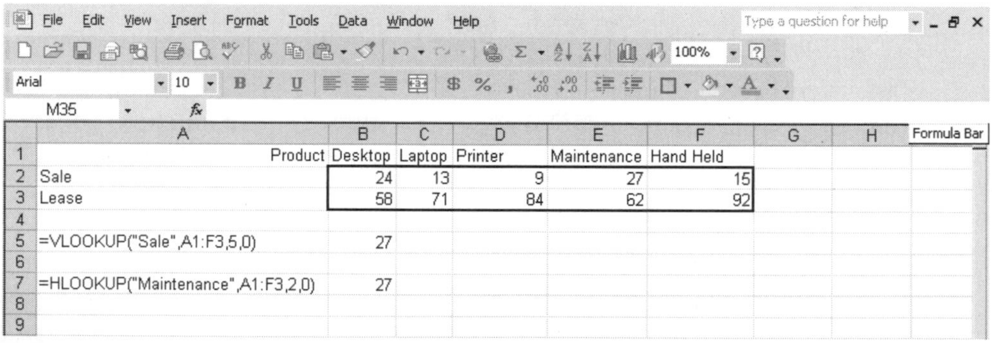

Figure 9-1. *By using a Lookup function, you can automatically find the correct commission amount*

returns the number 27 in cell B5. And you can tell by looking at the table that the commission for selling Product D is 27. In words, here is what the formula does:

- It invokes the VLOOKUP function. The *V* in VLOOKUP stands for *vertical*. The VLOOKUP function looks for a value in the first (vertical) column of the table.

- In this example, VLOOKUP looks for the value "Sale" in the table's first column, A1:A3. In Excel terms, VLOOKUP's first argument is *lookup_value*. When it finds "Sale", VLOOKUP knows which row to use.

- The table is found in cells A1:F3. In Excel terms, VLOOKUP's second argument is *table_array*.

- The argument *5* tells VLOOKUP which column to use. Excel terms this argument *range_lookup*.

- The argument *0* tells VLOOKUP to find an exact match for the lookup value "Sale".

VLOOKUP finds an exact match for "Sale" in the second row of the first column; its third argument tells VLOOKUP to use the fifth column. So VLOOKUP returns the value in the table's second row and fifth column, and VLOOKUP returns the value 27.

The function HLOOKUP works in almost the same way as does VLOOKUP. The difference is that HLOOKUP starts by looking in the first (horizontal) row of a table, instead of in the table's first (vertical) column. In Figure 9-1, the HLOOKUP function in cell B7 returns the same value as does the VLOOKUP function:

=HLOOKUP("Maintenance",A1:F3,2,0)

This formula invokes HLOOKUP. The function looks for the value "Maintenance" in the table's first row. It finds that value in the table's fifth column. Then it looks in the table's second row (that's the function's third argument, the number 2). The range_lookup argument *0* directs HLOOKUP to look for an exact match for the lookup value "Maintenance". And the function returns the value 27.

Whether you use VLOOKUP or HLOOKUP depends on whether you want the function to search for a value in a column or in a row. The VLOOKUP function locates a row by finding a value in a table's first column. The HLOOKUP function locates a column by finding a value in a table's first row.

You could, of course, arrange to always use VLOOKUP. You can rearrange a table so that its rows become columns and its columns become rows. But it frequently happens that layout considerations—especially in printed reports—dictate that you use one particular orientation for the table. Then you should keep that orientation, and choose VLOOKUP or HLOOKUP according to whether you need to look in the table's first column or in its first row.

Another useful function that searches for a value in a worksheet range is MATCH. The MATCH function looks for a value in a single column or in a single row. If it finds the value, it returns the position that the value occupies (see Figure 9-2).

Cell B5 of Figure 9-2 contains this formula:

=MATCH(27,A2:F2)

(The formula is shown as text in cell A5.) In words, here's what the formula does:

- It invokes the MATCH function.
- The MATCH function takes its first argument, 27, as the value to look for.
- The second argument, A2:F2, is a column or, as here, a row that tells MATCH where to look.

In this case, MATCH returns 5. Match finds the value 27 in the *fifth* column of the range A2:F2.

In Figure 9-2, MATCH also appears in cell B7 in the following guise:

=MATCH(27,E1:E3)

This time, MATCH returns 2. The function locates the value 27 in the *second* row of the range E1:E3.

More generally, MATCH(Value, Range) tells you the position in Range where it first finds Value. If Range is a column, MATCH returns a row offset: the number of rows into the column where it first finds Value. If Range is a row, MATCH returns a column offset: the number of columns into the row where it first finds Value.

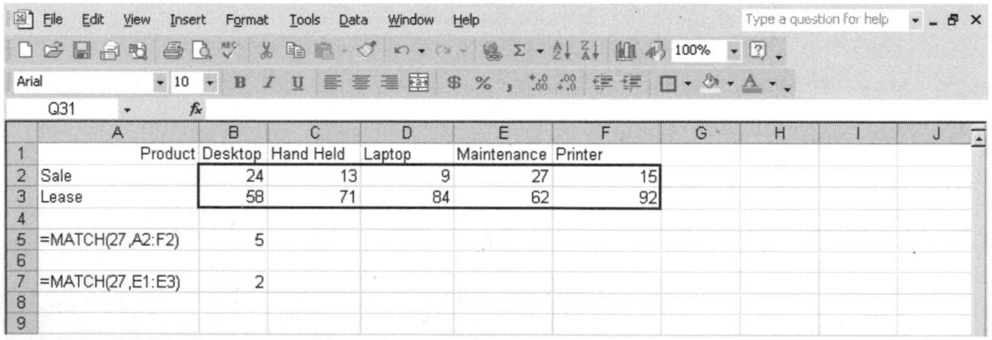

Figure 9-2. *The MATCH function tells how far from the beginning of a range it finds a particular value*

Notice these differences between VLOOKUP (or HLOOKUP) and MATCH:

■ VLOOKUP returns a value in a worksheet cell. MATCH returns a column offset (if it looks in a row) or a row offset (if it looks in a column).

■ VLOOKUP begins by looking in a table's first column; HLOOKUP begins by looking in a table's first. MATCH looks in either a row or a column, depending on the orientation of the worksheet range in its second argument.

The final argument, *range_lookup*, in VLOOKUP, HLOOKUP, and MATCH is optional. If you do not supply the *range_lookup* argument to VLOOKUP, HLOOKUP, or MATCH, the functions look for the exact value that you supply. This is the default situation and is the same as supplying the value 0 for the function's final argument:

=MATCH(27,E1:E3) is the same as =MATCH(27,E1:E3,0)

and

=HLOOKUP("Laptop",A1:F3,2) is the same as =HLOOKUP("Laptop",A1:F3,2,0)

But suppose that the lookup range is sorted, in either ascending or descending order (see Figure 9-3).

Notice in Figure 9-3 that the values in B1:F1 are sorted in ascending order. This fact enables the MATCH function to return the *largest* value that is *less than or equal to* the value to match. Cell B3 contains the formula

=MATCH(17,B1:F1,1)

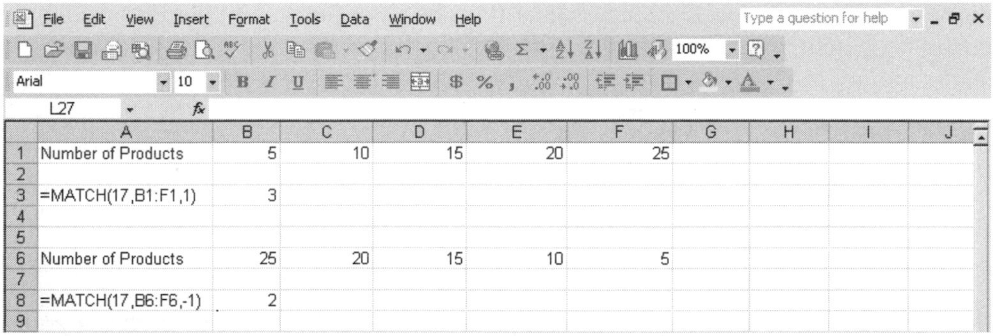

	A	B	C	D	E	F	G	H	I	J
1	Number of Products	5	10	15	20	25				
2										
3	=MATCH(17,B1:F1,1)	3								
4										
5										
6	Number of Products	25	20	15	10	5				
7										
8	=MATCH(17,B6:F6,-1)	2								
9										

Figure 9-3. *If the lookup range is sorted, you can call for an approximate match*

which returns 3. In this case, the final argument is 1 and has these consequences:

- MATCH is informed by the third argument that the range B1:F1 is sorted in ascending order.
- In B1:F1, there are three values that are less than or equal to 17, the lookup value. These three values are 5, 10, and 15.
- Of the values 5, 10, and 15, the largest is 15. 15 is found in the third column of B1:F1, so MATCH returns 3.

In contrast, the range B6:F6 in Figure 9-3 is sorted in descending order. You therefore can cause MATCH to return the *smallest* value that is *greater than or equal to* the lookup value. Compare the above example with this formula, in cell B8:

=MATCH(17,B6:F6,-1)

which returns 2. In this case, MATCH's final argument is –1 and has these consequences:

- MATCH is informed by the third argument that the range B6:F6 is sorted in descending order.
- In B6:F6, there are two values that are greater than or equal to 17, the lookup value. These two values are 20 and 25.
- Of the values 20 and 25, the smaller is 20. 20 is found in the second column of B6:F6, so MATCH returns 2.

The final argument to the VLOOKUP and HLOOKUP functions—in these, it's the fourth argument—works similarly. For example:

=HLOOKUP(17,B1:F3,3)

says to look for the value 17 (first argument) in the first column of the range B1:F3 (second argument) and return the corresponding value in the third row (third argument). This formula:

=HLOOKUP(17,B1:F3,3,1)

adds 1 as the fourth argument. With the fourth argument set to 1, HLOOKUP is also told that

- The first row in the range, B1:F1, is sorted in ascending order.
- HLOOKUP should look for the largest value in B1:F1 that is less than or equal to the lookup value of 17 (see Figure 9-4).

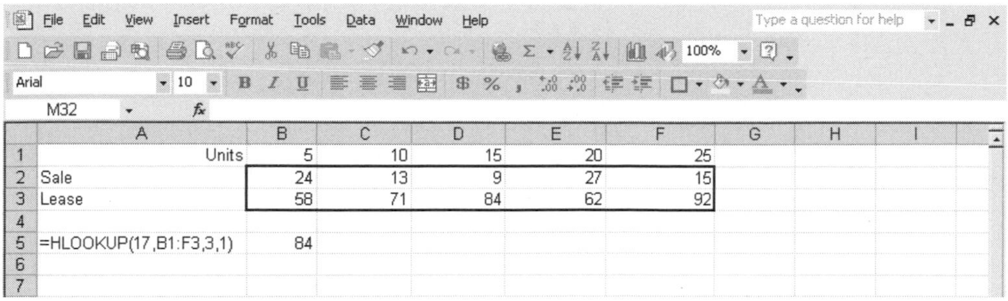

Figure 9-4.   *Approximate matches can be useful when categories embrace intermediate values*

Cell B5 in Figure 9-4 contains this formula:

=HLOOKUP(17,B1:F3,3,1)

HLOOKUP finds the largest value in B1:F1 that is less than or equal to 17. That value is 15, which is in the third column of B1:F1. HLOOKUP is told by its third argument, 3, to look in the third row of B1:F3. So HLOOKUP returns the value in the third column and third row of B1:F3, or 84.

Consider using sorted lookup ranges and approximate matches in situations such as commission calculations. Often, the commission will be the same for a range of values; for example, the commission for selling 11, 12, 13, 14, or 15 units might be $47. Using approximate matches, you could combine the commission of $47 for all five quantities into one row or column that is headed by the value 11. See "Lookup Functions Combined" later in this chapter for an example of this approach.

Statistical Functions

Some of Excel's statistical functions, such as AVERAGE, provide descriptive information about the distribution of some numbers. Others, such as LINEST, enable you to compare samples with hypothetical populations.

Suppose that you are interested in learning whether men and women differ in their attitude toward a new model of car. You park this new car near a downtown New York street corner and chance your arm by stopping pedestrians and asking them how much they like the car, on a scale of one to ten.

Using a table of random numbers to choose which people to approach, you get responses from 20 people. In your scoring method, a response of ten is the most favorable attitude; for the least favorable, you score zero. You put the data into an Excel worksheet, as shown in Figure 9-5.

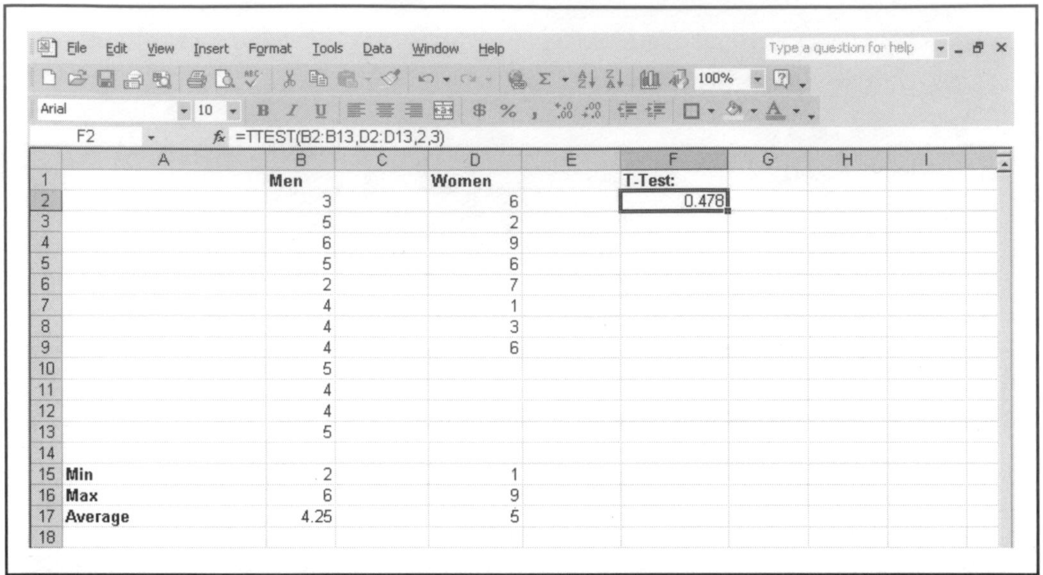

Figure 9-5. *Excel's statistical functions are useful only if you have gathered the data properly—in this example, that means taking random samples*

You can get an initial impression of the range of responses by using the MIN and MAX functions. In Figure 9-5, the minimum and maximum responses for men are shown in B15 and B16; for women, in D15 and D16. For example, the minimum value for men in B15 is returned by

=MIN(B2:B13)

and the maximum value for women in D16 is returned by

=MAX(D2:D13)

The MAX and MIN functions in D15:D16 use the range D2:D13 as their arguments, so the functions evaluate the empty cells D10:D13. Most mathematical and statistical functions in Excel ignore empty cells (as well as text values), which is the reason that MIN(D2:D13) returns one, not zero.

Since the range of responses among men is five (from two through six) and among women is nine (from one through nine), it's clear that women's attitudes toward this car are more variable than men's.

What you're really after, though, is information that bears on this question: On average, do men or women—or neither—like this car better? As implied by the question, you need to use the AVERAGE function. It's used in Figure 9-5 in cells B17 (for men) and D17 (for women). In D17, the formula is

=AVERAGE(D2:D13)

The AVERAGE function ignores empty cells, just as do the MIN and MAX functions.

The difference between an average value of 4.25 for men and 5 for women doesn't seem like much, in the context of a ten-point scale. And you would need to make a decision as to whether you regarded the difference as meaningful. If you didn't find it meaningful, you'd probably stop right there.

But if you thought it might be meaningful, your next step would probably be an inferential test. In this situation, that would involve Excel's TTEST function. It appears in Figure 9-5, cell F2:

=TTEST(B2:B13,D2:D13,2,3)

The arguments are as follows:

- The range B2:B13 contains the values for one group of observations—in this example, for men.

- The range D2:D13 contains the values for the other group of observations— in this example, for women.

- The third argument, 2, specifies a two-tailed test. This means that you have no prior hypothesis that men's average attitude would be higher than or lower than women's average attitude. If you had such a prior hypothesis, you could use 1 as the second argument and have a statistically more powerful test.

- The fourth argument, 3, specifies that you want to assume that variability in attitude among men might be different than variability in attitude among women.

The function returns the value 0.478. This means that if the population of men and the population of women have the *same* average attitude toward your car, you would still observe a difference as large as this one (5 − 4.25 = .75) in almost 48 percent of samples like the one you took. So the difference of .75 in average attitude does not support the notion that the attitudes in the populations of men and women are different.

To recap: the statistics category of Excel's functions includes:

- **Descriptive statistics** For example, the average, the minimum, and the maximum of a set of numbers.

- **Inferential statistics** For example, the t-test that helps you infer whether or not the observed difference between two samples is likely to occur in the population.

Text Functions

As the name implies, text functions are those that take text values as their arguments and that often return text values as their results. Here's a straightforward example.

You have been maintaining a list of employee names in an Excel worksheet. The list is starting to get long, and your reasons for using the list have become complex. It's time to move the list from the worksheet into a true database. But before you do so, you'll need to know the maximum length of the names.

When you create an Employee Name field in the database, you will need to specify how many characters the field should be able to contain. If you specify four characters, the field will store only the *Nixo* portion of the name *Nixon*. So you should find out the maximum number of characters in your current list of names, add (say) five characters to that as a fudge factor, and use the result as the field's length in the database.

Figure 9-6 shows how you could go about this by using Excel's LEN function.

Column A in Figure 9-6 shows the employee names. Cell B2 contains this formula:

```
=LEN(A2)
```

The LEN function returns the length of a text value as the number of characters. The name *John Smith* contains ten characters: one for each letter and one for the blank between the first and last name. So the formula in B2 returns 10, the number of characters in the text value found in cell A2.

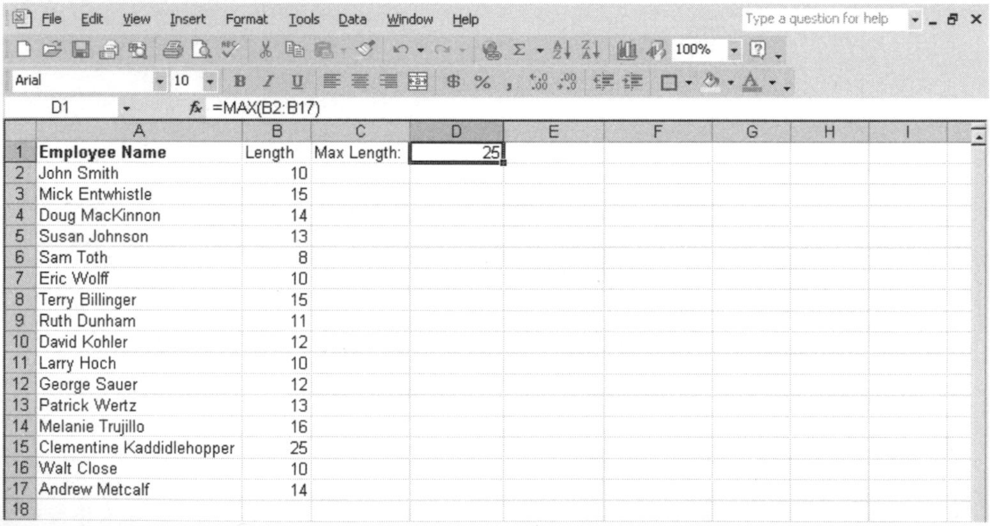
File Edit View Insert Format Tools Data Window Help
Type a question for help
100%
Arial
10
D1
=MAX(B2:B17)
A B C D E F G H I
1 Employee Name Length Max Length: 25
2 John Smith 10
3 Mick Entwhistle 15
4 Doug MacKinnon 14
5 Susan Johnson 13
6 Sam Toth 8
7 Eric Wolff 10
8 Terry Billinger 15
9 Ruth Dunham 11
10 David Kohler 12
11 Larry Hoch 10
12 George Sauer 12
13 Patrick Wertz 13
14 Melanie Trujillo 16
15 Clementine Kaddidlehopper 25
16 Walt Close 10
17 Andrew Metcalf 14
18

Figure 9-6. *Blank spaces between names count as part of the length of the text*

The formula in B2 is copied and pasted into B3:B17. Now the range B2:B17 contains the length of each employee name. You find the maximum length as shown in cell D1 of Figure 9-6, where the formula is

=MAX(B2:B17)

Using the statistical function MAX, you get 25, which is the number of characters in "Clementine Kaddidlehopper," the longest of the employees' names. You might now define the length of the Employee Name field in your database as 30, to make more sure of capturing all the characters in an even longer name.

What if someone had mistyped an employee's name, inadvertently adding a blank space somewhere? If that space were at the beginning of the name or somewhere within the name, it might be easy to see on the worksheet. But if the space is at the end of the name, it's very difficult to find. To take care of this possibility, you could use the TRIM function, as shown in Figure 9-7.

The employee names are as shown in Figure 9-6, but the formulas that calculated name length with the LEN function have been moved to column C. Cell B2 now contains

=TRIM(A2)

The TRIM function removes spaces at the beginning and the end of (but not within) a text value. So if someone had typed a blank space at the beginning or end

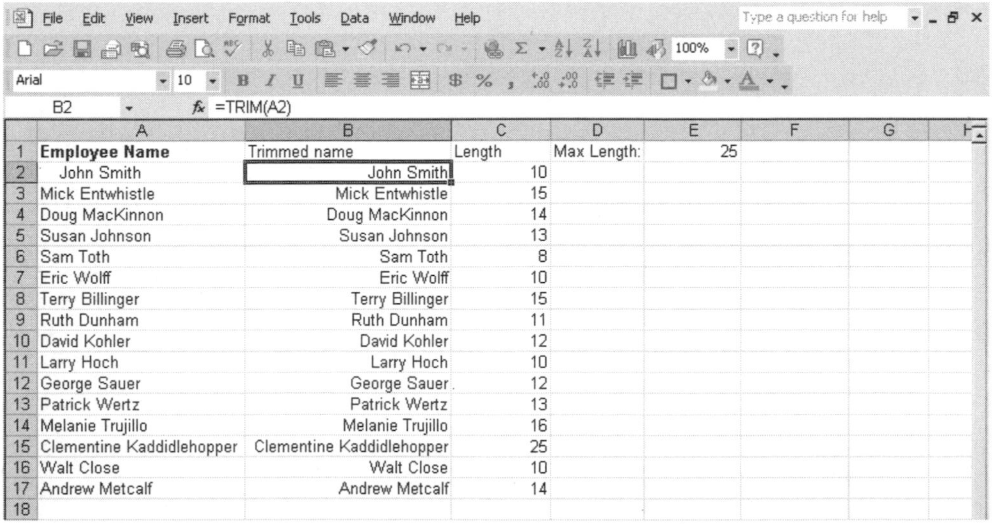

Figure 9-7.   *Use TRIM to guard against inadvertent leading or trailing blanks*

of an employee's name, the TRIM function would remove it and would return just the name's nonblank characters. In Figure 9-7, the LEN functions take the names, trimmed of leading and trailing spaces, as their arguments.

> **Note**   *The term* string *is often used to mean a series of consecutive characters, or even just a single character. A string is therefore a text value. Every word in this sentence—and the sentence itself, since spaces are characters—is an example of a string.*

Some text functions deal with individual characters in strings—for example, with the "N" in "JONES". The FIND function is one such:

=FIND("N","JONES",1)

This formula's components are as follows:

- **The FIND function itself**   Searches for a string within another string.
- **The character "N"**   The string that FIND will search for.
- **The string "JONES"**   The string that FIND will examine in its search for N.
- **The numeral 1**   Directs FIND to start its search with the first character, J, in JONES. If the function's fourth argument were 2 instead of 1, the search would start at the second character, O.

The string "N" is the third character in the string "JONES", so this example of FIND returns the value 3.

> **Note**   *Why might you want to start the search after the first character? Suppose that you wanted to find the last part of a UNC such as \\NTS01\User Data\Profiles. To find the rightmost folder name you would want to locate the final backslash. But the final backslash is preceded by three other backslashes, and in this instance you would want FIND to start looking at least nine characters into the string.*

When used in the FIND function, strings are case-sensitive; that is, the FIND function pays attention to uppercase versus lowercase. In contrast to the prior example, the formula

=FIND("n", "JONES",1)

returns the error #VALUE!, because there is no lowercase "n" in JONES. If you want to be case insensitive, use the SEARCH function. Both the formula

=SEARCH("n","Jones",1)

and this one:

=SEARCH("N","Jones",1)

return 3, because SEARCH doesn't distinguish between "n" and "N".

Two other very useful text functions are LEFT and RIGHT. These return some number of characters from the left or right end of a string. For example:

=LEFT("JONES", 3)

returns the string "JON", the three leftmost characters in the string "JONES", and the formula

=RIGHT("JONES", 4)

returns ONES, the four rightmost characters in JONES.

Are you wondering why you would ever use functions like these? Good—you should be. Used by themselves, their value is quite limited. But they are building blocks for more sophisticated and useful tasks. You shouldn't still be wondering by the end of Chapter 10.

Logical Functions

There are just a few functions that perform logical comparisons.

TRUE() and FALSE() are functions that you don't usually need. You might have use for them if you open a spreadsheet file that was created by an application other than Excel. If you want to use either of the Boolean values TRUE and FALSE, just enter them directly into the Excel worksheet.

The AND function requires that all its arguments evaluate as TRUE in order for AND to evaluate to TRUE. For example:

=AND(1<5,10>2)

evaluates to TRUE, because both arguments are TRUE. But

=AND(1>5,10>2)

evaluates to FALSE, because at least one of its arguments is FALSE.

In contrast to the AND function, the OR function requires that at least one of its arguments evaluate as TRUE in order for OR to return TRUE. For example, both

=OR(1<5,10>2)

and

=OR(1>5,10>2)

evaluate to TRUE, because at least one argument is TRUE in each case. But:

=OR(1>5,2>10,8<4)

evaluates to FALSE because all three of its arguments are FALSE.

The NOT function changes a TRUE outcome to a FALSE one, and vice versa. For example:

=NOT(10>2)

returns FALSE. The NOT function is often useful in combination with Excel's information functions such as ISERROR (see the next section).

The IF function is a particularly important one in Excel worksheets. It has three arguments: a condition that evaluates as either TRUE or FALSE, a value if the condition is TRUE, and a value if the condition is FALSE. For example, the formula

=IF(10>2, "Comparison is correct.", "Comparison is not correct.")

returns the string "Comparison is correct." The first argument, which is the condition to evaluate, returns TRUE. Therefore, the IF function returns the argument for a TRUE condition. This formula:

=IF(10<2, "Comparison is correct.", "Comparison is not correct.")

returns the string "Comparison is not correct." The first argument evaluates to FALSE, so the IF function returns the argument for a FALSE condition.

Information Functions

Functions in this category are generally concerned with values on the worksheet. For example, the ISTEXT function returns TRUE if you point it at a text value and FALSE otherwise:

=ISTEXT(A1)

would return TRUE if the string "Pi" were in A1, and FALSE if the numeric value 3.1416 were in A1.

There are many different error values that formulas can return. One is #DIV/0!, which is returned by any formula with a zero divisor. For example:

=1/(10-10)

returns #DIV/0!. A worksheet littered with error values is ugly; furthermore, if you use a cell containing an error value as an argument to another function, the latter function must also return an error value.

To anticipate the section on combining functions, consider this formula:

=IF(ISERROR(SUM(A1:A5)/COUNT(A1:A5)),"", SUM(A1:A5)/COUNT(A1:A5))

It's useful to break complex formulas like this one into component parts. The Formula Evaluation tool, described in Chapter 8, is useful for this purpose. Start with this component:

SUM(A1:A5)/COUNT(A1:A5)

If there are no numeric values in A1:A5, then COUNT(A1:A5) will return zero. Because that expression is a divisor, a zero will result in the error value #DIV/0!. To prevent that, deploy the ISERROR function:

ISERROR(SUM(A1:A5)/COUNT(A1:A5))

This component will return TRUE if the division results in any error value—of interest in this particular case is the error value #DIV/0!. ISERROR will return FALSE if the division results, as desired, in a number.

Recalling from the previous section the syntax of the IF function:

=IF(condition, value if condition is true, value if condition is false)

the ISERROR component is the condition. When ISERROR returns TRUE, the IF function in the example returns "", which is just a null string, visually the same as an empty cell. This keeps the potential #DIV/0! error value off the worksheet.

When ISERROR returns FALSE, the IF function in the example returns the result of this component:

SUM(A1:A5)/COUNT(A1:A5)

(that is, the average of the values in A1:A5). To review, the entire formula

=IF(ISERROR(SUM(A1:A5)/COUNT(A1:A5)),"", SUM(A1:A5)/COUNT(A1:A5))

says, in words: "If calculating the average of cells A1:A5 causes a division-by-zero error, return a null string. Otherwise, return the average of cells A1:A5."

Database Functions

This function category has a pretentious name. *Database Functions* conjures capabilities such as conditional SQL statements, external database retrievals, and the creation of one-to-many linkages among tables. In fact, Excel's database functions have a much shorter reach.

Suppose you have created several Excel lists: sets of values each occupying one column and each headed by a cell with a label. If the columns are contiguous, you have created a structure that Excel refers to as a *database*.

You might also create a range of cells that contain the contents of the lists' header labels. Below each cell in this range you might enter expressions such as <1 or <>Northeast. This is what Excel refers to as a *criteria range*.

Having created these two structures, you can enter a database function. These functions are mainly versions of other functions like SUM and AVERAGE. They are distinguished by an initial *D* for *database*. Thus:

=DSUM(A10:F20, "AGE", A1:F2)

returns the sum of the values in the AGE field in the database range A10:F20, subject to selection criteria found in A1:F2.

You will find that by combining functions such as SUM and AVERAGE with other functions such as IF, you can get the same results as with database functions, and you need not define a database or criteria range to do so. Furthermore, Excel's pivot tables enable you to get this type of information with much greater efficiency. Apart from the present section, this book neither discusses nor exemplifies the use of database functions.

Math and Trig Functions

The mathematical and trigonometric functions start to move Excel out of the realm of a strictly financial application. Of course, most of Excel's worksheet functions are mathematical in one way or another, but the functions in this category tend to have broader applicability than, for example, RATE or PMT.

Many functions in this category take a single number as their argument. For example:

=ABS(-90)

returns 90, the absolute value of –90, or

=LN(40)

returns 3.69, the natural logarithm of 40.

The Math and Trig category includes several functions that require special treatment by the user. These are the matrix algebra functions MINVERSE, which returns the inverse of a matrix, and MMULT, which returns the matrix product of two matrices. While Excel classes it as a Lookup and Reference function (see later in this chapter), the TRANSPOSE function is heavily used in matrix algebra and requires similar treatment.

This mysterious treatment consists of two steps:

1. These functions return more than one value: they return an array of values. So you need to begin by selecting not a single cell, but an array of cells. For example, instead of starting by selecting C5, you might need to start by selecting C5:E7 to contain the result.

2. After selecting the range of cells that will contain the function's result, you type the equal sign, the function name, and its arguments. But instead of pressing ENTER or clicking the Enter button, first hold down the CTRL and SHIFT keys. While holding them down, press ENTER.

Step 2 is termed *array-entering* the formula. When you do so properly, you see two results:

- If you began by selecting a range of cells (instead of just one) and entered a formula with a function that returns an array of results, you see the range of cells filled with different results.

- The formula that you array-entered appears in the formula bar with curly brackets around it. *Do not* type the curly brackets yourself—if you do, Excel interprets your formula as text.

Figure 9-8 provides examples of these matrix functions, array-entered.

Formulas entered in this fashion have broad applicability in Excel. There are many results that you can achieve with array formulas that would otherwise require you to write a VBA procedure. This book has much more to say about array formulas in Chapter 10.

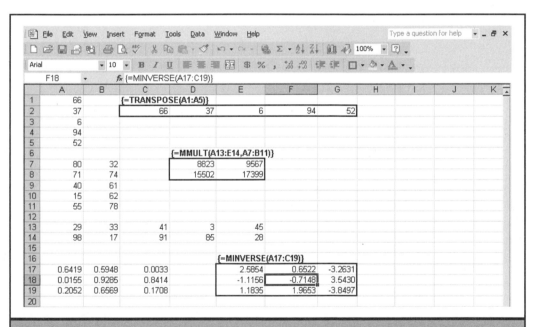

Figure 9-8.   *Excel supplies the curly brackets that surround an array-entered formula*

The trigonometric functions are concerned with angles. Each of these functions takes its argument in radians, not degrees. You can convert degrees to radians in one of two ways. Both

=PI()/180 * 90

and

=RADIANS(90)

return 1.57, and the formula

=SIN(1.57)

returns 1, the sine of a 90-degree angle. More concisely, the formula

=SIN(RADIANS(90))

returns 1. This type of formula construction is the topic of the next section, "Combining Functions."

Combining Functions

You know that you're starting to employ the full power of the Excel application when you start feeling comfortable with using functions in combination with one another. This is particularly true of using the result of one function as an argument to another function.

Keep in mind that the categories of functions discussed in the prior section are just convenient labels. Although this section focuses on combining functions from the same category, there's no reason that you couldn't validly combine a statistical function with a text function or a financial function with a lookup function.

Math Functions Combined

The example at the end of the last section:

=SIN(RADIANS(90))

is typical of how you combine functions to more concisely get the result you're after. In many cases, it's not just a matter of brevity but necessity: you *must* combine the functions to get the result you want. Here's a closer look at the present example.

The last section showed that RADIANS(90) returns 1.57 and that SIN(1.57) returns 1, the sine of a 90-degree angle. To see the intermediate results of the combined version, select the cell that contains SIN(RADIANS(90)) and verify that the formula appears in the formula bar. With your mouse pointer, drag across the RADIANS(90) portion of the formula so that it is highlighted in the formula bar (see Figure 9-9).

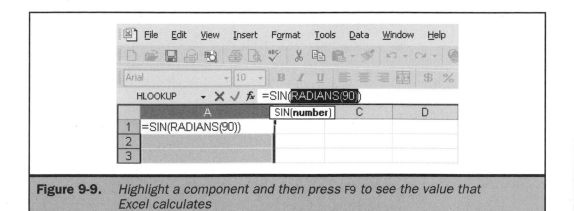

Figure 9-9. *Highlight a component and then press F9 to see the value that Excel calculates*

If you now press the F9 key, you will find that Excel calculates the portion of the formula that you highlighted. The formula bar will show how Excel has responded to the F9 key by calculating the highlighted portion. Now you're back to

=SIN(1.5707963267949)

which of course returns 1.

Note *Press the ESC key or click the Cancel button on the formula bar to leave a calculation as it was before you pressed F9. If you press ENTER or click the Enter Formula button, Excel accepts the calculation as part of the complete formula.*

Excel has handled the combination of the RADIANS and the SIN functions by calculating the result of the RADIANS function on its argument and using that result as the argument to the SIN function.

Note *The Formula Evaluation tool provided by Excel 2002 does not make the approach outlined in this section obsolete. On occasion, you'll want to evaluate a formula's component in some order other than the one forced on you by the Formula Evaluation tool. Furthermore, it's handy to get a quick peek at a formula's component by highlighting it and pressing F9.*

Text Functions Combined

An earlier example in this chapter (see Figure 9-7) first used the TRIM function on employee names to remove any leading or trailing blanks (Column B) and then the LEN function of the results of the TRIM function (Column C). By using the TRIM function as an argument to the LEN function, you can save a step:

=LEN(TRIM(A2))

Logical Functions Combined

You can also combine a function within another instance of the same function. One typical way to do so is with the IF function, where you want one outcome when the condition is true, and another outcome (another IF) when the condition is false. Figure 9-10 provides an example.

Given the schedule in B3:B4 and an actual amount in B7, this formula in C7:

=IF(B7>=B3,0.02*B7,IF(B7>=B4,0.01*B7,0.005*B7))

returns the amount of the executor's fee. Again, it's useful to break up complex formulas into their components. The first condition in the IF is

B7>=B3

This condition is true when the amount in cell B7 is greater than or equal to the amount in cell B3. B3 contains the value 2,000,000; if B7 is 2,000,000 or more, the condition is true. The IF returns the value of its second argument:

0.02*B7

(that is, 2 percent of the estate's value), and nothing further happens.

What if the value in cell B7 is less than 2,000,000? Then the condition B7>=B3 is false, and the IF returns its third argument. The third argument in this case is another IF:

IF(B7>=B4,0.01*B7,0.005*B7)

Suppose the amount in B7 is 1,750,000. Then the second IF's first argument:

B7>=B4

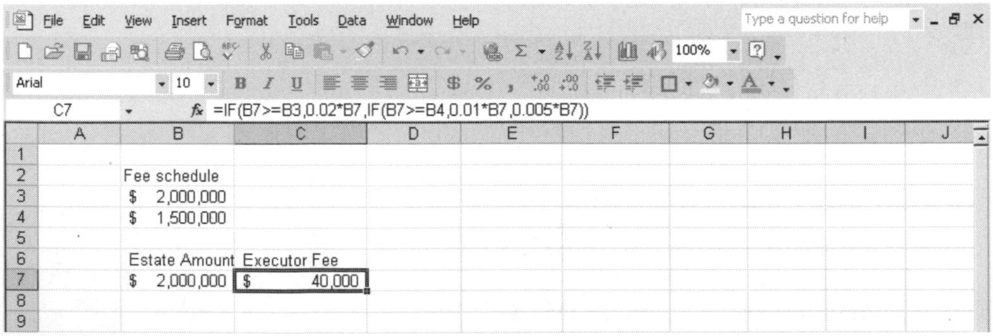

Figure 9-10. *Consider nesting IF functions when you need to account for different possible outcomes*

is true, and the IF returns the value of its second argument:

0.01*B7

(that is, 1 percent of the estate's value), and nothing further happens.

Finally, if the amount in B7 is less than 1,500,000, the second IF's first argument is false. Therefore, the IF returns the value of its second argument:

0.005*B7

(that is, one half of one percent of the estate's value).

The sort of function combination discussed so far in this section—one function used as an argument to another—is termed *nesting*. In Excel, you can nest up to seven levels of functions within the outermost function. The prior example nested one IF function. It could have nested an additional six IF functions:

=IF(A,B,IF(C,D,IF(E,F,IF(G,H,IF(I,J,IF(K,L,IF(M,N,IF(O,P)))))))))

Lookup Functions Combined

The examples of Lookup and Reference functions earlier in this chapter probably struck you as a little contrived. The usage of MATCH and VLOOKUP becomes more realistic when you combine them.

Prior examples of VLOOKUP required that you specify which column the function should obtain the result value from—for example:

=VLOOKUP(10,Q1:Z10,4)

where the third argument, 4, is supplied explicitly so as to return the value in the range's fourth column. You might as well look at the table yourself and find the value you're after. Combining the MATCH and VLOOKUP functions results in the (more realistic) situation shown in Figure 9-11.

In Figure 9-11, the VLOOKUP functions in C12:C16 take their arguments from columns A and B. For example, the formula in C12 is

=VLOOKUP(B12,$B$2:$G$7,MATCH(A12,$B$1:$G$1),1)

In words, here's what the formula does:

- It uses the MATCH function to find the value in A12, "Laptop", in the range $B$1:$G$1. "Laptop" is in the fourth column of that range, so MATCH returns 4. Therefore, the formula simplifies to

    =VLOOKUP(B12,$B$2:$G$7,4,1)

- VLOOKUP looks for the value in B12 in the first column of the range $B$2:$G$7, which is B2:B7. The function's final argument is 1, so VLOOKUP assumes that the first column is sorted in ascending order. VLOOKUP finds the largest value in B2:B7 that's less than or equal to the value in B12. B12 contains 14, so VLOOKUP uses the value 10 from B2:B7.

- VLOOKUP now has the column to use—the fourth column in the table—from the result of the MATCH function. It now has the row to use—the third row in the table—from finding 10 as the largest value that's less than or equal to 14, and 10 is in the third row of the table's first column. The value in the table's third row and fourth column is 57, which is the value returned by the formula.

Note *The VLOOKUP and MATCH example discussed here used an absolute reference for the range arguments and relative references for the lookup value arguments. (See Chapter 8 for a discussion of relative, absolute, and mixed references.) This arrangement made it easy to copy the formula originally entered into cell C12 in Figure 9-11 into C13:C16. The lookup values adjusted accordingly, while the lookup ranges remained constant.*

The combination of MATCH with VLOOKUP is a very useful tool. By using it, all you need do is enter the quantity sold and the product sold—in this example, you enter them in columns A and B. MATCH and VLOOKUP combine to return the resulting commission.

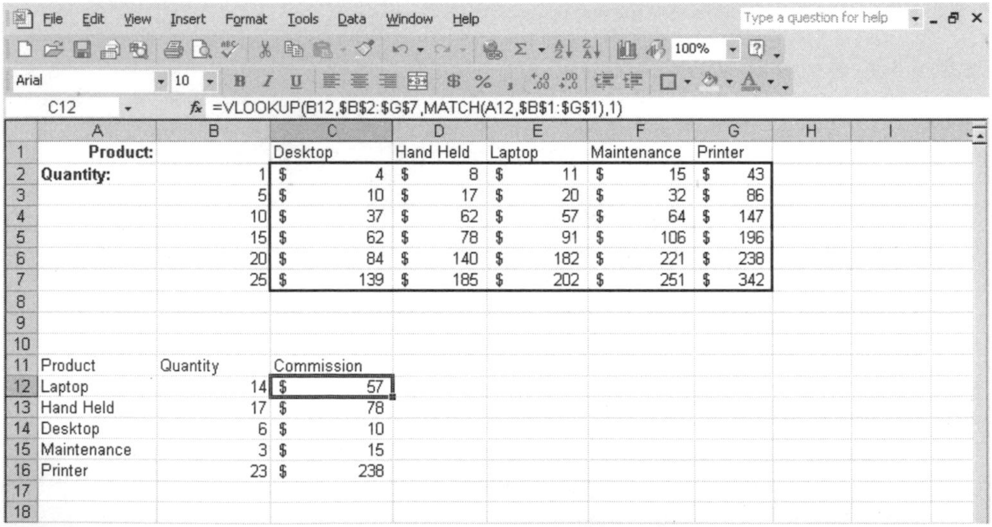

	A	B	C	D	E	F	G
1	Product:		Desktop	Hand Held	Laptop	Maintenance	Printer
2	Quantity:	1	$ 4	$ 8	$ 11	$ 15	$ 43
3		5	$ 10	$ 17	$ 20	$ 32	$ 86
4		10	$ 37	$ 62	$ 57	$ 64	$ 147
5		15	$ 62	$ 78	$ 91	$ 106	$ 196
6		20	$ 84	$ 140	$ 182	$ 221	$ 238
7		25	$ 139	$ 185	$ 202	$ 251	$ 342
8							
9							
10							
11	Product	Quantity	Commission				
12	Laptop	14	$ 57				
13	Hand Held	17	$ 78				
14	Desktop	6	$ 10				
15	Maintenance	3	$ 15				
16	Printer	23	$ 238				
17							
18							

Figure 9-11. *In this example, MATCH informs VLOOKUP which column to use*

Of course, commission calculations aren't the only reason to use these functions. Any situation that calls for finding a particular value in a table (tax rates, for example) is a good candidate for this approach.

Math and Reference Functions Combined

Suppose that you wanted to get the sum of the values in column A but only for cells in odd-numbered rows: row 1, row 3, row 5, and so on. This sort of situation sometimes arises when you have alternating values on your worksheet: for example, number of shares traded on the NYSE followed by number of shares traded on the NASDAQ. You could construct the formula

=A1+A3+A5+A7+A9

and that's not too onerous, but what if you had, say, 100 rows to deal with? That's too tiresome to type. Instead, consider the MOD function, which returns the remainder of a division. Thus, the formula

=MOD(5,2)

returns 1, the remainder after dividing 5 by 2. And the formula

=MOD(6,2)

returns 0, the remainder after dividing 6 by 2. In general, dividing any even number by 2 returns a zero remainder; dividing any odd number by 2 returns a remainder of 1.

The ROW function, with no argument, returns the number of the row where it is entered. So, entered in row 3, ROW() returns 3. The math function MOD and the reference function ROW are combined in Figure 9-12.

Cell C1 in Figure 9-12 contains the formula

=A1*MOD(ROW(),2)

Cell C1 is in row 1, so ROW() returns 1. The remainder from dividing 1 by 2 is 1. So the formula resolves to:

=A1 * 1

Cell C2 contains this formula:

=A2*MOD(ROW(),2)

Cell C2 is in row 2, so ROW() returns 2. The remainder from dividing 2 by 2 is 0. So the formula resolves to

=A2*0

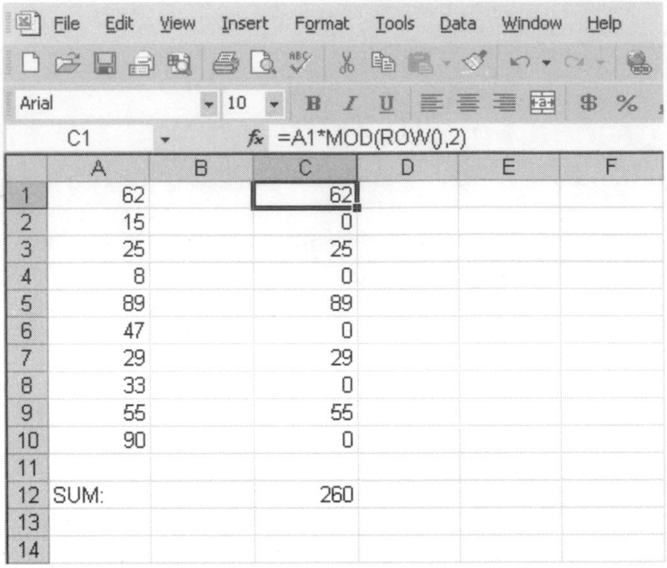

Figure 9-12.   *The ROW and COLUMN functions are a good way to automatically put ordered integers into your formulas or function arguments*

The results are similar in Rows 3 through 10. The combined MOD and ROW functions return zero in even-numbered rows, and they return 1 in odd-numbered rows. By taking the sum of the results in cell C12, you get the total of the values in column A's odd-numbered rows.

Insert Function

Except with functions that you use frequently, it's not easy to remember the arguments that different functions take—let alone the order that you must supply them. To ease that task, Excel provides a command called Insert Function. You invoke that command with the Insert Function button on the Formula Bar, or by choosing Insert | Function (see Figure 9-13).

When you use Insert Function, the dialog box shown in Figure 9-13 appears. Select a function category from the Or Select a Category drop-down. When you do so, the functions that belong to that category appear in the Select a Function list box. Click the function you want, and then choose OK. The dialog box appears as shown in Figure 9-14.

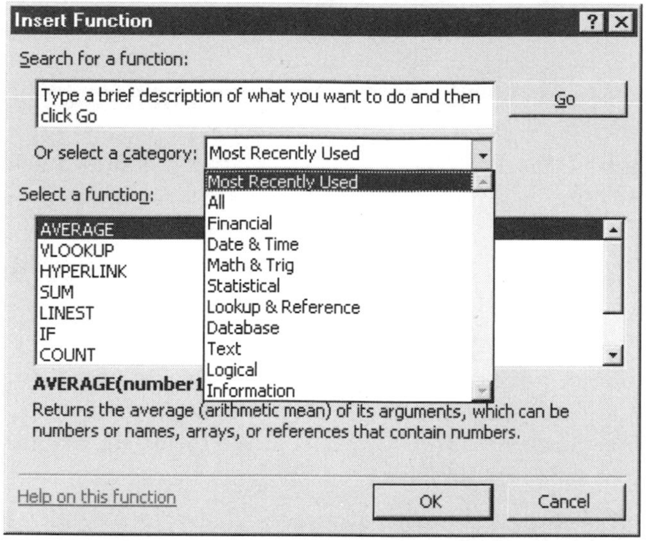

Figure 9-13. *When you click a function category in the dropdown, a list of the functions in that category appears in the list box*

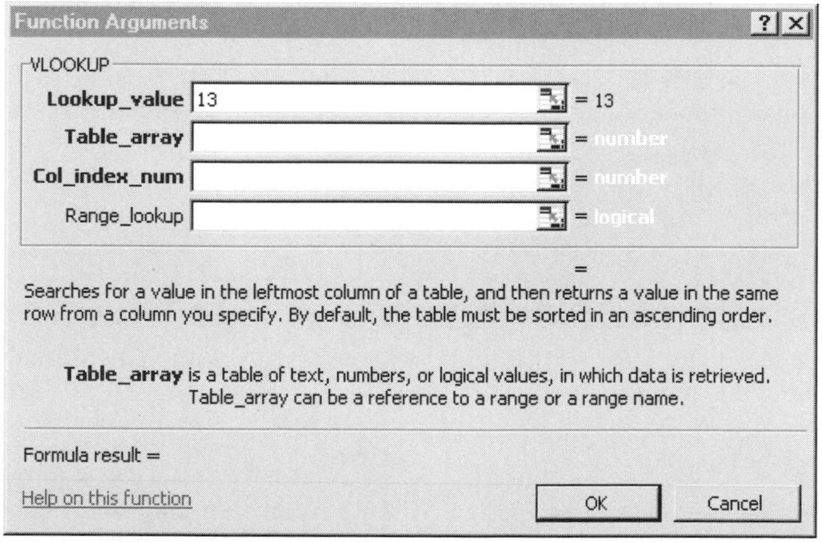

Figure 9-14. *The Insert Function button eases the use of unfamiliar functions*

Notice that Insert Function supplies you with the following features:

■ The function's arguments, with the names of required arguments in boldface and the names of optional arguments shown in the normal font.

■ An edit box to the right of the argument's name. You can type a value into the edit box, or you can click in a worksheet cell that contains the value you want to use for the argument. After clicking in the edit box, click in the cell or highlight a range of cells.

■ To the right of each edit box is a brief description of the type of data the argument should take; for example, a number, a text string, a logical value, and so on. Some arguments can take any type of data.

■ To enter another function as an argument—that is, to nest a function—click in the argument's edit box and then select a function from the drop-down Function Box at the left of the formula bar. Return to the original, outer function by clicking in the Formula Bar.

■ As you provide a value for each argument, that value replaces the data type. If you supply a worksheet range as an argument, the contents of that range appear as an array.

■ The text in the lower portion of the dialog box describes both the selected function and the currently selected argument.

■ When you have supplied enough arguments for the function to return a result, that result appears at the bottom of the dialog box.

■ When you have finished supplying arguments, click OK to paste the function and its arguments into the active cell, or click Cancel to abandon the task.

Hold down CTRL *and* SHIFT *simultaneously as you click OK in order to array-enter the function.*

Certification Skills Covered in This Chapter

If you're preparing for Microsoft Office User Specialist certification, here are the skills you learned in this chapter.

Skill Set	Activity
Creating and revising formulas	Use statistical, date and time, financial, and logical functions in formulas

The
Complete
Reference

Excel
2002

Chapter 10

Advanced Work
with Formulas

The prior chapters on formulas and functions introduced the basics of constructing formulas and using functions in formulas. These are the skills that enable you to use Excel to calculate results. But you can get more informative, more useful results more quickly if you learn some of the ways to enhance the basic formulas and functions. This chapter covers those enhancements, particularly the use of array formulas and defined names.

Array Formula Specifics

The mechanics of putting an array formula on the worksheet are different from those used with regular formulas: array formulas are entered not just with the ENTER key, but with CTRL-SHIFT-ENTER. When you have entered a formula in this way, Excel indicates that it interprets the formula as an array formula by curly braces in the formula bar. That is, if you array-enter the formula

=LINEST(A1:A30,B1:B30,,TRUE)

it appears in the formula bar as

{=LINEST(A1:A30,B1:B30,,TRUE)}

Don't try to add the curly braces yourself; Excel interprets the formula as text if you do so.

> **Note**   *To avoid implying that you should type the curly braces, this chapter omits them in subsequent examples.*

There is one other major difference between array formulas and regular formulas: when the array formula is intended to return different results in different cells, you need to begin by selecting those cells. For example, the LINEST function in the example above can return different information in each cell of a five-row by two-column range. If you want to see that information, you must begin by selecting that range: if you begin by selecting just one cell, LINEST does not automatically fill in the remaining nine cells for you.

Editing Array Formulas

Array formulas that span multiple cells require special handling when you want to edit, move, or delete them. Suppose that you have entered an array formula in A1:A5. Excel responds with the error message "You cannot change part of an array" if:

- You select any single cell, such as A3, in the range, edit its contents, and press ENTER.

■ You try to delete or move some but not all of the cells that contain the array formula.

There's no solution to the second condition. If you want to delete or move any part of the range that contains the array formula, you must delete or move the entire range.

If you want to edit a single cell of that range but leave the other cells as they are, again you're out of luck. But you *can* edit a single cell and have that change applied to the entire range of cells that contain the formula. Just select the cell, make the change, and then press CTRL-SHIFT-ENTER. The modification will take effect in each of the formula's cells.

Conditional Sums

Beyond question, the most frequent use of array formulas is to perform conditional calculations. Consider this simple example: you have a list of salespeople and sales dollars. Each record in the list represents a different sale. You would like to know the total sales dollars for the salesperson named Smith (see Figure 10-1).

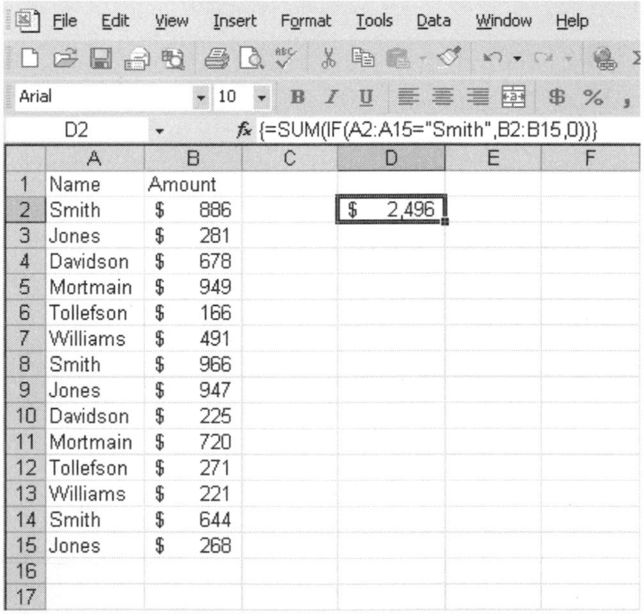

Figure 10-1.   *Notice the curly braces, added by Excel, around the array formula*

One way to get Smith's total sales would be to create a pivot table that uses salesperson as a Row field and the Sum of sales dollars as the Data field. Then you would look for Smith in the Row items and read across to find Smith's total sales dollars.

Here's an easier way. Array-enter this formula (in Figure 10-1, it's in cell D2):

=SUM(IF(A2:A15="Smith",B2:B15,0))

The formula returns the total of the sales dollars in column B for values of "Smith" in column A.

| Note | *Excel provides two worksheet functions that perform conditional arithmetic operations: SUMIF and COUNTIF. This book recommends that you not rely on those worksheet functions. They are neither as flexible nor as powerful as formulas that use the SUM and IF functions or the COUNT and IF functions explicitly and in combination.* |

Throughout this chapter it will be important to look inside formulas at intermediate calculations. In order to understand how to construct complex formulas so that they return the results you're after, you need to know how the formula assembles those results. As Chapters 8 and 9 have shown, Excel gives you two ways to get inside a formula:

■ Select the cell that contains the formula and choose Tools | Formula Auditing | Evaluate Formula, or click the Evaluate Formula button on the Formula Auditing toolbar. If you choose this method, Excel steps you through the formula, showing intermediate results in a window. That's handy because you need only click a button to see what's next. It's awkward because Excel chooses which portion of the formula to evaluate next.

■ Select the cell that contains the formula and highlight with the mouse pointer the portion of the formula that you want to evaluate. Then, press F9 to evaluate the highlighted portion. That's handy because you choose which portion to evaluate. It's awkward because you have to be precise about what you choose to highlight. Also, this method actually edits the formula, so you must remember to click the Cancel button or otherwise abandon the edit. Else, the result of the evaluation replaces that which was evaluated.

The examples in this chapter will illustrate both evaluation methods. In the present example, to see what's going on with the array formula, select the cell that contains it so that the formula appears in the formula bar. With your mouse pointer, drag across the A2:A15="Smith" portion of the formula so that it's highlighted, and then press F9 to calculate the highlighted portion. You will see an array of TRUE and FALSE values, depending on whether a value in column A equals the "Smith" value.

When Is Array Entry Necessary?

There are three fundamental reasons that you would need to array-enter a formula:

■ You are using a function that Excel requires be array-entered in order for it to return the correct results.

■ You are entering a formula whose components require that it be array-entered.

■ You are entering a formula whose results will occupy more than just a single cell.

Each of these reasons is explored in more detail in the next three sections.

Functions That Require Array Entry

Internet newsgroups that are concerned with spreadsheets in general and with Excel in particular constantly get questions that have headers such as "Help change rows to columns and columns to rows." This nearly always means that someone has lots of data entered in many columns that span a couple of rows and that the formatting of a report demands that the values occupy a couple of columns that span many rows. That is, the user needs to put the data that's now in F1:O4 into A1:D10.

You might be familiar with one solution. Select F1:O4. Choose Edit | Copy. Select A1. Choose Edit | Paste Special, fill the Transpose check box, and click OK. Excel transposes the 4-row by 10-column range to a 10-row by 4-column range.

The drawback to this approach is that you wind up with values in the new range—values that do not change in response to changes in the original range. Or, if the original data range consisted of formulas that depend on relative references to other cells, the transposed formulas almost always point to the wrong precedents.

Consider using the TRANSPOSE worksheet function. In this example, you would array-enter this formula (see Figure 10-2):

=TRANSPOSE(F1:O4)

But before you can get the results you're after, you need to make sure that:

1. You have selected the full worksheet range that will display the transposed data. In this case, that means that you need to start by selecting A1:D10. If you selected just A1, relying on Excel to fill in the rest of the data range, you'll get the result for A1 only, in A1 only.

2. You array-enter the formula by pressing CTRL-SHIFT-ENTER. If you just press ENTER or just CTRL-ENTER after selecting the range, you will obtain 40 instances of the #VALUE! error. TRANSPOSE is one of the worksheet functions that *must* be array-entered if you are to obtain the results you want.

ANALYZING DATA

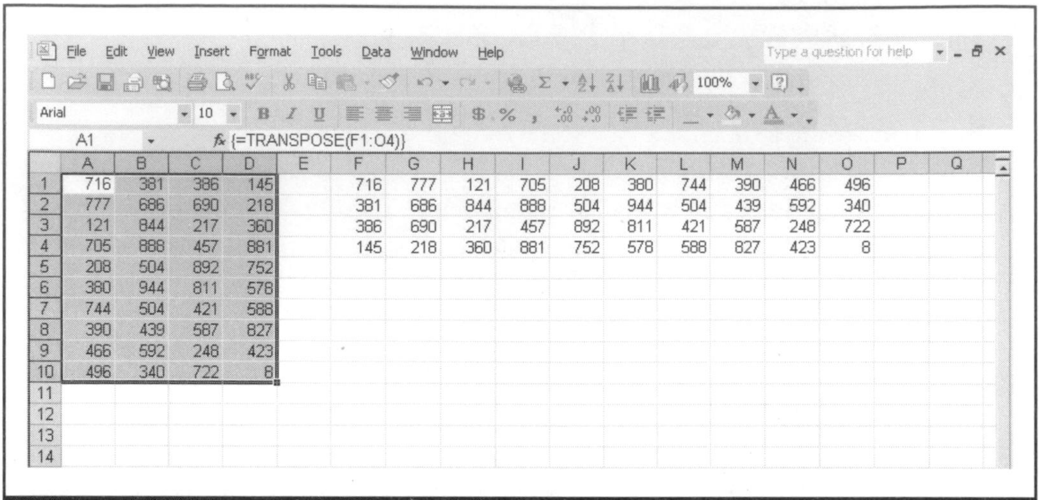

Figure 10-2. *The TRANSPOSE function is used for both matrix algebra and data orientation*

There are several other functions that require array-entry. These functions also require that you begin by selecting the full worksheet range that their results will occupy. The FREQUENCY function returns as many values as there are categories in what's known as the *bin range*, as shown in Figure 10-3.

The FREQUENCY function uses Figure 10-3's worksheet range D2:D7 as its bin range. The bin range establishes the upper bounds of a series of categories; the number of underlying values in each category is what FREQUENCY returns. Because there are six categories established by the six rows in the bin range, you must begin by selecting a range with six rows that will display the six values in the array that FREQUENCY returns. In Figure 10-3, that's E2:E7. Then, you must use CTRL-SHIFT-ENTER to enter the formula; so doing puts the six *different* values of the function's results into E2:E7. If you used ENTER only, you would get the same value in all six cells.

The statistical functions LINEST and LOGEST each return coefficients used in least-squares equations. They require similar treatment. In the case of LINEST and LOGEST, the number of columns returned by the function depends on the number of columns in its *known_x's* range, much as FREQUENCY's rows depend on the number of rows in its bins range. Complicating matters is that LINEST and LOGEST, at the user's option, return up to five rows of inferential statistics. So, to get the full benefit of the functions, you must begin by selecting as many columns as there are columns in the known_x's range, and five rows. Then, type the function's name and arguments and finish with CTRL-SHIFT-ENTER. (If you do not want to suppress the constant in the

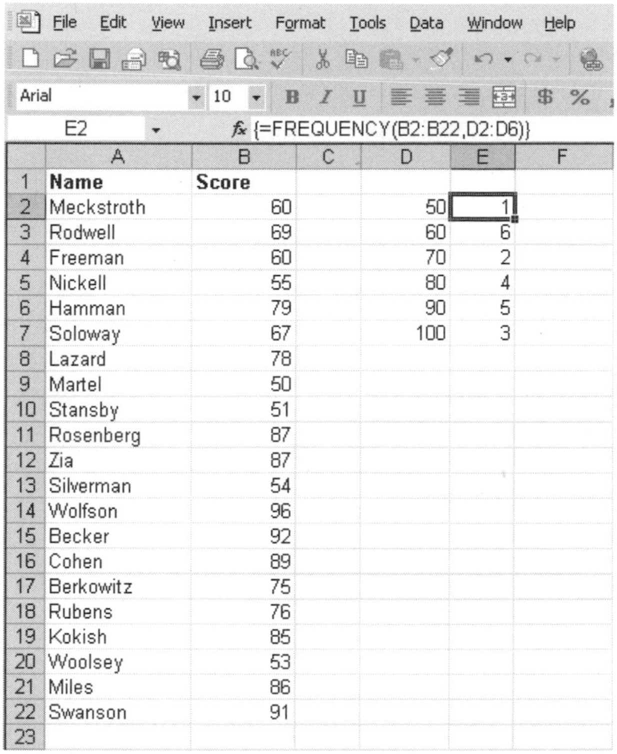

	A	B	C	D	E	F
1	**Name**	**Score**				
2	Meckstroth	60		50	1	
3	Rodwell	69		60	6	
4	Freeman	60		70	2	
5	Nickell	55		80	4	
6	Hamman	79		90	5	
7	Soloway	67		100	3	
8	Lazard	78				
9	Martel	50				
10	Stansby	51				
11	Rosenberg	87				
12	Zia	87				
13	Silverman	54				
14	Wolfson	96				
15	Becker	92				
16	Cohen	89				
17	Berkowitz	75				
18	Rubens	76				
19	Kokish	85				
20	Woolsey	53				
21	Miles	86				
22	Swanson	91				
23						

Figure 10-3. *The FREQUENCY function is useful for grouping numeric values into categories*

least-squares equation, begin by selecting one more column than you have in the range of known_x's.)

TREND and GROWTH are also statistical functions closely related to LINEST and LOGEST. Each has a known_x's range. But these functions return the results of applying the least-squares coefficients to the known_x's, instead of the coefficients themselves. So, you begin by selecting a range with one column and as many rows as in the range of known_x's. Then, enter the function and its arguments and finish with CTRL-SHIFT-ENTER.

MINVERSE and MMULT are mathematical functions used in matrix algebra. MINVERSE returns the result of dividing 1 by a matrix, and you begin by selecting a range with the same number of rows and columns as are in the divisor matrix. The definition of a matrix inverse requires that it be a square range, with as many columns as rows.

MMULT multiplies two matrices, multiplying the values in a row of one matrix by the values in a column of another matrix. The results of the multiplication are summed, and the sum is placed in a cell of MMULT's result array. Here's an example:

=MMULT(A10:B12,D10:G11)

A requirement of matrix multiplication is that the number of columns in the first array argument (here, A10:B12, which has two columns) must be the same as the number of rows in the second array argument (here, D10:F11, which has two rows).

But the result matrix has dimensions that depend on the number of rows in the first array argument and columns in the second array argument. So, before you enter the formula in the present example, you begin by selecting a range with three rows (as in the first array argument, A10:B12) and four columns (as in the second array argument, D10:G11). Finish with CTRL-SHIFT-ENTER.

Formulas Whose Components Require Array Entry

Not all formulas that are array-entered cover multiple cells. Single-cell array formulas are not only possible but common. Here's a typical example:

=SUM(IF(A2:A11="Payroll",B2:B11,0))

The result appears in Figure 10-4.

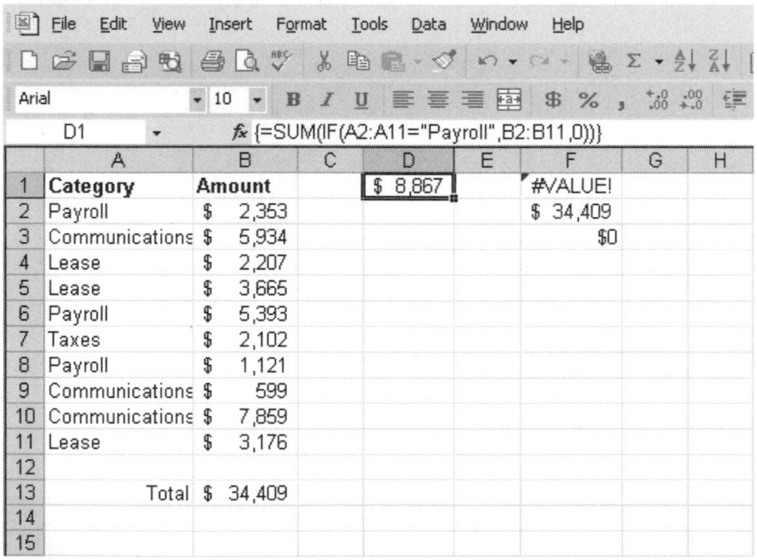

Figure 10-4. *The result of formulas that contain arrays can depend on their location*

The formula is entered four times. Consider first the instance in cell D1: it was entered by means of CTRL-SHIFT-ENTER. As entered in D1, the formula returns the correct result, $8,867. The formula looks to the values in A2:A11, and if any values equal "Payroll," the formula returns the corresponding values ($2,353, $5,393 and $1,121) from column B and sums them.

How does Excel know to return these figures? You can find out by selecting cell D1 and choosing Tools | Formula Auditing | Evaluate Formula. Then press the Evaluate button to see what happens to the expression A2:A11="Payroll". You will see this TRUE/FALSE array:

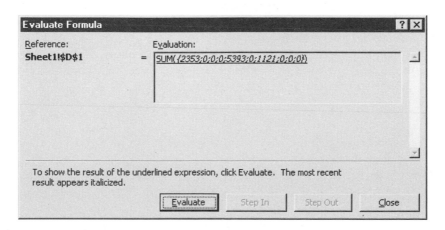

Recall from Chapter 9 that the IF function returns its second argument when its first argument is TRUE. Here, and in a formula that's array-entered, the IF finds that the first, fifth, and seventh values in the first array are TRUE, so it returns the first, fifth, and seventh values in the second array: $2,353, $5,393, and $1,121.

These values are interspersed with seven zero-values, which the IF returns when the first array contains FALSE. Press Evaluate again to see this new array.

Then the SUM function returns the total, $8,867. Press Evaluate a final time to see it.

What about the formulas in F1:F3 of Figure 10-4? They are each instances of the formula in D1, but they are entered normally—with ENTER instead of CTRL-SHIFT-ENTER. Because they refer to ranges but are entered as normal formulas, they become instances of the *implicit intersection*.

An implicit intersection comes about when you enter, using ENTER, a formula such as

=A1:A10

In this example, you would enter the formula somewhere outside Column A and in some row from Row 1 to Row 10. Your formula *implies*, by way of the row where you enter it, that it *intersects* A1:A10 at that row.

Another example:

=A1:J1

You would enter the formula somewhere below Row 1 and in some column from Column A to Column J. The formula implies, by way of the column where you enter it, that it intersects A1:J1 at that column.

So, an implicit intersection can be used with a range of many rows and one column or many columns and one row. It cannot be successfully used with both at once, as in this union:

=A1:A10,A1:J1

You also cannot successfully use the implicit intersection with a 3-D range (a 3-D range spans several worksheets).

In a formula that uses the IF function, as cells F1:F3 of Figure 10-4, the reference is in the IF's first argument, its condition:

A2:A11="Payroll"

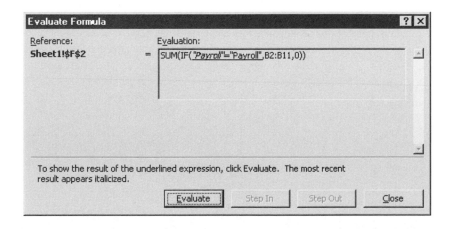

Cell C2 in the preceding illustration contains this formula:

=A1:A10

and because the formula is entered in row 2, it implicitly intersects row 2 of A1:A10. That cell, A2, contains $5,934, and that's what the formula in cell C2 returns. If the same formula were entered in cell C8 (or D8 or E8 or AF8), it would return the value in A8, $599.

Now consider cell F2 in Figure 10-4. It contains this formula:

=SUM(IF(A2:A11="Payroll",B2:B11,0))

just as does cell D1, but it is not array-entered. It is entered normally, with ENTER. That means that the formula intersects implicitly with the A2:A11 range. If you select cell F2, choose Tools | Formula Auditing | Evaluate Formula and click Evaluate, you will see this:

So the logical test is whether *"Payroll"* equals "Payroll". Because it does (Excel does not distinguish between formats when testing whether values are equal), the SUM function totals the values in B2:B11 and returns $34,409.

There is a difference, not readily apparent, in how the IF function in this example uses the range A2:A11 and the SUM function uses B2:B11:

- The IF function's first argument, its conditional, compares *one* value with another: for example, IF(C35 > 100, "Big", "Small"). When, as here, you present it with a range of values (A2:A11) to compare with "Payroll", the IF function resolves the apparent conflict by invoking the implicit intersection. Because it is entered in Row 2, the IF uses the one value it finds in A2 to compare with "Payroll".

- In contrast, the SUM function takes a range of values as its argument and so does not have to invoke the implicit intersection to find a single value.

The sole difference between the formulas in cells D1 and F2 of Figure 10-4 is that D1's formula is array-entered and F2's formula is not. In cell D1, the test value "Payroll" is compared to each value in the A2:A11 array. When they are equal, as is the case in cells A2, A6, and A8, the corresponding values in B2, B6, and B8 are totaled, and the result of $8,867 is returned by SUM. In cell F2, the test value "Payroll" is compared only to the value in the cell A2, due to the implicit intersection. Because A2 contains the value "Payroll", the IF test is met and *all* the values in B2:B11 are summed.

If you followed that, it will be clear to you why the same formula entered normally in cell F3 of Figure 10-4 returns 0. In this case, the test value "Payroll" does not equal the value in the implicit intersection cell A3. So the IF test is not met, and no values are totaled, resulting in the 0 you see in cell F3.

What about the #VALUE! error value in cell F1? If you select cell F1, choose Tools | Formula Auditing | Evaluate Formula, and click Evaluate, you will see this:

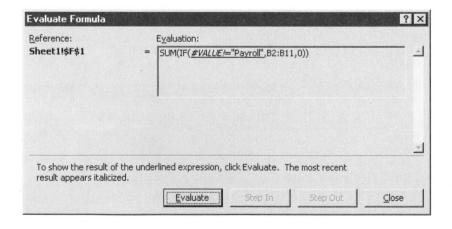

The reference to the range A2:A11 has been replaced with the #VALUE! error value. Excel attempts to invoke the implicit intersection and to find a value in the A2:A11 range that corresponds to the row where the formula is entered. The problem is that the formula is entered in row 1, and there is a null intersection with the range A2:A11.Excel resolves the problem by replacing the range reference with #VALUE!. Unless you make special arrangements (such as an ISERROR test), any time you have an error value in a formula, that formula returns an error value. That's the reason there is an error value displayed in cell F1 of Figure 10-4.

To recap:

■ The formula in F1 refers to A2:A11. Excel cannot find a cell in the reference that is in the same row as the formula itself, and Excel returns the #VALUE! error.

■ The formula in F2 again refers to A2:A11. It uses cell A2 because it is in the same row as the formula itself. Because the value in cell A2 satisfies the IF function's first argument, the IF function returns its second argument—the values in B2:B11. And the SUM function totals them.

■ The formula in F3 refers to A2:A11. It uses cell A3, in the same row as the formula itself. The value in A3 does not satisfy the IF function's first argument, so the IF function returns its third argument, zero. The SUM function totals zero and returns it.

Formulas That Require Multiple Cells

The following illustration shows a type of table that you often find in worksheets: two basis arrays (B1:F1 and B2:F2) that are multiplied together to return the result array in D4:H4. The result array must occupy multiple cells, just as do its basis arrays.

The range D4:H4 contains this array formula:

=$B$1:$F$1*$B$2:$F$2

There is no function in this formula, just simple range and arithmetic operations. If entered normally (as it is in D6:H6, with CTRL-ENTER), then Excel interprets the formula as invoking the implicit intersection. Because cells G6:H6 are outside the range of columns B:F referenced in the formula, the implicit intersection fails. So G6:H6 return the #VALUE! error, just as does cell F1 in Figure 10-4.

> **Note** *Just as you use* ENTER *to put data into a single selected cell, you can use* CTRL-ENTER *to put data into a selected range of cells.*

Therefore, when you create a formula that directly references a range of cells and you do not want the formula's result to depend on its location vis-à-vis the range, array-enter the formula.

Using Names

Names are nearly as important to the effective use of Excel as are rows and columns. Many users don't realize this, largely because names aren't as visible as other workbook and worksheet components. Nevertheless, using names effectively eases many tasks.

A name is a variable that can take on different values and different kinds of values. It's likely that the most frequent use of names is to identify worksheet ranges, such as in Figure 10-5.

You might give the name Revenues to the worksheet range B2:B13. Then you can use the name Revenues in place of the range address B2:B13. For example, these two formulas would return the same result:

=SUM(B2:B13)

=SUM(Revenues)

The first and most obvious result is that the formula becomes self-documenting. A year hence, when you've forgotten how you structured the worksheet, it might take you a few seconds to figure out what you were up to when you totaled the values in B2:B13. But when you see that a formula returns the sum of Revenues, its purpose is immediately apparent.

Naming Constants

You can also define a name that represents a constant value. Suppose that you use a worksheet to calculate your payroll. A constant in any payroll calculation is the FICA contribution. There are at least two good reasons to define a name that refers to the FICA rate: it helps to document the formulas that use the name, and it's much easier to remember than some number that has to be accurate to four decimal places.

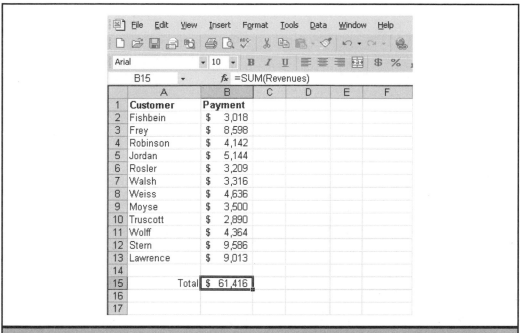

Figure 10-5. *You can use a range name anywhere you would use a range address*

To define a name that refers to a constant, take these steps:

1. Choose Insert | Name | Define. The dialog box in Figure 10-6 appears.

2. Type the name you want to use into the Names In Workbook edit box. In the present example, you would type **FICA**.

3. Clear the contents of the Refers To edit box, which will usually be the address of the cell that was active when you took step 1. Clear the contents by dragging across them and pressing DELETE.

4. Type an equal sign and the constant value in the Refers To box. In the present example, you might type **=.0765**.

5. Click OK to close the dialog box.

Note *There are rules for the characters you can use in names. A name's first character must be either a letter or an underscore. After the first character you can use letters, numbers, periods, and underscores. Spaces and special characters such as slashes and dashes are not allowed. Excel trims away any leading or trailing blanks for you.*

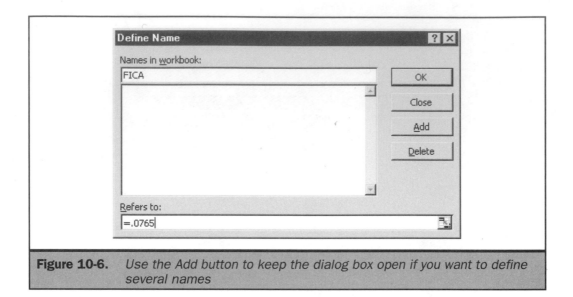

Figure 10-6.   *Use the Add button to keep the dialog box open if you want to define several names*

Now, if an employee's salary is in cell B3, you could enter the formula

=FICA * B3

to obtain the FICA contribution for that employee in the current salary period. Even better might be to give a name such as Smith_Salary to cell B3 and enter this formula:

=FICA * Smith_Salary

Range Names

The beginning of this section discussed the use of a named range, *Revenues*, to return the sum of a set of revenue figures in B2:B13. You could name this range using a technique similar to the one described for defining a FICA percentage:

1. Choose Insert | Name | Define and type the name **Revenues** into the Names In Workbook edit box.
2. You need not remove whatever is in the Refers To edit box. Just drag through the range B2:B13 on the worksheet—say, the worksheet named Sheet1.

Whatever was in the Refers To edit box is replaced by:

=Sheet1!$B$2:$B$13

There are two important aspects to the address that Excel puts into the Refers To box:

- The address names the worksheet—here, Sheet1—that contains the cells you dragged through. The Sheet name is separated from the cell designation by an exclamation point. However, there is no mention of Sheet1 in the name *Revenues* itself.

- Excel made the range reference absolute by preceding the column letters and row numbers with dollar signs.

These aspects are discussed in the next three sections.

Worksheet-Level Names versus Workbook-Level Names

Suppose that you maintain information about revenues and costs for each fiscal year in a separate worksheet. You might have a worksheet named 2002, one named 2003, and so on. In each worksheet there are lists containing monthly costs and monthly revenues.

You would like to define the name *Revenues* for each list of monthly revenues on each worksheet. However, you run into a snag: a particular name can be used once only in each workbook. You cannot use the name *Revenues* to refer to the revenues on both the 2002 worksheet and the 2003 worksheet.

Instead, give the ranges worksheet-level names. Structure the name by using the worksheet name and the descriptive name separated by an exclamation point just as in the Refers To box. For example, '2002'!Revenues and '2003'!Revenues are worksheet-level names that use the names of the worksheets to distinguish between the two instances of the name *Revenues*.

When a worksheet name begins with a number or contains a blank space and in some other situations, Excel surrounds its name with single quotes when it makes use of the worksheet name.

What's wrong with making the names unique by attaching the name of the year to the end of the name? For example, you might define the name *Revenues2002*.

The reason you shouldn't do this is that if you follow the *sheetname!rangename* structure, you need not use the sheet name when you refer to a name on its own sheet. That is, given that the names '2001'!Revenues and '2002'!Revenues exist, then on the sheet named 2001, you can use the formula

=SUM(Revenues)

to obtain the total of the numbers in the range named '2001'!Revenues. The same formula, if entered on the sheet named 2002, would return the total of the numbers in the range named '2002'!Revenues.

In other words, if you use a worksheet-level name in a formula but omit the worksheet name and the exclamation point, Excel uses the name as defined for the active worksheet.

If you wanted to get the total of '2002'!Revenues on a worksheet *other than* the 2002 worksheet, you would need to enter

=SUM('2002'!Revenues)

That is, you would need to qualify the name by that of its worksheet.

When you define a worksheet-level name, it subsequently appears in the Define Name dialog box, in the Names In Workbook list box (see Figure 10-7).

If you define a worksheet-level name and subsequently change the name of the worksheet, Excel changes any references to the old worksheet name with references to the new one.

Worksheet-level names do not appear in the Define Name dialog box when another worksheet is active. If you have already defined the worksheet-level name *2002!Revenues*, and if the worksheet named 2003 is active when you choose Insert | Name | Define, *2002!Revenues* will not appear in the Define Name dialog box.

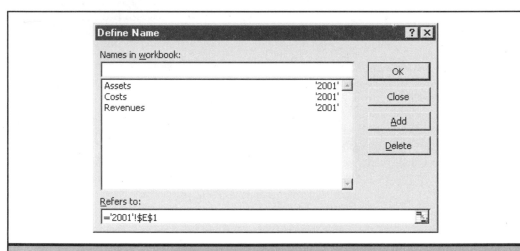

Figure 10-7. *Existing worksheet-level names appear in the Names In Workbook list box, with the range name on the left and the sheet name on the right*

Any defined name—whether it refers to a worksheet range, a constant value, or something else—that does *not* begin with a worksheet name is a workbook-level name. In contrast to worksheet-level names, workbook-level names

- Can be defined once only in a workbook at the workbook level.

- Can be referenced—for example, used in a formula—on any sheet in the workbook.

- Appear in the Define Name dialog list box no matter what sheet is active.

The Name box is a useful aid to definition and navigation. When the active cell or range has a defined name, that name appears in the Name box, as shown here.

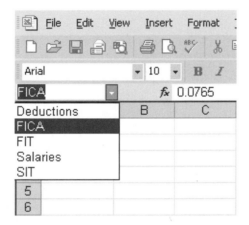

Notice that the active cell's defined name appears in the Name box. Click the down arrow at the right of the Name box to display a drop-down list of defined range names. When you select one of those range names, Excel makes it the active cell or the active range.

You can also type the address of a cell or range in the Name box in order to go there. For example, if you type **A3:B5** into the Name box and press ENTER, the range A3:B5 is selected.

Another use of the Name box is to quickly define a range name:

- If you click in the Name box and type **MyRange**, whatever cell or range was active when you clicked in the Name box is named *MyRange*.

- If Sheet1 is active when you click in the Name box and you type **Sheet1!MyRange**, you will create a worksheet-level name.

Absolute Range Names

By default, when you define a range name using either the Name box or the Define Name dialog box, Excel makes the address that the name refers to an absolute address.

Suppose that C16 is the active cell and you use the Name box to give that cell a name such as *Prime_Rate*. If you subsequently look at that name in the Define Name dialog box, you will see =*$C$16* in the Refers To edit box.

Similarly, you could choose Insert | Name | Define, type **Prime_Rate** in the Names In Workbook edit box, click in the Refers To edit box, and then click in cell C16. Excel inserts =*$C$16* in the Refers To edit box.

The result is that no matter where you are on the worksheet, the name Prime_Rate always refers to the cell C16. It's an absolute reference. This is similar to the formula

=SUM($A$1:$A$10)

No matter where you enter that formula on the worksheet, you can copy it to any other location and it returns the sum of the values in A1:A10. It's an absolute reference.

The virtue of defining the name in this way is twofold:

- You can use the name in different formulas and cause them to update properly when you change the value that the name takes on.

- When, as here, you cause the name to refer to a cell, the name returns whatever value is in the cell. This makes it easy to see the value associated with the name.

Relative Range Names

Now, suppose that the active cell is E6. You use Insert | Name | Define to define the name Five_Above. You click in the Refers To edit box and then drag through the cells E1:E5—five rows up from and in the same column as the active cell. But before you click Add or OK, you remove the dollar signs from the edit box reference =$E$1:$E$5. That is, you position the insertion point to the right of each dollar sign and press the BACKSPACE key so that the reference becomes =E1:E5. Then you click Add or OK.

You can also remove the dollar signs from an absolute or mixed reference by highlighting the reference and pressing F4. *This key cycles references through the pattern RC, R$C, $RC, RC.*

You have now created a relative range name. Excel interprets the name as relative to the active cell. When you began the process, E6 was the active cell and you defined the name Five_Above to refer to the range E1:E5, the five rows up from the active cell.

If you now select cell G8 and use the Name box to go to the range referenced by Five_Above, the range G3:G7—the five rows above the active cell and in its column—is selected.

Why bother? See the next section.

Naming Formulas

It's not too likely that you will frequently need to define a name that refers to a formula. There's little reason to create a formula that is named, for example, *Eight* that refers to the equation

=4*2

On occasion, though, you might want to define a name that combines an arithmetic operation (or a function) with a worksheet range. But there's little need even for this usage unless the range is *relative*. Making it relative, as described in the previous section, means that you can use it repeatedly, in different locations on the worksheet, returning different results. If the name referred to a range that was defined as absolute—the default arrangement—you could use it in various locations, but it would always return the same result.

Suppose that you have reason to analyze different quantitative characteristics of five products—say, buggy whips. You gather data on variables such as the length, the weight, the tensile strength, and the street price of each buggy whip. You enter the data as a list in an Excel worksheet as shown in Figure 10-8.

Interested as you are in the average of each characteristic, you select cell B7 and define the name Average_Five_Above as:

=AVERAGE('Buggy Whips'!B2:B6)

Note that you removed the dollar signs from the range address, rendering it a reference that's relative to the five cells directly above whatever cell is active.

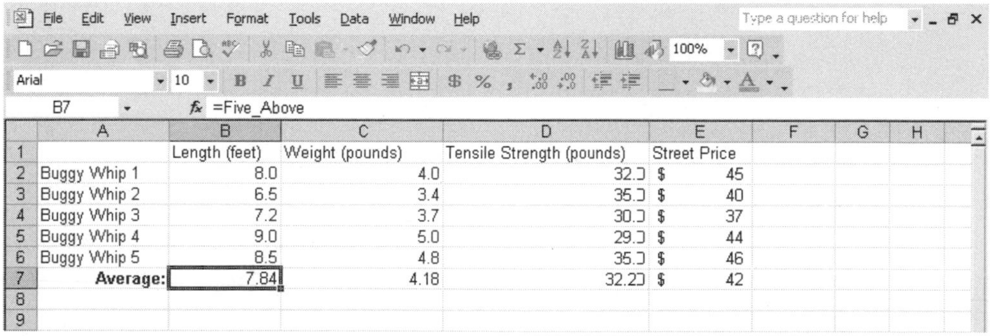

	A	B	C	D	E	F	G	H
1		Length (feet)	Weight (pounds)	Tensile Strength (pounds)	Street Price			
2	Buggy Whip 1	8.0	4.0	32.0	$ 45			
3	Buggy Whip 2	6.5	3.4	35.0	$ 40			
4	Buggy Whip 3	7.2	3.7	30.0	$ 37			
5	Buggy Whip 4	9.0	5.0	29.0	$ 44			
6	Buggy Whip 5	8.5	4.8	35.0	$ 46			
7	Average:	7.84	4.18	32.20	$ 42			
8								
9								

B7 = =Five_Above

Figure 10-8. *Cells B7:E7 each contain the formula =Average_Five_Above*

Having defined that name, you enter it in B7, C7, D7, and E7. Each time you enter it, the name evaluates to the average of the values in the five cells above the cell that contains the name.

In sum, you will very likely encounter your own reasons to define names that refer to formulas. But the formulas will probably be too restrictive and trivial if they don't refer to a range, or if they refer to a formula that uses an absolute range. A name that refers to a formula will have the greatest applicability if the formula acts on a relative range.

Dynamic Definitions for Named Ranges

It often happens that you must add data to an existing range. You would like to have objects in the workbook, such as charts and formulas, automatically update in response to the additional data.

For example, you might have a list of numbers in column B that represents your monthly revenues. The numbers at present extend from B2:B10, and that range of cells is named *Monthly_Revenues*. Elsewhere on the worksheet you keep the year-to-date total of revenues with this formula:

=SUM(Monthly_Revenues)

You also have a chart in the workbook that shows the monthly revenue stream.

When it comes time to add the next month's revenue figure in cell B11, you would like the formula that totals the revenues to update automatically. You would also like the revenue chart to automatically show the new revenue figure.

The problem is that the formula depends on the range name *Monthly_Revenues*, which refers to the range $B$2:$B$10. And the data series in the chart also refers to $B$2:$B$10. Just adding another number in cell B11 will change neither the formula nor the chart.

The solution lies in how you define the range that's named *Monthly_Revenues*. This chapter has already shown that you can define a name that refers to a range by putting the range's address in the Define Name dialog's Refers To box. You have also seen how you can define a name that refers to a constant value, by putting that value in the Refers To box.

You can also use formulas and functions in the Refers To box. To solve the present problem, you need to find a function that is sensitive to the presence of new data on the worksheet. Then you need to use that function to help define the range named *Monthly_Revenues*.

One such is the worksheet function COUNT. If you want to know how many numbers are in column B, you use this formula:

=COUNT(B:B)

> **Note**
>
> *When you use a reference such as B:B, omitting the row numbers, you refer to the entire column. Similarly, the reference 5:5 captures the entire row 5. If you use R1C1 notation, the references are to C2 and R5, respectively.*

In the present example, the COUNT function returns 9 when you have numbers in B2:B10 only. When you add the next month's revenue in B11, COUNT(B:B) returns 10.

Chapter 9 discusses, among others, the Lookup and Reference category of worksheet functions. One reference function is the OFFSET function, which has this syntax:

=OFFSET(reference, rows, columns, height, width)

OFFSET returns a range of cells. The anchor point of that range is OFFSET's *reference* argument.

The *rows* and the *columns* arguments indicate how far the returned range is from the anchor point. So the formula

=OFFSET(A1,3,5)

returns the range that is three rows below and five columns to the right of the anchor point A1—that is, it returns the cell F4.

> **Note**
>
> *The height and width arguments to the OFFSET function are optional and are not used in the previous formula. But this example will make use of them later on.*

The formula

=OFFSET(A1,0,0)

returns the range that is zero rows below and zero columns to the right of the anchor point A1—that is, it returns the cell A1 itself. This is not a trivial usage.

The *height* and *width* arguments to the OFFSET function indicate the number of rows and the number of columns to include in the returned range. So the formula

=OFFSET(A1,3,5,2,3)

shifts (that is, *offsets*) the returned range three rows down and five columns right of A1. Then it makes the returned range two rows high and three columns wide. Therefore, it returns the range F4:H5.

Getting close. You can use the COUNT function to determine how many numbers there are in a range, and you can use that result to determine the height, in rows, of a range. Therefore, the formula

=OFFSET($B$2,0,0,COUNT($B:$B),1)

returns a range that is shifted zero rows and zero columns from B2, that has as many rows as there are numbers in column B, and that has one column. If column B contains numbers in rows two through ten only, then there are nine numbers and the formula returns the range B2:B10.

As soon as you add a number in (say) B11, the formula recalculates, the COUNT function returns ten instead of nine, and the OFFSET function returns the range B2:B11. If you use the formula in the Refers To box of the Define Name dialog box, you will have defined a name whose reference depends on some number of numeric values (see Figure 10-9).

When you have defined the name *Monthly_Revenues* in this way, the formula

=SUM(Monthly_Revenues)

returns different results depending on how many numeric values there are in the range that's returned by the OFFSET function.

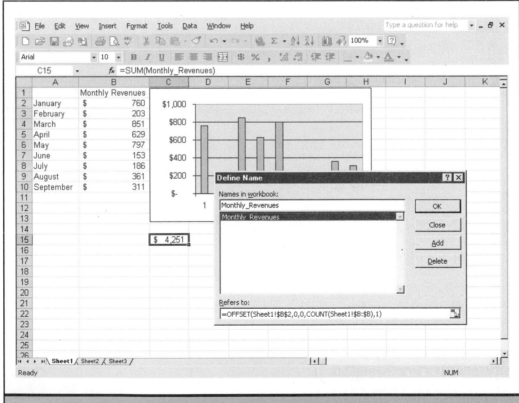

Figure 10-9. *Dynamic range names appear only in the Define Name dialog box, not in the Name Box*

To use the name *Monthly_Revenues* in a chart, follow these steps:

1. Create a chart (see Chapter 11 for specific instructions) that displays the revenue figures. In this instance, you might start out by charting the values in B2:B10.

2. Click on the charted data series. That is, if you created a Column chart, click on one of the columns; if a Line chart, click on the line or on one of the dots that the line connects.

3. Depending on the choices you made when creating the chart, you will see something very similar to the following formula in the formula bar:

=SERIES(,,Sheet1!$B$2:$B$10,1)

With your mouse pointer, drag across the portion of the formula that shows $B$2:$B$10 to highlight it. Then type the name **Monthly_Revenues** and press ENTER. The formula bar (see Figure 10-10) should now contain something similar to the formula

=SERIES(,,Book1! Monthly_Revenues,1)

When you add a new value to column B, the COUNT function in the name Monthly_Revenues recalculates, as does the OFFSET function in which COUNT

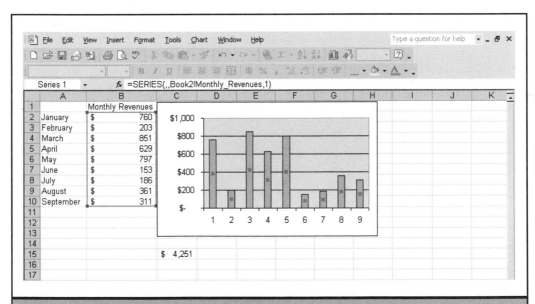

Figure 10-10.   *This chart redraws when you add a new numeric value to column B*

is nested. The name Monthly_Revenues then refers to a new range, and the chart displays the new revenue value, as shown here.

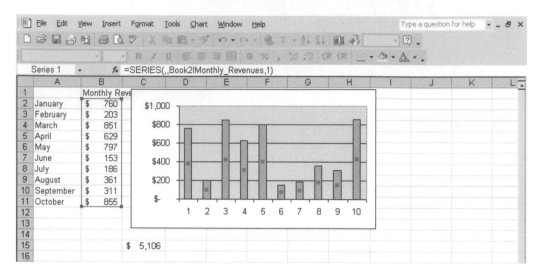

As useful as they are, though, dynamic range names aren't bulletproof. Notice in Figure 10-10 that the total of column B's revenue figures is given in column C. If it had been placed instead in column B, a circular reference would have resulted: the formula would depend on itself. And, had an extraneous number gotten into column B somewhere, that would have added another numeric value to the column, and COUNT($B:$B) would have returned a result one greater than the number of monthly revenue values.

In turn, that extra value returned by COUNT would have increased the number of rows in the dynamic range—spuriously. You want the number of rows in the range to depend solely on the number of monthly revenue values, not on something extraneous such as the sum of the revenues.

Nothing's free. If you want to avail yourself of the convenience of dynamic range names, as well as their protection against forgetting to include a new value in a chart or a summary formula, you'll just have to remember to keep extraneous values out of the range in question.

Using Functions in Array Formulas

Combining the power of worksheet functions with that of array formulas can bring about unique and elegant results. While it's often the case that some other approach, such as writing some VBA code, would have worked, you will find that you can get there faster with an array formula. If you spend some time expanding array formulas by using the formula bar in combination with the F9 calculation key, you'll find that these formulas act like miniature programs, complete with loops and function calls.

Locating Duplicate Values

Duplicate values can be troublesome in worksheet applications. You frequently create formulas whose correct answer assumes that there is only one instance of each value in a range. For example, when you're totaling expense reimbursements issued to employees, your formula might well assume that each employee is listed only once.

When a list with possibly duplicated values represents a problem, the situation is made more difficult if the list is a long one. And it's even worse when the values were entered manually—it's easy for a person's eye to wander and for the fingers inadvertently to type the same value twice.

Use Excel's worksheet functions to help guard against situations where duplicate values would pose a problem.

Duplicates in One Range

Excel's FREQUENCY function is intended to return the number of values in different ranges of values. This chapter briefly discussed the FREQUENCY function in the section on array formulas.

Figure 10-11 shows the FREQUENCY function in a guise that you might not find familiar.

Notice that there is only one range of values, A1:A10, and that the result in cell C1 is 2: the maximum number of times any value appears in A1:A10 (note that the number 8 appears twice).

The formula in cell C1 makes use of the FREQUENCY function and the MAX function as follows:

```
=MAX(FREQUENCY(A1:A10,A1:A10))
```

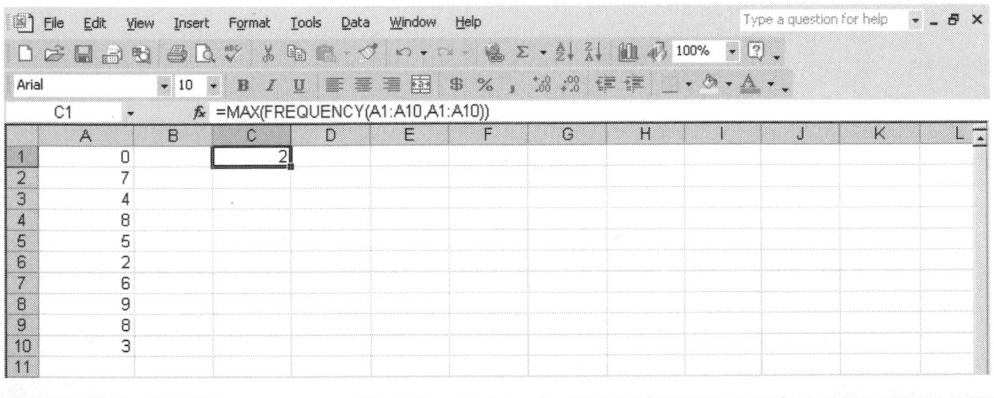

Figure 10-11. *FREQUENCY can use the same range as both the data array and the bins array*

What's different about the FREQUENCY function in the present example is that its first argument—the data array—is the same as its second argument—the bins array. The effect of the FREQUENCY function as used here is to return the number of times a value in the data array equals itself.

Each value in the data array must equal itself at least once, simply by virtue of being in the array. If the value appears twice in the array, then it can equal itself twice—once for each instance. If you enter the data and the formula as shown in Figure 10-11, you can click and drag across this portion of the formula to highlight it:

FREQUENCY(A1:A10,A1:A10)

If you then press F9, you will see this array:

1;1;1;2;1;1;1;0;1;0

There are three points to note about this result array:

■ The fourth value in the result array is 2. That fourth array element corresponds to the value 8 in cell A4. The value 8 also appears in cell A9, so the value 2 in the result array corresponds to the fact that there are two instances of the value 8 in the data array.

■ Since both 8s have already been counted, the ninth element in the result array is 0. The rule is that the position in the result array where a number first appears gives the total number of times it is found in the data array; subsequent positions that correspond to that number in the result array have the value 0.

■ The FREQUENCY function always returns one value more than the number of values in the bins array. This final value is there to account for any values in the data array that are larger than the largest boundary in the bins array.

So, by enclosing the FREQUENCY function and its arguments within the MAX function, you can determine whether any values are duplicated: if MAX returns a result greater than 1, you know that there is at least one duplicated value.

If instead of MAX you use SUM and IF, you can learn how many values are duplicated:

=SUM(IF(FREQUENCY(A1:A10,A1:A10)>1,1,0))

In Figure 10-11, only the value 8 is duplicated. Therefore, FREQUENCY returns only one value greater than 1. When you enclose the array returned by FREQUENCY within the IF function:

IF(FREQUENCY(A1:A10,A1:A10)>1,1,0)

you get this array:

0;0;0;1;0;0;0;0;0;0

And when you finally take the SUM of that array, you get 1 as a result: there is one value in A1:A10 that is duplicated.

The FREQUENCY function is useful in this context, but its drawback is that it doesn't work on strings. The function ignores both text strings and empty cells. By introducing a complication (see Figure 10-12), you can handle either numbers or text:

=SUM(IF(FREQUENCY(MATCH(A1:A9,A1:A9,0),MATCH(A1:A9,A1:A9,0))>1,1,0))

Figure 10-12 illustrates how the MATCH function enables you to compare a range to itself. In Chapter 9's incarnation, the MATCH function used one lookup value as its first argument. MATCH compared that single value to those in its second argument, the lookup range.

In the present version, entered in an array formula, MATCH uses an array of values as its first argument. It compares *each* of those values, in turn, to the values in its second argument. Because MATCH's third argument is zero, an exact match is required.

Working from the inside out, start with this fragment of the formula:

MATCH(A1:A9,A1:A9,0)

By dragging across it in the formula bar and then pressing F9, you can verify that it returns this array:

{1;2;3;4;5;2;7;8;9}

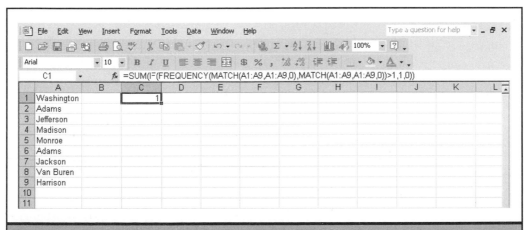

Figure 10-12.   *Nesting MATCH within FREQUENCY helps you locate duplicate strings*

Recall that with zero as its third argument, MATCH returns the position of the *first* instance of the lookup value in the lookup array. The above array indicates that the first value in A1:A9 matches the first value, the second value matches the second value, and so on until you reach the sixth value. That sixth value is Adams, which also appears as the second value in the array—so, 2 appears as the sixth value in MATCH's results.

The MATCH fragment appears twice in the full formula, so it evaluates to

=SUM(IF(FREQUENCY({1;2;3;4;5;2;7;8;9},{1;2;3;4;5;2;7;8;9})>1,1,0))

The FREQUENCY fragment, using the results of the MATCH functions, is

FREQUENCY({1;2;3;4;5;2;7;8;9},{1;2;3;4;5;2;7;8;9})

or:

{1;2;1;1;1;0;1;1;1;0}

In words: one value (1) in FREQUENCY's data array is less than or equal to the first value in the bins array. Two values (both equal to 2) in FREQUENCY's data array are less than or equal to the second value in the bins array. These two values correspond to the value Adams in the original data range, A1:A9 in Figure 10-12.

The original formula now evaluates to

=SUM(IF({1;2;1;1;1;0;1;1;1;0}>1,1,0))

Now use the IF fragment to test whether its arguments are greater than 1. If so, return 1; if not, return 0. Here's what the IF returns:

{0;1;0;0;0;0;0;0;0;0}

Finally, enclosing that array in the SUM function:

=SUM({0;1;0;0;0;0;0;0;0;0})

returns 1: the number of duplicated text values in cells A1:A9 of Figure 10-12.

Note *The worksheet range that is tested for duplicates in the present example can contain text strings, numeric values, or both. When you have text values only or a mix of some strings and some numbers, nest the MATCH function inside the FREQUENCY function as illustrated here.*

Duplicates in Different Ranges

The MATCH function was used in Chapter 9 to locate a value in a table as an aid to the VLOOKUP function. It was used in the prior section to help locate duplicate text strings in a single range. MATCH has its uses in other contexts, of course. Suppose that you must assign e-mail addresses to each of the employees at your company. You need to ensure that everyone has a unique address. In A1:A15 of Figure 10-13 are the first 15 addresses that you assign, and C1:C10 shows the next 10 addresses you assign.

One way to check for duplicate addresses would be to copy the addresses into one column, sort them, and visually scan the list looking for duplicates. That wouldn't be too tough with just 25 addresses, but it's a different story if there are 500 to check.

Instead, array-enter the formula

=COUNT(MATCH(A1:A15,C1:C10,0))

which appears in cell E1 of Figure 10-13.

Drag across the MATCH function and its arguments as used in this example. When you then press F9, you will see an array similar to this one:

#N/A;#N/A;#N/A;#N/A;#N/A;#N/A;#N/A;#N/A;#N/A;#N/A;#N/A;#N/A; 6;#N/A;#N/A

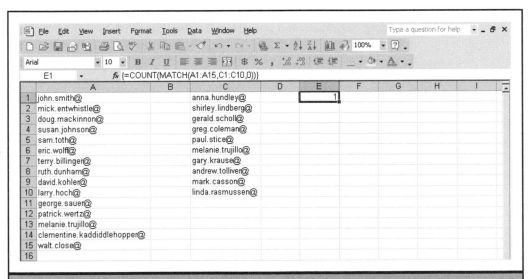

Figure 10-13.   *Entered in an array formula, MATCH tests each value in its first argument against its second argument*

The MATCH function returns the #N/A! error value, meaning None Available, when it cannot find a match. That's good news in this case—a match would mean that a value in the first range is duplicated in the second range.

The COUNT function is one of the few that do not return #N/A! when one of its arguments is #N/A!.

Figure 10-13 shows the MATCH function nested within the COUNT function in cell E1. The COUNT function returns 1 as its result, so there is one value in A1:A15 that's duplicated in C1:C10. Examining the array returned by MATCH, above, you see that there is one numeric value, 6, the thirteenth element of the array. And once your attention is drawn to it, you can see that the thirteenth value in A1:A15, melanie.trujillo@, is duplicated in cell C6—the sixth value in B1:B10.

String Handling

As the owner of a chain of video rental stores, you occasionally want to check on the number of days that a customer is entitled to keep a rented videotape. You want to ensure that the most popular titles come back soonest. Unpopular titles can stay out months at a time, for all you care.

Your stores keep an inventory of titles, structured as the title of the video, followed by the number of days that the customer may keep the tape. See Figure 10-14 for an example.

It's an unfortunate scheme, but it's built into the canned software that the previous owner bought. Lotus 6-6-6 or something. The pattern is to show the title, followed by the title's rental period, followed by at most one trailing blank. As shown in Figure 10-14, a customer can keep a rented copy of *Bonnie and Clyde* for 2 days or *Ishtar* for 60 days.

You would like to separate the number of days at the end of each title from the title itself for more convenient analysis. One way to do this is by means of Excel's Text To Columns item in the Data menu. The problem with that approach is that it would put each title's number of days in a different column, depending on how many words are in the title.

And you can't use something such as

=RIGHT(A1,LEN(A1)-FIND(" ",A1))

because that depends on the number of blank spaces in the cell. If there's just one space, fine. But in the case of *Wait Until Dark 8*, the formula would return *Until Dark 8*, because the function focuses on the first blank space only—the one between *Wait* and *Until*.

You need a way of finding the final blank space in the cell and then returning everything to its right. That's not easy, but here's how.

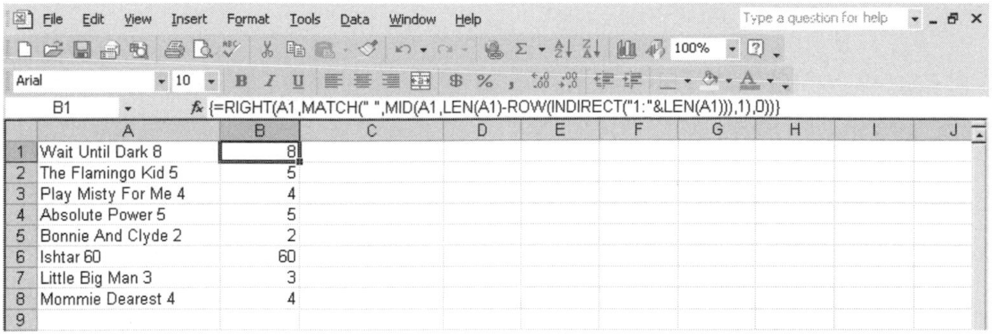

Figure 10-14. *This example obtains the numbers at the end of each value in Column A and puts them in Column B*

Note

This sort of situation—where you need to find some value at the end of a string—occurs frequently. You often need to isolate last names or the final directory in a path or a domain name in a URL.

It's a complex formula:

=RIGHT(A1,MATCH
(" ",MID(A1,LEN(A1)-ROW(INDIRECT("1:"&LEN(A1))),1),0))

Again working from the inside out, start with this fragment:

INDIRECT("1:"&LEN(A1))

Meet the INDIRECT function. It has various uses, but one of them is to assemble a cell address from a string. Here, the INDIRECT function takes as an argument the length of the string in cell A1, or 17. So it evaluates as

INDIRECT("1:17")

The expression "1:17" is, as discussed above in the section on range names, a reference to rows 1 through 17. So nesting the INDIRECT function within the ROW function as here:

ROW(INDIRECT("1:17"))

returns this array:

1;2;3;4;5;6;7;8;9;10;11;12;13;14;15;16;17

Notice that this technique returns a series of consecutive integers that is only as long as the length of the string in cell A1. Altering the fragment to

ROW(INDIRECT("1:"&LEN(A6)))

would return this array:

1;2;3;4;5;6;7;8;9

because the value in cell A6, *Ishtar 60*, has only nine characters.

Expanding the fragment another level:

LEN(A1)-ROW(INDIRECT("1:"&LEN(A1)))

becomes

17-{1;2;3;4;5;6;7;8;9;10;11;12;13;14;15;16;17}

which results in this array:

{16;15;14;13;12;11;10;9;8;7;6;5;4;3;2;1;0}

The result of all this formulaic hand waving is to create an array of integers that is in descending order and that is no longer than the length of the string of interest. Here's the full formula as it's simplified so far:

=RIGHT(A1,MATCH(" ",MID(A1,{16;15;14;13;12;11;10;9;8;7;6;5;4;3;2;1;0},1),0))

MID is another function that you might not have seen yet. It returns a string that's inside another string. So this formula:

=MID("mxyzptlk",4,1)

returns from the string "mxyzptlk" (first argument) the one character (third argument) that is fourth position (second argument) in the string—that is, it returns "z".

If you evaluate the MID function in the current formula by highlighting it and its arguments and pressing F9, you get this array:

{" ";"k";"r";"a";"D";" ";"l";"i";"t";"n";"U";" ";"t";"i";"a";"W";#VALUE!}

That's "Wait Until Dark " spelled backward, with #VALUE! at the end, because there's no zero-th position in the string.

Applying the MATCH function, you get this fragment:

MATCH(" ",{" ";"k";"r";"a";"D";" ";"l";"i";"t";"n";"U";" ";"t";"i";"a"; "W";#VALUE!},0)

which returns 1. In words, the final blank space in cell A1 comes one position before the final character (8) in cell A1.

At last, this is what was needed: a way to locate the final blank-space separator in the string. Using that as a locator, you can isolate the final nonblank character or characters in the string. The original formula has now simplified to:

=RIGHT(A1,1)

or 8. Applying the same formula to cell A6 simplifies to RIGHT(A6,2) and returns 60. Suppose that you have entered the formula, with its six nested functions, into B1:B8.You can now select the cells in columns A and B and sort ascending on column B: this will move the videos with the shortest rental periods to the top of the list.

Chapter 11

Charting Data

There is no potion so soporific as someone else's spreadsheet. Interpreting a mass of numbers arrayed in the familiar matrix, data instead of information, will drive you straight to Minesweeper. It's that bad.

But if you put the data in a chart, then you've got something. Unexpected trends jump out at you. Important points, otherwise lost in the morass of columns and rows, take shape in columns and curves. The signal emerges from the noise and you've begun to communicate.

Sounds grand, and it can be. But don't forget that it all starts with a mouse.

Using the Chart Wizard

Suppose you have some numbers in a worksheet. These numbers are related to one another in some fashion—for example, they might be annual revenues from 1992 to 2001. The numbers are arranged as a list: in contiguous cells, in a column, just as recommended in Chapter 5.

Starting the Wizard

To get these numbers onto a chart with the help of the Chart Wizard, follow these steps:

1. Use your mouse to select the cells that contain the numbers you want to chart.

2. Click the Chart Wizard button on the Standard toolbar (or choose Insert | Chart from the menu bar).

3. Choose a chart type in the Chart Wizard's first step (see Figure 11-1). Click Next to move to the next step.

Verifying the Data Selection for the Chart

The Chart Wizard's second step gives you a chance to modify the underlying worksheet data range. If you have oriented your data in rows (e.g., A2:J2), be sure that the Rows option button is chosen; if in columns (e.g., B1:B10), choose the Columns button. Then click the Series tab (see Figure 11-2).

You often intend the first row or column of the selected worksheet range as labels, not values. But if these values are numeric (as shown in cells A1:A5 of Figure 11-2), then the Chart Wizard can't tell that they are intended as labels—and it considers them a separate data series. When this occurs, correct it by first deleting the series (in Figure 11-2,

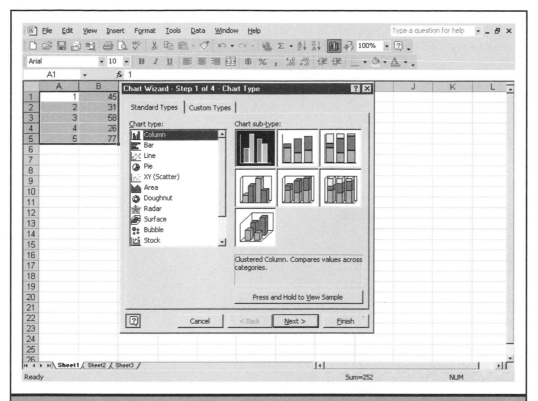

Figure 11-1. *Using the Press And Hold To View Sample button helps you make an initial choice from the available chart types*

it's Series1), and then entering the address of the range of labels into the Category (X) Axis Labels text box. Take these steps:

1. Select Series1 in the Series list box.
2. Click Remove.
3. Click in the Category (X) Axis Labels text box.
4. Drag through A1:A5 on the worksheet.
5. Click Next.

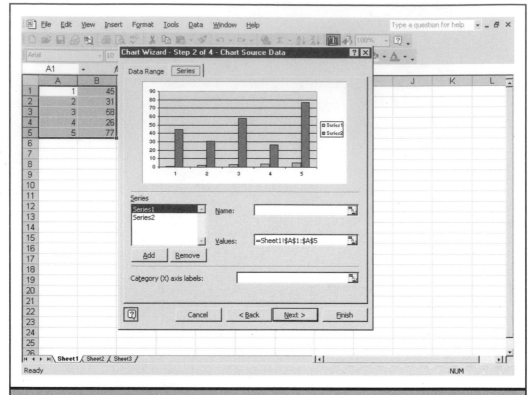

Figure 11-2.   Use the edit boxes on the Series tab to select or to modify range addresses

Selecting Chart Options and Location

The Chart Options dialog box appears as the Chart Wizard's Step 3. This chapter details the available choices in the section titled "Chart Options." For now, accept the default options by clicking Next.

The Chart Wizard's fourth and final step (see Figure 11-3) lets you choose between locating the chart on a new sheet or as an object in the active worksheet. Make your choice and click Finish.

After you complete Step 4 (or after you click Finish in any step), the chart appears and is automatically selected. When a chart is selected, the chart menu appears in the main menu bar. When you select something else, such as a worksheet cell, the chart menu disappears.

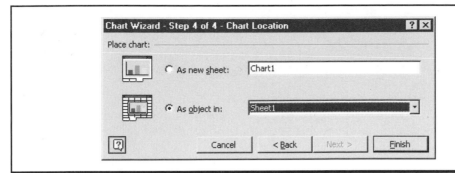

Figure 11-3.   *While a chart is under development, it's useful to locate the chart as an object in the worksheet*

Changing the Chart

All the choices that you make in the Chart Wizard are revocable decisions. You can change your mind later by using the Chart menu:

- Chart Wizard's Step 1 is the same as choosing Chart I Chart Type.
- Chart Wizard's Step 2 is the same as choosing Chart I Source Data.
- Chart Wizard's Step 3 is the same as choosing Chart I Chart Options.
- Chart Wizard's Step 4 is the same as choosing Chart I Location.

After creating a chart, you can add data to it by highlighting the range of data that you want to add and dragging it into the chart. Or you can choose Chart I Add Data and then select the range that you want to add to the chart.

Types of Charts

As the prior section suggests, the process of creating a chart in Excel appears simple and straightforward. But Excel offers 14 different standard chart types, some very similar to one another and some quite different in appearance, intent, and requirements. This section's discussion of the different standard chart types will help you choose the type that best conveys your intent and that conforms to the data you have available.

Understanding Chart Axes: Column, Bar, Line, and XY Charts

Figure 11-4 shows one set of data and how the numbers appear in a Column chart, a Bar chart, a Line chart, and an XY chart.

Apart from their orientation, the Bar and Column charts appear very similar. That's to be expected, since they are almost identical. There is no difference between a Bar and a Column chart, except that numeric values appear horizontally in a Bar chart and vertically in a Column chart.

The Line and the XY charts in Figure 11-4 also appear similar, but this is due to the nature of the values depicted on their horizontal axes. On a Line chart, the 1, 2, 3, 4, and 5 are just the first, second, third, fourth, and fifth data points: this is because the Line chart's horizontal axis just identifies different categories. In contrast, on an XY chart, the 1, 2, 3, 4, and 5 are shown as actual numeric values, and the chart's horizontal axis preserves the quantitative relationships between the values. To see this distinction more clearly, compare how the Line and the XY charts shown in Figure 11-5 treat the same five values.

Notice in Figure 11-5 that the horizontal axis values are spaced evenly in the Line chart. Regardless of their actual values, they are just the first, second, third, fourth, and

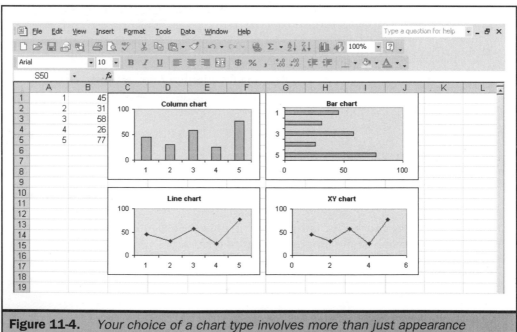

Figure 11-4.   *Your choice of a chart type involves more than just appearance*

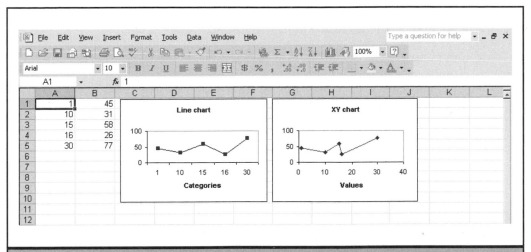

Figure 11-5. *The Line chart's horizontal axis is a Category axis; an XY chart's horizontal axis is a Value axis*

fifth data points. But in the XY chart, each position on the horizontal axis reflects its relative magnitude.

In Excel's terms:

- An XY chart has two value axes.
- A Line chart's vertical axis represents numeric values, while its horizontal axis represents categories.

Excel's charting terminology is a little idiosyncratic. To keep things straight and to conform to Excel's Help documentation, this book uses these definitions:

- A data series is a set of numeric values that are connected to one another on the chart, usually by a line or by the same color. The values in a data series are usually found on the worksheet in contiguous cells and oriented in either a single row or a single column.

- A data marker is the main visual element in a chart. In a Bar chart, it is a bar; in a Line or XY chart, it is a diamond, square, triangle, dash, or circle. Each data marker represents an individual point in the data series.

- A chart's Value axis displays numeric quantities and preserves their relative magnitude. Excel often uses the terms *Value axis* and *Y-axis* interchangeably.

- A chart's Category axis displays any scale of measurement using distinct categories. A Category axis implies neither serial order nor relative magnitude. For Category axis purposes, the categories "Ford," "Chevrolet," and "GM" might as well be "1," "2," and "3" or "98," "72," and "3." Excel often uses the terms *Category axis* and *X axis* interchangeably.

These definitions of category and value axes make statements about chart types a little more crisp:

- A Column chart has a vertical Value axis and a horizontal Category axis.
- A Bar chart has a vertical Category axis and a horizontal Value axis.
- A Line chart has a vertical Value axis and a horizontal Category axis.
- An XY chart has two Value axes.

No 2-D Excel chart has both a vertical and a horizontal Category axis.

Summing to 100 Percent: Pie, Doughnut, and Radar Charts

Particularly in business applications, you often work with percentages. For example, business analysts frequently common-size documents such as income statements to make comparisons easier. One way to common-size is by means of percentages: "This company's salaries are 68 percent of its revenue; the industry average is only 56 percent."

When you want to chart several categories whose percentages total to 100 percent, consider using a Pie or Doughnut chart.

Figure 11-6 shows a Pie chart and a Doughnut chart. Both charts have a category and a value dimension, and the distinctions between categories are represented by different slices of the pie or the doughnut. The relative values are represented by the different sizes of the slices. Since the charted values must all fit within the circumference of the chart's plot area, these chart types visually imply a sum-to-100 percent characteristic.

The main difference between the Pie and Doughnut types is that the Pie can display one data series only. The Doughnut type can display multiple data series. As shown in Figure 11-6, the Doughnut chart is useful for displaying changes in percentages over time, using a different data series for each year.

Comparing Dimensions: Area and Radar Charts

Like Column and Bar charts, both Area and Radar charts enable you to examine the contributions of different categories (say, companies) to different value measurements (say, expense dollars). The Radar chart is more useful when you are interested in *comparing* categories. The Area chart is more useful when you are interested in *summing* categories (see Figure 11-7).

There are drawbacks to both charts shown in Figure 11-7. Notice that it's barely possible to compare the 2001 with the 2002 Accounts Payable on the Radar chart, but you can't even see the 2001 Accounts Payable on the Area chart.

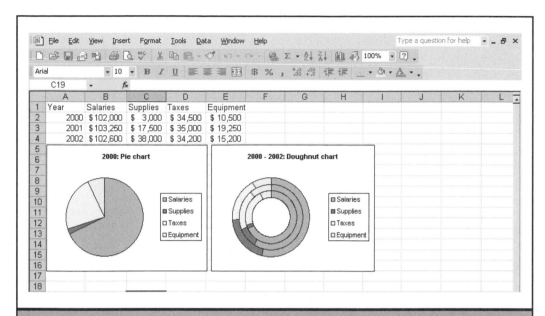

Figure 11-6.   *Pie and Doughnut charts emphasize differences between categories*

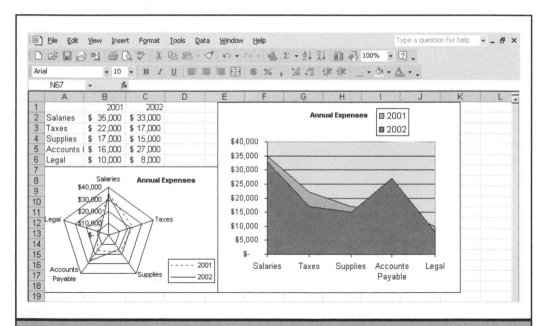

Figure 11-7.   *The unstacked area chart with two or more series usually obscures at least one data point*

Although the Radar chart enables comparisons between the two years, it's visually messy. Each additional category (Salaries, Taxes, Supplies, and so on) requires another axis extending from the chart's origin. Add the pentagonally shaped gridlines, the Value axis labels, and the category labels, and you have a chart that displays much and communicates nothing.

Suppose you wanted to emphasize the total of each expense type across the two-year period. Figure 11-8 shows the results.

The stacked Area chart in Figure 11-8 makes it easy to see the total of the expense types for the two-year period and helps you see the relative contribution of each year to the total. Visually disaggregating the relative contributions by way of the Radar chart is very difficult.

Creating Stock Charts

Use a Stock chart to display statistics about a given stock during some time period: often that period is a day, but it might also be a week, month, or year. Of course, you can use this chart type to plot anything you want, but the chart is intended to help track stock prices.

There are four Stock chart subtypes. In each case, you would usually supply a contiguous worksheet range of dates for display on the chart's Category axis.

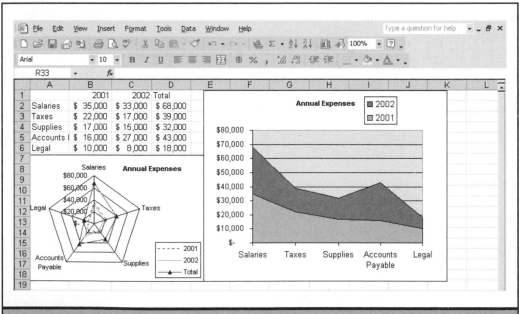

Figure 11-8.   *The Radar chart becomes cluttered very quickly*

- **High-Low-Close** This subtype requires that you supply, in order, the high, the low, and the closing price of the stock for each time period. "In order" means that the high prices are shown in the left-most column (or top-most row) of the data range, and the closing prices are shown in the right-most column (or bottom-most row) of the data range.

- **Open-High-Low-Close** In addition to high, low, and closing prices, you supply the opening price of the stock. The opening price must precede the high price on the worksheet.

- **Volume-High-Low-Close** Instead of the opening price, you supply the number of shares traded. The volume is charted against the chart's Primary Value axis, and the prices are charted against its Secondary Value axis.

- **Volume-Open-High-Low-Close** You supply all five statistics, in that specific order on the worksheet.

Figure 11-9 shows each of these charts.

In each time period, there is a vertical, or *High-Low*, line. The top point of the line represents the high price for the time period, and the bottom point represents the low price.

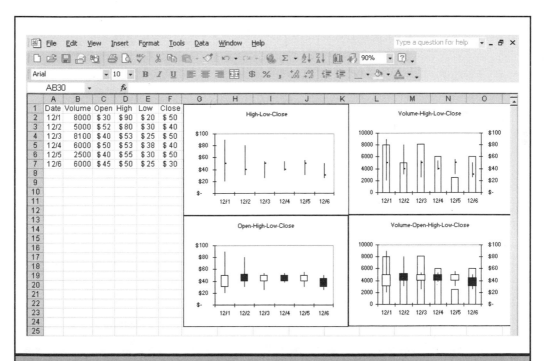

Figure 11-9. *The charts that show both volume and price put the volume scale on the primary axis and the price scale on the secondary axis*

There is a horizontal dash on the High-Low line in both the High-Low-Close and the Volume-High-Low-Close charts. This dash represents the closing price for that period.

There is a box, bounded by *Up-Down* bars, on the High-Low line in the Open-High-Low-Close and the Volume-Open-High-Low-Close charts. The top point of the box represents the higher of the opening and closing prices, and the box's bottom point represents the lower of the opening and closing prices.

If the box is white, the stock closed higher than it opened (it gained value during the time period). If the box is black, the stock closed lower than it opened (it lost value during the time period). These colors are defaults. You can change them by clicking the box and choosing Format | Selected Up Bars or Format | Selected Down Bars.

The Stock charts are unique in these respects: their High and Low data series are automatically formatted with neither data markers nor lines. Instead, the High-Low lines are used to indicate the high and the low values. Similarly, when both the Open and the Close prices are charted, their data series have neither markers nor lines. Instead, the Up-Down bars indicate the opening and closing values.

The absence of data markers causes a problem if you use one of the Volume subtypes. The Volume series is charted with Column markers, which have both areas and borders. The Column marker usually obscures the Low price and can obscure the Open, High, and Close prices as well. If you find that this happens, take these steps:

1. Select the Volume data series—the one that appears as columns—by clicking it.

2. Choose Format | Selected Data Series and click the Patterns tab.

3. In the Area box, choose the None option button. This makes the column transparent, while leaving its border visible.

4. Click OK. With the columns transparent but their borders visible, you can see the full range of the Up-Down bars and the High-Low lines. This is how the columns are shown in Figure 11-9.

You could instead format the pricing data series so that they use data markers as well as lines and bars. But doing so is time consuming and clutters up the chart.

Three Value Axes: the Bubble Chart

Bubble charts combine characteristics of XY and Area charts so as to offer visually informative depictions (see Figure 11-10).

The Bubble chart has three ways to depict quantitative values: the vertical and horizontal axes and the size of each bubble. Figure 11-10 shows partial results of a hypothetical political preference survey as a bubble chart where

■ The vertical axis shows the average attitude toward the proposition.

■ The horizontal axis shows the number of people in each bubble.

■ The size of each bubble shows the average likelihood that the people in that group will vote. The bubbles have been given data labels, discussed later in this chapter.

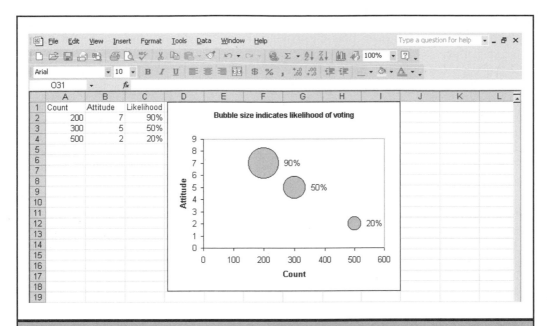

Figure 11-10.   *The size of the bubbles might be a guide to their relative importance*

Although the right-most bubble has the largest number of potential voters, they are the least likely to vote, as indicated by the size of the bubble. Therefore, you might conclude that the proposition is likely to pass.

Because bubbles take up so much room on a chart, the Bubble chart is best used to display aggregate data. There are only three observations (each with three values) that form the chart in Figure 11-10. Each observation is a different *group* of potential voters. Because each bubble represents an observation, a Bubble chart based on individual voters would have so many data markers that any trends would be obscured. A standard XY chart, even though it provides only two value axes, is better than a Bubble chart for the analysis of data about individuals: an XY's data markers are not so obtrusive.

Data Series and Data Points

In Figure 11-10, the bubble chart is based on the data found in the range A2:C4; the first row contains labels for the data series. This is the first instance in this chapter of a range with the same number of data series (three: Count, Attitude, and Likelihood) as there are data points in each series (three: one in row 2, another in row 3, and another in row 4).

It is typical of most charts that they contain more data points in a given data series than they have data series. Consider Figure 11-9. There, the High-Low-Close chart has three series (High, Low, and Close) and six data points per series (12/1 through 12/6). Even the Volume-Open-High-Low-Close chart has six data points per series and but five data series.

Excel uses this aspect of charts—that they typically have more data points per series than they have data series—to guess at the orientation of the underlying data. If the range of input data has more rows than columns, then Excel assumes that each column represents a data series, and that each data point within a column's data series is found in a different row. This is the orientation of the input data used in Figures 11-1, 11-2, 11-4, 11-5, 11-7, 11-8, and 11-9. If you create for yourself the charts shown in those figures and then choose Chart | Source Data, you will see that Excel shows Series in Columns on the Data Range tab.

Contrast those figures with Figure 11-6, which has five columns of data and three rows. If you create the chart shown in that Figure 11-6, the Data Range tab will show you that Excel shows Series in Rows. Because there are more columns than rows, Excel assumes that each series occupies a different row and places observations belonging to the same series in different columns. The assumption in this case is wrong; you need to correct it as described in the next section.

Reorienting Charts

Occasionally, you will have reason to create a chart that has more data series than data points per series: suppose, for example, that you had only three days worth of data and four data series for an Open-High-Low-Close chart. This type of chart requires four data series. But Excel assumes that you have more data points than data series.

So, if you selected the range C2:F4 and tried to create an Open-High-Low-Close chart, you would be presenting Excel with a conflict. This kind of chart requires four series. But you have selected three rows and four columns, so Excel's initial assumption is that you have three series and four data points. This conflicts with the expectation of four data series for this type of chart, and Excel will eventually complain to you with a message about how to set up your data.

To resolve the conflict, navigate to Step 2 of the Chart Wizard (or, if the Chart Wizard is not active, select the chart and choose Chart | Source Data). On the Data Range tab, click the Data Series in Columns button. This tells Excel that, contrary to its initial assumption and despite the fact that there are fewer data points than data series, your four data series are each located in a different column.

Now consider the bubble chart shown in Figure 11-10. It is built on the data found in the range A2:C4. That range has three columns and three rows, so Excel can't use its assumption about more data points than data series: they're identical in number. Excel's fall-back assumption is that data series are found in rows. Suppose you started the Chart Wizard with A1:C4 selected and created a Bubble chart with the markers labeled by bubble size. If you accepted Excel's fall-back assumption with the data oriented as in Figure 11-10, you would wind up with one bubble labeled 300, another labeled 5, and another labeled 50%. Your chart would have another data series, but it would be invisible because Excel would think its bubble sizes were all zero.

Again, the solution is to inform Excel that, with three data series in columns and three data points in rows, its assumption that series occupy rows is wrong. On Step 2 of the Chart Wizard, click the Data Series in Columns button.

Visual Variety: Cylinder, Cone, and Pyramid Charts

Figure 11-11 shows a Cylinder, a Cone, and a Pyramid chart. Although Excel offers these charts as standard types, they do not differ functionally from Bar and Column charts. All that's different is the shape of their data markers, which are round, tapering, or both. In order to show the shape of these markers, their associated charts are always 3-D.

If you prefer these shapes to standard bars or columns, keep in mind that you can orient them so that the Value axis is either vertical (like a Column chart) or horizontal (like a Bar chart).

Creating Surface Charts

Surface charts imply the combined effects of two variables on a third (see Figure 11-12).

To create a Surface chart, you need at least two (and preferably many more) data series, each consisting of numeric values. Figure 11-13 shows an example of how to lay

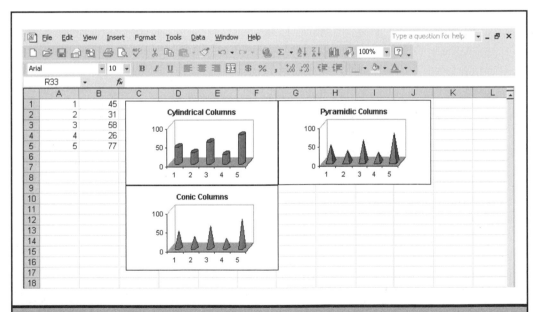

Figure 11-11. *These charts have different chart types, but they differ only in the shape of their markers*

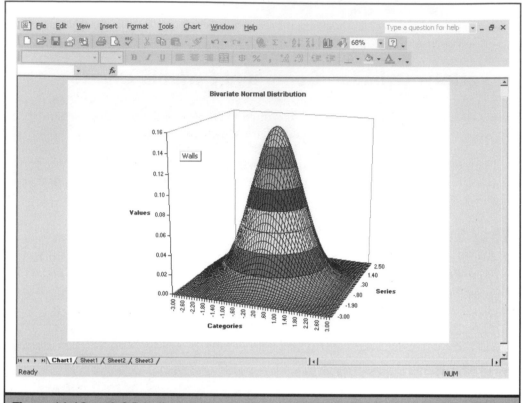

Figure 11-12. *A 3-D bell curve can be represented by a Surface chart*

out the worksheet. Row 2, starting in column B, contains the X-axis labels. Column A, starting with row 3, contains the Series names. Cells B3:BJ63 contain the values that are represented on the chart's Z, or height, axis.

The Surface chart is always a 3-D chart, with three axes:

- A Category axis that suggests width
- A Series axis that suggests depth
- A Z-axis that represents height

In Figure 11-12, the Series axis displays the series names shown in A3:A63 of the worksheet shown in Figure 11-13. The Category axis displays the labels found in B2:BJ2. And the height or Z-axis shows the value associated with the intersection of each category with each series, in the worksheet range B3:BJ63.

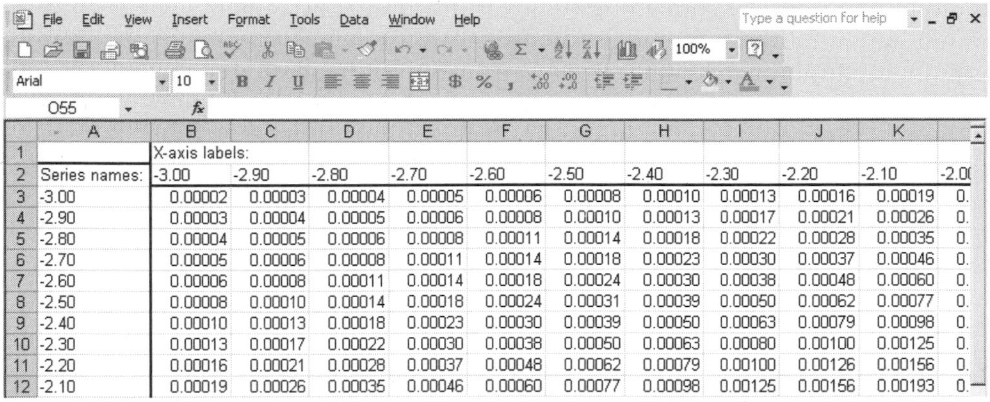

	A	B	C	D	E	F	G	H	I	J	K	
1		X-axis labels:										
2	Series names:	-3.00	-2.90	-2.80	-2.70	-2.60	-2.50	-2.40	-2.30	-2.20	-2.10	-2.0
3	-3.00	0.00002	0.00003	0.00004	0.00005	0.00006	0.00008	0.00010	0.00013	0.00016	0.00019	0.
4	-2.90	0.00003	0.00004	0.00005	0.00006	0.00008	0.00010	0.00013	0.00017	0.00021	0.00026	0.
5	-2.80	0.00004	0.00005	0.00006	0.00008	0.00011	0.00014	0.00018	0.00022	0.00028	0.00035	0.
6	-2.70	0.00005	0.00006	0.00008	0.00011	0.00014	0.00018	0.00023	0.00030	0.00037	0.00046	0.
7	-2.60	0.00006	0.00008	0.00011	0.00014	0.00018	0.00024	0.00030	0.00038	0.00048	0.00060	0.
8	-2.50	0.00008	0.00010	0.00014	0.00018	0.00024	0.00031	0.00039	0.00050	0.00062	0.00077	0.
9	-2.40	0.00010	0.00013	0.00018	0.00023	0.00030	0.00039	0.00050	0.00063	0.00079	0.00098	0.
10	-2.30	0.00013	0.00017	0.00022	0.00030	0.00038	0.00050	0.00063	0.00080	0.00100	0.00125	0.
11	-2.20	0.00016	0.00021	0.00028	0.00037	0.00048	0.00062	0.00079	0.00100	0.00126	0.00156	0.
12	-2.10	0.00019	0.00026	0.00035	0.00046	0.00060	0.00077	0.00098	0.00125	0.00156	0.00193	0.

Figure 11-13. *Be sure to include the category and series labels in your selection when you start the Chart Wizard*

If you don't select the category labels and the series labels before starting the Chart Wizard, you must either live with the default labels that Excel supplies, or change them one by one on the Series tab of the Chart Wizard's second step.

Further, you should make these labels text values before you begin charting. Otherwise, the Chart Wizard will interpret them as data series instead of as labels, and you'll have to make the appropriate adjustments on the Series tab.

Perhaps the quickest way to convert a range of numeric data to text is by way of the TEXT function. Suppose you have date values such as *12/9/2001* in column A. Enter this function in, say, B1:

```
=TEXT(A1,"m/d/yy")
```

to obtain this text value:

```
12/9/01
```

Then, copy and paste that function through the remaining cells in column B. You now have text values to use as labels, and Excel will not assume that they are another data series to be charted.

The 3-D bell curve shown in Figure 11-12 is called a *bivariate normal distribution.* Excel has no built-in function that creates this distribution, but it's easily created by multiplying the results of the NORMDIST function on two different values. For example, the second value in the first data series in Figure 11-12 could be calculated by

```
=NORMDIST(-3,0,1,FALSE)*NORMDIST(-2.90,0,1,FALSE)
```

Using Custom Chart Types

Both in Step 1 of the Chart Wizard and in the dialog box that appears when you choose Chart | Chart Type, there is a tab labeled Custom Types. These chart types are variations on the standard types, with different formatting options applied. The custom types can be visually attractive and, as such, you should consider using them if they meet your other charting criteria.

The custom types are also useful as examples of how you can modify different chart elements to achieve more interesting, or even more informative, effects. Try creating a chart that uses one of the custom types; then select different elements of the chart and examine the format of each selected element to see how the effect was achieved. For example, the Floating Bars chart type floats the bars by stacking them and then turning the first data series invisible.

You can also define your own chart type, name it, and cause it to appear on the Custom Types tab. You will find this process described later in this section.

Selecting the Right Chart Type

The preceding sections have emphasized the relationship between the type of chart and the kind of data it can display. For example, a Column chart must display categories on its horizontal axis and numeric values on its vertical axis, while an XY chart must display numeric values on both its horizontal and its vertical axis.

This implies that your first criterion for choosing a chart type is the nature of the data you want to display. If your data values include no categories, you should consider an XY or perhaps a Bubble chart. A data set with both categories and numeric values can be handled by a variety of charts: Column, Bar, Line, Pie, Doughnut, or Radar. If your data values sum to unity—as they would if you were charting each cost category's contribution to total costs—consider using a Pie chart or a Doughnut chart.

If several chart types pass your first criterion, keep traditional formats in mind. For example, process control charts traditionally use a format very much like Excel's Line chart. Pareto charts are constructed as a combination of a Column chart (for each category's frequency) and a Line chart (for the cumulative frequency). Project management charts, particularly those that display time schedules, can be emulated in Excel with stacked Bar charts. And keep in mind that most people expect times and dates to progress left to right, not up or down.

If you expect to print the chart, visualize how it will appear along with other figures and printed matter. Other things being equal, a Column or Bar chart uses the available chart area more efficiently than a Radar or a Pie chart.

User-Defined Chart Types

Suppose you have created a chart and painstakingly set its axis titles and fonts, decided on its plot area texturing, and chosen the proper border and area patterns for the data series—in short, you've created fine art. You'd prefer not to go through all those gyrations every time you want to re-create the chart with different data. One solution is to include it as a user-defined chart type.

To do so, take these steps:

1. Select the chart.

2. Choose Chart | Chart Type and click the Custom Types tab (see Figure 11-14).

3. In the Select From box, choose the User-Defined option button.

4. Click the Add button. The Add Custom Chart Type dialog box appears. Use it to give your chart type a name and a description. Click OK, and then click OK again in the Chart Type dialog box.

Subsequently, the chart characteristics that were in place when you added the custom chart type will be available for new charts. To access it, just click the Custom Types tab in Step 1 of the Chart Wizard (or choose Chart | Chart Type) and click the User-Defined option button.

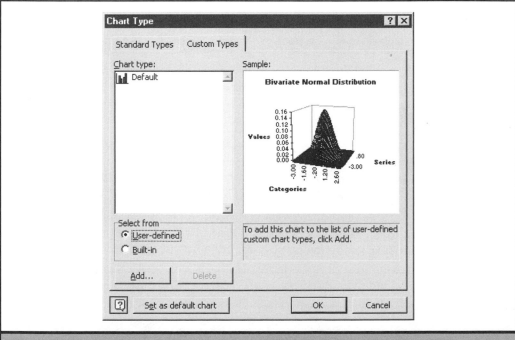

Figure 11-14. *Clicking Set As Default Chart means that you can subsequently click Finish in Step 1 of the Chart Wizard to get a chart of that type*

Previewing and Printing Charts

After you have created a chart—whether embedded in a worksheet or in its own sheet—you can preview how it will look when it's printed.

To do so, just select an embedded chart, or activate the chart sheet. Then choose File | Print Preview. You will see Excel's depiction of how the chart will appear in hard copy. If you're ready to print, click the Print button at the top of the preview window.

Otherwise, you might want to do some tinkering with the chart before printing it. To return to the workbook, click the Close button at the top of the preview window. Make whatever changes are needed. If you now want to print without previewing, make sure that the chart is still selected and choose File | Print.

Chart Options

Once you have created a chart, you can modify each of its components from the Chart menu. This menu appears on the worksheet menu bar when you select the chart, either by clicking on an embedded chart or by activating a separate chart sheet. Selecting Chart Options from the chart menu displays the dialog box shown in Figure 11-15.

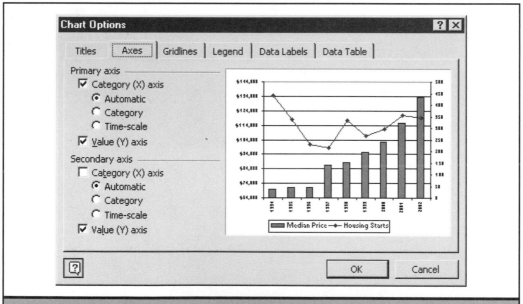

Figure 11-15.   *Use the Axes tab to specify the type of axis you want to display*

This section explores each chart option available from the dialog box. As usual, you access different options by clicking the appropriate tab on the main dialog box.

Axes

Figure 11-15 shows options for both Primary and Secondary axes. The Secondary Axis options are available only if your chart has more than one data series. Even then you must specifically call for the Secondary axis as described later in this section.

Suppose you want to chart both the number of new houses and the median home price over a period of several years. If your data values pertain to a medium-sized community, the number of new houses might be numbered in the hundreds of units, and the median home price in the tens or hundreds of thousands of dollars. The number of housing starts, relative to the home price figures, is so small that it would not be visible on the chart: you won't be able to distinguish a value of 900 on a scale whose maximum is 144,000.

One solution is to use a secondary Y-axis. As shown in Figure 11-16, the secondary Y-axis enables you to show two (or more) data series in their proper scales.

To get the Secondary axis shown in Figure 11-16, take these steps:

1. Ensure that the values in column A are text, not numbers.

2. Select the data on the worksheet. In Figure 11-16, select A1:C10.

3. Use the Chart Wizard to create a Column chart.

4. If you can see the secondary data series on the chart, select it by clicking.

Tip   *If you cannot see a chart element such as a data series, select the chart and use your keyboard's arrow keys to cycle through the available chart elements until you have selected the chart element you're after. This is also a good way to select a specific data point in a data series.*

5. Choose Chart | Chart Type. Set the selected data series to a Line chart type. Click OK.

6. Select the secondary data series again. Choose Format | Selected Data Series.

7. On the Axis tab, select Secondary Axis.

8. Click OK.

Once you have established a Secondary axis for a chart, you will find options for the Secondary axis available on the Chart Options Axes tab.

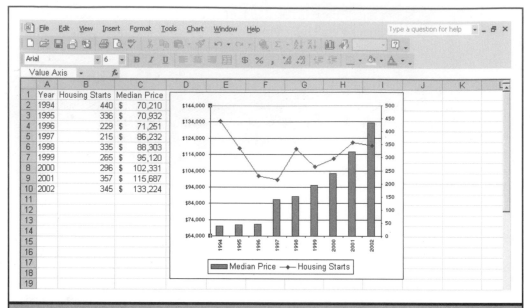

Figure 11-16. *Without a Secondary axis, you would have to show the number of new houses and the median price in two different charts*

> **Note**   *When you use a Primary and a Secondary Value axis on a Column or on a Bar chart, Excel overlays the data markers for one series on top of the data markers for the other series. This obscures the data markers of one of the data series. One way to improve its visibility is to select the fully visible data series, choose Format | Selected Data Series, and change the Gap Width on the Options tab.*

The Axes tab offers three options for scaling an X-axis: Automatic, Category, and Time-Scale (refer to Figure 11-15). Choosing Automatic lets Excel decide how to scale the X-axis: as a time-scale if the values are date-formatted on the worksheet, or as regular categories otherwise. You can use the Category or the Time-Scale option to make the decision yourself.

The time-scale capability causes some confusion among users, due in part to its name. Setting an axis to use a time-scale has consequences for how the chart treats *dates*, not *times*. If the values on the worksheet are date-formatted and you choose the Automatic option, or if you choose the Time-Scale option, then:

- Excel displays the data points on the chart in date order, regardless of their order on the worksheet.

- Excel leaves blank regions on the X-axis to represent missing dates.

- You can set days, months, or years as units for the X-axis by selecting the X-axis, choosing Format | Selected Axis and clicking the Scale tab (see Figure 11-17).

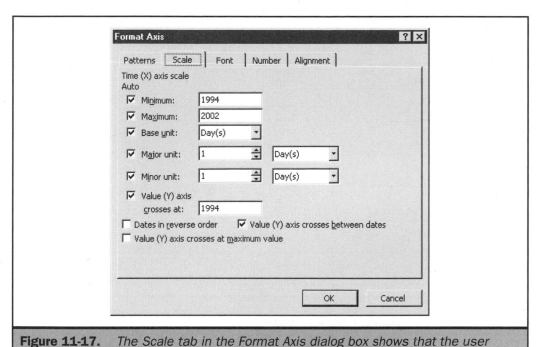

ANALYZING DATA

Figure 11-17.   *The Scale tab in the Format Axis dialog box shows that the user chose the Time-Scale option for the X-axis*

Including Titles

It's nearly always a good idea to provide a title for Value and Category axes, and it's often helpful to title the full chart. To do so, click the Titles tab on the Chart Options dialog box. On that tab you can enter a title for the chart, for the Primary Value and Category axes, and if applicable for the Secondary Value and Category axes (see Figure 11-18).

Once you have created a title, you will usually want to modify its appearance so that it helps explain the chart, rather than interfering with it. You will find that the title's font is often too large. To adjust it, click the title and adjust the font with the Font Size combo box on the Formatting toolbar, or choose Format | Selected title and adjust the font size on the Font tab.

You can split a title into two lines of text after creating the title. Click the title, and then click where you want the line break to appear. Press ENTER on your keyboard to break the line.

Link a chart or an axis title to a worksheet cell by clicking the title to select it. Then, type an equal sign in the formula bar's edit box, and click in the worksheet cell you want to link. Now, whatever value you put in the worksheet cell will appear in the title.

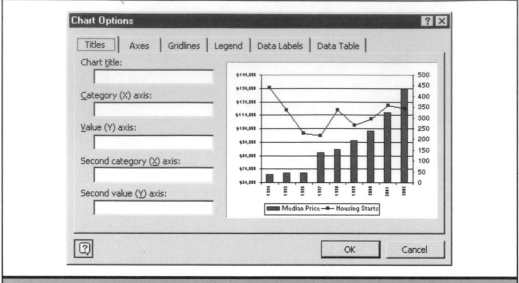

Figure 11-18.   *If your chart does not have Secondary axes, the Secondary Axis edit boxes are disabled*

Using Chart Legends

The Legend tab lets you choose to display a chart legend. As shown in Figure 11-19, you fill the Show Legend check box to display the legend. If you want to suppress the legend directly from the chart, just click the DELETE key after you have selected the legend. You will find little use for the legend placement options: you can exercise more control over the legend's location by dragging it around on the chart until it's placed to suit you.

By default, a chart legend always shows the names of the charted data series and a color-coded key to each series on the chart. You can click the name of a series in the legend and type a new, or more descriptive, name. You can also click the series' key in the legend and choose a different color.

A chart legend has a special function on a Surface chart. Suppose you want to change the color of a data series. To do so you must first select the data series. But you cannot select a data series directly on a Surface chart, as you can on other chart types, by clicking on it. Instead, follow these steps:

1. If the chart does not have a legend, use Chart | Chart Options and click the Legend tab. Then fill the Show Legend check box and click OK.

2. Click the legend. Handles appear on its box. Click the legend key that corresponds to the data series that you want to modify.

Note

The legend contains legend entries. In Figure 11-19, for example, the phrase "Median Price" and the rectangle to its left together comprise a legend entry. A legend entry consists of a legend key (that's the rectangle in the Median Price legend entry in Figure 11-19) and its label ("Median Price"). Be sure to select the legend key. If you select the full legend entry instead, Step 3 won't work.

3. Choose Format | Selected Legend Key. The Format Legend Key dialog box enables you to set the Border and Area characteristics, including color. You can also use this dialog box to change the series order, chart depth, and 3-D shading. Changes you make are applied both to the key and to the data series it represents.

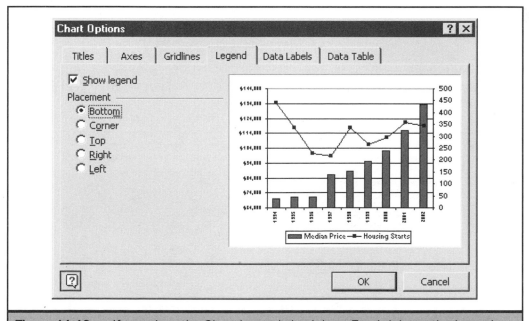

Figure 11-19.   *If you clear the Show Legend check box, Excel deletes the legend and then resizes the chart's plot area for you*

When to Use Gridlines

When you add a component to a chart, you complicate it. When you complicate a chart, you blur its visual impact. A useful chart conveys one or two main points but loses its visual effect if it's unnecessarily complex.

Overused, gridlines can make a chart all but unreadable. See Figure 11-20 for an example.

The gridlines distract the eye from the data series, which is charted as a Line. When the relationship of the data values to one another is more important than the numeric magnitude of a data value, it's usually best to dispense with gridlines. In Figure 11-20, the important point is that the data series is gradually increasing, and the gridlines are just a distraction.

When the absolute size of the data value is important, though, gridlines are very useful. They help you trace the numeric magnitude of each value on its associated axis.

Showing Error Bars

You've probably read about public opinion polls that report that their margin of error is some value such as plus or minus 3 percent. Excel enables you to display this kind of bracketing by means of error bars.

Figure 11-21 shows the Y Error Bars tab and the options it offers. The tab is labeled as Y Error Bars because error bars are available only for the chart's value dimension (and not for its category dimension, if any). You get to the tab only by selecting the data series and choosing Format | Selected Data Series—the tab is part of neither the Chart Wizard nor the Chart Options dialog box.

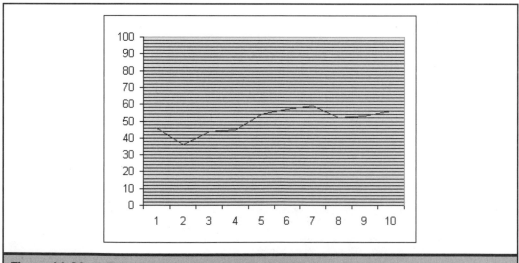

Figure 11-20.   *This chart's gridlines make it difficult to discern the pattern in the data*

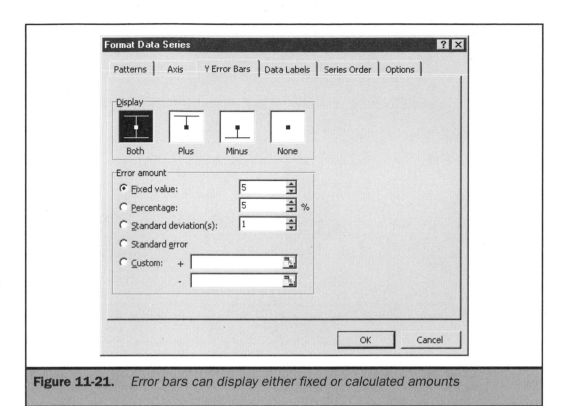

Figure 11-21.   *Error bars can display either fixed or calculated amounts*

Once created, error bars belong to the data series. You cannot attach one sort of error bar to some points in a data series and another type of error bar to other points in the same series.

Figure 11-22 shows the results of choosing three different types of error bars for the same data series.

Notice in Figure 11-22 that

- The Fixed Amount of +/−5 results in a bar 5 points above and 5 points below each data marker. This error bar was created by choosing the Fixed value option and entering 5 in the associated edit box.

- The Percentage of +/−5% results in longer bars for larger data point values. The error bars are nearly invisible for small data point values. If the data point's value is 8, then the error bar extends from 8 minus 5% of 8, to 8 plus 5% of 8. Therefore the error bar extends from 7.96 to 8.04. In contrast, the 5% error bar around a value of 100 extends from 95 to 105.

- The Standard Deviation error bars are centered around the mean of the data series. This type of error bar helps approximate a rudimentary statistical

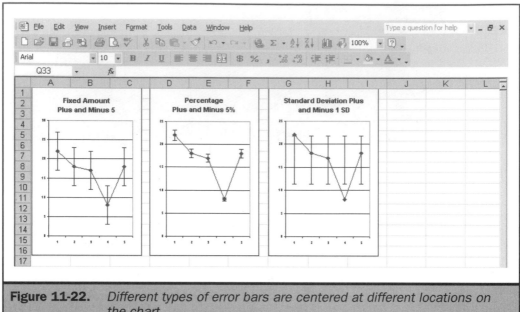

Figure 11-22. *Different types of error bars are centered at different locations on the chart*

process control (sometimes called a *Shewhart*) chart. You can choose any number of standard deviations for the size of the error bar.

Figure 11-23 shows the remaining two types of error bars.

■ The Standard Error error bars are centered on each data point. The standard error is the standard deviation of the data series divided by the square root of the number of data points. It is a measure of the variability of the mean across a distribution of sample means. If the individual data points are themselves averages, then the Standard Error error bar helps approximate a multiple comparison procedure following an analysis of variance. This type of error bar allows only one standard error above and below the data point. There is no sensible reason for this restriction.

■ The Custom error bars enable you to use error amounts from the worksheet. Begin by entering on the worksheet the error values, plus and minus, that you want to associate with each data point. Then on the Error Bars tab, choose the Custom option button, and click the text box labeled with a plus sign. Drag through the worksheet cells that contain the plus error amounts. Repeat this process for the minus error amounts.

If you begin by creating an XY chart—one with two value axes—then in addition to Y error bars you can also set error bars that parallel the chart's X-axis.

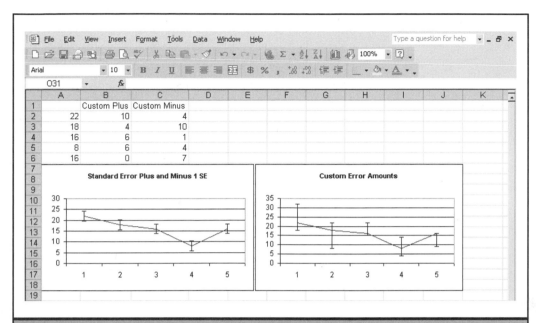

Figure 11-23.   *Decide on custom error amounts and enter them on the worksheet before choosing Custom error bars*

> **Tip**   *If you set up error bars for a data series but don't see them on the chart after you click OK, make sure that you did not leave None chosen on the Error Bars tab of the Format Data Series dialog box.*

Data Tables

If you find it absolutely necessary to show the numeric values that underlie a chart on the chart itself, you can insert a data table. The Data Table tab appears in Step 3 of the Chart Wizard and also on the Chart Options dialog box. There you can choose to show or to suppress the data table by, respectively, filling or clearing the Show Data Table check box.

The data table clutters up the chart, of course, and the data values are often visible on the worksheet. Very likely the only time you would find it necessary to include a data table on the chart is when you are including the chart but not the worksheet as part of a report, *and* the supporting numbers cannot be displayed in any other way.

After including a data table in your chart, be sure to take another look at what it displays. It can easily use a font that's too large for the cells in the data table, and you might see, for example, only the 6 in the value 65.

If you want the chart to look really disheveled, you can also fill the Data Table tab's Show Legend Keys check box (see Figure 11-24).

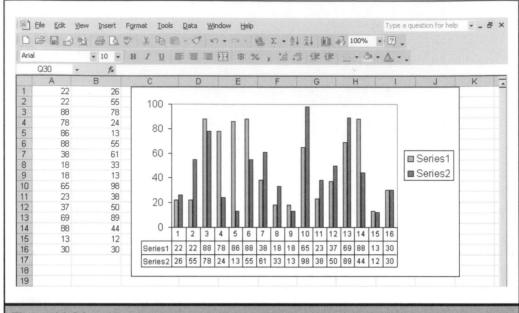

Figure 11-24.   *You need a compelling reason to put a data table on a chart*

Data Labels

At times it can be more informative to label a data marker with a value or with a category label than to rely solely on an axis to show that information. Figure 11-25 shows two charts: one that labels each data marker with its value, and one that labels each data marker with its category.

To label the data markers, use the Data Labels tab—accessible either from Step 3 of the Chart Wizard or from the Chart Options dialog box or by choosing Format | Selected Data Series.

Your choices in the Data Labels tab depend on the type of chart that is active. If the chart has a Category axis and a Value axis, as do most chart types, then you can choose to label each data point with its category name, with its value, and with the name of its data series. These are not mutually exclusive choices.

If the active chart has two value axes, as does the XY(Scatter) chart, you can choose to label each data point with its x value, its y value, and its data series name. Again, the choices are not mutually exclusive: you can use all three labels simultaneously if you want.

If you choose to label data points with values, the data points' numeric values appear next to their markers. In that case, you might want to dispense with gridlines and possibly suppress the Y-axis labels and tick marks.

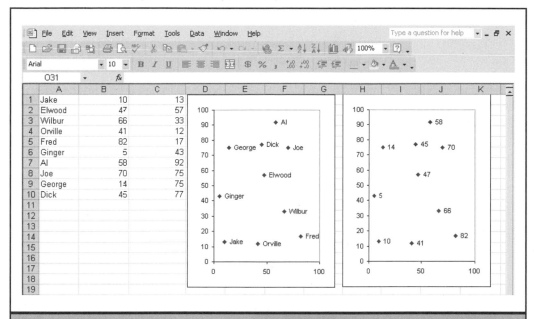

Figure 11-25. *Data labels work best when a chart has only a few data markers*

If you choose the Category name option button, the data points' category labels appear next to their markers. Then you might want to suppress the X-axis labels and tick marks.

A special problem arises with data labels on XY charts, where each data point represents the combination of a value on the X value axis with a value on the Y value axis. If you want to attach data labels, you can choose to show each point's *x* value, its *y* value or both.

None of these choices is particularly useful. In these cases, you usually have some third variable that identifies the data point. If you're charting salary against years of service, for example, that third variable might be employee name. Or if you're charting water temperature against depth, the third variable might be date of observation. You can't include that third variable as one of the data series, or the chart ceases to be an XY chart.

The only manual solution is to attach data labels—showing either the value or the label—to the XY chart. Then select each label in turn and type the text (employee name, perhaps) of the label you want in the formula bar. After you press ENTER, the label you typed will appear next to the data point.

This "solution" gets tiresome, and if you have many situations in which you need to attach third-variable labels to an XY chart, you should automate the process. See Chapter 18 on using VBA to do repetitive tasks on your behalf, for suggestions on how to manage this.

Trendlines

You sometimes want a chart to display both your actual data and a trend that's implied by the data. Chart trendlines can be a useful way to show the trend.

Your data usually comprise both signal and noise. For example, over several years your cost of goods sold might be gradually rising—some years by a lot, other years just a little. But the basic trend is for your costs to increase.

If your chart displays just the actual yearly costs, it might obscure the underlying trend. In 2001, there might have been enough competition among your suppliers to hold your costs down. In 2002, suppliers might try to recoup earlier losses by raising their prices.

Your actual data points reflect both the underlying trend—the *signal*—and the unpredictable yearly fluctuations—the *noise*. Chart trendlines seek to isolate the signal and display it. This can help you identify and quantify the underlying trend—and perhaps predict what will happen next, or what will happen under some other condition. (By the way, it can also be informative to examine the noise around the signal.)

Suppose you chart the amount of bacteria in a lake against its temperature. You want to show your actual measures, which consist of a mix of signal and noise. You also want to convey how the bacteria count varies with water temperature: the trend.

Here again the issue of category and value scales arises. If you choose a chart with a Category and a Value axis, your trendline will be in trouble.

Suppose the actual relationship between temperature and bacteria count is expressed by this equation:

Bacteria Count = 1.37 * Temperature – 18

An XY chart would show the temperature value against the associated bacteria count value. See Figure 11-26, where the trendline returns the equation just shown.

You can create a trendline such as the one shown in Figure 11-26 by means of these steps:

1. Select the chart by clicking on it.

2. Choose Chart | Add Trendline. The dialog box shown in Figure 11-27 appears.

3. Click the image of the trendline type that you want to use. If your chart contains more than one data series, select it in the Based On Series list box. Then click OK.

| Note | *To remove a trendline, click on it to select it and then choose Edit | Clear | Trendline. To edit a trendline, click on it to select it and then choose Format | Selected Trendline.* |

Now suppose you chose to use a Column chart to display the data. A Column chart assumes that the horizontal axis represents categories, not quantitative values. Such a chart assigns the value 1 to the first category, 2 to the second category, and so on. Your

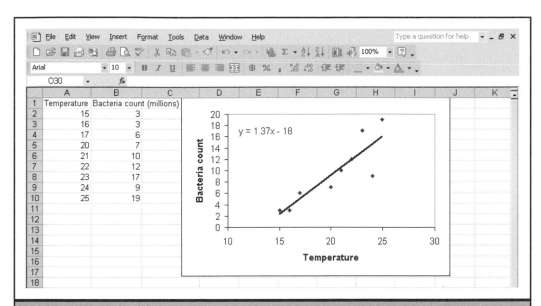

Figure 11-26. *A trendline that moves from lower left to upper right suggests a direct relationship between the x- and the y-values*

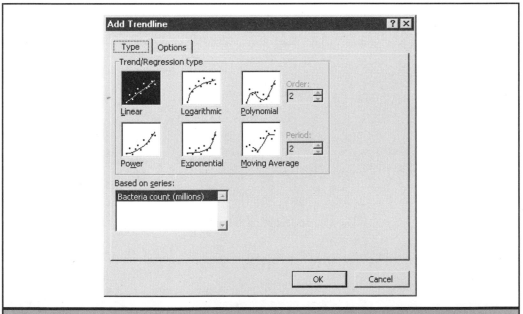

Figure 11-27. *You will find a check box on the Options tab that shows the least squares equation on the chart*

ANALYZING DATA

value of 15 degrees would be treated as 1, 17 degrees as 2, 22 degrees as 3, and so on. The trendline is therefore based on a different and erroneous set of values, and therefore on a different and erroneous equation (see Figure 11-28).

The lesson is that if you want to show a trendline, use an XY chart.

 An exception occurs when the values that will occupy the Category axis are date-formatted. Then you can use a Line chart. Excel recognizes the formatting and enables you to specify a horizontal axis time scale. As a consequence, the horizontal axis values are treated as quantitative, not categorical, and trendlines will be accurate.

Simulating a Trendline with the TREND Function

Although they are convenient, chart trendlines sometimes are ill behaved. The previous section described how they can mislead you: when the trendline is based on a chart's category scale.

Suppose you nevertheless want to display a trendline on a Column chart. You can manage this if you calculate the trendline values on the worksheet and then chart them as a Line series on the chart. By calculating them on the worksheet you can control how they are derived, and you can ensure that the trend is based on the actual numeric values, not on their serial order on the chart's Category axis.

As shown in Figure 11-29, you have actual data on advertising dollars and units sold in A2:B20. Figure 11-29 also shows the data in a Column chart.

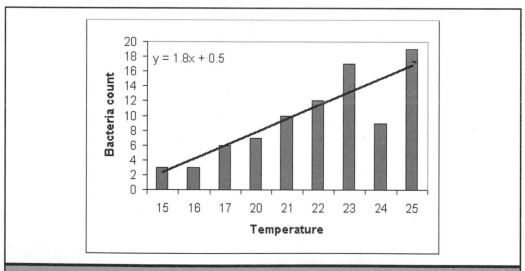

Figure 11-28. *A trendline based on categories is usually misleading*

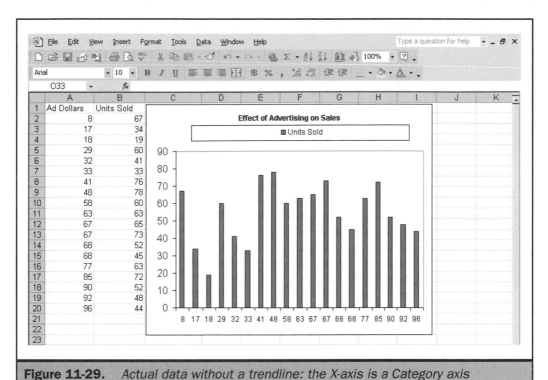

Figure 11-29. *Actual data without a trendline: the X-axis is a Category axis*

To get the correct trendline on the chart, take these steps:

1. In cell D2, enter the first Advertising Dollars value. In this case, that value is 8.

2. In cell D3, enter this formula:

    =($A$20-$A$2)/(COUNT($A$2:$A$20)-1)+D2

    and copy and paste the formula through cell D20. The values in D2:D20 are now the range of the Advertising Dollars, divided into equal increments. This step ensures that the calculated trendline will be a smooth one.

3. In C1, enter a label such as **Linear Trend**. Select C2:C20. Array-enter this formula:

    =TREND(B2:B20,A2:A20,D2:D20)

    (Recall that you use CTRL-SHIFT-ENTER, not just ENTER, to array-enter a formula.)

4. Select cells B1:C20. Start the Chart Wizard by clicking its button, or by choosing Insert | Chart from the worksheet menu bar.

5. In Step 1, select a Column chart.

6. In Step 2, click the Series tab, and then click the Category (X) Axis Labels edit box. Drag through cells A2:A20 to establish the labels for the Column chart's horizontal axis. Click Next.

7. In Steps 3 and 4 of the Chart Wizard, make whatever choices you want.

8. When you have completed the Chart Wizard, you will have a Column chart with two data series. On the chart, select the series that corresponds to the Linear trendline by clicking it.

9. Choose Chart | Chart Type. On the panel of available standard types, select a Line chart that has lines only, no data markers. Click OK.

Your chart will appear largely as shown in Figure 11-30.

You can now select the data series that represents the trendline and choose Format | Selected Data Series to make any other formatting changes that you want.

Note *In general, you can use Chart | Chart Type to specify a type for any single data series in a chart that contains multiple data series. This menu item does not necessarily apply to all the data series in a chart.*

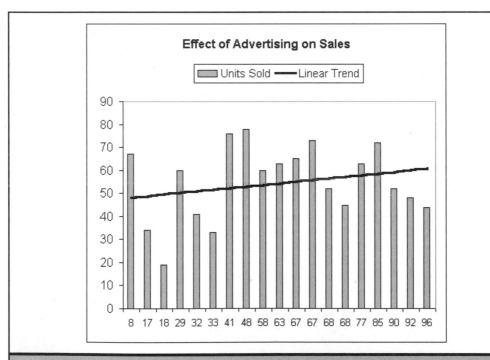

Figure 11-30. *The trendline, calculated on the worksheet, is drawn accurately. An automatic trendline would be based on the serial order, not the magnitude, of the data points*

Getting the Trendline Equation with LINEST

Users often try to build a worksheet formula from a chart trendline. Consider the earlier example of a lake's temperature and its bacteria count. You have complete measurements at 15, 16, 17, and 20 through 25 degrees. You would like to estimate the bacteria count at 18 and 19 degrees.

One approach would be to show the trendline equation on the chart. You can do so either by selecting that option when you create the trendline, or after the fact by selecting the trendline and choosing Format | Selected Trendline. Then fill the Display Equation On Chart box on the Options tab.

With the equation on the chart, you can type its coefficients into worksheet cells, and apply those coefficients to your new x-values of 18 and 19 degrees.

There are three problems with this approach:

- The chart's equation usually doesn't show enough significant figures in the coefficients. If it did, it would obscure the other visual elements in the chart.

- Entering the coefficients as constants on the worksheet means that they won't update as you acquire new data.

- It's a pain.

Instead of using the chart's equation for the trendline, calculate it directly on the worksheet. Suppose you chose a Linear trendline, and your data values are in A2:B10. To calculate the trendline equation on the worksheet, take these steps:

1. Select two adjacent cells consisting of one row and two columns, such as D1:E1.

2. Array-enter this formula: **=LINEST(B2:B10,A2:A10)**.

The first value in the LINEST results is the slope, and the second is the intercept. Assume that you entered the equation in D1:E1. To use the equation and obtain the y-value that would correspond to a new x-value in F1, you would enter in, say, G1:

=$D$1*F1+$E$1

By making the references to cells D1 and E1 absolute, you can copy and paste the formula as many cells down as you have new x-values, and the formulas will still refer to the coefficients returned by LINEST.

See Figure 11-31 for an example.

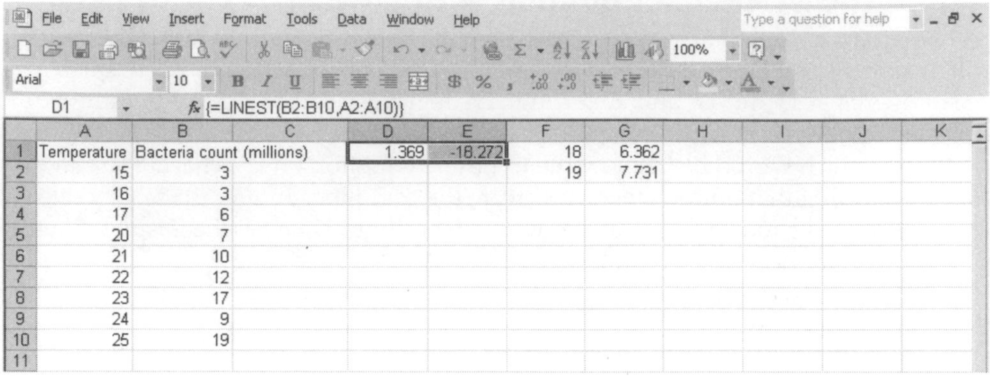

Figure 11-31. *To make sure of updating the equation as you acquire new values, use dynamic range names (see Chapter 10) in the LINEST function*

Certification Skills Covered in This Chapter

If you're preparing for Microsoft Office User Specialist certification, here are the skills you learned in this chapter.

Skill Set	Activity
Creating and modifying graphics	Create, modify, position, and print charts

Chapter 12

Drawing Objects

Excel provides a number of graphics tools, including one you can use to draw objects. You can take advantage of these graphical elements to draw attention to sections of a worksheet.

Using the Drawing Toolbar

To begin drawing, you need the Drawing toolbar, which isn't in your Excel window by default. Clicking the Drawing button on the Standard toolbar puts the Drawing toolbar on your window, below your worksheet and above the status bar. (Clicking the Drawing button again removes the Drawing toolbar; it's a toggle.)

Just so you can identify this array of buttons, here's what each tool does, moving from left to right on the toolbar. More discussion about using these tools is found throughout this chapter.

Draw   Click the Draw button to see a menu of options for manipulating the objects you've drawn and placed in the worksheet.

Some of the menu choices are inaccessible if you haven't selected a drawing that applies.

Select Objects   Click the Select Objects button (which has an Arrow icon); then select a graphic object. If you have multiple objects, you can click the button and drag a box around a group of objects, then use the menu choices available from the Draw button to create groupings.

AutoShapes   Clicking the AutoShapes button opens a menu of categories. Select a category to see all the shapes available for that category.

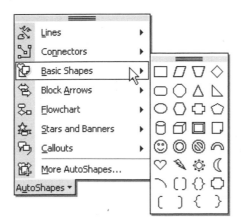

The AutoShapes menu is also a toolbar. Drag the top bar of the AutoShapes menu to any position in your window to position the toolbar. Also, each of the shape category choices is a toolbar, which you can drag anywhere on your window to keep them handy.

Line   Click the Line button; then click and drag to draw a line.

Arrow   The Arrow button works like the Line button, but the line has an arrow head at the end (the place where you release the mouse button).

Rectangle   The Rectangle button is really a Square/Rectangle button. Click it, then click to insert a square. Click it, then click and drag to draw a rectangle.

Oval   This is really a Circle/Oval button. Click it, and then click to insert a circle. Click and drag to create an oval.

Text Box   Use this button to insert a free-floating box that accepts any text you enter.

WordArt   Use this button to open the WordArt Gallery dialog box. You can use the features in WordArt to create striking titles.

Diagram   Use this button to open the Diagram dialog box, where you can create a diagram or an organization chart.

ClipArt   Click this button for access to the Microsoft ClipArt Gallery, which provides an enormous array of drawings, symbols, cartoons, and pictures.

Picture   Click this button to open the Insert Picture dialog to select a picture file to place in your worksheet.

Fill Color   Click the Fill Color button to select the color or pattern effect you want to use to fill a shape.

Line Color   Use this button to choose a color for a line you drew, or for the line around any shape.

Font Color   Click the Font Color button to choose a color for text objects.

Line Style   Use this button to specify the style or thickness of lines in an object.

Dash Style   Choose a dashed line from several possible styles.

Arrow Style   Use this button to see choices that can turn the arrow you created (with the Arrow button) into something dramatic and stylized.

Shadow   Make objects stand out by applying a shadow effect from the choices offered when you click the Shadow button.

3-D   Use the 3-D choices to turn simple objects into 3-D figures.

Creating Shapes

Now that you're familiar with the tools at your disposal, you can begin putting graphics, text, and other objects into your worksheets. However, that's just the beginning, because you're probably going to have to modify, decorate, enhance, and manipulate the objects you create.

The first section is about shapes—inserting them, modifying them, decorating them, and so on. Shapes are commonly added to worksheets to enhance cells or ranges. However, all the things you learn about manipulating shapes you can apply to other graphic objects.

Inserting a Shape

To insert a shape in a worksheet, you just have to click the drawing tool you want to use:

- Select the Rectangle or Oval tool.
- Select the AutoShapes tool; then point to a category and select one of the shapes.

Place the object on your worksheet by clicking or dragging. When you release the mouse button, there are a couple of things you should notice (see Figure 12-1):

- The object is selected, which is indicated by the sizing handles around it.
- Excel has given the object a name, which appears in the Name box to the left of the formula bar.

Click outside the object to deselect it. Click anywhere in the object to select it again. When the object is selected you can perform the following actions:

- Move it.
- Resize it.
- Manipulate it with the tools on the Drawing toolbar.

Modifying Shapes

You rarely keep an object looking the way it does when you first insert it; it's usually much too dull. Also, it frequently isn't positioned exactly where you want it, or it may not be the exact size you need.

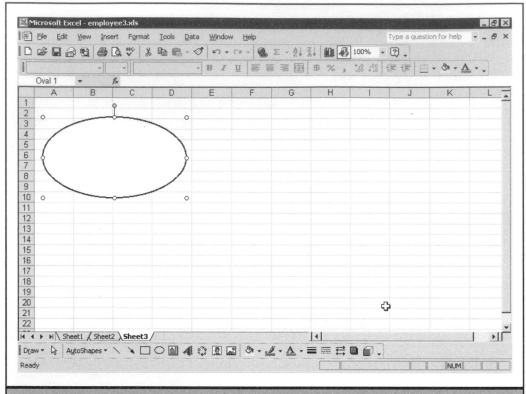

Figure 12-1. *Excel keeps track of graphic objects by assigning names*

Moving Shapes

To move your shape to a different position, place your pointer in the shape. The pointer turns into a four-headed arrow. Drag the shape to the new position.

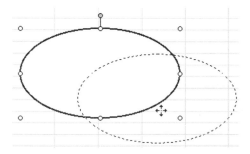

If you want to fine-tune the positioning, hold down the CTRL key and use the arrow keys to push the shape in small increments.

Resizing Shapes

If you need to resize the shape, you can use the sizing handles to drag it to its new dimensions, or use menu commands to add precision to your resizing action.

To resize a shape, position your pointer over a sizing handle (the pointer turns into a double-headed arrow). Then press and hold the left mouse button while you move the sizing handle in the appropriate direction.

- To resize the opposite side the same amount (including the opposite diagonal), hold down the CTRL key while you drag.

- To resize the opposite side and also keep the center of the shape in the same position, hold down the CTRL-SHIFT keys while you drag a corner sizing handle.

- To keep the proportions the same when you drag a corner sizing handle, hold down the SHIFT key while you drag.

If you need to be more precise when you resize, follow these steps:

1. Select the shape and choose Format | AutoShape from the menu bar.

2. In the Format AutoShape dialog box, move to the Size tab.

3. Use the Height and Width choices in the Size section of the dialog box to specify the measurements you need.

4. Use the Height and Width choices in the Scale section of the dialog box to specify a percentage of change in the size.

Here are some guidelines for using the Size tab:

- Whether you use the Size section or the Scale section, when you change one number, all the numbers change.

- If you want to maintain the proportions of the shape as you resize, select the Lock Aspect Ratio check box.

Coloring Shapes

You can add color to the shape by clicking the arrow next to the Fill Color tool to see a menu of choices.

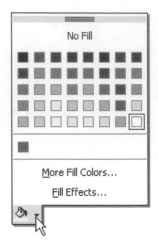

If nothing in the color palette strikes your fancy, choose More Fill Colors to open the Colors dialog box. On the Standard tab, drag your mouse around the color choices until you find the one you want to use.

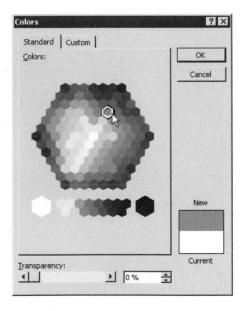

If you're comfortable with the scientific and mathematical aspects of creating colors, use the Custom tab where you can specify HSL or RGB values.

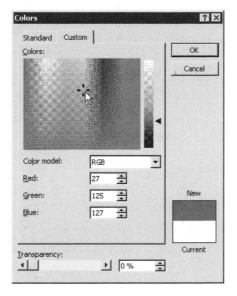

There's lots of fun in designing nifty effects, which you can reach by clicking the Fill Effects choice. Selecting this option opens the dialog box seen in Figure 12-2.

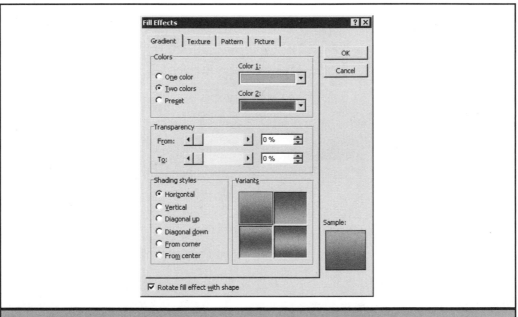

Figure 12-2. *Design textured surfaces or insert a color pattern*

Visit the other tabs to see all the available options for adding color, texture, patterns, and pictures (which stretch to fill the shape).

 After you select a fill color, that color becomes the new default for the Fill Color tool. If you want to use the same color for additional objects, just click the Tool button.

Coloring Lines Around Shapes

You can also colorize and enhance the line around a shape:

1. Select the shape.

2. Click the arrow next to the Line Color tool on the Drawing toolbar.

3. If you see a color you like in the palette that displays, select it.

4. Choose More Line Colors to custom mix a color.

5. Choose Patterned Lines to choose a pattern effect for the line around the shape.

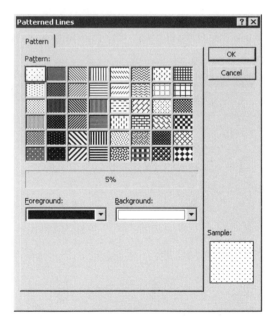

 After you select a line color, that color becomes the new default for the Line Color tool. If you want to use the same color for additional lines, just click the Tool button instead of opening the dialog box.

Modifying the Lines Around a Shape

You can change the thickness of the line around a graphic object with the Line Style tool on the Drawing toolbar:

- Click on More Lines to open the Format AutoShape dialog box (see Figure 12-3) where you can specify the style, thickness, and color.

- Click the Tool button and choose a different thickness or style.

If you want to substitute a dashed line for the shape's border, click the Dash Style tool and pick the dashed (or dotted) line style you prefer.

You can also add a shadow to the shape, extending the artistic look of a border.

Adding ClipArt

Microsoft includes a large selection of clip art you can use to enhance your worksheets.

Note   *Clip art takes a lot of disk space, so the common installation options for Microsoft Office omit the transfer of the entire clip art collection to your hard drive. Therefore, if you want to be able to select clip art from the entire assortment, be sure the CD-ROM that contains the clip art is in your CD-ROM drive.*

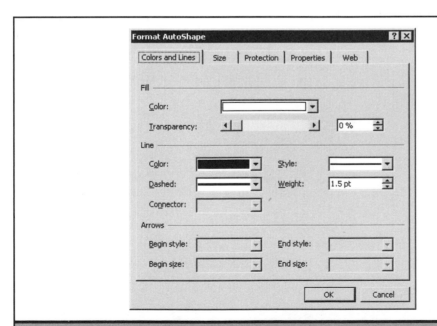

Figure 12-3.   *You can tweak the appearance of the line around a graphic object*

Selecting a Clip

To choose a clip, click the ClipArt tool on the Drawing toolbar. The first time you use clip art, you're asked to let the Microsoft Media Gallery collect and catalog any clip art on your system.

Choose Options to open a hierarchical display of your drives, with the folders most likely to hold clips already selected. You can select and deselect folders yourself; click Catalog to start the process.

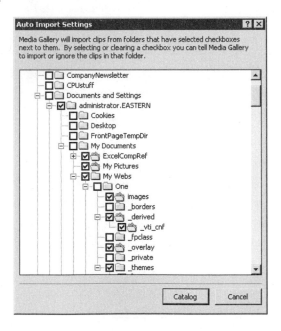

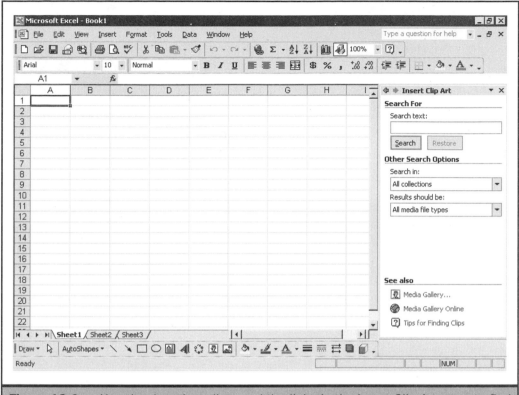

Figure 12-4. *Use the drop-down lists and the links in the Insert Clip Art pane to find artwork for your worksheet*

The key words that describe the clip art are also placed in the catalog (using the filenames) so you can search for specific types of artwork.

The Insert Clip Art pane opens on the right side of your screen so you can use its tools to search for artwork (see Figure 12-4).

The assembled collection includes all multimedia files (sound, pictures, movies, and clip art). Open a collection and scroll through the category list to find a category that matches the type of object you want to insert in your worksheet. Then scroll through the choices in that category to find the right object. When you find what you want, double-click it to insert it in your document (see Figure 12-5).

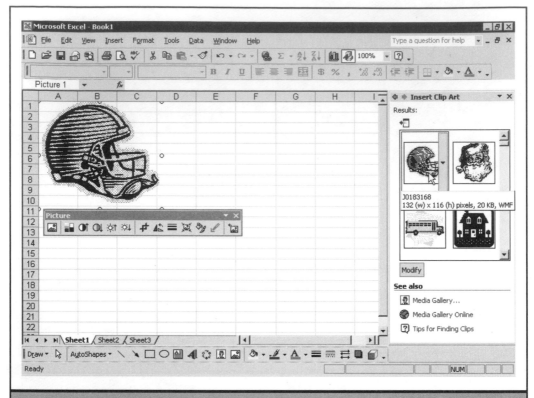

Figure 12-5. *Double-click to insert clip art in your document—the Picture toolbar automatically opens so you can work with the graphic object*

Instead of double-clicking, you can click the arrow to the right of the selection to see a menu of choices.

Manipulating Clip Art

You can use the Picture toolbar to manipulate the graphic, using the buttons on the toolbar from left to right:

- **Insert Picture From File** Click this button to insert another picture. An Insert Picture dialog box appears so you can move through the folders on your hard drive and find a picture.

- **Color** Click this button to manipulate the colors or black and white tones.

- **More Contrast** Each time you click this button, the contrast between dark and light colors is enhanced.

- **Less Contrast** Each time you click this button, the contrast between dark and light colors is reduced.

- **More Brightness** Each click lightens the depth of colors, making the picture brighter.

- **Less Brightness** Each click deepens the depth of colors, making the picture less bright.

- **Crop** Select the crop button and then drag a sizing handle inward. When you release the mouse button, the outside section of the picture is eliminated.

- **Rotate Left** Click the button to rotate the image 90 degrees left. To rotate the picture in other directions and in smaller increments than 90 degrees, click the green dot at the top of the picture. When your mouse pointer turns into a circular arrow, drag to rotate the graphic.

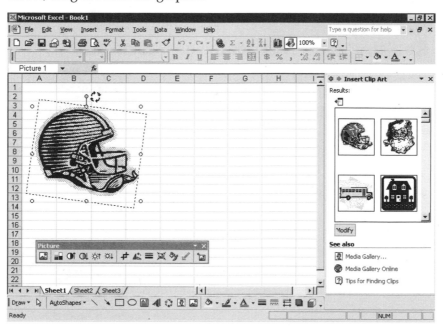

ANALYZING DATA

- **Line Style**   Choose a line to create a border around the clip.
- **Compress Pictures**   Opens the Compress Pictures dialog box, where you can apply options to compress graphics files to save disk space options. You can also delete the outside portion of pictures you've cropped.

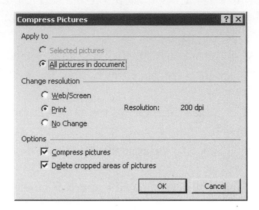

- **Format Picture**   This button opens the Format Picture dialog box, which has multiple tabs for modifying the picture. All the tools available via the buttons on the toolbar are available in the dialog box.

- **Set Transparent Color**   Use this feature to make colors in the graphic transparent so the cell contents behind the picture are seen.

- **Reset Picture**   Use this button to restore the original picture after you've messed around with all the tools on the Picture toolbar and you don't like the results.

Moving, Resizing, and Manipulating Pictures

You can use all the functions and tools described in the previous section on shapes to manipulate the clip art you put into your worksheet. Here's a quick summary:

- To move a picture, select it (your pointer turns into a four-headed arrow) and drag the object to a new location. Click outside the object to deselect it.

- To resize a picture object, select it and position your pointer over one of the sizing handles. Then drag the handle in the appropriate direction.

- To delete a picture object, select it and press the DELETE key.

Using WordArt

WordArt is a ton of fun! It's text as graphics and graphics as text, the best of both worlds when you need to insert a message, headline, or title and also want a terrific eye-catching graphic.

Creating a WordArt Graphic

Click the WordArt button on the Drawing toolbar to open the WordArt Gallery seen in Figure 12-6.

Click on the style you like and then click OK (it's easy to change to another style later if you decide you picked the wrong style). The Edit WordArt Text dialog box appears so you can get started.

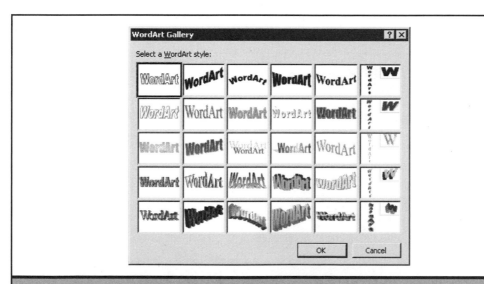

Figure 12-6.   *WordArt provides shapes and styles for text*

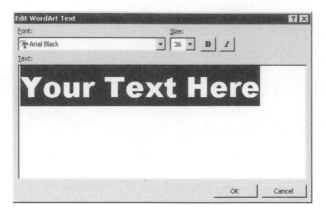

Enter the text for your WordArt graphic. You can use the ENTER key to create another line (WordArt works best with one or two lines of text). Use the toolbar on the dialog box to change the font, font size, and attributes (bold and italic).

Click OK to put the WordArt graphic into your worksheet, where it's accompanied by a floating WordArt toolbar (see Figure 12-7).

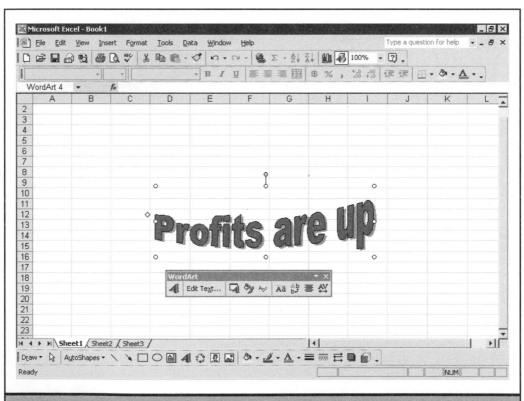

Figure 12-7. *Your text has the characteristics of the WordArt style you selected*

Modifying a WordArt Graphic

You can resize, move, border, and otherwise manipulate your WordArt graphic with the same tools described earlier for manipulating shapes.

In addition, there are some modifications unique to WordArt that you can access with the buttons on the WordArt toolbar:

- **Insert WordArt**   Adds another WordArt picture to your worksheet.
- **Edit Text**   Returns to the original dialog box so you can change the text or the font settings.
- **WordArt Gallery**   Opens the original gallery of styles so you can choose a different style.
- **Format WordArt**   Opens the Format WordArt dialog box, which provides lots of configuration options.

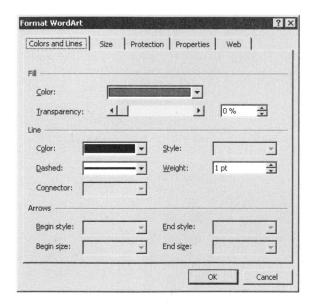

- **WordArt Shape**   Opens a gallery of shapes. You can choose a different shape for the WordArt graphic without changing all the other options attached to the style you chose.
- **Same Letter Heights**   Makes all the characters in your WordArt graphic the same height. Sometimes this makes the text easier to read.
- **Vertical Text**   Turns your WordArt graphic into a vertical graphic, with the text reading from top to bottom. If you have multiple lines of text, the second line appears to the right of the first line.

ANALYZING DATA

- **Alignment**   Produces a menu of alignment choices (by default, WordArt is aligned in the center of the graphic).
- **Character Spacing**   Offers menu options for changing the spacing between characters.

In addition to the tools on the WordArt toolbar, you can use the green circle at the top of the WordArt graphic to rotate the image in any direction.

Using 3-D Shapes

You can draw attention to cells, ranges, or titles with the dynamic look of a 3-D shape. Start with a standard shape or one of the shapes available through the AutoShapes menu choices.

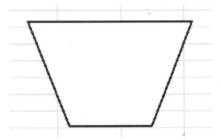

Select the shape; then click the 3-D button on the Drawing toolbar and choose one of the 3-D options.

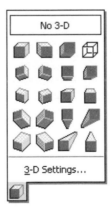

After you change the shape, use the tools described earlier in this chapter to modify its color, size, border, or other characteristics. The 3-D attributes change appropriately.

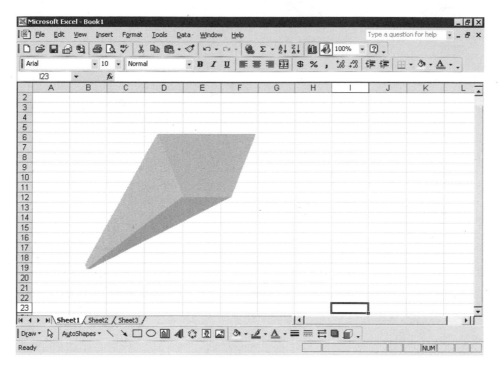

Remember that the 3-D effect is added on to the original shape, so when you select the graphic, sizing handles appear around the original shape only. Don't worry; when you finish moving or resizing the shape, the 3-D add-on changes too.

Adding Text to Shapes

If you want to use a shape to highlight part of a worksheet, it's frequently effective to add text (so the reference you're making is clear). Adding text to a shape is easy:

1. Right-click the shape and choose Add Text from the shortcut menu.

2. A text box appears, centered on the shape, with an insertion point inside.

3. Enter the text you want to use for this shape.

4. Use the text tools on the Formatting toolbar to change the font, font size, attributes, and alignment of the text.

You can see the shadow of the text box while you're entering text, but it won't show unless the shape is selected, so your final product will look as if the text is applied directly to the shape (see Figure 12-8).

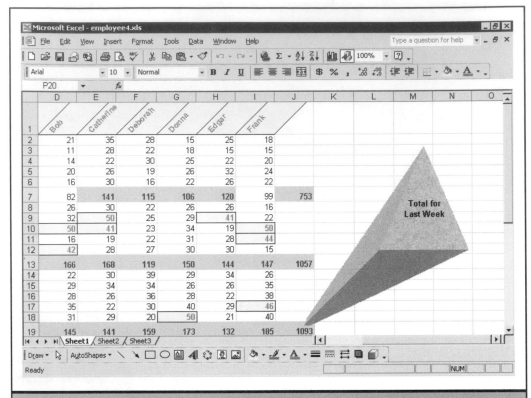

Figure 12-8. *Put text on a shape to enhance its effectiveness*

Working with Layers

You can overlap multiple graphics to create some nifty graphic effects (see Figure 12-9). All you have to do is drag one graphic to another. However, it's not always as straight-forward as it seems.

Each graphic element you place on your worksheet is on its own plane—there are layers that determine what goes on top of what. The pecking order is "first in gets the bottom" and then each additional graphic you add is positioned on top of the previous one.

This means sometimes you have to change the planes, or levels, of graphic elements in order to use them properly. Excel has a series of commands to handle this need. Those commands are available under the Order feature, which you can access by either of these methods after you select an object in your merged graphic:

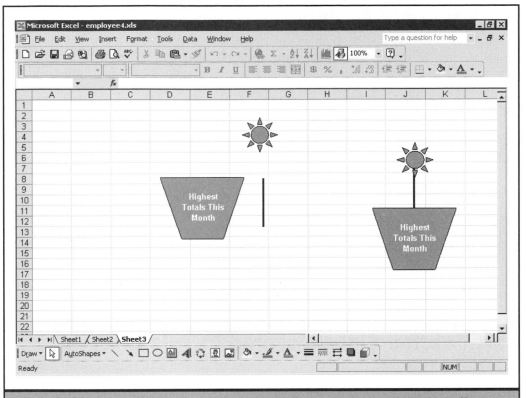

Figure 12-9. *Layer individual multiple graphic elements to create special effects*

- Right-click the graphic element you want to change and choose Order from the shortcut menu.

- Click the Draw button on the Drawing toolbar, and choose Order from the menu.

The Order commands that display let you move graphic elements to different planes:

- **Bring To Front**   Puts the selected graphic element at the front of the stack.

- **Send To Back**   Puts the selected graphic element at the back of the stack.

- **Bring Forward**   Puts the selected graphic element one step closer to the front.

- **Send Backward**   Puts the selected graphic element one step back.

Working with Groups

Excel uses a grouping feature to let you combine multiple graphic elements. You can take advantage of the group to move multiple elements (if you move them one at a time, it's almost impossible to maintain the relationship between them), or resize all the elements by the same amount. Use these steps to create a group:

1. Click the Select Objects button on the Drawing toolbar (it looks like an arrow).

2. Drag a box around all the elements you want to include in the group. When you release the mouse button, all the individual objects are selected (there are sizing handles on every object).

3. To move the group, place your pointer on any element in the group so your pointer turns into a four-headed arrow. Then drag the element and watch the rest of the group come along.

4. To resize all the elements in the group proportionately, use the sizing handle on any element. The other elements change as you drag.

Click anywhere outside the group to ungroup the elements.

Certification Skills Covered in This Chapter

If you're preparing for Microsoft Office User Specialist certification, here are the skills you learned in this chapter.

Skill Set	Activity
Creating and modifying graphics	Create, modify, and position graphics

Excel
2002

Chapter 13

Pivot Tables

C hapter 7 devoted considerable attention to the topic of *lists*. Lists are worksheet ranges that contain data, with different variables occupying different columns headed by the variable name and different records occupying different rows. You learned that this structure makes tasks such as sorting and filtering much easier.

Pivot tables also make use of lists. Lists show details, and pivot tables summarize details. Suppose that you have records on the age and political party membership of 400 people. You organize the data in a list: one column for age, one column for party membership, and 400 rows for each of the 400 people.

You can use a pivot table to coalesce all that detail into a summary that shows, for example, the average age of the members of each political party. That's the power that pivot tables give you: the ability to summarize large amounts of data in a simple, clear framework.

Pivot Table Components

That simple pivot table—average age by party membership—is illustrated in Figure 13-1, with two different orientations.

You'll find it helpful to understand how Excel refers to the different components of a pivot table. (Actually, Excel terminology prefers the single-word neologism *PivotTable*, but the usage seems excessively cute and this book employs *pivot table*, except when quoting screen syntax.)

Fields and Items

In Figure 13-1, the pivot table in cells D1:E6 has a *row field* and a *data field*. The row field identifies the political parties, and it occupies cells D2:D6, including the Grand Total. The data field shows the average age of those who identify themselves with each party, and it occupies cells E2:E6—again including the Grand Total.

The other pivot table in Figure 13-1 is in cells D10:H12. It has a *column field* in cells E11:H11. Its data field is in cells E12:H12.

Each value in a row or column field is termed an *item*. In Figure 13-1, the values *Democrat, Independent,* and *Republican* are items.

Every field in a pivot table has an associated button labeled with the name of its field. As you will see, double-clicking these buttons has an effect that depends on the sort of field they represent.

Comparing the two pivot tables helps explain the term *pivot table*. You can change the orientation of a row field to a column field—and vice versa—simply by clicking on the field's button and dragging it. This action is called *pivoting the table*.

Although the capability of reorienting fields is convenient, the name implies that to pivot is the primary function of the table. That implication is unfortunate at best. The pivot table is the most powerful means of data aggregation and analysis available in Excel.

In Figure 13-2, two more fields have been added to the pivot table: Sex (Male and Female) and Voted (Yes and No—whether or not the person voted in the prior election). In the upper pivot table, in cells G1:J8 the Sex field is a *page field*. A page field is a means of selecting a subset of records to use in the pivot table. You can use the page

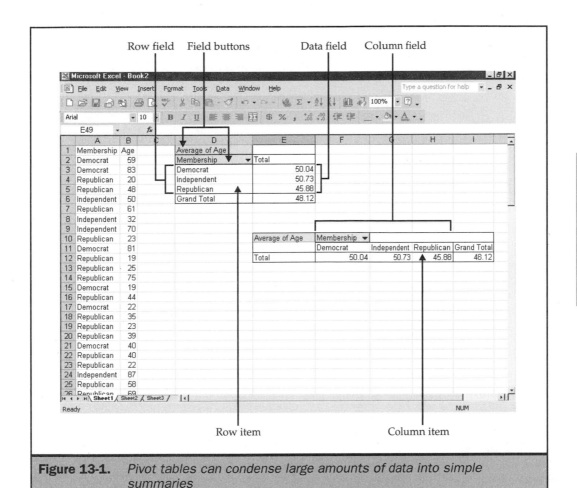

Figure 13-1. *Pivot tables can condense large amounts of data into simple summaries*

field's drop-down arrow to display the possible values: in this case, Female, Male, or All. If you choose Male, that value is shown next to the field's button, and the summary values—here, Average of Age—are based on the Male records only. You can do the same with the Female item. If you choose All, no distinction is made between the items in the page field, and the entire set of data is used in calculating the averages.

Also notice that the pivot table in G1:J8 uses, in addition to the page field, both a row field, Membership, and a column field, Voted. By building a table with all three fields, you can summarize Age by each possible combination of party membership, sex, and voting status.

Now consider the pivot table in cells F11:J21 in Figure 13-2. It has no page field; instead, it has two row fields. The pivot table is structured so that each Membership item appears within each Sex item. In Excel's terminology, this pivot table uses Sex as an *outer* row field and Membership as an *inner* row field.

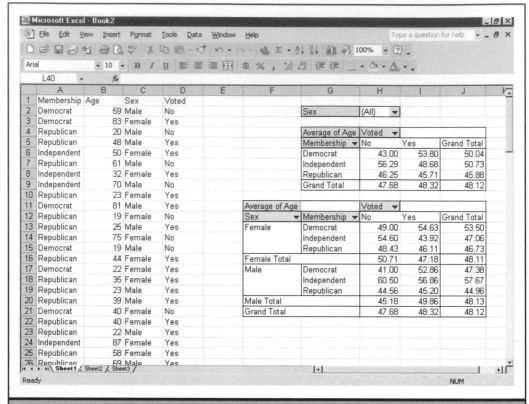

Figure 13-2. *Use page fields to filter the records shown in a pivot table*

Custom Subtotals for Inner Fields

There is something special about inner row fields. Notice in Figure 13-2 that you can see a Grand Total for all Females (cell J16), all Males (cell J20), all Voted—No (cell H21), and all Voted—Yes (cell I21) but not for the Membership items.

Note *Excel refers to the summary cells as Totals, even though that implies that the data field has been summed, or totaled. You may have chosen a different means of summarizing the data field—the current example uses the Average. Don't be misled by the terms Total and Grand Total into thinking that the summary method is therefore the Sum.*

In order to see a total for Democrat, Independent, and Republican—items in the inner row field—you need to call for a custom subtotal (see Figure 13-3).

Figure 13-3 shows the pivot table used in Figure 13-2, except that it now displays the inner row field's item totals (cells J11:J13). You arrange for this by taking these steps:

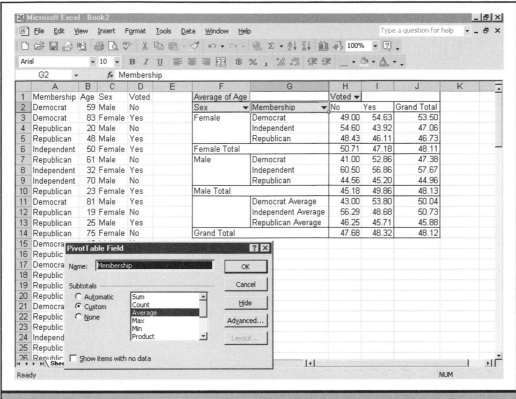

Figure 13-3.   *Totals for inner fields are called* block totals

1. Double-click the Membership button (in general, the button for an inner row or inner column field).

2. The dialog box labeled PivotTable Field, shown in Figure 13-3, appears. Click the Custom button for subtotals.

3. Choose the summary method you want to show. In the current example, it's Average. Then choose OK.

Hiding Items

You have probably noticed the down arrows on the row and column field buttons. Use these to choose to display or hide selected items from a given field.

This chapter has already discussed the use of a page field's drop-down. Using that control, you select any one of the page field's items to restrict the pivot table to those records—or you select the All item to show all records. Used this way, the page field acts as a selection criterion.

The drop-down for row and column fields acts differently. Figure 13-4 shows what the drop-down for the Membership button looks like.

Use the check boxes in the drop-down to hide (unchecked) or display (checked) any single item or combination of items. If you have previously hidden one or more items, you can fill the Show All check box to fill all the check boxes in the drop-down. Notice in Figure 13-4 that the Democrat item is unchecked in the drop-down. If the drop-down did not hide the field's items, it would be possible to see that the Democrat item is absent from the pivot table.

Summary Options

How should you choose to summarize your detail records? Excel provides you 11 different summary methods:

- **Sum**   This is the default option if the data field is numeric. Each cell in the pivot table shows the sum of the data field for a particular item (e.g., Male) or combination of items (e.g., Democrat and Female).

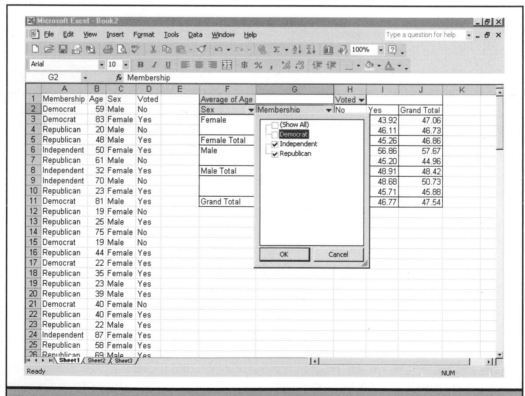

Figure 13-4.   *Use the drop-down associated with any row or column field to display any combination you want*

- **Count** This is the default option if the data field is text or a mix of text and numeric. Each cell in the pivot table shows the count of records for a particular item or combination of items. Closely related to Count is *Count Nums*, which counts the numeric records and ignores text records in a mixed numeric-text data field.

- **Average** The average is the arithmetic mean—not the median, not the mode. It is the result of dividing, for a particular item or item combination, the sum of the data field's numeric values by their count.

- **Max and Min** You can choose to display the largest or smallest numeric value for that item or item combination.

- **Product** This summary method returns the product of all numeric values for the item or item combination. If the only three records for Republican, Male, and Did Not Vote had ages of 25, 30, and 40, then Product would return 25 * 30 * 40 = 30,000.

- **StdDev and StdDevp** The standard deviation of the records for the item or item combination. The StdDev statistic assumes that the records are a sample from a population (n–1 in the denominator), and the StdDevp statistic assumes that the records constitute the population (n in the denominator). The square root of Var or Varp.

- **Var and Varp** The variance of the records for the item or item combination. Again, the "p" at the end of "Var" indicates the assumption that the records constitute the population. The square of StdDev or StdDevp.

If you're unfamiliar with the meaning and use of standard deviations and variances, don't worry. They're nice to have available, but far from necessary to the effective use of pivot tables.

When would you use these summary options? They can be used to answer questions such as:

- What were the total dollars spent in each of several expense categories? Use Sum.

- How many units of Product A were sold during each quarter? Depending on how you have laid out your source data, you might answer this question with either Sum or Count.

- What was the average cost of the raw material units that were purchased to inventory? Use Average.

- In dollars, what was the largest single sale this quarter? Use Max. The smallest? Use Min.

- Is the variability in birth weight among newborns different during winter months than it is during the remainder of the year? Use StdDev or Var.

Use the PivotTable Field dialog box, shown in Figure 13-3, to make your choice of summary method. You can refine the method by right-clicking a cell in the data field, choosing Field Settings from the shortcut menu, and clicking the Options button on the PivotTable Field dialog box. More choices appear there, as shown in Figure 13-5.

In Figure 13-5 you see several of the summary options available to you; not all of them are visible in the Show Data As drop-down. In each of the following five pivot tables, the summary method is Sum: each data cell in each pivot table displays in one way or another the sum of the net profit for different product lines during different quarters.

This pivot table shows a standard way to analyze profits: the sum of the raw dollars broken down by quarter and by product line. No special options are needed to get this result:

	A	B	C	D
1				
2				
3	Sum of Net Profit	Product		
4	Quarter	Desktops	Laptops	Grand Total
5	Q1	$4,941	$5,088	$10,029
6	Q2	$3,947	$3,455	$7,402
7	Q3	$4,181	$8,655	$12,836
8	Q4	$5,845	$5,968	$11,813
9	Grand Total	$18,914	$23,166	$42,080
10				

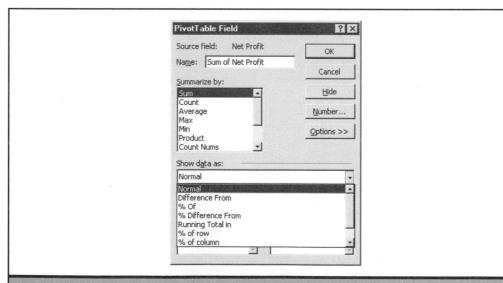

Figure 13-5. *The Number button on the PivotTable Field dialog box sets data field formats*

The next pivot table shows the sum of profits for each product and for each quarter, expressed as percent of row. For example, Quarter 2 had a total of $7,402 in net profits: $3,947 for Desktops and $3,455 for Laptops. In terms of row percentages, Desktops accounted for 53 percent and laptops for 47 percent of the Quarter's profits. To get this result, choose % of Row from the Show Data As drop-down in the PivotTable Field dialog box shown in Figure 13-5.

	A	B	C	D
1				
2				
3	Sum of Net Profit	Product ▾		
4	Quarter ▾	Desktops	Laptops	Grand Total
5	Q1	49%	51%	100%
6	Q2	53%	47%	100%
7	Q3	33%	67%	100%
8	Q4	49%	51%	100%
9	Grand Total	45%	55%	100%
10				

Of course, you can also cause the pivot table to express profits in terms of column percentages. Of the $18,914 in profits for Desktops, 26 percent came during Quarter 1, 21 percent during Quarter 2, and so on. To get this result, choose % of Column from the Show Data As drop-down in the PivotTable Field dialog box shown in Figure 13-5.

	A	B	C	D
1				
2				
3	Sum of Net Profit	Product ▾		
4	Quarter ▾	Desktops	Laptops	Grand Total
5	Q1	26%	22%	24%
6	Q2	21%	15%	18%
7	Q3	22%	37%	31%
8	Q4	31%	26%	28%
9	Grand Total	100%	100%	100%
10				

You could also choose % of Total so that the percentage shown in each cell is the sum of profits for that product and quarter divided by the sum of all profits.

The next pivot table again shows profits expressed in dollars, but this table displays running totals. For example, the table shows that profits for Desktops at Quarter 2 are $8,888—the sum of Quarter 1 ($4,941) and Quarter 2 ($3,947). This is a useful way to obtain cumulative, or running, totals. It's typically used when the totals are across sequential time periods. To get this result, choose Running Total In from the Show

Data As drop-down. This option requires that you identify a base field; click Quarter to get a running total by Quarter.

	A	B	C	D
1				
2				
3	Sum of Net Profit	Product ▾		
4	Quarter ▾	Desktops	Laptops	Grand Total
5	Q1	$4,941	$5,088	$10,029
6	Q2	$8,888	$8,543	$17,431
7	Q3	$13,069	$17,198	$30,267
8	Q4	$18,914	$23,166	$42,080
9	Grand Total			
10				

Here's another example of using a base field. This time the net profits are expressed as differences. Notice that the profits for Desktops during Quarter 2 are $994 less than during Quarter 1: $3,947–$4,941 = –$994. The approach makes it easy to compare, in this case, quarter-to-quarter results. To get this result, choose Difference From in the Show Data As drop-down, choose Quarter as the base field and (Previous) as the base item. Notice that the choice of Previous as the base item results in empty cells for the first item; it has no previous item to base itself on.

	A	B	C	D
1				
2				
3	Sum of Net Profit	Product ▾		
4	Quarter ▾	Desktops	Laptops	Grand Total
5	Q1			
6	Q2	($994)	($1,633)	($2,627)
7	Q3	$234	$5,200	$5,434
8	Q4	$1,664	($2,687)	($1,023)
9	Grand Total			

Other options available to you in the Show Data As drop-down are:

- **% Of (you specify a base field and base item)**   You might use this if you wanted to view net profits as a percentage of Product (the base field) and Laptops (the base item). This would display net profit for Desktops as a percentage of the net profits for Laptops.

- **% Difference From (you specify a base field and base item)**   This is similar to the Difference From option discussed above, but the difference is expressed as a percentage instead of in the original units.

- **Index**   This option is useful primarily when you display the data field as a Count. It results in a sort of weighted average:

    Index = (Cell Count * Total Count) / (Row Count * Column Count)

The Index is typically used in statistical inference, where the analyst wants to know the likelihood that there's a dependable relationship between the column field and the row field.

Calculated Fields and Items

Sometimes it's useful to create new fields—called *calculated fields*—in an existing pivot table. And you sometimes want to add a new item—called a *calculated item*—to an existing field in the pivot table. Recall that in pivot table terminology, an *item* is a value that belongs to a field. When you create a calculated field, it's usually one that you will use in the pivot table's data area—that is, you will summarize it according to items in the table's row, column, and page fields. When you create a calculated item, it's one that will be part of a row, column, or page field.

Defining a Calculated Field

There are times that you will want to include a field in a pivot table that does not exist in the data source. For example, a worksheet might contain a list with the fields Month, Revenues, and Costs. You could create a pivot table that sums both the revenues and the costs for each month.

If you also want to put a Profit Margin field in the pivot table, it would be easy to add a new column to the data source and from there to the pivot table. An alternative is to add a Profit Margin field to the pivot table as a calculated field, perhaps by expressing profit as a percentage of revenue. As this section explains, there are reasons to choose one method over the other: it isn't always true that adding the field to the data source will provide the result you're after.

You define a calculated field in a pivot table sometime after the table has been created. Click the PivotTable button on the PivotTable toolbar and choose Formulas | Calculated Field (see Figure 13-6).

Create the calculated field Margin by typing the name **Margin** into the Name edit box. Then type this equation into the Formula edit box:

= (Revenues – Costs)/Revenues

(You can also assemble the formula by clicking field names in the Fields list box and placing them in the formula by means of the Insert Field button.) This equation is a standard way of expressing profits as a percentage of revenues.

When you finish typing the equation, click the Add button, and then click OK. The calculated field is inserted into the pivot table, as shown in Figure 13-7.

Notice that each instance of Margin equals the difference between Revenues and Costs, divided by Revenues. The field has been set to the Percentage number format.

You can also enter the Margin formula directly on the worksheet. This has been done in Figure 13-8, which also shows a pivot table with the Margin field taken from the worksheet instead of as the calculated field shown in Figure 13-7.

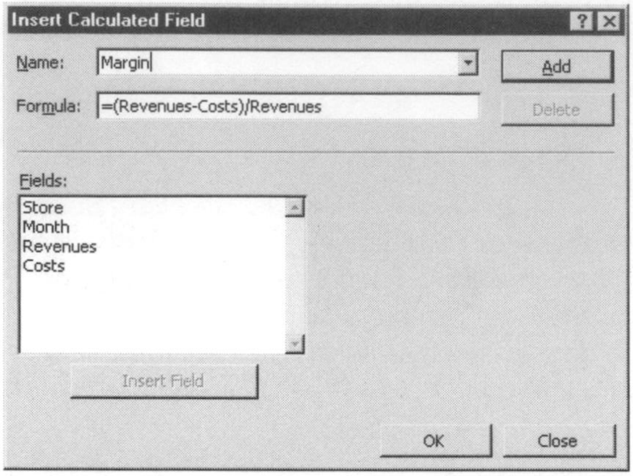

Figure 13-6. A calculated field is used only in the Data area

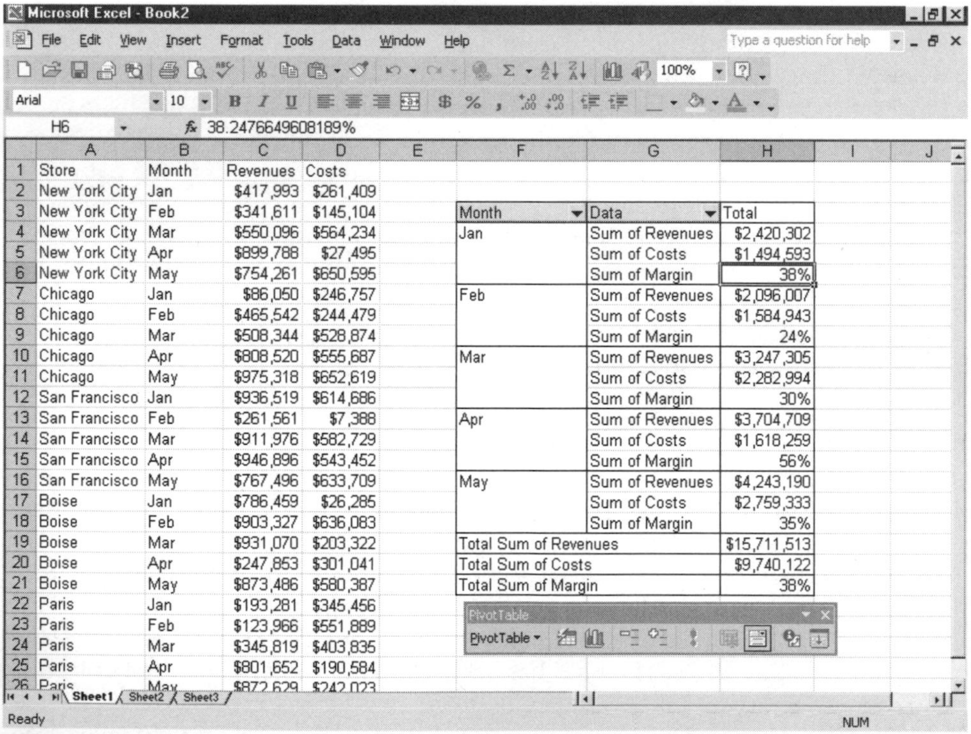

Figure 13-7. The calculated field combines all instances of the row field's item

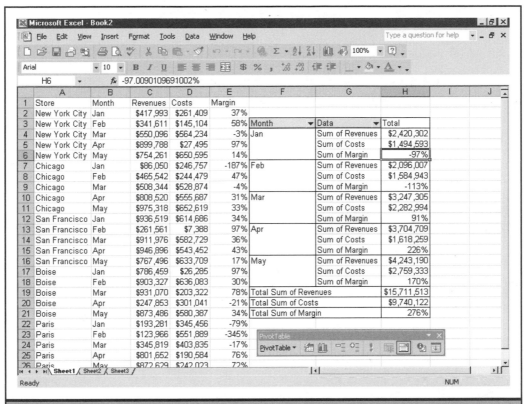

Figure 13-8. *Be wary of problems induced by different orders of calculation*

The pivot table in Figure 13-8 reports very different figures for Margin than does the table in Figure 13-7 because the order of calculation is different. When you include Margin as a calculated field, the pivot table sums the revenues for a month and the costs for a month. Then it applies the (Revenues – Costs)/Revenues formula to those sums.

In contrast, when you calculate Margin on the worksheet, Excel begins by calculating Margins for each record in the source data range. Then these Margin figures are included in the pivot table and are summed for each month.

The result isn't very informative and almost surely isn't what you want. It makes a difference whether you do the addition and then divide (as does the calculated field), or do the division and then the addition (as occurs when you calculate Margin in the source data). In the more general case, there's usually a difference between the approach taken by the calculated field:

$$(SUM(Revenues) - SUM(Costs))/SUM(Revenues)$$

and the approach taken by calculating the Margin on the worksheet and letting the pivot table summarize it:

SUM((Revenues – Costs)/Revenues)

There isn't always a difference, though. If you calculate profit as the simple difference between Revenues and Costs, it doesn't matter whether you subtract and then sum (from the data source), or sum and then subtract (via the calculated field).

Defining a Calculated Item

You define a calculated item in an existing row or column field. In fact, if you have selected any part of a pivot table other than a row or column field, Excel will not let you create a calculated item.

Suppose that your existing pivot table summarizes Revenues for the first five months of the year: the data field is Revenues and the row field is Month. You would like the pivot table to show an estimate of Revenues for the sixth month, June—perhaps, 5 percent greater than May's Revenues. One way to do so is to put the item, June, explicitly on the worksheet and include it in the pivot table's data source. That's a problem, though, if your pivot table uses an external data source: you don't want to include forecast estimates in a database of actual values. (See Chapter 16 for a discussion of using a database as input to a pivot table.)

The solution is to create a calculated item. Select an existing row or column item in your pivot table, click the PivotTable button on the PivotTable toolbar, and choose Formulas | Calculated Item (or right-click a row or column item and use the shortcut menu). The Insert Calculated Item dialog box appears (see Figure 13-9).

In the Name box, enter **June**. In the Formula box, enter **=1.05 * May**. When you click Add and then OK, your new item is added to the Month field and its value for Revenues is 105 percent of May's Revenues:

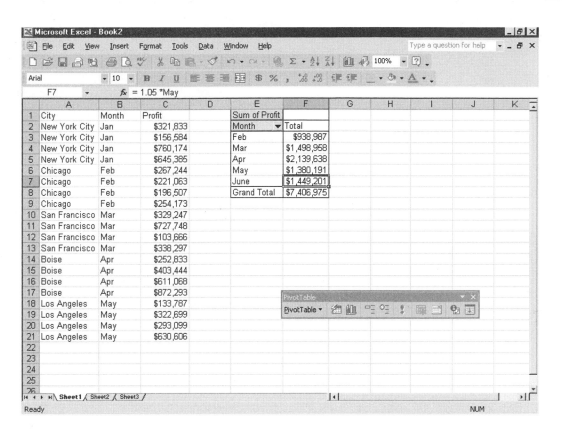

You could also assemble the formula for the new item by using the Items list box in conjunction with the Insert Item button, shown in Figure 13-9. Although it wouldn't help in the present example, you might also use existing fields, shown in the Fields list box, as part of the new item's formula.

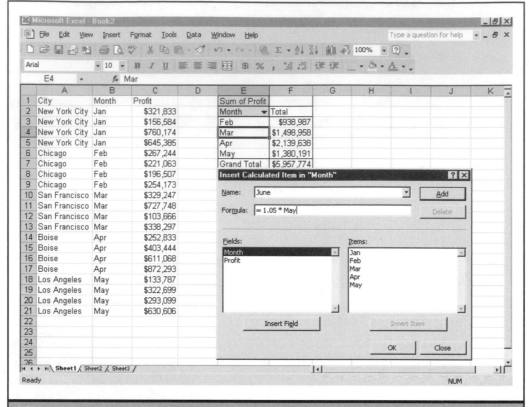

Figure 13-9. *Calculated items apply to row and column fields only*

PivotTable Wizard

With the foregoing in mind as an introduction to a pivot table's components, it's time to look at how to create one. The process is driven by the PivotTable Wizard—a series of dialog boxes similar to the Chart Wizard.

Before you begin, you must have your source data accessible. This is often a worksheet list, such as the ones that earlier examples in this chapter have analyzed. It might be a range of data that spans several worksheets, termed a *multiple consolidation range*. Other possible data sources are an external data source (in practice, this is typically a true relational database) and another, existing pivot table.

When you choose Data | PivotTable and PivotChart Report, the dialog box shown in Figure 13-10 appears.

This is Step 1 of the wizard. Subsequent steps depend on where you have placed your source data. For clarity, the present tour of the wizard assumes that the source data is in a worksheet list. In that case, you accept the default option of Microsoft Excel List or Database.

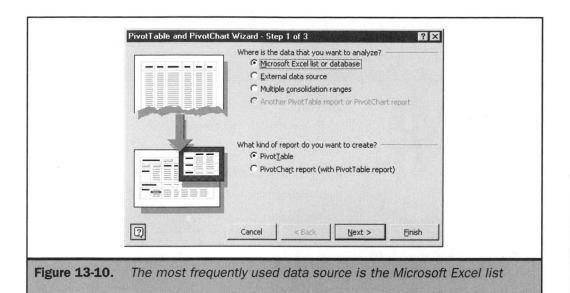

Figure 13-10. *The most frequently used data source is the Microsoft Excel list*

Note   *An Excel database is just a list. The term is a legacy from earlier versions of Excel.*

Also in Step 1, you choose whether you want to create a pivot table by itself or a pivot table that's accompanied by a chart. Again for clarity, this example creates only the pivot table. Later in this chapter you will see an example of the pivot chart.

When you have made your two choices in Step 1, click Next to continue to Step 2.

Both the function and the appearance of Step 2 depend on the choice you make in Step 1. If, as here, you choose a Microsoft Excel list or database, you next need to identify where the list is found.

The most straightforward way to do so is to drag through the complete list. When Step 2 appears, you should see a flashing cursor in the Range edit box; if you don't, just click once in the edit box. Then click in the upper-left cell of the list and drag through the complete range while holding down the mouse button. You can also make this selection before you invoke the PivotTable Wizard.

Tip   *If your source data range occupies many rows, use a keyboard shortcut to select the full range. Begin by dragging through just the first row. Then release the mouse button, hold down CTRL and SHIFT, and press the DOWN ARROW key. This will select down until Excel reaches an empty row.*

Be sure that you have included the first row of the list, which should contain the list headers, in your selection. Then click Next. The PivotTable Wizard's third step appears:

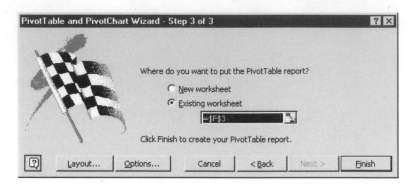

If you selected the source data range before invoking the Wizard, the default option is to put the pivot table on a new worksheet.

If an empty cell was active when you started the Wizard, the default option is that existing worksheet. In that case, if the active cell is in row 1 or row 2, the proposed starting cell is two cells below the active cell to leave room for a page field.

If you are just beginning to develop the pivot table, you will probably want to put it on the existing worksheet. This makes it easier to refer to the source data as you're refining the functionality and the appearance of the pivot table.

To put the table on the existing worksheet, click that option button and then, with the vertical bar flashing in the edit box, click in the cell where you want to place the upper-left corner of the pivot table.

If you select a cell in row 1 or row 2, it won't be as easy to establish a page field as it is if you select a cell in row 3 or below.

The additional buttons at the bottom of Step 3 are helpful. This chapter discusses the Options button in the next section. If you click the Layout button, the dialog box shown here appears:

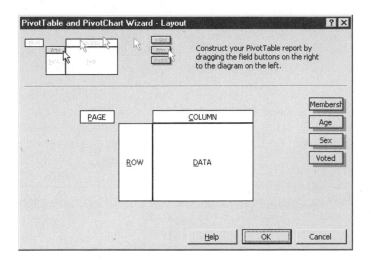

If you have created pivot tables in earlier versions of Excel, you recognize the dialog box shown above as what once was Step 3 of the PivotTable Wizard. You might then feel more comfortable using this method of designing the pivot table.

Note

Using the off-worksheet layout window can also be useful if you are using an external data source with a large number of records or with a slow network connection. If you design the pivot table in this window, Excel defers its retrieval of records until you have finished using the PivotTable Wizard. If you design the pivot table directly on the worksheet, Excel retrieves records each time you create a new page, column, or row field.

ANALYZING DATA

Designing the pivot table directly on the worksheet has some advantages. Instead of using the Layout button, click Finish on Step 3. The worksheet now appears much as shown in Figure 13-11.

Excel puts the outline of a pivot table on the worksheet for you, with a place to put the data field and places for row, column, and page fields. To use these areas, notice in the figure that both the PivotTable toolbar and the PivotTable Field List appear when you have completed the wizard. On the Field List are the names of the fields—the list headers from your source data range. You have three ways to put a field into the pivot table:

- Use your mouse to drag the button to the appropriate area. For example, if you want Voted to be a row field, click on its name in the Field List, hold down the mouse button, and drag it to the rectangle that's labeled Drop Row Fields Here on the worksheet.

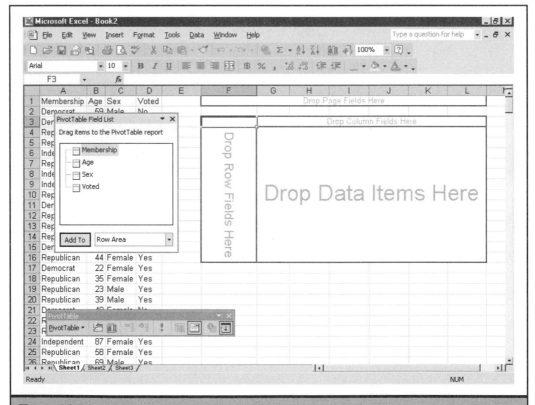

Figure 13-11. *Arranging the layout on the worksheet makes it easy to visualize the results*

■ Select an area from the drop-down at the bottom of the Field List (you can choose from Row Area, Column Area, Page Area, or Data Area). Then click the Add To button.

■ Select an area from the drop-down and double-click the field's button in the Field List.

When a field has been placed in the pivot table, its name in the Field List box appears in boldface.

You can put as many fields as you want to the outline of the pivot table. But as soon as you put a field into the data area (Drop Data Items Here) the outline collapses and you see the pivot table that you have constructed so far. See Figure 13-12, which assumes that you have used Voted as a column field, Membership as a row field, Sex as a page field, and that you are about to drop Age into the data area.

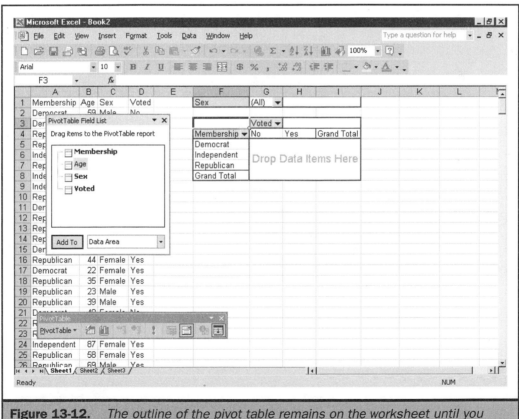

Figure 13-12. *The outline of the pivot table remains on the worksheet until you put a field into its Data Area*

Notice one of the advantages of structuring the pivot table on the worksheet instead of on the Layout dialog box: it's easier to tell if you already have data on the worksheet that will be in the way of the pivot table: the pivot table will overwrite existing data if it is in cells that the pivot table will occupy. Structuring the pivot table on the worksheet can enable you to switch row and column fields so that you can preserve existing data without having to start the PivotTable Wizard from scratch.

When you have dropped a field into the data area, the outline disappears and the pivot table completes (see Figure 13-13).

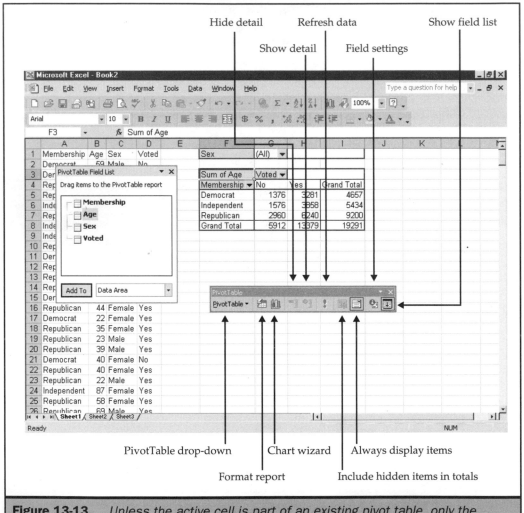

Figure 13-13. *Unless the active cell is part of an existing pivot table, only the PivotTable drop-down is enabled on the toolbar*

After you have finished with the PivotTable Wizard, the PivotTable toolbar appears by default (refer to Figure 13-13). After you have selected a cell or range of cells in the pivot table, the toolbar controls are enabled:

- **PivotTable drop-down**   Click the drop-down for a shortcut menu that repeats the other buttons on the toolbar and gets you to calculated fields and items and to table options.

- **Format Report**   Click this button to autoformat the pivot table.

- **Chart Wizard**   Click this button to create a pivot chart based on the pivot table. See the section "Pivot Charts" in this chapter for more information.

- **Hide Detail and Show Detail**   The Hide Detail button collapses an inner row (or column) field and leaves only the outer row (or column) items visible.

- **Refresh Data**   This button updates the pivot table on the basis of changes to information in the data source.

- **Include Hidden Items in Totals**   If you are not using an OLAP data source, this button is disabled. If you are using one, this button toggles between including and excluding the data associated with hidden items in the pivot table's totals. For example, if you hide the item (or level) named March from a Month field, you can choose whether or not to include March's revenues in the total of Revenues.

- **Always Display Items**   Suppose that your data source, instead of existing in your workbook, is a database, perhaps one that you connect to across a relatively slow network. In that case, it can take a long time for Excel to retrieve the necessary data every time you put another field into the row or the column area. Excel needs to establish access to the database and find the field in question. Excel must also determine the unique values that the field takes on because they will become row or column items in the pivot table. You can make Excel wait to make those determinations by turning off the Always Display Items button. (It's turned off if it looks dimmed on the toolbar.) Then, Excel waits until you put a field into the Data Area before it goes to the data source to determine what items to display. Note that this has an effect only during the initial design of the pivot table.

- **Field Settings**   This button enables you to change such field properties as the nature of its subtotals and its number format.

- **Hide Field List and Show Field List**   This toggle button either hides or displays the PivotTable Field List box.

At this point—after the pivot table has been created—you might want to change some of the options that apply to the entire table. The next section discusses these options.

Setting Pivot Table Options

If you chose not to set options for the pivot table in Step 3 of the PivotTable Wizard, or if you want to modify any options, use the PivotTable toolbar to display the Table Options dialog box. Be sure that you have selected a cell in the pivot table, then click the PivotTable drop-down arrow on the toolbar, and click Options. The dialog box shown in Figure 13-14 appears.

The first option available on the PivotTable Options dialog box is the Table Name. The default value is PivotTable1 or PivotTable2 or however many pivot tables you've created during the current session. You'll find it useful to give a pivot table a name you can easily recognize when you want to base several pivot tables on one base table. (See this chapter's section on the pivot table cache for more information.) If you give that table a name such as Base Table, it's easier to be sure that all the pivot tables use the same base.

The Table Options dialog box provides you many options to choose among. Fortunately, you will usually want to accept the default options. On occasion, though, the defaults don't fill the bill. Then you can change one or more of either the Format options or the Data options.

| **Figure 13-14.** | *Use field buttons to manage field settings; use PivotTable Options to manage settings for the entire pivot table* |

Pivot Table Format Options

The format options available to you on the PivotTable Options dialog box pertain to the entire table, not just to a particular field or fields.

Grand Totals for Columns, Grand Totals for Rows   Default: filled. Showing these totals is the default. It's useful to show them if you need to recover the source data as a list (again, see this chapter's section on the cache). Sometimes, though, when you're desperate for space on the screen or on a report, you might want to suppress the Grand Totals. This is particularly true when you are displaying percentages that are constrained to add up to 100 percent.

AutoFormat Table   Default: filled. Excel supplies 21 autoformats for pivot tables. To apply one of them, click the Format Table button on the PivotTable toolbar. To remove an autoformat, clear the check box on the Table Options dialog box.

Subtotal Hidden Page Items   Default: cleared. Suppose that you have created a page field. Subsequently, you either use the Field Settings button on the PivotTable toolbar or double-click its field button so as to hide one or more of the page field's items. That item will not appear in the page field's drop-down. By filling the Subtotal Hidden Page Items check box, you can arrange for the records that belong to that hidden item to appear in the pivot table's subtotals.

Merge Labels   Default: cleared. This check box causes row and column item labels to be merged and centered across cells. It is principally an alignment setting.

Preserve Formatting   Default: filled. Leave this check box filled if you want the pivot table to retain any formatting characteristics when you pivot the table or refresh its data.

Repeat Item Labels on Each Printed Page   Default: filled. This option is useful when you will print the pivot table, when it spans more than one printed page, and when it has multiple row fields or multiple column fields. When a page break comes before all the items of an inner field have completed printing, then the outer field's item does not appear on the subsequent page. Filling this check box causes the outer field's current item to repeat on the next page. This distinction is easier to see than to describe. Next is the top of a printed page that contains a pivot table, when the Repeat Item Labels checkbox has been cleared.

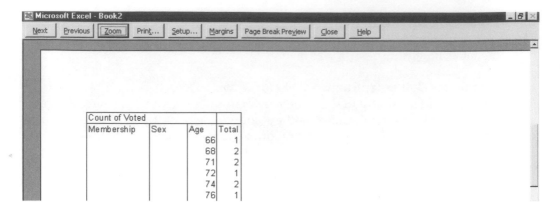

The same printed page when the Repeat Item Labels check box has been filled is shown next.

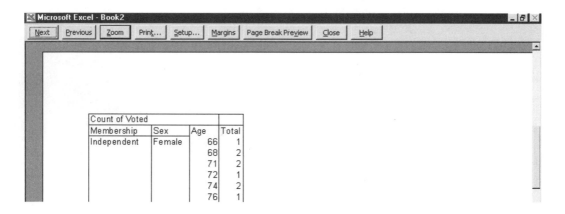

Mark Totals with *   Default: filled. This option is available only if your pivot table is based on an OLAP data source. Even then, it is disabled unless you click the Include Hidden Items in Totals button on the PivotTable toolbar. If both conditions are met, then you could arrange a situation in which certain row (or column or page) items are hidden on the pivot table but their data field values are included in subtotals and grand totals.

If you want a visual reminder that this might be the case, fill the Mark Totals with * check box. If you don't want that reminder, clear it.

Keep in mind that if you fill the check box, you will see an asterisk in the subtotal and grand total cells whether there are hidden items or not. The asterisk does *not* mean, "A hidden item is contributing to this total." It does mean "If an item is hidden, it is contributing to this total."

Page Layout   Default: Down, Then Over. This option applies to pivot tables that have more than one page field. You can choose to have the page fields stacked vertically (Down, Then Over) or side by side (Over, Then Down). See Figure 13-15.

Fields per column or Fields per row   Suppose that you chose Down, Then Over as the page layout. Use the Fields Per Column spinner to indicate the number of page fields that will occupy a column before Excel starts another column of page fields. Similarly, if you chose Over, Then Down as the page layout, you would use the Fields Per Row spinner to indicate the number of page fields on a row before Excel starts another row of page fields.

For Error Values, Show   Default: cleared. You will have some difficulty creating an error value in a pivot table. In earlier versions, pivot tables would return the #DIV/0! error value for the average when a combination of row and column items had no records. With no records, the average would have a zero denominator and you would get #DIV/0! in that pivot table cell. Now, though, Excel returns an empty cell in that

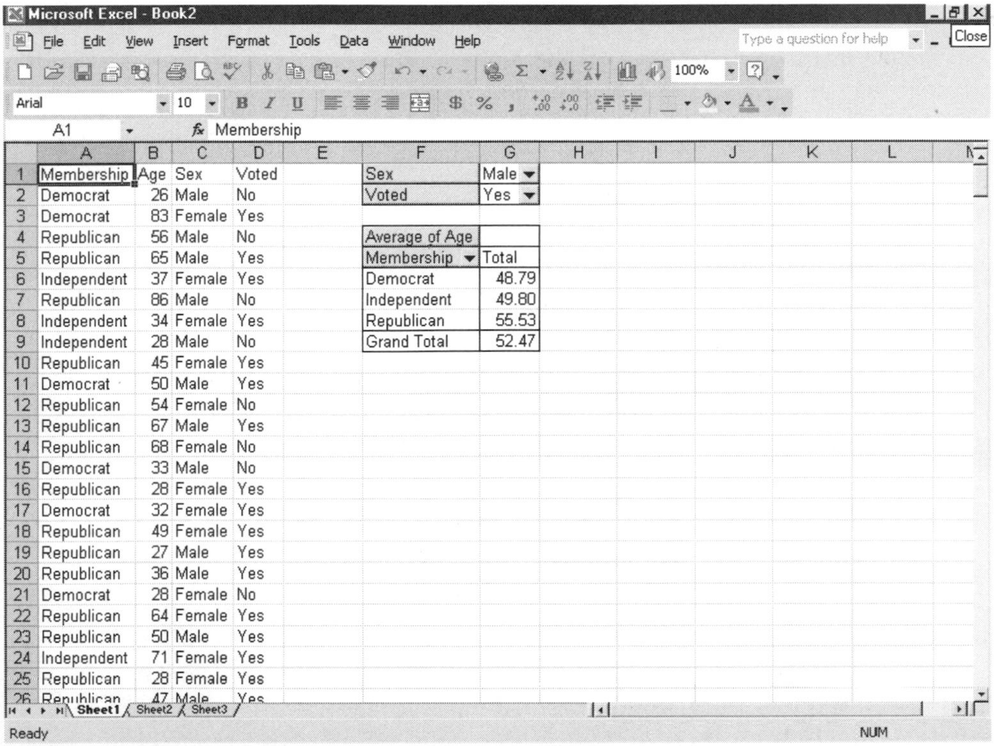

Figure 13-15.   *Stacked page fields usually make for a more compact layout*

and similar cases. But if there are error values in the source data, they flow through to the pivot table and appear there. It's usually better to remove them from the source data, but if you want you can check the For Error Values, Show check box and either leave the edit box empty or type something such as **Error** in it.

For Empty Cells, Show   Default: cleared. Use this check box and edit box in the same way as the For Error Values, Show check box, to replace an empty cell with a message such as **No Data Available**.

Set Print Titles   Default: cleared. You might want to fill this check box if you want to print the pivot table and if, when printed, it will span more than one page. Pages following the first will then repeat the pivot table's column headers and row headers. This makes it easier to follow the pivot table's results across multiple printed pages. Take care to clear any print titles on the Page Setup dialog box before you invoke this pivot table option. And keep in mind that if there is more than one pivot table in the print area, only one of them can repeat its headers on multiple printed pages.

Pivot Table Data Options

The data options that apply to a full pivot table pertain to the ways that the pivot table obtains data from its source—a worksheet range, a multiple consolidation range, an external data source, or another pivot table. There are three options that apply only if you use an external data source. When you use a data source that is located in the active workbook, the External Data Source options are disabled.

Save Data with Table Layout   Default: filled. Later in this chapter you will learn how the pivot table works with a special copy of the source data called the *cache*. If the Save Data with Table Layout check box is checked when you save the workbook, the cache is also saved. If it is cleared when you save the workbook, it is not saved. Failing to save the cache causes the workbook file to be a little smaller. But when you reopen the workbook, you must click the Refresh Data button on the PivotTable toolbar (or choose Data | Refresh Data) before you can modify the table's structure.

Enable Drill to Details   Default: filled. At times you will find that it's useful to look at a pivot table's source data in the form of a worksheet list, particularly if the data source is an external one such as a true database. You can do that by double-clicking a cell in the pivot table's data area if both the Save Data with Table Layout and the Enable Drill to Details check boxes are checked.

Refresh on Open   Default: cleared. If a pivot table's data source is external to its workbook, you might want to automatically refresh the pivot table's data when the workbook is opened. This helps ensure that the pivot table summaries are based on the most current information. To refresh automatically when you open the workbook, check this check box. The check box is cleared by default because you might not want to wait a long time for the refresh to occur when there is a substantial amount of data in the pivot table's source.

Refresh Every *x* Minutes   Default, if the pivot table uses an external data source: cleared, 60 minutes. If the pivot table does not use an external data source, this control is disabled. The option is nearly identical to the Refresh on Open option, but it allows you to specify how frequently Excel should refresh the pivot table from its external source.

Save Password   Default: cleared. An external data source may be password protected. When you create the pivot table, you will be required to supply the password. Subsequently you will probably want to refresh the pivot table's data to make sure it's using current information. If you want Excel to save the password that you supplied originally and to use it when it accesses the data source, fill the Save Password check box.

Filling the Save Password check box does not, as can happen in other contexts, cause the password to be saved in an unencrypted fashion. An unencrypted password can be stolen and misused. But you're safe if you save the password by means of this pivot table option.

Background Query   Default: cleared. If your pivot table's external data source is a large one, it can take some time for the query to fully execute. If the Background Query check box is cleared, the query must complete execution before control is returned to Excel (and to you). In that case, you cannot perform any work until the query is completed. Check the Background Query check box to allow the query to complete in the background and to let you continue to work while the query executes. This option works only with external data sources that support asynchronous queries.

Optimize Memory   Default: cleared. If you fill the Optimize Memory check box, Excel takes certain intermediate steps as it originally obtains the external data, and when you modify the table's structure or refresh its data. These intermediate steps are concerned with conserving available memory by determining, early on, how many unique items there are in a row or column field. That information is used to conserve memory and make it less likely that Excel will run out of resources before the pivot table is completed. The trade-off is that you might notice a minor performance slowdown as Excel carries out these optimization procedures.

Pivot Table Data Sources

There are four primary sources of data for a pivot table: a list, a multiple consolidation range, an external data source, and another pivot table. This section has shown how you use a list as the pivot table's data source. External data sources are treated in detail in Chapter 16. The remaining two options are discussed briefly here.

ANALYZING DATA

Another Pivot Table

When the active workbook already contains a pivot table, the Another PivotTable Report or PivotChart Report option on Step 1 of the PivotTable Wizard is enabled. When you select that option and click Next, Step 2 appears as shown in Figure 13-16.

When you base a pivot table on another, existing pivot table, the new pivot table has access to all the fields that are in the existing pivot table. As discussed in this chapter's section "Refreshing Data and the Cache," this approach can be efficient and useful.

Figure 13-16 makes it apparent why it's often wise to use the PivotTable Options to give a descriptive name to each pivot table. If you had to choose among PivotTable1, PivotTable2, PivotTable3, and so on, you might soon find it difficult to remember which pivot table contained which fields.

Multiple Consolidation Ranges

Suppose that you have several worksheets, each sheet representing a different month, a different product line, a different region, or something else that you find convenient to keep as related instances on separate sheets.

Further suppose that each worksheet has a similar list. For example, if each worksheet represents a different month, then each worksheet might have a list with data on product, region, and revenue for that product, in that region, during that month. Or if each worksheet represents a different product, each worksheet might have a list with data on month, region, and revenue.

With the data set up as described here, you can use a pivot table to summarize these different lists. You would use a pivot table to consolidate the information that's found in multiple worksheet ranges—hence the term *multiple consolidation ranges*.

Selecting that option in the PivotTable Wizard's first step brings up Step 2a, shown in Figure 13-17.

The effects of choosing between the two options in Step 2a are as follows.

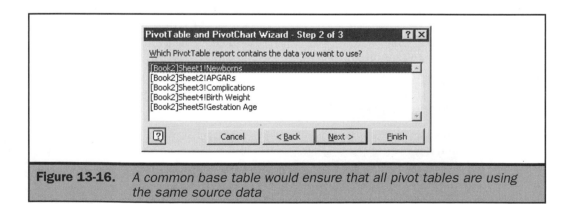

Figure 13-16.   *A common base table would ensure that all pivot tables are using the same source data*

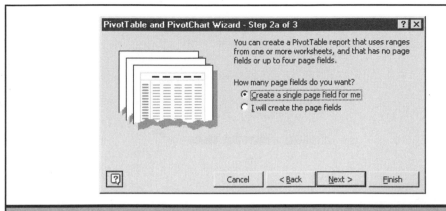

Figure 13-17.   *The Page field will have a different item for each consolidation range*

Create a Single Page Field for Me   If you choose this option, Excel puts one page field in the pivot table. The page field has one item for each range in the multiple consolidation range. So if you have one range with data for Product 1 and another range with data for Product 2, your page field will have an item for Product 1, another item for Product 2, and an All item that embraces Product 1 and Product 2. You can use this page field to view data for all the products or for one product at a time.

I Will Create the Page Fields   If you choose this option, you can create as many as four page fields (or none at all). This is a useful way to create different combinations of the multiple consolidation ranges. For example, you might have four different ranges each representing a region: North, East, South, and West. By creating your own page fields, you could have one page field that combines North and East, another page field that combines South and West, and another page field with each of the four regions. The result is that you can use the pivot table to view each region by itself, all regions together, a combined Northeast region, and a combined Southwest region.

When you click Next on Step 2a, Step 2b appears (see Figure 13-18).

Use Step 2b to indicate where the consolidation ranges are found. For each range, click in the Range edit box. Then click the tab of the worksheet that contains the range. Drag through the range to indicate the rows and columns it occupies. Then click the Add button and continue with the next range.

Note   *It's not necessary that the ranges occupy the same addresses on each worksheet. It is necessary that the ranges be laid out as lists and that each list have the same field names, also termed column headers. If the first list contains fields named Product, Quarter, and Revenue, then each other list must also contain fields named Product, Quarter, and Revenue.*

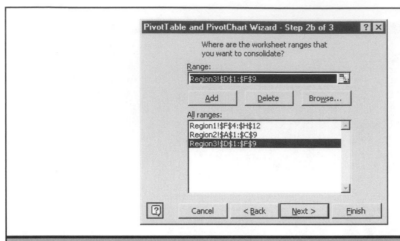

Figure 13-18.   *Use the worksheet Window menu to identify a consolidation range in another open workbook*

This is a good opportunity to use named ranges. Suppose you define sheet-level names such as Region1!ConsolidationRange and Region2!ConsolidationRange. You can use these names instead of cell addresses in Step 2b of the PivotTable Wizard. When new data is added to these ranges, just redefine the names accordingly, and refreshing the pivot table will cause the new data to enter the pivot table. See Chapter 10 for a discussion of named ranges.

When you have finished identifying the location of the consolidation ranges, click Next to go to Step 3. The Multiple Consolidation Ranges option has no effect on the appearance or functionality of the third step.

A sample result of using the Multiple Consolidation Ranges option appears in Figure 13-19.

Notice two anomalies in the pivot table shown in Figure 13-19:

■ The Row field (and, if it were shown, the Column field) does not have the name that's used as the header in the underlying consolidation ranges. Instead, the names Row, Column, and Value (for the Data field) are used. The first column in the consolidated lists is treated as the Row field.

■ The Page field's items are named Item1, Item2, and so on.

You can rename the fields after the fact by double-clicking on each button to invoke the PivotTable Field dialog box and entering a new name for the field.

If, in Step 2a, you choose to create your own page fields, you can override the default labels Item1, Item2, and so on.

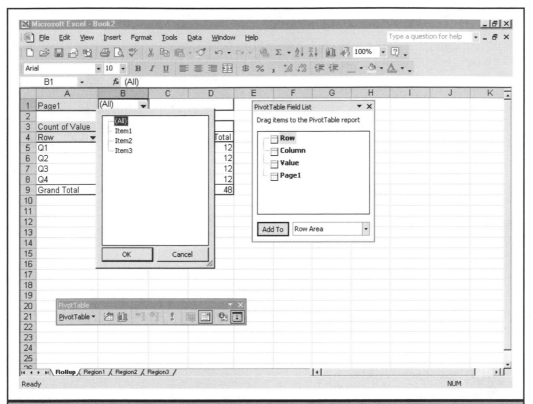

Figure 13-19. *A single page field is easy to create but is usually too rigid for useful analysis*

Manipulating Pivot Tables

After you have created a pivot table, it's likely that you'll want to modify it. The modifications most often take the form of changes to the structure of the pivot table: you want to change a column field to a page field or change a page field to an outer row field or group items in some way.

These structural changes are often dictated by the focus and clarity of the pivot table: you believe you can understand the data better by viewing it from a different perspective. On other occasions you find that you must change the pivot table's layout to accommodate the formatting requirements of a report, a Web page, or a presentation.

Pivoting a Table

You *pivot* a table whenever you change the role of a field: from a page field to a row field, from a row field to a column field, from an outer row field to an inner row field, and so on. In each case, the act of pivoting the table is carried out in much the same way.

To change a column field to a row field, for example, start by placing your mouse pointer over the column field's button. Hold down the left mouse button and drag the field button down and to the left until it is in the row field area. Then release the mouse button. The result is that the field items that had each occupied a different column now occupy a different row: the column field has become a row field.

You make other, similar changes—a column field to a page field, a page field to a row field—in the same way. Just drag the button from its present area to a different one.

If you want to remove a field from the pivot table entirely, drag its button completely outside the pivot table area. When you do so, a large X will appear over the field button. Now, when you release the mouse button, the field is removed from the pivot table. The field is still available as a button on the Field List, however, so you can always drag it back into the pivot table.

Another instance of pivoting a table changes a field's status to an inner or an outer field. To make a field an inner row field, drag its button to the right of the outer row field's button. To make a field an inner column field, drag its button to the right of the outer column field's button. See Figure 13-20 for an example.

Maintaining Formats

When you pivot a table or refresh its data, it's possible to lose any special formatting that you have applied. For example, if you have specified a currency format for a data field and subsequently pivot the table or refresh its data, the data field can revert to its original format. There are three ways to prevent this:

- Ensure that the Preserve Formatting check box on the PivotTable Options dialog box is filled.

- Double-click a field's button. On the PivotTable Field dialog box, click the Number button to bring up the Format Cells dialog box. Choose a format and then click OK buttons until you return to the pivot table.

- Use a PivotTable autoformat.

Any one of these actions is sufficient to preserve the formatting you have applied to a pivot table when you pivot the table or refresh its data.

To apply an autoformat, first select a cell in the pivot table. Then do either of the following:

- Choose Format | AutoFormat.

- Click the Format Report button on the PivotTable toolbar.

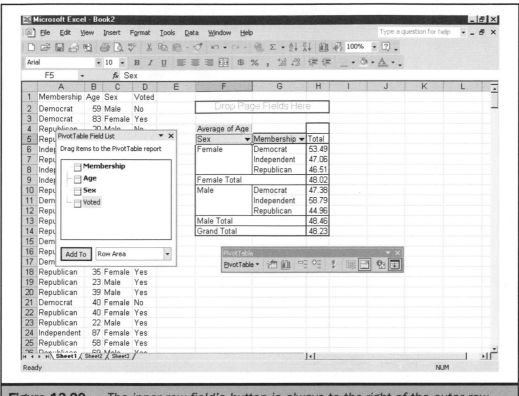

Figure 13-20. *The inner row field's button is always to the right of the outer row field's button*

You will see a dialog box with ten sample autoformats resembling reports, another ten that are tabular in appearance, a "classic" PivotTable format, and a choice labeled None that you can use to remove an existing autoformat.

Grouping Items

One of the most powerful capabilities offered by pivot tables is that of grouping items. Suppose that you have created a pivot table that displays the total rainfall during each of 12 months, where Month is the row field and Rainfall is the data field. You would like to examine the total rainfall during each of the four quarters comprised by the 12 months. By grouping the Month field into three-month chunks, you can view quarterly data.

Or you might have information about the number of newborns in a hospital and their birth weight. You would like to view the number of newborns whose birth weight is between 2000 and 2500 grams, between 2500 and 3000 grams, and so on. You can do so by grouping the birth weight field in 500-gram increments.

You can group on fields that represent dates or times and on other numeric fields. Consider the situation in Figure 13-21. There the source data is in columns A and B and reports rainfall by date. A pivot table has been created and redundantly shows rainfall by date.

To group the Date field by Month, take these steps:

1. Click on any item in the pivot table's Date field and choose Data | Group and Outline | Group. Or right-click any item in the Date field and, from the shortcut menu, choose Group and Show Detail | Group. The dialog box shown in Figure 13-22 appears.

2. You will usually want to accept the default starting and ending dates. Click Months in the By list box. If any other item in the By list box is selected, click on it to deselect it.

3. Click OK. The result appears in Figure 13-23.

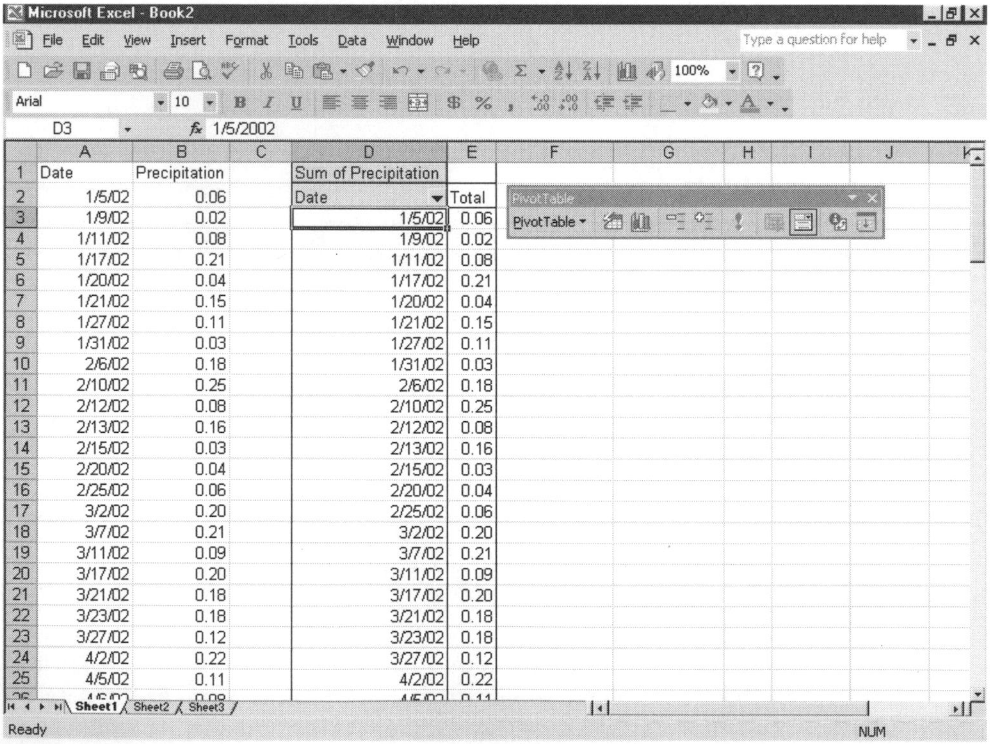

Figure 13-21. *If any source data record lacks a value on a date field, you won't be able to group on that field*

ANALYZING DATA

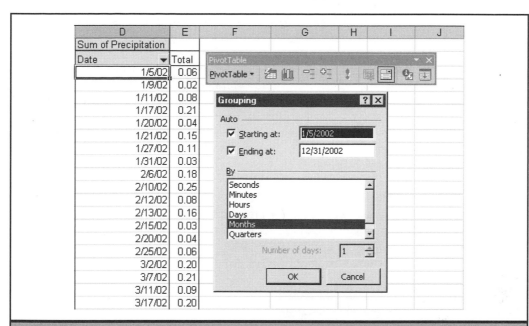

Figure 13-22. *Establish a week-long group by choosing Days in the By box and setting the Number of Days spinner to 7*

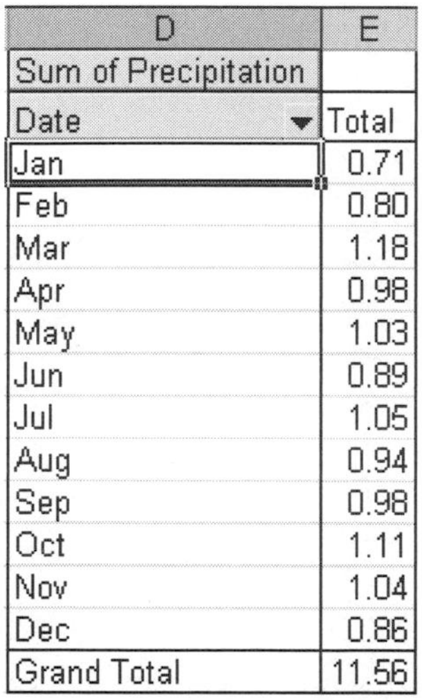

D	E
Sum of Precipitation	
Date ▼	Total
Jan	0.71
Feb	0.80
Mar	1.18
Apr	0.98
May	1.03
Jun	0.89
Jul	1.05
Aug	0.94
Sep	0.98
Oct	1.11
Nov	1.04
Dec	0.86
Grand Total	11.56

Figure 13-23. *Use a grouped field's drop-down to display or hide a group in the pivot table*

You can group on more than one time period. Perhaps your data spans several years. By clicking both Month and Years in the By list box, you could display each month of 2001, each month of 2002, and so on.

This kind of grouping that spans multiple years can require a little care. Suppose that you selected Month only. Then, the data from January in 2001 would be combined with January in 2002, February in 2001 would be combined with February in 2002, and so on. This type of grouping might or might not be what you're after.

If your data spans more than one year and you want to view months separately, according to the year in which they occur, group on months *and* years. But if you want to view months together, regardless of the year in which they occur, group on months only. You might do this if, for example, you wanted to view a seasonal or cyclical pattern in the data. (These comments apply to a quarterly grouping as well as a monthly grouping.)

If the field that you want to group on is a numeric field but does not represent dates or times, the grouping dialog box looks different (see Figure 13-24).

Suppose that you wanted to group on, say, birth weight in grams, and create categories of 500 grams each. You might accept the default Starting and Ending values and enter 500 in the By box.

To ungroup a field, just right-click on one of its items, select Group and Show Detail from the shortcut menu, and click Ungroup.

Refreshing Data and the Cache

Select a data cell in a pivot table and look at the Formula Bar. You do not see a formula, or a function such as SUM, COUNT, or AVERAGE. You see an actual value.

This means that, unlike a formula, a pivot table does not automatically update when its source data changes. To get a pivot table to change in response to a change in the source data, you must click the Refresh Data button on the PivotTable toolbar or choose Data | Refresh Data.

Count of Weight		Grouping
Weight ▼	Total	Auto
1048-1547	11	☑ Starting at: 1048
1548-2047	9	☑ Ending at: 4392
2048-2547	8	By: 500
2548-3047	4	
3048-3547	11	OK Cancel
3548-4047	4	
4048-4547	6	
Grand Total	53	

Figure 13-24.   *Grouping can be important when a row field represents a continuous variable*

When you refresh data, something is happening behind the scenes. Each pivot table depends directly on a *cache*. The cache is an invisible, inaccessible data storage area that's attached to any workbook that contains a pivot table.

The cache maintains information about the fields in the pivot table, and it is optimized to respond very quickly when you modify a table—by pivoting it, by changing summary methods or options, by hiding or displaying items, and so on. When you refresh a pivot table, you're actually refreshing the cache. The most current information in the source data is put into the cache, and in turn the pivot table that depends on the cache is updated.

There are a couple of consequences to this structure that can be of importance to you.

Clearing a Source Data Range

For a variety of reasons, such as a worksheet's visual appearance and the size of an Excel file, it can be convenient and desirable to clear a pivot table's source data range.

Because the source data has already been stored in the cache, you lose nothing by clearing the source range. Make any changes you want in the pivot table: the data is in the cache and the source range is no longer needed.

But suppose you need to refresh the cache: for example, you obtain additional data that you want to put in the pivot table. Without the original source data, you have nothing to append the new data to.

The solution is to double-click the pivot table's Grand Total cell. When you do so, a new worksheet is inserted in the workbook and the source data is written onto it. Fields occupy columns, records occupy rows, and each column is headed by the field name.

You can now add or change information in the retrieved source data and then redirect the pivot table's attention to the new data range—which might now have more rows or columns than it did originally.

In order to bring the original source data back, there are three requirements, as follows.

The Pivot Table Must Have a Grand Total Cell   If a pivot table has both row and column fields, a row field must have a Grand Total column and a column field must have a Grand Total row. Double-clicking the Grand Total cell returns all the records. If you double-click some other cell, only a subset of the records—those that belong to the cell you double-clicked—is returned. If you began by suppressing Grand Totals, use the PivotTable toolbar to get to Table Options and fill the Grand Totals check boxes.

The Enable Drill to Details Check Box on the Table Options Dialog Box Must Be Filled   Otherwise, no double-click anywhere in the pivot table will return source data, whether the entire data set or a subset.

The Save Data with Table Layout Check Box, also on the Table Options Dialog Box, Must Be Filled   Otherwise, the cache is not saved.

ANALYZING DATA

Multiple Pivot Tables, One Cache

The first step in the PivotTable Wizard asks for information on the location of the source data: Microsoft Excel list or database, multiple consolidation ranges, external data source, or another pivot table.

When you choose Another Pivot Table, you are in effect saying that the new pivot table will use the same cache as an existing one.

So doing saves some file storage space, but at a time when local hard disks are routinely multigigabyte in stature, this is not a major consideration.

More important is the refresh time. Suppose that you have a variety of pivot tables that all depend on the same external database. Each pivot table provides a different view of the information in the database.

If each pivot table has its own cache, you must update each cache when the external database changes. This means that each cache must reexecute the database query with which it's associated, possibly bring data back across the network, store it in the cache, and then update the pivot table accordingly. And this must happen for each pivot table every time you open the workbook if you choose Refresh on Open.

But suppose that you base only one pivot table on the external source and all the others on this first, primary pivot table. Then the refresh, including the query execution, the data communication, and updating the cache, needs to occur once only. All the "subsidiary" pivot tables look to that one cache for their data. It still takes a little time to update the remaining pivot tables, but you've saved a lot of time by not having to update the putative individual caches.

Pivot Charts

Pivot charts represent the marriage of charts to pivot tables. Pivot charts give you nearly all the power of displaying data on an Excel chart, plus the convenience and flexibility of the pivot table report. By choosing a pivot chart instead of a traditional chart, you lose very little:

- The ability to create XY (Scatter) charts, Bubble charts, and Stock charts. But you can create these by using the Chart Wizard in the traditional way, with a pivot table as the data source.
- The ability to manually move chart objects such as titles and legends. But you can move a legend by specifying a different placement: Choose Chart | Chart Options | Legend.

Figure 13-25 shows a pivot chart.

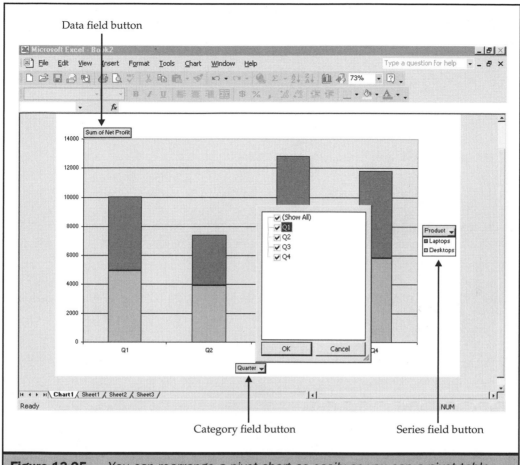

Data field button

Figure 13-25. *You can rearrange a pivot chart as easily as you can a pivot table*

Category field button   Series field button

The pivot chart has a button for the Category axis and for the Value axis. It is shown with the Category axis button's drop-down arrow clicked to display the items in the Category axis. You can hide an item on the chart by clearing its check box, or display it on the chart by filling its check box.

Tip *Many of the procedures described in this section require that the field buttons be visible on the pivot chart. After the pivot chart is complete, however, you might want to suppress the buttons. To do so, click the PivotChart drop-down arrow on the toolbar and click the Hide PivotChart Field Buttons menu item. So doing also hides boxes that say Drop Page Fields Here and Drop Series Fields Here. You can display the buttons again by repeating the process.*

You create a pivot chart by choosing PivotChart (with PivotTable) on Step 1 of the PivotTable Wizard. All proceeds as usual with the wizard until you click Finish. Then you see a new chart sheet, the PivotTable Field List box and the PivotTable toolbar (see Figure 13-26).

At this point, you can drag buttons from the Field List onto the chart into one of four areas:

- **Drop Category Fields Here** Dropping a field into this box defines that field as the Category axis variable.

- **Drop Page Fields Here** Dropping a field into this box defines a page field. Use the page field to filter the data on the chart—your choice of page field item restricts the chart to data belonging to that item. You can, of course, choose All to chart all the data.

- **Drop Data Items Here** This is where you place one or more variables that are charted against the Value axis. After you have placed a data item, a Data Item button appears just above the plot area.

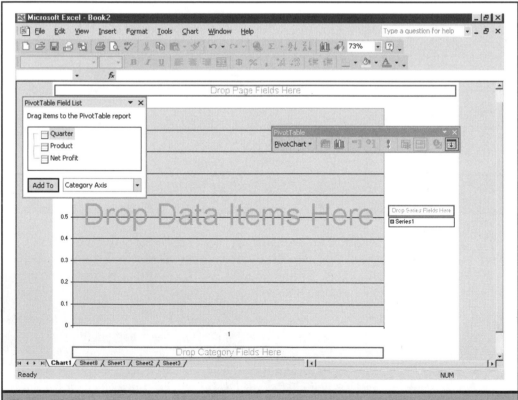

Figure 13-26. *Notice that the Chart menu appears along with the new chart sheet*

■ **Drop Series Fields Here**   Dropping a button from the Field List into the Series Field area has these effects: it divides the data items into series that represent the series field's items, it adds a legend so that you can interpret the series' color coding, and it establishes the button on the chart so that you can later make it a page field or an additional category field.

That phrase *additional category field* highlights a capability of pivot charts that's not available in traditional Excel charts. Compare Figure 13-27 with Figure 13-25.

In Figure 13-25, Quarter was the variable on the chart's Category axis, and Product was used as a series field. In Figure 13-27, Product has joined Quarter on the Category axis: it was dragged from the series field area to the Category axis area. Notice that the arrangement of items on the Category axis resembles the arrangement of items on a pivot table: each item of the Product field is associated with each item of the Quarter field.

This enables you to disaggregate the data field according to each combination of field items. The only way that you could manage this with a traditional chart would be to create a new category variable to represent the combination of items in the existing fields.

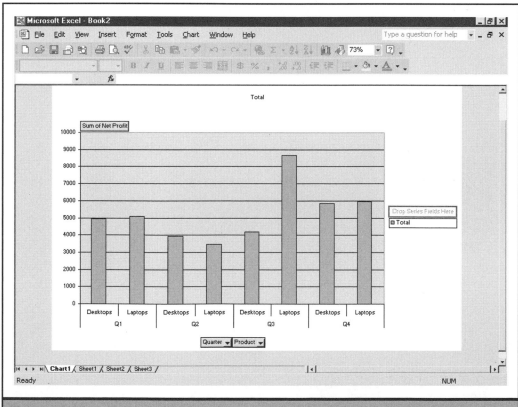

Figure 13-27.   *The combined Category axis changes the stacked column to a simple column*

ANALYZING DATA

Chapter 14

Goal Seek and Solver: Reaching Solutions with Brute Force

Sometimes you already know the answer that you're looking for. Then, it's not the answer that's interesting: you already have that. What's interesting is the set of values that gets you to the answer.

Perhaps you recall taking your first algebra class back in elementary or junior high school. The teacher put up an equation such as this:

$$y = 3x$$

and asked you that if y was 12, what was x?

If this was your second week in algebra class, you probably rearranged the equation like this:

$$x = y / 3$$

Then you replaced y with 12 and reported that x was 4.

If this was just your first day in algebra class, you might have tried substituting different values for x until you found one that satisfied the teacher's condition that y equals 12.

Welcome back to algebra class. This time, though, you're the teacher and Excel's the student. The problem is that while Excel is very fast and very accurate, it's not creative. It can't see that the most straightforward way to find x is to rearrange the equation. It does see that it can substitute different values for x until it satisfies your requirement that y equal 12.

There are many problems that relate several x quantities to a single y quantity by means of an equation. Some of those equations get pretty complicated, and rearranging them to solve for an unknown—such as x in the first equation in the chapter—can take a while.

If you turn Excel loose on the problem, it can try tens of thousands of possible values in the equation, and probably solve it, before you finish writing it down. That's what the chapter title means by *brute force*. All the intelligence resides in how you set the problem for Excel. The rest is just Do loops. Okay, sophisticated Do loops.

The brute force comes in two guises: Goal Seek and Solver.

Using Goal Seek

Goal Seek is a single-cell problem solver, which means you must know (and fill in) information about every aspect of the problem except one cell. Goal Seek will fill in that single cell for you.

Defining the Problem

Suppose that you want to buy a new car. You've gone to one of the fixed-price dealerships and picked out the one you want. It lists for $29,000. The dealer is offering you a five-year loan with an annual percentage rate of 9.6 percent, which works out to 0.8 percent each month.

You tell the salesperson that you don't want the undercoat, and he says he has to talk to his manager. Having gotten him out of the room, you fire up Excel on your laptop and enter the information shown in Figure 14-1.

The figures in cells A2:D2 of Figure 14-1 are fixed: it's a fixed price for the car, both the annual and the resulting monthly percentage rates are fixed, and the 60-month term of the loan is fixed. Given those constants, you enter this formula in cell E2 to determine your monthly payment:

=PMT(C2,D2,A2)

If you haven't already, meet the PMT function. It determines the loan payment that you must make in each period, given the periodic rate (here, that's in cell C2), the number of payments (in D2) and the amount of the loan (in A2).

Note *PMT is a member of a family of Excel financial functions that include RATE (the interest rate), NPER (number of periods), and PV (present value, or principal). These functions, and the values they return, are interdependent: change the loan rate, hold other things equal, and the payment changes. Change the present value, hold other things equal, and the rate changes. Because of the way they're defined, at least one value must be negative. It's conventional to let that be the payment.*

You decide that you don't want to spend $610 per month for five years. Because of your current bank balance and of how you're projecting your future monthly budgets, you'd like to keep the monthly payment right at $400.

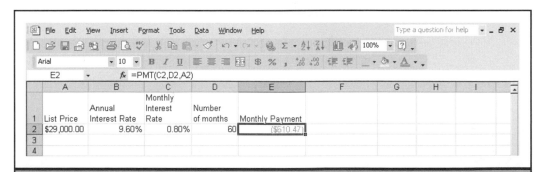

Figure 14-1. *When you're using a financial function, make sure to base the interest rate on the same schedule as the payments*

You're not in a position to change the interest rate or the number of payments, but you could change the principal amount of the loan by making a sizable down payment. You begin by plugging in new values for the principal in cell A2: you try $28,000, then $27,000—these result in monthly payments that are still too high.

Then you remember that you read this chapter, and you turn it over to Goal Seek. You take these steps:

1. You select columns B and C by dragging with your mouse pointer across their column headers, and choose Insert | Columns. This gives you two new columns to work with.

2. In cell B1 you enter **Down Payment**, and in cell B2 you enter **$1,000**. This is just a starting point—you already know you'll have to put more than that down.

3. In cell C2 you enter this formula:

    =A2 – B2

    That gives you the amount of the loan, after you subtract your down payment from the list price.

4. Because you inserted two new columns, the formula that was in E2 is now in G2. Instead of using the list price in A2, you now want it to use the balance after making a down payment. That's in C2, so you change G2 from:

    =PMT(E2,F2,A2)

    to:

    =PMT(E2,F2,C2)

5. Now you invoke Goal Seek. You select cell G2, which contains the monthly payment. Then you choose Tools | Goal Seek. The dialog box shown here appears.

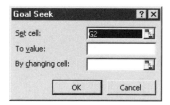

Because you began by selecting G2, Goal Seek makes that the Set Cell by default. The Set Cell box contains the address of the *cell* that you want to *set* to a target value—in this case, that's the $400 you want for your monthly payment. It is often termed the *target cell*.

6. In the To Value box, enter –400. (Recall that it's conventional to make the payment part of financial functions a negative number.)

7. Click in the By Changing Cell box to activate it. Then click in worksheet cell B2. This is the cell that Goal Seek will change as it seeks your goal of a $400 monthly payment. It is often termed the *changing cell*.

What you are asking Goal Seek, in words, is "How large a down payment must I make in order to reduce the loan principal so that my monthly payment is $400?" Goal Seek answers the question, as shown here:

	A	B	C	D	E	F	G	H	I	J	K
1	List Price	Down Payment	Principal	Annual Interest Rate	Monthly Interest Rate	Number of months	Monthly Payment				
2	$29,000.00	$9,998.31	$19,001.69	9.60%	0.80%	60	($400.00)				
3											
4											

G2 = =PMT(E2,F2,C2)

Goal Seek quickly puts the value $9,998.31 in cell B2. By making that large a down payment, you reduce the principal from $29,000 to $19,001.69. And with that as a loan amount, and 0.8 percent as the monthly rate for 60 months, your monthly payment is $400.

When to Use Goal Seek

You can use Goal Seek for something really trivial, if you want. Suppose A1 contains the value 10, and A2 contains the formula =A1–5. You could use Goal Seek to find a value for A1 such that the result of the formula in A2 is 7. But so doing is overkill and a waste of time. Use Goal Seek when you don't see a simple, straightforward way to get a formula to return a specific value.

There's another way to solve the car purchase example given earlier in this chapter. Initially, you were looking for a loan amount that would satisfy the constraints of the interest rate, number of payments, and size of payment. The PV function (the letters stand for Present Value) would return that. In effect, Excel's developers have taken this formula:

$$PV*(1 + RATE) \wedge NPER + PMT * (1 + RATE * Type) * ([1 + RATE]^{\wedge}NPER - 1)/RATE + FV = 0$$

and rearranged it several times: once to define the function PV(), once to define RATE(), once to define PMT(), and so on. (*Type* refers to whether the payment is made at the beginning or at the end of the period, and *FV* refers to the future value or cash balance.) If you're paying off a loan, the future value is zero. If you're saving toward a purchase, the future value is what the purchase will be worth when you're ready to acquire it.

So, you could have used the PV() function to return the amount of the loan, and then subtracted that from the list price of the car to arrive at the amount of your down payment. It's your call whether that's the easier way, or that it's easier to get the down payment with a formula, as in the preceding example, and let Goal Seek solve for it.

Here are a few things to keep in mind when you consider using Goal Seek:

Put a Formula in the Target Cell   Your target cell—the one whose address you provide in Goal Seek's Set Cell box—must contain a formula. Otherwise, it cannot respond to changes in the cell that you specify in the By Changing Cell box. And if it can't respond to changes, it can't reach your target value.

Put a Value in the Changing cell   The cell you specify in the By Changing Cell box must contain either a value or nothing at all. If it contains a formula, Goal Seek will complain that it must contain a value, so first select the cell and then choose Edit | Clear | Contents. Goal Seek substitutes trial values in the changing cell, and if you start with a formula in that cell then it would be overwritten. Goal Seek won't do that.

Point the Target Cell at the Changing Cell   Your target cell must depend, at least indirectly, on your changing cell. In the present example, the target cell G2 represents your monthly payment. It depends directly on the monthly interest rate in E2; the number of payments in F2; and the present value, or loan amount, in C2. In turn, the loan amount depends on the list price in A2 and the down payment in B2. So, in this case, the target cell G2 depends indirectly on the changing cell B2, by way of C2.

Using a Different Changing Cell

Suppose that you didn't have $10,000 available as a down payment. Your next realistic option might be to look into a loan with a longer term. (The longer the term, the more risk that the lender incurs, so you might have to accept a higher interest rate. For the present, though, assume that the interest remains at a 9.6 percent annual percentage rate.)

All you need to do is select a new changing cell:

1. Click in G2, to make it the default target cell. Make sure that it contains the formula =PMT(E2, F2, C2). Also make sure that B2 contains $0, so that C2 contains $29,000.

2. Choose Tools | Goal Seek. Notice that G2 is by default the target cell.

3. If necessary, enter –400 in the To Value box. Goal Seek will set the monthly payment to that value.

4. Instead of using B2, the down payment, as the changing cell, use F2, the number of payments. Click in the By Changing Cell box and then click cell F2.

5. Click OK.

	A	B	C	D	E	F	G	H	I	J	K	
				Annual Interest	Monthly Interest	Number	Monthly					
1	List Price	Down Payment	Principal	Rate	Rate	of months	Payment					
2	$29,000.00	$0.00	$29,000.00	9.60%	0.80%	108.8707	($400.00)					
3												
4												

G2 = PMT(E2,F2,C2)

This time, Goal Seek informs you that if you pay $400 per month for 108.87 months, you can make a $29,000 purchase at a 9.6 percent annual percentage rate. Maybe you should get the undercoat.

Troubleshooting Goal Seek Failures

Sometimes Excel reports that it cannot find a solution to your Goal Seek problem. Frequently this means you made an error in data entry in the Goal Seek dialog box, or there's a problem with one or more cells. Here are some things to check:

■ Make sure your formula cell really is dependent on the changing cell. The Formula Auditing toolbar is handy for this purpose.

■ Choose Tools | Options and click the Calculation tab. Make sure that you *don't* have Precision As Displayed checked.

Sometimes Excel reports that it can't arrive at a solution. That's because the number of tries is limited by a maximum number of iterations. There are two solutions you can try for this:

■ Change the current value in the changing cell to a number you think is closer to the solution, and try the Goal Seek command again.

■ Change the Maximum Iterations setting for your Excel software. This value is stored in the Calculation panel of the Options dialog box, and the default value is 100 iterations.

The Goal Seek command actually uses guesses, albeit intelligent ones. It starts with a random guess about the value of the changing cell (the cell in the By Changing Cell field of the dialog box) and calculates the formula to see the result on the *target* (the number you entered in the To Value field). Subsequent guesses alternate on the positive or negative side, and Excel notices which guesses bring it closer to the target.

With that information available, future guesses head in the same direction. The process continues, so the changing cell is changed constantly until the formula's results converge on the target value. If the maximum number of iterations is reached before the solution, an error message appears. The reason it can be helpful to put an "educated guess value" in the changing cell before starting is so Excel doesn't have to start all the way out in left field.

Using Solver

As useful as Goal Seek is, there may be times when the limitations of the feature get in your way. Goal Seek solves for just one cell and allows you to specify only one changing cell. For those times when you need more power, Excel offers *Solver*, which differs from Goal Seek in a variety of ways. Among them:

- You can specify more than one changing cell.
- You can impose limits on the values the changing cells can take on.
- Solver can arrive at multiple solutions.

Installing Solver

Solver is an add-in supplied with Office, and if you didn't install it when you first set up Office, you have to install it. To do so, start the Office Setup program and expand the Microsoft Excel options section. Expand the Add-ins section, select Solver and choose either Run from My Computer or Installed on First Use.

After you install the Solver files, you still won't find Solver on the Tools menu. Add-ins work differently from other Excel features: you must first install them on your computer using Setup, and then you must make them available to Excel using Tools | Add-Ins.

Choose Tools | Add-Ins to open the Add-Ins dialog box. Scroll to the Solver Add-in listing and select it, placing a check mark in the check box. This puts the Solver command on the Tool menu. Solver is loaded each time you start Excel until you uncheck Solver in the Add-Ins dialog box.

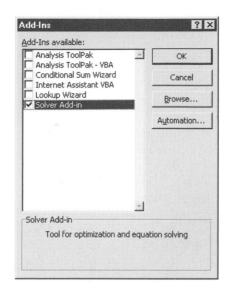

ANALYZING DATA

Setting Up the Worksheet for Solver

You use Solver to find values for variables in a model you establish on a worksheet. These values must take into account any constraints that you establish. The model worksheet you use for Solver contains input values. It also contains formulas, which depend on the input values or on other formulas.

The input values are found in cells, of course, and these cells are directly analogous to the changing cell used in Goal Seek. The most obvious difference is that you can direct Solver to modify the values in several changing cells, whereas Goal Seek is limited to changing one cell only.

There are several types of information you need to identify for Solver:

- **Fixed Input Values**   These are values that are fixed numbers that you've associated with the problem you're solving. They usually represent constraints on the solution. For example, you might need to tell Solver that it may not reach a target figure for Profit by lowering Costs below some minimum value.

- **Changing Cells**   These are the values that Solver changes while calculating the target cell.

- **Target Cell**   This is the cell that holds the value Solver returns. It must contain a formula, and the formula must depend on the changing cells. Otherwise, the value returned by the formula would never change and Solver wouldn't be able to reach a solution.

Creating a Plan for Solver

It's important to understand what you want to know, and even know why you want to know it, before creating your Solver worksheet. This makes it easier to design the worksheet properly.

It's probably easier to translate all the information about cell data into real numbers with an example. So let's build one.

A candidate is running for the United States Congress. The district he wants to represent covers six counties. He raised about $400,000 from supporters, and his campaign manager has put together a budget worksheet, which you can examine in Figure 14-2.

The worksheet helps to allocate advertising costs to each county in the congressional district. So that you have a complete understanding of this worksheet, here are the numbers and formulas it contains:

- **Column A** The list of counties.
- **Column B** The amount of money the campaign expects to spend for each campaign advertisement in each county.
- **Column C** The number of voters in each county.
- **Column D** The number of campaign advertisements to run in each county. These will be the changing cells.
- **Column E** The total advertising expense for the county. This is the product of columns B and D, the expense per ad times the number of ads. Therefore, the formula in cell E6 is =B6 * D6.

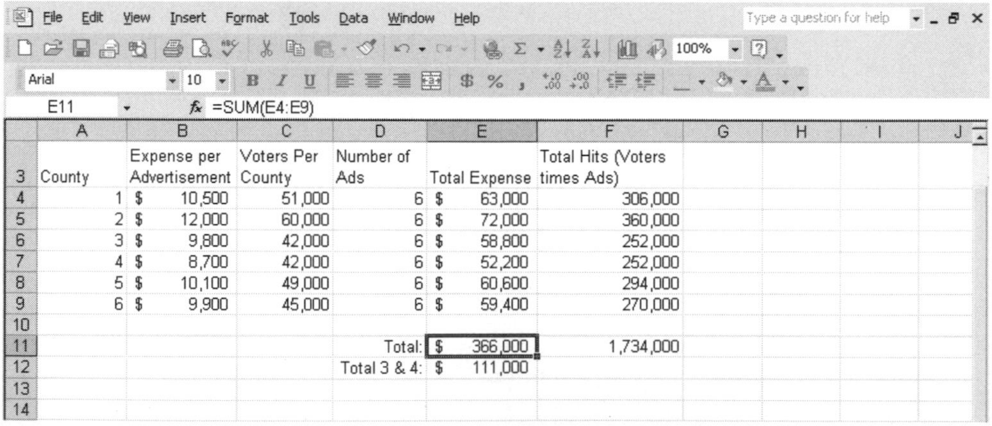

E11 =SUM(E4:E9)

	A	B	C	D	E	F
3	County	Expense per Advertisement	Voters Per County	Number of Ads	Total Expense	Total Hits (Voters times Ads)
4	1	$ 10,500	51,000	6	$ 63,000	306,000
5	2	$ 12,000	60,000	6	$ 72,000	360,000
6	3	$ 9,800	42,000	6	$ 58,800	252,000
7	4	$ 8,700	42,000	6	$ 52,200	252,000
8	5	$ 10,100	49,000	6	$ 60,600	294,000
9	6	$ 9,900	45,000	6	$ 59,400	270,000
10						
11				Total:	$ 366,000	1,734,000
12				Total 3 & 4:	$ 111,000	
13						
14						

Figure 14-2. *The campaign plans its advertising budget*

■ **Column F** The maximum number of hits that can be made in each county with its advertising budget. The maximum number of hits is the product of the number of voters per county times the number of advertisements run. So the formula in cell F6 is =C6 * D6.

■ **Cell E11** The sum of the numbers in column E: the total advertising dollars across counties.

■ **Cell F11** The sum of the numbers in column F: the total number of contacts across counties.

There is an assumption implicit in the formulas in Column F: that an ad won't reach voters outside the county's boundaries. Violating the assumption probably doesn't do much harm, though: an underestimate for a given county is probably balanced by a compensating overestimate in a neighboring county.

After the press conference announcing the opening of the campaign, checks from some political action committees arrived at campaign headquarters. With $1,000,000 at his disposal, the candidate told the campaign manager to redo the budget, arranging new ads and spreading the money equally around the counties.

The campaign manager demurred, explaining there were some political realities to consider. Here are those political realities—those who use Solver call them *constraints*.

■ The voters in County 3 and County 4 are party loyalists and would vote for Mickey Mouse as long as he ran on the party's ticket. Therefore, you can limit the number of advertisements in those counties: just show enough ads to get the vote out. This limit will constrain the changing cells D6 and D7, indirectly by way of cells E6 and E7.

■ Each county needs at least six advertisements, if only because six have already been bought in each county. It would be unwise to cancel any of them: financially, because the campaign would lose the benefit of expenses already incurred, and politically, because the county's residents would think the campaign was taking them for granted. The lower limit of six ads per county also constrains the changing cells.

■ The campaign cannot run a partial advertisement. The number of ads in each county must be an integer: the campaign can run 10 ads in a county, but not 10.368. The requirement that the number of ads be an integer is a constraint on the changing cells.

■ The total advertising expense across all six counties may be no more than $1,000,000. This is a constraint that does *not* operate directly on the changing cells. It operates on a formula that depends indirectly on the changing cells' values. In words, the constraint says that you cannot show so many ads that their total cost exceeds $1,000,000.

■ The budget must have a goal of at least four million hits. This is another constraint that operates only indirectly on the changing cells.

Building a Solver-Ready Worksheet

The campaign manager built a worksheet that is designed for using Solver. You can view it in Figure 14-3.

Here are the additional values and formulas the campaign manager entered to get ready for Solver:

- **Cell F18** The number of hits that the campaign wants to reach—the goal.

- **Cell E12** The formula =SUM(E6,E7), the total expenses for Counties 3 and 4, where the party loyalists are found. It's there for two reasons: to show the current total for these counties, and to check that Solver used the constraint properly.

- **Cell F15** The amount of money available.

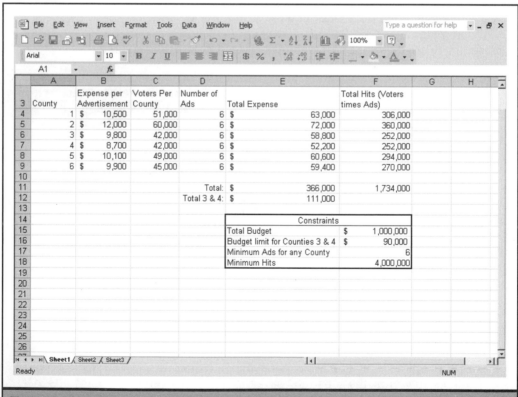

Figure 14-3. *The rebuilt worksheet, ready for Solver*

■ **Cell F16**   The amount of money the campaign is willing to spend for Counties 3 and 4.

■ **Cell F17**   The minimum number of ads for each county.

Using the Solver Parameters Dialog Box

In effect, the campaign manager is asking Solver, "What will it take to reach four million hits, given the constraints I've imposed?"

Now it's time to use Solver. You can follow along. Choose Tools | Solver from the menu bar to open the Solver Parameters dialog box.

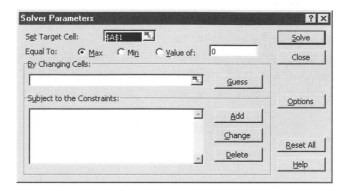

Note   *Solver opens assuming the target cell is the selected cell. In this case, the selected cell happened to be the first cell in the worksheet, but you can click the target cell before opening Solver to make the right selection automatic.*

Enter the Target Information

The target, or goal, of this Solver exercise is to see how much money we need to spend ("what does it take to get the job done?"). In this worksheet, that's cell E11 (the total of the per-county advertising budget). Remember that in the definitions listed earlier in this chapter you learned that the target cell must contain a formula, and this cell has the formula =SUM(E4:E9).

In this case, Solver is asked to calculate a maximum amount (remember, there will be a constraint on the maximum because we know how much money is actually available).

The reason Solver is asked to return a maximum is that we want to spend as much of the available money as we can (the law says that candidates for federal offices can't pocket any leftover money after election day, so they might as well spend it all to try to win). For your own Solver exercises, you may ask for a minimum amount (especially if you're trying to reduce costs) or for an exact amount.

Enter the Changing Cells

The changing cells for this Solver exercise contain the number of advertisements per county that the campaign can afford, given the new budget amount. Because we know the number of voters in each county, the number of advertisements gives us a new estimate of hits, or times that voters see an advertisement. Therefore, the entry in the By Changing Cells box is D4:D9.

You can enter the cell range manually in the By Changing Cells box, or select cells by dragging your mouse pointer through the range. If you are entering individual cell addresses manually, use a comma between each cell address. Whether you enter the addresses manually or by dragging with the mouse pointer, Solver converts them to absolute references.

Sometimes it's handy to click the Guess button to let Solver decide which cells should change. Cells that are "guessed" cannot contain formulas.

Enter the Constraints

Now you must tell Solver of any limitations, or constraints, you're imposing on the calculations. In this case, we have several constraints to enter. Click Add to begin adding the constraints in the Add Constraint dialog box.

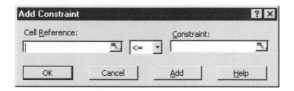

Enter the Cell Reference, the operator, and Constraint for each constraint. Continue to click Add until all the constraints have been entered. Then click OK.

Here are the constraints we're entering for this Solver exercise:

- **$D$4: $D$9 >= $F$17** The number of advertisements run in each county must be greater than or equal to the value of cell F17. Cell F17 (currently containing the value 6) is the minimum number of advertisements that must run in a county.

- **$D$4: $D$9 = integer** The campaign cannot run fractional advertisements. To constrain the values that Solver tries in changing cells D4:D9 to integers, enter D4:D9 as the cell reference, then choose "int" as the constraint's operator, and click Add.

- **$E$6: $E$7 <= $F$16** Neither County 3 nor County 4 may spend more than the amount in cell F16 (which currently has a value of $90,000).

- **$E$11 <= $F$15** The new total budget amount (the target cell, E11) must be less than or equal to the amount in cell F15 (which currently has a value of $1,000,000). The campaign is not allowed to budget more than this amount for advertising. Solver should arrive at a number that's close to, but less than, the amount in cell F15. The reason is that we've called for Solver to maximize the value in E11, given the current constraint that it be less than or equal to the value in F15.

■ **$F$11 >= $F$18**   The total number of hits in cell F11 (currently holding the formula **=SUM(F4:F9)**, which is the maximum number of voters reached) must be at least the value in cell F18 (currently holding the value 4,000,000).

After entering the last constraint, click OK. The Solver Parameters dialog box lists all your parameters.

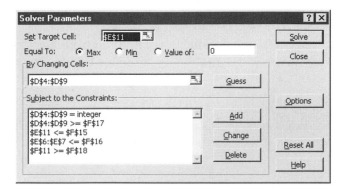

Note   *If you enter your final constraint and click Add, Solver expects you to provide at least one more constraint. This is awkward if you're through entering constraints, because Solver complains if you click OK when the Cell Reference box or the Constraint box is empty. If this happens, just click the Close button—the × box in the upper right corner of the Add Constraint dialog box—to close the dialog box and return to the Solver.*

You can select any constraint and click Change or Delete to fix any mistakes. When everything looks right, click Solve.

Viewing the Results

While staying within your constraint, Solver tries new values in the changing cells (and updates any formulas that reference the changing cells). This can take some time. When the calculations are complete, Solver displays the Solver Results dialog box.

Drag the Solver Results dialog box out of the way to look at the new totals (Solver recalculates the worksheet with its solution). Figure 14-4 shows the new totals for this sample Solver exercise.

If Solver found a solution you can use, click OK. If you don't like the solution and you want to make changes in the way you set up the problem, select Restore Original Values and then click OK.

Saving the Solver Parameters

Solver automatically saves the entries you made in the Solver Parameters dialog box when you save your workbook. The next time you use the Solver command with the same worksheet active, the dialog box displays the parameters you entered for the Solver.

If you want to use totally different Solver parameters on a worksheet, copy the original worksheet to another sheet so you have a way to attach a different Solver setup to the new worksheet.

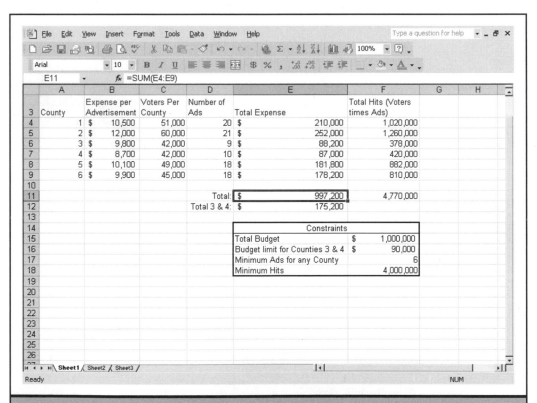

Figure 14-4. *Solver created a budget that spends nearly all the money and complies with all the constraints*

ANALYZING DATA

Saving Solver Parameters as a Scenario

You can save the values of the changing cells from a successful Solver operation as a scenario, which gives you an opportunity to play what-if games in the future. Click the Save Scenario button to open the Save Scenario dialog box and enter a name for the scenario. (You can learn about using scenarios in Chapter 7.)

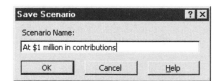

Saving Solver Parameters as a Model

If you want more than one set of Solver parameters saved to a single worksheet, you need to configure Solver to do that. Open Solver, and in the Solver Parameters dialog box click on the Options button to open the Solver Options dialog box. Then click the Save Model button to display the Save Model dialog box.

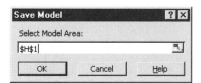

You can specify either a single cell or a range in the Select Model Area box. The location you name is where Excel stores the Solver parameters for this exercise. Here are the guidelines to use when you enter the information:

- If you specify a cell, Solver pastes the information by starting in that cell and using as many cells beneath that cell as it needs. Therefore, be sure you choose a cell that has empty cells below (in fact, it's best to choose a blank column).

- If you specify a range, Solver pastes the information into the cells in that range, but if there are more parameters than cells in the range, some of the parameters won't be saved.

After you click OK to save the model, you can use it again by opening Solver and clicking the Load Model button. Solver shows you a list of ranges containing your saved models. Herein lies a potential problem, of course. It's going to be hard to remember which range has which model. After you save your model, select the range that Solver used to store the parameters and name the range. Then, when you open the Load Model dialog box, you see a list of names. If you name each saved model's range in a way that reminds you of the Solver exercise, loading saved models is much easier.

Using Solver Reports

The Solver Results dialog box displays a list of reports, and you can choose one to view details about the exercise. Each report you select is placed on a separate worksheet.

After you select whether or not to keep the solution or return to the original values, select a report. You can select multiple reports by holding down the CTRL key as you click the name of each report you want. Then click OK.

- **Answer Report**   Lists the target cell and displays both the original and changed values of the adjustable cells. Information about the constraints that were applied against those cells is also available.

- **Sensitivity Report**   Provides information about the sensitivity level of the target cell to changes in your constraints.

- **Limits Report**   Displays the values, upper and lower limits, and target values of the target and adjustable cells. The limits are the values (lowest and highest) the cell can accept and still satisfy the terms of your constraints.

Handling Solver Failures

Occasionally, Solver reports that it couldn't find a solution. The dialog box that imparts this information qualifies the failure with a message; here are the common ones:

- **Solver Could Not Find A Feasible Solution**   Usually this message means there's been a problem meeting all your constraints. You should look at the settings because you might find that you used *equal* instead of *greater than or equal to*, or that you entered conflicting constraints, such as *greater than 6* and *less than 5*.

- **The Maximum Iteration Limit Was Reached, Continue Anyway?**   This message indicates that Solver is pausing to let you know that it has performed the maximum number of iterations without reaching a solution. Click Continue to keep going, using more than the maximum number of iterations configured for Excel. Solver continues until it finds a solution or runs up against the Maximum Time Limit (see the next item). You can change the Maximum Iteration number by opening Solver and clicking the Options button. Then change the Iterations specification.

- **The Maximum Time Limit Was Reached, Continue Anyway?**   This is like the previous message, except the Maximum Time Limit was reached. Open the Solver Options dialog box and change the Max Time specification.

Tip   *If you get a lot of messages about reaching maximum iteration or time limits, change the way you design your worksheets for Solver. You might want to alter the initial values in the changing cells so they're closer to the place you think Solver will land.*

The
Complete
Reference

Excel
2002

Part III

The Outside World

The
Complete
Reference

Excel
2002

Chapter 15

Acquiring Data

There are many ways to enter data into an Excel worksheet. You can type numbers and words into specific cells. You can use data forms to add and edit data in lists. You can construct VBA code that collects data from the user by way of a custom dialog box.

Useful as these devices are, you didn't learn Excel for the opportunity to enter data. Almost surely your purpose was to analyze data, to look for relationships, and to summarize the data in meaningful ways. From that perspective, data entry is no more than a necessary obstacle in the route to understanding a data set.

Fortunately, there are means of acquiring data from existing sources and placing it in Excel worksheets. These techniques are largely automated—they get some instructions from the user as to where the data is located, whether to return all the data or just some of it to Excel, whether to sort the data on some field, and so on. Once the user has made these decisions, the data is copied from the external data source and into the Excel worksheet, ready for analysis, synthesis, charting, and so on.

In this chapter you'll learn the techniques of returning external data directly to an Excel worksheet, how to use Microsoft Query, and how to control the way that data is refreshed.

Returning Data to the Worksheet

Suppose that you have a Microsoft Access database that contains a daily hospital census. Each record contains the following information:

- The date
- The shift: day, evening, or night
- The care unit: intensive care, oncology, orthopedics, and so on
- The number of patients at different levels of acuity (acuity is a measure of the degree of attention a patient requires).

You have anecdotal evidence that acuity has been increasing in recent months: that is, more patients seem to be requiring more concentrated care from the hospital staff. To see whether the anecdotal information is supported by empirical evidence from the database, you want to bring the data into an Excel workbook. That way, you can take advantage of Excel's analysis tools: statistical functions such as AVERAGE and LINEST and charts that help you visualize change over time.

A pivot table or pivot chart (see Chapter 13) might be the way to go. Excel makes it possible to retrieve external data such as this directly into a pivot table, but it's best to reserve that approach until you're more familiar with the nature of the information. As yet, for example, you have no idea whether you would want a pivot table to summarize by week, month, or quarter.

You decide, therefore, to bring the Access data into an Excel worksheet and defer the question of analysis method until later. In general it's a good plan to learn something about the data before you start outlining an analysis.

The process of bringing the data into the worksheet consists of two general steps: specifying the type and location of the data source, and specifying the query that actually returns records from the data source. If you follow the steps described in the next sections, you will actually be using Microsoft Query to obtain the external data. Microsoft Query is a program that accompanies Microsoft Office, and Excel starts Microsoft Query on your behalf when you import external data.

Specifying the Data Source

With a blank worksheet active, you choose Data | Import External Data and click New Database Query on the submenu. The Choose Data Source dialog box shown in Figure 15-1 appears.

Note   *Chapter 13 deferred a discussion of basing a pivot table on external data until this chapter. If you start the PivotTable Wizard and opt to base the table on an external data source, Step 2 appears with a Get Data button. Clicking that button displays the Choose Data Source dialog box shown in Figure 15-1, and you proceed exactly as described here.*

Note   *If, when you choose New Database Query, you see an error message that Microsoft Query is not available, you will need to run Office Setup again and specify that you want to install Microsoft Query. It is found in the Office Tools component.*

Because you are making a connection between Excel and this particular Access database for the first time, you select <New Data Source> on the Databases tab. When you click OK, the Create New Data Source dialog box appears (see Figure 15-2).

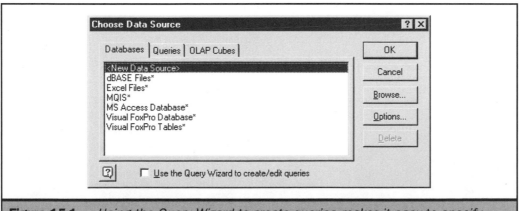

Figure 15-1.   *Using the Query Wizard to create queries makes it easy to specify data filters and sorts*

THE OUTSIDE WORLD

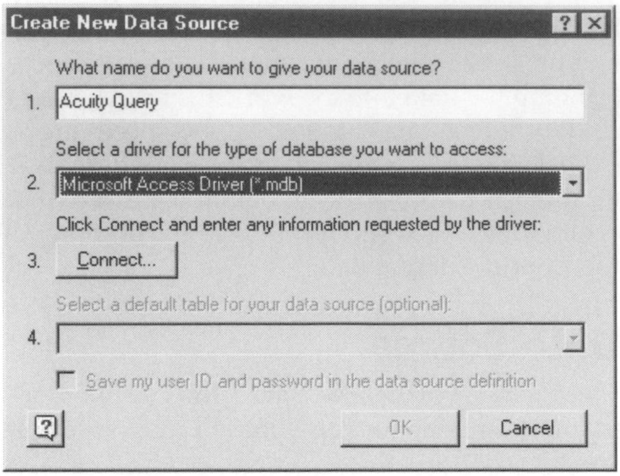

Figure 15-2. *The Driver drop-down is enabled after you enter a data source name*

The reason to provide a name for the data source is that you often want to obtain data from it repeatedly—for example, after new information has been added to it. By naming the data source, you can distinguish it from other data sources that you might create. Name it by typing a short phrase in the first text box shown in Figure 15-2. This example names the data source *Acuity Query*.

After naming the data source, select a database driver from the drop-down. You can select among Access, Dbase, FoxPro, and SQL Server databases; text files; and other Excel workbooks. In this case, the information you want is stored in an Access database, so you select that driver option from the drop-down. The drop-down denotes the driver as Microsoft Access Driver (*.mdb).

You then click the Connect button, to navigate to the location of the database. The ODBC Microsoft Access Setup dialog box appears, as shown in Figure 15-3. When you click the Select button on the ODBC Microsoft Access Setup dialog box, the Select Database dialog box appears (also see Figure 15-3).

When you click a folder in the Directories list box, files in that folder with the required extension appear in the Database Name list box. Access database files have the extension *mdb*. This example uses an Access database named *Acuity Staffing.mdb*.

When you have found the database, click on its name in the Database Name list box. Then click OK on the Select Database dialog box and then on the ODBC Microsoft Access Setup dialog box. You are returned to the Create New Data Source dialog box (refer to Figure 15-2).

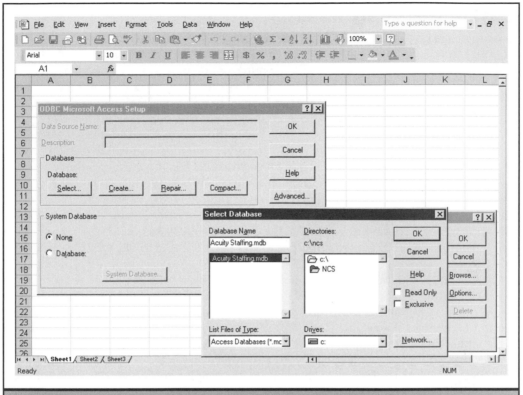

Figure 15-3. *The Select Database dialog box enables you to browse to the folder that contains the database you want to query*

You decide not to identify a default table for the data source, and also not to save your user ID and password in the data source definition. The Data Source Options section, later in this chapter, discusses the rationale for these decisions.

After you click OK, you are returned to the Choose Data Source dialog box, where your newly named data source now appears on the Databases tab.

You have now completed the first step, specifying the data source. You could stop now if you wanted to, because the data source definition has been saved and will in the future appear in the Create New Data Source dialog box when you choose Data | Import External Data | New Database Query. This data source will also be available when you choose Data | Import External Data | Import Data.

You haven't defined the query yet—that's the next step—but you have defined the data source that you will point the query at.

Specifying the Query Itself

Now that you have defined your new data source, its name now appears in the Choose Data Source dialog box. Fill the check box labeled Use the Query Wizard to Create/Edit Queries on the Choose Data Source dialog box. Then, click on the name of your data source and click OK. Because you filled the check box, the Choose Columns step of the Query Wizard appears on your screen (see Figure 15-4).

If you hadn't filled the Query Wizard check box, instead of the Query Wizard you would see the Microsoft Query data pane. Using the Query Wizard makes it easier to construct a simple query; using the data pane gives you more control over the process.

Databases have, among several other structures, tables. It's the tables that contain the actual data: in this case, it's fields such as date, acuity, and unit, and the individual records that represent particular shifts. It's conventional to show different fields in different columns and different records in different rows—for example, Excel lists use this arrangement. This is the reason that the Query Wizard asks you to select the columns that will appear in your query: at this point, you're identifying fields, which are shown in columns.

Besides tables, databases usually have queries. Queries display data from tables, but they are normally used to display the data in special ways. For example, queries might filter out certain records or display the records in a different order than they're found in the table. Queries also link tables together in order to show data from two or more tables simultaneously.

Because you might want to base your new query on a table *or* on an existing query, the Query Wizard enables you to choose from both tables and queries. It does not distinguish between them but refers to both types as tables.

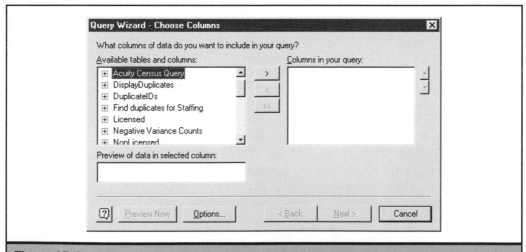

Figure 15-4. *Use the double left-arrow button to remove all columns from a query*

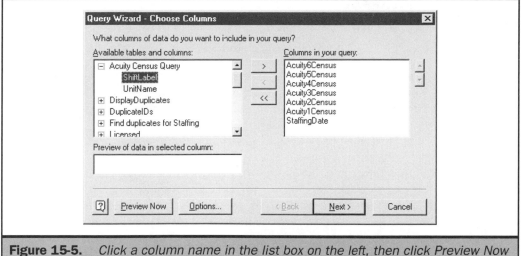

Figure 15-5. *Click a column name in the list box on the left, then click Preview Now to see records from that column*

You begin by selecting the query that contains the data you're after: Acuity Census Query. You click on the plus sign next to its name in the list box. When you do so, the fields—the columns—in the Acuity Census Query appear below its name.

You now need to move field names from the Available Tables and Columns list box into the Columns in Your Query list box. You scroll through the list box until you find the field named Acuity6Census. You click on it and then click the right-arrow button to move Acuity6Census into the Columns in Your Query list box. Then you repeat these actions with the fields named Acuity5Census, Acuity4Census, …, Acuity1Census. You also add the field named StaffingDate to the query. The Choose Columns step now appears as shown in Figure 15-5.

You have now identified the fields that your query will return. When you click Next, the Filter Data step of the Query Wizard appears (see Figure 15-6).

After you have specified the fields to return, the Query Wizard directs your attention to the question of which records to return. You decide to retrieve only those records that have a value on the StaffingDate field greater than 6/1/2000. To arrange that, take these steps:

1. Click StaffingDate in the Column to Filter list box, as shown in Figure 15-6.

2. Select Is Greater Than from the left hand drop-down.

3. Select 2000-06-01 00:00:00 from the right hand drop-down.

    Although you can specify only one field in this step, you can subject the field to as many as three criteria. Suppose that you wanted to limit the records you retrieve to only those in June and July of 2000. After taking the first three steps, you could then take these steps:

THE OUTSIDE WORLD

4. Click the first And button.

5. Choose Is Less Than from the left hand drop-down in the second row.

6. Choose 2000-08-01 00:00:00 from the right hand drop-down in the second row.

Using the Query Wizard, you cannot create more complex criteria involving multiple fields, such as StaffingDate is greater than 6/1/00 and Acuity1Census is greater than 5. To create criteria such as that, you need to bypass the Query Wizard and use Microsoft Query itself, which is discussed later in this chapter.

When you click Next, the Query Wizard's Sort Order step appears, as shown in Figure 15-7.

Figure 15-7 shows that you choose to return the records sorted in ascending order according to their value on the StaffingDate field. This will make it easier to scan the records visually when they are returned to the worksheet. It's worth noting here that if you were returning records directly to a pivot table—instead of directly to the worksheet—there wouldn't be much sense to the use of a sort order in the query. In a pivot table you can quickly sort and re-sort information, so it's usually a waste of time to sort records in the query that feeds the pivot table.

When you click Next, the Query Wizard's final step appears (see Figure 15-8). You have completed the definition of a query. At this point you can choose to:

■ **Return the data identified by your query to the worksheet**

■ **View the data, or edit the query, using Microsoft Query**   You might want to view the data to ensure that you have called for the information that you're after. If you need to make changes, you can then edit the query. In both cases, you would use Microsoft Query's data pane, mentioned earlier and discussed in more detail later in this chapter.

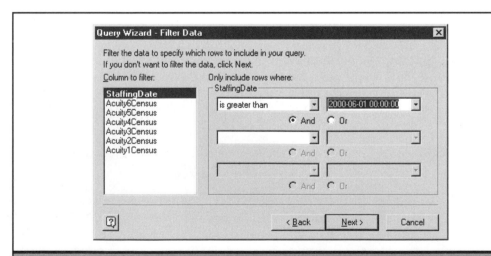

Figure 15-6.   *The drop-downs are disabled until you click a field in the Column to Filter list box*

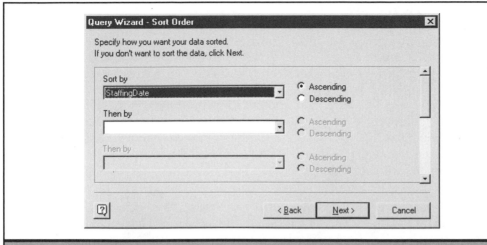

Figure 15-7.   *Click a blank row in the drop-down to remove a field from the Sort specification*

- **Create an OLAP cube**   *OLAP* stands for On Line Analytic Processing. *Very* briefly, an OLAP cube is a source of data that has been prespecified, often with certain data summaries already executed (for example, the sum of first quarter sales might have already been calculated). OLAP cubes are often very useful as partial summaries of data sets so large that applications such as Excel would have difficulty capturing every individual record. Choose this option to create an OLAP cube using the field and record information that you have already supplied.

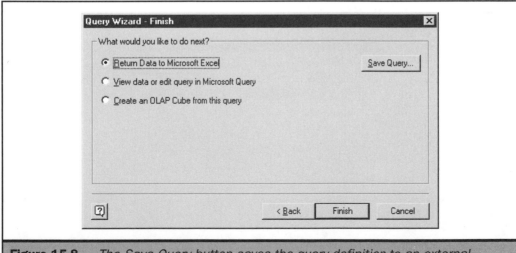

Figure 15-8.   *The Save Query button saves the query definition to an external text file*

THE OUTSIDE WORLD

■ **Save the query**   When you created the data source, it was automatically saved as a file with the default extension .dsn: this example creates a data source definition file named *Acuity.dsn*. Your query is *not* automatically saved as a file. If you want to use this query again—in a different workbook, perhaps—you need to click the Save Query button. Doing so displays a dialog box where you can name the query and specify its saved location. The file you save will have the extension .dqy. It will contain all the information that's in the data source definition file. It will also contain the Structured Query Language (abbreviated as *SQL*; pronounce the abbreviation as "sequel") statements that define your query: which table to use, the fields to return, the filtering criteria, and the sort order.

Note   *The query definition is by default saved as part of the active workbook. See "External Data Range Properties" later in this chapter for more information.*

Assuming that you choose to return the data to the Excel worksheet, when you click Finish you see the dialog box shown in Figure 15-9.

This dialog box lets you choose to return the fields and individual records to the worksheet that was active when you started the process, or to a new worksheet. You can also change your mind about returning individual records to the worksheet and invoke the PivotTable Wizard instead.

Recapping the External Data Process

The steps involved in getting data out of a database and into an Excel worksheet probably appear circuitous and confusing at this point. It's helpful to stay focused on the two general steps: specifying a data source and defining a query.

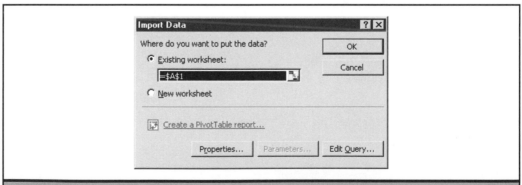

Figure 15-9.   *Use the Properties button to set options for the range of cells that the records will occupy on the worksheet*

Specifying the Data Source

If you were to follow the steps outlined in the previous section, you would:

1. Choose to create a new data source.

2. Identify the nature of that data source: this example used an Access database.

3. Identify the name and location of the data source: this example identified a database named Acuity Staffing in a folder on the user's local disk drive.

These three steps create a file with the extension .dsn, which stands for Data Source Name. The name of that file, less its extension, appears in the Databases tab when you subsequently choose Data | Import External Data | New Database Query. The file contains information such as the type of data source to use, the path to and the name of the data file, and other information that is needed to open the data file. It's available for you to use as a basis for more queries—perhaps queries that specify different tables in the database or different fields in the same table or a different subset of records. Using the data source name that you have already defined means that for this data file, you need not repeat steps 1 through 3, just shown.

Constructing the Query

If you filled the check box labeled Use the Query Wizard to Create/Edit Queries, the Query Wizard guides you through these actions:

1. Identify the table that contains the data you want. Display its fields. Move the fields you want into the query.

2. Choose if and how to filter the records that the query will return.

3. Choose if and how to sort the records that the query will return.

4. Choose to return the data directly to the worksheet or view the query's results and edit the query if necessary or create an OLAP cube.

In the Query Wizard's final step, if you click the Save Query button, the query is saved and the name that you give it will subsequently appear on the Queries tab of the Choose Data Source dialog box. The query is saved as a file with the extension .dqy. Such files repeat the information in the .dsn file—the file type, the filename and location, and so on—and also save information about which tables and fields to return, which records to get, if and how to sort them, and so on. Saved as it is, you can use the query repeatedly in other workbooks.

Understanding the Effects of Query Options

The previous section walked you through the creation of a database query and the retrieval of data from a database to a worksheet. The section ignored many of the options available to you, as well as their effects. This section fills in those details.

Data Source Options

Options that you set for the data source pertain to Excel's treatment of the source file, not to the query. Query options pertain to the query, regardless of the data source to which the query is applied.

User ID and Password

On the Create New Data Source dialog box (refer to Figure 15-2), you can fill a check box labeled Save My User ID and Password in the Data Source Definition. If you do so, you immediately see a message warning you that your password will not be encrypted.

That means the password will not be secure. Recall that the information you provide for the data source name is saved in a .dsn file. If you choose to save the query, the .dsn file's information is repeated in a .dqy file. These files are pure ASCII—that is, unformatted text. Anyone with access to the subdirectories that store the .dsn and .dqy files can open a file with any text editor and read your ID and password.

So, if your data source contains information that's at all sensitive and if it's password protected, you should consider very carefully whether you want the data source information to store your ID and password. If you don't fill that check box, the only downside is that you'll have to supply the password yourself when you run queries that use password-protected data sources. (You'll be prompted to supply the password.)

Note   *You cannot execute a query against a closed and password-protected Excel workbook.*

Selecting a Default Table

Also on the Create New Data Source dialog box is a drop-down that lists the names of tables in the data source you have identified and located. If you want, you can select a table in that drop-down that is used not only as the default, but as the only available table.

This option might be useful if your data source has many tables and if you plan to create several queries that use only one table. Then identifying a default table will ease the next step, where you select a table from among those available.

You lose nothing, except perhaps a little convenience, by ignoring the default table option. In contrast, if you do select a default table, you restrict your options later in the process of developing queries.

    If your data source is another Excel workbook, you need to create named ranges in that workbook. It is these named ranges that Microsoft Query will recognize as tables. See Chapter 10 for information on naming ranges.

Query Wizard Options: Choose Columns

In the first step of the Query Wizard (refer to Figure 15-4), clicking the Options button displays the dialog box shown in Figure 15-10.

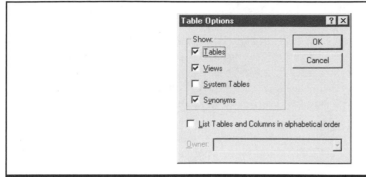

Figure 15-10.   *The list of Available Tables in the Query Wizard can become unwieldy if you choose too many objects in this dialog box*

By filling or clearing these four check boxes you can control which objects—objects that contain fields—are displayed in the Query Wizard:

- **Tables**   Fill this check box to show the names of tables stored in the database.

- **Views**   In the case of Microsoft Access, a view is a query. Fill this check box to show the names of queries that have been stored in an Access database.

- **System Tables**   There are some tables in any database that are normally hidden from the user (although they are not by default further protected, as by means of a password). Unless you are an administrator responsible for the maintenance of the database in question, it's unusual to want access to these tables. But if you do, fill the check box.

- **Synonyms**   Databases often use linkages to other databases. For example, two departments in the same company might share the same set of vendors but use two different databases to record their operations. One database would contain a table named Vendors, and the other would contain a link to that table. In this way, changes to the table's data need not be made in both databases, and both databases nevertheless have access to exactly the same data. In Microsoft Access, these are termed *attached* (or *linked*) *tables*. In Microsoft Query, so that the option encompasses the terminology used by other database management systems, they are termed *synonyms*. Fill the check box to display them in Microsoft Query.

Using the Microsoft Query Data Pane

In the example that was detailed in this chapter's first section, the Query Wizard was used to create the query itself after the data source had been specified. Once you have some experience with the Query Wizard and have begun to understand more fully its options and capabilities, you might want to use Microsoft Query's data pane instead of the Query Wizard. The data pane gives you more control over the structure of the query, as well as a much greater range of options. But because you are not answering questions posed by a wizard, you have to know what to specify and how to specify it.

You call for Microsoft Query by clearing the Query Wizard's check box on the Choose Data Source dialog box (refer to Figure 15-1). You can also get to Microsoft Query by choosing the option labeled View Data or Edit Query in Microsoft Query on the Query Wizard's final step.

Suppose that, on the Choose Data Source dialog box, you opt not to use the Query Wizard. In that case, the Microsoft Query window appears in place of the Query Wizard (see Figure 15-11). (If you choose a .dsn instead of a .dqy file, and if there is more than one table or query, you will first see the Add Tables dialog box. Use it to select the tables or queries you want to use.)

The correspondence between actions you take with Microsoft Query and the steps of the Query Wizard is as follows.

Choose Columns on the Query Wizard   Using Microsoft Query, drag a field name from a table in the Table pane into a field name box in the Data pane—or, just double-

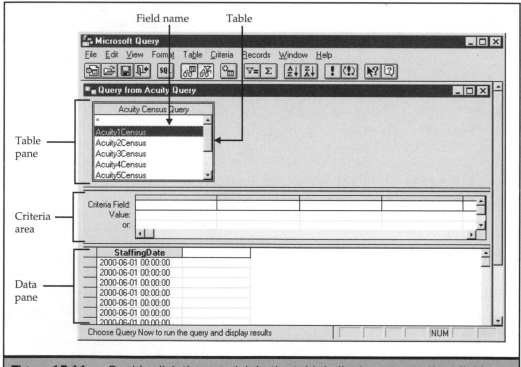

Figure 15-11.   *Double-click the asterisk in the table's list box to put all available fields into the query*

click the field name in the Table pane. You can rearrange the order of the fields in the Data pane by clicking on a field name and dragging it to the right or to the left.

If you're familiar with the structure of the tables in the database you're using, you can also use the Table pane to link tables that share a common field. Choose Table | Add Tables to place a new table in the Table pane. Then click and drag from a field in one table to the corresponding field in the other table. When you release the mouse button you will see a new join line between the tables. Double-click the join to control its characteristics: you can specify an inner, a left outer, or a right outer join in this manner. The Query Wizard isn't sophisticated enough to support the creation of new joins.

Sort Order on the Query Wizard   Using Microsoft Query, choose Records | Sort. The dialog box shown in Figure 15-12 appears. Choose a column from the drop-down list, select Ascending or Descending, and click Add. When you execute the query, records will be returned, ordered by their values on the field to which you assigned a sort order. To establish a sort order for more than one field, select another field from the drop-down, choose Ascending or Descending, and again click Add. The records are sorted by the first field you added from the drop-down; records that have the same value on the first field are sorted within that value according to their values on the subsequent field or fields.

Filter Data on the Query Wizard   If you don't see the Criteria pane, choose View | Criteria. Then drag a field that you want to use as a filter from the Table pane to the Criteria Field row of the Criteria pane. (You can also click in the Criteria Field row to view a drop-down list of available fields.)

On the Criteria pane, click the Value row below the name of the filter field. Then type in the value—the criterion—that the field should equal or type an operator such as > or < followed by a value to establish a range criterion.

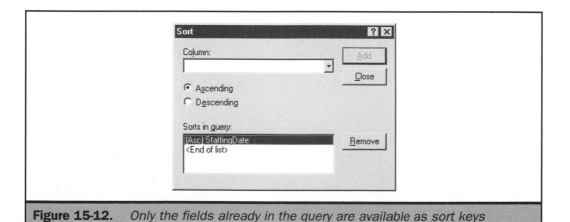

Figure 15-12.   *Only the fields already in the query are available as sort keys*

THE OUTSIDE WORLD

For example, to return only records where the StaffingDate field equals 12/15/2001, enter **12/15/2001** in the StaffingDate column in the Value row (Microsoft Query adds pound signs around the date value that you enter). Or, to return records where the StaffingDate field is greater than 12/14/2001, enter **>12/14/2001** in the StaffingDate column in the Value row. To filter on multiple fields, put the criteria on the same row to connect them with an AND; put the criteria on different rows to connect them with an OR. See Figure 15-13 for an example. When you have completed your work with Microsoft Query, choose File | Return Data to Microsoft Excel.

External Data Range Properties

Whether or not you choose to use the Query Wizard, the final step invoked by Import External Data is the Import Data dialog box (refer to Figure 15-9). If you choose to return data to a worksheet, you can use the Properties button to specify different useful characteristics. The properties in question belong to the worksheet range to which the external data is returned—it's termed the *external data range*.

The External Data Range Properties dialog box appears in Figure 15-14.

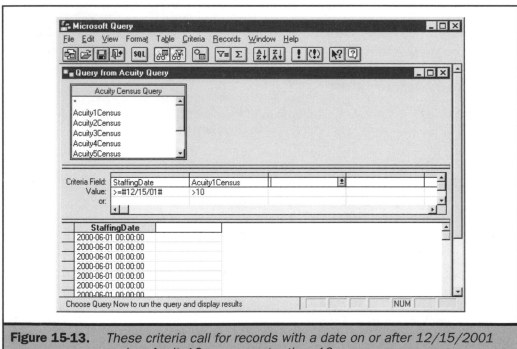

Figure 15-13.   *These criteria call for records with a date on or after 12/15/2001 and an Acuity1Census greater than 10*

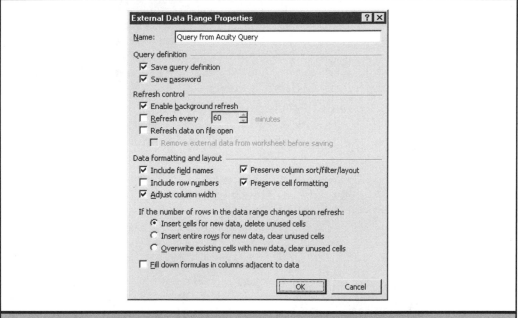

Figure 15-14. *You can get to these options at any time by right-clicking a cell in the external data range and choosing Data Range Properties*

The options of note in this dialog box are:

■ **Save Query Definition** This is different from saving the .dsn and the .dqy files discussed earlier in the chapter. Filling this check box saves the query definition in hidden names on the worksheet. Saving the query definition in this way makes it easy to refresh the data—either on command with Data | Refresh Data (you must have selected a cell in the range of returned data for this command to be enabled) or when you open the workbook. Clearing the check box does *not* affect the .dsn and .dqy files. The Save Query Definition check box is filled by default.

■ **Save Password** Again, this option has nothing to do with the .dsn and .dqy files. Filling the box means that if the data source is password protected, you need supply the password only the first time you refresh the external data range. Subsequent refreshes during the same session do not require you to supply the data source's password. If you clear the check box, you will have to supply the password each time you refresh the external data range. The Save Password check box is filled by default.

- **Enable Background Refresh**   Filling the check box means that you have control of Excel while a (possibly time-consuming) query is executing. Clearing the check box means you'll have to wait until the data has been returned from the data source before you can do anything else in Excel. However, the actual time it takes for the query to complete may be shorter than it would be with a background refresh. This check box is filled by default.

- **Refresh Every x Minutes**   Fill the check box and set the number of minutes to automatically refresh the data every so often. This is useful if your data source frequently gets new data or deletes existing data. This check box is cleared by default.

- **Refresh Data on File Open**   This option makes it unnecessary for you to remember to refresh the external data range whenever you open the workbook. If you fill the Refresh Data on File Open check box, the Remove External Data from Worksheet Before Saving check box is enabled. This check box is cleared by default.

- **Remove External Data from Worksheet Before Saving**   Filling this check box clears the external data range when you save the file. However, the query definition is retained so that you can refresh the external data range when you next open the workbook. This check box is cleared by default.

- **Include Field Names**   Filling the check box puts the names of the fields as row headers at the top of their columns—just like an Excel list structure. This check box is filled by default.

- **Include Row Numbers**   Filling the check box adds a column to the external data range with the number of each record. This option can be useful if you start the external data range somewhere other than Row 1. Keep in mind that Access numbers its records such that the first record is Record Number Zero. This check box is cleared by default.

- **Adjust Column Width**   This makes each column in the external data range wide enough to fully display its longest value (including that of the row header). This check box is filled by default.

- **Preserve Column Sort/Filter/Layout**   If, after a refresh, you make changes to the sort order of the external data range or to data filters or to the order of its columns, filling this check box retains those changes when you next refresh the external data range. Suppose that your query sorts records by Invoice Date. After executing the query, you re-sort the data using another field— say, Account Number. If this check box is filled, when you next refresh the data the range will still be sorted by Account Number, not necessarily by the query's Invoice Date sort order. This check box is filled by default.

- **Preserve Cell Formatting**   Similar to the Preserve Column Sort/Filter/Layout option, but applies to individual cells, not to columns. This check box is filled by default.

The following three options are mutually exclusive:

- **Insert Cells for New Data, Delete Unused Cells**   Suppose the external data range occupies cells A1:D20. Another five records are added to the data source. When you refresh the data and this option is selected, new *cells* are inserted from A21:D25, and the new records occupy those cells. Any value that had been in, say, cell E22 remains there, because cells were inserted only in columns A:D. Suppose that five records were removed from the data source. When you refresh the data, the external data range becomes A1:D15 and any value in, say, C21 moves up to C16 because the unused cells were deleted. This button is selected by default.

- **Insert Entire Rows for New Data, Clear Unused Cells**   Selecting this button causes full *rows* to be inserted in order to accommodate new records. If the original range A1:D20 increases to A1:D25, a value in cell E22 would be moved down to cell E27 because the inserted rows span all columns. If the range shrinks by five records, a value that was in C21 would stay there because the cells that are no longer needed are cleared, not deleted. This button is deselected by default.

- **Overwrite Existing Cells with New Data, Clear Unused Cells**   New records arriving from the data source do not result in the insertion of cells or rows. They just overwrite any information that's already on the worksheet below the existing external data range. If the range shrinks, the cells are cleared, not deleted. (A cleared cell loses its data but not its formatting characteristics.) This button is deselected by default.

- **Fill Down Formulas in Columns Adjacent to Data**   Suppose that your external data range is in A1:B50. In column C you have placed formulas that calculate the sum of column A and column B—for example, =A2+B2, =A3+B3, and so on. When you next refresh the data, the query returns five more records, in A51:B55. If you have filled this check box, Excel automatically extends those formulas from their current terminus at C50 into C51:C55. This check box is cleared by default.

Importing Data from Existing Sources

This chapter has been largely concerned with the New Database Query command on the submenu that appears when you choose Data | Import External Data. There is another command on that submenu that you will find useful from time to time: Import Data.

The Import Data command works with existing data sources, and you can also use it to create new data sources. You cannot use it to create a new query, as you can with the New Database Query command, which invokes Microsoft Query. But it allows you to connect to a broader range of data sources than does Microsoft Query.

Microsoft Query can connect Excel to ODBC data sources, including Access, Excel, FoxPro, dBASE, and SQL Server. It can also use queries that you have created and saved as .dqy files, data sources that you have saved as .dsn files, and OLAP cubes.

Using Import Data, you can connect to each of the data sources offered by Microsoft Query. You can also connect to these other data sources:

- **Web pages**   For example, files with .htm, .html, and .asp extensions.

- **Text files**   For example, files with .txt and .prn extensions (although you can open these directly with File | Open).

- **Office Database Connections**   This type of file has an .odc extension. It is the type of file that is created if you create a new data source from Import Data.

When you choose Data | Import External Data | Import Data, you see the Select Data Source window shown next:

If you click the New Source button, you initiate the Data Connection Wizard. Completing this four-step wizard results in a new .odc file, which subsequently appears in the Select Data Source window. Here's a quick tour of the Data Connection Wizard. Its first step looks like this:

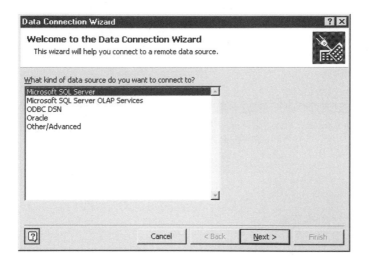

If you don't see the type of data source that you're looking for, you need either to obtain and install the proper driver, or to check with your system administrator if you're trying to get to a data source that's on a network. Various OLE (Object Linking and Embedding) providers are found in the Other/Advanced category, and ODBC-compliant drivers are of course found in the ODBC DSN category.

Suppose that you choose ODBC DSN and click Next. The wizard's second step is shown next:

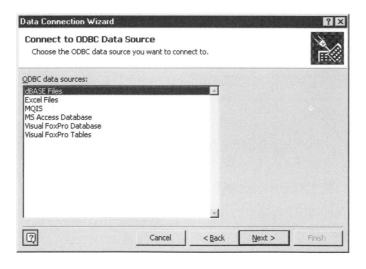

The wizard's third step depends on the type of ODBC source you choose. Selecting MS Access Database displays a dialog box that you can use to browse to the file's location. Once that file is located and selected, the wizard displays the available tables and queries (views) in that file:

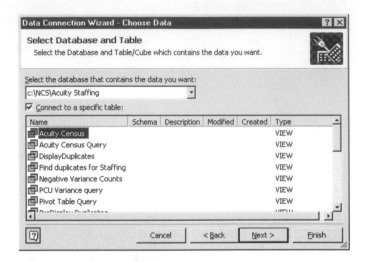

If you clear the Connect to a Specific Table check box, the entries in the list box are dimmed and disabled. All tables and queries will be available when you use this data connection. If you fill the check box, you can select a particular table or query, and the data connection will later present only that table or query. Click Next to get to the wizard's final step.

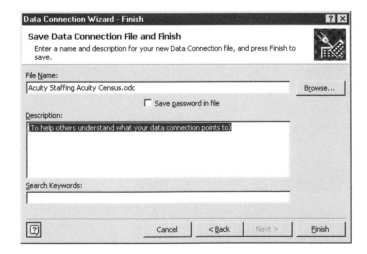

Here you can rename the data connection file, using the Browse button if you wish to locate it in a different folder. You can also type a description of the data connection; that description will appear in the Comments box on the Summary tab that appears when you view the data connection's properties. Notice the Save Password in File check box. Your decision to save a password should be guided by the same security considerations that apply to saving a .dsn or .dqy file (see the "Data Source Options" section earlier in this chapter).

When you click Finish, the Data Connection Wizard again displays the Select Data Source window, with your new .odc file shown. Click its name and then click the Open button. You will see the Import Data dialog box (refer to Figure 15-9). This is the dialog box that appears if you choose Data | Import External Data | Import Data, select an existing data source that connects to only one table or query, then click Open. You can return the data into a range starting with the active cell or to a new worksheet.

> **Tip**   *Returning the data to a new worksheet is the safest means of preventing the overwrite of existing data.*

You can return the data into a pivot table report or as a list onto a worksheet. If the data source was created using Microsoft Query, you can also edit the underlying query. Click the Edit Query button to start Microsoft Query. An interesting feature of .odc data connection files is that they are actually markup language files—a mix of HTML and XML. To demonstrate this, right-click on an .odc file in the Select Data Source window that appears when you choose Data | Import External Data | Import Data. The default option is View in Browser. If you choose that option, your default Web browser opens and displays the data in a static mode.

Notice that nowhere in the process of creating a new data connection did you have the opportunity to create a new query. To do that, you need to use Microsoft Query by choosing Data | Import External Data | New Database Query.

You can also create and run queries that obtain data from Web sites. To do so, you choose Data | Import External Data | New Web Query. For information on that process, see Chapter 17, "Using Web Technology."

THE OUTSIDE WORLD

The Complete Reference

Excel 2002

Chapter 16

Sharing Workbooks

Excel supports the feature known as *shared workbooks*, which permits multiple users to work on the same workbook file simultaneously. In addition, you can let other users access your workbooks without turning on the sharing features. The functions necessary to keep this feature under control, without totally destroying the workbook, are at your fingertips. They include a variety of methods for protecting your work when other users access your workbooks.

This chapter covers all the features available for both methods of sharing workbooks—passing them to one user at a time and permitting simultaneous access by multiple users.

Enabling Security for Workbooks

There are lots of occasions in which you're asked to add your own input to another user's workbook. And you probably ask the same of users for workbooks you've created. When a workbook starts moving around the company, there are some security issues that accompany the movement. To make sure you don't end up with total chaos, you should approach sharing with some controls. You must have control over

- Which users can make changes
- Which users can look at the workbook, even if they aren't permitted to make changes

Some of the worksheets you create may need to be checked, approved, examined, or added to by other users. This is typical of budgets, financial reports, scenarios, and other types of workbooks that are created by combining data from several sources. If you use a network to provide access to other users, you risk exposing the workbook contents to any user who sees the filename on a network drive. In fact, even if you pass a file around on a floppy disk, anyone who picks up the disk could access the workbook.

There are two levels of security you can use to lock a workbook. You can permit only authorized users to

- Open the workbook
- Make changes to the workbook

You can also lock the workbook against modifications, even if the entire world is permitted to view it, by changing the file attributes to read-only. However, any user who knows how could eliminate the read-only attribute.

Securing workbooks against access and modification is accomplished with the file password feature. Password protection is available in the dialog box that appears when you choose File | Save As from the menu bar. Remember that the first time you save a workbook, even if you choose File | Save or click the Save button on the Standard toolbar, you see the Save As dialog box.

Here's how to password-protect your workbook in the Save As dialog box:

1. If this is the first time you're saving the workbook, select a folder for the file and name the file. If this is an existing workbook, there's no reason to change its folder or filename.

2. Click the Tools button on the toolbar and choose General Options from the drop-down menu.

3. In the Save Options dialog box, select the password protection level(s) you need (described next).

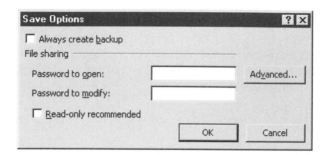

Creating a Password to Open a Workbook

You can require the user to supply a password to open a workbook by entering a password in the Password To Open text box. When you type the password, the screen echoes asterisks instead of the characters you type (in case anyone is peeking over your shoulder).

- Passwords can be from 1 to 15 characters.
- Use letters, numbers, or a combination of both.
- Passwords are case-sensitive. The password **StayOut** is not the same as **stayout**.

After you enter the password, click OK, which brings up the Confirm Password dialog box. Enter the same password again and click OK. If you enter it incorrectly, a message displays to tell you that your entry is not identical to the original password, and you're returned to the original Save Options dialog box to repeat the process.

Note *If you have trouble typing the password in the confirmation dialog box, maybe you've created a password that's too complicated. Remember that you, too, have to enter the password to open this workbook, so be sure to use characters you can enter without a high risk of error.*

After you successfully enter and confirm the password, click Save in the Save As dialog box to save the workbook and its password.

THE OUTSIDE WORLD

If you forget the password, you won't be able to open your own workbook. Excel has no "override the password" feature, and Microsoft support offers no help for forgotten passwords. There are some third-party programs that claim to be able to break into password-protected documents.

Using a Password to Open a Workbook

After you create the password, share it with anyone you think should be allowed to see this workbook.

 There are some common-sense rules about sharing a password, and sometimes common-sense rules bear repeating. Don't leave a note with the password on somebody's desk or taped to a monitor. Don't yell it down the hall. An e-mail message usually works well unless the recipient commonly lets other users open his or her mailbox. And beware of birth dates and names spelled backwards: they're the first things that snoops try.

When you or anyone else selects this workbook to open it, the Password dialog box appears. Enter the password and click OK.

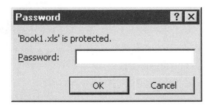

If the password you enter is incorrect, a message appears to let you know. Click OK to get rid of the error message. Then reopen the Open dialog box and start again.

If you don't know the password (which is the case for everyone except those people to whom you gave the password), you cannot open the file. Nor can you successfully try something sneaky like linking to the file from another workbook or program. You need to have the password.

Creating a Password to Modify a Workbook

Whether you password-protect the document or not, you can require a password before letting a user make any changes to a workbook. If you do password-protect the act of opening the document, doing so produces the Document Password dialog box, followed by the Modification Password dialog box.

To establish password protection against modification, click the Tools button on the Save As dialog box and choose General Options.

When the Save Options dialog box opens, enter a password in the Password To Modify text box and click OK. Then reenter the password in the Confirm Password dialog box and click OK. Finally, save the file.

Don't use the same password for opening a file and modifying it. And don't forget, *you'll* have to enter both passwords when you subsequently open the file.

Using a Password to Modify a Workbook

When you open a file that has a password for modifications, a dialog box appears to explain that if you don't have the password, you must open the file in read-only mode.

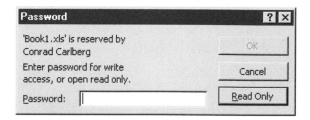

As soon as anyone begins to enter a password, the OK button is available.

If the user doesn't know the password, choosing Cancel stops the file open process, and choosing Read Only opens the file as a read-only document (changes cannot be saved).

Actually, anyone can make all sorts of changes to a read-only file, but the changes won't be saved under the original filename in its original folder. Clicking the Save button (or choosing File | Save from the menu bar) produces an explanatory message.

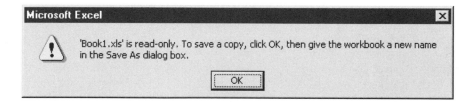

Click OK to open the Save As dialog box, and save the workbook with a different filename or to a different location. (Excel offers to give the workbook a default filename; if you opened it as Book1.xls, Excel will propose that you save it as Copy of Book1.xls.)

Changing Passwords

If you want to change either or both passwords, go through all the same steps you used to create the passwords. Delete the current password and enter a new one. After you confirm it and save the file, the new password is in effect. Don't forget to notify the appropriate users.

Protecting Workbooks and Worksheets

If you want more people to be able to use your workbook but you want to limit their activities, Excel provides an additional level of password protection. You can use it whether or not you employ the security methods discussed in the previous section. The feature, called *protection*, gives you a way to specify the elements in your workbook that you want to keep as is. Other users can't manipulate those elements. This is a method of specifying protection that is more focused than the no-holds-barred password-protection schemes.

Using the Excel Protection Menu

Access the protection feature by choosing Tools | Protection from the menu bar, which displays the following three choices on the submenu:

- **Protect Sheet**   Offers protection for several elements in a worksheet.
- **Protect Workbook**   Offers protection for the workbook structure and window configuration.
- **Protect and Share Workbook**   Configures protection for a shared workbook and also shares the workbook. (See the section "Using Shared Workbooks" later in this chapter.)

Protecting a Worksheet

If you want to protect the current worksheet, choose the Protect Sheet command from the Protection submenu. The Protect Sheet dialog box appears so you can take advantage of the options you need.

You have much more flexibility in deciding how to protect a worksheet than you did in earlier releases of Excel. Use the Protect Sheet dialog box to set the actions that all users of the worksheet can take. If you are using Windows 2000 as your operating system, you can set worksheet permissions for specific users.

Understanding Locked and Hidden Items

Before you proceed with worksheet protection, it's important to understand what the options mean and how they work.

By default, cells are locked, but the locking means nothing unless you enforce it. Applying protection does just that. If there are cells you're willing to let other users manipulate, you must unlock them before protecting your worksheet.

For example, you might want to allow an employee to change data in cells that contain her name, phone, and mailing address but not cells that contain her salary or her job performance rating.

In addition, you can hide formula cells, but the hidden attribute doesn't take effect unless you apply the protection feature.

Here's how to unlock cells and hide formulas:

1. On your worksheet, select the cell(s) you want to unlock or the formulas you want to hide.

2. Choose Format | Cells from the menu bar.

3. In the Format Cells dialog box, go to the Protection tab. (You won't see this tab if the worksheet is already protected.)

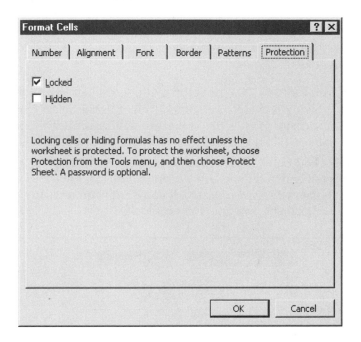

4. To unlock the cell(s), click the Locked check box to deselect the option.

5. To hide formulas, click the Hidden check box.

When you hide a formula, you aren't hiding its result. Suppose that cell A1 contains this formula:

= 9 / 3

You see the result in the cell and the formula in the formula bar. You then hide the formula as described above and then protect the worksheet. You still see the result in the cell, but you no longer see the formula in the formula bar.

Note   *If you choose Tools | Options and fill the Formulas check box on the View tab, you see formulas instead of results in the cells. Then, hiding a formula and protecting the worksheet hides the formula in the cell as well as in the formula bar.*

Graphics are also locked by default, and like cells, the locking is meaningless until you apply protection. To unlock any graphical element before you protect the worksheet, select the graphic and choose Format | <graphic type> (for instance, Autoshape, Text Box, and so on). Then go to the Protection tab and unlock the item.

Now you're ready to proceed with protecting your work.

Using the Protect Worksheet Options

When you choose Tools | Protection | Protect Sheet, the Protect Sheet dialog box appears, as shown in Figure 16-1.

You can tailor the actions that all users can take by filling or clearing the check boxes in the Allow All Users Of This Worksheet To list. Here are the effects of selecting the different check boxes:

- **Select Locked Cells**   Users can select a cell that is locked, but they can't modify it. Filling this check box automatically fills the Select Unlocked Cells check box: the assumption is that if you are willing for users to select locked cells, you are also willing for them to select unlocked cells.

- **Select Unlocked Cells**   Any cells you unlocked before opening this dialog box can be selected and manipulated by users. If you clear this check box, the Select Locked Cells check box is also cleared. If you don't want users to select an unlocked cell, you surely don't want them to select locked cells.

Figure 16-1.   *Clearing the Protect Worksheet and Contents of Locked Cells check box disables the OK button*

Tip   *If you've unlocked a group of cells because you want users to enter data in them, the* TAB *key moves from unlocked cell to unlocked cell, skipping the locked cells.*

Note   *If you clear both the Select Locked Cells and the Select Unlocked Cells check boxes, you make it impossible for the user to select anything on the worksheet, including columns and rows. This restricts other activities that you might allow, such as Format Cells: you need to select a cell to format it.*

- **Format Cells**   Fill this check box to allow users to change a cell's format. (But recall that the Protection tab is suppressed if the worksheet is protected. This prevents the user from unlocking cells or unhiding formulas.)

- **Format Columns and Format Rows**   Fill the Columns check box to allow users to change a column's width and to hide or unhide it. Fill the Rows check box to allow users to change a row's height and to hide or unhide it. (Read Chapter 5 to learn how to hide and unhide columns and rows.)

- **Insert Columns and Insert Rows**   Fill the appropriate check box to allow users to insert new columns and rows.

- **Insert Hyperlinks**   Fill this check box to allow users to insert hyperlinks.

- **Delete Columns and Delete Rows**   Fill the appropriate check box to allow users to delete existing columns and rows.

In addition to the options just discussed, the following options are available but are not visible in Figure 16-1:

- **Sort**   Filling this check box allows users to sort data *in unlocked cells*. When you have selected one cell only and choose Data | Sort, Excel tries to include in the sorting range any adjacent cells that contain data. (If A1:A5 only contain data, if you select A3 and choose Data | Sort then Excel expands the selection to A1:A5.) If a cell adjacent to the selected cell is locked, Excel will not complete the sort. The solution is to select a range of unlocked cells before beginning the sort.

- **Use AutoFilter**   Despite this check box's label, filling the check box allows the user to employ both AutoFilter and Advanced Filter.

- **Use PivotTable Reports**   If this check box is filled, the user can manipulate— that is, refresh, pivot, and otherwise modify—any pivot tables on the worksheet.

Caution   *It is possible that you could overwrite data in a locked cell on a protected sheet by pivoting a portion of a pivot table over that cell. Excel displays a warning if you are about to do so, but this behavior is nevertheless in conflict with the protection of a locked cell.*

- **Edit Objects**   If the worksheet contains objects (for example, text boxes, pictures, or files created by other applications), then filling this check box enables the user to perform actions such as editing, moving, or deleting them.

THE OUTSIDE WORLD

- **Edit Scenarios**   Scenarios are associated with the worksheet. Fill this check box to enable the user to modify or delete them. Clear the check box to prevent users from viewing hidden scenarios, changing locked scenarios, and deleting locked scenarios. They can, however, create new scenarios.

Selecting Password Protection

The Password option in the Protect Sheet dialog box is for this protection scheme only; it is not the same as a general password that must be entered in order to open the workbook or modify it.

Enter a password in the Protect Sheet dialog box to prevent users from turning off protection. Otherwise, they can go to the Protection command and remove the protection options you've established.

Removing Worksheet Protection

When you turn on worksheet protection, the submenu item Protect Sheet changes to Unprotect Sheet. Select it to turn off the protection feature. You'll be prompted for a password if one was specified when the worksheet was protected.

Permitting Specific Users to Access Protected Cells

If your operating system is Windows 2000, you can allow different users to get at different cells, or ranges of cells, in a worksheet. To do so, take these steps:

1. If it is protected, unprotect the sheet.

2. Choose Tools | Protection | Allow Users To Edit Ranges.

3. Click New. A dialog box appears where you can enter a name for the range, supply the cell addresses for the range, and enter a password to access the range.

4. Click the Permissions button, and then click the Add button. Click on any users who should have access to this range. When you're through, click OK.

5. Click OK again to return to the Allow Users To Edit Ranges dialog box. You can repeat steps 1 through 4 to define user access for a new range.

6. Fill the Paste Permissions Information Into A New Workbook check box if you want Excel to record the information you entered. The new workbook will contain, for each range you specified, its title, its address, whether it is password protected, and the users who have access to it.

7. Click OK if you prefer to protect the worksheet later. Click Protect Sheet if you want to protect it now.

Protecting a Workbook

To protect elements of a workbook, choose Tools | Protection | Protect Workbook. In the Protect Workbook dialog box, select the options you need.

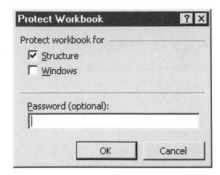

By default, the Structure item is selected and the Windows item is not.

Protecting Workbook Structure

The Structure option prevents users from performing any of the following tasks:

- View hidden worksheets.
- Move worksheets.
- Delete worksheets.
- Hide worksheets.
- Rename worksheets.
- Insert new worksheets.
- Insert chart sheets.
- Move worksheets to another workbook.
- Copy worksheets to another workbook.
- Display the source data for a cell in the data area of a pivot table.
- Display a pivot table's page field pages on separate worksheets.
- Create a summary report by using the Scenario Manager.

Note   *Users are able to add embedded charts to existing worksheets with the Chart Wizard.*

Protecting Workbook Windows

Selecting the Windows check box prevents users from changing the size or position of the workbook's windows.

The Password Protection option is the same as described for protecting worksheets.

 # Using Shared Workbooks

Sharing a workbook in simultaneous access with other users is a way to *collaborate* on a workbook. There are some workbooks that benefit from sharing. A workbook that tracks a project is frequently updated, and multiple users may be opening the file at the same time. A budget workbook often has the same fate, especially if various departments are entering specific data. In fact, any workbook that requires frequent updating by several people should be shared because there's probably no way to avoid multiple simultaneous access.

Understanding Shared Workbook Limits

To make sharing viable, Excel has limits on the type of manipulation you can apply to a shared workbook. Here's the list of the things you cannot do when a workbook is marked for sharing:

- Merge cells.
- Insert or delete blocks of cells.

 You can insert or delete columns and rows.

- Make changes to menus.
- Insert hyperlinks.
- Delete worksheets.
- Create conditional formats.
- Create or change data validation restrictions.
- Create or change graphical objects (in fact, you cannot use the drawing tools).
- Create or change hyperlinks.
- Assign, remove, or alter passwords.
- Create or change scenarios.
- Group or outline data.
- Create automatic subtotals.
- Create data tables.

- Create or change a pivot table.
- Record, change, or assign macros, or make changes to user forms.

This seems to be a long list, but the truth is there aren't many restrictions on sharing when you consider the reasons for sharing. Almost always, the reason for sharing a workbook is to view and add cell data.

Configuring a Shared Workbook

To share a workbook, you must designate it as shared and configure the options for sharing. Choose Tools | Share Workbook to open the Share Workbook dialog box.

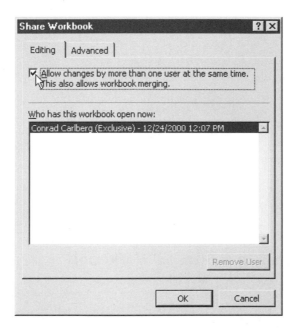

First, turn on the simultaneous user feature so you can access the options in the Advanced tab of the dialog box. Do so by filling the check box labeled Allow Changes By More Than One User At The Same Time. Notice that your name is in the list of people who are working with this workbook. After you complete the sharing configuration and the notebook is available to network users, every user who opens this workbook will be listed.

Note   *To unshare a workbook, open that workbook, choose Tools | Protection, and click Unprotect Shared Workbook. Then choose Tools | Share Workbook and clear the Allow Changes … check box. If another user has the workbook open when you unshare it, he sees a message that you made it exclusive when he attempts to save his copy.*

Caution *Unsharing a workbook erases the change history.*

In the Advanced tab of the dialog box, select the features you want to use for your shared workbook.

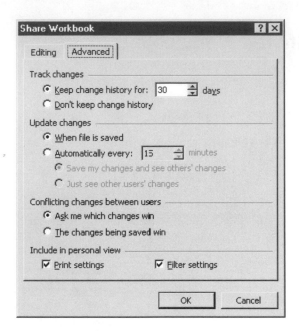

Tracking Changes in a Shared Workbook

By default in a shared workbook, tracking changes is turned on and a history of changes made during the last 30 days is kept. You might want to change the number of days. However, if you select the option to turn off the change history, you won't be able to merge changes from multiple copies of the workbook.

There are some changes that Excel doesn't track, even with changes tracked and history kept. These include:

■ The insertion or deletion of a worksheet

■ Formatting cells

■ Hiding or unhiding columns or rows

■ Entering or changing cell comments

■ A formula recalculation (due to a change to a precedent cell)

You have some options as to how Excel tracks the changes. Choose Tools | Track Changes | Highlight Changes to display this dialog box:

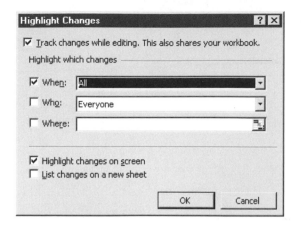

Points to note about the Highlight Changes dialog box:

- When the dialog box appears for the first time with the current worksheet active, all the controls except the Track Changes While Editing check box are disabled. Fill the check box to enable them.

- When Excel highlights changes on the screen, it does so by putting a border around the cell and a comment symbol in the cell's upper left corner. To establish this highlighting, fill the appropriate check box.

- If you also (or instead) want to keep a log of changes on a separate worksheet, fill the List Changes On A New Sheet check box. Excel adds a worksheet named History to the workbook and maintains a change log there. This check box is enabled only after the workbook has been shared and saved.

Note   *Excel deletes the History worksheet when you save the workbook. To get it back you must again use the Highlight Changes dialog box. The reason for this is that Excel does not continuously update the History sheet once you've displayed it. To make sure it's kept current, Excel deletes it and forces you to redisplay it.*

- You can use the Highlight Changes dialog box to establish a workbook as shared. That is, if you fill the Track Changes While Editing check box and subsequently click OK, Excel configures the workbook as shared and displays the Save As dialog box. To set advanced sharing options, though, you still need to choose Tools | Share Workbook. (See the following list for information on these options.)

You can choose to highlight changes that have been made since another event. Your choices in the When drop-down are

- **All**   Highlight the entire saved change history.
- **Since I Last Saved**   Highlight only those changes since your last save.

- **Not Yet Reviewed**   Highlight only those changes that you have not reviewed by means of Tools | Track Changes | Accept Or Reject Changes.

- **Since Date**   Highlight changes that have been made since a date that you specify.

You can choose to highlight changes made by certain users. Your choices in the Who drop-down include

- **Everyone**   Highlight all users' changes.

- **Everyone But Me**   Highlight other users' changes.

- **Specific Users**   The names of current simultaneous users appear in the drop-down. You can select one of them and only one. That user's changes are highlighted.

Lastly, you can use the Where reference edit box to establish a range of cells. Excel will highlight only changes to cells in that range.

The three highlighting criteria—When, Who, and Where—are not mutually exclusive. That is, you can specify one, two, three, or no highlighting criteria.

There are many different possible outcomes if you choose more than one highlighting criterion. For example, suppose you chose All for When, Everyone for Who, and cleared the Where check box. A change you make would then be highlighted.

In contrast, suppose you chose All for When, and Everyone But Me for Who, leaving the Where check box cleared. Everyone But Me (Who) would override the All (When), and a change you make would *not* be highlighted.

Updating Changes in a Shared Workbook

You have several configuration options for the manner in which you want to save changes as you and a group of other users are working on the workbook simultaneously. Here's how the options work:

- **When File Is Saved**   You receive updates about the changes made by other users whenever you save the workbook. The definition of "changes made" means the other users must save the workbook to record the changes.

If you're afraid that the option to receive changes on save isn't frequent enough to keep up with the changes being made to the workbook, all you have to do is save often. Make sure the other users are also saving often.

- **Automatically Every**   This option saves changes you have made at the interval you specify. If you select this option, you must indicate what occurs when changes are received. You can tell Excel to save your own changes automatically when you receive the changes made by other users, or just display the changes made by other users.

Handling Conflicting Changes

Sometimes, when the changes are written you may find that you and another user (or a bunch of other users) made changes to the same cell. You have a conflict unless everyone made the same change to the cell—that's unlikely. The sequence of events that results in a conflict are as follows:

1. In a shared workbook, John makes a change to, say, cell A1. Jane also makes a change to cell A1. The order in which these changes are made doesn't matter.

2. Jane saves the workbook.

3. John performs some action such as clicking the Save button that begins to save the workbook.

   Step 3 triggers the conflict. It is only then, at the time of the *second* save, that one user attempts to make a permanent change to another user's data.

You have to tell Excel how to handle the conflict, and you have two choices:

- **Ask Me Which Changes Win**   Choose this option to see a dialog box where you (that's John in the previous example) can declare a winner.
- **The Changes Being Saved Win**   Select this option to tell Excel to keep the changes you save (again, you're John). Essentially, this is telling Excel "I win."

Configuring Your Own View of a Shared Workbook

You can decide what you want to use for your own view of the worksheet as you use it and save it. You can keep your own print settings and filters, deselect either one, or deselect both.

Note   *Information about print settings is in Chapter 6; information about filters is in Chapter 7.*

After you've configured the Share Workbooks dialog box, click OK. Excel tells you that it is going to save the workbook. Click OK in the Save As dialog box and your title bar displays the designation [Shared].

Incidentally, you should make sure you save shared workbooks on a server or a computer that's designated to hold shared documents. Otherwise, you have to permit users to access your hard drive, and they may have to hunt through subfolders on your local drive to find the file.

Using Shared Workbooks

You perform tasks on a shared workbook in the same manner that you do in any workbook. The way your changes are saved when you're competing for the same cell depends on the configuration options for the way changes are saved. If you aren't the "winner," Excel lets you know.

There is a mildly complicated relationship between how you choose to handle conflicting changes between users and the nature of the conflict. Suppose that you are using a shared workbook simultaneously with John. At the time that you both opened the workbook, cell A1 contained the value 5.

John enters 12 in cell A1 and saves the workbook. What happens next depends on what you enter in cell A1 and on what conflict resolution option you have chosen on the Share Workbook dialog box's Advanced tab.

Ask Me Which Changes Win

If you choose this option there are three possible outcomes when you save your copy of the workbook:

■ You enter 15 in cell A1 and click the Save button. This establishes a conflict with John's entry of 12. Because you have selected Ask Me Which Changes Win, the Resolve Conflicts dialog box appears. If there are multiple conflicts displayed, you can decide on each change separately or make a wholesale decision.

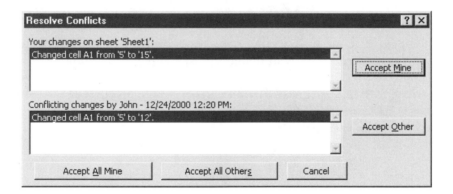

■ You make no change to cell A1, leaving it with its original value of 5. You save the workbook. *No conflict is established.* Because you made no change to cell A1, Excel assumes that you're willing to accept whatever value a simultaneous user saved. The value 12 that John entered and saved is put into cell A1 of your copy of the workbook, your copy is saved, and you see this message:

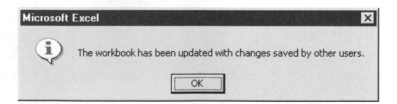

Also, the cell is highlighted on your copy of the workbook. Positioning the mouse pointer over the cell displays more information.

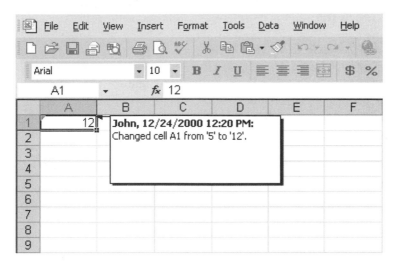

- You make the same change that John did, entering 12 in cell A1. No conflict is established. Nevertheless, when you save your copy of the workbook, you see the same message box informing you that the workbook has been updated with changes made by other users.

The Changes Being Saved Win

If you choose this option instead of the Ask Me Which Changes Win option, there are again three possible outcomes when you save the workbook:

- You enter 15 in cell A1 and click the Save button. This establishes a conflict with John's entry of 12. Because you have selected The Changes Being Saved Win, you see no Resolve Conflicts dialog box and no The Workbook Has Been Updated message box. All that happens is that Excel obeys the option you selected and saves your changes. Of course, this overwrites the 12 that John entered in cell A1.

- You make no change to cell A1, leaving it with its original value of 5. You save the workbook. No conflict is established, and therefore Excel has nothing to ask you to resolve. But Excel does display the The Workbook Has Been Updated message box, and your workbook's cell A1 is updated to the value that John entered and saved.

- You make the same change that John did, entering 12 in cell A1. No conflict is established. You see no message, and Excel saves your change. This is in contrast to the outcome with the Ask Me Which Changes Win option, where Excel displays the The Workbook Has Been Updated message box.

The general rule that you can derive from these examples is that Excel decides that there is a conflict if two users change the same cell in a shared workbook and each saves the change. Unless you override another user's change, your version of the workbook is updated to reflect the other user's change when you save your copy.

Deciding to Share a Workbook

If all this seems complicated, it is. The reason is that Excel was not originally designed to be a multiuser application. The shared workbook feature was tacked on in Excel 97. Despite all its ins and outs, it works just fine for a few users.

But if you have many users, or if one or two of the simultaneous users have the workbook open much of the time, you should give some thought to using something that was designed as a multiuser application. Microsoft Access is one possibility. The tradeoff, of course, is that Excel's worksheets provide a familiar interface for most users. Fewer users are familiar with the Access interface.

The Complete Reference

Chapter 17

Using Web Technology

W e speak and read about the World Wide Web so much and so often that it's easy to forget that it's only one of many thousands of Webs in existence. Corporations, for example, use Webs for both external and internal communications. Information about the company, its products and services, is distributed to the world via Web sites. Information for the company employees may be disseminated via an *intranet*, a Web site with more limited access.

When you're preparing documents for a Web site, it doesn't matter whether it is an Internet or intranet site, because the sites use very similar technology.

Working with HTML Workbooks

You can save your Excel files in Hypertext Markup Language (HTML) format, just as you save them as workbooks, as text files, or in database formats. You can also preview how a worksheet will look in a browser, and you can open HTML documents directly into Excel. In fact, when you use the Open dialog box, you'll see .htm and .html listed as Excel file types, and you can open an HTML file directly in Excel.

> *The reason there are two choices for the file extension is that different Web host sites require different file extensions.*

Previewing HTML

Before you save your workbook as a Web document, you should preview it in your browser. This helps you make design decisions about fonts, size, and so forth, because most people try to make Web pages a bit more spiffy than a plain document.

Choose File | Web Page Preview from the menu bar to open your browser and see your document as a Web page (see Figure 17-1).

Close the browser window to return to the Excel window.

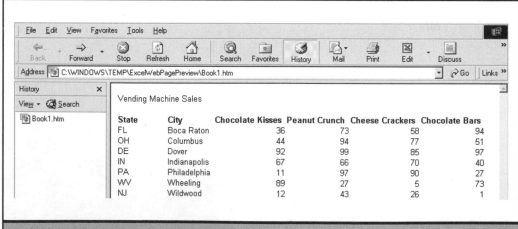

Figure 17-1.   *This worksheet definitely needs some design work to make it a slick Web page*

Saving as HTML

You can save your work as an HTML file, which means you can share the contents with anyone who has browser software (which includes almost everybody running a PC), even if they don't have Excel.

Note *You cannot save an Excel workbook as an HTML file if it is password protected.*

To save your workbook as an HTML document, use one of these methods:

- Choose File | Save As from the menu bar; then choose Web Page in the Save As Type text box.
- Choose File | Save As Web Page from the menu bar.

When the Save As dialog box appears (see Figure 17-2), choose from these options and command buttons:

- **Entire Workbook**   Saves the whole workbook, including all the sheets (removes any sheets you're not using).
- **Selection**   Saves only the current selection. The current selection is *Sheet* if, when you choose File | Save As Web Page, only one cell is active or if a range of noncontiguous cells is active or if all cells are active because you clicked the Select All button. The current selection is a range of cells if more than one contiguous cell is active.
- **Add Interactivity**   Makes the Web document interactive, so that viewers can work with the workbook. Without interactivity, the document is a static item that can only be viewed.

Note *Interactivity requires Microsoft Internet Explorer Version 4.01 or higher. It also requires the Office Web Components, which together constitute an option found under Office Shared Features in Microsoft Office Setup.*

- **Publish**   Publishes this document directly to a Web site. Successfully doing so usually requires that you have permission (in practice, this is a password) from a Webmaster or network administrator.
- **Save**   Saves the document in HTML format to a local or network accessible folder.
- **Change Title**   Lets you supply a title for your Web document instead of using the filename.

Tip *Before you save the file as a view-only Web document, you should convert to pictures any charts that are linked to data. The links between the chart's data series and the source data aren't hyperlinks and aren't built for Web processes.*

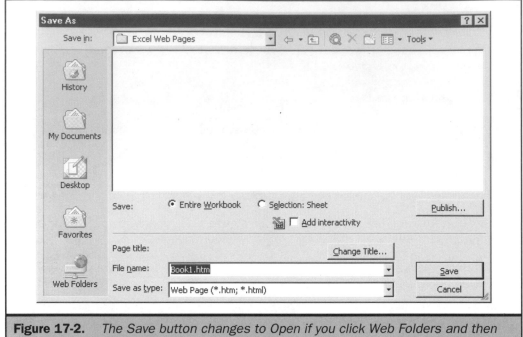

Figure 17-2. *The Save button changes to Open if you click Web Folders and then select one*

Adding interactivity can be very useful, but don't expect full Excel functionality. A user who opens a Web page containing an Excel document with interactivity can edit data, change formulas, and switch from worksheet to worksheet. But when that user closes the browser, any changes that the user made disappear. The page reverts to its original version, and that's what the user will see the next time it's opened.

To save the changes in an Excel file, click the Export To Excel button on the Spreadsheet toolbar. The Excel window opens with the HTML file loaded, but the file is marked read-only. Use File | Save As to save the file with a different filename in the Excel file format.

If you want the user to be able to modify data and make it stick in the HTML file format, consider using Access in conjunction with Active Server Pages or Data Access Pages.

Saving Graphics in HTML

If you have graphics in your worksheet, Excel converts them to the appropriate format when you save the sheet as an HTML file. You can use clip art, shapes, text boxes, and so on. Depending on the original graphic type, the conversion process usually results in .gif or .jpg images. Keep in mind that if you have a graphic that's not embedded but instead is linked to a graphic image, that link must point to a file on your Web server so it's accessible to the viewer.

Setting Web Options

You can exert a fair amount of control over how Excel saves your workbook as an HTML document. Beyond the general options available through File | Save As Web Page, there is another, larger group of settings that pertain to the HTML code. These settings are found by choosing Tools | Options, selecting the General tab, and clicking the Web Options button. When you do so, the dialog box shown here appears. The Web options available to you are discussed next.

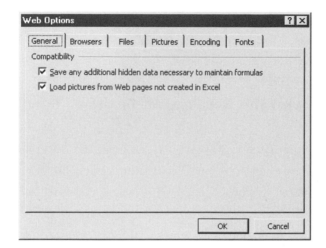

Web Options: General Tab

On the Web Options General tab, you can choose whether to save hidden data into a Web page and whether to load pictures when you open a Web page in Excel.

Save Any Additional Hidden Data Necessary To Maintain Formulas   This option concerns hidden data and formulas on interactive Web pages. Suppose that cell A1 contains the formula = B1 * Z1. You select the range A1:E5 and publish that selection to an HTML file, adding interactivity. In that file, the formula in A1 would not normally recalculate following a change to cell B1 because Z1 is not part of the published range.

The intent of this option is to enable the recalculation of a formula that has precedent data that is not published to the HTML file. If you clear the check box, the formula will be saved instead as a static value.

Load Pictures From Web Pages Not Created In Excel   Fill this check box to include pictures as well as data when you open a Web page in Excel.

Web Options: Browsers Tab

The Browsers tab of the Web options dialog box is shown next. Use it to cause Excel to tailor HTML to the capabilities of different browsers.

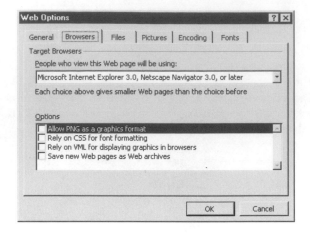

What People Who View This Web Page Will Be Using   In this drop-down you can choose

- Internet Explorer version 3.0 and Navigator version 3.0, or later versions
- Internet Explorer version 4.0 and Navigator version 4.0, or later versions
- Internet Explorer version 4.0, 5.0, or 6.0 (each is a distinct item in the drop-down list box)

Options   The options in the list box are

- **Allow PNG As A Graphics Format**   PNG stands for Portable Network Graphics. It is an alternative to GIF.
- **Rely On CSS For Font Formatting**   Early versions of popular browsers did not support the use of cascading style sheets (CSS). If the users of your Web pages might be using these early versions, you can accommodate them by clearing this check box.
- **Rely On VML For Displaying Graphics In Browsers**   VML stands for Vector Markup Language. It is a means of defining graphic images by means of vectors, or paths described with connected lines and curves.
- **Save New Web Pages As Web Archives**   When you save an Excel file in HTML format, you create a new folder with the same name as the .htm file itself. This folder contains supporting files that contain information and graphics needed to display the Web page properly. The .htm file contains pointers, relative links to the supporting files. These links contain the path to and name of the folder that contains the supporting files. If you move either the supporting folder or the .htm file so that the supporting files are no longer accessible to the .htm file, browsers cannot open the file properly. If you use this option to save as an archive, all the information is written to a single file, termed a *Web Archive*.

A Web archive has the file extension .mht. Using this format, you can (for example) e-mail to another location one file with all the required information contained in it. Web archives are typically much larger than the combination of .htm and supporting files combined.

Browsers and Default Options   Different versions of different browsers have different capabilities, and those differences show up in the check boxes that are filled by default when you choose different browser levels in the Target Browsers drop-down. You can override the defaults by filling or clearing check boxes. The defaults are

- **Internet Explorer 3.0 and Netscape 3.0**   No options selected
- **Internet Explorer 4.0 and Netscape 4.0**   Rely On CSS For Font Formatting
- **Internet Explorer 4.0**   Rely On CSS For Font Formatting and Save New Web Pages As Web Archives
- **Internet Explorer 5.0**   Rely On CSS For Font Formatting, Rely On VML For Displaying Graphics In Browsers, and Save New Web Pages As Web Archives
- **Internet Explorer 6.0**   All four options selected

Web Options: Files Tab

The options you can set for saving Web files are located on this tab. It appears here:

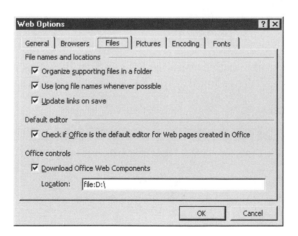

Organize Supporting Files In A Folder   As noted, supporting files are placed in a folder with the same name as the .htm file. If you clear this check box, those files will be placed in the same folder as the .htm file.

Use Long File Names Whenever Possible   If some users have Windows 3.1 as an operating system, they will not be able to locate .htm files that have long (that is, longer than the 8.3 standard) file names. Clear this check box if you think you will need to accommodate them.

Update Links On Save   Selecting this option helps prevent the link breakage that can occur when you move an .htm file so that it can't locate the support files. Filling this check box means that if you resave an existing .htm file to a new location, its links' addresses are updated to reflect the new positioning. This does not prevent link breakage, however: the addresses may be updated but the links will still be broken if the .htm file cannot access their location.

Check If Office Is The Default Editor For Web Pages Created In Office
Suppose that a non-Office application is registered on your computer as the default editor of Web pages. If you use Excel to save a Web page, a message will appear on your screen asking if you want to make Excel the default editor. If you don't want to see that message, clear this check box.

Download Office Web Components   If you are running Excel in a network environment, the system administrator might not have called for Office Web Components to be available to you during the Office setup procedure. When you subsequently take some action that requires one or more Office Web Components, Excel will automatically download the required files if you have filled this check box. You also must supply the server and path in the Location edit box; you can get that information from the system administrator.

Web Options: Pictures
Before you save a final version of a Web page, it's a good idea to view it in different browsers to make sure that it will look the way you want it in each one. Similarly, you should test the page with different screen size settings. The size of the screen itself, measured in pixels, as well as the resolution, can affect the placement of text and graphics. You can try different combinations by changing the settings on the Pictures tab, shown next:

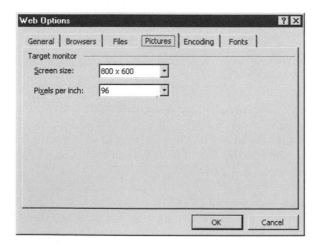

After changing a setting, save the file again as a Web page and then open it in a browser.

Web Options: Encoding

Web pages have an attribute termed *encoding* that determines the character set that's displayed. You can exert some control over that attribute by using the Encoding options, shown here:

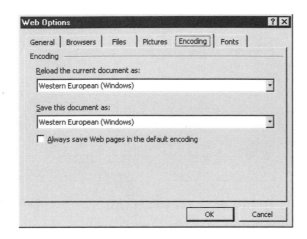

Reload The Current Document As   When it opens a Web page, Excel tries to determine the encoding used by that page. If Excel makes the wrong determination, the characters may look wrong to you. When you click another encoding in this drop-down, Excel reloads the Web page using the encoding you chose. By looking at the resulting characters you may be able to choose the correct language.

Save This Document As   Select the language you want to use for encoding the Web page you're about to save.

Always Save Web Pages In The Default Encoding   Suppose that you open Web pages in Excel that were created using languages other than the one you want to use, and then you re-save them. You can use this option in conjunction with the selection you make in the Save This Document As list box. Filling the check box means that when you save or re-save a Web page, it will use the encoding you selected in the list box. Clearing the check box means it will be saved with the encoding that was in effect when you opened it.

Web Options: Fonts

It is possible for Excel to apply not only the wrong encoding but the wrong font when you open a Web page. After you have selected an encoding, the associated character set is highlighted in the Character Set list box, shown here:

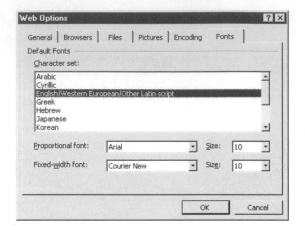

You may also need to select fonts associated with that character set. You can do so using the Proportional Font and the Fixed-Width Font drop-downs.

Opening an HTML Worksheet

When you receive an HTML worksheet, you can view it in a browser. However, you'll find some differences between browsers in the way the document looks. Although a browser might not display formatting characteristics such as bold and italic fonts, the worksheet information is all there so you can examine the figures.

If you don't receive the HTML file directly, but it's on your company's intranet server or application server, you can open it from your browser. Choose File | Open and enter the address for the file in the appropriate dialog box. Some browsers may use the command File | Open File In Browser, and the text box in which you enter the address may be named Open, or File Name. The way you enter the filename depends on whether you're dialing in to the Internet or accessing a company intranet server over a network. For example, you may have to enter **http://companyserver/filename**.

Opening an Interactive HTML Worksheet

When you open an HTML worksheet that was saved as an interactive document, you can manipulate the values. You must be running Internet Explorer 4.01 or higher, but your Office XP software includes IE 5 and the necessary Web components, so you shouldn't have any problems. If you send the file to someone who opens it in a browser that can't handle the file, an error message explains that the document cannot be used interactively.

With the right software, the worksheet opens and you can manipulate the data. You can open the file by double-clicking on it in Explorer, or by choosing File | Open on the IE toolbar. Figure 17-3 shows a worksheet loaded in Internet Explorer 5.0.

Manipulating Contents in a Browser

The first thing you notice when you work with an HTML version of a worksheet is that there's no formula bar, which means you can't tell which values are entered and which are calculated. Additionally, there's no menu bar with commands that match the functions available to you when you work in Excel. However, manipulating the document is quite easy once you understand how everything works.

Editing Cell Contents

If you double-click on a cell, the cell takes on some of the functionality of the formula bar in Excel.

	A	B	C	D	E	F
1	Vending Machine Sales					
2						
3	State	City	Chocolate Kisses	Peanut Crunch	Cheese Crackers	Chocolate Bars
4	FL	Boca Raton	93	80	40	80
5	OH	Columbus	61	54	51	73
6	DE	Dover	54	31	30	74
7	IN	Indianapolis	31	24	31	71
8	PA	Philadelphia	75	97	57	67
9	W V	Wheeling	87	30	90	52
10	NJ	Wildwood	10	52	16	10

Figure 17-3. *The browser spreadsheet has tools for manipulating cell contents*

THE OUTSIDE WORLD

	A	B	C	D	E	F
1	Vending Machine Sales					
2						
3	State	City	Chocolate Kisses	Peanut Crunch	Cheese Crackers	Chocolate Bars
4	FL	Boca Raton	93	80	40	80
5	OH	Columbus	61	54	51	73
6	DE	Dover	54	31	30	74
7	IN	Indianapolis	31	24	31	71
8	PA	Philadelphia	75	97	57	67
9	W V	Wheeling	87	30	90	52
10	NJ	Wildwood	10	52	16	10
11						
12			=SUM(C4:C11)			
13						
14						
15						
16						
17						
18						
19						

Double-clicking means you can see whether the data is a value or a formula. In addition, you can edit all or some of the contents. You merely have to position your cursor at the point where you want to make a change. Use the DELETE or BACKSPACE key to remove information, and enter any new characters you desire. To turn the cell back into a cell (instead of a formula bar), you must press ENTER—clicking another cell doesn't do it.

On the other hand, if you single-click on a cell, any character you type replaces all of the original contents of the cell. Indeed, you could replace a formula with a value and you won't see a warning message.

Inserting and Deleting Rows and Columns

There's no menu item or toolbar button for inserting additional rows and columns, but you can accomplish those tasks by right-clicking and using the commands on the shortcut menu.

Changing Column and Row Size

You can change the width of columns and the height of rows by dragging the separator bar between the column and row buttons. You can also double-click the separator bar to expand the column or row to accommodate the widest (or tallest) cell.

Using Commands and Options Dialog Box

When you're working on an interactive spreadsheet in your browser, the Commands and Options Dialog Box provides tools, features, and functions. To open it, click the Commands and Options button on the toolbar.

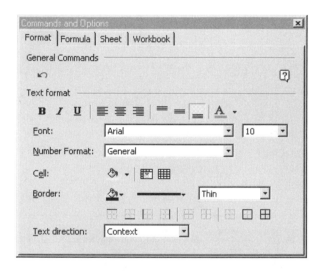

- **Format Tab**   Includes many of the tools and commands you've learned to rely on when you work in Excel. You can format text, cells, and numbers. You can also merge and unmerge cells.

- **Formula Tab**   Displays the value in the active cell and the formula (if any). Use this tab to add and remove names that refer to ranges, formulas, or constants.

- **Sheet Tab**   On this tab you'll find a Find command, along with options to match case and to match an entire cell only. There are also controls to show or hide row or column headers, to show or hide gridlines, and to display the worksheet right to left instead of left to right.

- **Workbook Tab**   Use this tab to set calculation to automatic or manual and to insert, delete, or hide worksheets. You can also choose to show or hide scrollbars, the sheet selector, and the toolbar.

THE OUTSIDE WORLD

Using Hyperlinks

Although it's easy to understand how and why you'd want to use hyperlinks for the workbooks you publish to the Web, what's more interesting is that you can use hyperlinks in your standard, regular workbooks. This is an effective way to use this Web technology.

Using Hyperlinks to Move Around a Workbook

You can jump quickly from one location to another in a workbook by creating a hyperlink. The hyperlink works in Excel and also in the HTML file you view in your browser. To prepare for the hyperlink, you need to understand these choices:

- The target location can be a name (which you must define) or a cell reference.

- The hyperlink itself can be attached to text or to a graphic (which you must insert).

Here's how to create a hyperlink to jump to another location in your workbook:

1. Right-click the text or graphic you're using for the hyperlink.

2. Choose Hyperlink from the shortcut menu to open the Insert Hyperlink dialog box seen in Figure 17-4.

3. If you are using text, fill in the Text To Display box (which automatically inserts the current text in the cell, but you can change it). If you are using a graphic, this field is unavailable.

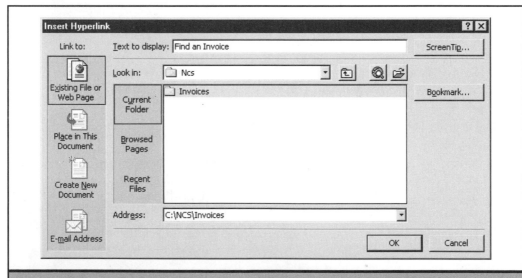

Figure 17-4.   *Use the Insert Hyperlink dialog box to create and configure a hyperlink*

4. Click the Screen Tip button to open the Set Hyperlink ScreenTip dialog box and enter the text you want to use on the screen tip. Click OK to return to the Insert Hyperlink dialog box.

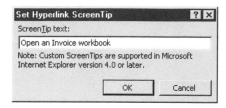

5. In the Link To column, click the icon named Place In This Document.

6. Enter a cell reference, or select a defined name. If the cell is on a sheet other than the currently selected sheet, select that sheet first.

7. Click OK.

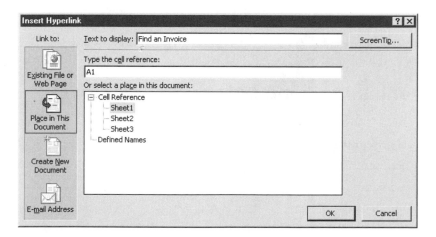

When you position your mouse pointer over the hyperlink, the pointer turns into a hand and the Screen Tip displays.

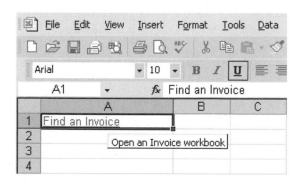

If your hyperlink is text, the text is underlined. If your hyperlink is a graphic, there's no indication that it's a hyperlink, so you may want to put text on the graphic. See Chapter 12 for information about drawing graphics.

- To edit a hyperlink, right-click on it and choose Edit Hyperlink from the shortcut menu.

- To remove a hyperlink, right-click on it and choose Remove Hyperlink from the shortcut menu.

- To copy a hyperlink, right-click on it and choose Copy from the shortcut menu. If you paste it into another worksheet cell, keep in mind that it's not a relative address. Suppose the hyperlink in A1 has A20 as its target. You copy the hyperlink and paste it into C1. The hyperlink in C1 still has A20 as its target: hyperlinks in worksheets don't use relative addressing.

When you copy and then paste a hyperlink into another cell, the hyperlink's text or graphic, its screen tip, and the linkage itself are pasted. When you remove a hyperlink, only the screen tip and the linkage are removed, and the text or graphic stays put.

I use a cell near (usually next to) the target cell to insert a hyperlink that sends the viewer back to the original cell. Having "back buttons" makes it easier to use hyperlinks.

Using Hyperlinks to Jump Outside the Workbook

You can also use a hyperlink to jump to these other targets:

- Another workbook
- A document file
- A Web page
- An e-mail message form
- A new document you create when you create the hyperlink

Open Another Workbook with a Hyperlink

If you want your link to open another Excel workbook, click the Existing File Or Web Page button. Then enter the path and filename to the workbook in the Address box. You can, of course, browse to the file by using the Look In drop down and list box.

Try clicking the Recent Files button to locate the workbook. Of course, if you haven't worked on that file in months, it probably isn't listed and you'll have to use the Browse feature.

Open a Document with a Hyperlink

You're not restricted to Excel files; you can use the Existing File or Web Page button to open a file created in another software application. Of course, in order to open the document, you must have the appropriate software. Clicking the link opens the software application associated with the document, and the document is loaded into the software window.

Open a Web Page with a Hyperlink

You can link to a Web page from your workbook by putting the URL in the Insert Hyperlink dialog box. Click the Browsed Pages button to see the Web pages you've recently visited, in case the target page is listed there.

Clicking on the link opens your browser, which travels to the target Web page.

Open an E-mail Message Form with a Hyperlink

This is really designed for workbooks you're using on the Web, but technically it works anywhere. You can use this to let viewers contact you—perhaps they have a question about some data in your worksheet.

Click the E-mail Address button and fill in the address of the recipient (probably you). You can also fill in the subject line if you wish.

Clicking on the link opens your e-mail software application.

Create a Document for a Hyperlink

If you need a new document for your link, click the Create New Document button on the Edit Hyperlink dialog box.

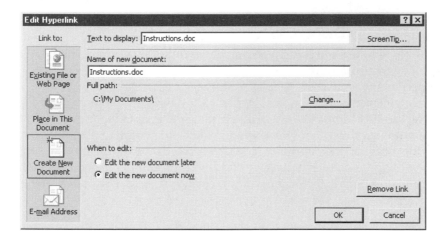

Fill out the dialog box as follows:

1. Enter the name of the new document. If you do not enter a file extension, Excel assumes you want to create a new workbook. If you enter a file extension, the associated software application launches so you can create your document.

2. If you want to change the default path for the storage location for the document, click the Change button and enter a new path.

3. Select Edit The New Document Later or Edit The New Document Now, depending on your mood.

4. Click OK. If you opted to edit the document now, the appropriate software opens so you can create your file. Otherwise, the software opens the first time you use the link.

Using Hyperlinks for Commands and Tool Buttons

You can assign a hyperlink to a toolbar button or to a menu command. Your hyperlink replaces the current command for that button or menu command listing. This process works with any button that does not have a menu connected to it (some buttons display a menu of choices when you click them).

In many cases, hyperlinks for commands and tool buttons have the same end result as creating a macro and assigning it to a button or command, but the amount of work involved in creating a macro is a heck of a lot more than accomplishing this via a hyperlink.

The truth is, turning the existing commands and buttons into hyperlinks has a rather limited advantage (you lose an existing command), but there may be some situations that warrant it. For instance, you may want to replace a shape on the Drawing toolbar with a specific graphic file. Or there may be a menu item you know for sure you are never, ever going to use—making it acceptable to turn it into a hyperlink. It's usually more useful to create new buttons or commands, as you would with macros, and assign hyperlinks to them.

Here's a convenient way to assign a hyperlink to a new, custom button, and if you're so inclined, you can use the instructions to do the same thing, or to replace an existing Excel button (the process is the same). This exercise creates a hyperlink to the Microsoft Word document that provides the information needed to work on a complicated workbook—it's the company budget, and each department adds information to the document. There are comments and questions in the document (for instance, some departments offered several budget figures with explanations, and it's necessary to decide which figure goes into the company's final budget).Before you begin, be sure the toolbar that will contain the Hyperlink button is in your Excel window. Then follow these steps:

1. Choose Tools | Customize from the menu bar to open the Customize dialog box.
2. Click the Commands tab.
3. Scroll to the Macros listing.

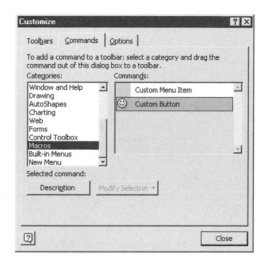

4. Drag the Custom Button to the target toolbar.
5. Right-click on the button and choose Assign Hyperlink | Open from the shortcut menu.
6. In the Assign Hyperlink: Open dialog box, enter the location you want to open.
7. Close the dialog box.

You can tweak your hyperlink button by right-clicking it and choosing Customize from the shortcut menu. This opens the Customize dialog box again, and it also changes the shortcut menu for the button. With the Customize dialog box still open, right-click the hyperlink button to see the new shortcut menu and give the button a name, change the icon, change the appearance (many people like both text and icon), edit the hyperlink, and so on.

Incidentally, Excel automatically displays a default screen tip for all your Hyperlink buttons. The screen tip's text depends on which button you used and on what the Hyperlink's target is.

 You cannot assign to a button on a toolbar a hyperlink that points to a place in the active workbook.

Using Web Queries

You can retrieve text, a table, or multiple tables from a Web document and then use the functions and tools in Excel to work with the data. To accomplish this, you need to create a *Web query*.

A Web query has some limitations, so you should use it only when you need specific data from a Web page. It does not fetch all the contents of a Web page: in particular, it retrieves graphic images.

Configuring a Web Query

To create a Web query, choose Data | Import External Data | New Web Query. The New Web Query window seen in Figure 17-5 opens.

 Before you carry out the import itself, you will probably want to set, or at least check, the query options discussed in the next section.

Enter in the Address box the URL for the Web page you need, and click Go. When the Web page appears, locate the table (or tables) that you want to import and click the

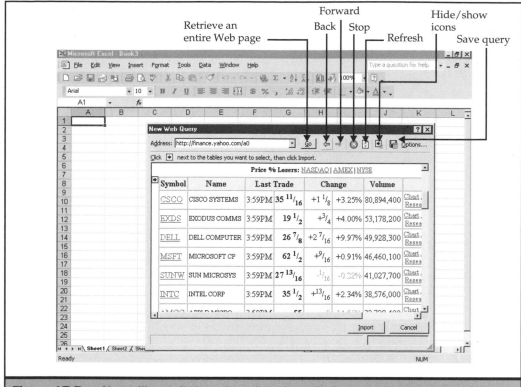

Figure 17-5. *You will usually be taken directly to the home page you selected for your browser*

arrow button at its upper left corner. This action selects the table. When you click the Import button, the data in the selected tables will be imported into the active worksheet. When the data is placed in your worksheet, the range that it occupies is automatically given a range name. That name depends on the name of the site from which you executed the query. Check the Name Box, or use Insert | Name | Define, to find out what that range name is.

Later, you can select any cell in that range and choose Data | Refresh Data to re-execute the query.

Configuring the Data Formatting

Your decision about whether or not you want to keep the Web page formatting (which includes colors and fonts) depends on the look you want for your worksheet. If you do decide to opt for formatting, then you next must decide whether you're going to retrieve all the HTML formatting or just the RTF. Incidentally, it may help you to know as you make this decision, that Excel usually works with RTF more accurately than with HTML formatting.

THE OUTSIDE WORLD

If you plan on retrieving any preformatted text, click the Options button to select the options you need.

Choose the type of formatting you want to keep with the data you retrieve. The three choices are all self-explanatory: None, Rich Text Formatting Only, or Full HTML Formatting.

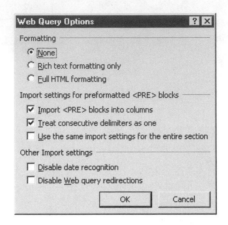

There are three available options that pertain to preformatted blocks. Each option is dependent upon the previous one:

- **Import <PRE> Blocks Into Columns**   This option retrieves preformatted sections divided by columns, using the delimiters available on the Web page. If you deselect this option, each row of the data you retrieve is placed in its own cell.

- **Treat Consecutive Delimiters As One**   This option is available only if you selected the previous option. It means that consecutive delimiters won't produce a blank cell.

- **Use The Same Import Settings For The Entire Section**   This option is available only when you've chosen to treat consecutive delimiters as one. It instructs Excel to use your choice on all the preformatted sections on the Web page. Deselecting this option sets your choices for the first preformatted block; then Excel determines the best options for any other preformatted blocks. (Of course, the "best options" may turn out to be that consecutive delimiters are treated as one.)

In addition to the three options for handling preformatted blocks of text, there are two other import settings:

- **Disable Date Recognition**   Use this option if you expect to encounter numbers on the Web page that Excel will incorrectly interpret as a date. For example, the data may have a column of identification numbers that have dashes or slashes (for instance 10-4-80) that you don't want translated into a date.

■ **Disable Web Query Redirections**   If the Web site contains a redirection attribute, your query might be redirected to a different site when you execute it again at a later time. You can disable any redirecting activity by filling this check box.

Sending the Query and Handling the Retrieved Data

When your configuration options are set, click OK to return to the New Web Query window. Then click Import to send the query. Excel examines the Web page and your options, and then retrieves the relevant data. When the data is ready, Excel needs to know how to handle it.

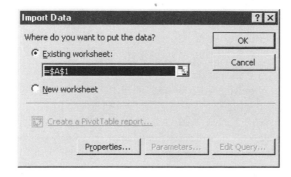

Choose whether you want to place the retrieved data in the existing worksheet or in a new worksheet and indicate the cell you want to use as the first cell.

Click the Properties button to view and manipulate the way Excel handles the query results (see Figure 17-6).

■ In the Name box, Excel automatically inserts the name (from the Web page). You can change the name to something that reminds you of the contents.

■ The Save Query Definition box is checked by default. This saves the query as part of the worksheet so you can refresh the data.

■ Use the options in the Refresh Control section of the dialog box to configure the method you want to use for refreshing.

■ The Data Formatting And Layout section has options you can use to configure the way the data displays in Excel. The available options change depending on the type of data you retrieved.

Click OK to return to the original dialog box; then click OK again to place the data in your worksheet.

THE OUTSIDE WORLD

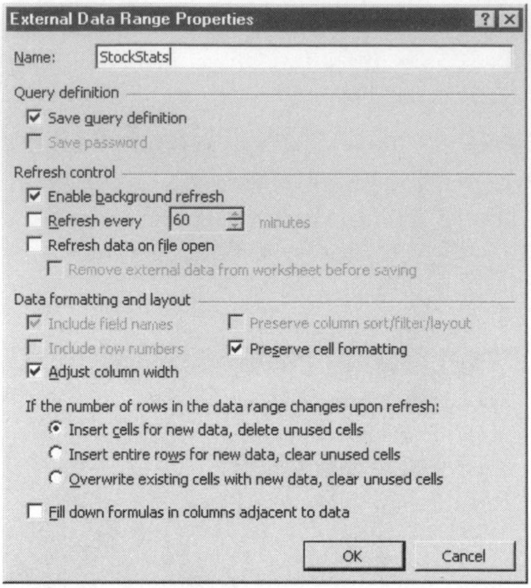

Figure 17-6. *You can tweak your data query after the data is retrieved*

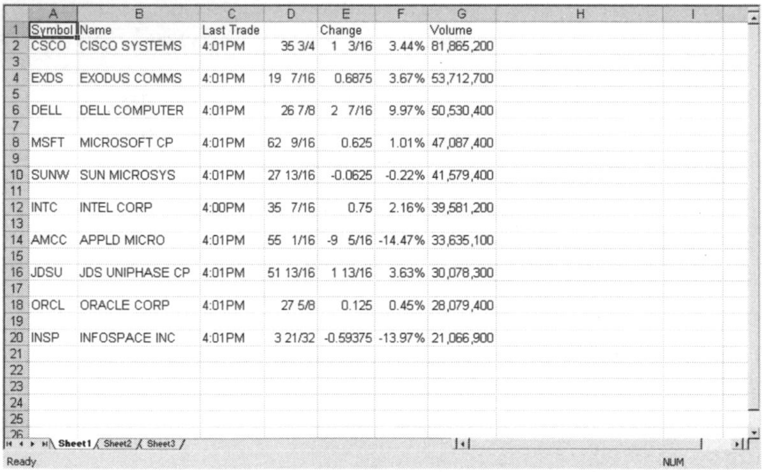

	A	B	C	D	E	F	G
1	Symbol	Name	Last Trade		Change		Volume
2	CSCO	CISCO SYSTEMS	4:01PM	35 3/4	1 3/16	3.44%	81,865,200
4	EXDS	EXODUS COMMS	4:01PM	19 7/16	0.6875	3.67%	53,712,700
6	DELL	DELL COMPUTER	4:01PM	26 7/8	2 7/16	9.97%	50,530,400
8	MSFT	MICROSOFT CP	4:01PM	62 9/16	0.625	1.01%	47,087,400
10	SUNW	SUN MICROSYS	4:01PM	27 13/16	-0.0625	-0.22%	41,579,400
12	INTC	INTEL CORP	4:00PM	35 7/16	0.75	2.16%	39,581,200
14	AMCC	APPLD MICRO	4:01PM	55 1/16	-9 5/16	-14.47%	33,635,100
16	JDSU	JDS UNIPHASE CP	4:01PM	51 13/16	1 13/16	3.63%	30,078,300
18	ORCL	ORACLE CORP	4:01PM	27 5/8	0.125	0.45%	28,079,400
20	INSP	INFOSPACE INC	4:01PM	3 21/32	-0.59375	-13.97%	21,066,900

Now you can work with the data, using the Excel tools and features you're used to.

Saving Web Queries

The option to save a Web query discussed in the previous section only saves the query definition in hidden names that belong to the worksheet. You can also save a query definition so that it's a discrete file in your system, which means you can use it with other worksheets. To do so, click the Save Query button in the New Web Query (or the Edit Web Query) window's toolbar. When you save the query file, it becomes accessible for any workbook. To open it, choose Data | Import External Data | Import Data. When the Run Query dialog box opens (see Figure 17-7), select the query you want to use.

Using Microsoft Query Files

Your Excel software came with several preconfigured query files from Microsoft (refer to Figure 17-7). They use a special type of query—one that contains parameters.

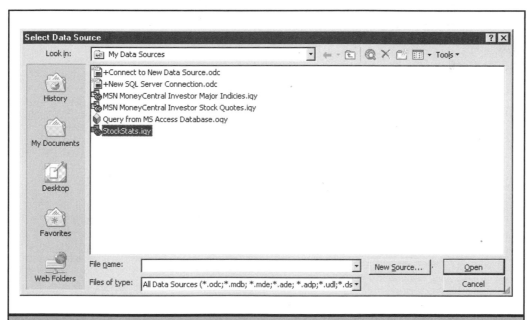

Figure 17-7. *You can open a saved query from any worksheet, not just the worksheet used to create it*

Parameters are data, and you use them in a query to retrieve the data that matches the parameters you set. For instance, the Microsoft Investor Stock Quotes query lets you enter stock symbols so you can retrieve data for specific stocks.

You cannot set parameters in the New Web Query dialog box. The only way to build a Web query with parameters is to use HTML code to set your parameters and configure the query. In addition, the Web page that holds the data you seek must be configured to accept your parameter input.

Certification Skills Covered in This Chapter

If you're preparing for Microsoft Office User Specialist certification, here are the skills you learned in this chapter.

Skill	Activity
Workgroup collaboration	Create Hyperlinks

The Complete Reference

Excel
2002

Part IV

Extending Excel's Reach with VBA

The
Complete
Reference

Excel
2002

Chapter 18

Repeating Tasks Automatically

The first experience that most Excel experts have with Visual Basic for Applications (VBA) comes in response to the mind-numbing boredom of doing the same task over and over. That task might be a standard analysis whose preparation takes little thought but great exactitude. Or it could be the process of combing through data obtained from a remote database throwing out the records that are irrelevant and keeping those that are pertinent.

After you've performed the same task several times with no prospect that it will go away, your mind turns to ways of automating the task. Excel has plenty of tools—particularly the Redo button and the Edit | Replace command—that help you repeat certain tasks. But the scope of these tools is limited. When you need something tailored to your situation, VBA is often the answer.

You needn't be skilled in VBA to take advantage of it. Excel provides you with something called a *macro recorder*. You turn on the recorder, carry out the task that you want repeated, and turn off the recorder. In the meantime, Excel has recorded a macro—that is, some commands in VBA, a dialect of the BASIC programming language—that can mimic the actions you took while the recorder was on.

Later, you "play" that recording—that is, you run the program—and Excel repeats exactly your sequence of actions. You can, if you want, edit that program so that it fits a group of situations similar, but not necessarily identical, to the conditions when you recorded the macro.

Incidentally, that's the first step toward becoming a VBA expert. You may never want to become one. The user's manual for Release 1 of Lotus 1-2-3 introduced macro programming by asking the naïve yet boldface question: "Do you sincerely want to be a programmer?" No one *wants* to be a programmer. You learn to program in self-defense.

But you can benefit from VBA without ever writing or editing a line of code. Just about all you need to know is how to turn the recorder on and off.

Recording, Storing, and Running Macros

Creating a macro with the macro recorder is a two-step process: actually recording the macro and deciding how to store it for later use. Storing the macro is necessary in order to retrieve it later: if you weren't going to run the macro later, there would be little point to recording it. This section details the actions involved in recording, storing, and using a new macro.

Recording a Macro

As part of an ongoing quality control process, you routinely obtain information from a database that captures the ambient temperature in a manufacturing environment. The data set includes the date and time that the measurement was taken (see Figure 18-1).

It makes no difference, of course, where the data comes from—it could just as easily be from a CSV (comma-separated values) file. You need to prepare the data for use in a process control chart. That means that the date in column A needs to show the year as

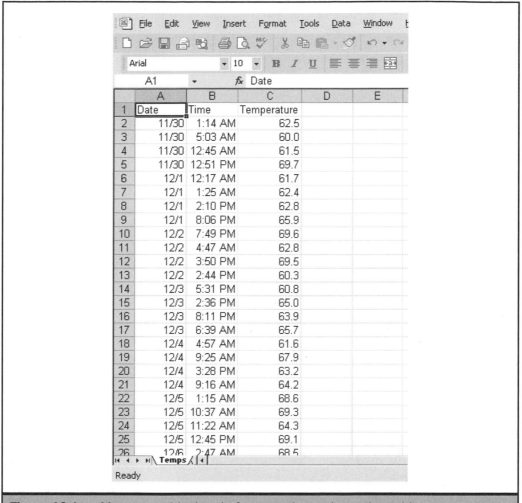

Figure 18-1.   *Macros are ideal tools for repeating tasks such as this data conversion*

well as the month and day, and the time of day in column B needs to appear in 24-hour notation. Also, the Fahrenheit temperature in column C needs to be converted to Celsius.

These tasks take only a couple of minutes. But because you do this once a week, that's about an hour and a half per year that you can save yourself. So, with the worksheet in Figure 18-1 active, you begin by choosing Tools I Macro I Record New Macro. The dialog box shown in Figure 18-2 appears.

The choices that you make in the Record Macro dialog box are important. They are discussed in detail later in this section. You can move ahead using the defaults, though,

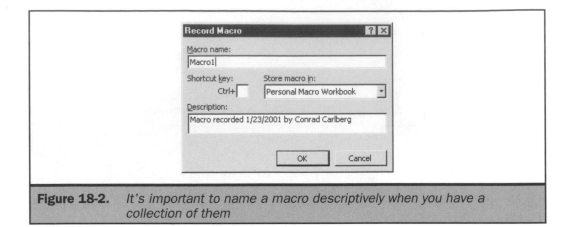

Figure 18-2. *It's important to name a macro descriptively when you have a collection of them*

so for now you just accept them and click OK. When you do so, the Stop Recording toolbar appears (see Figure 18-3).

If the Stop Recording toolbar does not appear when you expect it to, choose View | Toolbars and fill the Stop Recording check box. If you do not see the Stop Recording check box in the toolbar list, you are not recording a macro.

Using the Stop Recording toolbar, you can turn off the macro recorder by clicking the Stop Recording button; you can, instead, choose Tools | Macro | Stop Recording.

With the Relative Reference button, you can toggle between recording absolute cell references such as $C$12, which is the default, and relative cell references such as C12 that depend on the location of the active cell. It is seldom that you will want or need to change to relative referencing, but when you do it's very handy. There is no menu alternative to the Relative Reference button.

Now record the tasks. Take these steps:

1. Click column A's heading to select the entire column. Choose Format | Cells | Number and select the Date category. In the Type list box, choose the 3/14/98 type. Then click OK.

2. Click column B's heading. Choose Format | Cells | Number and select the Time category. In the Type list box, choose the 13:30 type. Then click OK.

3. Select cell D2. Enter this formula:

   =5/9*(C2-32)

   to convert the Fahrenheit temperature to Celsius.

4. With D2 selected, position the mouse pointer over its fill handle and hold down the left mouse button. Drag down to autofill the formula in D2 through the final used cell in column C. (It does not show in the figures, but suppose that is cell C36.) Release the mouse button.

5. Position the mouse pointer on the border of the selected range in column D. Hold down the right mouse button and drag one column left, into column C. Release the right mouse button, and click Copy Here As Values Only. This step replaces the Fahrenheit values with Celsius values.

6. Choose Format | Cells | Number and select the Number category. Choose 1 decimal in the Decimal Places edit box. Then click OK.

7. Click the Stop Recording button on the Stop Recording toolbar or choose Tools | Macro | Stop Recording.

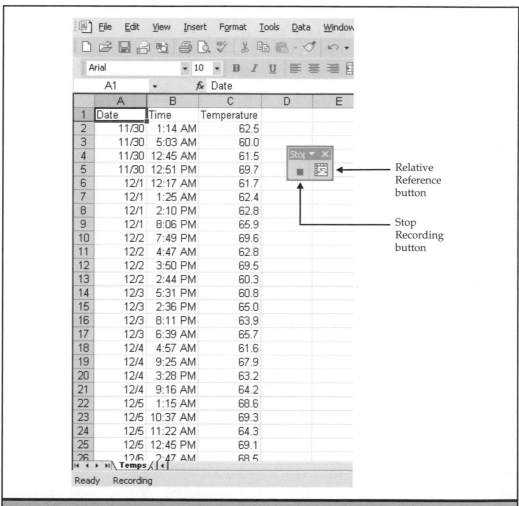

Figure 18-3.   *You can dock the Stop Recording toolbar if it's in the way of your work*

You have now recorded a macro that will take exactly the same actions—format column A to m/d/yy format, format column B to h:mm format, convert Fahrenheit values in C2:C36 to Celsius, and format those values to display one decimal place. This macro will be useful whenever your incoming data has dates in column A, times in column B, and Fahrenheit temperatures in C2:C36. Later sections in this chapter explain how to generalize the macro so that it isn't so finicky about the placement of data.

Using the Record Macro Options

As shown in Figure 18-2, you have four choices to make when you begin to record a new macro: name, shortcut key, storage location, and description. These options become important when you are preparing a macro that you intend to use repeatedly.

Naming and Describing the Macro

The name of a macro is important if you store very many macros. To run—that is, to replay—the macro, you must identify which macro you have in mind by choosing it from a list. A list consisting of Macro1, Macro2, Macro3, and so on is unhelpful, but that's what you get by default.

A possible name for the macro described in the previous section is *Convert_Temperature_Data*. Notice the underscores in the name: the only characters allowed in a macro name are letters, numbers, and underscores— in particular, spaces are disallowed. The macro name must begin with a letter.

During the development process and to make a macro easily accessible, some people start the macro's name with the letters *aa*: for example, *aaConvert_Temperature_Data*. The list of macro names that you can run is sorted alphabetically. Temporarily beginning a macro's name with *aa* helps ensure that it will head the list.

There's no great need to be too wordy in specifying a name. You can supply a description of the macro in another option, and you can make it verbose if you want. The temperature conversion macro might have a description such as "Reformat data to 24-hour clock and mm/dd/yy; convert Fahrenheit to Celsius." When you want to run the macro, this description appears at the bottom of the Macro dialog box.

Selecting a Shortcut Key

If you've come this far in this book, you are surely familiar with shortcut keys. Assigning a shortcut key to a macro means that you can run the macro by pressing CTRL and whatever key you choose. This approach can be faster than the menu method (i.e., Tools | Macro | Macros, select the macro you want, and click Run).

But assigning shortcut keys to macros has two disadvantages: you have to remember the keystrokes, and you need to be careful not to override an existing shortcut that you need.

For example, many users find it convenient to use CTRL-C to copy something. It's a keyboard sequence that crosses Office and other Windows applications and is even similar to the COMMAND-C sequence on an Apple. To enter **C** into the Shortcut Key edit box as a Record Macro option is to override CTRL-C as a keyboard shortcut for Copy. Because 20 letters are already yoked to the CTRL key for special purposes, you should ensure that you're not losing a shortcut that you need. You can, of course, specify a numeral instead of a letter, but some are already in use (for example, CTRL-1 to format cells), and numerals seldom have the mnemonic properties that letters do.

If you have recorded a macro that you're certain to use with great frequency, assigning a shortcut key is probably a good idea. For example, if you run that macro twice for every time that you insert a hyperlink into a worksheet, it might be smart to assign CTRL-K to your macro.

But there are many other ways to conveniently run a macro—auto-open and auto-close procedures (which automatically run when you open or close a workbook), key sequences such as ALT-T-M-M, and toolbar buttons, which are discussed later in this chapter. If you have any doubt, don't specify a shortcut key for the macro. Instead, use another means of invoking it.

Storing the Macro

Macros are stored with workbooks. That's why you sometimes see Excel's warning message that you are opening a workbook that contains macros. When you record a macro, you need to decide what workbook to store it in. This is not an irrevocable decision: you can copy or move a macro to another workbook at any time.

On the Record Macro dialog box shown in Figure 18-2, there is a drop-down labeled *Store Macro In*. It gives you three choices, as follows.

This Workbook

The macro will be stored in the active workbook. In order to run or modify the macro later, you must first open the workbook that is active at the time you record the macro.

New Workbook

Excel keeps the current workbook active but opens a new workbook. When you finish recording the macro, Excel stores it in that new workbook. Later, you must open that new workbook in order to run or modify the macro.

Personal Macro Workbook

Excel stores the macro in a special workbook named Personal.xls. Personal.xls is stored in a subdirectory named XLSTART. When you start Excel, it automatically opens any workbook found in the XLSTART subdirectory—including, of course, Personal.xls (which Excel opens as hidden; to view it, choose Window | Unhide). Storing the macro in this Personal Macro Workbook is a convenient way to make a set of macros accessible whenever you start Excel.

When you close Excel, don't be surprised if you're asked if you want to save changes in Personal.xls. The change you're being asked about is the addition of the macro to that workbook.

Microsoft has long stored the XLSTART folder, by default, in C:\Program Files\\ Microsoft Office\XLSTART. Beta releases of Office XP created that folder. But when Personal.xls was used to store a macro, Excel created another XLSTART in C:\Windows\Application Data\Microsoft\Excel\XLSTART. If you need to find Personal.xls, you should probably use the Windows Find tool to search for it.

Running a Macro

Actually running the macro is the simplest part of the whole macro creation process. If you assigned a shortcut key to the macro—CTRL-E, perhaps—you just press that combination and the macro runs.

Or you can use the menu approach, which doesn't require you to set up anything special such as a shortcut key or a toolbar button. Choose Tools | Macro | Macros to get to the dialog box shown in Figure 18-4.

Click on the name of the macro you want to run. If you gave the macro a description, you might glance at the bottom of the dialog box to make sure you've selected the macro you want. Then click the Run button; when you do so, the macro runs. It carries out the exact actions that you did when you recorded it (unless you have edited the macro in the meantime, as discussed in the section "Editing Macros").

The other command buttons shown in Figure 18-4 require a brief overview:

- **Cancel**   "Never mind, I don't want to run you."

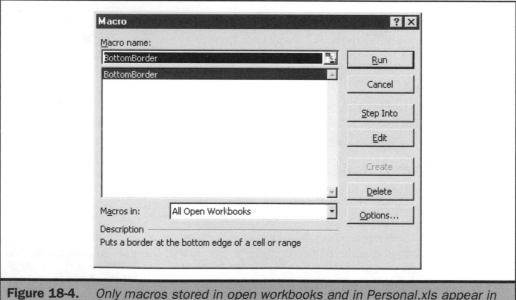

Figure 18-4.   *Only macros stored in open workbooks and in Personal.xls appear in the list box*

- **Step Into** You will find that you have great use for this button. It runs the macro but one step at a time instead of all at once. This enables you to look at the line of code that's about to execute, press a key that means *take the next step only*, and then see what effect the step had. Stepping through a macro like this (discussed in detail later in the chapter) is a wonderful learning tool as well as an aid to debugging.

- **Edit** This is one way to get at the macro's code so as to modify it. One typical reason to modify code is to broaden its scope beyond the specific conditions that existed when you recorded it. Another reason is to make the macro do things that you can't record (such as looping through a series of statements).

- **Create** This button is enabled only when no macros appear in the list box (therefore no workbook that contains macros is open) and you have entered the name of a macro to create in the Macro Name edit box. Once you have done so, clicking Create takes you to the Visual Basic Editor, where you can type your own code instead of recording it.

- **Delete** You know what this does. Be careful, though: this is one Delete you can't Undo.

- **Options** This button brings up the Macro Options dialog box, where you can assign or change a shortcut key and enter or change the macro's description.

All you need to do in order to run—to play back—the macro is click the Run key. Still, setting the stage properly takes a little thought.

At the beginning of this chapter, running a macro was described in this way: *Later, you "play" that recording—that is, you run the program—and Excel repeats exactly your sequence of actions.* At this point, it's fair to tack this phrase on: *in the conditions that apply when you run the macro.*

Suppose that Sheet1 is active, and you record a macro that enters the text string "Phone Number" in cell C1. Later on, with Sheet2 active, you run the macro. You might well think, "Sheet1 was active when I recorded the macro, and I recorded the action of entering 'Phone Number' in C1 on Sheet1. Therefore, running the macro should enter that string on Sheet1 even though Sheet2 is active."

But that's wrong. Running the macro enters the text string in the *active cell*, not necessarily in C1 on Sheet1. There's no reason that distinction should be apparent to you, and you learn this sort of thing only through the experience of recording a macro and then examining what Excel has recorded. Whereas you might intuitively expect Excel to record something like

```
[Book1]Sheet1!$C$1 = "Phone Number"
```

what it actually records is

```
ActiveCell.FormulaR1C1 = "Phone Number"
```

So when you run the macro, the value Phone Number is entered in whatever cell is active.

> **Note** *FormulaR1C1 means that if you had entered a formula, it would have been recorded in R1C1 instead of A1 notation. When you enter a constant value, Excel records FormulaR1C1 even though it's irrelevant. You will encounter many similar irrelevancies in recorded code. The macro recorder attempts to be comprehensive and therefore records much that is not needed.*

After you have been a few times through the process of recording a macro and examining the resultant code, the distinctions between what you might expect and what Excel actually records become clearer.

Creating Your Own Macros

When you are ready to create your own VBA code, instead of using the macro recorder to get things started, take these steps:

1. With the Visual Basic Editor active, choose Insert | Module.

2. A new window appears. It represents the newly inserted module, which is where your code will be stored. Begin by typing the keyword *Sub*.

3. Press the SPACEBAR once, and then type the name you want to give your subroutine—perhaps that's *TopBorder*.

4. Press ENTER. The Visual Basic Editor responds by placing a pair of empty parentheses following the name of the subroutine, a blank line, and an End Sub statement. You should see something similar to this:

   Sub TopBorder()

   End Sub

5. Your flashing cursor should be on the blank line between the Sub and the End Sub statements, so you can just start typing your code.

6. When you have finished, choose File | Save. You can also switch to the Microsoft Excel window and choose File | Save from there. If you do save from the Excel window, be sure that the workbook containing your code is active.

Editing Macros

The prior section discussed how the macro recorder can include unnecessary information in the code it produces—unnecessary, that is, to the task you mean to accomplish. As another example, suppose that with the recorder turned on you format a cell to give it a bottom border. Excel records this:

```
With Selection.Borders(xlEdgeBottom)
   .LineStyle = xlContinuous
   .Weight = xlThin
   .ColorIndex = xlAutomatic
End With
Selection.Borders(xlEdgeRight).LineStyle = xlNone
```

Notice first that the final line in the code gives the border on the right edge of the selection (identified by xlEdgeRight) a linestyle of xlNone—that is, no linestyle and therefore no border. Similar lines of code that the recorder provides—for the top edge, the left edge, and up-and-down diagonals—are omitted from this example; you can find them later in this section. All they do is say, in effect, "Nope, no border here." They're superfluous.

Also superfluous are the .Weight and the .ColorIndex statements between the With and the End With. (This particular With structure says "Between the With and the End With are statements that should all apply to the border at the bottom edge of the selection: its linestyle, its weight, and its colorindex.") During the recording process, all you did was specify a continuous line as a border on the bottom edge of the cell. But so as to be comprehensive, the macro recorder included code for things you didn't set—here, those are the weight and the color of the border.

Because these statements are superfluous, you want to dispense with them. Their presence slows things down, however imperceptibly. More important, they interfere with maintaining the code. When you are fine-tuning a macro, the last thing you need is to be fighting your way through a thicket of superfluous statements.

Getting rid of statements like these is one reason to edit a macro. Another is to broaden its applicability, to make the code work in a variety of contexts. Whatever the reason, you get to the recorded code by choosing Tools | Macro | Macros and clicking the Edit button. The Visual Basic Editor appears, as shown in Figure 18-5.

When you record a macro in Excel, the resulting code is in the language called Visual Basic for Applications. You use the Visual Basic Editor to edit code (of course), to create code from scratch instead of via the macro recorder, to debug the code, and to take other actions such as creating custom user forms. Once you have reached the Visual Basic Editor, you can start modifying the code to suit your purposes. The full code listing that is created by recording a macro to put a border on the bottom edge of a cell is as follows:

```
Sub BottomBorder()
'
' BottomBorder Macro
' Adds a border to the bottom edge of a cell
'
    Selection.Borders(xlDiagonalDown).LineStyle = xlNone
```

```
        Selection.Borders(xlDiagonalUp).LineStyle = xlNone

        Selection.Borders(xlEdgeLeft).LineStyle = xlNone
        Selection.Borders(xlEdgeTop).LineStyle = xlNone
        With Selection.Borders(xlEdgeBottom)
            .LineStyle = xlContinuous
            .Weight = xlThin
            .ColorIndex = xlAutomatic
        End With
        Selection.Borders(xlEdgeRight).LineStyle = xlNone
    End Sub
```

Under the assumption that you have not already added borders to a cell—
borders that you want to remove—the statements that end with the keyword *xlNone*

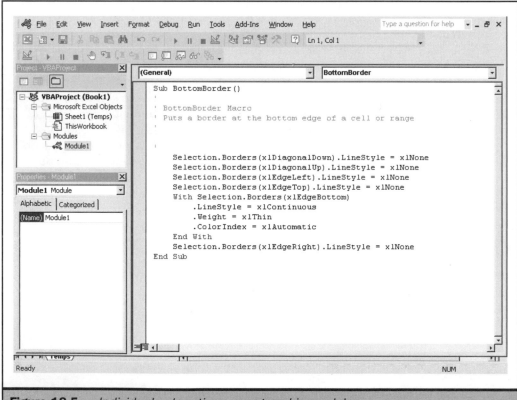

Figure 18-5.   *Individual subroutines are stored in modules*

are irrelevant and can be deleted. To do so, just drag across them with the mouse pointer to select them and press the DELETE key. That will leave you with this code:

```
Sub BottomBorder()
'
' BottomBorder Macro
' Adds a border to the bottom edge of a cell
'
    With Selection.Borders(xlEdgeBottom)
        .LineStyle = xlContinuous
        .Weight = xlThin
        .ColorIndex = xlAutomatic
    End With
End Sub
```

All you want the macro to do is put a border with a continuous (that is, not dashed or dotted) line at the bottom edge of the cell. That means it's okay to delete the statements that define the border's weight (above, xlThin) and its color (above, xlAutomatic). Deleting those statements leaves this code:

```
Sub BottomBorder()
'
' BottomBorder Macro
' Adds a border to the bottom edge of a cell
'
    With Selection.Borders(xlEdgeBottom)
        .LineStyle = xlContinuous
    End With
End Sub
```

Because there's now only one statement inside the block of code between With and End With, that structure no longer helps. Get rid of it as follows:

```
Sub BottomBorder()
'
' BottomBorder Macro
' Adds a border to the bottom edge of a cell
'
    Selection.Borders(xlEdgeBottom).LineStyle = xlContinuous
End Sub
```

EXTENDING EXCEL'S
REACH WITH VBA

Deleting all the extraneous code makes it easier to deal with what's left. Notice first the Sub and the End Sub statements. These statements indicate where the code begins and where it ends and provide the name of the macro. They also indicate that the macro is a *sub*routine, not a function (about which Chapter 21 has more to say). While the statements do little more than act as boundaries here, they are nevertheless necessary: the code would fail to run without them.

The four statements following the Sub statement each begin with an apostrophe. That mark indicates that the line of code is to be skipped—it's a comment. Comments are crucial to good code: the developer uses them to explain what's going on in the code, to annotate changes, to separate blocks of code, and so on. It's up to you whether you would want to delete the four comment lines in the macro as it now stands.

The critical line of code is this one, the only statement left in the macro that actually does something:

```
Selection.Borders(xlEdgeBottom).LineStyle = xlContinuous
```

Notice what's called *dot notation* in the statement. Anything that follows a dot belongs to whatever precedes the dot. In this case, the selection is a cell—the cell that's selected when the macro runs—and a cell has borders: the borders (following the first dot) belong to the selected cell (preceding the first dot).

Similarly, a border has a linestyle: continuous, dashed, or dotted. The linestyle (following the second dot) belongs to the border (preceding the second dot).

But which border? A cell has several. The border in question is identified in parentheses following the *Borders* keyword. This macro has to do with the bottom edge of the selected cell.

Finally, the assignment carried out by the equal sign gives the current selection's bottom border a continuous linestyle.

Consider the keyword *Selection*. As briefly discussed, the macro recorder adopts the convention that its code refers not to the address of the cell that was active when the border was created, but to a less specific object: the *Selection*. Later, when you run the macro and VBA encounters the *Selection* object in the code, it does something with that *Selection*. And the *Selection* depends on what is active when you run the macro.

To recapitulate: cell C1 was active when you recorded the macro. The macro recorder creates code that calls for the bottom border of the *Selection* to be a continuous line. Later, when you run the macro, cell AC42 might be active and therefore selected. If so, cell AC42 gets a bottom border.

A *Selection* can be more than one cell: it can be a range of cells. If the range C1:F1 were selected when you run the macro, each of the cells in that range would get a bottom border. In this case, the range rather than the single cell is the selection.

Suppose that, with cell A1 active, you started the macro recorder and put a bottom border on each of an apparently random set of cells—say, C1, F13, and A10. Shorn of its extraneous statements, the resulting code would look like this:

```
Sub BottomBorder()

    Range("C1").Select
    Selection.Borders(xlEdgeBottom).LineStyle = xlContinuous

    Range("F13").Select
    Selection.Borders(xlEdgeBottom).LineStyle = xlContinuous

    Range("A10").Select
    Selection.Borders(xlEdgeBottom).LineStyle = xlContinuous

End Sub
```

The macro recorder faithfully takes down each of your steps. You selected C1 and gave it a border; you selected F13 and gave it a border; you selected A10 and gave it a border.

Note the statements that select the individual cells. A cell is just a special case of a range: that is, a range that has one cell only. By putting the cell's address within double quotes and the quoted address within parentheses, you can tell VBA which cell you're referring to. A simple extension like this:

```
Range("A1:A10").Select
```

tells VBA that you're interested in a range that contains multiple cells.

Presumably, your purpose in recording this macro is not to both select cells and give them borders, but merely to give borders to certain cells. When you run the macro, you're not interested in selecting the cells. You're just want to make sure that they have borders on their bottom edges.

So the macro can be further simplified (and incidentally made to run faster) by eliminating the statements that select cells and just assigning the border to the cells directly. It's still necessary to tell VBA on which cells to put the borders:

```
Sub BottomBorder()

    Range("C1").Borders(xlEdgeBottom).LineStyle = xlContinuous
    Range("F13").Borders(xlEdgeBottom).LineStyle = xlContinuous
    Range("A10").Borders(xlEdgeBottom).LineStyle = xlContinuous

End Sub
```

As a revealing exercise, try recording a macro while you select and put a border on the bottom edge of three different cells. Stop the macro recorder, and then view the macro by means of the menu sequence Tools | Macro | Macros | Edit. Compare the code you see with the five lines of code just shown.

The macro recorder is an excellent means of teaching yourself VBA. It's also a fine way to develop the first draft of a macro. Whether you use it as a learning tool or as a development device, it's important to know how to reduce the recorded code to its necessary statements. And simpler code is easier to step through, as discussed in the next section.

Stepping Through Macros

As you gain more confidence and experience with VBA, you start causing it to accomplish more complicated tasks. Inevitably your code gets longer and more complicated itself.

As the code gets longer, as you intervene by editing more and more, and as you add more and more code from scratch, the opportunities to make mistakes become inevitable. At some point you will introduce a syntax error, or perhaps a logical error.

Syntax errors are the more easily caught and corrected. One sort of syntax error is

```
Rnge ("A1") = 2
```

where you have simply failed to type "Range" correctly in your attempt to put the value 2 in cell A1. Another sort of syntax error is

```
Range ("A1) = 2
```

where you neglected to supply the closing quote mark around the cell address. In either case, VBA will flag the location of the error for you. In the case of the misspelled "Range," VBA will object when it tries to execute the statement. VBA can recognize the missing quote mark when your cursor moves to another line. With your attention directed to the offending statement, it's up to you to figure out what error VBA found and how to correct it.

Logical errors are often harder to spot. A gruesome error in logic on which I once stubbed my toe concerned the active sheet. I had developed a workbook that has a different worksheet for each day of the year. One of the housekeeping functions in the associated VBA code is to look at the name (such as "Oct 1 2002") of the first sheet in the workbook and determine if the sheet's date precedes the current date; if so, delete the sheet.

The workbook also has a hidden worksheet where various constants are stored. These constants are used in financial calculations on the visible, nonhidden worksheets. That hidden worksheet is named Constants.

One day while opening the workbook, I got a type mismatch error. I looked at the problem statement and saw

```
If DateValue(ActiveSheet.Name) < Date Then ActiveSheet.Delete
```

Looking more closely, I determined that the active sheet was my Constants worksheet. Over time, as each successive first sheet in the workbook was deleted, Constants had worked its way up to being the first sheet. And DateValue("Constants") creates a type mismatch error—it's as though you tried to evaluate SUM("Fred").

But I knew that in the normal course of events, the hidden sheet Constants could not be the active sheet. Without help, Excel does not make a hidden sheet active.

My ego is healthy enough that for a while I thought I'd discovered a bug. But it's also scarred enough to know that I should check it out thoroughly. I stepped through the code, statement by statement and found, buried in a routine that had already executed, this statement:

```
Sheets(1).Activate
```

My own code had induced the error. All the code was syntactically correct, and because VBA cannot divine my intentions, it had nothing to warn me of. That stray Activate statement caused no problems until my hidden Constants sheet became the first sheet in the workbook. Then, as the active sheet, Constants brought my carefully constructed application to its knees.

I never would have found the problem if I hadn't stepped through the code one statement at a time. I'll tell you how to do that next.

Have a workbook open with one or more macros in it. Choose Tools | Macro | Macros and click on the name of the macro that you want to step through (refer back to Figure 18-4). Then click the Step Into button. The Visual Basic Editor appears, as shown in Figure 18-6.

If you do not see the Debug toolbar on your screen, choose View | Toolbars and click Debug in the submenu.

When you get to the Visual Basic Editor by means of the Step Into button on the Macro dialog box, the first line of the selected macro is highlighted. That's always the statement that names the macro. You're ready to start stepping through the statements in the code.

To step through the code is to execute one statement at a time. After that statement has executed, the code pauses—allowing you to examine the effects of that statement—until you call for the next statement to execute. In most cases, that means either clicking

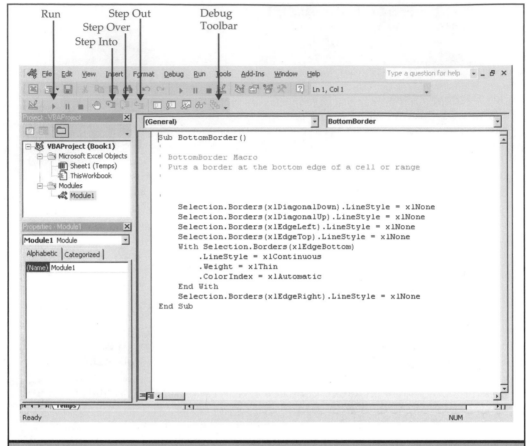

Figure 18-6. *Change the Editor's display properties with Tools | Options and click the Editor Format tab*

the Step Into button on the Debug toolbar (shown in Figure 18-6) or pressing the F8 key (or, if you must, choose Debug | Step Into). You can always tell which statement is the next one to execute: it is highlighted in the Visual Basic Editor.

Suppose that you are testing code that's structured something like this:

```
Sub EnterAndFormatData()
    Range("A1").Select
    ActiveCell = 5
    FormatThisCell
    Range("C2").Select
```

```
    ActiveCell = 24
    FormatThisCell
    Range("B5").Select
    ActiveCell = 7
    FormatThisCell
End Sub

Sub FormatThisCell()
    Selection.Style = "Currency"
    Selection.Font.ColorIndex = 5
End Sub
```

The code has two subroutines. The main subroutine is named EnterAndFormatData. It selects three cells (A1, C2, and B5) in turn and enters numeric values in them. After each value is entered, the main subroutine executes the subroutine named FormatThisCell.

The subroutine named FormatThisCell applies the Currency format to the active cell, and then sets its font color to Blue (a ColorIndex of 5 identifies Blue). Then control returns to the main subroutine, which selects the next cell, enters a numeric value, calls FormatThisCell, and so on.

This is one standard way to duplicate a result. Instead of repeating the two formatting statements for each of the three cells, the main subroutine calls one subsidiary subroutine that encompasses both formatting statements. Once you have the subsidiary subroutine working properly, you don't need to be concerned with it.

But if you're stepping through your code, you will repeatedly step through the subroutine named FormatThisCell. That's a waste of your time. It's a particular problem in a more typical setting, where the secondary subroutine might contain 10 or 20 statements. You don't want to be stepping through all those statements each time the subroutine is called.

Instead of using the Step Into command or button, use Step Over. Refer back to Figure 18-6 for the location of the Step Over button on the Debug toolbar. You can also press SHIFT-F8, or use the Debug menu. When you are stepping through a subroutine and arrive at a statement that calls another subroutine (FormatThisCell, in the preceding sample code), use Step Over to execute the subroutine without stepping into each statement individually.

It's easy to forget to do that, though. There's little more frustrating than to step into a 50-statement subroutine for the second or third time when you never wanted to step through it even once. To avoid that, you could use Step Over all the time. Stepping over an individual statement has the same effect as stepping into that statement. So, using Step Over instead of Step Into is one way to avoid having to step into each statement of a subsidiary subroutine.

But you might want to step partway through a subsidiary subroutine. In that case you can use Step Out (also found on the Debug toolbar, or the Debug menu, or via CTRL-SHIFT-F8). When you have stepped as far as you want into the subroutine, use Step Out to execute the remainder of the subroutine and return control back to the main subroutine, if any.

To illustrate these concepts, here are shortened versions of the preceding example code.

- Step Into:

```
Sub EnterAndFormatData()
    Range("A1").Select
    ActiveCell = 9
'(1)USE STEP INTO HERE:
    FormatThisCell
    Range("C2").Select
End Sub


Sub FormatThisCell()
'(2)TO CONTINUE STEP EXECUTION HERE:
    Selection.Style = "Currency"
    Selection.Font.ColorIndex = 5
End Sub
```

- Step Over:

```
Sub EnterAndFormatData()
    Range("A1").Select
    ActiveCell = 9
'(1)USE STEP OVER HERE:
    FormatThisCell
'(2)TO CONTINUE STEP EXECUTION HERE:
    Range("C2").Select
End Sub


Sub FormatThisCell()
    Selection.Style = "Currency"
    Selection.Font.ColorIndex = 5
End Sub
```

■ Step Out:

```
Sub EnterAndFormatData()
    Range("A1").Select
    ActiveCell = 9
    FormatThisCell
'(2)TO CONTINUE STEP EXECUTION HERE:
    Range("C2").Select
End Sub

Sub FormatThisCell()
'(1)USE STEP OUT HERE:
    Selection.Style = "Currency"
    Selection.Font.ColorIndex = 5
End Sub
```

Running Macros from Toolbar Buttons

When you have created a macro that you use very frequently, you want to speed up access to it. This chapter has already discussed the drawbacks associated with assigning shortcut keys to macros. A good alternative is a toolbar button.

For a variety of reasons, I frequently need to put a set of random integers on a worksheet.

To do this manually, I would have to take these steps:

1. Select a range of cells.

2. Enter the formula **=TRUNC(RAND()*100)**.

3. Choose Edit | Copy. Then choose Edit | Paste Special | Values. Or I could right-drag the range, release the mouse button, and choose Copy Here As Values Only from the shortcut menu.

I much prefer to select a range of cells and then click a toolbar button to run this code:

```
Sub RandomValues()
Dim cel As Range

For Each cel In Selection.Cells
   cel = CInt(Rnd * 100)
Next cel
End Sub
```

Don't worry about the syntax or logic in this code. It will be much clearer after you have completed this book's chapters on VBA. The point is that I use it so often that to me it's worth assigning it to a toolbar button. You very likely have some similar tasks—here's how to associate them with buttons:

1. Your macro should be stored either in an open workbook or in Personal.xls.

2. Choose View | Toolbars and click Customize in the Toolbar submenu. The Customize dialog box appears.

3. If necessary, click the Toolbars tab in the Customize dialog box. Then click the New button. The New Toolbar dialog box appears (see Figure 18-7).

4. Either enter a descriptive name for the new toolbar or accept the default name. (If you plan to create several toolbars, keep in mind that names like Custom1 and Custom2 are not rich in intuitive meaning.) Then click OK.

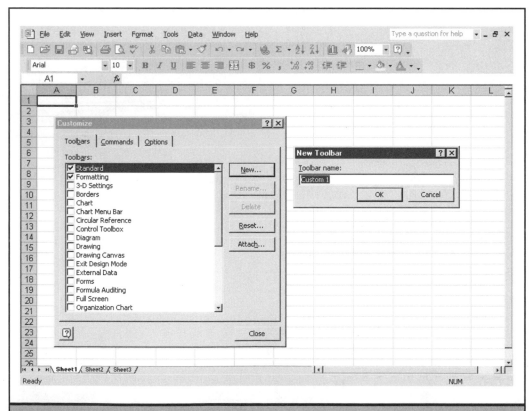

Figure 18-7. *The name you assign to the toolbar will subsequently appear in the Toolbars list box*

5. A new, empty toolbar appears. This is where you will place your toolbar button. Click the Commands tab on the Customize dialog box (see Figure 18-8). Select a command category from the Categories list box by clicking it. The commands that are available for that category appear in the Commands list box.

6. Select a command in the Commands list box by putting the mouse pointer over it. Hold down the left mouse button and drag the command onto the new, custom toolbar. Release the mouse button.

Tip *To avoid confusion, it's best to choose a button that does not appear on the toolbars that you normally use. But the same button image can have different functions. The Save button on the Standard toolbar saves a workbook; the same button image on a custom toolbar could be made to close the workbook without saving it.*

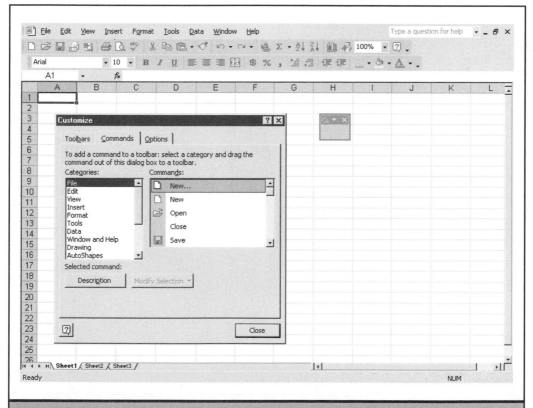

Figure 18-8. *Click the Description button to see what each command does*

7. Either click Modify Selection on the Commands tab, or right-click the new toolbar button on the custom toolbar. Choose Assign Macro. The Assign Macro dialog box appears (see Figure 18-9).

8. Choose the appropriate location of your macro in the Macros In drop-down. Then click the name of the macro that you want to assign to the button.

9. Click OK to return to the Customize dialog box, and then click Close. Dock the new toolbar, if you want, by dragging it to an edge of the Excel window.

Your macro is now assigned to the toolbar button. The macro will run whenever you click its button.

Figure 18-10 shows the shortcut menu that appears when you click Modify Selection on the Commands tab of the Customize dialog box.

Notice in Figure 18-10 the submenu of button images from which you can choose. These are images that are not associated with buttons on any of the built-in toolbars.

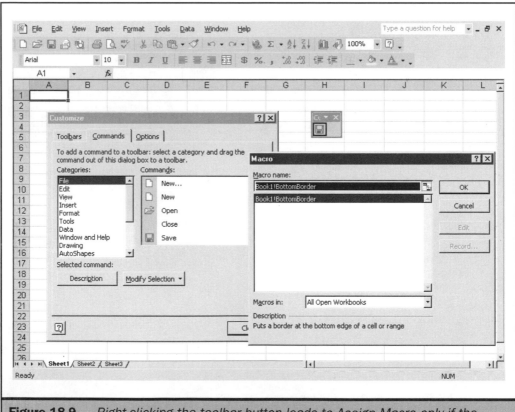

Figure 18-9.   *Right-clicking the toolbar button leads to Assign Macro only if the Customize dialog box is open*

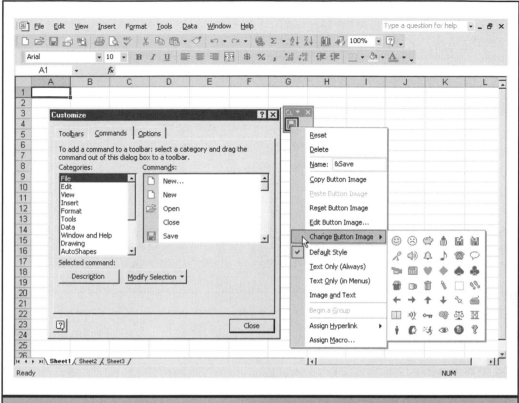

Figure 18-10.   *Using an image from the submenu helps prevent confusion with a standard button*

If you prefer not to use a standard button—such as the Open File or the Chart Wizard button—begin by selecting a standard button and then use this submenu to change the image to something more apt.

You are probably familiar with the screen tips that appear when you place your mouse pointer over a toolbar button for a second or two. A box appears with the button's name and disappears when you move your pointer away from the button. You can set a screen tip by entering a name for your custom toolbar button on the submenu shown in Figure 18-10: where that figure shows *&Save*, type the text of your screen tip, such as *Enter Random Integers*.

A toolbar can belong either to the application—Excel—or to a particular workbook. When you create a custom toolbar, it belongs by default to Excel. Whenever you start Excel, the toolbar is available and appears automatically if you have filled its check box in the View | Toolbars list box.

You can also assign a custom toolbar to a particular workbook (if you do so, it surely makes sense to store the toolbar's macro in the same workbook):

1. Open the workbook to which you want to assign the toolbar.

2. Invoke the Customize dialog box either by right-clicking the toolbar or choosing View | Toolbars and clicking Customize.

3. On the Toolbars tab there is an Attach button (refer to Figure 18-7). Click Attach to display the Attach Toolbars dialog box (see Figure 18-11).

4. Click the name of the toolbar in the Custom Toolbars list box. Then click the Copy button to attach the toolbar to the workbook.

5. Click OK, and then click Close on the Customize dialog box. Save the workbook.

The custom toolbar is now associated with the workbook and will appear whenever you open that workbook. With that workbook closed, you can even delete the custom toolbar using View | Toolbars. If you do so, the toolbar will not be available—not to Excel, not to any other workbook—unless you open the workbook to which it's been assigned.

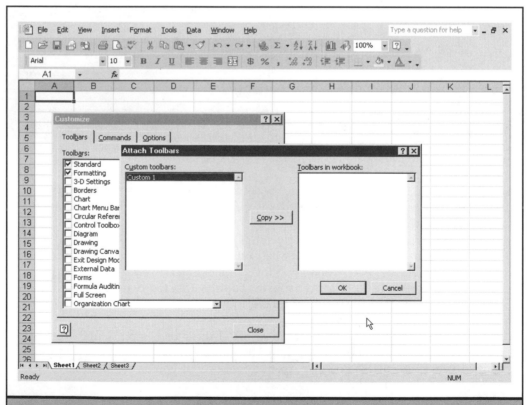

Figure 18-11. *You also use this dialog box to delete an attached toolbar from a workbook*

Chapter 19

The Visual Basic
Editor and the
Excel Object Model

A s you do more and more work with VBA, you will need to use the Visual Basic Editor (VBE) more frequently. And because all Office applications use the same VBE, you can apply your knowledge of the VBE, as it appears in Excel, to Word, to Access, and so on—that's one reason that Microsoft refers to the VBE as an Integrated Development Environment.

There are several ways to look at projects that you have under development, and this chapter begins by discussing those viewpoints. This chapter also provides an introduction to two broad groups of elements that you work with in the VBE: modules (which contain VBA code) and forms (which contain controls such as option buttons, check boxes and list boxes).

Viewing and Using VBE Windows

The VBE provides you with several windows where you can look at and control different aspects of your developing project: among them are the Project Explorer, the Properties window, the UserForm window, and the Code window. Before you can use these windows, you need to get to the VBE from Excel's workbook window: choose Tools | Macro | Visual Basic Editor, or use ALT-F11 (see Figure 19-1).

The Project Window

A *project*, in VBA terminology, is usually considered to consist of modules, forms, and sheets. The Project Explorer works much like the Windows Explorer: by using it properly you can select and activate any element in any active project. Notice in Figure 19-2 that the Project Explorer displays two different projects.

As in Windows Explorer, you click the plus sign on the left of a folder to open the folder and see its contents. Or click a minus sign to close the folder. There are three different objects that the Project Explorer organizes into their own folders:

- **Objects** These consist of the worksheets and chart sheets that are in the workbook that contains the project. There is also a special object called ThisWorkbook. It is a useful way to refer to the entire workbook that contains the project.

- **Forms** A project's forms are any custom user forms that you have developed for use with the project. These are usually dialog boxes that appear on the user's screen under conditions that you have specified (for example, the user clicks a custom menu item). You customize these forms by placing buttons, check boxes, list boxes, spinners, text boxes, combo boxes—in short, almost anything you'd see on a dialog box that's built into Excel itself.

- **Modules** As noted above, modules contain your VBA code.

By selecting—that is, by single-clicking—in the Project Explorer any Excel object, form, or module, you make it active in the Properties window, where you can view and change its properties.

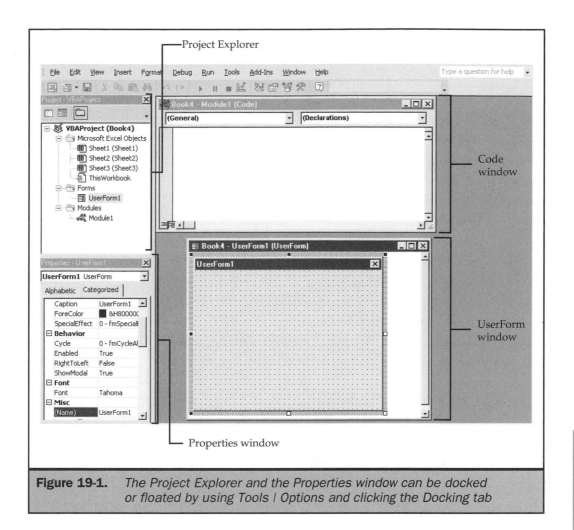

Figure 19-1.   *The Project Explorer and the Properties window can be docked or floated by using Tools | Options and clicking the Docking tab*

By double-clicking a form or module in the Project Explorer, you cause it to appear in its own window. And by double-clicking an object—again, a worksheet or the ThisWorkbook object—you cause a new module to appear in the Code window: the module can contain code that pertains to the selected object.

The Properties Window

Once you have used the Project Explorer to select a sheet, a form, or a module, you can control its properties in the Properties window. Although there are various properties that you can set in other ways, there are some that can be set only by using VBA or by means of the Properties window.

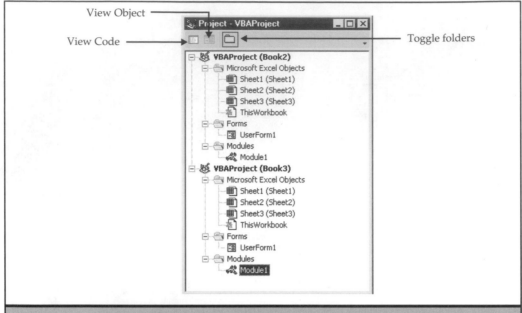

Figure 19-2.   *Click the Toggle folders button to display or suppress the folder icons in the Project window*

For example, you're familiar with how to hide a worksheet in Excel: you select the worksheet and choose Format | Sheet | Hide. You might supply a password to protect the hidden sheet against being opened by someone who shouldn't do so.

A drawback to this approach is that if you now choose Format | Sheet, the Unhide menu item is enabled. This tells anyone who cares that there is a hidden worksheet in the workbook. You might not want anyone to be aware of that fact.

When you hide a worksheet in this way, you are setting its Visible property: the property's value is xlSheetHidden. If you did the same thing using VBA, the statement would be something very much like this:

```
ActiveSheet.Visible = xlSheetHidden
```

But VBA gives you another value for the Visible property: xlSheetVeryHidden. You can't make a worksheet Very Hidden from the Excel window, but from the VBE you can write a VBA statement like this:

```
ActiveSheet.Visible = xlSheetVeryHidden
```

Making a worksheet Very Hidden does not enable the Unhide menu item from Format | Sheet. So there's no clue from the Excel window that a Very Hidden worksheet exists. The only way to make visible a worksheet that is Very Hidden is through the VBE.

You can also set a worksheet's Visible property from the Properties window. With a worksheet selected in the Project Explorer, just click in the Visible row of the properties grid. A drop-down arrow appears; when you click it, you can choose among the three values for the Visible property: xlSheetVisible, xlSheetHidden, and xlSheetVeryHidden.

Of course, you can also set other properties by using this window: a worksheet's name, the standard width of columns on the worksheet, the font for text that appears on a form, where in a window a User Form appears when it's called, and so on.

> **Note**   *The Properties window shows two instances of the Name property for a worksheet: Name and (Name). The property that's not enclosed in parentheses is the name that appears on the worksheet's tab in the Excel window. The property that is enclosed in parentheses is termed the CodeName and is an alternative way to refer to that worksheet in VBA code. For example, a worksheet's tab might show the name Sheet1, while its CodeName might be AuthorizedUsers.*

The Properties window has two tabs: Alphabetic and Categorized. On the Alphabetic tab, properties are displayed in alphabetic order without regard to their category. On the Categorized tab, properties are listed alphabetically within categories.

For worksheets and for the ThisWorkbook object, there is only one category of properties: Miscellaneous. Because the properties are listed alphabetically within that category (and a Module has only one property, its Name), there's nothing to be gained by using the Categorized tab.

But User Forms (for example) have several categories: among them are Appearance, Behavior, Position, and Scrolling. Within these categories are a total of 35 properties. So the Categorized tab can be useful in this case: if you don't know the name of the User Form property that you want to set, but you can guess that it belongs to a particular category, then it will be easier to find on the Categorized tab.

The Code Window

The main portion of the Code window contains the module that you are editing. When a module is active, the combo box in the upper-right corner of the Code window contains a list of the macros that are located in that module; click its drop-down arrow to see their names. Because macros are also termed *procedures*, this combo box is called the Procedure box (see Figure 19-3).

By clicking on the name of a macro in the Procedure box, you can jump directly to the first statement in that procedure.

The Code window also contains two icons in the lower-left corner of the window: Procedure view and Full Module view. In Procedure view, only one procedure in the module is visible at a time; to go to another procedure, you must use the Procedure box. In Full Module view, all procedures in the module are visible, and you can get to another procedure either by means of the Procedure box or by scrolling up or down until the procedure comes into view.

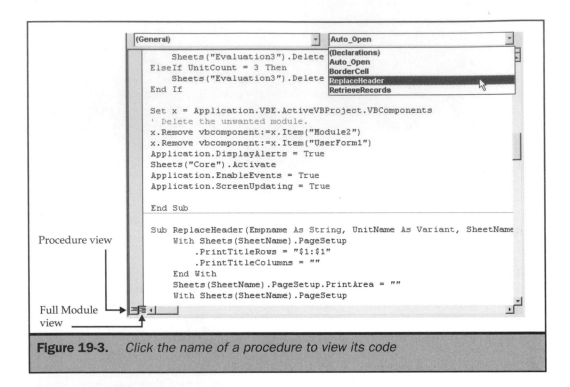

Figure 19-3. Click the name of a procedure to view its code

The UserForm Window

In the VBE, when you choose Insert | UserForm, the UserForm window appears. The Control Toolbox by default also appears (see Figure 19-4).

Later in this chapter, and in Chapter 23, you will learn about the controls that are available to you by way of the Toolbox. You can use them to establish, on your form, familiar elements such as text boxes, command buttons such as OK and Cancel, combo boxes, reference edit boxes, tab strips, and so on.

Use the sizing handles at the corners and the sides of the form to make it wider or narrower, taller or shorter.

When a UserForm window is active, the View Code and the View Object icons in the Project Explorer become useful. It often happens that your form has VBA code associated with it—for example, code that defines what to do when the user selects an option button on the form, or when an item is chosen from a list box, or when the user clicks a command button such as OK. This code doesn't appear in the Modules folder in the Project Explorer—it's kept "behind" the form where it's out of the way.

This method of storing the code makes good sense, because the code usually has no purpose beyond reacting to controls on the form. So you probably don't need to get at that code unless the form is active in the VBE.

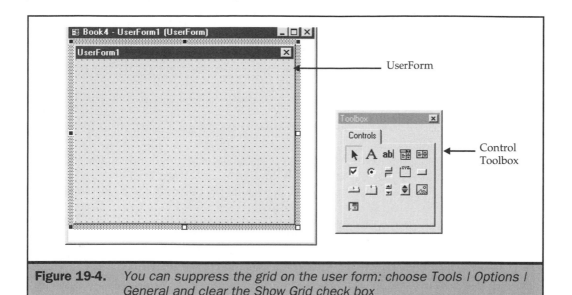

Figure 19-4. *You can suppress the grid on the user form: choose Tools | Options | General and clear the Show Grid check box*

In that case, you can toggle back and forth between the form and its code by clicking the Project Explorer's View Object icon to view the form and its View Code icon to view the code behind the form. In either case, you must have first opened the form by double-clicking its icon in the Project Explorer.

 While the code that's associated with a control on the user form doesn't appear in a module, that code can make reference to other procedures that are in modules.

Other Windows

Two other windows that are available to you in the VBE are the Immediate window and the Locals window. Their applicability is more limited than that of the windows already discussed in this chapter—they are most often useful when your code is either running or in Break Mode. (Break Mode occurs when you have interrupted the code such that the next statement will not execute until you cause it to do so.)

Nevertheless, it's difficult to get along without these windows when you're developing and debugging a project.

The Immediate Window

You can use the Immediate window to execute a command or to return a value immediately, and this applies whether or not code is running. To invoke the Immediate window, either choose View | Immediate Window or click the Immediate Window button on the VBE's Debug toolbar.

Suppose that you are working in the VBE and you want to add a worksheet to the active workbook. You could click in the Immediate window and type the following VBA statement:

```
Sheets.Add
```

This VBA statement has the same effect as choosing Insert | Worksheet from Excel's main menu.

Now suppose that you have written some VBA code that creates an array of values—this might be a memory array with three rows and three columns. As you are stepping through your code, statement by statement, you come to a point where you'd like to check the values that are in the array. One useful way to do this is via these two statements in the Immediate window:

```
Sheets.Add
Range("A1:C3") = MyArray
```

After you type each statement, you press ENTER to execute that statement in the Immediate window. Because your code is running, even though you're stepping through the code in Break Mode, the array named MyArray contains the values that have been assigned to it. (If the code is not running, its variables have no values.) Assigning MyArray to A1:C3 on the active sheet—the one that you added with Sheets.Add—writes the values in MyArray to that range. Now you can switch from VBE to Excel to look at those values on the new worksheet, and later switch back to VBE to continue execution of your code.

Another way to view the values in MyArray, or of any variable that has a printable value, is to use the question mark in the Immediate window. For example, you could check the value in the first row, second column of MyArray with this:

```
? MyArray(1,2)
```

The value that you requested then appears in the Immediate window when you press ENTER. This is a useful way to check individual values, but if you have an array of values to check, then it's best to add a worksheet and write the array to that sheet.

Another use for the Immediate window is to capture values as code is running normally. For example, you might find that your code is taking an unexpectedly long time to execute, and you're not sure which part of the code causes the delay. You could sprinkle this statement in a few locations in the code:

```
Debug.Print Time
```

(Be sure you understand that to have the desired effect of timing the execution of your code, this statement must be in the code itself, not typed into the Immediate window.) Whenever VBA encounters that statement, it writes the current time to the Immediate window. Even better:

```
CurrentPoint = CurrentPoint + 1
Debug.Print CurrentPoint, Time
```

By incrementing the variable named CurrentPoint by 1 each time you execute Debug.Print, you make it easier to associate elapsed time with different points in your code. And if your code consists of several procedures, you might print the name of the procedure along with the time.

The Locals Window

The Locals window is a great help when you are testing or debugging code. It displays information about variables that are *local* to the procedure that is active. The Locals window in Figure19-5 shows this information:

- The name of each variable declared within the procedure
- The value of that variable as the current statement is being executed
- The type of that variable

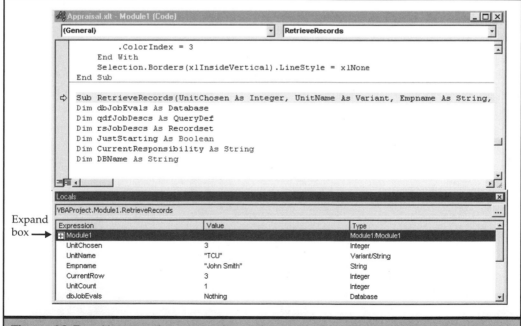

Figure 19-5.   *You see the expression, value, and type in the Locals window only when you are stepping through a procedure*

In addition, the Locals window can display similar information about any variables that have been declared at the module level, outside any procedures that the module contains. To display module level variables, click the Expand box beside the name of the module in the Locals window; to suppress them, click the Collapse box.

How can this information be of value to you? When you are testing your code, it's often by stepping through it, one statement at a time. As you do so, you know what values different variables *should* take on. If there's a problem with your code, it often shows up in an unexpected value for some variable. Keeping an eye on the value of variables that are local to a procedure, and that are available to the procedure because they're defined in the procedure's module, is a good way to keep track of what's going on as the procedure executes.

The Watch Window

The Watch window is similar to the Locals window, except that you choose the expressions that you want to watch. These expressions may be local to the active procedure or they may be module level variables or they may belong to some other procedure. In the latter case, the expression is said to be *out of context*, and that is what is displayed in the Value column of the Watch window (see Figure 19-6).

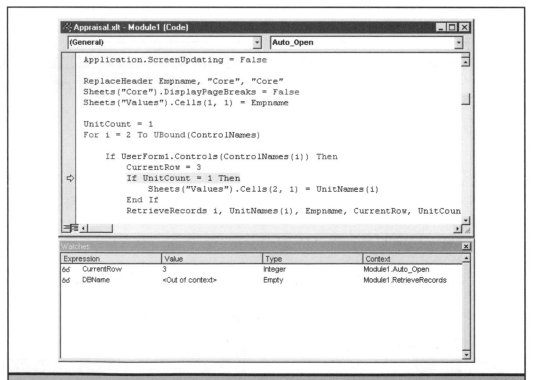

Figure 19-6. *Watches can be used to conditionally suspend execution of your code*

To add a watch expression, either choose Debug | Add Watch or right-click in the Watch window and select Add Watch from the submenu. When you do so, the dialog box shown in Figure 19-7 appears.

Your choice of Watch Type depends on what you are trying to accomplish. If you are stepping through your code statement by statement, you might want to simply watch what happens to the value of the expression as statements execute. You would choose Watch Expression.

But if you are actually running the code rather than stepping through it, you might want to stop the code as it's running—that is, to enter Break Mode—when something special happens. For example, you might be having trouble with a variable named TotalCosts. You could arrange to enter Break Mode when the value of TotalCosts changes: choose TotalCosts as the Watch Expression, and choose Break When Value Changes as the Watch Type. Then run your code. You don't need to examine each and every statement that executes: your attention will be drawn only to those statements that result in a change to the value of TotalCosts.

Yet another use of the Watch window is to define new expressions based on existing variables. Suppose that your code uses, among many others, variables named TotalSalaries and TotalCosts. The value of the TotalSalaries variable *shouldn't* exceed the value of the TotalCosts variable, but something's wrong with your code and you find that at completion TotalSalaries is greater than TotalCosts.

To trace what's going wrong, you could enter this in the Expression box of the Add Watch dialog box:

TotalSalaries > TotalCosts

Then choose Break When Value Is True as the Watch Type. As you run the code, VBA keeps track of whether TotalSalaries exceeds TotalCosts. When a statement executes that causes the expression to be True, VBA breaks execution of the code and highlights

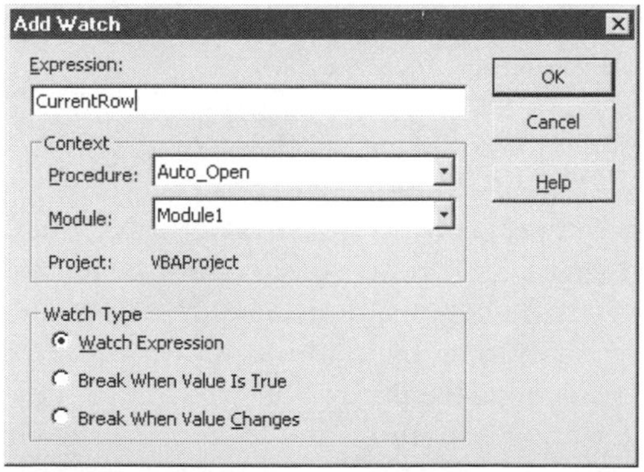

Figure 19-7.   *To watch a nonlocal variable, choose the All Procedures option in the Procedure drop-down*

EXTENDING EXCEL'S
REACH WITH VBA

the current statement. This normally helps you isolate the cause of the erroneous condition.

To delete or edit an existing Watch Expression, choose one of those options from the Debug menu or from the submenu that appears when you right-click in the Watch window.

The Object Browser

When you are developing a VBA project in Excel, you have access to objects. Many of these objects belong to Excel: worksheets, toolbars and menus, rows, columns, charts, and so on; other objects, such as the Office Assistant, belong to Office; other objects, such as check boxes, belong to Forms; still other objects belong to your VBA project— for example, the worksheets in its workbook and the workbook itself.

These objects have methods, properties, and events that are associated with them. For example, the worksheet object has a Name property, an Activate method, and a Calculate event. A worksheet alone has over 80 associated properties, methods, and events.

A property is an aspect of an object that you can control. You could, for example, think of a car as having a Color property. You can change the value of that Color property by having the car painted. Similarly, a worksheet has a Visible property. You can change the value of the Visible property by hiding the worksheet.

A method is a procedure that acts on an object. If you are driving that newly painted car, you might apply the SteerLeft method to turn a corner. If you want to remove a worksheet from a workbook, you apply the worksheet's Delete method.

An event is a procedure that occurs when something happens to an object. If you drive that newly painted car into a tree, the car's InflateAirBag event might occur. If you change a value on a worksheet, the worksheet's Change event would occur. Then, you can make use of the occurrence of the Change event to cause other things to happen.

The difference between a method and an event is a little subtle. A method occurs when your code calls for it to occur. Embedded in your code might be this statement:

```
Sheets("Sheet1").Delete
```

When the execution of your code reaches this statement, VBA applies the Delete method to remove Sheet1 from the workbook.

In contrast, an event can occur regardless of whether or not code is running. A worksheet has a Change event, and you write code for that event; that code, also known as an event handler, then runs when the worksheet changes. The worksheet can change because a user entered something or because other VBA code changes it.

It's difficult to keep track of all the things you can do with an object by manipulating its properties, invoking its methods, and firing its events. The Object Browser helps you do so.

For example, suppose that you are developing a project that calls for the user to enter some data using a Data Form. Rather than relying on the user to choose Data | Form from the worksheet menu, you want your code to display the Data Form on the user's behalf. But you don't know whether you use a property or a method to show the Data Form; nor do you know which property or method to use.

One solution is to use the Object Browser. You can click its button on the VBE's Standard toolbar, or choose Object Browser from the View menu. When you do so, the window shown in Figure 19-8 appears.

To solve the current example, you would scroll through the Classes list until you come to Worksheet. When you click on the Worksheet class, the Members list displays the properties, methods, and events that belong to the Worksheet class. Scrolling through the associated members, you come to the ShowDataForm member and intuit that it's the member that you wanted. And you enter this statement in your code:

```
Worksheets(1).ShowDataForm
```

The Object Browser makes it easy to get Help for a class or for a member of that class. With a class or a member selected, click the Object Browser's Help button; the Help information for the selection is displayed.

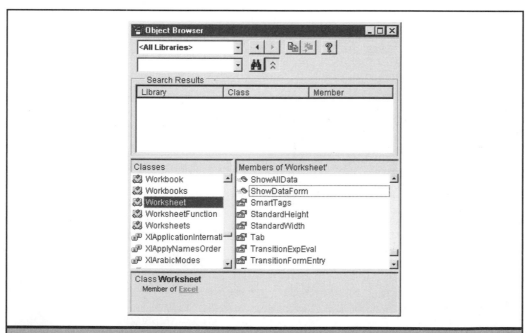

Figure 19-8.   *The Object Browser is a roadmap to the entire Excel object model*

The Object Browser can also ease the task of determining what values a property can take on. For example, recall that you can use VBA code to set the Visible property of a worksheet. To find out what values you can use for that property, you start by clicking Worksheet in the Class list. In the Members list, you scroll down until you come to the Visible property. When you click on that property, further information appears at the bottom of the Object Browser: you see Property Visible As XlSheetVisibility. When you click on the word XlSheetVisibility, the Object Browser enumerates the values that this property can take on: xlSheetHidden, xlSheetVeryHidden, and xlSheetVisible (see Figure 19-9).

Modules

A *module* is a place where you store VBA code. If you have written more than just one procedure, you can store them all in one module. But if you have quite a few procedures to store, it's best to classify them in some fashion and then store each set of the procedures in a different module. This helps you locate a particular procedure.

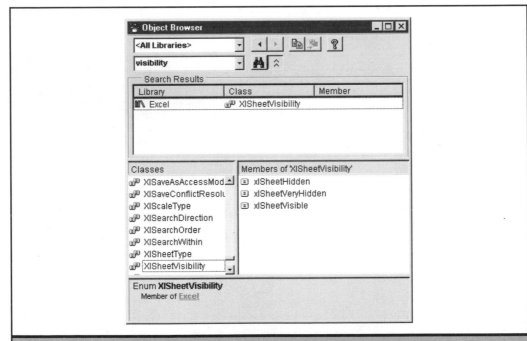

Figure 19-9. *Type a word in the combo box by the binoculars, then click the binoculars to search for related classes and members*

Unless you began by recording a macro (doing so automatically creates a module to store the recorded code) you need to establish a module to contain your code. With the VBE active, choose Insert | Module. A new module appears in the Code window, ready for you to enter your code.

If you expect to have more than one module in your project, it's helpful to give the module a descriptive name. With the module active, notice that it is the active object in the Properties window. Drag across the module's default name on the (Name) row—the default name will be Module1 unless there were already modules in the project—and enter in its place a more descriptive name for the module. The VBE renames the module as soon as you click elsewhere.

VBA recognizes two kinds of modules: Standard and Class. There's little you can do with a standard module other than to put VBA code in it—but that's plenty. When you are creating a major VBA project, one that requires hundreds or even thousands of lines of code, consider dividing your subroutines and functions into categories and putting each category onto a different module. Giving the different modules descriptive names then helps you locate subroutines for testing, editing, and so on. For example, you might put the subroutines that run when the project is opened and closed in a module named OpenAndClose; housekeeping procedures that clear ranges, set options, name worksheets, and perform similar tasks might go into a module named Utilities.

Class modules are a different matter. Recall from the prior section that, in VBA, you have access to classes—the Object Browser displays all the classes that are available, as well as the members that belong to those classes. Classes include objects such as Charts, and a class has members—properties, methods, and events. So the Chart class includes the ChartArea property, the Delete method, and the Resize event.

On a class module, you can define your own class. That class can have its own properties and methods. Suppose that you run a public library. You could create a class of Books. Each book in the class of Books could have some properties—for example, the name of the book, whether it is checked out, and the date that it was last checked out.

To get at that information—a book's name, its availability, and its checkout date—each book could have a method that displays the book's status. Here's how you can arrange all that.

With the VBE active, choose Insert | Class Module. Using the Properties window, give the class module the name *Book*. This establishes the name of the class, just as the class of worksheets is named Worksheet.

At the top of the class module, in the Code window, declare these three variables:

```
Public BookTitle As String
Public ShelfStatus As String
Public LastCheckedOut As Date
```

When you have entered these three declarations, you have defined three new properties that belong to the Book class. Below the declarations, and still in the class module, enter the following code to establish a new subroutine:

```
Public Sub DisplayStatus()
MsgBox "The book named " & Me.BookTitle & " is " & _
    Me.ShelfStatus & ". It was last checked out on " & _
    Me.LastCheckedOut & "."
End Sub
```

This subroutine, DisplayStatus, is a new method that belongs to the Book class, just as the PrintOut method belongs to the Worksheet class.

With the new class defined, along with its properties and a method, you can begin to use it in your standard modules. You can use an existing module or choose Insert | Module to establish a new standard module. Then enter this code:

```
Sub BookStatus()
Dim FirstBook As Book, SecondBook As Book
Set FirstBook = New Book
Set SecondBook = New Book

With FirstBook
    .BookTitle = "'King Lear'"
    .ShelfStatus = "available"
    .LastCheckedOut = #10/7/00#
End With

With SecondBook
    .BookTitle = "'Endocrinology'"
    .ShelfStatus = "checked out"
    .LastCheckedOut = #4/6/00#
End With

FirstBook.DisplayStatus
SecondBook.DisplayStatus

End Sub
```

Notice first that the subroutine named BookStatus declares two variables (FirstBook and SecondBook) whose type is the class Book. Using the New keyword, these two variables are set to new instances in the Book class. You could create many more instances if you wanted.

Then the three properties of each book are assigned values: each book gets a name, a shelf status, and a date on which it was last checked out. Because each property belongs to the same class, the code can use the With structure to save time.

Finally, the DisplayStatus method is called for each book. This method, which you defined on Book's class module, displays a message box that gives the book name, its shelf status, and its checkout date. For example, when the DisplayStatus method executes for the instance FirstBook, the message box contains this verbiage: "The book named 'King Lear' is available. It was last checked out on 10/7/00."

Notice how powerful this capability is. To create a new class, complete with new properties and its own method, required only six statements on a class module (granted, this is an extremely simple example). But you can copy a class module to many different VBA projects—once you have defined your new class, its procedures, and its methods, the heavy lifting is done and you can reuse it wherever it suits your purposes.

User Forms

Your code frequently needs to obtain information from the person who is running it. User forms are one way to get that information. In the context of user forms, this information usually *isn't* data that's stored on a worksheet, such as financial results, manufacturing specifications, and data from experiments. In these and similar cases, the volume of information is too great to put it on a user form. Nor does this sort of information include simple Yes–No decisions, such as whether or not to continue processing: for this sort of thing you usually use a simple message box, which requires much less handling.

User forms are ideal for situations where your code needs the user to do some decision making and, perhaps, to supplement information found on the worksheet. Examples of this sort of data include:

- What range of worksheet cells your code should obtain data from
- Whether your code should store its output in a new workbook
- Which account an expense should be charged to
- What title to display on a chart's vertical axis
- What range of dates the code should attend to
- When to remove the user form from the screen and continue by running your code

You can obtain this sort of information most effectively from a user form. Chapter 23 goes into this topic in much more detail; for now, simply keep in mind that a user form gives you much more control over events than does a simple message box, and that a user form is nearly always more convenient for the user than are alternatives such as worksheet cells and message boxes.

It's easy to establish a new user form in your VBA project. With the VBE active, just choose Insert | UserForm. When you do so, a blank user form appears in the VBE window, along with a special toolbar called the Toolbox. The Toolbox contains controls such as option buttons, list boxes, and tab strips that you can put on your form (see Figure 19-10).

Chapter 23 details the uses of the Toolbox's controls. (Your computer probably has other controls available to it; to see what they are, make a UserForm active and then choose Tools | Additional Controls.) The next section describes the physical process of getting controls from the Toolbox onto your new user form.

Using the Toolbox

As you can see from Figure 19-10, the Toolbox offers 15 controls that you can place on a user form, plus the Select Objects tool that enables you to select, move, and resize controls that are already on the user form.

To put a control on the user form, click that control on the Toolbox. When you then move your mouse pointer over to the user form, notice that the mouse pointer is accompanied by an icon that represents the control you have chosen. Once over the user form, hold down the left mouse button to establish the location of the control, and drag diagonally on the user form to establish the control's height and width. When you release the mouse button the control has been placed on the user form.

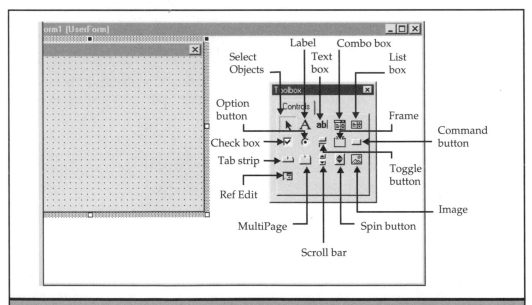

Figure 19-10.   *You can write event handlers for the controls you put on a user form*

To select a control that you've already put on the user form, first click the Select Objects control on the Toolbox—this ensures that you won't accidentally establish yet another control on the user form. Then click the control on the user form. Use the selection handles that appear on the control to resize it, drag the control to relocate it, or press the DELETE key to remove the control from the form.

The functions of the controls in the Toolbox are as follows:

- **Label** Use this control to provide instructions to the user or to help distinguish among different parts of the User Form. You seldom use a label for another control, such as an Option button: they come with their own labels. But you might use a label to tell the user to select an item in an adjacent list box.

- **Text box** This control enables the user to enter textual information, such as the title for a chart.

- **List box** You normally use a list box to display a list of choices from which the user selects. It's often the control to use when the list of choices is so long that it's inconvenient to show each one separately on the user form with its own option button or check box. A short list, such as Male and Female, is better handled with option buttons.

- **Combo box** A combo box is so named because it combines the functions of a text box and a list box. The user can make a choice from the list box and it appears in the text box portion of the combo box. If the user's desired choice does not appear in the list box portion, the user can type it into the text box portion of the combo box.

- **Check box** Combined with labels, check boxes enable the user to select among a few different options. The function of check boxes is very similar to that of Option buttons. It's conventional to use check boxes when the user might choose more than one (for example, Breakfast, Lunch, and Dinner) or when the user might choose no option at all. In contrast, it's conventional to use Option buttons where the user would choose exactly one (for example, Male or Female). Check boxes can have three states: checked (True), unchecked (False), and shaded (Null). A Null value can be useful when a meaning such as Not Applicable is needed.

- **Option button** Use this control when you want the user to choose exactly one of several options. You can restrict the user to one choice by placing a frame (see the next page) on the User Form, and then putting option buttons inside that frame. Of a set of option buttons in a frame, exactly one at a time can be selected.

- **Toggle button** Use a toggle button to give the user an either-or choice: for example, a toggle button might let the user choose between closing and saving, or closing without saving, a new workbook created by your code.

- **Frame** Frames are generally placed on User Forms for two purposes: to group option buttons so that only one can be chosen, and to set off visually the different portions of the User Form.

- **Command button** Command buttons are most frequently used as OK and Cancel buttons. In either case, they dismiss the User Form from the screen; the OK button usually means to continue processing, given the information that's been entered on the User Form. The Cancel button usually means that the user doesn't want the code to continue. Command buttons are also used in Wizards (such as the Chart Wizard or the Text Import Wizard) to help the user navigate to and fro (that is, Next and Back).

- **Tab strip** Conceptually, a tab strip is similar to the worksheet tabs that Excel displays near the bottom of its window. No matter which worksheet tab you select, you are confronted by the same arrangement of rows and columns. A tab strip works in much the same way. You place a tab strip on a User Form and then put one or more controls on one of the tabs: as a result, each tab on the tab strip displays the same controls. By default, new tab strips come with two tabs. To add a tab, select the tab strip, and then left-click one of the tabs. A rectangle appears around the tab's caption and the Toolbox is hidden— to get the Toolbox back, just click the UserForm somewhere other than on the tab strip. Right-click on the tab to display a shortcut menu that lets you add, delete, rename, or move a tab (the shortcut menu refers to the tabs as *pages*, but don't let this throw you). You use a tab strip when there are several different items— such as people or days of the week or rooms in a building—that have different values on the same variables. Then each tab represents a different person or day or room. You might have a text box on the tab strip where the name of the person or day or room is entered.

- **MultiPage** Although a MultiPage looks like a tab strip, the two controls have very different functions. Different tabs on a tab strip have the same controls, and each tab represents a different item. MultiPage controls have several pages, each of which has a different set of controls, much like a Wizard. Use a MultiPage when there are so many variables required to describe a person (or a product or a service or some other item) that you can't show all the needed controls at once. In that case, you can create as many pages as necessary to account for all the controls you need.

- **Scroll bar** It's unusual to put a scroll bar on a User Form. On a User Form, a scroll bar doesn't have the same function as it does on, say, a worksheet— which is to navigate through that worksheet. You can use a scroll bar on a User Form to help the user enter numeric values. It may seem easier to dispense with the scroll bar and let the user enter numbers with the keyboard. But many users prefer to use either the keyboard or the mouse and avoid switching back and forth between the two input devices. If your User Form is designed with lots of controls such as list boxes, check boxes, and Command Buttons—which are easily controlled via the mouse—then it's considerate to let the user enter numbers by means of scroll bars. (If you do so, it's usual to pair a scroll bar, which controls numeric values, with a text box which displays the current value as set by the scroll bar.)

- **Spin button**   A spin button is used in much the same way as a scroll bar, to set a numeric value. But spin buttons increment and decrement by only one value: that is, you can use a spin button to change 9 to 10 (increment of 1) or 18 to 25 (increment of 7), but not both. In contrast, you can have two different increments with a scroll bar: you might set it to increment by 1 if its arrow is clicked, or by 5 if the bar itself is clicked.

- **Image**   There's little for you to do with an image control other than to let the user look at it and click it. You can attach code to the image (as you can with nearly all controls) that will run if the user clicks it, but the image has none of the special characteristics offered by other controls. After you establish an image on a User Form, you will need to locate, on an available drive, a graphics file that contains the image you want to display. It's typical to use a .gif, a .bmp, or a .jpg file as the source of the image.

- **Ref Edit**   The Ref Edit control enables the user to select a worksheet cell, or range of cells, that your code will subsequently use to do its job. The cells identified by the user often contain data that will be analyzed, or constitute a range where results will be output. While these latter two uses are typical, there are many other reasons that you might ask a user to select a cell: for example, the cell uses a format that your code will replicate in its output.

Accessing Additional Controls

Depending on what other software you have installed on your computer—and depending on downloads you have performed from various Web sites—you have access to other controls, and you can place them on your User Form. To see a list of those controls and to arrange to put them in the Toolbox, right-click on the Toolbox and choose Additional Controls from the submenu. You will see a list similar to that shown in Figure 19-11.

When you fill a check box next to the name of a control in the list, and then click OK, a new icon appears on the Toolbox. Use that icon just as you use the icon for one of the standard Toolbox controls. Figure 19-12, for example, shows the Toolbox with the Calendar control's icon installed and a User Form with the Calendar control itself attached to the Form.

EXTENDING EXCEL'S
REACH WITH VBA

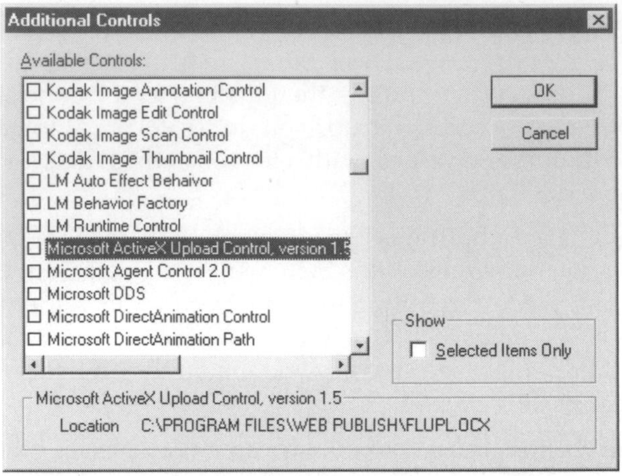

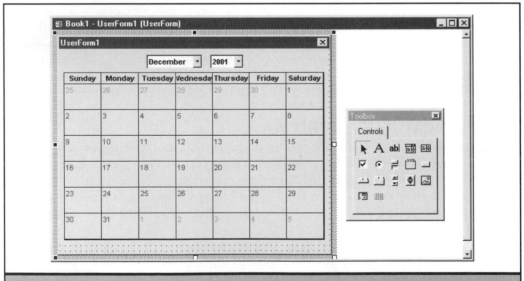

Figure 19-11. *You can sometimes find here useful controls that were not supplied with Office*

Figure 19-12. *Compared to typing into a text box, clicking the Calendar Control is a much easier way for a user to specify a date*

Chapter 20

Writing Subroutines

Subroutines are the heart of the code you create with VBA. It's no accident that when you record a macro, Excel records it as a subroutine: subroutines written in VBA are capable of doing almost everything that you can do in Excel. This chapter shows you some of the techniques that help you write efficient VBA code.

First, it's useful to clear up some terminology. If you haven't already, you will encounter the terms *macro, procedure, function,* and *subroutine.* The terms are similar in that each is a way of referring to VBA code. Here's how to distinguish among them.

The term *macro* is just an alternate way of referring to VBA code that you have recorded or written. The menu items in the Excel worksheet menu that refer to macros are, in a sense, a legacy of the Excel Version 4 macro language that predated VBA. A macro can be a subroutine or a function or a set of related subroutines and functions.

The term *procedure* is a more definitive term than *macro,* which is sometimes used to mean code written in the Excel Version 4 language. A procedure is a single subroutine or a single function written in VBA.

You can use a *subroutine* to automate nearly anything that you can do manually in the Excel window. You, the user, can insert rows, format cells, enter formulas, open and close workbooks—and so can a subroutine. A subroutine begins with the Sub statement and concludes with the End Sub statement.

As you will see in Chapter 21, *functions* can be used in two ways: by referring to them in other procedures and by entering them directly on the worksheet. Suppose that you frequently need to convert temperatures from Fahrenheit to Celsius on the worksheet. You could write a function in VBA that performs the conversion and then enter it on the worksheet just as though it were a built-in function such as SQRT(). A function used in this way can return a calculated value to the cell where it's entered, *and that's all it can do.* Functions entered on the worksheet can't insert rows, delete worksheets, or open workbooks—those tasks are the province of subroutines. A function begins with the Function statement and concludes with the End Function statement.

When to Use Subroutines

The simplistic notion about using subroutines is that their purpose is to help you repeat a task many times. For example, you might track investments daily and find it useful to chart them over time. Every day, you could enter stock prices, select the range that contains them, start the Chart Wizard, select a chart type, select among various chart options, and finally create the chart.

As long as you need to perform essentially the same task time after time, you probably would do better to create a subroutine that carries out these tasks on your behalf. The advantages, of course, are that the subroutine works much faster than do your fingers and that a well-written subroutine acts the same way time after time.

But the value of subroutines goes well beyond the simple issue of repetition. Following are some of the other reasons to write subroutines.

Getting Input from the User

Many people write VBA code not just for their own use but for friends, coworkers, or customers. When the code does something even a little more complex than entering some formulas, creating a chart, or formatting a worksheet, you generally want the user to make some choices or to supply some information. That's where forms, sometimes called UserForms, come into play.

It takes a procedure to display a form: most often that procedure is a subroutine rather than a function. Among the typical uses of forms are

- To get from the user a range of cell addresses containing data that the subroutine will manipulate.

- To enable the user to select among some options: choosing a chart type or choosing to put results on an existing or on a new worksheet or choosing among several different types of analysis.

- To enter new information, such as the name of a new workbook or a chart title or a phone number.

Along the same lines, you use subroutines to display message boxes that communicate information to the user: warning of a possible problem, informing that some condition has made it impossible to continue or conveying something as simple as the location where a workbook will be saved.

Conditional Outcomes

Many users want Excel to respond automatically when some condition is met: for example, to turn a cell's font red when a number is negative or to insert a new row when a certain date has passed.

Excel's worksheet capabilities enable some of this. For example, you can set conditional formatting for a cell, such that the cell's font is one color if the cell's value is negative, another color if its value is zero, and another color if its value is positive. But there's no function- or menu-driven way to set the font for cell A2 on the basis of the value in cell A1.

To accomplish objectives like those just suggested, you need subroutines like this:

```
Sub ResetFontColor()
If Range("A1").Value < 0 Then
    Range("A2").Font.ColorIndex = 3
ElseIf Range("A1").Value > 0 Then
    Range("A2").Font.ColorIndex = 50
Else
    Range("A2").Font.ColorIndex = 0
End If
 End Sub
```

This simple subroutine is bounded by its beginning statement, Sub ResetFontColor(), and its end statement, End Sub. The Sub statement names the subroutine; that there is nothing between the parentheses means that the subroutine receives no information from elsewhere. See "Passing Variables to Subroutines," later in this chapter, for more information.

When it runs, the subroutine checks the value in cell A1. If the value is negative, it sets the color of the font for cell A2 to 3 (in this context, *3* means *red*) and the subroutine ends. If the value in A1 is not negative, the subroutine then checks to see if the value is greater than zero. If so, it sets the color of the font in A2 to 50 (*50* means *green*) and the subroutine ends. Finally, if neither condition is true—if the value in A1 is neither negative nor greater than zero—it sets the font in A2 to 0 (the default font color) and the subroutine ends.

Simplifying the User's Life

For the user who is new to Excel, even its standard interface can appear intimidating. There's a worksheet menu, a Standard toolbar, row and column headers, gridlines that demark the individual cells, scroll bars with split boxes, sheet tabs and tab scrolling buttons, a formula bar, a Name Box, a status bar—it's a little much until you get used to it.

Many developers take this into account when they create something new for their users. If that something new doesn't require a scroll bar or sheet tabs, the developer uses VBA to suppress them. For example, here's a snippet of code taken from a complete subroutine:

```
With Application
    .CommandBars("Standard").Visible = False
    .CommandBars("Formatting").Visible = False
    .DisplayFormulaBar = False
End With
With ActiveWindow
    .DisplayGridlines = False
    .DisplayHeadings = False
    .DisplayHorizontalScrollBar = False
    .DisplayVerticalScrollBar = False
    .DisplayWorkbookTabs = False
End With
```

This bit of code uses blocks bounded by With and End With statements. VBA expects that whatever statements come between the With statement and the End With statement apply to the object identified by the With statement. So these two statements:

```
ActiveWindow.DisplayGridlines = False
ActiveWindow.DisplayHeadings = False
```

are equivalent to these four statements:

```
With ActiveWindow
    .DisplayGridlines = False
    .DisplayHeadings = False
End With
```

That is, the DisplayGridlines property and the DisplayHeadings property both belong to the ActiveWindow object. Therefore, you need not mention ActiveWindow more than once: in the With statement itself. Any statements that follow the With statement and precede the End With statement are assumed to apply to the object in the With statement: here, that's the ActiveWindow object.

It may look profligate to use four statements instead of just two, and a With/End With block always calls for two more statements than does equivalent code that doesn't use that structure. Nevertheless, there's a net gain.

In the Excel model, objects belong to other objects, in a hierarchy. Borders belong to ranges, which belong to worksheets, which belong to workbooks. And VBA is in some ways remarkably obtuse: you can't just tell it to set a border around a range. No, you have to tell VBA to look at the workbook to find a particular worksheet, to look at that worksheet to find a particular range, and to set the border for that range.

If VBA had to traverse that entire hierarchy every time you refer to, say, a range, it would slow the processing down. But by using the With structure, you can tell VBA, in effect, "Okay, now that you've found this particular range, here are several things to do with it. They all apply to the range you've already found, so there's no need to start over at the top of the hierarchy."

The gain in processing time that you obtain by using blocks bounded by With and End With depends on what occurs between those two statements and the length of the trail of bread crumbs specified in the With statement. The gain may be very small, but it's real, and in some cases it can be significant. Furthermore, using With and End With statements gives structure to your code that makes it easier to trace, document and debug.

Here's another example:

```
With ThisWorkbook.Sheets("Sheet1").Range("C6:D8")
    .Borders(xlDiagonalDown).LineStyle = xlNone
    .Borders(xlDiagonalUp).LineStyle = xlNone
    .Borders(xlEdgeLeft).LineStyle = xlContinuous
    .Borders(xlEdgeTop).LineStyle = xlContinuous
    .Borders(xlEdgeBottom).LineStyle = xlContinuous
    .Borders(xlEdgeRight).LineStyle = xlContinuous
    .Borders(xlInsideVertical).LineStyle = xlNone
    .Borders(xlInsideHorizontal).LineStyle = xlNone
    .Font.ColorIndex = 3
```

```
      .Interior.ColorIndex = 5
      .Style = "Percent"
      .Font.Size = 12
End With
```

In this example, the code sets properties for a particular range in a particular sheet in the active workbook. It sets borders around the range, the font color, the interior (fill) color, the number format, and the size of the font. There are 12 statements that actually set properties. In the absence of the With structure, VBA would have to traverse the hierarchy of objects, from workbook to worksheet to range, 12 times before it finished setting the properties. Using the With structure, VBA need find the range only once: when found, it keeps setting properties for that range until it encounters an End With.

Back to the notion of simplifying the user interface. As a developer, you can't tell exactly how each of your users has set up the Excel window: someone might already have suppressed scroll bars, someone else might not want any toolbars showing, and so on. It behooves you to account for the preexisting status of any settings you intend to change. Then, when your user has finished using your code, you should return those settings to their original state.

You do this by creating some variables to store the settings. Here's an example that's more considerate than the one you saw earlier:

```
With ActiveWindow
    Grids = .DisplayGridlines
    .DisplayGridlines = False
    Heads = .DisplayHeadings
    .DisplayHeadings = False
    HBar = .DisplayHorizontalScrollBar
    .DisplayHorizontalScrollBar = False
    VBar = .DisplayVerticalScrollBar
    .DisplayVerticalScrollBar = False
    Tabs = .DisplayWorkbookTabs
    .DisplayWorkbookTabs = False
End With
```

This code stores the current values of properties, such as whether or not to display gridlines, in variables; then the code sets each property to False. For example, suppose that at present the user wants to see gridlines on the worksheet. In that case, the active window's DisplayGridlines property has a value of True. When the statement

```
Grids = .DisplayGridlines
```

executes, VBA assigns the value for .DisplayGridlines, which is True, to the variable Grids. The next statement sets .DisplayGridlines to False, thus suppressing their display.

Later, the code returns the properties to the states that the user had settled on, prior to running the code:

```
With ActiveWindow
    .DisplayGridlines = Grids
    .DisplayHeadings = Heads
    .DisplayHorizontalScrollBar = Hbar
    .DisplayVerticalScrollBar = Vbar
    .DisplayWorkbookTabs = Tabs
End With
```

Passing Variables to Subroutines

There was a time when developers thought nothing of writing code that stretched to hundreds and thousands of statements. The code was sprinkled with complicated GO TO statements and implicit branching statements such as

```
IF (M) 10, 10, 30
```

which meant, in FORTRAN: If M is negative or zero, go to Statement 10; and if M is positive, go to Statement 30.

This sort of thing created an intolerable situation: you were dealing with very lengthy code, shot through with statements such as GO TO 150, and IF statements that told you nothing about what they were intended to do. The development process was hard enough. Tracing and debugging someone else's code was a nightmare.

To name variables on the fly creates other problems. That is, you might write or encounter a statement such as this:

```
NetWorth = Assets - Liabilities
```

without ever having specified anything about the NetWorth variable. When you wanted to have a variable named NetWorth, you just used it in a statement such as the one just shown.

There are problems with that go-as-you-please approach. What if, elsewhere in your code, you used NetWorth again, in an entirely different context? The value stored in the original NetWorth would get overwritten, and that's probably not a good thing. And what if you elsewhere entered this statement:

```
NetWerth = 0
```

If you intended that statement to put a value of zero into the variable NetWorth, you'd have a problem. You mistyped the name of the variable, thus creating a new one, and the variable NetWorth, the one you meant to zero out, still contains the difference between Assets and Liabilities.

Over time, the people who wrote the compilers and interpreters allowed for, and in some cases enforced, a more structured approach to coding. Some languages such as Pascal began to require you to declare variables before you could use them. VBA lets you use the declaration Option Explicit in your code to force the explicit declaration of variables. This means that mistyping a variable name causes an error message ("Variable not defined") instead of the inadvertent creation of a new variable.

And you began to see statements such as FormatTheOutput instead of statements such as GO TO 150—that is, people began to write and call separate subroutines, instead of writing what was called spaghetti code. (You understand the aptness of that term if you've ever tried to flowchart one of those nightmares.) And the If-Then-Else structures became clearer. Instead of this:

```
IF (M) 10, 10, 20
```

you began to see this:

```
If Materials <= 0 Then
   GetMoreMaterials
Else
   SellSomeMaterials
End If
```

If these two examples of If statements look equally easy to write, trace, and debug, you probably have a flair for programming in assembly language. The rest of us find it easier to understand that if the variable named Materials is less than or equal to zero, a subroutine named GetMoreMaterials executes next; otherwise, when Materials is greater than zero, a subroutine named SellSomeMaterials runs.

That's straightforward enough, but what if the two subroutines need to know the value of the Materials variable in order to run properly? Because of the way the subroutines are called, GetMoreMaterials knows that Materials is less than or equal to zero, and SellSomeMaterials knows that Materials is greater than zero. But if the subroutines need to know the magnitude of Materials, you need to make some other provision. This provision is termed *passing variables*.

Procedure-Level and Module-Level Variables

Suppose that you have a module that contains the following code:

```
Option Explicit
Dim Materials As Integer, Cash As Integer

Sub Main()
Cash = InputBox("Enter an integer value for Cash.")
Materials = InputBox("Enter an integer value for Materials.")

If Materials <= 0 Then
    GetMoreMaterials
Else
    SellSomeMaterials
End If

MsgBox "Cash = " & Cash & ", Materials = " & Materials
End Sub

Sub GetMoreMaterials()
Materials = Materials + Cash
Cash = 0
End Sub

Sub SellSomeMaterials()
Cash = Cash + Materials
Materials = 0
End Sub
```

The Option Explicit declaration means that all variables must be explicitly declared before they can be used; this affords you the protection against typos and the other mistakes described. The Dim statement declares variables: that is, it informs VBA that variables exist, what their names are, and what type of value the variables can take on. In the preceding example, the Dim statement is *outside* any procedure, and it is, therefore, at the module level. When variables are declared at the *module level*, they are available to any procedure in that module.

Now suppose that the Dim statement, instead of preceding the subroutine named Main, occurs inside it:

```
Option Explicit
Sub Main()
Dim Materials As Integer, Cash As Integer
```

In this case, the Dim statement is within a procedure. That makes the variables Materials and Cash *procedure-level* variables. They are available only within the procedure that declares them. If you made that change—that is, relocating the Dim statement from outside any procedure to inside the Main procedure—then when either the SellSomeMaterials or the GetMoreMaterials procedure runs, you get an error message that a variable hasn't been defined. Materials and Cash are now procedure-level variables and are unavailable outside the procedure that declares them.

The placement of the Dim statement inside a procedure, or outside a procedure at the module level, illustrates the concept of *scope*. When you declare a variable within a procedure, its scope does not extend to other procedures. When you declare a variable outside a procedure at the module level, its scope extends to other procedures in that module.

If you declare a variable at the module level, you might well want to control its scope beyond that module—that is, to determine whether it is available to procedures in *other* modules. You can restrict a variable's scope to the module by declaring it with the Dim statement, but you can make things clearer by using *Private* instead of *Dim* at the module level. For example:

```
Option Explicit
Private Materials As Integer, Cash As Integer

Sub Main()
```

Using the keyword *Private* means that the variables named Materials and Cash are not available outside the module. You can instead use the keyword *Public* to make them available outside the module:

```
Option Explicit
Public Materials As Integer, Cash As Integer

Sub Main()
```

Declared in this fashion, the variables Materials and Cash are available to procedures in other modules in the same project. (You can't use *Private* and *Public* inside subroutines—only at the module level.)

Why restrict yourself unduly? Why not declare all variables at the module level and declare them as Public rather than with Private (or, equivalently, with Dim)? The reason is that when you declare a variable so that it's available to many procedures, it can be hard to tell what's going on with that variable when you're tracing and debugging code.

Suppose you have a module that contains subroutines named RecordPayments, TotalReceivables, TotalPayables, CalculateCashFlow, PrepareIncomeStatement, and PrepareBalanceSheet. Some of these subroutines are concerned in one way or another with a company's cash assets.

You declare a variable named Cash at the module level. Then something goes wrong with the code—the balance sheet that the code produces shows that assets don't equal liabilities, which by definition they must. Looking more closely, you see that something is wrong with the Cash variable.

Now, in order to trace and locate the error, you have to step through the code one statement at a time, looking for the problem that is throwing your balance off. Worse, you have to look at all of the subroutines. Because Cash was declared at the module level, it's available to any of the subroutines in that module. Therefore, any of the subroutines might have modified Cash erroneously, and you have to step through all of them.

But if you had declared Cash inside a subroutine, then its scope is limited. Not all procedures would have access to the variable, and your debugging task is made much easier.

The problem, as you've no doubt seen, is this: If you declare Cash inside a subroutine, you protect it from erroneous alteration by subroutines that shouldn't change it. Don't you also protect it from subroutines that *should* change it?

No, not if you manage things properly. You can *pass* the Cash variable to subroutines that need it and keep it away from subroutines that don't.

Passing by Reference

The code shown next gives an example of how you might pass procedure-level variables to another procedure that needs them:

```
Sub Main()
Dim Materials As Integer, Cash As Integer
Cash = InputBox("Enter an integer for Cash.")
Materials = InputBox("Enter an integer for Materials.")

If Materials <= 0 Then
    GetMoreMaterials Materials, Cash
Else
    SellSomeMaterials Materials, Cash
End If
End Sub

Sub GetMoreMaterials(Materials As Integer, Cash As Integer)
Materials = Materials + Cash
Cash = 0
End Sub

Sub SellSomeMaterials(Materials As Integer, Cash As Integer)
Cash = Cash + Materials
Materials = 0
End Sub
```

By naming the variables in the statement that calls for a procedure to execute (here, one such is the statement GetMoreMaterials Materials, Cash), you pass the variables explicitly—rather than willy-nilly—to the procedure than needs them. Contrast this call for the GetMoreMaterials sub with that of the prior example, where the variables were not named and therefore were not passed.

In another part of the forest, where the procedure that was called picks up the variables that were passed, the variables must be named in parentheses and their types must be declared:

```
Sub GetMoreMaterials(Materials As Integer, Cash As Integer)
```

If you don't mention the variables in parentheses in the Sub statement, VBA notifies you with the error message "Wrong Number of Arguments." (The term *Arguments* is just a fancy way of referring to what's getting passed to the procedure.)

It's not necessary for the procedure that's been called to give the same names to its arguments. In the preceding example, the calling statement could be

```
GetMoreMaterials PaperGoods, Dollars
```

and the called sub could begin with

```
Sub GetMoreMaterials(Materials As Integer, Cash As Integer)
```

This can give you some useful flexibility in how you name variables in called subroutines. They are often called in different contexts by different procedures. In this case, the variable PaperGoods is treated in GetMoreMaterials as Materials, and the variable Dollars is treated in GetMoreMaterials as Cash.

In these examples, variables are passed to the called subroutine *by reference*. It is the variable itself that is passed to the called procedure. Variables can vary: their values can change. The called procedure can change the variable, and it does so in the preceding examples. When the procedure has finished processing, the variable is returned to the calling procedure and any change to the variable is still in place.

This is termed *passing by reference*, because although a value is passed, you refer to that value by using the name of the variable that contains it.

Passing by Value

Passing by value, as the term implies, means that you pass the variable's value, rather than the variable itself, to the called procedure. The called procedure may, and often does, modify that value. But the changed value is *not* returned to the variable in the calling procedure. Therefore, from the viewpoint of the calling procedure, the variable's value remains unchanged.

I have written an application that performs statistical process control. It contains many subroutines, and here is how I call two of them:

```
MakeXChart ByVal XBar, ByVal MRBar, XBarLimits
MakeRChart XBar, MRBar, RLimits
```

Notice the use of ByVal in the first statement, which calls the subroutine MakeXChart. Two variables are passed *by value* to MakeXChart: XBar and MRBar. The procedure MakeXChart can change the values of these variables, and I don't want these changes used when the code next calls MakeRChart. I pass them by value to MakeXChart to ensure that it's the value, not the variable, that gets passed. So, when it's time to call MakeRChart, I know I'm using the same values as I did when I called MakeXChart. If I passed the variables by reference instead of by value, I couldn't be sure that I was passing the same values to MakeRChart that I passed to MakeXChart.

Also note that I use ByVal explicitly. In VBA, passing by reference is the default situation: if you use neither ByVal nor ByRef, VBA passes by reference. To pass by value, you need to use the ByVal keyword.

And you need to use it in both the calling statement and the called procedure. Given that I call MakeXChart like this:

```
MakeXChart ByVal XBar, ByVal MRBar, XBarLimits
```

the subroutine MakeXChart must begin like this:

```
MakeXChart (ByVal XBar As Double, ByVal MRBar As Double, XBarLimits
As Integer)
```

So if the calling statement specifies ByVal for a variable, the called statement must do so also.

Types of Variables

Thus far, this chapter has mentioned, without explanation, terms such as Integer and Double. These are two types of variables. A variable that's declared as Integer:

```
Dim CountWorksheets As Integer
```

can take on integer, nonfractional values only. A variable that's declared as Double:

```
Dim AverageRate As Double
```

can take on integer values, but it can also take on values with decimal places. A variable declared as Double can accurately represent values up to 15 digits. This is regarded as very precise, and indeed the term *Double* is short for *double precision*. The values can range from about −1.7 * 10^308 to about 1.7 * 10^308. Note that the possible range of values involves numbers with many more than 15 digits. While a double-precision variable can store numbers within that range of values, it can do so within only 15 digits of precision. That means that very large or very small numbers, numbers that require more than 15 digits to denote, will be represented inaccurately.

There's a less precise type of variable, single precision, that's declared like this:

```
Dim InterestRate As Single
```

A single-precision variable can take on values ranging from about −3.4 * 10^38 to about 3.4 * 10^38. It's precision is limited to about seven digits.

Why not just declare all variables as Double? The principal reason is that it's wasteful. Double-precision variables occupy more memory than do integers or single-precision variables. This probably doesn't seem important today, when personal computers routinely have 512MB or more of memory available, but it is. Resources are still limited, and double-precision variables are processed more slowly than integer or single-precision variables. When your code is processing thousands of values that have been declared, unnecessarily, as double precision, you'll see things slow down markedly.

VBA provides you with several data types besides Integer, Single, and Double:

- **Long (short for Long Integer)**   An Integer variable can take on values from −32,768 to 32,767, with no decimal portion. A Long variable can take on integer values from −2,147,483,648 to 2,147,483,647. A variable that's declared as Long is useful when you need to represent the rows in an Excel worksheet, which run from 1 to 65,536. That latter value is too large for an Integer variable, but it's well within the capabilities of a Long variable.

- **Byte**   A Byte variable can take on integer values from 0 to 255. Coders sometimes go wrong by using Byte instead of Integer, thinking that they are programming efficiently when the values that they need to represent don't exceed 255. But it often happens that they need to represent a *negative* value, and then they get an error message because a Byte variable's value can't be less than zero.

- **Currency**   A Currency variable can take on values from −922,337,203,685,477.5808 to 922,337,203,685,477.5807. A variable of this type is useful when you need to do financial calculations that won't take you over 922 trillion units or below −922 trillion. (It is a fixed-point data type, so it won't carry as many possible decimal values as a Single or Double variable.)

- **Boolean**   A Boolean variable can take on just two values: True and False. You've seen Boolean variables used earlier in this chapter, to capture the settings for certain properties of the ActiveWindow.

- **Date**   Despite its name, a Date variable captures information about both the calendar date and the time of day. The possible range of dates is from January 1, 100 to December 31, 9999. Times can be any value on a 24-hour clock. A Date variable works by assigning its integer portion to represent a particular day, and its decimal portion to represent a particular time on that day. Positive values start on December 31, 1899: a Date variable with a value of 1 represents December 31, 1899, 2 represents January 1, 1900, and so on. Negative values move backward from December 31, 1899: a Date value of –1 represents December 29, 1899, –2 represents December 28, 1899, and so on. In the decimal portion, .0 represents midnight and .5 represents noon. So the value 36,156.74, when assigned to a Date variable, would represent December 27, 1998 (which is 36,156 days following December 31, 1899) at 5:45:36 PM (which is 74 percent of the way through the 24-hour day).

Note   *Although VBA is capable of handling dates with negative values, the worksheet cannot. Be aware of this before you try to write negative date values to worksheet cells that use a date format.*

- **String**   Use a String variable to represent alphanumeric text values, such as "Beth" or "3UZW816."

There are three other data structures that are particularly important and are discussed in the following sections: the Variant type, the Object type, and the array variable.

The Variant Data Type

A variable that's declared as Variant can represent any type of data: String, Boolean, Double, Date, and so on. You might expect that so polymorphous a data type would require more resources than do other types, and it does. Whereas a Byte variable requires only 1 byte of storage, a Boolean requires 2 bytes, and even a Double requires only 8 bytes, a Variant that contains a numeric value requires 16 bytes. A Variant that contains a string—a text value—requires 22 bytes plus the length of the string itself.

Recall from earlier in this chapter that if you don't use Option Explicit as a declaration in your code, you need not declare a variable explicitly: you can declare it implicitly just by using it, usually in an assignment statement such as

```
QualityOfMyCode = "Sloppy"
```

When you declare a variable in this fashion, you haven't defined its type, whether Single, Double, Currency, String, whatever. Therefore, VBA assumes the most flexible data type, Variant. As a result, the variable uses anywhere from 3 to 22 times (or more) the storage space that it would use if you had just declared it explicitly with a Dim, Private, or Public statement.

That's the downside. The advantage is that a Variant variable can store values whose size and type you can't predict. The most typical situation occurs when you want to obtain a value entered by a user onto a worksheet and you haven't controlled what the user has done (or you haven't wanted to do so). Because there's no telling whether the user has entered a large number, a small one, a positive, a negative, an error value such as #DIV/0!, or a string value, you use a Variant variable to capture the value from the worksheet. For example:

```
Dim UserData As Variant
UserData = ActiveSheet.Range("C10")
```

Using code such as the preceding example, you can put any value that the user might have entered into cell C10 into your UserData variable because you declared its type as Variant.

A related, and also typical, use of a Variant variable is to create an array of values from a range of worksheet cells. Suppose that your code requires that the user highlight a range of cells, and you would like to store the values of those cells in a memory array. Code such as this does the trick:

```
Dim UserRange As Variant
UserRange = Selection
```

Note *Selection is a keyword that identifies the cell, or range of cells, that the user has selected.*

If, at the time the preceding code ran, the user had selected the range B2:C4, then the UserRange variable would become an array of values. It would have three rows and two columns, just like the worksheet range it is based on. The value in the first row of its first column would be the value in cell B2 on the worksheet. The value in the first row of its second column would be the value in cell C2 of the worksheet, and so on: the value in the third row of the second column of the array would be the value in cell C4 on the worksheet.

Object Variables

VBA uses an *object model* specific to the application where VBA is running. This chapter has already referred, if only obliquely, to that model. The model is a hierarchy of objects, starting at the top with the Application object (in this case, that object is Excel itself, although it could be Word or Access or some other application). The Application object subsumes all the other objects in the model.

In this context, an object is just some *thing* that exists in Excel. Given that definition, a workbook is an object, a worksheet is an object, a range is an object (and, as a special case of a range, so is a cell), a chart is an object, and so on.

Objects have characteristics. For example, a worksheet might be hidden or it might be visible: the worksheet's visibility is a characteristic of it. Or a cell has an assigned numeric format: the format is a characteristic of the cell. VBA refers to these characteristics as *properties*: VBA would say that a worksheet's Visible property is xlSheetHidden, or xlSheetVisible, depending on whether you have chosen to hide or unhide that worksheet. Similarly, VBA might say that a cell's NumberFormat property is Percent, or Date, or some other numeric format. More generally, Excel objects have properties, and the values of those properties define how the objects appear and behave.

Objects also have things done to them. You *close* a workbook. You *delete* a row. You *copy* a range of cells. VBA refers to these as *methods*. They are actions that happen to objects. Other actions that belong to objects are *events*—things that occur when something happens to an object.

It can be difficult to know, without looking them up in the Help documentation, which is a property, which a method, and which an event. Your best guide is experience. Fortunately, it's not crucial to know when you write lines of code such as

```
If ActiveSheet.ProtectContents Then
ActiveWorkbook.Close
```

that you have invoked first a property (ProtectContents) and then a method (Close).

The point of this disquisition is that VBA enables you to declare a special kind of variable termed an *object variable*. Instead of representing a numeric quantity or a text value as follows:

```
MyCost = 1000
MyCity = "Far Rockaway"
```

an object variable represents an object such as a workbook, a worksheet, a range, a toolbar—in short, any object in an Excel workbook can be represented by a variable. There are two requirements.

The first is that you must declare the object variable as the appropriate type. Suppose you want to declare an object variable to represent worksheets and another object variable to represent ranges on worksheets. You would declare them like this (the variable names are, as always, up to you):

```
Dim Wks As Worksheet
Dim Rng As Range
```

The second requirement is that you use the special *Set* keyword when you assign a particular object to the object variable. For example:

```
Set Wks = ActiveWorkbook.Sheets("Sheet1")
```

EXTENDING EXCEL'S
REACH WITH VBA

The Set keyword is peculiar to statements that assign a value (here, a specific worksheet) to an object variable (here, the variable named Wks).

There are several good reasons to use object variables. Three of them are discussed in the next sections.

Object Variables and With Blocks

The With structure is useful when you want to do several things in succession to an object that's a ways down the object hierarchy. By specifying that object—say, a cell—in your With statement, you can set its number format, its font, its text alignment, its borders, and its color pattern, and then delete the cell just for spite.

But suppose that you know you'll want to set some cell properties at one point in the code, and other properties later in the code: perhaps after the user has made some choices, or after your code has returned some intermediate results. To build another With structure identical to the first is to lose at least some of its efficiency. For example:

```
With ActiveWorkbook.Sheets("Sheet1").Range("A1")
    .NumberFormat = "0.00%"
    .HorizontalAlignment = xlCenter
    .Font.Name = "Times New Roman"
    .Font.Size = 12
    .Borders(xlEdgeBottom).LineStyle = xlContinuous
    .Borders(xlEdgeBottom).Weight = xlThick
End With
```

After the preceding code executes, some condition determines the color that you want to apply to the cell. At that point you execute this statement:

```
ActiveWorkbook.Sheets("Sheet1").Range("A1").Interior.ColorIndex = 42
```

Notice that this approach requires VBA to traverse the hierarchy twice: once in the With statement, and once to set the cell's color.

But what if you declare an object variable that refers to the cell in question, and then set properties for the cell represented by the variable:

```
Dim TheCell As Range
Set TheCell = ActiveWorkbook.Sheets("Sheet1").Range("A1")
With TheCell
    .NumberFormat = "0.00%"
    .HorizontalAlignment = xlCenter
    .Font.Name = "Times New Roman"
    .Font.Size = 12
    .Borders(xlEdgeBottom).LineStyle = xlContinuous
```

```
.Borders(xlEdgeBottom).Weight = xlThick
End With
```

And later on you use

```
TheCell.Interior.ColorIndex = 42
```

Notice that you traverse the hierarchy once only: when you assign cell A1 on Sheet1 in the active workbook to the object variable *TheCell*. Subsequently, VBA knows not only that a cell is needed, but which cell it is.

Object Variables in For Each Loops

A *loop* is a way of doing something several—perhaps very many—times in your code. Loops are an important feature of VBA, and there are several types of loop that you can use. Usually you know how many times to do something. For example, you might want to open a new workbook with 12 worksheets, each identified by a month number:

```
Sub NewWorkbookForMonths
Dim KeepNewSheetCount As Integer, SheetCounter As Integer
KeepNewSheetCount = Application.SheetsInNewWorkbook
Application.SheetsInNewWorkbook = 12
Workbooks.Add
Application.SheetsInNewWorkbook = KeepNewSheetCount

For SheetCounter = 1 To 12
    Sheets(SheetCounter).Name = "Month " & SheetCounter
Next SheetCounter
End Sub
```

This subroutine does the following:

1. Stores, in KeepNewSheetCount, the user's preferred number of sheets in a new workbook.

2. Sets the number of sheets in a new workbook to 12.

3. Opens a new workbook. Because of step 2, this new workbook has 12 sheets.

4. Resets the number of sheets in a new workbook to the user's original preference.

5. Loops through the numbers 1 to 12. Each time the loop runs, another sheet is named. The loop uses the variable SheetCounter both to keep track of the loops and to help name the worksheets as *Month 1, Month 2,..., Month 12.*

This sort of looping structure has broad applicability in VBA. But sometimes you don't know how many times the loop should execute. When the loop involves an object, you can make good use of an object variable. Suppose, in the preceding example, that you don't know how many worksheets are in a workbook. You could use code like this:

```
Dim Wks as Worksheet, SheetCounter As Integer
SheetCounter=1
For Each Wks In ActiveWorkbook.Worksheets
   Wks.Name = "Month " & SheetCounter
   SheetCounter=SheetCounter + 1
Next Wks
```

This time, the loop is based on what the Excel object model terms a *collection*: in particular, the collection of worksheets in the active workbook. The loop is controlled by an object variable, Wks. Each time the loop executes, the object variable is set to another worksheet in the collection of worksheets in the workbook. During each instance of the loop, Wks represents a different worksheet, and the name of that worksheet is set to the text string "Month" and the current value of SheetCounter. The loop stops when it has accounted for each worksheet in the collection of worksheets in the active workbook.

 The object variable that controls the For Each loop can be declared as a specific object (in the example, as Worksheet), or as a Variant, or as a generic object (e.g., Dim Wks as Object).

Objects from Other Applications

Excel's object model contains virtually every object that you can manipulate in Excel. But what if you need to get at some other application's objects? For example, Microsoft Access has databases that contain tables—analogous to Excel's workbooks that contain worksheets.

Using VBA in Excel, you can manipulate Access databases. By using object variables, you can bring another application's objects into your VBA code and use them as if they were native to the Excel object model. Here's a very brief example:

```
Dim BirthsFile As Database, BirthData As Recordset
Set BirthsFile = OpenDatabase("C:\Workfiles\Births.mdb")
Set BirthData = BirthsFile.TableDefs("NewBorns").OpenRecordset(dbOpenTable)
```

In the Dim statement, two objects that belong to the Access object model are used: Database and Recordset. Two object variables are declared: BirthsFile, which will be used to represent a database, and BirthData, which will represent a set of records.

You need to make a reference to Access's object library before you can use these types of variables. Take these steps:

1. From the Visual Basic Editor, choose Tools | References.
2. In the Available References list box, scroll down until you see Microsoft DAO 3.6 Object Library. Fill its check box.
3. Click OK.

You can now declare object variables that represent objects in the Access model, including Database and Recordset.

As usual with object variables, the Set keyword is used to assign an existing database, Births.mdb, to the object variable BirthsFile. Then the TableDefs property of the Database object identifies a table of data in BirthsFile, opens that table with the OpenRecordset method, and assigns the table's records to the object variable BirthData: a recordset.

When these two object variables have been assigned objects to represent, you can use them in various ways: for example, you can add, edit, or delete records in the database directly from Excel, and you can retrieve records from the database directly into an Excel worksheet.

Array Variables

So far in this chapter you've seen many examples of variables: numeric variables such as InterestRate that store decimal values, string variables such as MyCity that store text values, object variables such as Wks whose values can be actual objects—among them, worksheets.

Mostly, these examples have been of single-value variables. Declared as it was earlier in this chapter, the variable MyCity can take on one value at a time:

```
MyCity = "Far Rockaway"
MyCity = "Pacoima"
```

Variables can also take on multiple values at once. Such a variable is termed an *array variable*. It's helpful to visualize an array as though it were a range of cells on a worksheet. An array might consist of a single row and several columns, much as the range A1:E1 consists of one row and five columns. Or the array might consist of several rows and one column, as does the range C2:C8. Or you might have several columns and several rows in the array, as the range A1:E6. An array variable represents many values which are organized into an array of rows and columns.

An array can go beyond the two dimensional structure of a worksheet. A three dimensional array, for example, might be three rows high, three columns wide and three layers deep—for instance, 3^3 = 27 cells.

If you are to work with arrays, it's necessary to know how to declare them and how to access their individual elements.

Declaring Arrays

You declare an array variable using the Dim, the Private, or the Public keyword, just as you do with a single-value variable. But if you supply parentheses after the name of the variable, you indicate to VBA that you are declaring an array variable. For example:

```
Dim Months(1 To 1, 1 To 12) As Integer
```

declares an array variable with 1 row and 12 columns. The values within the parentheses are termed the array's *subscripts*. In this case, the array has one row, identified by the subscript 1. It has 12 columns, each identified by a subscript between 1 and 12, inclusive.

You can assign a value to a cell in an array with a simple assignment statement. For example, to assign the number 84 to the first (and only) row, and the sixth column, of Months, you would use:

```
Months(1, 6) = 84
```

Using an Array Variable in a Subroutine

Arrays lend themselves beautifully to For loops. Suppose that you wanted to copy the contents of cells A1:A100 on Sheet1 into an array variable. You know that these cells will contain numeric values, possibly with decimals. This code would do it for you:

```
Dim CellContents(1 To 100, 1 To 1) As Single, i As Integer
With ActiveSheet
   For i = 1 to 100
      CellContents(i, 1) = .Cells(i, 1)
   Next i
End With
```

The code begins by declaring an array variable, CellContents, that has 100 rows and 1 column. It also declares an integer variable, *i*, that will act as a counter in a loop.

A With block is established. Its object reference is the active worksheet. Belonging to that object reference is a collection of cells, denoted by .Cells. Because the loop executes 100 times, the With block saves VBA the time and trouble of locating the active sheet 100 times. Only the cell reference changes.

The .Cells syntax is used here for the first time in this chapter. Earlier examples have referred to individual cells by using the Range object: Range("A5") refers to cell A5. Certainly that usage is familiar, in terms of worksheet notation. But it requires that the cell reference be a text value. You could assemble that reference in the current example with something such as this:

```
CellContents(i, 2) = .Range("A" & i)
```

But that's clumsy and it slows things down. Using the .Cells object, you refer directly to the row number and the column number you're interested in. So, when *i* equals 5, the reference .Cells(i,1) identifies cell A5.

The loop executes 100 times, as the counter variable *i* runs from 1 to 100. Each time, a different cell is identified (A1, then A2, then A3, and on through A100), and its value is placed in a different location in the array variable CellContents: CellContents(1,1), then CellContents(2,1), and on through CellContents(100,1).

Using With Blocks, Loops, Functions, and Cells in a Subroutine

Why would you want to read the contents of cells into an array variable? There are quite a few reasons, most of them pertaining to speed of execution. VBA can manipulate values in array variables much faster than it can manipulate values in worksheet ranges.

Suppose that the 100 cell values in the preceding example represented sales dollars for each of 100 sales representatives and you wanted to convert those figures into percentages. Then you would report certain commission amounts based on the percentage of total revenue each salesperson generated.

Certainly you could do all this on the worksheet, entering the proper formulas manually. But that approach is prone to error, and if the task had to be performed regularly, you'd soon tire of it. (You'd also tire of having bricks thrown at you by angry salespeople. Never screw up a sales commission.)

You might cause VBA to write the proper formulas to the worksheet: first to calculate the percentages, then to run the percentages through IF functions that calculate the commission amounts, then to convert the commissions from formulas to values, and finally to delete the formulas that calculate percentages—the latter formulas are just an intermediate step and you wouldn't want them in a report.

It's faster to do all this in an array variable. Here's one way:

```
Sub CalculateCommissions()
Dim SalesResults(1 To 100, 1 To 2) As Single, i As Integer
Dim TotalSales As Single, CommPct As Single
With ActiveSheet
   For i = 1 To 100
      SalesResults(i, 1) = .Cells(i, 1)
   Next i
   TotalSales = Application.WorksheetFunction.Sum(SalesResults)
   For i = 1 To 100
    SalesResults(i, 2) = SalesResults(i, 1) / TotalSales
    If SalesResults(i, 2) > 0.03 Then
       CommPct = 0.05
```

```
        ElseIf SalesResults(i, 2) > 0.02 Then
            CommPct = 0.03
        Else
            CommPct = 0.01
        End If
        .Cells(i, 2) = CommPct * SalesResults(i, 1)
    Next i
    .Range(Cells(1, 2), Cells(100, 2)).NumberFormat = "$0.00"
End With
End Sub
```

Walk through this subroutine, line by line. The first statement just names the subroutine. The name, CalculateCommissions, is (as always) followed by parentheses. The fact that in this case there's nothing within the parentheses indicates that no variables are being passed to the subroutine.

Note   *One way to run a subroutine when the Excel window is visible is to choose Tools | Macro | Macros and click the name of the procedure that you want to run. Only those procedures that have no variables passed to them are visible in the list of available procedures.*

Two statements declare the variables used in the subroutine. SalesResults is dimensioned (that's where the keyword Dim comes from, by the way) as an array variable with 100 rows and two columns and can take on single-precision values. A counter variable, i, is declared. To represent the total of the sales values, TotalSales is declared, and CommPct is also declared: it will represent the commission percentage.

A With block is started; using that block, VBA needs to identify the active sheet only once. The For loop, which immediately follows, uses the members of the Cells collection 100 times, and so the With block saves VBA the effort of identifying the active sheet 100 separate times. This instance of the For loop just picks up the values in cells A1:A100 of the active sheet.

The next statement calculates the value of TotalSales by taking the sum of the array variable SalesResults. Notice that VBA gets that sum by using Excel's worksheet function, SUM. You can use nearly all of Excel's worksheet functions in VBA by preceding the name of the function with the construct Application.WorksheetFunction. The exceptions are those functions for which VBA has its own versions, such as Rnd (instead of RAND) and Sqr (instead of SQRT).

Another For loop now begins. Its first task is to calculate the fraction of total sales attributable to each individual salesperson; then VBA puts that fraction into the appropriate row of the second column in the array variable *SalesResults*.

Also inside the For loop is an If-Then-Else structure that tests each fraction in the second column of SalesResults. If the fraction is greater than .03, the sales commission is set to 5 percent; if the fraction isn't greater than .03 but is greater than .02, then the sales commission is set to 3 percent; in all other cases, the sales commission is 1 percent.

The final step taken during the For loop is to multiply the sales commission percentage times the actual results, for the current row in column 1 of the array variable. That value is written to the current row, second column on the worksheet.

After the second of the two For loops has completed, it remains to format cells B1:B100 on the worksheet in currency format. That range is identified with this VBA reference:

```
.Range(Cells(1, 2), Cells(100, 2))
```

The Range keyword is preceded by a dot, indicating that the range in question belongs to the current With block's object, which is ActiveSheet. Following the keyword are references to two cells: the first row, second column; and the 100th row, second column—that is, B1:B100. This construct is one typical way that VBA refers to a range of cells on a worksheet.

Finally, the With block is terminated and the subroutine ends. As just mentioned, one way that you could run this subroutine is by using Tools | Macro | Macros from the Excel window. If you were to run the subroutine often, you might prefer to attach the macro to its own toolbar button. To do so, take these steps:

1. From the Excel window, choose View | Toolbars | Customize. Click the Commands tab.

2. Click on a category in the Categories list box. Then click a command in the Commands list box and, without releasing the mouse button, drag that command onto an existing toolbar.

3. Release the mouse button. The Modify Selection button in the Customize dialog box becomes enabled.

4. Click Modify Selection and change the appearance of the toolbar button, if you want, by choosing Change Button Image and selecting another image from the palette.

5. The Modify Selection menu also has an Assign Macro item. Click it, and then click on the name of your subroutine in the Macro Name list box. Click OK, and then click Close in the Customize dialog box.

You can now run your macro by clicking the toolbar button that you just placed on the toolbar.

EXTENDING EXCEL'S REACH WITH VBA

Chapter 21

Writing Functions

C hapter 20 stressed that if you want to use VBA to modify some aspect of an Excel workbook, you must use a subroutine. Subroutines are the way to go if you want your code to do things such as adding worksheets, moving data around, formatting ranges of cells, and deleting columns.

You can write a function in VBA like this one, which deletes Column E on a worksheet:

```
Function DeleteAColumn()
Columns("E:E").Delete
End Function
```

but unless that function is called by a subroutine, it won't have any effect. Entering this function directly on the worksheet, as you would with the SUM function, just gives you a zero in the cell where you enter it, and Column E stays stubbornly in its place.

If functions are so limited as to their usage, why bother with them at all? The reason is that functions that you write can do one thing that subroutines can't. When you enter the name of your function directly on the worksheet, it can return a value in that cell—just as though you had entered one of Excel's built-in worksheet functions such as AVERAGE or MAX. You can do that with a subroutine only by going through such gyrations as establishing a Change event handler for a worksheet and then writing code that responds to a change by returning a value to the cell.

A function that you write is termed a *user-defined function*, usually abbreviated *UDF*. Written correctly, your UDF can have all the features of a built-in function: range arguments, optional arguments, automatic recalculation, availability in Insert Function, usage in an array formula, and so on. This chapter shows you how to structure your UDF so as to take advantage of each of these capabilities. The chapter's final section discusses how to improve your subroutines by including in them calls to UDFs.

Writing UDFs for Use on the Worksheet

There are three principal issues involved in creating a UDF that can be used on the worksheet:

- The UDF's basic structural components
- Returning an array of values (as does, say, the built-in function FREQUENCY)
- Integrating the UDF with the Insert Function command and button

The UDF's Structure

Functions that you write can range from something as simple as dividing an argument by 2 to one that duplicates the functionality of the built-in LINEST function while correcting its errors. But the issues involved in structuring a function have little to do with the function's complexity. This section discusses the basic characteristics of a UDF.

Setting the Function Name to Its Own Result

The one absolute requirement for any function that returns a value is that the *name* of the function be assigned the value of the *result* of the function. Here's the basic code for a function that returns the square of a number:

```
Function SquareThis(N)
SquareThis = N * N
End Function
```

The calculation performed by the function is to multiply N times itself. Notice that the result of the calculation is assigned to SquareThis—the name of the function itself. This characteristic is typical of all functions that return values to the worksheet.

Although the function's code assigns a value to the function's name, the name does not subsequently act as a variable with an assigned value. Something such as this:

```
FourthPower = SquareThis * SquareThis
```

does not work. You still need to supply the function's arguments. So, this would work just fine:

```
FourthPower = SquareThis(N) * SquareThis(N)
```

Giving the UDF a Type

Just as it's smart to declare variables with the most efficient type, it's smart to assign a type to a UDF. Functions can take on the same types that variables can—that is, Byte, Boolean, Integer, Single, Double, String, and so on. And, like variables, if you don't assign a type to a function, VBA assumes the most flexible type, Variant. As Chapter 20 discussed, Variant is also the most expensive type in terms of resources required.

You assign a type to the function by means of the *As* keyword followed by the type you have in mind. If, for example, you want the function SquareThis to return a single precision value, you would declare it like this:

```
Function SquareThis(N) As Single
```

Or if for some reason you wanted it to return an integer value, you would use this declaration:

```
Function SquareThis(N) As Integer
```

What if you typed your function as Integer and then asked it to return the square of a number such as 5.2? The square of 5.2 is 27.04. Typed as Integer, your function would return 27. The function is constrained to return a value that corresponds to the function's type; typed as Integer, it cannot return a result's decimal component. So it rounds the result to the nearest integer. At times, this can be a useful characteristic—for example, you might find it expedient to declare a function as Integer instead of declaring it as Single and subsequently rounding its result with the built-in ROUND function.

Arguments and Argument Types

The calculation performed by the function must correspond to the type that you assign to it. In particular, you can't ask functions to perform numeric calculations on nonnumeric values. For example:

```
Function SquareThis(N As String) As Single
SquareThis = N * N
End Function
```

If you passed, say, the letter A to SquareThis, it would return the error value #VALUE!.
Most frequently, a UDF that's intended to be used on the worksheet takes one or more cells as its argument. This is consistent with the structure of the built-in functions: when you use the function AVERAGE or MAX or VLOOKUP, for example, you usually supply a range of cells as an argument: for example, =AVERAGE(A1:A30). Should you, then, declare your UDF's arguments as ranges?

```
Function SquareThis(N As Range) As Single
SquareThis = N * N
End Function
```

This example works, but it's unnecessarily limited. If you pass a cell to it, as in =SquareThis(A1), the UDF will return the square of whatever value is in A1. But if you pass a value to it, as in =SquareThis(4.4), it will again return the error value #VALUE!.

To enable the function to deal correctly with the argument that you pass to it, you should usually avoid typing the argument as a Range (or as a Cell, which is a special case of a Range). The default property of a range is the values it contains. So if you start your UDF like this:

```
Function SquareThis(N As Single) As Single
```

you can pass a cell to it; the UDF will square and return the cell's value. Of course, you can also pass a value to it directly, as in =SquareThis(4.4), to obtain the square of that value.

What if your UDF expects a range of values instead of just one? If you declare the argument as Variant, then your UDF can handle both an array of specified values and an array of values passed as a range of worksheet cells.

Using Other Functions in a UDF

A general rule is that a UDF entered on the worksheet cannot modify the Excel environment other than by returning a value. As this chapter has already pointed out, you can't enter a UDF on the worksheet and expect it to delete a row or add a worksheet.

But in some cases you can make use of an existing function to *appear to* modify the cell or range that the UDF occupies. Here's an example:

```
Function MyPercent(Top As Single, Bottom As Single) As String
MyPercent = Format(Top / Bottom, "#.##%")
End Function
```

This example uses the VBA *Format* function to return a string value, formatted as a percentage. The cell in which it is entered will display the result of dividing *Top* by *Bottom*, and the result will show two decimal places and the percent sign. Note that the function does not change the cell's format. The value that the function returns contains a character that is normally associated with the cell's format.

The drawback is that the result is a string value, necessarily in this case because the Format function returns a string. If you constrain the result to a numeric value, perhaps by adding zero or multiplying by one, your UDF will lose the percentage formatting.

Don't neglect existing functions in your UDFs (or, for that matter, in your subroutines). I have several UDFs that, for different reasons, need to perform matrix algebra operations on the way to returning a result to the worksheet. These operations are fairly easy to write in VBA. But to do so is to reinvent the wheel, as well as to slow down the speed of my UDF. Instead, I use the built-in matrix functions. For example:

```
Dim NewMatrix As Variant
NewMatrix = Application.WorksheetFunction.MMult(MatrixA, MatrixB)
```

If I were to provide VBA code that does matrix multiplication, the UDF would run slower: it would be uncompiled code. Using the built-in MMult worksheet function, I can take advantage of the extra speed it provides because it has already been compiled.

Array UDFs

If you have used functions such as LINEST, TREND, TRANSPOSE, or FREQUENCY, among others, you are probably familiar with the notion of array-entering a formula. Formulas that use these functions require that they be array-entered in order to return the required results. As Chapter 10 explained, you array-enter a formula by pressing CTRL-SHIFT-ENTER, instead of only ENTER.

You might well have a reason to write a UDF that should be array-entered. Perhaps you want to parse a value that contains a complete name—for example, first name, middle initial, and surname—into its constituents, each in a separate cell. Or you might find fault with one of Excel's built-in functions that returns an array of values; although your UDF will run more slowly than the built-in version, it's a price you're willing to pay for the enhancement.

There are a couple of added requirements you need to observe in order to write a UDF that returns an array of values:

■ You must declare the UDF as type Variant. For example:

```
Function MyUDF(InputValue As Double) As Variant
```

■ In your UDF, you must declare an array variable with as many elements as necessary to capture the results that you want to return. When your code has populated the cells in the array variable, set the function equal to that array variable.

It's unusual to know in advance how many cells your function will need to fill. That's where Excel's ReDim statement comes in handy.

Using ReDim to Change an Array Variable's Dimensions

Recall from Chapter 20 that you can declare an array variable with a statement like this:

```
Dim Names(1 To 1, 1 To 10) As String
```

The declaration just shown creates an array variable with one row and ten columns that can take on text values. In contrast, this declaration:

```
Dim Names() As String
```

declares an array variable that can take on text values—but with an unknown dimensionality. It's not yet known how many rows or columns it will have. Before your code can use it, you'll need to determine what dimensions it needs and how many elements to give each dimension.

Suppose that the logic of your code and the nature of your data dictate that the array variable have one row and three columns. Early processing determines that a variable named LastRow equals 1, and one named LastColumn equals 3. After you have learned that, you use this statement to redimension the array variable that you have already declared:

```
ReDim Names(1 To LastRow, 1 To LastColumn)
```

Because you have already declared the array variable as String, there's no need to respecify its type. Using the ReDim statement enables you to declare the array variable at the beginning of the function (always a good practice) and to define its dimensionality only after you've learned how large it needs to be.

Note *You can use ReDim only on an array variable that was originally declared with empty parentheses: for example, Dim MyArray() As Single.*

A useful quality of ReDim is that you can use a variable to redimension the array. You just saw this at work, in the LastRow and LastColumn example. For another example, suppose that you have declared an Integer variable named CharacterCount and that your code has already set that variable equal to 7. This statement:

```
Dim Characters(1 To CharacterCount)
```

is not legal: your code will end with an error if you attempt to use it. The reason is that you can't use a variable to help set the dimensions of an array variable in a Dim statement. But you're free to do so in a ReDim statement; that is, the syntax in these statements is legal:

```
Dim CellValues() As Double
RowCount = Selection.Rows.Count
ReDim CellValues(1 To RowCount)
```

In the examples shown thus far, the lower and the upper bound of an array variable's dimensions have been given explicitly. In the previous example, suppose that the user's worksheet selection contains 12 rows. Then the variable RowCount equals 12. When the array variable CellValues is redimensioned, it has a lower bound of 1 and an upper bound of 12. There is, then, no CellValues(0) and no CellValues(13).

When you use ReDim on an array variable you lose the array's data values. For example:

```
Dim MyArray() As Integer, i As Integer
ReDim MyArray(1 To 5)
For i = 1 To 5
   MyArray(i)=i
Next i
ReDim MyArray(1 To 6)
```

Both ReDim statements initialize the contents of MyArray. Because MyArray is declared as a numeric type, initializing the array sets each element to zero. A variable-length String type is initialized to a zero-length string.

But there's a keyword, *Preserve*, that can help you keep existing data in an array that you redimension. In the preceding example, using this version of ReDim would retain the values that were assigned in the For loop:

```
ReDim Preserve MyArray(1 To 6)
```

Given the For loop that precedes the ReDim, the values in MyArray are now 1, 2, 3, 4, 5, and 0.

The *Preserve* keyword carries some limitations. If you use it:

- You can resize only the final dimension: that is, the rightmost dimension within the ReDim statement's parentheses. These two statements are legal (they are also strange, but are chosen as illustrative):

```
ReDim MyArray(1 To 5, 1 To 5)
ReDim Preserve MyArray(1 To 5, 1 To 6)
```

  However, the second of these two statements:

```
ReDim MyArray(1 To 5, 1 To 5)
ReDim Preserve MyArray(1 To 6, 1 To 6)
```

  results in a "Subscript out of range" error, because it attempts to resize a dimension that is not the final dimension in the array while using the *Preserve* keyword.

- You cannot change the lower bound of the final dimension while using the *Preserve* keyword. The second of these two statements is not legal:

```
ReDim MyArray(1 To 5)
ReDim Preserve MyArray(3 To 5)
```

  and causes a "Subscript out of range" error.

- You cannot change the number of dimensions while using *Preserve*. Again, the second of these statements causes a "Subscript out of range" error:

```
ReDim MyArray(1 To 5)
ReDim Preserve MyArray(1 To 5, 1 To 5)
```

Using Option Base 1

You're not required to specify the lower bound of an array's dimension, whether you're using Dim or ReDim. Both these statements are correct:

```
Dim InputValues(12) As Double
ReDim CellValues(RowCount)
```

But by default, if you omit the lower bound in the statement, it is zero. Making no other provision, the preceding two statements cause the elements in InputValues to be indexed from 0 to 12 and those in CellValues to be indexed from 0 to the value of RowCount, respectively.

If you want to make the default lower bound 1 instead of 0, use the Option Base 1 declaration at the beginning of a module. Then all array variables that are declared or redimensioned without an explicit lower bound will get 1 as their lower bound. For example:

```
Option Base 1
Dim InputValues(12) As Double
ReDim CellValues(RowCount)
```

In contrast to the prior example, the two declarations just shown cause the elements in the array variables to run from 1 to 12 and from 1 to the value of RowCount, respectively.

> **Note** *Keep in mind that this information about array variables, redimensioning, and lower bounds applies equally to both user-defined functions and to subroutines.*

Applying ReDim in a UDF

The function that follows parses a name into its constituent parts. For example, suppose that the name *William Henry Harrison* were in cell C15. You could array-enter the function into, say, F3:H3 and get *William* in F3, *Henry* in G3, and *Harrison* in H3.

```
Option Explicit
Option Base 1

Function ParseNames(FullName As String) As Variant
Dim Names() As String, i As Integer
i = 1
ReDim Names(1)
Do While InStr(i, FullName, " ") <> 0
    i = InStr(i, FullName, " ")
    Names(UBound(Names)) = Left(FullName, i - 1)

    FullName = Right(FullName, Len(FullName) - i)
    ReDim Preserve Names(UBound(Names) + 1)
    i = 1
Loop

Names(UBound(Names)) = FullName
ParseNames = Names
End Function
```

Here's a step-by-step tour of the code:

1. There are two module-level declarations: Option Explicit and Option Base 1. Option Explicit is used as good coding practice. Option Base 1 is used to keep the lower bound of all array variables at 1, even though the lower bound is unstated in its declarations.

2. The function is named and is given a string value as an argument. The user can pass the string either directly, like this:

   =ParseNames("William Henry Harrison")

   or by passing a string value that's in a cell such as B5, like this:

   =ParseNames(B5)

3. Because the function is to be array-entered on the worksheet, it must be declared as type Variant.

4. Two variables are declared. *Names()* is an array variable and will be populated with the constituent parts of the full name. The variable *i* will be used as a counter and is set to 1.

5. *Names()* is redimensioned to have an upper bound of 1—its lower bound is implicitly set, also to 1, by the Option Base 1 declaration.

6. A Do loop is entered. The InStr function returns the position where a sought-for string value is found inside a searched string value, given a starting point inside the searched string. Using values instead of variables, this statement:

   ```
   InStr(1, "William Henry Harrison", " ")
   ```

   searches for a blank space (the third argument) within *William Henry Harrison* (the second argument) starting with the first letter (the first argument) of *William Henry Harrison*. The InStr function with these values returns 8—the eighth character in *William Henry Harrison* is a blank space. As part of the controlling condition in the Do loop, the InStr function causes the loop to continue as long as InStr does not return zero—indicating that there are no more blank spaces to be found. Inside the Do loop, the counter variable *i* is set to the position of the first blank space that InStr encounters. This position will be used to find the end of the first name within the full name.

7. The UBound function returns the upper bound of a dimension in the named array. The first time through the loop, UBound(*Names*, 1) returns 1, because at present the first (and in this case, the only) dimension in *Names* has an upper bound of 1. So this statement:

   ```
   Names(UBound(Names)) = Left(FullName, i - 1)
   ```

   puts the leftmost *i - 1* characters in FullName (that is, the characters that precede the position at which InStr found the first blank space) into the first element in the *Names* array.

8. The string that has been extracted from *FullName* and placed in the *Names* array is removed from *FullName*. At present, that means that *William Henry Harrison* becomes *Henry Harrison*. That task is accomplished by this statement:

```
FullName = Right(FullName, Len(FullName) - i)
```

Consider the portion *Len(FullName)–i*. The variable *i* is the position at which the first blank space was found in *William Henry Harrison*—that is, 8. The Len function returns the number of characters in a string—applied to *FullName*, that is 22. Because 22 – 8 equals 14, the statement reduces to

```
FullName = Right(FullName, 14)
```

which replaces *FullName* with the rightmost 14 characters in *FullName*, or *Henry Harrison*. At this point in the loop, the first element of the *Names* array is *William*, and *FullName* has been reduced to *Henry Harrison*.

9. The ReDim *Preserve* statement is used to redimension the *Names* array:

```
ReDim Preserve Names(UBound(Names) + 1)
```

Regardless of how many times the code has executed the loop, this statement finds the upper bound of the Names array, adds 1 to that, and redimensions the array so that it has one more element than it did before. As it performs this feat, the statement preserves the existing values in the array.

10. The last statement inside the loop resets *i* to 1. This is done so that when the InStr function is next used to find a blank space, it will begin its search with the first character of the searched string.

11. Then the Loop statement is encountered; this transfers control back to the Do statement, the first one in the loop. In the case of *William Henry Harrison*, the second time the loop executes, it evaluates *Henry Harrison*, because the first name has already been trimmed off and placed in the first element of the *Names* array. So the second time through the loop finds *Henry*, stores that value in the second element of the *Names* array, and trims the variable *FullName* down to *Harrison*.

12. The third time the code encounters the Do statement, it again tests whether InStr returns a zero. By this time, *FullName* contains only *Harrison*, and there are no blank spaces in that value. So the test finally fails, the looping terminates, and control passes to the first statement following the Loop statement. That is:

```
Names(UBound(Names)) = FullName
```

13. At the end of the second iteration through the Do loop, the code redimensioned the *Names* array and gave it a new, empty element. The loop did not execute again, so the last element in *Names* is still empty. The preceding statement assigns the current value of *FullName* to that element. In this case, *FullName* has been trimmed down to *Harrison*, and that's the value that's placed in the final element of the array *Names*. Finally, the function ParseNames is set equal to the array *Names*, and the function terminates. The following illustration shows the result.

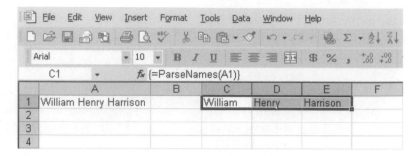

Notice the curly brackets in the formula bar: the UDF has been array-entered.

Putting UDFs into Insert Function

When you have written a UDF, it automatically appears in the list of functions available in Insert Function. You can find it both in the User Defined category and, of course, in the All category.

Specifying a Description for the UDF

Until you specify a description of your UDF, however, the Insert Function dialog box doesn't provide you or anyone else information about the purpose of the UDF. Insert Function offers descriptive information about built-in functions: the RATE function, for example, is described in part as, "Returns the interest rate per period of a loan or an investment." Until you provide a description, Insert Function describes your UDF with "No help available." Unhelpful.

To enter a description that Insert Function displays when a user chooses your UDF, take these steps:

1. If necessary, open the workbook that contains your UDF. Press ALT-F11 to start the VBE.

2. In the Project Explorer, click on the name of the workbook that contains your UDF. For example, if your workbook is named MyUDF.xls, in the Project Explorer you would click on VBAProject (MyUDF.xls).

3. Click the Object Browser button, or choose View | Object Browser.

4. In the Object Browser's Project/Library drop-down, choose VBAProject. (The Project/Library drop-down is the one in the upper left corner of the Object Browser window.)

5. If your project has more than one module, click in the Classes list on the module that contains your UDF.

6. The name of your UDF appears in the Members list. Right-click on the UDF's name, and choose Properties from the shortcut menu.

7. The Member Options dialog box appears (see Figure 21-1).

8. In the Description box, enter a brief description of what your UDF accomplishes. For the ParseNames UDF discussed in the previous section, you might enter as a description, "Parses multi-word names into multiple cells."

9. Click OK to close the Member Options dialog box.

Now, when you select your UDF in Insert Function, the description you entered in the Object Browser appears in the Function Arguments dialog box (see Figure 21-2).

If you find that you cannot set a UDF description as outlined here, the next section shows how you can do so programmatically.

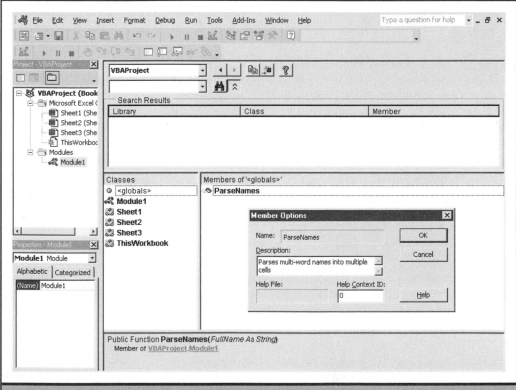

Figure 21-1. *This is where you would establish a reference to a Help file for your UDF*

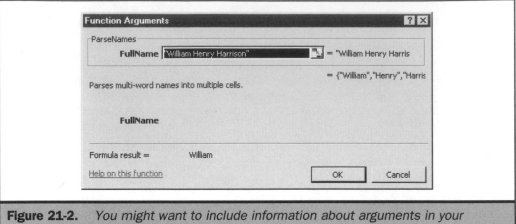

Figure 21-2. *You might want to include information about arguments in your description*

Specifying a Function Category for the UDF

The User Defined category in Insert Function is a handy catchall for available UDFs. But you often want to classify your UDF according to one of the established function categories—Logical, Financial, Mathematical, Statistical, and so on. Excel versions that preceded Office 97 allowed you to classify UDFs from a Macro Options dialog box. In subsequent versions you need to establish those options programmatically, using the MacroOptions method.

Here's the full syntax:

```
Application.MacroOptions(Macro, Description, HasMenu, MenuText, _
    HasShortcutKey, ShortcutKey, Category, StatusBar,
    HelpContextID, HelpFile)
```

You can use these named arguments to set any or all available options for a subroutine procedure or a function procedure. To set a function category, use the Category option. For example, to assign the ParseNames function to the Text category—and also to set its function description—you could use

```
Application.MacroOptions Macro:="ParseNames", _
    Description:= "Parses multi-word names into multiple cells.", _
    Category:=7
```

Note *Notice the use of the := operator in this example. It is used to assign a value to a named argument. Named arguments, such as Macro, Description, and Category, are useful because they don't need to conform to a particular order. Also, as here, you can simply omit arguments that you don't need. The alternative, positional arguments, require that you supply commas to indicate missing arguments, and that the arguments be supplied in a specified order.*

You assign a function category by means of a number. The correspondence between the categories and their associated numbers is

Financial: 1

Date & Time: 2

Math & Trig: 3

Statistical: 4

Lookup & Reference: 5

Database: 6

Text: 7

Logical: 8

Information: 9

After you establish Text as the function category for ParseNames, the UDF appears in Insert Function's Text list as shown in Figure 21-3.

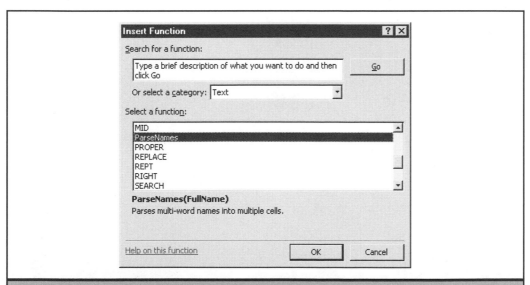

Figure 21-3. *Capitalization helps distinguish between built-in functions and UDFs*

You need to decide where—that is, in what workbook and in what procedure—to put your usage of the MacroOptions method. It's almost surely best to put the code in the same workbook that contains the UDF itself. Consider putting the MacroOptions code in a subroutine named Auto_Open() or Workbook_Open(), so that the UDF's characteristics will be established as the workbook that contains the UDF opens.

UDFs Solely for Use in Code

A UDF has a definite place in your VBA code, even if you intend never to use the UDF directly on the worksheet. Typical uses of this type of UDF include

- Mathematical conversions that Excel and VBA don't provide.
- Calculations that must be coded and that are used frequently in your application.
- Utilities that you use in several different projects.

An example of the latter usage, writing a function that has a home in more than one project, is a method of determining how to proceed if a file isn't found where it's supposed to be. The following code assigns a path and a database name to a string. Then the string is passed to a UDF that looks for the database; if it can't find the database it asks the user for assistance in finding it. If the user declines to assist or if the database just can't be found, the code terminates.

Once the function, here named *FoundTheFile*, is written, it can be used in any VBA project that needs to locate and open a file. In the next example it's used to open an Access database.

```
Option Base 1
Sub Main()
Dim DatabaseName As String, FileType As String
Dim PromptText As String, TitleText As String

DatabaseName = ThisWorkbook.Path & "\Resources.mdb"
PromptText = "Could not find the database file. Do you want to help " _
 & "locate it?"
TitleText = "Couldn't find database"
FileType = "Access Files(*.mdb), *.mdb"
If FoundTheFile(DatabaseName, FileType, PromptText, TitleText) Then
    OpenTheDatabase(DatabaseName)
Else
    MsgBox Prompt:="Application ending.", Buttons:=vbOKOnly
    CleanUpAndTerminate
```

```
End If
End Sub

Function FoundTheFile(FileToOpen As String, FileType As String, _
   PromptText As String, TitleText As String) As Boolean

If Dir(FileToOpen) <> "" Then
   FoundTheFile = True
Else
   If MsgBox(Prompt:=PromptText, Buttons:=vbYesNo, Title:=TitleText) = vbYes _
    Then
      FileToOpen = Application.GetOpenFilename(FileType)
      If FileToOpen = "False" Then
         FoundTheFile = False
      Else
         FoundTheFile = True
      End If
   Else
      FoundTheFile = False
   End If
End If
End Function
```

The code that calls the function begins by assigning values to four string variables:

- *DatabaseName* is assigned the path of the workbook that contains the VBA project—that is, ThisWorkbook. It uses the ampersand, VBA's concatenation operator, to tack a backslash and Resources.mdb onto the path.

Note   *VBA's Path function does not return a final backslash, so if you want to add a filename at the end of the path, you must supply your own backslash.*

- *PromptText* and *TitleText* may be used in a message box: this is for convenience. These two string variables are not strictly necessary because their values could be supplied directly by the MsgBox function, which actually displays the message. But it's easier and less error-prone to change their values in the assignment statements than to change them in the statement that invokes the message box.

- The string variable *FileType* may be used if the user will try to locate the database. This variable defines the kind of file the user will look for: the application the file belongs to and its filename extension.

Then these four string variables are passed to the UDF that's named FoundTheFile. After the UDF has executed, the main code continues by opening the database when FoundTheFile returns a True value; it alerts the user and terminates processing when FoundTheFile returns a False value.

The UDF's Function statement itself names the function, specifies its arguments' names and data types, and declares the function as Boolean—that is, one that returns a True or a False.

The UDF continues with three nested If structures. The main If calls VBA's Dir function, using FileToOpen as its argument. The Dir function returns an empty string ("") if it cannot find the specified file in the specified path. In this example, the value of FileToOpen might be "C:\Temp\Resources.mdb". If the file Resources.mdb exists in the path C:\Temp, Dir returns "C:\Temp\Resources.mdb". Otherwise, Dir returns the empty string.

The UDF FoundTheFile continues on the basis of what the *Dir* function returns. If Dir does *not* return the empty string, FoundTheFile is set to True. The main If function is satisfied and terminates, and the value True is returned to the main code, which continues by opening the database.

What if the Dir function *does* return an empty string? This means that Dir wasn't able to find the specified file in the specified location. But just because it wasn't found where it was expected doesn't mean that the file is really missing: files get moved all the time. Sometimes they stay where they were but are renamed. Sometimes network servers get reimaged and the pathname changes.

So the function asks the user for help by displaying a message box. The message in the box explains that the file wasn't found where it was expected and asks the user if he wants to help locate it. (It makes that explanation, and asks that question, by using the Prompttext variable that was passed from the main code.) Clicking the Yes button causes the MsgBox function to return the value vbYes; clicking the No button causes it to return the value vbNo.

When the user clicks the Yes button in the message box, the UDF displays a built-in dialog box named GetOpenFileName. This dialog box looks just like the one you see when you choose File | Open in any Office application. You can use the dialog box to browse to the location of a file, click on the filename, and then click OK to open the file. By supplying arguments as shown to GetOpenFileName—and notice that the arguments are passed as a variable from the main code—you provide a description of the kind of file to look for (here, Access files) and a combination of wildcards and extensions (here, *.mdb) that suppress the display of other types of files. Figure 21-4 shows what the GetOpenFileName dialog box looks like when it's given the argument used here.

As used in this UDF, the dialog box doesn't actually open a file, but returns a string that contains the path and the name of the file. So, when the user browses to the file's location, clicks the filename, and then clicks OK, the UDF receives a string that identifies the file's actual location. It assigns that string to the variable DatabaseName. Because that variable was passed to the function by reference, the revised value for DatabaseName is returned to the main code, and that's the path and name that the code uses to open the database.

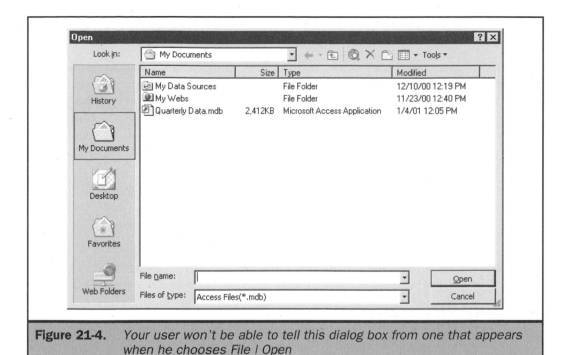

Figure 21-4.   *Your user won't be able to tell this dialog box from one that appears when he chooses File | Open*

What if the user can't find the database file with the help of GetOpenFileName? Then the user will have clicked Cancel on the dialog box; this causes GetOpenFileName to return the string value "False", which is assigned to DatabaseName.

The UDF then tests DatabaseName: if it's "False", the UDF itself is set to False. When control subsequently returns to the main code, processing will end. If DatabaseName is not "False", the UDF itself is set to True, and processing in the main code will continue using the new value of DatabaseName.

You may find this UDF, as written, useful in your own code. More important is to see that the UDF can be used, unchanged, in any VBA project. All you have to do to use it is supply a call to the function; the call used in the example just shown is

```
If FoundTheFile(DatabaseName, FileType, PromptText, TitleText) Then
```

By changing the values of DatabaseName, FileType, Prompttext, and Titletext (and perhaps the names of the variables as well), we can generalize the use of the UDF to any situation in which VBA code needs to open a file before it can continue—for example, another Excel workbook, or a text file, a Word document, and so on.

The point is that if you write a UDF that could be used in another VBA project, make the UDF as general as possible:

- Avoid giving names to its arguments that are unnecessarily specific: if this sample UDF had received a variable that it called DatabaseName, that name could be misleading when used in a context that opens an Excel workbook.

- Rather than assigning values in the function itself, pass those values to the function. This helps keep the function more generally applicable, and it also tends to shorten the number of statements in the function itself—always a desirable outcome.

- Don't cause the project to terminate processing by means of something such as an End statement inside the function. If a condition forces you to unconditionally terminate processing, take care of that outside the function. More generally, limit the tasks that a function performs to those it *must* perform.

It's also important to keep in mind that this UDF displays a message box and a built-in dialog box. Therefore, it cannot successfully be entered in a worksheet cell.

Chapter 22

Controlling Input
with User Forms

A *user form* is a dialog box that you create and display on the screen with VBA. There are two broad situations that call for user forms:

- You have designed your VBA code to act in different ways, depending on what the user wants it to do. A user form is an effective means of determining which choices your user wants to make.

- Your code needs the user to supply data. You can use a user form to collect data directly from the user, or to get the user to indicate a worksheet location that contains the data.

A side benefit of user forms is that they can make the application you have designed look more attractive, even more professional. Users typically appreciate that.

This chapter discusses the general issues involved with the design of user forms, as well as the techniques used to collect information by means of user forms as efficiently as possible.

Designing the Form

Figure 22-1 shows a portion of a completed user form. It includes several of the controls that you might want to use on a form.

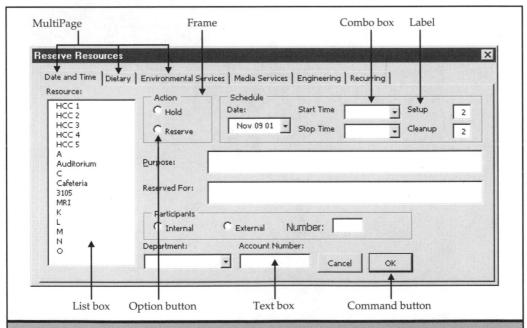

Figure 22-1.   *Shown is the first Page in a MultiPage control, with other controls installed*

Chapter 19 discusses how to establish an empty user form, and how to place controls on that form by means of the Toolbox. This section shows you how to get the form to work the way you want it to.

Showing, Hiding, and Unloading User Forms

There are fifteen methods associated with user forms, but in practice there are three methods that you almost always need when you are going to employ a user form. These methods pertain to loading the user form into memory, thereby making it accessible to your VBA code, and displaying the user form on the screen, thereby making it accessible to the user.

You also need to remove the form from the screen when the user is finished with it, and to remove it from memory when your code is finished with it.

The Show Method

You use the Show method to display the user form on the user's screen. If the user form has not already been loaded into memory, the Show method first loads and then displays it. *Showing the form stops your code from running* until the user dismisses the user form, usually by clicking an OK or a Cancel button. You provide the code that runs when the user clicks a button. Often, but not always, you will decide to have an OK button invoke the Hide method.

 Keep in mind as you read this chapter that VBA code stops running while a user form is on the screen. Once the form is removed from the screen, control returns to the code and use can be made of the information that the user entered on the form.

The Hide Method

The Hide method removes the user form from the screen but leaves it in memory. While it's still in memory, your code can access it. Your code accesses the user form in order to obtain, and to store in variables, the information that the user supplied. This also gives your code a chance to validate the information that the user entered—for example, a password. Once your code has finished examining data on the user form, it's a good idea to use the Unload method.

The Unload Method

The Unload method removes from memory the user form and all the controls on it. Once it's unloaded, your code cannot obtain any information from the user form. Unloading the form is useful because it frees up the memory the form occupied.

Putting the User Form Methods Together

The sequence of events usually runs along these lines:

1. Show the form. This is often done in a Do loop that tests for some condition on the user form, such as the accuracy of a password entered by the user.

2. Hide the form in response to the user clicking an OK button. This returns control to VBA, and you can now validate the information that the user has supplied. It may be, of course, that some of that information is not valid—an incorrect password, for example. In that case the Do loop mentioned in step 1 might show the user form again, refusing to continue any further processing until the user gets the password right. Once any test in the Do loop has been passed, the user form is not automatically shown again by the Do loop, and your code can continue its tasks.

3. After your code has finished examining the information supplied by the user and (probably) storing much of that information in its variables, it can unload the user form and free up some memory.

This chapter's examples illustrate the use of these three methods.

Controls on User Forms

The controls on the form shown in Figure 22-1 have some special aspects. Each one is detailed in the following sections.

The List Box

You can arrange for a list box to give the user only one choice or multiple choices. If you want the user to be able to select only one item in the list, make sure that the list box's MultiSelect property is set to *fmMultiSelectSingle*. This is the default setting. If you want the user to be able to select more than one of the items in the list, set the MultiSelect property to *fmMultiSelectMulti*.

To set any of the properties discussed in this chapter, first make sure that the VBE's Properties window is visible. Then select the control in question. Find the property that you want to set in the Properties window. Then either enter the property's value to the right of the property's name, or click the drop-down to select among the available choices.

The list box shown in Figure 22-1 has its MultiSelect property set to *fmMultiSelectExtended*. This enables the user to select any single resource by clicking it. The user can select, for example, resources HCC 3 and K by clicking on HCC 3, and then holding down the CTRL key and clicking K. Finally, the SHIFT key helps the user select several adjacent resources: for HCC 1 through HCC 5, the user could click on HCC 1, hold down SHIFT, and click HCC 5.

Option Buttons and Frames

A typical use of option buttons is to force the choice of one option from a group of two or more: for example, option buttons would be the standard way for the user to indicate Male vs. Female, Resident vs. Nonresident, or Paper vs. Plastic.

The user form in Figure 22-1 shows two uses of option buttons: one to distinguish between Hold and Reserve, and one to distinguish Internal from External. Notice that the option buttons are surrounded by frames. One frame is labeled Action, and one frame is labeled Participants. Frames are useful to help visually set off sections of a form from one another, but they also exert control over option buttons. When there are two or more option buttons inside a frame, only one of the buttons can be selected at once.

In Figure 22-1, for example, the user might click Hold. The button would then be filled to indicate that Hold has been selected. If the user then clicked Reserve, its button would be filled and the Hold button would again be blanked.

To arrange option buttons in a frame, begin by establishing the frame on the user form. Then place the buttons one by one within the frame's boundaries. If you place the buttons first and then drag a frame around them, the frame will obscure the buttons.

You can also use the framing technique with check boxes—of several check boxes in a frame, only one can be chosen. It's conventional, though, to reserve option buttons for use when the user should choose exactly one option and to use check boxes to allow the user to make more than one choice.

Combo Boxes

A *combo box* is a combination of a text box—one in which you can type information—and a list box. Figure 22-1 shows four combo boxes, labeled Date, Start Time, Stop Time, and Department.

Notice that each combo box has a drop-down arrow. The user clicks that arrow to view the entire list of available items (see Figure 22-2).

Once an item is clicked, it appears in the text box portion of the combo box. The user can also type a value directly into the text box portion.

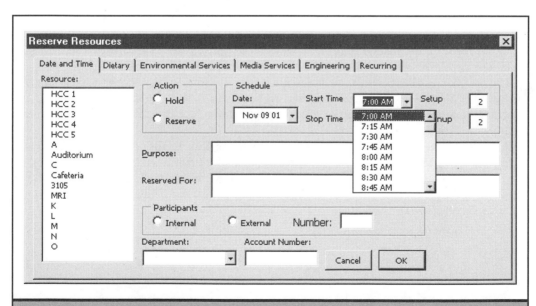

Figure 22-2. *Use a combo box's ListRows property to control the number of rows that appear*

You normally use a list box when it will not obscure something else on the form and a combo box when you need its list to be out of the way. Notice in Figure 22-2 that the box that contains the Resource list doesn't obscure anything. But the Start Time combo box, for example, has so many times in it that to display even a subset of them in a list box would take up too much room on the form.

Using Text Boxes and Labels

When you can't present the user with an abbreviated list of choices, as you do with option buttons and list boxes, a text box is often the right control. In Figure 22-2 there are six text boxes: Setup(number of setup periods), Cleanup (number of cleanup periods), Purpose (of a reservation), Reserved For (who the reservation was made for), Number (of participants), and Account Number. In each case, the user types some alphanumeric information into the text box.

Some controls come with their own captions. For example, when you create an option button on a user form, both the button itself and a caption appear on the form. You use these captions both to define the option for the user and to establish accelerator keys.

When you choose File | Save As in Excel, one of the choices you can make in the resulting dialog box is Save As Type. If you look at that choice, you will see that the letter *T* in *Type* is underlined. This is termed an *accelerator key*. If you hold down the ALT key and then press the accelerator key, the associated control is activated.

If a control has an accelerator key property, you can set that property in the Properties window. Text boxes, however, do not have the Accelerator property. To establish an accelerator key for a control that doesn't have that property, use a label.

Labels do have an Accelerator property. In Figure 22-2, notice that the *P* in *Purpose* is underlined. A label has no particular function other than as a caption, but if you set the tab order for a form such that the label immediately precedes a control, then using the label's accelerator key activates the associated control (see Figure 22-3).

The text box for Purpose has no accelerator key. But setting the Accelerator property for the Purpose label to P, and then setting the tab order so that the label immediately precedes the text box, has the same effect. Holding down ALT and pressing the P activates the associated text box.

Accelerator keys are partly case-sensitive. Setting the Accelerator property to P in *Purpose* would mean that the uppercase *P* would be underlined on the user form. Setting its Accelerator property to p would mean that the lowercase *p* would be underlined. But if it were set to P, holding down ALT-SHIFT-P would have no effect: you would still use ALT-P.

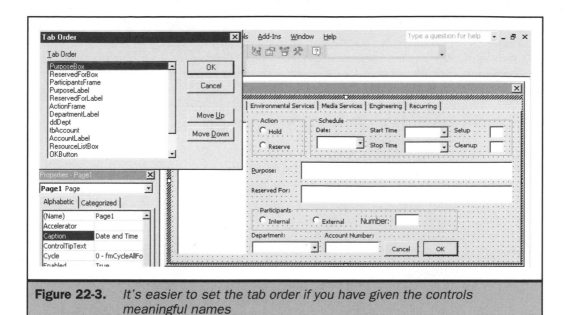

Figure 22-3. *It's easier to set the tab order if you have given the controls meaningful names*

Text Boxes and Passwords

You have probably noticed what happens when Excel or some other application asks that you enter a password. If you have started to open a workbook that is password-protected, or if you have tried to unprotect a worksheet that someone has password-protected, you are confronted by a dialog box similar to the one shown next.

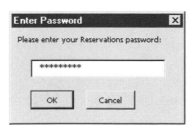

You are expected to enter the correct password in the text box. As shown in the illustration, whatever you type appears as asterisks. This feature prevents someone who might be looking over your shoulder from seeing what you typed. To obtain the password illicitly, that someone would have to watch which keys your fingers press.

If your application uses information that should stay confidential, or that only certain people should be able to edit, consider protecting it with a password scheme. A fairly simple, but not simpleminded, approach is to structure a user form to look like the one shown in the preceding illustration. Then select the text box on the user form and use the Properties window to set the text box's PasswordChar property to some character—conventionally, this is an asterisk but you can use any character you want. If you have some other use for that user form, you can reset the PasswordChar property in your code. Here's an example:

```
Sub GetPasswordAndAge()
With UserForm1
   .Caption = "Please enter your password."
   With .TextBox1
      .SetFocus
      .Value = ""
      .PasswordChar = "*"
   End With

   Do While UCase(.TextBox1.Value) <> "SHIBBOLETH"
      .Show
   Loop

   .Caption = "Please enter your age."
   With .TextBox1
      .SetFocus
      .Value = ""
      .PasswordChar = ""
   End With
   .Show
End With
End Sub
```

This code begins by establishing a With block, so that subsequent objects in that block belong to the user form. It then sets the caption of a user form to ask the user to enter the password.

A nested With block is established and refers to the text box that itself belongs to the user form that governs the outer With block. In the nested With, three actions occur:

- The text box gets the focus. That is, it will be the active control when the user form appears on the screen.

■ The text box's value is set to an empty string. This clears any value that might remain in the text box from an earlier session—in particular, a password.

■ The text box's PasswordChar property is set to an asterisk. Each character the user types into the text box now appears as an asterisk.

A loop is then entered. The user form continues to be shown until the user types SHIBBOLETH. Note the use of the *UCase* function. This converts whatever the user typed in the text box to all uppercase letters, and relieves the user of having to provide the letters of the password in precise upper- and lowercase.

You could make arrangements more strict by requiring the user to type, for example, an uppercase *S* and the remainder in lowercase. If you do so, your code should remind the user to check the status of the CAPS LOCK key, because the user might have typed sHIBBOLETH.

When the user clicks a button on the form, that button executes a UserForm.Hide statement in the button's On Click event handler. Hiding the user form turns control back over to VBA. The next statement to execute is the Loop statement, which loops back to the Do While statement. The Do While statement evaluates the password supplied by the user. If it's incorrect, the user form is shown again and the process repeats.

If it's correct, though, the loop terminates and the caption on the user form is changed to ask the user to enter an age. The text box is again given the focus, its value is cleared, and the PasswordChar property is set to a blank string. So doing allows the user to see the characters that are typed into the text box. Finally, the user form is shown again, so that the code can obtain the user's age.

Scroll Bars and Spin Buttons

As noted in Chapter 20, a scroll bar gives the user more ways to enter and increment a number than does a spin button. With a scroll bar, the user can click the scroll arrow at either end of the bar or between the scroll box and the scroll arrow, or the user can drag the scroll box in either direction. In contrast, a user can click only one of the two arrows on a spin button.

A scroll bar has a SmallChange property and a LargeChange property. These properties identify the amount that the value changes when the user clicks the scroll bar. Suppose the SmallChange property is set to 1. In that case, the value associated with the scroll bar increases by 1 when the user clicks the upper scroll arrow (or, if the scroll bar is oriented horizontally, the right scroll arrow), and decreases by 1 if the user clicks the lower (or the left) scroll arrow. A spin button also has a SmallChange property. It is the amount that the value changes when the user clicks one of its arrows.

Similarly, if you set the LargeChange property to 10, the value increases by ten if the user clicks between the scroll box and the upper (or the right) scroll arrow, and decreases by ten if the user clicks between the scroll box and the lower (or the left) scroll arrow.

Spin buttons and scroll bars do not themselves display their values. Usually, the values appear in text boxes, but it's also feasible to use a spin button to control the selected item in a single selection list box. You use the spin button's or the scroll bar's Change event to change the value displayed in, say, an associated text box. Here's an example:

```
Private Sub ScrollBar1_Change()
UserForm1.TextBox1.Value = ScrollBar1.Value / 2 & "%"
End Sub
```

Suppose your form contains a scroll bar named ScrollBar1 and a text box named TextBox1. Right-click on the scroll bar and choose View Code from the shortcut menu. In the code window you see the Private Sub and the End Sub statements shown in the preceding code. You add the command that executes when the user clicks the scroll bar or clicks a scroll arrow or drags the scroll box (see Figure 22-4).

You might have set the scroll bar's SmallChange property to 1 and its LargeChange property to 10. If the scroll bar's value starts at zero, then clicking the right scroll arrow displays .5% in the text box. Again, if the scroll bar's value starts at zero, then clicking in the space between the scroll box and the right scroll arrow displays 5% in the text box.

To limit the values shown in this example's text box to the range 0 percent to 100 percent, use the Properties window to set the scroll bar's Min property to 0 and its Max property to 200. If, as is almost certain, you intend to use the value in the text box for some numeric purpose, be sure to divide that value by 100 before applying it. All the text box is doing is accepting a value between 0 and 200, dividing it by 2, tacking a percent sign onto that value, and then displaying the result.

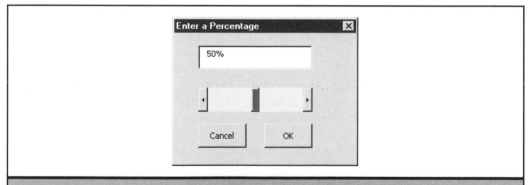

Figure 22-4.   *It's important to have a control that displays the scroll bar's current value*

Notice that this example handles fractional values in the code by dividing the scroll bar's value by 2. The reason is that the SmallChange and LargeChange properties can take only integer values: that is, you cannot successfully set the SmallChange property to .5 or the LargeChange property to 10%. Therefore, if you want to account for fractional values, you must do so after the user has, by clicking, set the value of the scroll bar or spin button.

The Calendar Control

The Calendar Control is a sophisticated tool and is surprisingly easy to handle in your code. You can always have the user enter or modify dates by using text boxes, and if you have very little room available on your form, you might want to take that approach.

But text boxes cause problems for some users. For example, if you display a date in the text box using a short date format—so *March 16 1999* would appear as *3/16/99*— then if the user wanted to change the day from 16 to 17, it would be necessary to use the mouse pointer very precisely.

In contrast, consider the layout shown in Figure 22-5.

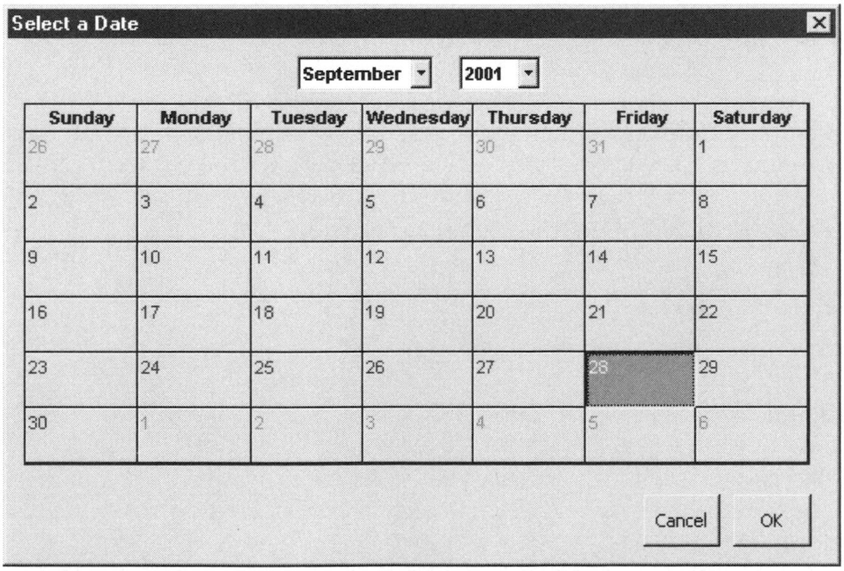

Figure 22-5. *Setting a date with the Calendar Control is much easier than with text boxes*

Here, the user might need to select a month and a year from their respective drop-down lists, and then click on a day. The code that you use to control the calendar might look like this:

```
Dim WhichDate As Date, CaptureCaption As String
With DateForm
   CaptureCaption = .Caption
   .Calendar1.Value = Date
   .Caption = "Select a date"
   .Show
   WhichDate = .Calendar1.Value
   .Caption = CaptureCaption
End With
```

The code assumes that you have placed a Calendar Control on a form named DateForm and that you have kept the default name of this instance of the Calendar Control, Calendar1. The form's current caption is saved in the CaptureCaption variable and is returned to that value at the end of the With block.

Note   *The Calendar Control is not one placed on the Control Toolbox by default. You need to choose Tools | Additional Controls. The procedure is shown in Chapter 19.*

Before the user form appears on the screen, the code uses the VBA Date function to set the calendar's value to the system date. After the user has chosen a date on the calendar, the user clicks the button that hides the user form, control is returned to VBA, and the variable WhichDate is set to the user's selection.

Initializing Controls

Before your code displays the form on the screen, it's good practice to set the form's controls to certain values. This process is termed *initializing* the form.

You should determine which controls should be cleared and which ones could be given default values to save the user a little time. For example, you might want to clear all text boxes on the form. Because text boxes are typically used to get free-form information from the user, there's often no way to predict what the user might enter, or to supply a default value.

When there is a typical value, though, you should supply it for the user. Your form might have a text box where the user can enter a date. If that date is usually the same as the system date, you can save time and errors by setting that control's value on the user's behalf. For example:

```
MainForm.DateBox.Value = Date
```

Some controls—a list box, for example—require special handling. In an initialization routine, you might want to populate a list box with your code, rather than assigning some particular worksheet range to the list box. Here's an example:

```
With UserForm.ResourceListBox
    .Clear
    For i = 1 To NumberOfResources
        .AddItem (Sheets("ResourceNames").Cells(i, 1).Value)
    Next i
End With
```

This code establishes a With block, so that the Clear and the AddItem methods that follow, as well as the Selected property, are taken to belong to the list box on the user form cited in the With statement. The first statement in the With block, the Clear method, removes all items that might be there from the list box.

A loop that's governed by the counter variable i then runs and executes once for each resource. Each time through the loop, another item is added to the list box. In this case, the names of the resources are found in cells A1:A16 on a worksheet named ResourceNames. The code picks up each of those 16 values and puts them into the list box.

How you later determine which list box item the user has selected depends on whether the list box is a single- or multiselection box—that is, it depends on how you set the list box's MultiSelect property. If it's a single-selection box, you can use either the Value property or the ListIndex property. So, if the ResourceListBox in the preceding code is a single-selection box, either of these two statements would get the index of the item that the user selected:

```
UserSelection = UserForm.ResourceListBox.ListIndex
UserSelection = UserForm.ResourceListBox.Value
```

Be careful, though: list boxes number their items starting at zero. So, if the user chooses the first item in the list, both the Value and the ListIndex properties return zero; if the user chooses the 22nd item, they return 21.

If the list box allows multiple selections, you can't use the ListIndex or the Value property. Instead, you must use the Selected property, which returns an array of values. These values are True or False, depending on whether the user chose the associated list box item. Again, the items in the array are numbered starting with zero. You also use this property to deselect items in a multiselection list box. For example:

```
For i = 1 to NumberOfResources
    UserForm.ResourceListBox.Selected(i - 1) = False
Next i
```

EXTENDING EXCEL'S
REACH WITH VBA

On Events for Controls

Two of the most important controls on a form are the OK button and the Cancel button. Together, these buttons enable the user to indicate that the user has completed entering information on the form and to return control to VBA, or that the user wants to stop the code from running. It's your responsibility to associate the proper events with those buttons.

Keep in mind, though, that "OK" and "Cancel" are just convenient designations and are used here because of their familiarity. A user form needs a button for the user to click when he's finished using the form and wants your code to continue processing. That button is often named OK Button and often has "OK" as its caption. But you've probably seen a button with the same function captioned "Finish." And you may have seen a button that cancels processing captioned "Quit."

The Cancel Button

You should give careful consideration to what you want to happen when the user clicks a Cancel button on your form. It's often inappropriate to simply terminate processing with an End statement. Executing an End statement in VBA destroys all variables that have been declared and makes all processing in the active project stop. This means that if you have created code that supports an orderly termination, that code won't run when End is executed.

Suppose you have used the Toolbox to put a command button on your form. Now right-click on the command button to display the shortcut menu and choose View Code. A window appears with these statements already in it:

```
Private Sub CommandButton1_Click()

End Sub
```

If you really want the execution of your code to unconditionally end when the user clicks this command button, you can enter the single End statement, as follows:

```
Private Sub CommandButton1_Click()
End
End Sub
```

Perhaps, though, you have written another subroutine that performs tasks such as closing files, updating information about when the code was run and who ran it, terminating applications that your code started, and closing connections to databases. If that subroutine were named CloseDown, then the subroutine that's attached to the Cancel button might look more like this:

```
Private Sub CommandButton1_Click()
Unload UserForm1
CloseDown
End Sub
```

Notice the use of the Unload statement. Because it uses UserForm1 as an argument, it removes UserForm1 from memory—and thus removes it from the screen. Once this Unload executes, UserForm1, its controls, and their values are unavailable to your code. Then your CloseDown procedure executes.

> **Note**
>
> *If you are a member of a team that's developing a VBA project, it's considered very bad practice to use the End statement. Some other team member might have written code that must execute before the code stops running. That person will get a nasty surprise when a user does something, such as clicking a Cancel button, that makes the code stop prematurely.*

There are two properties that are sometimes set to True for Cancel buttons: the Cancel property and the Default property. Their names are a little misleading.

Setting a button's Cancel property to True does not by itself cause the button to dismiss a user form when the button is clicked. (To dismiss the form, you must put a command such as Unload or Hide in a subroutine that runs when you click the button.) All that setting the Cancel property to True does is to associate the ESC key with that button: pressing the ESC key then has the same effect as clicking the button.

If you set a button's Default property to True, then you have associated the ENTER key with that button. So long as no other button has the focus, pressing ENTER has the same effect as clicking that button.

Only one control on a form can have its Default property set to True or its Cancel property set to True.

The OK Button

Usually you want your code to progress normally when a user clicks an OK button on your form. (Of course, that button can have any caption you want, but *OK* is a conventional and unambiguous choice.)

On the user form is a command button, probably labeled *OK*. The developer has associated this subroutine with the OK button by right-clicking the button, choosing View Code, and entering the UserForm.Hide statement:

```
Private Sub CommandButton1_Click()
UserForm.Hide
End Sub
```

The portion of code that displays the user form might look much like this:

```
Sub ShowTheForm()
Dim ResponsesValid As Boolean
ResponsesValid = False
Do While ResponsesValid = False
    UserForm.Show
    CheckResponses ResponsesValid
Loop
End Sub


Sub CheckResponses(ResponsesValid As Boolean)
With UserForm
    If .OptionButtonMale = True Or .OptionButtonFemale = True Then
        ResponsesValid = True
    Else
        MsgBox "Please choose either Male or Female."
    End If
End With
End Sub
```

The subroutine ShowTheForm first sets a Boolean variable, ResponsesValid, to False. The idea is to keep showing the user form until that variable becomes True. The subroutine enters a loop that continues to run until the user has provided the necessary information. The loop shows the user form. When the user clicks the OK button, the user form is hidden but is still available in memory. The loop then calls the subroutine CheckResponses, passing the Boolean variable along by reference.

The subroutine CheckResponses examines the user form. If it finds that the user has chosen one of two option buttons, it sets ResponsesValid to True; otherwise, it leaves ResponsesValid as False. Then control returns to ShowTheForm, and the loop continues to first show and then hide the user form until the user has chosen one of the two option buttons.

Notice the distinction between the UserForm.Hide and Unload UserForm. Both statements remove a form named UserForm from the screen, but UserForm.Hide leaves the user form in memory. It can be reshown, and the values of its controls remain available to the VBA code. Unload UserForm removes the user form both from the screen and from memory, so you would usually want first to hide the user form, waiting to unload it until your code has finished checking the user's responses and assigning the values of the form's controls to other variables.

Conditionally Hiding and Displaying Controls

Figure 22-6 shows a different page on the user form that was introduced in Figure 22-1.

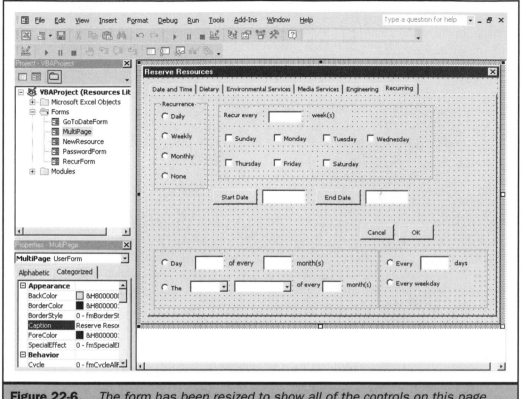

Figure 22-6.   *The form has been resized to show all of the controls on this page*

There are four frames used on this tab. One contains four option buttons: Daily, Weekly, Monthly, and None. Because these four option buttons are within the same frame, only one of them can be chosen at a time.

The other three frames establish different patterns of recurrence: again, daily, weekly, and monthly. Of the latter three frames, only one is visible at a time. Their visibility is controlled by the option buttons. For example, Figure 22-7 shows what the tab looks like when the user clicks the Monthly option button.

There are a couple of reasons to show only one of the three frames at a time. One is room: given the size of the user form, there isn't enough space on the tab to show all the frames. The other reason is that two frames will always be irrelevant. For example, if the user wants to establish a weekly recurrence pattern, there's no reason to confront the user with options for daily or monthly patterns.

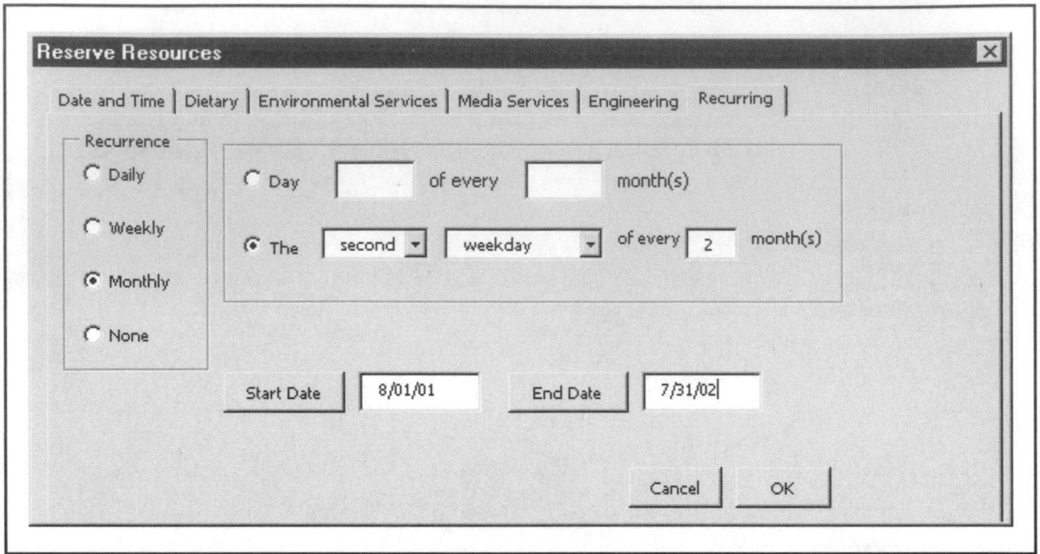

Figure 22-7. *The form is shown in its normal size, hiding several controls on the page*

The visibility of the frames is controlled by code that's associated with the four option buttons. For example, when the user clicks the Monthly button, this code executes:

```
Private Sub MonthlyOptionButton_Click()
With Me.DailyFrame
    .Visible = False
    .Top = 168
End With
With Me.WeeklyFrame
    .Visible = False
    .Top = 168
End With
With Me.MonthlyFrame
    .Top = 12
    .Left = 78
    .Visible = True
End With
End Sub
```

This subroutine pushes the top margin of the Daily frame and the Weekly frame down below the visible portion of the user form; for good measure, it also sets their Visible properties to False. In moving these frames and in making them invisible, the code has the same effect on the controls located in the frames: the controls are moved and made invisible.

Then the code pulls the Monthly frame up into the visible portion of the user form, adjusts its left margin, and makes it visible. The controls that are located on the Monthly frame are moved and made visible along with their frame.

The other option buttons—Daily and Weekly—have similar code associated with them. For example, the Daily button's code moves down and makes invisible the Monthly frame and the Weekly frame, and then moves up and makes visible the Daily frame.

To determine the position that you want a control to occupy, first use your mouse pointer to drag the control to a location. In the Properties window you will find the Height, Left, Top, and Width properties. Make a note of their values, and then use those values in any code that you use to position the control.

Chapter 23

Techniques for Handling VBA Arrays

605

A n Excel worksheet—more generally, any spreadsheet—is an array. It has rows and columns, and it has cells that represent the intersections of the rows and columns. Extending the concept to three dimensions, an Excel workbook is an array of its worksheets' rows and columns, plus the layer of worksheets in the workbook.

Excel offers a variety of techniques for handling the data in that array. You can copy columns from one part of a worksheet to another. You can cut a row from one worksheet and paste it into another worksheet. You can sort data on up to three fields at once. You can create pivot tables using multiple consolidation ranges. All of these techniques are readily accessible from the Standard worksheet menu.

Chapters 20 and 21 touch on the use of VBA arrays, and Chapter 24 discusses their use in temporarily storing data from an external database. If you haven't yet covered the material on arrays in those chapters, you'll find the necessary concepts summarized here. This chapter shows you how to extend the array concept, persistent and visualized on the worksheet, to the more transient and often invisible context of the VBA array. Depending on how you declare them, VBA arrays can have rows and columns, just as worksheets do, and they can also have a depth dimension, just as workbooks do. You will find, if you haven't already, that it helps to visualize a VBA array as though it were an Excel worksheet.

VBA arrays are memory locations. Their structure and contents disappear as soon as the VBA code that declares and populates them stops running. It's in part *because* of this transience that VBA arrays can be so efficient. Your VBA code can write to a VBA array, read from it, and perform calculations on it—usually much faster than it can perform the same operations on worksheet cells.

Declaring and Populating Arrays

In most cases you must declare an array as such before you can use it. (One major exception, discussed later in this chapter, occurs when you assign an existing array to a Variant variable.)

Dimensioning the Array

Declaring an array is a matter of naming it and defining its type. The declaration also might indicate its dimensions. For example, this declaration

```
Dim MyArray(1 To 5, 1 To 10) As Integer
```

creates an array named *MyArray*, consisting of two dimensions. The first dimension's index starts at 1 and ends at 5; the second dimension's index starts at 1 and ends at 10. The array can contain integer values.

Suppose you want to declare an array that has ten rows and two columns. You could do that with this statement:

```
Dim MyArray(1 To 10, 1 To 2) As Integer
```

This declaration means that MyArray has ten rows, which are numbered 1 to 10, and two columns, numbered 1 to 2; MyArray can store integer values only. You would refer to the intersection of the first row and the first column with a statement like this one:

```
SomeValue = MyArray(1,1)
```

You could also declare the array as follows:

```
Dim MyArray(-5 To 4, 0 To 1) As Integer
```

This array also has ten rows, but they are numbered –5 to 4. Its two columns are numbered 0 to 1. You would refer to the intersection of the first row and the first column with this statement:

```
SomeValue = MyArray(-5,0)
```

It would take an idiosyncratic situation to get you to dimension the array in this way, but it's not impossible to imagine one.

In the declaration of the array, you're not required to specify the lowest and highest value of a dimension, as is done in the previous examples. If you omit the lowest value (also termed the *lower bound*), VBA supplies a default value. Consider this declaration:

```
Dim MyArray (10, 2) As Integer
```

The default lower bound for both rows and columns is 0. So the previous declaration is equivalent to

```
Dim MyArray (0 To 10, 0 To 2) As Integer
```

If you want to avoid having to declare each dimension's lower bound, and if you want the lower bound to default to 1 instead of 0, use this option statement:

```
Option Base 1
```

at the beginning of any module to which it should apply. Then the declaration

```
Dim MyArray (10, 2) As Integer
```

is the same as

```
Dim MyArray (1 To 10, 1 To 2) As Integer
```

Letting the lower bound of a dimension equal 0 can ease some situations—for example, when you return indexed field names from a Microsoft Access database, they begin with Field(0), then Field(1), and so on. But for most situations, it's easier to set the lower bound to 1. If you do so, you know that the expression MyArray(5,1) refers to the value in the fifth row, first column of the array.

As noted, when you declare an array to have two dimensions, the first dimension represents rows and the second represents columns. So it's counterintuitive to learn that the declaration

```
Dim MyArray(10) As Integer
```

has ten columns and one row. You would think that the first (and only) dimension would represent rows. But it represents columns. To convince yourself, run this code:

```
Dim MyArray(10) As Integer, i As Integer
For i = 1 to 10
   MyArray(i) = i
Next i
Range(Cells(1,1), Cells(10,1)) = MyArray
Range(Cells(15,1),Cells(15,10)) = MyArray
```

The result is shown in Figure 23-1.

Note that cells A1:A10 all contain the same value, 1. This is because the statement

```
Range(Cells(1,1), Cells(10,1)) = MyArray
```

which puts values in cells A1:A10—that is, ten rows and one column—puts the value in the first column of MyArray in each cell. In contrast, cells A15:J15 contain the integers 1 through 10, the full range of MyArray. So each column in MyArray has been written to a different column on the worksheet.

This bit of array esoterica has little practical value, but you need to be aware of it. Otherwise, you will write code that you expect to put different values in different rows but in fact puts the same value in different rows. For this reason, many developers declare the row and column orientation of an array explicitly. For example, the code

```
Option Base 1
Dim MyArray(10,1)
```

unambiguously results in an array with ten rows and one column.

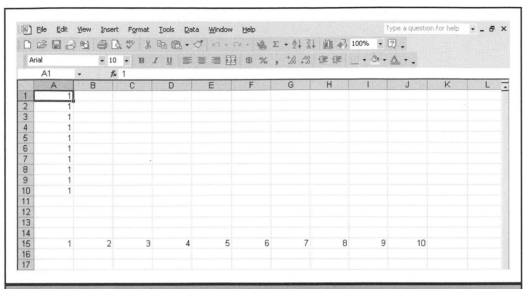

Figure 23-1.   *A single-dimension VBA array has one row and at least one column*

Populating the Array

In practice, you populate (that is, fill with values) most VBA arrays from the worksheet. Your VBA code reads values from a worksheet and inserts them into an array. At times, though, you want to put into an array values that you specify in your code. VBA has a function, Array, that enables you to do that. Here's an example:

```
MyArray = Array(1, 3, 5, 7, 9)
```

For this assignment statement to work, you must declare MyArray as type Variant, and you must *not* provide it with dimensions. So you would declare MyArray with this statement:

```
Dim MyArray As Variant
```

You're not restricted to specific values when you populate an array in this way. You can use variables, too:

```
QuarterlyCostArray = Array(JanCosts, FebCosts, MarchCosts)
```

Because you must declare the variable that will contain the array as Variant, you can mix different types of data:

```
EmployeeArray = Array(EmpName, HireDate, Salary)
```

In the previous example, EmpName might contain a string, HireDate a date value, and Salary a single-precision value.

Getting Data from the Worksheet

There would be little point to using VBA arrays at all if you didn't have data to put in them. Often, though not always, the data comes from the worksheet. There are two main ways to move data from the worksheet and into a VBA array, and (necessarily) both require that you use VBA code to accomplish the move. One method moves the data cell by cell, and the other moves the data en masse.

Looping Through Cells in the Range

Suppose you have a worksheet that's set up as shown in Figure 23-2.

Note that every other row in the range A1:D25 is blank. You want to put the data in this range into a VBA array, but you don't want to bother with the empty rows; similar considerations would apply if every other column were empty. A nested loop is an ideal solution to this sort of problem. Here's one way to do it:

```
Option Explicit
Option Base 1
Sub ReadRevenues
Dim Revenues(12,4) As Single
Dim i As Integer, j As Integer, k As Integer
k = 1
For i = 3 To 25 Step 2
   For j = 2 To 4
      Revenues(k,j) = Cells(i,j).Value
   Next j
   k = k + 1
Next i
End Sub
```

The preceding code indexes the worksheet rows in increments of 2. That is, the outer For loop first sets i equal to 3, then equal to 5 (because of the Step 2 argument), then to 7, and so on. The result is that the rows with empty cells—the even-numbered rows, in this example—are skipped.

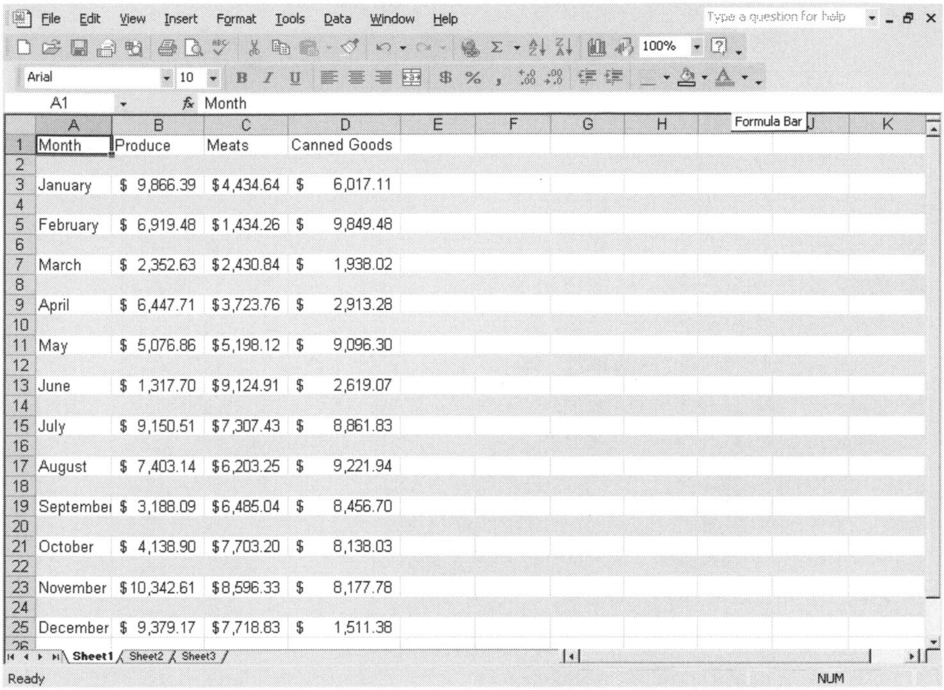

	A	B	C	D
1	Month	Produce	Meats	Canned Goods
2				
3	January	$ 9,866.39	$4,434.64	$ 6,017.11
4				
5	February	$ 6,919.48	$1,434.26	$ 9,849.48
6				
7	March	$ 2,352.63	$2,430.84	$ 1,938.02
8				
9	April	$ 6,447.71	$3,723.76	$ 2,913.28
10				
11	May	$ 5,076.86	$5,198.12	$ 9,096.30
12				
13	June	$ 1,317.70	$9,124.91	$ 2,619.07
14				
15	July	$ 9,150.51	$7,307.43	$ 8,861.83
16				
17	August	$ 7,403.14	$6,203.25	$ 9,221.94
18				
19	Septembei	$ 3,188.09	$6,485.04	$ 8,456.70
20				
21	October	$ 4,138.90	$7,703.20	$ 8,138.03
22				
23	November	$10,342.61	$8,596.33	$ 8,177.78
24				
25	December	$ 9,379.17	$7,718.83	$ 1,511.38

Figure 23-2. *Intermittent blank rows represent a common setup for reports*

Although every other worksheet row is skipped, every row in the VBA array is used. So the third row on the worksheet goes into the first row in the VBA array, the fifth worksheet row goes into the second row in the VBA array, and so on. This means that the code must use different variables to index the worksheet rows and the VBA array rows.

The example uses *i* to index the worksheet rows, and *k* to index the VBA array rows. Each time that *i* increments (by 2), *k* increments (by 1). The technique of using one variable to keep your place in an array and another to keep your place on a worksheet has applicability in many situations—for example, when you reverse the present example by writing from an array to a worksheet, and you want to leave some rows empty.

Another example of this concept occurs when you need to apply a condition to reading the data. Consider the worksheet shown in Figure 23-3.

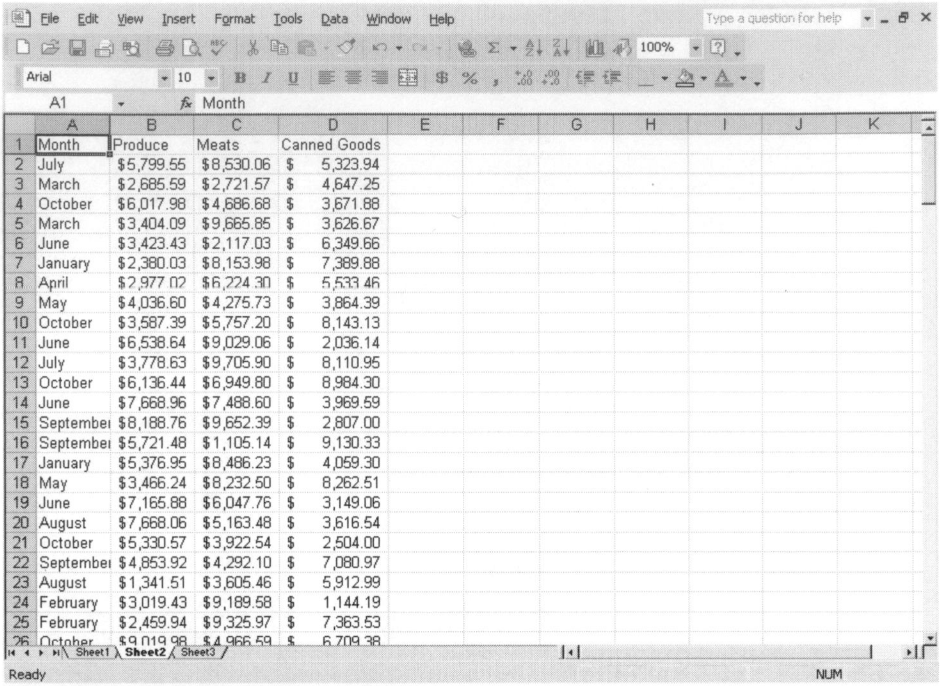

Figure 23-3. *Unsorted data ranges often call for conditional processing*

Suppose that part of the task you set for your code is to select sales made during the year's first quarter. You need to look at the value in column A: if it is January, February, or March, you want to use that row, and to skip it otherwise. Code such as this would work:

```
Option Base 1
Option Explicit
Sub ReadSalesIntoArray()
Dim ArrayOfSales() As Currency, NumberOfRows As Integer
Dim i As Integer, j As Integer, k As Integer
k = 1
NumberOfRows = Cells(65536, 1).End(xlUp).Row
```

```
ReDim ArrayOfSales(4, k)
For i = 2 To NumberOfRows
   If Cells(i, 1) = "January" Or Cells(i, 1) = "February" Or _
     Cells(i, 1) = "March" Then
        For j = 2 To 4
           ArrayOfSales(j, k) = Cells(i, j).Value
        Next j
      k = k + 1
      ReDim Preserve ArrayOfSales(4, k)
   End If
Next i
End Sub
```

This code is complicated enough to require some comment. After setting options, the code declares some variables, notably ArrayOfSales. This variable is declared with an empty pair of parentheses; so doing indicates that it is a *dynamic* array: one whose dimensions can be changed while the code is running. To declare the array as something such as

```
Dim ArrayOfSales(100,4) As Currency
```

where its dimensions are given specific upper and lower bounds, would prevent you from redimensioning the array later in the code.

The code then sets the value of NumberOfRows, which defines how many worksheet rows are to be examined. It does this by starting with the cell in the 65536th row, first column. The code then applies the End property to that cell. When you invoke a cell's End property, you must also specify a direction. Here the direction used is xlUp—a VBA constant meaning "the up direction on a worksheet."

This has the same effect as if you had selected cell A65536, the final row in column A, held down the CTRL key, and pressed the UP ARROW key. The active cell would become the bottommost cell in column A that contains a value.

Once the code has found that cell, it notes the number of that cell's row and puts the row number in the variable NumberOfRows. Now the code knows how far down the worksheet to go in its search for sales made during the first quarter.

A loop is entered, indexed by *i* and terminated after *i* has become equal to NumberOfRows. The first step within the loop is to find out whether the current row belongs to the first quarter: that is, if the value in column A is January, February, or March. If not, nothing happens inside the loop—the index *i* is incremented and the loop starts over at the next worksheet row.

But when the value in the current row of column A passes that If test, the data in that row is read into the current column of ArrayOfSales. This occurs by means of this simple loop:

```
For j = 2 To 4
    ArrayOfSales(j, k) = Cells(i, j).Value
Next j
```

The loop might read the values in cells B45:D45 into these array locations: (2,11), (3,11), and (4,11). This procedure—reading a row of worksheet data into a column of a VBA array—is not there just to make life difficult. It is to conform to the requirements of the ReDim Preserve statement.

At the beginning of this code, it's not known how many worksheet rows contain data from the first quarter. Therefore, the code doesn't know how many elements to reserve in the VBA array for sales that meet that criterion. The code takes the approach that it will create another element in the VBA array each time it encounters another worksheet row that qualifies to go into the array.

The code creates that additional element by means of the ReDim statement. Each time the index variable k is incremented by 1, the array is redimensioned to have an additional element. The statement

```
ReDim Preserve ArrayOfSales (4, k)
```

means "Redimension the array so that it has four rows and as many columns as the value of k, and preserve the data that's already in the array." (See Chapter 21 for a full explanation of the use of the Preserve keyword, but be aware that the use of ReDim alone reinitializes an array, thus losing any data it contains.) It is the use of Preserve that requires the code to add new columns instead of adding new rows. When you redimension an array and you want to preserve its contents, you can change the limits of the array's final dimension only—that is, the rightmost dimension in the ReDim statement.

What about column A? The loop that actually populates the array skips column A and reads the values in columns B, C, and D. The loop also populates rows 2, 3, and 4 of the VBA array, ignoring row 1. The reason is that the code declares ArrayOfSales as type Currency. Trying to place a text string, read from column A, into the array would result in a type mismatch error, so the loop bypasses it when it populates the array.

An alternative would be to dimension ArrayOfSales with three instead of four rows and use a loop like this one:

```
For j = 2 To 4
    ArrayOfSales(j - 1, k) = Cells(i, j).Value
Next j
```

Notice that as *j* runs from 2 to 4, its usage as an index to ArrayOfSales runs from 1 to 3. Where possible, I prefer to avoid doing calculations inside a loop that could execute thousands of times, so in this example I dimension the array with four rows and ignore the first row of the array along with the first column on the worksheet.

Another alternative would be to declare ArrayOfSales as type Variant instead of Currency. Then the array could take on virtually any sort of value. But as was discussed in Chapter 20, a Variant array requires considerably more memory than other array types. See this chapter's section "User-Defined Data Types" for a more elegant solution to the problem of mixing data types in an array.

After *k* is incremented and the array is redimensioned, the loop executes again, and it continues to execute until its counter, *i*, exceeds the value of *NumberOfRows*. When that occurs, all the rows have been tested, those that belong to the first quarter have been read into the array, and both the loop and the subroutine terminate.

Assigning a Range to an Array

At times, the worksheet range whose values you want to put into a VBA array will consist of a group of contiguous columns and contiguous rows. If you don't need to apply a criterion to the data you put into the array, you can perform the worksheet-to-array transfer in one step. The key is to declare the array properly.

Suppose you want to assign, in one step, the currency values in worksheet range A1:D100 to an array named ArrayOfSales. You must declare ArrayOfSales in this way:

```
Dim ArrayOfSales As Variant
```

(It's not recommended, but if you fail to use Option Explicit and fail to declare ArrayOfSales at all, then the approach discussed here also works. Not explicitly declaring a variable causes it to default to type Variant when you first use it.)

If you declare the array in any of the following ways, you won't be able to assign the range of values in one step:

- **Dim ArrayOfSales As Currency**   Currency is the wrong data type. You must declare the variable as Variant.

- **Dim ArrayOfSales(100,4) As Variant**   Even though ArrayOfSales will contain 100 rows and four columns, you can't specify the dimensions in the declaration and later assign the range to the array.

- **Dim ArrayOfSales() As Variant**   While ArrayOfSales will eventually be an array, you can't make it so with the empty pair of parentheses, as you would to declare a dynamic array.

After declaring the variable as Variant, you can populate it with a statement such as

```
ArrayOfSales = Sheets(1).Range(Cells(1,1),Cells(100,4))
```

When you do so, the VBA array has exactly the same dimensions as the worksheet range whose values you assign to it: in the previous example, ArrayOfSales would automatically be dimensioned to have 100 rows and four columns. You would find precisely the same values in the array's cells as you find in the range's cells. That is, if C85 on the worksheet contains 1.234, so does the cell in the 85th row of column 3 of ArrayOfSales.

This technique can be clumsy when you aren't working with a range of relevant and contiguous rows and columns—then you have to account for the blank or irrelevant rows or columns in the VBA array. It also requires more of your computer's memory, because data of type Variant nearly always requires more memory than do other data types.

But when your worksheet data is laid out in a way that supports this approach, it can be much faster than executing a couple of potentially lengthy loops. Further, it's easier to write a single assignment statement than it is to write two loops, making sure that the counters controlling the loops are consistent with the dimensions of the VBA array that the loops populate.

Putting Data on the Worksheet

Many of the same considerations apply when you're determining how best to move data from a VBA array to a worksheet range. You can do so in one statement, or by means of loops. Again, the choice is usually dictated by how you want the worksheet range to appear.

Writing to the Full Range in One Statement

Suppose you want to move an entire VBA array to a worksheet range, and you don't have any special requirements for the worksheet layout: for example, you don't require any intervening rows or columns. A statement like this one could work:

```
Sheets(1).Range(Cells(1,1),Cells(100,4)) = ArrayOfSales
```

If ArrayOfSales has 100 rows and four columns, the previous assignment statement will do the trick. But it's a good idea to be wary of statements that rely on numeric constants. What if the upper limits of the dimensions of the array are not 100 and 4?

The UBound and LBound functions are useful in situations like this. UBound returns the largest subscript of an array's dimension, and LBound returns the lowest subscript. So, if you declare an array as follows:

```
Dim MyArray(-10 To 15)
```

LBound(MyArray) returns –10, and UBound(MyArray) returns 15. If an array has more than one dimension, you should include the dimension you're interested in as the second argument to LBound and UBound, as follows:

```
Dim MyArray(-10 To 15, 1 to 8)
```

With this declaration, LBound(MyArray,1) returns –10 and UBound(MyArray,2) returns 8.

You can use these functions to generalize your code. For example:

```
Dim NRows As Long, NCols as Integer
NRows = UBound(MyArray,1) - LBound(MyArray,1) + 1
NCols = UBound(MyArray,2) - LBound(MyArray,2) + 1
Sheets(1).Range(Cells(1,1),Cells(NRows, NCols)) = MyArray
```

The number of rows, NRows, in the array is found by subtracting the lower bound of the array's first dimension from its upper bound and adding 1. The number of columns, NCols, in the array is found by subtracting the lower bound of the array's second dimension from its upper bound and adding 1. This approach makes it possible to adjust the size of the worksheet range according to the size of the array.

Special treatment is needed when the worksheet range that you are writing to is not on the active sheet. Suppose Sheets(1) is the active sheet and Sheets(2) is the one where you want to write the contents of your VBA array. You might well expect this statement to work:

```
Sheets(2).Range(Cells(1,1),Cells(Nrows,Ncols)) = MyArray
```

But it doesn't. The reason is that in this construction, the Cells object refers to cells on the active sheet. If Sheets(2) is not the active sheet, you won't get what you're after—writing the array to Sheets(2). Instead, use the dot notation to make sure that the Cells object you refer to belongs to Sheets(2):

```
With Sheets(2)
    .Range(.Cells(1, 1), .Cells(Nrows, NCols)) = MyArray
End With
```

> **Note**   *This situation, writing to one sheet when another is active, occurs frequently. You might be updating all the sheets in a workbook, for example. Then it's usually a waste of time to activate each sheet in turn. Or your code might be running in response to an event triggered by an action the user took. Then you might not want to activate a sheet other than the one the user is looking at.*

Consider the situation described previously in the section titled "Looping Through Cells in the Range." There, using the Preserve keyword meant you had to reverse rows and columns in your array: a row on the worksheet became a column in the array. When it comes time to write the array to the worksheet, you could use nested loops to reverse the process, to convert a column in the array to a row on the worksheet. But if you want to write the array in just one statement, you can make use of the worksheet function TRANSPOSE to reverse the orientation of the rows and columns:

```
With Sheets(2)
    .Range(.Cells(1, 1), .Cells(Nrows, NCols)) = _
        Application.WorksheetFunction.Transpose(ArrayOfSales)
End With
```

Without using the TRANSPOSE function, the array would be written to the worksheet, as shown in Figure 23-4.

With the TRANSPOSE function, the array is written, as shown in Figure 23-5.

And Figure 23-5 shows the proper orientation, one that mirrors the orientation of the data on its source sheet.

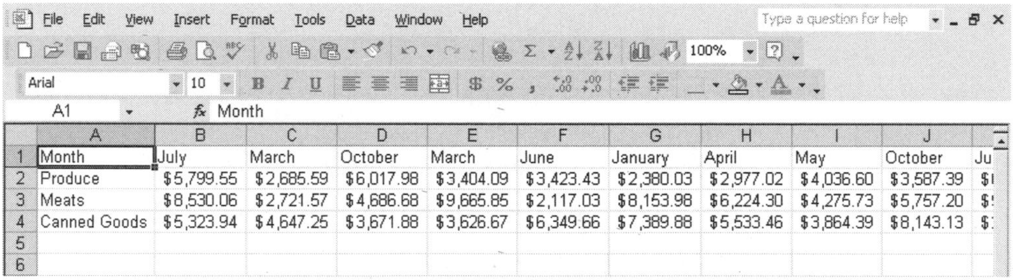

Figure 23-4.   *This is the original orientation of the array*

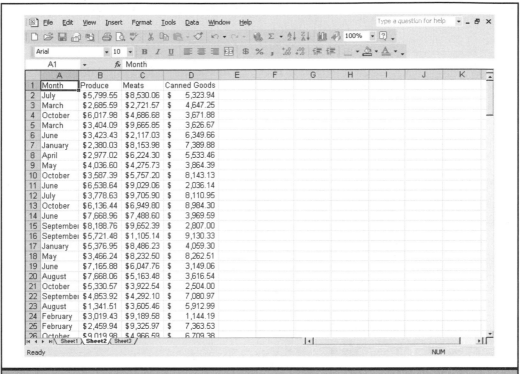

Figure 23-5. *This is the orientation that Paste Special Transpose would provide*

Writing the Array with Loops

Continuing the example from the previous section, if you wanted to transpose the array
to the worksheet value by value, a nested loop is the right approach.

```
Sub WriteTheArray(ArrayOfSales() As Currency)
Dim NRows As Long, NCols as Integer
Dim i As Integer, j As Integer
NRows = UBound(ArrayOfSales,1) - LBound(ArrayOfSales,1) + 1
NCols = UBound(ArrayOfSales,2) - LBound(ArrayOfSales,2) + 1
With Sheets(1)
```

```
      For i = 1 To Nrows
         For j = 1 to NCols
             .Cells(j, i) = ArrayOfSales(i, j)
         Next j
      Next i
End With
End Sub
```

There are three points to note in the previous code:

■ When the array is passed to the procedure, the argument to the Sub statement indicates that it is an array by means of the empty parentheses.

■ The With block is used to avoid referencing the destination worksheet during every cycle through the loops.

■ The indexes, *j* and *i*, are switched in the cell assignment statement so as to transpose the array.

User-Defined Data Types

We've all seen or written code such as this:

```
Source = Income(i, 2)
Amount = Income(i, 3)
```

where a particular value was believed to be stored in a particular column of the array named Income. (Presumably, the array Income was declared as Variant, or the values in both the second and third columns of the array are numeric.) This approach is workable but it has some disadvantages. As the developer of the code, or as a person who must maintain it, how confident are you that the second column of the array contains the source of the income? Or that the third column really contains its amount? At some point during the development process, or during a subsequent edit, it's entirely possible that the contents of those two columns might have been moved to other columns.

Unless the person who moved them also accounts for the move in the two statements just shown, then the variables Source and Amount will be assigned some value other than the one you're expecting. Employing user-defined variable types can solve this sort of problem.

Declaring a User-Defined Type

Consider this declaration:

```
Type Revenue
    Source As String
    Amount As Currency
    SaleDate As Date
End Type
```

Statements such as these, placed at the top of a module, enable you to declare your own data type. So doing augments the standard data types—integer, string, date, object, variant, and so on—with a type that facilitates your tasks and adds safeguards to your code.

A data type that you declare is assembled using the standard data types. Notice in the previous example that each element of the user-defined type is one of those supplied by VBA. With a type named Revenue declared, you can use code such as this to make more certain that values are where they should be:

```
Dim CurrentSale As Revenue
CurrentSale.Source = "Catalog"
CurrentSale.Amount = 42.56
CurrentSale.SaleDate = #9/28/02#
```

You can even use With blocks on user-defined data types:

```
Dim CurrentSale As Revenue
With CurrentSale
    .Source = "Catalog"
    .Amount = 42.56
    .SaleDate = #9/28/02#
End With
```

Perhaps best of all, you can declare an array as your user-defined data type:

```
Dim SalesData(100) As Revenue
```

The previous statement shown declares an array with 100 elements as the Revenue type. Now the coding problem that this section started with, repeated here:

```
Source = Income(i, 2)
Amount = Income(i, 3)
```

could be replaced with this code:

```
Source = CurrentSale(i).Source
Amount = CurrentSale(i).Amount
```

The difference is that meaningless column numbers (in the example, 2 and 3) have been replaced by meaningful element names (.Source and .Amount). This makes your code much easier to write, understand, and edit—and much less error prone.

User-defined data types lend themselves well to situations in which you are dealing with records: information about employees, for example, or products. It's often the case in these situations that a given record is described by several variables that have different types. So you might declare these types:

```
Type Employee
    LastName As String
    FirstName As String
    BirthDate As Date
    SSN As String
    Salary As Currency
    Allowances As Byte
End Type
Type Car
    Brand As String
    Model As String
    Year As Integer
    Price As Currency
    NumberOfDents As Long
End Type
```

With these, you can set each element to a given value (for example, Car.Brand = "Ford" or Employee.FirstName = "David") and so create a full description of each employee on the staff, or of each car on the lot.

Limitations to User-Defined Types

User-defined data types provide an elegant solution to many problems that you encounter as a developer. But there are some limitations to their use, detailed in the following sections.

User-Defined Types and Variant Types

You cannot directly assign a variable that has a user-defined type to a Variant variable. For example, this code results in a type mismatch error:

```
Type EmpType
    Name As String
    Salary As Currency
End Type
Option Base 1
Sub AssignARecord()
Dim NewHire As Variant
Dim Employee As EmpType
Employee.Name = "Fred"
Employee.Salary = 1000
NewHire = Employee
End Sub
```

You can, however, use the Array function to create an array of values that you assign to the Variant variable. For example, this statement could replace the NewHire = Employee statement just shown:

```
NewHire = Array(Employee.Name, Employee.Salary)
```

The Array function returns a variant that contains an array. Using this statement, the Variant named NewHire contains an array of two elements. NewHire(1) equals Fred and NewHire(2) equals 1000. Its lower bound is determined by the Option Base statement: it is one if Option Base 1 is used, and zero otherwise.

For Each Loops and User-Defined Types

The For Each loop is intended to cycle through objects in collections and, more rarely, elements in arrays. A For Each loop such as the following is legal and often useful:

```
Dim Wks As Worksheet
i = 1
For Each Wks In ActiveWorkbook.Worksheets
```

```
    Cells(i, 1) = Wks.Name
    i = i + 1
Next Wks
```

This For Each loop is also legal:

```
Dim Employee(2) As String, EmpName As Variant
Employee(1) = "Dick"
Employee(2) = "Jane"
For Each EmpName In Employee
    MsgBox EmpName
Next EmpName
```

So long as the iteration element—in the example, EmpName—is declared as Variant, you can use the For Each structure to loop through an array. But if the array itself is declared as a user-defined type, the For Each structure will cause a syntax error. This would occur if the Employee array were declared not as String but as the user-defined type EmpType.

The solution is to use a normal For loop. Before executing the loop, you will need to determine how many times to run it. For example, if the Employee array is declared as a user-defined type, you could use this code:

```
EmpCount = UBound(Employee)
For i = 1 to Empcount
    MsgBox EmpName(i)
Next i
```

Constants and User-Defined Types

In VBA you can declare constants, and it's often smart to do so. For example:

```
Const CurrentYear As Integer = 2002
```

This could be a useful declaration if your code uses the value 2002 frequently, perhaps as a test for valid data. When the year changes, it's easy to change the value of CurrentYear where it's declared, and you needn't change 2002 to 2003 throughout your code.

But you can't declare a constant as a user-defined type. If WhenType is a user-defined type, this statement would fail:

```
Const CurrentYear As WhenType = 2002
```

Passing Arguments by Value

You can't pass by value to another procedure a variable whose type is user-defined. So this is not legal:

```
Type ArgType
    Element1 As String
End Type
Sub CalledSub (ByVal TheArgument As ArgType)
```

The previous code would fail at compile time: a user-defined type cannot be passed by value.

Sorting Arrays

You can sort data in a VBA array just as you do on the worksheet. Text, numbers, date values (which are actually numbers)—all can be sorted in a VBA array.

Using the worksheet sort capability can be more effective than doing the sort on a VBA array. Certainly, multiple sort keys can make the situation complex enough that you might want to write the array contents to the worksheet as described earlier in this chapter. Then sort the array on the worksheet—you can do so from within VBA by calling the Sort method of the Range object. After the sort is complete, and if necessary, you can read the contents back into the array, again as described in earlier sections of this chapter.

That said, there are reasons that you might want to do the sort using a VBA array anyway. For example, Excel offers you no way to sort the order of the worksheets in a workbook. When they need to be sorted, you must sort them manually. After describing a basic approach to array sorts, this section provides you with a subroutine that will sort a workbook's sheets for you.

Simple Exchange Sorts

The sorting method that's easiest to understand is the *exchange sort*. It's the most basic approach to sorting—and usually the slowest. But its theme can be found in the most sophisticated and fastest algorithms.

The idea behind an exchange sort is to work through an array of values from the first to the last. Each time you find a pair of values that's out of order, you switch them. For example, if the fifth value is 9 and the tenth value is 2, an ascending sort would call for their positions to be switched—the fifth value would become 2 and the tenth value would become 9.

It's easy enough to say "switch the positions of these values," and it's only a little more difficult in practice. Suppose the array is named Values, you want to sort it in ascending order, and the fifth value is 9 and the sixth value is 2. You can't start with the statement

```
Values(6) = Values(5)
```

because then both positions in the array would equal 9—you've lost the 2. And of course if you start with the statement

```
Values(5) = Values(6)
```

you've lost the 9. The solution is to use a holding place, a variable of the same type as the array that you're sorting. The current example would look something like this:

```
TempValue = Values(5)
Values(5) = Values(6)
Values(6) = TempValue
```

In words:

1. Put 9 into TempValue.

2. Put 2 into Values(5).

3. Put 9 into Values(6).

These three steps swap the values in positions 5 and 6 of Values, and it's what happens in an exchange sort whenever two values are out of order. One value is put in temporary storage, the other value is made to occupy both positions in the array, and then the first value is copied from temporary storage into its proper position.

Of course, code like this example is useless in practice, because the indexes of the array are frozen at 5 and 6. To work properly, the sort needs to step through all the positions in the array, and that implies the use of a loop.

Sorting the Array with Loops

An exchange sort uses two loops, one nested within the other. The outer loop steps through the array once, starting with its first value and ending with its next-to-last value.

The inner loop steps through the array once for each instance of the outer loop, but it starts farther into the array each time. The inner loop compares its current value with the value that's current in the outer loop. If the sort calls for those two values to be swapped, then the switching logic described in the prior section comes into play.

At a minimum, exactly nine statements are needed, as follows:

```
For i = 1 to UBound(Values) - 1
   For j = i + 1 To UBound(Values)
      If Values(i) > Values(j) Then
         TempValue = Values(j)
         Values(j) = Values(i)
         Values(i) = TempValue
      End If
   Next j
Next i
```

Suppose the array Values contain three values: in order, they are 5, 8, and 1. You want to sort them in ascending order, so that after the sort they are in the order 1, 5, and 8. The code just given would take the following steps:

1. The outer loop is governed by i. There are three values in the array, so i will run from 1 to 2.

2. The inner loop is governed by j, which always starts at $i + 1$. The first time the outer loop executes, j will run from 2 to 3. The second time the outer loop executes, j will run from 3 to 3—that is, the inner loop will execute once only when i equals 2.

3. At the outset, $i = 1$ and $j = 2$. The If test asks if Values(i) is greater than Values(j): that is, given that it's an ascending sort, are they out of order? They are not. Values(i) equals 5, which is less than the 8 found in Values(j). So the statements in the If block are skipped, and the inner loop executes again.

4. The second time through the inner loop, $i = 1$ and $j = 3$. This time the If statement finds that the two values are not in ascending order. Values(i) equals 5, which is more than the 1 found in Values(j). So the If test is satisfied and the values are swapped, making use of the TempValue holding place. After the switch, *Values(1)* = 1 and *Values(3)* = 5. *Values(2)* was not involved in the comparison or the swap and remains with its original value, 8. The order in the Values array is now 1, 8, and 5.

5. The inner loop's counter, j, equals 3, which is the upper bound of Values. Therefore, the inner loop has executed as many times as it is supposed to. Control reverts back to the outer loop, where i still equals 1. The outer loop is not to terminate until i is greater than 2, the upper bound of Values minus 1. So i is incremented to 2 and the inner loop begins again. The inner loop's counter, j, is set to $i + 1$ or 3. Because that's also the inner loop's final value, the inner loop will execute just once more.

6. With $i = 2$ and $j = 3$, the If test checks to see if Values(2) is greater than Values(3). That is the case: 8 is greater than 5. So the swapping code kicks in and the 8 and the 5 switch positions. Values(2) now equals 5, and Values(3) now equals 8.

7. At the end of the If block, j equals 3 and the inner loop terminates. The outer loop also terminates because i equals 2, its final value. The nested loops have completed, and the array has been sorted in ascending order: 1, 5, and 8.

Beware of using a simple exchange sort on arrays that are large. It is a grind-it-out approach that invokes no shortcuts, and therefore can take a long time to complete if there are, say, a few hundred values to sort. In these cases, it can be better to write the array to a worksheet and use VBA code to invoke the worksheet's Sort command. After the worksheet has finished sorting the values, read them back into the VBA array.

As a practical matter, a sort on two or three keys is often more easily done on the worksheet than directly on a VBA array. However, because of its simplicity, an exchange sort is often ideal when the array is smaller, or when there is only one sort key.

Using VBA Arrays with Workbooks

A neglected area in books about VBA and Excel is the use of VBA arrays in conjunction with objects that belong to workbooks and worksheets. Although the arrays themselves are transient, disappearing along with their contents as soon as the code stops running, their effects can be made to persist. The array-handling techniques such as sorting that are discussed in this chapter are well suited to this type of use.

Sorting a Workbook's Sheets

One collection of objects that you can't sort on the worksheet, but that you might well want sorted, is the group of worksheets in a workbook. This section discusses a subroutine that sorts worksheets into ascending order according to their names.

The approach used by the subroutine is to put the worksheets' names into an array named SheetNameArray. Each cell in the array is assigned the name of a sheet, in the existing sheet order.

Then the array is sorted in ascending order, using the worksheet names as the sort key. After the loops that perform the sort have completed, a final loop puts the worksheets themselves in the same order as the names are found in the array. Here's the code:

```
Option Explicit
Option Base 1
Sub SortSheets()
Dim i As Integer, j As Integer
Dim SheetNameArray() As String
Dim TempName As String, SheetCount As Integer
```

```
SheetCount = ActiveWorkbook.Sheets.Count
ReDim SheetNameArray(SheetCount)
'Get the sheet names:
For i = 1 To SheetCount
    SheetNameArray(i) = Sheets(i).Name
Next i
'Sort the sheet names alphabetically:
For i = 1 To SheetCount - 1
    For j = i + 1 To SheetCount
        If SheetNameArray(i) > SheetNameArray(j) Then
            TempName = SheetNameArray(i)
            SheetNameArray(i) = SheetNameArray(j)
            SheetNameArray(j) = TempName
        End If
    Next j
Next i
'Rearrange the sheets themselves:
For i = 1 To SheetCount
    Sheets(SheetNameArray(i)).Move Before:=Sheets(i)
Next i
End Sub
```

The dimensioning of the array, the placement of the worksheet names into the array, and the sort itself are routine. Take a brief look at the rearrangement of the worksheets themselves. Suppose there are three sheets named C, B, and A that are in that order in the workbook. After the sort has taken place, they are in ascending order A, B, and C in the array. When the final loop starts to actually rearranges the worksheets, its counter i equals 1. So the statement

```
Sheets(SheetNameArray(i)).Move Before:=Sheets(i)
```

evaluates to this:

```
Sheets("A").Move Before:=Sheets(1)
```

Because Sheets(1) is the sheet named C, A is moved before C. When C scoots to the right, it becomes Sheets(2). SheetNameArray(2) contains "B". So, when i equals 2, the statement evaluates to this:

```
Sheets("B").Move Before:=Sheets(2)
```

So doing pushes the sheet named C one more position to the right, into the third slot. When the statement executes for the third and final time, it evaluates to this:

```
Sheets("C").Move Before:=Sheets(3)
```

The statement causes nothing to happen, because as a result of the prior statements, sheet C is already in position 3. And indeed the final loop could have run from 1 to SheetCount – 1. It was terminated at SheetCount only for clarity.

What if you wanted to sort the sheets in descending order, rather than ascending order? Just change the If test so that it uses a less-than instead of a greater-than operator:

```
If SheetNameArray(i) < SheetNameArray(j) Then
```

Using Workbook Functions with Arrays

With a very few exceptions, any worksheet function such as SUM, AVERAGE, or VLOOKUP can be used on an array. The exceptions are those functions for which there is a VBA version, such as Len. There is a worksheet function LEN, which returns the length of a string value. VBA has its own Len function, and to try to use the worksheet version in VBA code results in an error.

To invoke an Excel worksheet function in VBA, use the WorksheetFunction property of the Application object. For example, to obtain the sum of the values in an array named Costs, you could use something like this:

```
TotalCost = Application.WorksheetFunction.Sum(Costs)
```

Keep an eye out for opportunities to use worksheet functions in your VBA code. Because they are part of the compiled application, they almost always execute faster than the VBA counterpart that you might write. Suppose that you needed to calculate the average of the values in an array. You could use code such as this:

```
ValCount = UBound(MyArray)
TotalVals = 0
For i = 1 To ValCount
    TotalVals = TotalVals + MyArray(i)
Next i
MeanVals = TotalVals / ValCount
```

But it's easier and faster—often *much* faster—to use this:

```
MeanVals = Application.WorksheetFunction.Average(MyArray)
```

Some worksheet functions need special handling. Consider those functions that themselves return arrays, such as FREQUENCY, TRANSPOSE, or LINEST. The previous example assigns the result of the AVERAGE function to a variable, and there need be nothing special about the way that variable is declared, so long as it's a type consistent with a numeric result. But if you are to assign an array to a variable in the following way, you must declare that variable as a Variant.

```
Dim HorizontalArray(1, 5) As Integer
Dim VerticalArray As Variant
For i = 1 To 5
    HorizontalArray(1, i) = i
Next i
VerticalArray = _
    Application.WorksheetFunction.Transpose(HorizontalArray)
```

If you declare VerticalArray as an array, the code will fail with a compile error. In particular, even though you can predict the dimensions of VerticalArray, either of the following declarations will result in a compile error at the point that VerticalArray is populated by the function:

```
Dim VerticalArray(5, 1) As Integer
Dim VerticalArray(5, 1) As Variant
```

Both declarations result in the compile error "Can't assign to an array." Only if you declare VerticalArray as Variant, and only if you fail to declare it as an array, will the assignment statement work as intended.

In general, if a function will return an array, then the assignment statement that uses the function must assign its result to a Variant variable.

Using VBA Arrays with Charts

At some point you have probably clicked a data series in a chart and seen something like this in the formula bar:

=SERIES(Sheet1!$C$1,,Sheet1!$C$2:$C$20,1)

That's the way charts show the location of the source data for the charted series. In this example, the name of the data series, as shown in the chart's legend, is found on Sheet1 in cell C1. The data series has no values for its X-axis (their address would appear between the consecutive commas in the example), and the values for its Y-axis are in cells C2:C20 on Sheet1.

What if you don't want to chart specifically the data that's on the worksheet? There are many situations in which you would prefer to manipulate the data before committing it to a chart. For example, you might want to omit the largest and the smallest values in a series before you chart it. Or you might want to rescale the data before you chart it, in order to maintain a particular minimum and maximum on the chart's Y-axis.

You can do that on the worksheet, of course, but if you want to preserve the original values on the worksheet and chart the manipulated values, a VBA array is often the right answer.

Suppose that your worksheet contains a range of values in A1:A7. You would like to chart them, but you want to constrain the values to a range that runs from 0 to 5. So doing means that you don't need to recast the scale of the Y-axis on the chart, which your audience expects to have a minimum of 0 and a maximum of 5. The following VBA code would do it for you:

```
Option Base 1
Option Explicit
Sub ReScaleAndChart()
Dim OldVals(7) As Single, NewVals As Variant
Dim i as Integer, Mean As Single, SD As Single
For i = 1 To 7
    OldVals(i) = Sheets("Sheet1").Cells(i, 1)
Next i
Mean = Application.WorksheetFunction.Average(OldVals)
SD = Application.WorksheetFunction.StDev(OldVals)
For i = 1 To 7
    OldVals(i) = 3 + (OldVals(i) - Mean) / SD
Next i
NewVals = Array(OldVals(1), OldVals(2), OldVals(3), _
    OldVals(4), OldVals(5), OldVals(6), OldVals(7))
Charts.Add
ActiveChart.ChartType = xlLine
ActiveChart.SetSourceData Source:=Sheets("Sheet1").Range("A1:A7")
ActiveChart.Location Where:=xlLocationAsObject, Name:="Sheet1"
ActiveChart.SeriesCollection(1).Values = NewVals
End Sub
```

This code rescales the values in cells A1:A7 to a 0–5 range and charts them. The two main points of interest are

- The statement that populates the array *NewVals* by means of the Array function.

- The statement that sets the Values of the chart's SeriesCollection to the array NewVals.

When the subroutine has finished running, you will find that the data series formula in the formula bar no longer refers to a worksheet range, but to an array of constant values such as this:

=SERIES(,,3.36,4.42,3.09,1.81,1.56,3.57,3.15,1)

Therefore, although the code has stopped running and the array named NewVals no longer exists, the data series now refers to an array of constants. The chart's appearance is maintained even though the source of the array has disappeared.

The Complete Reference

Excel 2002

Chapter 24

Using Data Access Objects

W hen it comes to retrieving data into Excel from a database, it may seem as though you have more options than you really need. For example, as you have seen in Chapter 15, you can use the Query Wizard or Microsoft Query itself to return information from a database directly to the worksheet, into a pivot table, or into a pivot chart.

The different methods have different advantages, and understanding the trade-offs is key to choosing the most effective way to get at the data. The methods discussed in this chapter are used by VBA code and enable two-way data transfer: to the workbook from the database, and from the workbook to the database.

Manipulating Data with DAO

DAO—short for Data Access Objects—is undoubtedly the most efficient means of moving data in both directions, back and forth, between Excel and a database.

| **Note** | *The Access in* Data Access Objects *is a little misleading. DAO is not limited to Microsoft Access databases. You can use DAO to exchange data between Excel and databases created by a variety of database management applications, such as dBASE and FoxPro.* |

You can use DAO only in a VBA context, by referring to DAO in your VBA code. DAO is not directly available to any of Excel's built-in commands or functions.

This may seem to restrict the usefulness of DAO, but it really doesn't. VBA enables you to use Excel objects such as Worksheets and Ranges. Those objects have methods such as Activate and Copy, and they also have properties such as Name and Row.

DAO is just an extension of the objects, methods, and properties that are available to you. DAO gives you additional objects such as Recordsets, which are closely analogous to what Excel terms *lists*. DAO objects, like Excel objects, have methods and properties. You would use the AddNew method of the Recordset object to add a new record to a recordset. You might use the RecordCount property to determine the number of records presently in the recordset.

To use DAO at all, you need to make the DAO library accessible to your VBA code. To do so, take these steps:

1. With Excel active, switch to the Visual Basic Editor by choosing Tools | Macro | Visual Basic Editor.

2. With your VBA project active, choose Tools | References. The dialog box shown in Figure 24-1 appears.

3. Scroll through the Available References list box until you come to Microsoft DAO 3.6 Object Library. Fill its check box.

4. Click OK to close the dialog box.

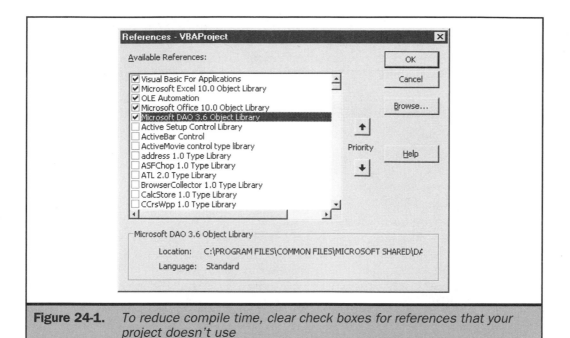

Figure 24-1. *To reduce compile time, clear check boxes for references that your project doesn't use*

The DAO object library is now available to the VBA code in the project that was active when you established the reference. If you want DAO to be available to some other VBA project, you must establish the reference again, with that other project active.

Understanding Recordsets

When you use DAO to move data to Excel from a database, or when you modify records in a database from the Excel environment, you do so by means of *recordsets*. From the point of view of DAO, a recordset is an object, a member of the DAO object model. Once created, it refers to a group of one or more database records that have one or more fields.

To use a recordset in VBA, you must declare it first. For example:

```
Dim MyRecordSet As Recordset
```

After declaring the recordset, you assign it to an object in much the same way that you assign objects to any other object variable. For example:

```
Set MyDatabase = OpenDatabase("C:\Inventory.mdb")
Set MyRecordSet = MyDatabase.OpenRecordset("Equipment", _
    dbOpenDynaset)
```

It's not the purpose here to discuss the entire DAO model in all its awful intricacy. But recordsets are so integral to moving data back and forth between Excel and a database that it's necessary to examine them in some detail.

There are three basic types of recordsets: the dynaset, the snapshot, and the table-type.

Using the Dynaset Recordset

In this assignment statement:

```
Set MyRecordSet = MyDatabase.OpenRecordset("Equipment", _
    dbOpenDynaset)
```

the dbOpenDynaset argument causes MyRecordSet to be a dynaset. The *dynaset* recordset is the most flexible of three basic types. Its basis can be a table or a query. If you assign it to a query—that is, if the Equipment argument in the previous example is the name of a query that exists in the database—then MyRecordSet can contain fields that belong to different tables, because the query itself can combine fields from different tables.

And if you change the values of data in the dynaset, the changes can take effect in the underlying data source (the table or query). Generally, you can perform the same operations on a dynaset as you would on a table either directly, or indirectly by means of a query.

For example, consider this fragment of code:

```
Set MyRecordSet = MyDatabase.OpenRecordset("Employees", _
    dbOpenDynaset)
With MyRecordSet
    .AddNew
    .Fields("LastName") = "Smith"
    .Update
    .Close
End With
```

This code performs these actions:

- Adds a new record to the recordset, by invoking the AddNew method.

- Gives that record the value Smith in the field LastName, by a simple assignment statement.

- Updates the new record—the Update command saves the new record with any changes that you have made. The Employees table, as the basis of the recordset, gets that new record.

- Closes the recordset—that is, removes it from memory.

```
Set MyRecordSet = MyDatabase.OpenRecordset("Employees", _
    dbOpenDynaset)

With MyRecordSet
    .Edit
    .Fields("LastName").Value = "Smith"
    .Update
    .Close
End With
```

This code changes again the value of the recordset field named LastName to Smith. The change is made to a record in the Employees table (as the code is written, this is the first available record). Notice that the Edit method is used, instead of the AddNew method, to make the change in the LastName field to an existing record rather than to a new record. The Update method is again used in order to save the change that has been made.

You use a dynaset type of recordset when you want to update records (by adding, editing, or deleting) in a recordset that involves one or more tables. If you didn't want to update records—perhaps you just want to return them, as is, from the recordset to a worksheet—you might use a snapshot recordset on one or more tables (see the next section, "Using the Snapshot Recordset").

If you wanted to update records from one table only, you could use the table-type recordset (see the section "Using the Table-Type Recordset").

The snapshot and the table-type recordsets are much less flexible than the dynaset. But because they can't do as much as the dynaset, they needn't do as much, and therefore they can be faster and make more effective use of resources. This is particularly true in a networked environment, where it can be important to limit the number of times that a workstation accesses a server. As you will see in the next sections, different recordset types interact differently with the source database.

Using the Snapshot Recordset

The *snapshot* type of recordset consists of a read-only group of records. Once you have opened a snapshot recordset, you can't change the values of its fields, nor can you add records to it or delete records from it.

Suppose you defined a recordset in this way, so that the recordset is a snapshot:

```
Set MyRecordSet = MyDatabase.OpenRecordset("Employees", _
    dbOpenSnapshot)
With MyRecordSet
    .AddNew
    .Update
    .Close
End With
```

This VBA code would halt with a run-time error at the .AddNew line, which would add a new record to a dynaset recordset. The snapshot recordset is read-only, so it won't permit you to add a record.

```
Set MyRecordSet = MyDatabase.OpenRecordset("Employees", _
    dbOpenSnapshot)
With MyRecordSet
    .Edit
    .Fields("LastName").Value = "Smith"
    .Close
End With
```

This code would halt with a run-time error at the .Edit statement. You can't change the value of a field in a snapshot recordset, and VBA won't even let you get ready to do so by means of Edit. Why the term *snapshot*? Because the recordset is a copy of the fields and records in the basis table or query at the time the recordset is opened. Any changes to the underlying records that occur after opening the recordset are not reflected in the snapshot.

Suppose the basis table for MyRecordSet is the Employees table. At 10:01:15 your code opens MyRecordSet, and at 10:01:20 your code retrieves the record in MyRecordSet for the employee named Smith.

At 10:01:17 another user changes the rate of pay field for Smith from $20 per hour to $30 per hour. At 10:01:20 you are looking at Smith's record, in particular at his rate of pay. What you see depends on whether you created MyRecordSet as a dynaset or as a snapshot.

■ If MyRecordSet is a dynaset, it will show $30 per hour as the rate of pay for Smith, reflecting the change that was made *after* you opened MyRecordSet. The dynaset, when it is first created, contains only bookmarks, which are pointers that uniquely identify each record in the underlying table. Only when the full record is needed—for editing, reporting, and so on—are all the fields retrieved. So the change in Salary that was made after you opened the recordset will show up when you subsequently get to that record and arrange to see the Salary field. Note that if you will be working with many records in a dynaset, one at a time, your code will need to access the source database each time you need another full record. This can result in delays if the data must cross a network that is slow to respond.

■ If MyRecordSet is a snapshot, it will show $20 per hour as the rate of pay for Smith. The snapshot, when created, contains the values for all the fields that are in its source. This means that the process that manages the recordset need not worry about multiple users, record locking, and so on. By declaring MyRecordSet to be a snapshot, you have said that you're willing to live with the data as it exists when you open MyRecordSet. You have taken responsibility for the possibility that some data will change after the recordset opens. You are not concerned that any changes made *after* you retrieve the data will not show up in your recordset.

The snapshot uses more memory and perhaps more disk space than does the dynaset. This is because all the fields of all the records (not just the bookmarks, as is the case with a dynaset) are obtained when the recordset is opened as a snapshot.

Using the Table-Type Recordset

Like the dynaset, you can use a *table-type* recordset to add, delete, or edit records. In this way, both the dynaset and the table-type recordsets differ from the snapshot recordset.

Unlike both the dynaset and the snapshot, the table-type recordset can deal with only one table—that is, you cannot use a table-type recordset to access fields from multiple tables, as is possible with both the dynaset and the snapshot, by basing them on queries instead of directly on tables.

But by using a table-type recordset, you can take advantage of any indexes that have been stored for the table. You cannot use these indexes with a dynaset or with a snapshot.

An index is a fascinating and valuable tool. It is a way to set the order of a table's records without physically sorting them. Suppose you have a table that contains information about employees. Among many other fields, there is a LastName field and a DateHired field.

You frequently need to process the employee data for a couple of different reasons: to create distribution lists for internal e-mail and to verify premiums paid to the company that carries your group health policy. To create distribution lists, you want to retrieve records from the database sorted by last name; to verify premiums, you want to retrieve records from the database sorted by the employee's hire date.

Using indexes properly, you can retrieve the data in either order without actually sorting the records. It's helpful to think of an index as a database's table that contains two fields: a record's primary key—the field that uniquely identifies a particular record—and the field that defines the index's order. Suppose these were three records in the employee table:

Record	Field 1: PrimaryKey	Field 2: LastName	Field 3: DateHired
1	1	Smith	9/28/95
2	2	Jones	8/14/94
3	3	Allen	3/5/98

When you set the table's index to the field LastName, the database uses an index that looks something like this to return the records:

Field 1: PrimaryKey	Field 2: LastName
3	Allen
2	Jones
1	Smith

EXTENDING EXCEL'S REACH WITH VBA

The database gets the first item in the index, which itself *is* sorted by LastName. Then it gets that primary key value, finds the record with that primary key in the table, and returns the full record that was the first one in the index. Then it moves to the next item in the index, takes its primary key, finds that record in the table, and returns that record—and so on.

Then, by setting the table's index to DateHired, you retrieve the data in the order specified by that index:

Field 1: PrimaryKey	Field 3: DateHired
2	8/14/94
1	9/28/95
3	3/5/98

Using these indexes is a way to retrieve data from tables in certain orders without actually doing a physical sort. An index is a way of saying, "If the table were physically sorted by, say, LastName, here's the order in which the records would be found."

Most database management systems enable you to specify that an index accept unique values only. In the previous example, you would be able to specify that the index based on the employees' last names accept only one instance of Smith, only one of Allen, and so on. In that particular example it would probably be unwise to require unique values, but smart if the index were based on Social Security Number. In many situations it's good to know that a field in the recordset contains unique values only, and often the best way to ensure that is to use a uniquely valued index.

Because any given table can have several indexes, with only one in use at a time, it's good practice to determine which one is in use and to set the index that you want to use explicitly. The following code shows how to do that.

```
Dim Engineers As Recordset, Staff as Database, ExistingIndex As _
    String
Set Staff = OpenDatabase("C:\Staff.mdb")
Set Engineers = Staff.OpenRecordset("Employees",dbOpenTable)
ExistingIndex = Engineers.Index
Engineers.Index = "LastName"
```

After declaring three variables, the code opens a database and assigns the variable Staff to represent the database. Then the code assigns the database table Employees to the recordset variable named Engineers; as it does so, it uses the keyword dbOpenTable to specify a table-type recordset. The string variable ExistingIndex is used to store the name of the index that the Employees table currently has. Finally, the code assigns the field LastName as the recordset's index (and because the recordset represents the table, LastName becomes the index of the Employees table itself).

Subsequently, you could return the Employees table to its original index with this statement:

```
Engineers.Index = ExistingIndex
```

With the index set to order the records as you want, you can bring them into Excel in that order. This chapter discusses that process in the next section.

Note *It is possible to have one or more linked tables in one database that are linked to one or more tables in other databases. You cannot open a linked table as a table-type recordset, and therefore cannot use Seek with a linked table.*

Basing Recordsets on Queries

This chapter has already referred, without much further explanation, to *queries*. Like a database table, a query is a collection of records. Also like a database table, each record in the query has a value on one or more fields.

Unlike a table, a query can contain records with values on fields that come from more than one table. It's by way of a query that you can tie together, for example, a table that contains information on mothers with a table that contains information on those mothers' children.

The records in those two tables would be joined by means of a key field, perhaps named MothersID. Each record—that is, each Mother—in the Mothers table would have a unique value on the MothersID field. In the Children table, each record—that is, each child—would also have a value on the MothersID field. But you want to be able to associate multiple children in the Children table with one mother in the Mothers table. Therefore, the MothersID field in the Children table would not require unique values.

Suppose that Jane Smith has two children, Thomas and Ann. Jane Smith's record in the Mothers table has a value on the MothersID field of 124. The Mothers table has been set up so that its MothersID field will accept only one value of 124.

Jane Smith's son Thomas has a value of 124 on the Children table's MothersID field. The same is true of Jane Smith's daughter Ann. The Children table has been set up so that its MothersID field will accept more than one value of 124.

Queries are written: that is, their operation is defined in words. The words come from *Structured Query Language*, usually abbreviated *SQL* and pronounced "sequel." A query that joins the Mothers and the Children tables might be defined like this, using SQL:

```
SELECT Children.MothersID, Children.FirstName, Mothers.MothersID,
    Mothers.FirstName, Mothers.LastName
FROM Mothers INNER JOIN Children ON Mothers.MothersID =
    Children.MothersID;
```

Note	*Notice the trailing semicolon. The SQL needs it to terminate the SELECT statement.*

This query says to do the following:

1. Select the fields MothersID and FirstName from the table named Children.
2. Select the fields MothersID, FirstName, and LastName from the table named Mothers.
3. Join the table named Mothers to the table named Children. Use an *inner join*—that is, display a record from Mothers only when it has a matching record in Children, and vice versa.
4. Consider that a record in Mothers matches a record in Children when both records have the same value on their respective MothersID fields.

This query would return the following data about the Smith family:

Children. MothersID	Children. FirstName	Mothers. MothersID	Mothers. FirstName	Mothers. LastName
124	Thomas	124	Jane	Smith
124	Ann	124	Jane	Smith

This is an example of a *one-to-many* relationship. In this case, there is one record in the Mothers table that can join to many (by which is meant *at least one*) records in the Children table. The ability to manage one-to-many relationships is one of the foundations of relational database management systems.

Using DAO, you can base a recordset on a query. The following VBA code establishes the query described previously and returns the records in a recordset. The records and fields in the recordset are copied to a range that starts in cell A1 of the active worksheet. Finally, the recordset and database are closed.

```
Dim BirthData As Database
Dim RetrieveCurrent As QueryDef
Dim RecordsToRetrieve As Recordset
Dim SqlString As String

SqlString = "SELECT Children.MothersID, Children.FirstName, " _
    & "Mothers.MothersID , Mothers.FirstName, Mothers.LastName " _
    & "FROM Mothers INNER JOIN Children ON Mothers.MothersID = " _
    & "Children.MothersID;"
Set BirthData = OpenDatabase("C:\Births.mdb")
```

```
Set RetrieveCurrent = BirthData.CreateQueryDef(Name:="", _
   sqltext:=SQLString)
Set RecordsToRetrieve = _
   RetrieveCurrent.OpenRecordset(dbOpenDynaset)
ActiveSheet.Cells(1, 1).CopyFromRecordset RecordsToRetrieve
RecordsToRetrieve.Close
BirthData.Close
```

Notice the statement that sets the value of the query definition RetrieveCurrent. It executes the CreateQueryDef method of the database object—here represented by the object variable BirthData. The query is based on the SQL string just shown, but the query definition that is created is not given a name: rather, its name is the null string identified by two consecutive quotation marks.

Had the code given the query definition a name, such as BirthQuery, the query would have been saved with the database. Failing to provide it with a name makes it a temporary query, one that is not saved with the database. When you create and execute a query in your VBA code, consider whether you want it to be saved with the database. You might not want to clutter the database with a lot of ad hoc queries.

On the other hand, if the preceding code *had* named the query and thus saved it with the database, then the next time the code was run, it could have been simplified along these lines:

```
Dim BirthData As Database
Dim RecordsToRetrieve As Recordset

Set BirthData = OpenDatabase("C:\Births.mdb")
Set RecordsToRetrieve = BirthData.QueryDefs("BirthQuery") _
   .OpenRecordset(dbOpenDynaset)
ActiveSheet.Cells(1, 1).CopyFromRecordset RecordsToRetrieve
BirthData.Close
```

Notice these differences in the code, due to the fact that the query named BirthQuery has been saved in the database:

- There's no need to specify the SQL string in the VBA code: it's already in the database, defining BirthQuery.

- There's no need to declare or set a query definition variable. The recordset can be created directly by referring to the existing BirthQuery.

- The code will execute a trifle faster because the query already exists in the database.

Specifying the Order of Records in Queries

Using indexes is the principal advantage to using table-type recordsets. You can't use them with dynasets or with snapshots. When you open a dynaset or snapshot recordset, the records are not accessed in any particular order. The main reason to use a dynaset or snapshot, instead of a table-type recordset, is to gain access to multiple joined tables, and to do so you need to base the recordset on a query.

Because you often need to use a query anyway, for these two types of recordset you might well give the query an ORDER BY clause, so as to set the order in which the records are returned from the database to the recordset. For example, the Births.mdb database discussed in the previous section, if it is to have any value at all, would need to contain records on many families. To return the data to Excel in alphabetical order by last name, you could convert the query in this fashion:

```
SqlString = "SELECT Children.MothersID, Children.FirstName, " _
    & "Mothers.MothersID , Mothers.FirstName, Mothers.LastName " _
    & "FROM Mothers INNER JOIN Children ON Mothers.MothersID = " _
    & "Children.MothersID " _
    & "ORDER BY Mothers.LastName;"
```

Note the simple addition of an ORDER BY clause. To return the records in descending alphabetical order, that clause could be

```
& "ORDER BY Mothers.LastName DESC;"
```

Getting Around in a Recordset

There are two ways to bring information into Excel from a DAO recordset. One, which returns data en masse, is by means of the CopyFromRecordset method. The other obtains data on a field-by-field, record-by-record basis. The latter approach requires that you move among the records and specify which fields to return. This section discusses both approaches.

Getting Data Record by Record

Once a recordset has been established, you can move from record to record. There are five types of moves:

- **Move**   Use this move to go forward or backward a specific number of records. For example, MyRecordSet.Move 20 takes you 20 records forward, toward the end of the recordset. MyRecordSet.Move –20 takes you 20 records back, toward the beginning of the recordset.

■ **MoveFirst**   This move takes you to the first record in the recordset. It can be used in combination with Move to get to a specific record number. For example, this code:

```
MyRecordSet.MoveFirst
MyRecordSet.Move 31
```

gets you quickly to the 32nd record. It doesn't happen very often that you want to move to a specific record number. But if you really do, another way is by means of the AbsolutePosition property:

```
MyRecordSet.AbsolutePosition = 31
```

Note   *Record numbers in recordsets are zero-based. That means that the first record is record number zero. Therefore, going to record number 31 gets you to the 32nd record regardless of the method you use to go there.*

■ **MoveLast**   This move is frequently used to get a count of the number of records in a dynaset or snapshot recordset. The property RecordCount tells you how many records are in these recordset, but it returns the correct number only after you have moved to the end of the recordset. Use code like the following to get to the end of a dynaset or snapshot recordset, obtain a count of its records, and then return to its beginning for further processing:

```
MyRecordSet.MoveLast
NumberOfRecords = MyRecordSet.RecordCount
MyRecordSet.MoveFirst
```

■ **MoveNext**   This move takes you one record closer to the end of the recordset. A typical usage occurs when you want to obtain all the values for a particular field in a recordset. Here's an example:

```
Option Base 1
Option Explicit
Sub GetNames()
Dim ArrayOfNames() As String, NameCount As Long, i as Long
Dim BirthData As Database, Names As Recordset
Set BirthData = OpenDatabase("C:\Births.mdb")
Set Names = BirthData.QueryDefs("MomsQuery")._
   OpenRecordset(dbOpenDynaset)
Names.MoveLast
```

```
NameCount = Names.RecordCount
Names.MoveFirst
ReDim ArrayOfNames(NameCount)
i = 1

Do While Not Names.EOF
    ArrayOfNames(i) = Names.Fields("LastName")
    Names.MoveNext
    i = i + 1
Loop
End Sub
```

After declaring and assigning some variables, this code gets the number of records in the recordset and uses that figure to redimension the array named ArrayOfNames. Then it uses a loop to put the value of the field LastName into ArrayOfNames, with an instance for each record in the recordset. Notice that the loop is controlled by the EOF property of the Names recordset (EOF means *end of file*). The loop continues to execute until the MoveNext method has taken the code to the end of the recordset—that is, until Names.EOF has become True.

Note   *EOF becomes True when an attempt is made to retrieve yet another record after the last record has been retrieved. This is unlike some systems which set EOF to True as soon as the last record has been retrieved. If your code attempts a MoveNext when EOF is True, it terminates with a No Current Record error.*

■ **MovePrevious**   This move takes you one record closer to the beginning of the recordset. It's useful when a loop, such as the one shown in the preceding code, has taken you one record past where you want to be. For example, the loop shown earlier concludes when it has moved past the final record in the recordset. To get back to that final record, you might use Names.MovePrevious after the loop concludes.

The VBA code shown previously returns data from a field into an array. You could just as easily return the data to a worksheet. The code might look like this:

```
Option Base 1
Option Explicit
Sub GetNames()
Dim BirthData As Database, Names As Recordset, i as Long
Set BirthData = OpenDatabase("C:\Births.mdb")
Set Names =
BirthData.QueryDefs("MomsQuery")._
```

```
_OpenRecordset(dbOpenDynaset)

i = 1
With Sheets("Sheet1")
   Do While Not Names.EOF
      .Cells(i,1) = Names.Fields("LastName")
   Names.MoveNext
   i = i + 1
   Loop
End With
End Sub
```

Because it returns data to the worksheet instead of to an array, this code is a little more straightforward: it need not concern itself with managing the dimensions of the array.

Getting Data En Masse with the CopyFromRecordset Method

The CopyFromRecordset method belongs to Excel's Range object. This method is part of the Excel object model and therefore does not itself belong to the DAO model. However, the method acts on DAO recordsets by returning their fields and records into a worksheet range. So you need to have established a DAO context in order to use CopyFromRecordset—otherwise, there's no recordset to return.

CopyFromRecordset is a swift way to get data out of a database and into a worksheet. For example, on a 233MHz computer, CopyFromRecordset can return over 13,000 records and ten fields in under two seconds:

```
Range("A2").CopyFromRecordset MyRecordSet
```

In contrast, using the same computer and the same recordset, the following loop requires just over 45 seconds to return those ten fields and 13,000 records.

```
With MyRecordSet
   For i = 2 to RecordCount + 1
      For j = 1 To .Fields.Count
         Cells(i, j) = .Fields(j - 1)
      Next j
      .MoveNext
   Next i
End With
```

You might wonder why these two examples start to return the data beginning in cell A2. It's useful to reserve the first worksheet row for the field names. So it's also useful to precede either the CopyFromRecordset or the loop approach with another loop that returns the field names and puts them into the first row. Here's an example:

```
For j = 0 to MyRecordSet.Fields.Count - 1
    Cells(1, j + 1) = MyRecordSet.Fields(j).Name
Next j
```

Why does this loop begin with zero? The fields in a recordset are numbered starting at zero, so the first field is Field Number 0, the second field is Field Number 1, and so on. When you write a loop similar to the one just shown, don't forget to account for unintended consequences. The code adds the number 1 to the current value of the index j. That prevents the code from trying to write the name of the first field in the zero-th column.

It's important to bear in mind that CopyFromRecordset applies to the Range object. So while you can bring an entire recordset into a worksheet range using the methods described in this section, you can't use CopyFromRecordset directly on a memory array. If you want to return data from a recordset into a VBA memory array, one way is to do so on a record-by-record, field-by-field basis:

```
With MyRecordSet
    .MoveFirst
    For i = 1 to 50
        MyArray(i,1)=.Fields("FirstName")
        MyArray(i,2)=.Fields("LastName")
        .MoveNext
    Next i
End With
```

But with a really large recordset, that's a lot of looping. An alternative is to write the recordset to a worksheet using CopyFromRecordset. Then write the range on the worksheet into a variant array:

```
Option Base 1
Option Explicit
Sub GetDataFromDatabase()
Dim MyArray As Variant
Dim NRows as Long, NCols as Integer
Dim MyDB As Database, MyRecords As Recordset
Set MyDB = OpenDatabase("C:\Births.mdb")
```

```
Set MyRecords = MyDB.OpenRecordset("Births", dbOpenDynaset)
With MyRecords
   .MoveLast
   NRows = .RecordCount
   .MoveFirst
   NCols = .Fields.Count
End With
With Sheets(1)
   .Range("A1").CopyFromRecordset MyRecords
   MyArray = .Range(.Cells(1, 1), .Cells(NRows, NCols))
End With
End Sub
```

Using DAO to Locate Records

Sometimes you need to find particular records, either singly or as a group. You can manage this in several ways; two of the best are by means of parameter queries, which specify records in the SQL definition, and by means of DAO's Seek command, which requires that you use an indexed table.

Using Parameter Queries

It often happens that you want a query to return a set of records that conform to some criterion, but that you can't define the value of that criterion in advance. For example, you might have a database whose records define when certain measurements are taken. Some of the measurements have already occurred, and the remainder are scheduled to occur in the future. You would like to obtain information about the future measurements only—such as who will take the measurement, what is to be measured, the scheduled date and time for the measurement, and so on.

Fair enough, but your code has to accommodate many different dates. If you run the code today, you want it to return all records for today through the final scheduled measurement. If you run it tomorrow, you don't want it to return information about measurements scheduled to take place today.

You handle this situation by means of one or more *parameters*. The parameter is part of the SQL statement that defines the query. When you use VBA and DAO, you usually pass the value or values for the parameters to the query before executing it. (In other situations, you sometimes wait for the query to prompt you for the parameter values.) Here's an example:

```
Dim SQLString As String, MeasureDataBase As Database
Dim RetrieveMeasures As QueryDef, RecordsToRetrieve As Recordset
SQLString = "PARAMETERS StartDate DateTime, StopDate DateTime; " _
```

```
      & "SELECT Measures.StaffName, Measures.ScheduleDate, " _
      & "Measures.ItemMeasured " _
      & "FROM Measures " _
      & "WHERE (((Measures.ScheduleDate) >= StartDate And " _
      & "(Measures.ScheduleDate) <= StopDate));"
Set MeasureDataBase = OpenDatabase ("C:\db2.mdb")
Set RetrieveMeasures = MeasureDataBase.CreateQueryDef(Name:="", _
    sqltext:=SQLString)
RetrieveMeasures.Parameters("StartDate") = Date
RetrieveMeasures.Parameters("StopDate") = #12/31/01#
Set RecordsToRetrieve = _
    RetrieveMeasures.OpenRecordset(dbOpenDynaSet)
```

This code starts by declaring the necessary variables. It then creates a SQL statement that has two parameters: StartDate and StopDate. The idea is to return records from the database only if their ScheduleDate is equal to or greater than the date when the code is run, *and* if their ScheduleDate is equal to or less than December 31, 2001. Notice that SQL declares a date or time variable with the keyword DateTime, whereas VBA declares this variable type with the keyword Date, tacitly incorporating time values.

After declaring the two parameters StartDate and StopDate, the SQL statement goes on to name the three fields to return: the staff member who is scheduled to take the measure, the date the measure is to be taken, and the item to be measured. The SQL statement includes a WHERE clause; this clause specifies how to use the parameters in deciding whether to return a record.

Then the query definition itself is created. It is assigned to the RetrieveMeasures object variable and is defined by the SQL statement. The query is given a null string ("") as a name, which ensures that it is not saved in the database.

The two parameters are given values. The StartDate parameter is given a value determined by the Date function, which returns the current system date. So, if this code is run on March 15, Date returns that date, and it is therefore assigned to the StartDate parameter. No records will be returned if their value on the field ScheduleDate precedes whatever value is assigned to StartDate.

The parameter StopDate is given a value corresponding to December 31, 2001. So doing ensures that no records will be retrieved from the database if their value on the field ScheduleDate comes after 12/31/01.

Finally, the recordset named RecordsToRetrieve is assigned to the fields and records that are returned by the SQL statement and its parameters. At this point, the code could retrieve the fields in the qualifying records to the worksheet or into a VBA memory array.

Other Actions with Recordsets

Retrieving records from a database into VBA arrays or to worksheets is a useful capability, but DAO enables you to do more than that with records. You can use DAO to edit records, as well as to add them to and delete them from the database. If you intend to edit or to delete a record, you need to first locate the record you want. To do so, you can use any of the methods outlined in this chapter—for example, with a SQL query's WHERE clause, or by using the Seek method with an indexed table.

Sometimes it can be expedient to locate a record in a recordset by means of that recordset's index, instead of with a query's WHERE clause. First, consider the limitations on the use of an index for locating a record:

- If you use an index, your recordset must be based on a table, not on a query. You must have opened the recordset as a table-type recordset, using dbOpenTable in the OpenRecordset statement.

- As noted earlier in this chapter, the recordset's table cannot be a table that is linked to another database. However, you might be able to assign the other database to an object variable and open it, along with its tables, directly with DAO. Then you can use the table's index.

Note *That waffling "might" in the previous bullet point means that there are possible obstacles. Before you can assign the other database to an object variable, you need to know its name and location. And if the other database has a database password, you'll have to supply it in the assignment statement. (When you create a linkage to a table that is in a database that has a password, you supply the password when you create the linkage. You need not supply it later, when you open the linked table.)*

- If the table's index is allowed to have nonunique values, then this approach returns the first record that qualifies. For example, if the table is indexed on LastName, then it's quite possible that more than one record will have the value Smith. In that case, the index must allow nonunique values. It follows that when you use the index to seek for a record where the LastName field equals Smith, you will get the first Smith in the recordset, and that might not be the one you want. Of course, this problem applies equally to a SQL WHERE clause. But you can specify, say, both last name and first name in a WHERE clause. If the table is indexed on last name alone, you're out of luck, but bear in mind that an index can contain more than one field.

Despite these limitations, you should try to use an index if your recordset is very large because retrieval is much faster with an index. As an example, a computer with a 66MHz processor twice retrieved a record near the end of a recordset with one million records. The first time, with no index in place, the retrieval took eleven seconds. The second time, using an index, the retrieval took less than one second.

Some DAO documentation recommends that where possible you use the Seek method on an indexed table. The implication is that to get the benefit of the index when you are retrieving a record, you must use Seek. That implication is wrong, though. Other means, such as a SQL WHERE clause or the FindFirst method, also benefit from the presence of an index. For the index to speed things up, though, it must apply to the field that you are searching.

Adding Records

Suppose you have a database that contains information about vendors, and you want to add information about a new vendor. You could use code similar to the following:

```
Dim VendorDB As Database, VendorRecs As Recordset
Set VendorDb = OpenDatabase ("C:\Vendors.mdb")
Set VendorRecs = _
    VendorDb.OpenRecordset(Name:="Vendor",Type:=dbOpenTable)
With VendorRecs
   .AddNew
   .Fields("PrimaryKey").Value = 76
   .Fields("Name").Value = "Freds Ice Cream Cones"
   .Fields("City").Value = "Petaluma"
   .Update
End With
VendorDB.Close
```

There are a few points to note about the preceding code:

- It uses the AddNew method of the Recordset object. You always use this method when you are adding a new record.

- It sets the values for three of the fields available to the recordset—here, the PrimaryKey field, the Name field, and the City field. When you are adding a new record, you must supply values for any required fields. It's wise to check the design of the database's underlying table to determine which, if any, fields have had their Required property designated as True. If you don't supply a value for a required field, your code will terminate with a run-time error.

- It uses the Update method after setting values for the fields. You must always use the Update method when you are adding a new record. If you don't, the record will not be added to the table.

- The new record is *not* the active record once you have added it. Whatever record was current when you started the process is still active when you complete the process.

Editing Records

Having added a new vendor to your database, you subsequently find that you must correct some of the information that you supplied. To do so, you use the Edit method. But first you need to ensure that you activate the proper record. Code such as the following is what you need:

```
Dim VendorDB As Database, VendorRecs As Recordset
Set VendorDb = OpenDatabase ("C:\Vendors.mdb")
Set VendorRecs = _
    VendorDb.OpenRecordset(Name:="Vendor",Type:=dbOpenTable)
With VendorRecs
   .Index = "PrimaryKey"
   .Seek "=", 76
   If .NoMatch Then StopProcessing (76)
   .Edit
   .Fields("City").Value = "Fremont"
   .Fields("State").Value = "CA"
   .Update
End With
VendorDB.Close
```

Notice these points about this example:

- A specific record is located before any editing is done. It's your responsibility to make sure that the record you're editing is the one that should be changed. Just because an index is *named* PrimaryKey doesn't necessarily mean that it allows unique values only. Assuming, though, that PrimaryKey is a uniquely valued index, the Seek method locates the one and only record that has a value of 76 on PrimaryKey.

- You must explicitly set an index for the recordset before you use the Seek method.

- Because Index and Seek are in use, the recordset must be opened as a table-type.

- The NoMatch property is invoked to determine whether the Seek was successful. If that record for some reason couldn't be found, the NoMatch property would equal True. In that event, the code calls a procedure named StopProcessing, with the missing key value as an argument. You should include a check of NoMatch any time you use a method such as Seek or a SQL clause such as a WHERE clause.

EXTENDING EXCEL'S REACH WITH VBA

■ The Edit method is invoked, and then certain fields are assigned values.

■ The Update method is called. As is the case when you are adding a new record, you must invoke the Update method to ensure that the new values are saved in the table.

Deleting Records

After some experience with your new vendor, you find that the vendor supplies really lousy ice cream cones and decide to delete the vendor from your database. This code would do that:

```
Dim VendorDB As Database, VendorRecs As Recordset
Set VendorDb = OpenDatabase ("C:\Vendors.mdb")
Set VendorRecs = _
    VendorDb.OpenRecordset(Name:="Vendor",Type:=dbOpenDynaset)

With VendorRecs
   .FindFirst "PrimaryKey=76"
   If .NoMatch Then StopProcessing (76)
   .Delete
End With
VendorDB.Close
```

Notice these aspects of this code:

■ It uses yet another way of locating a record, the FindFirst method. Again, the code assumes that there is only one record that has a value of 76 on the PrimaryKey field. A dynaset type of recordset allows you to use the FindFirst method of record location.

■ After attempting to locate the record in question, it checks the value of NoMatch. If NoMatch is False, it calls the Delete method to remove the record from its table.

■ In contrast to the processes of adding and editing records, it does not use the Update method. When you delete a record, you need not call the Update method to make sure of actually deleting it.

The examples of adding, editing, and deleting records as given here are not entirely realistic. To focus on the main points—how to use the methods that DAO provides you so as to manipulate records in a database—some associated issues were oversimplified.

For example, it's very unlikely that you would ever put specific field values (such as *Fremont*, as was done in the example on editing) into your code. More often you would get the data directly from the user by way of a user form or an input box. Or you might read data from a worksheet, by way of a loop, into a VBA array. Subsequently you could loop through that array and add new records to the database, or edit the fields of existing records, from that VBA array.

Notice also that none of the examples of adding, editing, or deleting records used the snapshot type of recordset. This is because a snapshot is a read-only recordset type. You can't use it to add, modify, or remove records from a database.

The Complete Reference

Excel 2002

Part V

Appendixes

Appendix A

Excel Functions

F unctions are predefined formulas. Excel 2002 is loaded with functions, which means you don't have to reinvent the wheel when you need to make a certain type of calculation. In this appendix we'll give you information about those functions.
You use functions by specifying *arguments* (values), and the type of arguments you use are specific to the function you're using.

The order in which you position the elements in a function is called the *syntax*. The standard syntax is:

    =FunctionName(arguments)

Most functions are built into Excel, but some are part of the Analysis ToolPak. That means you must install the ATP to have access to the function. In this appendix, we'll indicate functions that are part of the ATP.

Some functions can be used in VBA, which makes writing VBA code easier. In this appendix, we'll indicate whether or not a function is available to VBA.

Database Functions

Database functions are used when you need to analyze values in a list (which is the term for a worksheet database). For instance, in a list of company employees, you may want to count all the records (rows) in which the current salary is more than $50,000 but less than $100,000.

Most database function names start with the letter *D* and they're called Dfunctions. Most Dfunctions have three arguments:

- **Database** This is the range that contains the list (defines the database), and it must include the row that holds the column labels (usually the first row).

- **Field** This is the label for the column you want to summarize. You can use the text of a column label (put quotation marks around the text) or use a number that represents the position of the column in your database (the column furthest to the left of the database range is 1, the column to the right is 2, and so on).

- **Criteria** This is the range that has the criteria you're using. It must include one column label and a minimum of one cell below that label.

DAVERAGE

Use DAVERAGE to get the average of the values in a database, using criteria you specify.

DAVERAGE(Database,Field,Criteria)

Not available to VBA.

DCOUNT

Use DCOUNT to count the cells that contain numbers in a database that matches your criteria.

DCOUNT(Database,Field,Criteria) or

DCOUNT(Database, Criteria)

 You can omit the Field argument if you want to count all the records in the database that match the criteria.

Not available to VBA.

DCOUNTA

Use DCOUNTA to count all the cells that are not empty in a database that matches your criteria.

DCOUNTA(Database,Field,Criteria) or

DCOUNTA(Database,Criteria)

 You can omit the Field argument if you want to count all the nonblank cells in the database.

Not available to VBA.

DGET

Use DGET to extract a single value from a column in a database that matches your criteria.

DGET(Database,Field,Criteria)

Note *If no record meets the criteria, DGET displays the #VALUE! error; if multiple records match the criteria, DGET displays the #NUM! error.*

Not available to VBA.

DMAX

Use DMAX to find the largest number in a column in a database that matches your criteria.

DMAX(Database,Field,Criteria)

Not available to VBA.

APPENDIXES

DMIN

Use DMIN to find the smallest number in a column in a database that matches your criteria.

DMIN(Database,Field,Criteria)

Not available to VBA.

DPRODUCT

Use DPRODUCT to multiply values in a column in a database that match your criteria.

DPRODUCT(Database,Field,Criteria)

Not available to VBA.

DSTDEV

Use DSTDEV to calculate the standard deviation of a group based on a sample, using the numbers in a column in a database, matching your criteria.

DSTDEV(Database,Field,Criteria)

Not available to VBA.

DSTDEVP

Use DSTDEVP to compute the standard deviation of a group, based on the entire group, using the numbers in a column in a database, matching your criteria.

DSTDEVP(Database,Field,Criteria)

Not available to VBA.

DSUM

Use DSUM to add the numbers in a column in a database that matches your criteria.

DSUM(Database,Field,Criteria)

Not available to VBA.

DVAR

Use DVAR to estimate the variance within a group, based on a sample, using the numbers in a column in a database, matching your criteria.

DVAR(Database,Field,Criteria)

Not available to VBA.

DVARP

Use DVARP to find the variance of a population, using the numbers in a column in a database, matching your criteria.

DVAR(Database,Field,Criteria)

Not available to VBA.

GETPIVOTDATA

Use GETPIVOTDATA to retrieve data that's stored in a pivot table.

GETPIVOTDATA(Pivot_table,Name)

- Pivot_table is a cell or range that has the data you need to retrieve.
- Name is text (enclose the text in quotation marks) that describes the cell that has the value you're retrieving.
- When Pivot_table is a range that holds multiple pivot tables, the data is retrieved from the pivot table that was created last.
- When Name is a cell, the value of the cell is retrieved, regardless of its type (number, text, and so on).

Not available to VBA.

Date and Time Functions

Excel's Date and Time functions are designed to help you work with date and time values in formulas you build and use.

Dates are maintained as serial numbers in your computer and converted to date formats when they're displayed.

DATE

Use the DATE function to find a date based on arguments that may exist in multiple cells. For example, if you have separate columns for months, dates, and years, you can retrieve a specific date.

DATE(year,month,day)

Not available to VBA.

DATEVALUE

Use DATEVALUE to convert a date that is represented as a string into the form of a serial number.

DATEVALUE(date_text)

■ The date_text argument must be enclosed in quotation marks ("23-july-99").

Not available to VBA.

DAY

Use DAY to retrieve the day of the month for a date.

DAY(serial_number)

■ The argument serial_number means as it corresponds to the serial_number, which allows you to use any allowed form of the data. For example, if a cell contains the value 7/23/99, the serial number conversion returns 23 as the day.

Not available to VBA.

DAYS360

Use DAYS360 to compute the number of days between two dates. The assumption is that you're basing your dates on a 360 day year (12 months of 30 days each).

DAYS360(start_date,end_date,method) or

DAYS360(start_date,end_date)

■ The arguments start_date and end_date are the two dates between which you need to know the number of days.

■ If start_date is later than end_date, the result is a negative number. If start_date and end_date are equal, the result is zero.

■ Method is a logical value (TRUE or FALSE) that indicates whether to use the U.S. calculation method. TRUE=U.S. FALSE=European. (If method is omitted from the arguments, it's assumed to be TRUE). The difference in methods between the U.S. and European calculations involves the way the 31st day of a month is handled.

   ■ U.S. calculation (as defined in Excel's help file): If the starting date is the 31st of a month, it becomes equal to the 30th of the same month. If the ending date is the 31st of a month and the starting date is less than the 30th of a month, the ending date becomes equal to the 1st of the next month, otherwise the ending date becomes equal to the 30th of the same month.

■ European calculation: Dates that occur on the 31st of the month become equal to the 30th of the month.

Not available to VBA.

EDATE

Use EDATE to retrieve a date that is a specified number of months before or after a date you establish as the criteria.

EDATE(start_date,months)

■ To calculate a date in the past, use a negative number for the months argument.

An ATP function.

Not available to VBA.

EOMONTH

Use EOMONTH to retrieve the last day of the month that is a certain number of months before or after a specified date.

EOMONTH(start_date,months)

■ To calculate a date in the past, use a negative number for the months argument.

An ATP function.

Not available to VBA.

HOUR

Use HOUR to retrieve the hour for a time entry, using a 24-hour clock. For instance, if a cell contains the data 9:15:00am, this function returns 9. If the cell contains the data 9:15:00pm, the function returns 21.

HOUR(serial_number)

■ The serial_number argument can be in any format that the serial number conversion recognizes, including the serial number itself.

Not available to VBA.

MINUTE

Use MINUTE to retrieve the minute for a time entry.

MINUTE(serial_number)

Not available to VBA.

MONTH

Use MONTH to retrieve the name of the month from date data.

MONTH(serial_number)

Not available to VBA.

NETWORKDAYS

Use NETWORKDAYS to calculate the number of whole working days between two dates. Whole working days are days between Monday and Friday, excluding holidays. (Excel has a feature in which you can identify holidays.)

NETWORKDAYS(start_date,end_date,holidays) or

NETWORKDAYS(start_date,end_date)

- Omit the holidays argument if you don't want to include local holidays (state, city, or company).

An ATP function.

Not available to VBA.

NOW

Use NOW to retrieve the current date and time.

NOW()

- The function requires no arguments.
- The data retrieved from the NOW function is updated when you recalculate the worksheet.

Not available to VBA.

SECOND

Use SECOND to retrieve the seconds from a time entry.

SECOND(serial_number)

Not available to VBA.

TIME

Use TIME to display a time retrieved from information in the worksheet (each element of the time may be in a separate cell or calculated from separate cells).

TIME(hour,minute,second)

Not available to VBA.

TIMEVALUE

Use TIMEVALUE to convert time from a string representing time to a serial number.

TIMEVALUE(time_text)

- The time_text argument is enclosed in quotation marks. Any date information in the cell or calculation is ignored.

Not available to VBA.

TODAY

Use TODAY to retrieve the current date.

TODAY()

- The function requires no arguments.

Not available to VBA.

WEEKDAY

Use WEEKDAY to retrieve the day of the week from date data.

WEEKDAY(serial_number,return_type)

■ The argument return_type specifies the way in which you want the retrieved data to display:

```
1       Numbers, where Sunday is 1 and Saturday is 7.
2       Numbers, where Monday is 1 and Sunday is 7.
3       Numbers, where Monday is 0 and Sunday is 6.
```

■ Omitting the return_type argument is the same as indicating type 1.

Not available to VBA.

WORKDAY

Use WORKDAY to retrieve a serial number that is a specific number of working days before or after a specified date.

WORKDAY(start_date,days,holidays)

Not available to VBA.

YEAR

Use YEAR to get the year corresponding to an entry that contains the year.

YEAR(serial_number)

Not available to VBA.

YEARFRAC

Use YEARFRAC to retrieve the fraction of a year, which is calculated from the number of days between two dates.

YEARFRAC(start_date,end_date,basis) or

YEARFRAC(start_date,end_date)

■ Basis is the type of counting you want the function to use:

```
0       US 360
1       Actual based on actual days
2       Based on 360 days
3       Based on 365 days
4       European 360
```

■ Omitting the basis argument is the same as type 0.

An ATP function.

Not available to VBA.

Engineering Functions

Engineering functions are useful for the following types of tasks:

- Working with complex numbers.
- Converting values between different systems such as decimal, octal, binary, and hexadecimal.
- Converting values between different systems of measurement.

Discussing engineering functions requires the use of terminology that is technical and connected to the functions. In fact, most of the function names involve the technology with which they're connected. We are not defining those terms in this appendix, because those of you who need the functions understand the terminology.

All of the engineering functions are ATP functions and none of them are available to VBA.

Table A-1 describes the Engineering functions and syntax.

Function	Arguments
BESSELI	Value at which to evaluate Bessel, order of Bessel
BESSELJ	Value at which to evaluate Bessel, order of Bessel
BESSELK	Value at which to evaluate Bessel, order of Bessel
BESSELY	Value at which to evaluate Bessel, order of Bessel
BIN2DEC	Binary number
BIN2HEX	Binary number, *places*
BIN2OCT	Binary number, *places*
COMPLEX	Real coefficient, imaginary coefficient, *suffix*
CONVERT	Value to convert, original unit, result unit
DEC2BIN	Number, *places*
DEC2HEX	Number, *places*
DEC2OCT	Number, *places*
DELTA	First number, *second number*
ERF	Lower bound for integration, *upper bound for integration*

Table A-1.   *Engineering Functions and Syntax*

Function	Arguments
ERFC	Lower bound for integration
GESTEP	Value to test against threshold value, *Threshold value*
HEX2BIN	Number, *Places*
HEX2DEC	Number
HEX2OCT	Number, *Places*
IMABS	Complex number
IMAGINARY	Complex number
IMARGUMENT	Complex number
IMCONJUGATE	Complex number
IMCOS	Complex number
IMDIV	Complex numerator or dividend, Complex denominator or divisor
IMEXP	Complex number
IMLN	Complex number
IMLOG10	Complex number
IMLOG2	Complex number
IMPOWER	Complex number, Exponent
IMPRODUCT	From 1 to 29 complex numbers
IMREAL	Complex number
IMSIN	Complex number
IMSQRT	Complex number
IMSUB	Complex number from which to subtract, Complex number to subtract
IMSUM	From 1 to 29 complex numbers
OCT2BIN	Number, *Places*
OCT2DEC	Number
OCT2HEX	Number, *Places*

Table A-1. *Engineering Functions and Syntax* (continued)

Financial Functions

Financial functions provide methods for calculating business formulas related to investment and loan values.

Table A-2 describes the common arguments for financial functions.

ACCRINT

Use ACCRINT to retrieve the accrued interest for a security that pays interest periodically.

ACCRINT(issue,first_interest,settlement,rate,par,frequency,basis)

- issue is the issue date for the security.
- first_interest is the first interest date for the security.
- settlement is the date when the security is traded to the buyer.
- rate is the annual coupon rate.
- par is the par value.
- frequency is the per-year number of coupon payments.
- basis is the type of day count you want to use:

0	US 30/360
1	Actual/Actual
2	Actual/360
3	Actual/365
4	European 30/360

Argument	Name	Description
Fv	Future value	Value after all payments
Nper	Number of periods	Total number of payments or periods
Pmt	Payment	Amount of each payment
pv	Present value	Value at the beginning
rate	Rate	Interest or discount rate
type	Type	Interval for payments (start of month, end of month, and so on)

Table A-2. *Common Arguments for Financial Functions*

- Omitting the basis assumes type 0.
- Omitting par assumes $1000.00.

An ATP function.

Not available to VBA.

ACCRINTM

Use ACCRINTM to get accrued interest for a security that only pays that interest at maturity.

ACCRINTM(issue,maturity,rate,par,basis)

- issue is the issue date for the security.
- maturity is the maturity date.
- rate is the annual coupon rate.
- par is the value.
- basis is the count basis.

0	US 30/360
1	Actual/Actual
2	Actual/360
3	Actual/365
4	European 30/360

- Omitting the basis assumes type 0.
- Omitting par assumes $1000.00.

An ATP function.

Not available to VBA.

AMORDEGRC and AMORLINC

These functions are used for French accounting systems. They calculate depreciation.

COUPDAYBS

Use COUPDAYBS to get the number of days between the beginning of the coupon period and the settlement date.

COUPDAYBS(settlement,maturity,frequency,basis)

- settlement is the settlement date (when the security is traded to the buyer).

- maturity is the maturity date.
- frequency is the number of coupon payments each year.
- basis is the type of day count to use.

0	US 30/360
1	Actual/Actual
2	Actual/360
3	Actual/365
4	European 30/360

- Omitting the basis assumes type 0.

An ATP function.

Not available to VBA.

COUPDAYS

Use COUPDAYS to get the number of days within the coupon period that contain the date of settlement.

COUPDAYS(settlement,maturity,frequency,basis)

- settlement is the settlement date (when the security is traded to the buyer).
- maturity is the maturity date.
- frequency is the number of coupon payments each year.
- basis is the type of day count to use.

0	US 30/360
1	Actual/Actual
2	Actual/360
3	Actual/365
4	European 30/360

- Omitting the basis assumes type 0.

An ATP function.

Not available to VBA.

COUPDAYSNC

Use COUPDAYSNC to get the number of days from settlement to the next coupon date.

COUPDAYSNC(settlement,maturity,frequency,basis)

- settlement is the settlement date (when the security is traded to the buyer).

- maturity is the maturity date.
- frequency is the number of coupon payments each year.
- basis is the type of day count to use.

```
0       US 30/360
1       Actual/Actual
2       Actual/360
3       Actual/365
4       European 30/360
```

- Omitting the basis assumes type 0.

An ATP function.

Not available to VBA.

COUPNCD

Use COUPNCD to get the number that represents the first coupon date after the settlement. You can display this number as a date by changing the format of the cell to the date type.

COUPNCD(settlement,maturity,frequency,basis)

- settlement is the settlement date (when the security is traded to the buyer).
- maturity is the maturity date.
- frequency is the number of coupon payments each year.
- basis is the type of day count to use.

```
0       US 30/360
1       Actual/Actual
2       Actual/360
3       Actual/365
4       European 30/360
```

- Omitting the basis assumes type 0.

An ATP function.

Not available to VBA.

COUPNUM

Use COUPNUM to get the number of coupons payment between settlement and maturity. The number is always rounded up to a whole number.

COUPNUM(settlement,maturity,frequency,basis)

- settlement is the settlement date (when the security is traded to the buyer).
- maturity is the maturity date.
- frequency is the number of coupon payments each year.
- basis is the type of day count to use.

```
0       US 30/360
1       Actual/Actual
2       Actual/360
3       Actual/365
4       European 30/360
```

- Omitting the basis assumes type 0.

An ATP function.

Not available to VBA.

COUPPCD

Use COUPPCD to retrieve the number that represents the coupon date immediately previous to settlement. You can display this number as a date by changing the format of the cell to the date type.

COUPPCD(settlement,maturity,frequency,basis)

- settlement is the settlement date (when the security is traded to the buyer).
- maturity is the maturity date.
- frequency is the number of coupon payments each year.
- basis is the type of day count to use.

```
0       US 30/360
1       Actual/Actual
2       Actual/360
3       Actual/365
4       European 30/360
```

- Omitting the basis assumes type 0.

An ATP function.

Not available to VBA.

CUMIPMT

Use CUMIPMT to calculate the cumulative loan interest paid between the starting and ending dates.

CUMIPMT(rate,nper,pv,start_period,end_period,type)

- type is the payment timing:

    0   payment at end of period
    1   payment at beginning of period

An ATP function.

Not available to VBA.

CUMPRINC

Use CUMPRINC to retrieve the cumulative principal paid on a loan.

CUMPRINC(rate,nper,pv,start_period,end_period,type)

- type is the payment timing:

    0   payment at end of period
    1   payment at beginning of period

An ATP function.

Not available to VBA.

DB

Use DB to calculate depreciation for a specific period, using the fixed-declining balance method.

DB(cost,salvage,life,period)

- cost is the initial cost.
- salvage is the value at the end of the depreciation.
- life is the number of periods over which depreciation is calculated (useful life).
- period is the period for which you're calculating depreciation.
- month is the number of months in the first year.

Not available to VBA.

Note *The unit you use for period must be the same unit you use for life.*

DDB

Use DDB to calculate depreciation for a specific period, using the double-declining balance method. You can also use this function for a different declining balance method.

DB(cost,salvage,life,period,factor)

DB(cost,salvage,life,period)

- cost is the initial cost.
- salvage is the value at the end of the depreciation.
- life is the number of periods over which depreciation is calculated (useful life).
- period is the period for which you're calculating depreciation.
- factor is the rate at which the balance declines (if omitted, it's assumed to be 2).

Not available to VBA.

DISC

Use DISC to compute the discount rate for a security.

DISC(settlement,maturity,pr,redemption,basis)

- settlement is the settlement date (when the security is traded to the buyer).
- maturity is the maturity date.
- pr is the price per $100 of face value.
- redemption is the redemption value per $100 of face value.
- basis is the type of day count:
  ```
  0      US 30/360
  1      Actual/Actual
  2      Actual/360
  3      Actual/365
  4      European 30/360
  ```
- Omitting the basis assumes type 0.

An ATP function.

Not available to VBA.

DOLLARDE

Use DOLLARDE to convert a dollar amount expressed in the form of a fraction to a dollar amount expressed as a decimal number.

DOLLARDE(fractional_dollar,fraction)

- fractional_dollar is a number expressed as a fraction.
- fraction is the number to use in the denominator of a fraction.

An ATP function.

Not available to VBA.

DOLLARFR

Use DOLLARFR to convert a dollar amount expressed as a decimal to a fraction (the opposite of DOLLARDE).

DOLLARFR(decimal_dollar,fraction)

- decimal_dollar is a decimal number.
- fraction is the number to use in the denominator of a fraction.

An ATP function.

Not available to VBA.

DURATION

Use DURATION to return the Macauley duration, assumed to be calculated for a par value of $100. The definition of the duration is a weighted average of the current cash flow value. This is useful to measure a bond price in response to changes in the yield.

DURATION(settlement,maturity,coupon,yld,frequency,basis)

- settlement is the settlement date (when the security is traded to the buyer).
- maturity is the maturity date.
- yld is the annual yield.
- coupon is the annual coupon rate.
- frequency is the number of coupon payments each year.
- basis is the type of day count to use.

0	US 30/360
1	Actual/Actual
2	Actual/360

3	Actual/365
4	European 30/360

■ Omitting the basis assumes type 0.

An ATP function.

Not available to VBA.

EFFECT

Use EFFECT to determine the effective interest rate, taking the nominal annual rate and the number of compounding periods in a year.

EFFECT(nominal_rate,npery)

■ nominal_rate is the interest rate.

■ npery is the number of compounding periods for each year.

An ATP function.

Not available to VBA.

FV

Use FV to calculate the future value of an investment. The investment must return periodic, constant payments at a constant rate of interest (an annuity is a good example).

FV(rate,nper,pmt_pw,type)

■ rate is the interest rate (per period).

■ nper is the total number of payment periods in the annuity.

■ pmt is the payment made on each period.

■ pv is the present value.

■ type is the payment due:

0	end of period
1	beginning of the period

Not available to VBA.

FVSCHEDULE

Use FVSCHEDULE to get the future value after applying compound interest rates.

FVSCHEDULE(principal,schedule)

■ principal is the current value.

- schedule is an array of the interest rates you're applying.

Not available to VBA.

INTRATE

Use INTRATE to calculate the interest rate for a security.

INTRATE(settlement,maturity,investment,redemption,basis)

- settlement is the settlement date (when the security is traded to the buyer).
- maturity is the maturity date.
- investment is the amount you've invested in the security.
- redemption is the redemption value (per$100 face value).
- basis is the type of day count you're using:

```
0      US 30/360
1      Actual/Actual
2      Actual/360
3      Actual/365
4      European 30/360
```

- Omitting the basis assumes type 0.

An ATP function.

Not available to VBA.

IPMT

Use IPMT to get the interest payment for an investment a specific period. The investment must offer periodic, constant payments and a constant rate of interest.

IPMT(rate,per,nper,pv,fv,type)

- rate is the interest rate for each period.
- per is the period for which you're calculating the interest.
- nper is the total number of payment periods.
- pv is the present value.
- fv is the future value.
- type is the time when payments are made:

```
0      at the end of the period
1      at the beginning of the period
```

Not available to VBA.

IRR

Use IRR to get the internal rate of return for cash flows. The cash flow must occur on a regular interval, but the interval doesn't have to be even.

IRR(values,guess)

- values is an array (or reference to cells) that hold numbers for which you want to calculate the IRR.
- guess is a number that you guess is close to the result of IRR.

 You can omit the guess, but if you can supply it the process goes more quickly. Excel goes through a vast number of iterations to calculate IRR.

Not available to VBA.

MDURATION

Use MDURATION to get the modified duration for a security that has an assumed par value of $100.00.

MDURATION(settlement,maturity,coupon,yld,frequency,basis)

- settlement is the settlement date (when the security is traded to the buyer).
- maturity is the maturity date.
- coupon is the annual coupon rate.
- yld is the annual yield.
- frequency is the number of coupon payments in a year.
- basis is the type of day count you're using:

0	US 30/360
1	Actual/Actual
2	Actual/360
3	Actual/365
4	European 30/360

- Omitting the basis assumes type 0.

An ATP function.

Not available to VBA.

MIRR

Use MIRR to get the modified IRR, considering both investment cost and interest received on reinvestment of proceeds.

MIRR(values,finance_rate,reinvest_rate)

- values is an array representing payments and income that occur at regular intervals.
- finance_rate is the interest rate you pay on the money used in cash flows.
- reinvest_rate is the interest rate you get on the cash flows when reinvesting them.

Not available to VBA.

NOMINAL

Use NOMINAL to get the nominal annual interest rate, which takes into consideration the effective rate along with the number of compounding periods in a year.

NOMINAL(effect_rate,npery)

- effect_rate is the effective interest rate.
- npery is the number of compounding periods in a year.

An ATP function.

Not available to VBA.

NPER

Use NPER to determine the number of periods for an investment. This figure is based on constant periodic payments and a constant rate for interest.

NPER(rate,pmt,pv,fv,type)

- rate is the periodic interest rate.
- pmt is the consistent payment made each period.
- pv is the present value.
- fv is the future value.
- type is the time when payments are due:

```
0      at the end of the period
1      at the beginning of the period
```

Not available to VBA.

NPV

Use NPV to calculate the net present value of an investment. This function uses a discount rate and future payments (which are negative values) and income.

NPV(rate,value1,value2,value...)

- rate is the rate of discount for one period.
- value1,etc. represent payments and income.

Not available to VBA.

ODDFPRICE

Use ODDFPRICE to get the price (per $100 face value) for a security that has a first period (shorter or longer than subsequent periods).

ODDFPRICE(settlement,maturity,issue,first_coupon,rate,yld,redemption, frequency,basis)

- settlement is the settlement date (when the security is traded to the buyer).
- maturity is the maturity date.
- issue is the issue date for the security.
- first_coupon is the first coupon date.
- rate is the interest rate.
- yld is the annual yield.
- redemption is the redemption value (per$100 face value).
- frequency is the number of coupon payments in a year.
- basis is the type of day count you're using:

0	US 30/360
1	Actual/Actual
2	Actual/360
3	Actual/365
4	European 30/360

- Omitting the basis assumes type 0.

An ATP function.

Not available to VBA.

ODDFYIELD

Use ODDFYIELD to determine the yield for a security that has an odd first period.

ODDFYIELD(settlement,maturity,issue,first_coupon,rate,pr,redemption, frequency,basis)

- settlement is the settlement date (when the security is traded to the buyer).
- maturity is the maturity date.
- issue is the issue date for the security.
- first_coupon is the first coupon date.
- rate is the interest rate.
- pr is the price of the security.
- redemption is the redemption value (per$100 face value).
- frequency is the number of coupon payments in a year.
- basis is the type of day count you're using:

0	US 30/360
1	Actual/Actual
2	Actual/360
3	Actual/365
4	European 30/360

- Omitting the basis assumes type 0.

An ATP function.

Not available to VBA.

ODDLPRICE

Use ODDLPRICE to calculate the price per $100 face value for a security that has an odd last coupon period.

ODDLPRICE(settlement,maturity,last_interest,rate,yld,redemption,frequency,basis)

- settlement is the settlement date (when the security is traded to the buyer).
- maturity is the maturity date.
- last_interest is the last coupon date.
- rate is the interest rate.
- yld is the annual yield.
- redemption is the redemption value (per$100 face value).

- frequency is the number of coupon payments in a year.
- basis is the type of day count you're using:

0	US 30/360
1	Actual/Actual
2	Actual/360
3	Actual/365
4	European 30/360

- Omitting the basis assumes type 0.

An ATP function.

Not available to VBA.

ODDLYIELD

Use ODDLYIELD to get the yield for a security that has an odd last period.

ODDLYIELD(settlement,maturity,last_interest,rate,pr,redemption,frequency,basis)

- settlement is the settlement date (when the security is traded to the buyer).
- maturity is the maturity date.
- last_interest is the last coupon date.
- rate is the interest rate.
- pr is the price of the security.
- redemption is the redemption value (per$100 face value).
- frequency is the number of coupon payments in a year.
- basis is the type of day count you're using:

0	US 30/360
1	Actual/Actual
2	Actual/360
3	Actual/365
4	European 30/360

- Omitting the basis assumes type 0.

An ATP function.

Not available to VBA.

PMT

Use PMT to calculate the payment for a loan. The calculation assumes a constant interest rate and constant payments.

PMT(rate,nper,pv,fv,type)

- rate is the interest rate.
- nper is the total number of payments.
- pv is the present value (principal).
- fv is the future value (balance after last payment), which can be omitted if the value is zero.
- type is a number that indicates when payments become due:

```
0      at beginning of the period
1      at the end of the period
```

- Omitting type assumes 0.

Not available to VBA.

PPMT

Use PPMT to get the principal payment for a specific period for an investment. The investment must be based on constant periodic payments and a constant rate of interest.

PPMT(rate,per,nper,pv,fv,type)

- rate is the per period interest rate.
- per specifies the period of interest.
- nper is the total number of payment periods.
- pv is the present value.
- fv is the future value (cash balance after last payment).
- type is a number that indicates when payments become due:

```
0      at beginning of the period
1      at the end of the period
```

- Omitting type assumes 0.

Not available to VBA.

PRICE

Use PRICE to calculate the price per $100 face value for securities that pay periodic interest.

PRICE(settlement,maturity,rate,yld,redemption,frequency,basis)

- settlement is the settlement date (when the security is traded to the buyer).
- maturity is the maturity date.
- rate is the interest rate.
- yld is the annual yield.
- redemption is the redemption value (per $100 face value).
- frequency is the number of coupon payments in a year.
- basis is the type of day count you're using:

0	US 30/360
1	Actual/Actual
2	Actual/360
3	Actual/365
4	European 30/360

- Omitting the basis assumes type 0.

An ATP function.

Not available to VBA.

PRICEDISC

Use PRICEDISC to get the price per $100 face value for a discounted security.

PRICEDISC(settlement,maturity,discount,redemption,basis)

- settlement is the settlement date (when the security is traded to the buyer).
- maturity is the maturity date.
- discount is the discount rate.
- redemption is the redemption value (per $100 face value).
- frequency is the number of coupon payments in a year.
- basis is the type of day count you're using:

0	US 30/360
1	Actual/Actual

```
2       Actual/360
3       Actual/365
4       European 30/360
```

- Omitting the basis assumes type 0.

An ATP function.

Not available to VBA.

PRICEMAT

Use PRICEMAT to determine the price per $100 face value for a security that pays interest upon maturity.

PRICEMAT(settlement,maturity,issue,rate,yld,basis)

- settlement is the settlement date (when the security is traded to the buyer).
- maturity is the maturity date.
- issue is the issue date.
- rate is the interest rate (at day of issue).
- yld is the annual yield.
- basis is the type of day count you're using:

```
0       US 30/360
1       Actual/Actual
2       Actual/360
3       Actual/365
4       European 30/360
```

- Omitting the basis assumes type 0.

An ATP function.

Not available to VBA.

PV

Use PV to calculate the present value of an investment. The definition of present value takes into consideration future payments. For instance, if you're the borrower, the amount of the loan is the present value to the lender.

PV(rate,nper,pmt,fv,type)

- rate is the per-period interest rate.
- nper is the total number of payment periods.

- pmt is the payment made each period.
- fv is the future value (the value after the last payment is made); if it's omitted it's assumed to be zero.
- type is a number that indicates when payments become due:

```
0       at beginning of the period
1       at the end of the period
```

- Omitting type assumes 0.

Not available to VBA.

RATE

Use RATE to calculate the per period interest rate for an annuity.

RATE(nper,pmt,pv,fv,type,guess)

- nper is the total number of payment periods.
- pmt is the payment made for each period (a constant).
- pv is the present value.
- fv is the future value (balance after last payment).
- type is a number that indicates when payments become due:

```
0       at beginning of the period
1       at the end of the period
```

- Omitting type assumes 0.
- guess is your guess for the rate; if omitted it's assumed to be 10 percent.

 Note   *Excel tries 20 iterations before giving up, which is why an educated guess improves the chance of a response.*

Not available to VBA.

RECEIVED

Use RECEIVED to get the amount that will be received upon maturity of a fully invested security.

RECEIVED(settlement,maturity,investment,discount,basis)

- settlement is the settlement date (when the security is traded to the buyer).
- maturity is the maturity date.

- investment is the amount invested.
- discount is the discount rate.
- basis is the type of day count you're using:

```
0       US 30/360
1       Actual/Actual
2       Actual/360
3       Actual/365
4       European 30/360
```

- Omitting the basis assumes type 0.

An ATP function.

Not available to VBA.

SLN

Use SLN to calculate straight-line depreciation for one period.

SLN(cost,salvage,life)

- cost is initial cost.
- salvage is the value at the end of depreciation.
- life is the number of periods over which you're depreciating the asset.

Not available to VBA.

SYD

Use SYD to get the sum-of-years depreciation for a specific period.

SYD(cost,salvage,life,per)

- cost is the initial cost.
- salvage is the value after depreciation.
- life is the number of periods over which you're depreciating (useful life).
- per is the specified period.

Not available to VBA.

TBILLEQ

Use TBILLEQ to calculate the bond-equivalent yield for treasury bills.

TBILLEQ(settlement,maturity,discount)

- settlement is the settlement date (when the security is traded to the buyer).
- maturity is the maturity date.
- discount is the discount rate.

An ATP function.

Not available to VBA.

TBILLPRICE

Use TBILLPRICE to get the price (per $100 face value) for treasury bills.

TBILLPRICE(settlement,maturity,discount)

- settlement is the settlement date (when the security is traded to the buyer).
- maturity is the maturity date.
- discount is the discount rate.

An ATP function.

Not available to VBA.

TBILLYIELD

Use TBILLYIELD to get the yield for treasury bills.

TBILLYIELD(settlement,maturity,pr)

- settlement is the settlement date (when the security is traded to the buyer).
- maturity is the maturity date.
- pr is the price per $100 face value.

An ATP function.

Not available to VBA.

VDB

Use VDB to calculate depreciation for a period you specify. You can include partial periods. Any depreciation method is acceptable.

VDB(cost,salvage,life,start_period,end_period,factor,no_switch)

- cost is the cost of the asset.
- salvage is the value at the end of depreciation.
- life is the number of periods over which depreciation occurs (useful life).
- start_period is the starting period for which you want to calculate depreciation.
- end_period is the last period for which you want to calculate depreciation.
- factor is the rate at which the balance declines; if omitted it is assumed to be 2 for double-declining.
- no_switch is a logical value that specifies whether to switch to straight-line depreciation if that is greater than declining balance:

  True   Excel does not switch to straight-line depreciation

  False   Excel switches to straight-line depreciation
- Omitting no_switch assumes False.

Not available to VBA.

XIRR

Use XIRR to calculate the internal rate of return for cash flows that are not periodic.

XIRR(values,dates,guess)

- values is a series of cash flows that can be matched to a schedule of payments (in dates).
- dates is the schedule of payment dates.
- guess is a number you guess to help Excel reach a solution quickly.

An ATP function.

Not available to VBA.

XNPV

Use XNPV to get the net present value for a schedule of cash flows that is not regular (periodic).

XNPV(rate,values,dates)

- rate is the discount rate.
- values is a series of cash flows that can be matched to a schedule of payments (in dates).

■ dates is a schedule of payment dates.

An ATP function.

Not available to VBA.

YIELD

Use YIELD to calculate the yield for a security that pays interest periodically.

YIELD(settlement,maturity,rate,pr,redemption,frequency,basis)

■ settlement is the settlement date (when the security is traded to the buyer).

■ maturity is the maturity date.

■ rate is the interest rate.

■ pr is the price per $100 face value.

■ redemption is the redemption value (per $100 face value).

■ frequency is the number of coupon payments in a year.

■ basis is the type of day count you're using:

```
0      US 30/360
1      Actual/Actual
2      Actual/360
3      Actual/365
4      European 30/360
```

■ Omitting the basis assumes type 0.

An ATP function.

Not available to VBA.

YIELDDISC

Use YIELDDISC to calculate the annual yield for discounted securities.

YIELDDISC(settlement,maturity,pr,redemption, basis)

■ settlement is the settlement date (when the security is traded to the buyer).

■ maturity is the maturity date.

■ pr is the price per $100 face value.

■ redemption is the redemption value (per $100 face value).

■ basis is the type of day count you're using:

```
0       US 30/360
1       Actual/Actual
2       Actual/360
3       Actual/365
4       European 30/360
```

- Omitting the basis assumes type 0.

An ATP function.

Not available to VBA.

YIELDMAT

Use YIELDMAT to calculate the annual yield for securities that pay interest at maturity.

YIELDMAT(settlement,maturity,issue,rate,pr,basis)

- settlement is the settlement date (when the security is traded to the buyer).
- maturity is the maturity date.
- issue is the issue date.
- rate is the interest rate.
- pr is the price per $100 face value.
- basis is the type of day count you're using:

```
0       US 30/360
1       Actual/Actual
2       Actual/360
3       Actual/365
4       European 30/360
```

- Omitting the basis assumes type 0.

An ATP function.

Not available to VBA.

Information Functions

Information functions are handy for determining the data types of cells. You can determine whether the data meets specifications you describe or just determine whether a cell has data (or is empty). See Microsoft Excel documentation for a complete list of info_types. Table A-3 provides an overview of the Information functions.

Function	Built-In or ATP?	Available to VBA?	Arguments
CELL	Built-in	No	Type of information, Cell reference
ERROR.TYPE	Built-in	No	Error value
INFO	Built-in	No	Type of information
ISBLANK	Built-in	No	Cell reference
ISERR	Built-in	Yes	Cell reference or error value
ISERROR	Built-in	Yes	Cell reference or error value
ISEVEN	ATP	No	Cell reference or value
ISLOGICAL	Built-in	Yes	Cell reference or value
ISNA	Built-in	Yes	Cell reference or error value
ISNONTEXT	Built-in	Yes	Cell reference or value
ISNUMBER	Built-in	Yes	Cell reference or value
ISODD	ATP	No	Cell reference or value
ISREF	Built-in	No	Cell reference or value
ISTEXT	Built-in	Yes	Cell reference or value
N	Built-in	No	Cell reference or value
NA	Built-in	No	None
TYPE	Built-in	No	Cell reference or value

Table A-3.   *Information Functions in Excel*

Logical Functions

Use Logical functions when you need to learn whether a condition is true or false for values in your spreadsheet. All of the Logical functions are part of Excel and do not require the Analysis ToolPak. Table A-4 has descriptions of the Logical functions.

Function	Available to VBA?	Arguments
AND	Yes	1 to 30 arguments that evaluate to logical values
FALSE	No	None
IF	No	Condition, *Value if condition is True, Value if condition is False*
NOT	No	Condition
OR	Yes	1 to 30 arguments that evaluate to logical values
TRUE	No	None

Table A-4. *Logical Functions in Excel*

Lookup and Reference Functions

Use these functions to find values in your spreadsheet. None of these functions require the Analysis ToolPak. Table A-5 describes the Lookup and Reference functions.

Math and Trigonometry Functions

The Math and Trigonometry functions are used to perform calculations. The functions are extremely powerful, enabling you to perform some very complex mathematical operations. On the other hand, if you're not a rocket scientist, you can use these functions to perform more mundane calculations, such as getting the totals for a range of cells that meet some criteria. Table A-6 describes the Math and Trigonometry functions.

Statistical Functions

Statistics are so important to researchers but so involved and (in my opinion) boring to extract that having a robust collection of preconfigured statistical functions is one of the best reasons to buy and use Excel.

In describing these statistical functions, I assume you're familiar with the jargon and terminology of the trade.

Function	Available To VBA?	Arguments
ADDRESS	No	Row number, Column number, *Reference type, Reference style, Worksheet name*
AREAS	No	Reference to range or ranges or range name
CHOOSE	Yes	Which value, 1 to 29 cell references or values
COLUMN	No	Range reference to evaluate
COLUMNS	No	Range reference or array or array formula to evaluate
HLOOKUP	Yes	Value to search for, Range to search, Row to return from, *Type of match*
HYPERLINK	No	Path and filename, *Value to display*
INDEX	Yes	(Array form) Array or range reference, Row number, *Column number; (*Reference form*)* Range reference, Row number, *Column number, Area number*
INDIRECT	No	Range reference as text, *Reference style*
LOOKUP	Yes	(Vector form) Value to search for, Range to search, Range to return from; (Array form) value to search for, Range to search
MATCH	Yes	Value to search for, Array to search, *Type of match*
OFFSET	No	Range reference, Number of offset rows, Number of offset columns, *Number of rows high, Number of columns wide*
ROW	No	Range reference to evaluate
ROWS	No	Range reference or array or array formula to evaluate
TRANSPOSE	Yes	Range reference or array to transpose
VLOOKUP	Yes	Value to search for, Range to search, Column to return from, *Type of match*

Table A-5.   *Lookup and Reference Functions in Excel*

Function	Built-in or ATP?	Available to VBA?	Arguments
ABS	Built-in	No	Cell reference or value to convert
ACOS	Built-in	Yes	Cell reference or value to evaluate
ACOSH	Built-in	Yes	Cell reference or value to evaluate
ASIN	Built-in	Yes	Cell reference or value to evaluate
ASINH	Built-in	Yes	Cell reference or value to evaluate
ATAN	Built-in	No	Cell reference or value to evaluate
ATAN2	Built-in	Yes	X-coordinate, Y-coordinate
ATANH	Built-in	Yes	Cell reference or value to evaluate
CEILING	Built-in	Yes	Number to round, Multiple for rounded value
COMBIN	Built-in	Yes	Number in population, Number chosen
COS	Built-in	No	Cell reference or value to evaluate
COSH	Built-in	Yes	Cell reference or value to evaluate
DEGREES	Built-in	Yes	Angle to convert
EVEN	Built-in	Yes	Cell reference or value to round
EXP	Built-in	No	Cell reference or value for base
FACT	Built-in	Yes	Cell reference or value for basis of factorial
FACTDOUBLE	ATP	No	Cell reference or value for basis of double factorial
FLOOR	Built-in	Yes	Number to round, Multiple for rounded value
GCD	ATP	No	Range reference or array of 1 to 29 values
INT	Built-in	No	Cell reference or value to convert

Table A-6. *Math and Trigonometry Functions in Excel*

Function	Built-in or ATP?	Available to VBA?	Arguments
LCM	ATP	No	Range reference or array of 1 to 29 values
LN	Built-in	Yes	Cell reference or value to evaluate
LOG	Built-in	Yes	Cell reference or value to evaluate, *Base*
LOG10	Built-in	Yes	Cell reference or value to evaluate
MDETERM	Built-in	Yes	Cell reference or array of values with equal number of rows and columns
MINVERSE	Built-in	Yes	Cell reference or array of values with equal number of rows and columns
MMULT	Built-in	Yes	Two range references or arrays; Number of columns in Array 1 equals number of rows in Array 2
MOD	Built-in	No	Number to divide, Divisor
MROUND	ATP	No	Number to round, Multiple for rounded value
MULTINOMIAL	ATP	No	Range reference or array of 1 to 29 values
ODD	Built-in	Yes	Cell reference or value to round
PI	Built-in	Yes	None
POWER	Built-in	Yes	Base, Exponent
PRODUCT	Built-in	Yes	Range reference or array of 1 to 30 values
QUOTIENT	ATP	No	Numerator, Denominator
RADIANS	Built-in	Yes	Cell reference or value for angle
RAND	Built-in	No	None

Table A-6. *Math and Trigonometry Functions in Excel* (continued)

Function	Built-in or ATP?	Available to VBA?	Arguments
RANDBETWEEN	ATP	No	Lower limit of range, Upper limit of range
ROMAN	Built-in	Yes	Cell reference or value, Form of Roman numeral
ROUND	Built-in	Yes	Cell reference or value, *Significant digits*
ROUNDDOWN	Built-in	Yes	Cell reference or value, *Significant digits*
ROUNDUP	Built-in	Yes	Cell reference or value, *Significant digits*
SERIESSUM	ATP	No	Base, Exponent, Step, Coefficients
SIGN	Built-in	No	Cell reference or value to evaluate
SIN	Built-in	No	Cell reference or value for angle
SINH	Built-in	Yes	Cell reference or value to evaluate
SQRT	Built-in	No	Cell reference or value to evaluate
SQRTPI	ATP	No	Cell reference or value to evaluate
SUBTOTAL	Built-in	Yes	Type of subtotal, 1 to 29 ranges to subtotal
SUM	Built-in	Yes	1 to 30 range references or values
SUMIF	Built-in	Yes	Range to evaluate, Criteria, *Range to sum*
SUMPRODUCT	Built-in	Yes	2 to 30 range references or arrays
SUMSQ	Built-in	Yes	1 to 30 range references or values
SUMX2MY2	Built-in	Yes	2 arrays or range references
SUMX2PY2	Built-in	Yes	2 arrays or range references
SUMXMY2	Built-in	Yes	2 arrays or range references

Table A-6.   *Math and Trigonometry Functions in Excel* (continued)

Function	Built-in or ATP?	Available to VBA?	Arguments
TAN	Built-in	No	Cell reference or value for angle
TANH	Built-in	Yes	Cell reference or value to evaluate
TRUNC	Built-in	No	Cell reference or value to truncate, *Significant digits*

Table A-6.   *Math and Trigonometry Functions in Excel* (continued)

AVEDEV

Use AVEDEV to calculate variability. The function finds the average of all the absolute deviations from the mean.

    AVEDEV(number1,number2,number3...)

■   number is a data point for which you want to get the average of the absolute deviations.

Note   *You can use numbers, names, or arrays in the arguments, and you can have up to 30 arguments.*

Available to VBA.

AVERAGE

Use AVERAGE to find the average (arithmetic mean) of a list of numbers.

    AVERAGE(number1,number2...number30)

■   number is a number.

Available to VBA.

AVERAGEA

Use AVERAGEA to get the average of values in a list of arguments, including data other than numbers (logical values and text).

    AVERAGEA(value1,value2,value3...value30)

- value must be an array, name, number, or reference.
- Arguments that contain FALSE are evaluated as 0, TRUE as 1.

 Arguments that contain text are treated as 0.

Not available to VBA.

BETADIST

Use BETADIST to find the cumulative beta probability density function. This function is usually applied to the study of variations (by percentage) in samples (such as the fraction of a week people spend commuting to work).

BETADIST(x,alpha,beta,A,B)

- x is the value between A and B that you want to use to evaluate the function.
- alpha is a parameter for the distribution.
- beta is a parameter for the distribution.
- A is the lower boundary for x.
- B is the upper boundary for x.
- If A and B are omitted, Excel evaluates A as 0 and B as 1.

Available to VBA.

BETAINV

Use BETAINV to get the inverse of BETADIST.

BETAINV(probability,alpha,beta,A,B)

- probability is a probability associated with the beta distribution.
- alpha is a parameter for the distribution.
- beta is a parameter for the distribution.
- A is the lower boundary for x.
- B is the upper boundary for x.
- If A and B are omitted, Excel evaluates A as 0 and B as 1.

Available to VBA.

BINOMDIST

Use BINOMDIST to get an individual term binomial distribution probability. It's used for fixed numbers of trials where the outcome of each trial can be either success or failure.

BINOMDIST(number_s,trials,probability_s,cumulative)

- number_s is the number of successes.
- trials is the number of trials.
- probability_s is the probability of success for each trial.
- cumulative is a logical value that affects the form of the function.
- If cumulative is TRUE, then BINOMDIST will return the cumulative distribution function. If FALSE, it returns the probability mass function.

Available to VBA.

CHIDIST

Use CHIDIST to get the one-tailed probability of a chi-squared distribution.

CHIDIST(x,degrees_freedom)

- x is the value at which you want to make your evaluation.
- degrees_freedom is the number of degrees of freedom.

Available to VBA.

CHIINV

CHIINV is the inverse of CHIDIST.

CHIINV(probability,degrees_freedom)

- probability is the probability of the chi-squared distribution.
- degrees_freedom is the number of degrees of freedom.

Available to VBA.

CHITEST

Use CHITEST to get the test for independence, in order to determine whether or not hypothesized results of a chi-squared distribution can be verified.

CHITEST(actual_range,expected_range)

APPENDIXES

- actual_range is the range of data that holds observations you want to test against expected values.
- expected_range is the range of data that holds the ratio of [row totals x column totals] to the grand total.

Available to VBA.

CONFIDENCE

Use CONFIDENCE to get the confidence interval for the mean of a population.

CONFIDENCE(alpha,standard_dev,size)

- alpha is the significance level you use to compute the confidence level.
- standard_dev is the standard deviation for the range (it's assumed to be a known value).
- size is the size of the sample.

Available to VBA.

CORREL

Use CORREL to get the correlation coefficient of two cell ranges (containing arrays).

CORREL(array1,array2)

- array1 is the first range of values.
- array2 is the second range of values.

Available to VBA.

COUNT

Use COUNT to count the number of cells in a list that contains numbers or count numbers presented as arguments.

COUNT(value1,value2...value30)

- value1, etc. are arguments that contain numbers or reference cells that contain numbers.

Available to VBA.

COUNTA

Use COUNTA to determine the number of cells that aren't empty and any values contained in the arguments.

COUNTA(value1,value2...value30)

■ value is an argument that represents a cell that is not empty, including values in arrays or references in those cells.

Available to VBA.

COVAR

Use COVAR to get covariance, which is the average of the products of deviations for pairs of data points.

COVAR(array1,array2)

■ array1 is the first range.

■ array2 is the second range.

Note *Cells in the range are expected to contain integers.*

Available to VBA.

CRITBINOM

Use CRITBINOM to get the smallest value for cumulative binomial distribution when the distribution is equal to or greater than a criterion value.

CRITBINOM(trials, probability_s,alpha)

■ trials is the number of Bernoulli trials.

■ probability_s is the probability of such for each trial.

■ alpha is the criterion value you're using.

Available to VBA.

DEVSQ

Use DEVSQ to get the sum of squares of the deviations of data points from their sample mean.

DEVSQ(number1,number2...number30)

APPENDIXES

- number1, etc. are the arguments you use to calculate the sum of squared deviations.

 You can use an array instead of individual arguments.

Available to VBA.

EXPONDIST

Use EXPONDIST to get exponential distribution.

EXPONDIST(x,lambda,cumulative)

- x is the value of the function.
- lambda is the value of the parameter.
- cumulative is a logical value used to indicate the form of the exponential function.

 For the cumulative argument, TRUE returns the cumulative distribution function; FALSE returns the probability density function.

Available to VBA.

FDIST

Use FDIST to get the F probability distribution.

FDIST(x,degrees_freedom1,degrees_freedom2)

- x is the value at which you want to evaluate the function.
- degrees_freedom1 is the numerator degrees of freedom.
- degrees_freedom2 is the denominator degrees of freedom.

Available to VBA.

FINV

Use FINV to get the inverse of FDIST.

FINV(probability,degrees_freedom1,degrees_freedom2)

- probability is a probability for the F cumulative distribution.
- degrees_freedom1 is the numerator degrees of freedom.

■ degrees_freedom2 is the denominator degrees of freedom.

Available to VBA.

FISHER

Use FISHER to get the Fisher transformation at X.

FISHER(x)

■ x is the numeric value for which you want the Fisher transformation.

Available to VBA.

FISHERINV

Use FISHERINV to get the inverse of the Fisher transformation.

FISHERINV(y)

■ y is the value at which you want to perform the inverse.

Available to VBA.

FORECAST

Use FORECAST to predict a future value, using existing values.

FORECAST(x,known_y's,known_x's)

■ x is the data point for which you are predicting a value.
■ known_y's is the dependent range of data.
■ known_x's is the independent range of data.

Available to VBA.

FREQUENCY

Use FREQUENCY to calculate how often values appear in a range of values and to get a vertical array of numbers.

FREQUENCY(data_array,bins_array)

■ data_array is a range or reference to a set of values for which you want to count frequencies.

■ bins_array is a range or reference to intervals into which you want to assemble the values in data_array.

Available to VBA.

FTEST

Use FTEST to get the result of an F-test.

FTEST(array1,array2)

■ array1 is the first range of data.
■ array2 is the second range of data.

Available to VBA.

GAMMADIST

Use GAMMADIST to get the gamma distribution.

GAMMADIST(x,alpha,beta,cumulative)

■ x is the value that you want to assess the distribution.
■ alpha is a parameter to the distribution.
■ beta is a parameter to the distribution.
■ cumulative is a logical value which specifies the function's form.

Available to VBA.

GAMMAINV

Use GAMMAINV to get the inverse of the gamma distribution.

GAMMAINV(probability,alpha,beta)

■ probability is the probability for the gamma distribution.
■ alpha is a parameter to the distribution.
■ beta is a parameter to the distribution.

Available to VBA.

GAMMALN

Use GAMMALN to get the natural logarithm of the gamma function.

GAMMALN(x)

■ x is the value for which you're calculating GAMMALN.

Available to VBA.

GEOMEAN

Use GEOMEAN to get the geometric mean of a range of positive data.

GEOMEAN(number1,number2...number30)

■ number1,number2...number30 are arguments to calculate the mean.

Available to VBA.

GROWTH

Use GROWTH to calculate predicted exponential growth.

GROWTH(known_y's,known_x's,new_x's,const)

■ known_y's is the set of y-values which are known in the relationship $y = b*m^x$.
■ known_x's is an optional set of x-values that might already be known in the relationship $y = b*m^x$.
■ new_x's are new x-values to which you want GROWTH to return similar y-values.
■ const is a logical value pointing out whether to force the constant b to equal 1.

Available to VBA.

HARMEAN

Use HARMEAN to get the harmonic mean (reciprocal of the arithmetic mean of reciprocals) of a data set.

HARMEAN(number1,number2...number30)

■ number1,number2...number30 are arguments to calculate the mean.

Available to VBA.

HYPGEOMDIST

Use HYPGEOMDIST to get the hypergeometric distribution.

HYPGEOMDIST(sample_s,number_sample,population_s,number_population)

- sample_s specifies the number of successes in the sample.
- number_sample specifies the size of the sample.
- population_s specifies the number of successes in the population.
- number_population specifies the population size.

Available to VBA.

INTERCEPT

Use INTERCEPT to calculate the point where a line will intersect the y-axis, using existing x-values and y-values.

INTERCEPT(known_y's,known_x's)

- known_y's specifies the dependent set of observations or data.
- known_x's specifies the independent set of observations or data.

Available to VBA.

KURT

Use KURT to get the kurtosis of a data set.

KURT(number1,number2...number30)

- number1,number2... are arguments to calculate kurtosis.

Available to VBA.

LARGE

Use LARGE to get the *k*th largest value in a data set.

LARGE(array,k)

- array is a range of data to use to determine the *k*th largest value.
- k is the position (from the largest) in the cell range of data to return.

Available to VBA.

LINEST

Use LINEST to figure the statistics for a line using the "least squares" method to figure a straight line that fits your data and returns a range that describes the line.

LINEST(known_y's,known_x's,const,stats)

- known_y's specifies the set of y-values already known in the relationship $y = mx + b$.
- known_x's is an optional set of x-values that might already be known in the relationship $y = mx + b$.
- const is a logical value denoting whether to force the constant b to equal 0 value.
- stats is a logical value denoting whether to reinstate additional regression statistics.

Available to VBA.

LOGEST

Use LOGEST, in regression analysis, to figure an exponential curve that is suitable to your data and returns a range of values that depicts the curve.

LOGEST(known_y's,known_x's,const,stats)

- known_y's specifies the set of y-values already known in the relationship $y = b*m^x$.
- known_x's is an optional set of x-values that might already be known in the relationship $y = b*m^x$.
- const is a logical value denoting whether to force the constant b to equal 1.
- stats is a logical value denoting whether to reinstate additional regression statistics.

Available to VBA.

LOGINV

Use LOGINV to get the inverse of x's lognormal cumulative distribution function, where $\ln(x)$ is ordinarily distributed with parameters mean and standard_dev.

LOGINV(probability,mean,standard_dev)

- probability specifies a probability which is comparable with the lognormal distribution.
- mean specifies the mean of $\ln(x)$.
- standard_dev specifies the standard deviation of $\ln(x)$.

Available to VBA.

LOGNORMDIST

Use LOGNORMDIST to determine x's cumulative lognormal distribution, where ln(x) is ordinarily distributed with parameters mean and standard_dev.

LOGNORMDIST(x,mean,standard_dev)

- x denotes the value to evaluate the function.
- mean denotes the mean of ln(x).
- standard_dev denotes the standard deviation of ln(x).

Available to VBA.

MAX

Use MAX to get the largest value in a set of values.

MAX(number1,number2...number30)

- number1,number2... are arguments to find the maximum value.

Available to VBA.

MAXA

Use MAXA to get the largest value in a list of arguments. The arguments must be numbers or references, but the references may include text and logical values; these are ignored.

MAXA(value1,value2...value30)

- value1,value2... are arguments to find the largest value.

Not available to VBA.

MEDIAN

Use MEDIAN to get the median of the given numbers.

MEDIAN(number1,number2...number30)

- number1,number2... are 1 to 30 numbers for which you want the median.

Available to VBA.

MIN

Use MIN to get the smallest number in a set of values.

MIN(number1,number2,...number30)

- number1, number2... are 1 to 30 numbers for which you want to find the minimum value.

Available to VBA.

MINA

Use MINA to get the smallest value in the list of arguments. The arguments must be numbers or references, but the references may include text and logical values; these are ignored.

MINA(value1,value2...value30)

value1,value2... are 1 to 30 values for which you want to find the smallest value.

Not available to VBA.

MODE

Use MODE to get the most frequently occurring, or repetitive, value in a range of data. Excel returns #N/A if no most frequent number exists.

MODE(number1,number2...number30)

number1, number2... are 1 to 30 arguments that you want to figure the mode.

Available to VBA.

NEGBINOMDIST

Use NEGBINOMDIST to get the negative binomial distribution.

NEGBINOMDIST(number_f,number_s,probability_s)

- number_f specifies the number of failures.
- number_s specifies the threshold number of successes.
- probability_s specifies the probability of a success.

Available to VBA.

NORMDIST

Use NORMDIST to get the normal cumulative distribution for the specified mean and standard deviation.

NORMDIST(x,mean,standard_dev,cumulative)

- x specifies the value for which you want the distribution.
- mean specifies the arithmetic mean of the distribution.
- standard_dev specifies the standard deviation of the distribution.
- cumulative specifies the form of the function.

Available to VBA.

NORMINV

Use NORMINV to get the inverse of the normal cumulative distribution for the specific mean and standard deviation.

NORMINV(probability,mean,standard_dev)

- probability specifies a probability relating to the normal distribution.
- mean specifies the arithmetic mean of the distribution.
- standard_dev specifies the standard deviation of the distribution.

Available to VBA.

NORMSDIST

Use NORMSDIST to get the standard normal cumulative distribution function.

NORMSDIST(z)

- z is the value for which you need to get the distribution.

Available to VBA.

NORMSINV

Use NORMSINV to get the inverse of the standard normal cumulative distribution.

NORMSINV(probability)

- probability specifies a probability relating to the normal distribution.

Available to VBA.

PEARSON

Use PEARSON to get the Pearson product moment correlation coefficient (r), which is a dimensionless index that ranges from –1.0 to 1.0 inclusive.

PEARSON(array1,array2)

- array1 specifies a set of independent values.
- array2 specifies a set of dependent values.

Available to VBA.

PERCENTILE

Use PERCENTILE to get the *k*th percentile of an array's value.

PERCENTILE(array,k)

- array specifies the range of data that defines relative standing.
- k specifies the percentile value in the range 0...1 inclusive.

Available to VBA.

PERCENTRANK

Use PERCENTRANK to get the percentage rank of a value in a data set.

PERCENTRANK(array,x,significance)

- array specifies the range of data with numeric values which define relative standing.
- x specifies the value of the rank which you are seeking.
- Significance is an optional value that specifies the number of digits in the returned value (omitting this returns three digits).

Available to VBA.

PERMUT

Use PERMUT to get the number of permutations for a certain number of objects which can be selected from a number objects.

PERMUT(number,number_chosen)

- number describes the number of objects.
- number_chosen is an integer that describes the number of objects per permutation.

Available to VBA.

POISSON

Use POISSON to get the Poisson distribution.

POISSON(x,mean,cumulative)

■ x specifies the number of events.

■ mean specifies the expected numeric value.

■ Cumulative is a logical value that affects the form of the function

If cumulative is TRUE, them POISSON returns the cumulative poisson probablility that the number of random events will be between O and X. If cumulative is FALSE, it returns the probability mass function that the number of events will be x.

Available to VBA.

PROB

Use PROB to get the probability which determines that values in a range are between two limits.

PROB(x_range,prob_range,lower_limit,upper_limit)

■ x_range specifies the range of numeric values of x with which there are comparable probabilities.

■ prob_range specifies a set of probabilities comparable with values in x_range.

■ lower_limit specifies the lower bound on the value that you want a probability.

■ upper_limit specifies the optional upper bound on the value that you want a probability.

Available to VBA.

QUARTILE

Use QUARTILE to get the quartile of a data set.

QUARTILE(array,quart)

■ array specifies the cell range of numeric values for which you want the quartile value.

■ quart specifies which value to return.

Available to VBA.

RANK

Use RANK to get the rank of a number in a list.

RANK(number,ref,order)

- number specifies the number whose rank you are seeking.
- ref specifies a range of, or a reference to, a list of numbers.
- order specifies a number distinguishing how to rank numbers.

Available to VBA.

RSQ

Use RSQ to get the square of the Pearson product moment correlation coefficient using data points in known_y's and known_x's.

RSQ(known_y's,known_x's)

- known_y's specifies a range of data points.
- known_x's specifies a range of data points.

Available to VBA.

SKEW

Use SKEW to get the skewness of a distribution.

SKEW(number1,number2...number30)

- number1,number2... are 1 to 30 arguments for which you're calculating skewness.

Available to VBA.

SLOPE

Use SLOPE to get the slope of the linear regression line using data points in known_y's and known_x's.

SLOPE(known_y's,known_x's)

- known_y's specifies a cell range of numeric dependent data points.
- known_x's specifies the set of independent data points.

Available to VBA.

SMALL

Use SMALL to get the *k*th smallest value in a data set.

SMALL(array,k)

- array specifies a range of numerical data for which you want to determine the *k*th smallest value.
- k specifies the position (from the smallest) in the range of data to return.

Available to VBA.

STANDARDIZE

Use STANDARDIZE to get a normalized value from a distribution distinguished by mean and standard_dev.

STANDARDIZE(x,mean,standard_dev)

- x specifies the value you want to normalize.
- mean specifies the arithmetic mean of the distribution.
- standard_dev specifies the standard deviation of the distribution.

Available to VBA.

STDEV

Use STDEV to get estimates of standard deviation based on a sample.

STDEV(number1,number2...number30)

- number1,number2... are 1 to 30 arguments relating to a sample of a population.

Available to VBA.

STDEVA

Use STDEVA to get estimates of standard deviation based on a sample (text and logical values are included).

STDEVA(value1,value2...value30)

- value1,value2... are 1 to 30 values relating to a sample of a population.

Not available to VBA.

STDEVP

Use STDEVP to figure standard deviation based on the whole population given as arguments.

STDEVP(number1,number2...number30)

- number1,number2... are 1 to 30 arguments relating to a population.

Available to VBA.

STDEVPA

Use STDEVPA to figure standard deviation based on the whole population given as arguments, together with text and logical values.

STDEVPA(value1,value2...value30)

- value1,value2... are 1 to 30 values relating to a population.

Not available to VBA.

STEYX

Use STEYX to get the standard error of the foreseen y-value for each x in the regression.

STEYX(known_y's,known_x's)

- known_y's is a range of dependent data points.
- known_x's is a range of independent data points.

Available to VBA.

TDIST

Use TDIST to get the Student's t-distribution.

TDIST(x,degrees_freedom,tails)

- x specifies the numeric value to use to evaluate the distribution.
- degrees_freedom specifies an integer denoting the number of degrees of freedom.
- tails specifies the number of distribution tails to return.

Available to VBA.

TINV

Use TINV to get the inverse of the Student's t-distribution for the distinguished degrees of freedom.

TINV(probability,degrees_freedom)

- probability specifies the probability corresponding with the two-tailed Student's t-distribution.
- degrees_freedom specifies the number of degrees of freedom to identify the distribution.

Available to VBA.

TREND

Use TREND to get values along a linear trend.

TREND(known_y's,known_x's,new_x's,const)

- known_y's specifies the set of y-values already known in the relationship $y = mx + b$.
- known_x's specifies an optional set of x-values that might already be known in the relationship $y = mx + b$.
- new_x's specifies new x-values for which you want TREND to return relative y-values.
- const specifies a logical value denoting whether to force the constant b to equal 0.

Available to VBA.

TRIMMEAN

Use TRIMMEAN to get the mean of the inside of a data set.

TRIMMEAN(array,percent)

- array specifies a range of values to trim and average.
- percent specifies the fractional number of data points to leave out of the calculation.

Available to VBA.

TTEST

Use TTEST to get the probability associated with a Student's t-test.

TTEST(array1,array2,tails,type)

- array1 specifies the first data set.
- array2 specifies the second data set.
- tails specifies the number of distribution tails.
- type specifies the kind of t-test to carry out.

Available to VBA.

VAR

Use VAR to estimate the variance based on a sample.

VAR(number1,number2...number30)

- number1,number2... are 1 to 30 arguments relating to a sample of a population.

Available to VBA.

VARA

Use VARA to estimate the variance based on a sample, including text and logical values in the calculation.

VARA(value1,value2...value30)

- value1,value2... are 1 to 30 value arguments relating to a sample of a population.

Not available to VBA.

VARP

Use VARP to figure the variance based on the entire population.

VARP(number1,number2...number30)

- number1,number2... are 1 to 30 arguments relating to a population.

Available to VBA.

VARPA

Use VARPA to figure the variance based on the entire population, including text and logical values in the calculation.

VARPA(value1,value2...value30)

- value1, value2... are 1 to 30 value arguments relating to a population.

Not available to VBA.

APPENDIXES

WEIBULL

Use WEIBULL to get the Weibull distribution.

WEIBULL(x,alpha,beta,cumulative)

- x specifies the value at which to evaluate the function.
- alpha specifies a parameter to the distribution.
- beta specifies a parameter to the distribution.
- cumulative is the form of the function.

Available to VBA.

ZTEST

Use ZTEST to get the two-tailed P-value of a z-test.

ZTEST(array,x,sigma)

- array specifies the range of data against which to test x.
- x specifies the value to test.
- sigma specifies the population standard deviation.

Available to VBA.

Text Functions

Text functions let you investigate and manipulate text strings that are in formulas. You can find text, change its case, see how long it is, and join a date to a text string.

CHAR

Use CHAR to get the character specified by a number.

CHAR(number)

- number specifies a number between 1 and 255 designating a character.

Not available to VBA.

CLEAN

Use CLEAN to remove all nonprintable characters from text.

CLEAN(text)

■ text specifies worksheet information from which you want to remove nonprintable characters.

Available to VBA.

CODE

Use CODE to get a numeric code for the first character in a text string.

CODE(text)

■ text specifies the text for which you need the code.

Not available to VBA.

CONCATENATE

Use CONCATENATE to combine various text strings into one text string.

CONCATENATE (text1,text2...text30)

■ text1,text2... are 1 to 30 text items to be combined into a single text item.

Not available to VBA.

DOLLAR

Use DOLLAR to convert numbers to text using currency format, rounding the decimals to a specified place. The format used is $#,##0.00_);($#,##0.00).

DOLLAR(number,decimals)

■ number specifies a number, a reference to a cell consisting of a number, or a formula that evaluates to a number.

■ decimals specifies the number of digits to the right of the decimal point.

Available to VBA.

EXACT

Use EXACT to compare two text strings and return TRUE when exactly the same, FALSE otherwise (ignores formatting).

EXACT(text1,text2)

- text1 specifies the first text string.
- text2 specifies the second text string.

Not available to VBA.

FIND

Use Find to find one text string (find_text) within another (within_text) and also to return the number of the starting position of find_text, from the leftmost character of within_text.

FIND(find_text,within_text,start_num).

- find_text specifies the text you want to find.
- within_text specifies the text consisting of the text you want to find.
- start_num denotes the character at which to start the search.

Available to VBA.

FIXED

Use FIXED to round a number to a specific number of decimals place, put the number in decimal format using a period and commas, and return the result as text.

FIXED(number,decimals,no_commas)

- number specifies the number you want to round and convert to text.
- decimals specifies the number of digits to the right of the decimal point.
- no_commas specifies a logical value that, if TRUE, stops FIXED from having commas in the returned text (if FALSE or omitted, then the returned text allows commas as usual).

Available to VBA.

LEFT

Use LEFT to get the first (or leftmost) character(s) in a text string.

LEFT(text,num_chars)

- text specifies the text string containing the characters you want to remove.
- num_chars denotes how many characters you want LEFT to remove.

Not available to VBA.

LEN

Use LEN to get the number of characters in a text string.

LEN(text)

■ text specifies the text whose length you are seeking.

Not available to VBA.

LOWER

Use LOWER to transform all uppercase letters to lowercase.

LOWER(text)

■ text specifies the text needed to be transformed to lowercase.

Not available to VBA.

MID

Use MID to get a certain number of characters from a text string, starting at the position you have specified.

MID(text,start_num,num_chars)

■ text specifies the text string containing the characters you want to remove.
■ start_num specifies the position of the first character you want to remove in text.
■ num_chars denotes the number of characters to return from text.

Not available to VBA.

PROPER

Use PROPER to capitalize the first letter in a text string and any other letters in text that follow any character other than a letter. Transforms all other letters to lowercase letters.

PROPER(text)

■ text specifies text within quotation marks, a formula that returns text, or a reference to a cell having the text you want to partially capitalize.

Available to VBA.

REPLACE

Use REPLACE to replace a portion of a text string with a different text string.

REPLACE(old_text,start_num,num_chars,new_text)

- old_text specifies text for which you want to replace particular characters.
- start_num specifies the position of the character in old_text that you want replaced with new_text.
- num_chars specifies the number of characters in old_text that you want replaced with new_text.
- new_text specifies text that replaces characters in old_text.

Available to VBA.

REPT

Use REPT to repeat text a given number of times.

REPT(text,number_times)

- text specifies the text you want repeated.
- number_times specifies the number of times to repeat text.

Available to VBA.

RIGHT

Use RIGHT to get the rightmost character(s) in a text string.

RIGHT(text,num_chars)

- text specifies the text string containing the characters you want to know about.
- num_chars indicates how many characters you want to know about.

Not available to VBA.

SEARCH

Use SEARCH to get the number of the character where it is first found, reading from left to right.

SEARCH(find_text,within_text,start_num)

- find_text specifies the text you are seeking.

- within_text specifies the text in which you want to search for find_text.
- start_num specifies the character number in within_text, counting from the left, where you want to start searching.

Available to VBA.

SUBSTITUTE

Use SUBSTITUTE to substitute new text for existing text.

SUBSTITUTE(text,old_text,new_text,instance_num)

- text specifies the text or cell reference containing text for which you want to substitute other characters.
- old_text specifies the text you want to replace.
- new_text specifies the new text.
- instance_num indicates which occurrence of old_text you want to substitute with new_text (omit to replace all instances).

Available to VBA.

T

Use T to get the text referred to by value. This function is provided for compatibility with other spreadsheet software.

T(value)

- value specifies the value you want to test.

Not available to VBA.

TEXT

Use TEXT to transform a value to text in a specific number format.

TEXT(value,format_text)

- value specifies a numeric value, a formula which evaluates to a numeric value, or a reference to a cell with a numeric value.
- format_text specifies a number format in text form from in the Category box on the Number tab in the Format Cells dialog box.

Available to VBA.

TRIM

Use TRIM to remove all spaces from text aside from single spaces between words.

TRIM(text)

■ text specifies the text from which you want to eliminate spaces.

Available to VBA.

UPPER

Use UPPER to transform text to uppercase.

UPPER(text)

■ text specifies the text you want transformed to uppercase.

Not available to VBA.

VALUE

Use VALUE to transform a text string representing a number to a number.

VALUE(text)

■ text specifies the text inside quotation marks or a reference to a cell with the text you want to transform.

Not available to VBA.

Functions and Visual Basic

It pays to take some care when you plan to use an Excel worksheet function in a Visual Basic for Applications (VBA) procedure. There are several issues that you might need to attend to, which are discussed in this section.

The Application.WorksheetFunction Object

Chapter 22 urges you to make use of worksheet functions in your VBA code when appropriate. To do so, you employ the Application.WorksheetFunction object. For example:

```
Mean = Application.WorksheetFunction.Average(Range("A1:A10"))
```

This approach is almost always much better and much faster than calculating a result by means of your own code, such as this:

```
Total = 0For i = 1 To 10  Total = Total + Cells(i, 1)Next iMean = Total / 10
```

However, some worksheet functions are not members of VBA's WorksheetFunction object. For example, this line of code would fail:

```
RandomNumber = Application.WorksheetFunction.Rand
```

The WorksheetFunction object does not include Excel's worksheet function RAND() as a member. This is because VBA has its own method of generating a random number, the Rnd function. To get a random number in VBA you would use something such as this:

```
RandomNumber = Rnd
```

In almost all cases where an Excel worksheet function does not appear as a member of the WorksheetFunction object, the reason is that VBA has another way of accomplishing the same objective. Often, VBA has its own function that has the same name as the worksheet function. Entered on the worksheet, this formula

=COLUMN(B1:E5)

returns 2 as its result because the range starts in the second column. To get the same result in VBA, you need to use VBA's Column function:

```
TheColumn = Range("B1:E5").Column
```

Other worksheet functions can cause confusion because VBA has its own version and uses the same name, and yet the worksheet function belongs to the WorksheetFunction object. Consider the worksheet function LOG(). You can use it in your VBA code in this fashion:

```
TheLog = Application.WorksheetFunction.Log(20)
```

But which logarithm does that return? The LOG() function assumes base 10 unless you specify a different base. Executing the above line of code would set the value of TheLog to 1.30.

However, VBA has its own Log function. If your code looked like this:

```
TheLog = Application.Log(20)
```

then the value of TheLog would be set to 2.996, because VBA's Log function returns the *natural* logarithm—that is, the base is assumed to be 2.718. So, these two statements would return the same value of 2.996 to TheLog:TheLog = Application.WorksheetFunction.Log(20, 2.718)TheLog = Application.Log(20)

The lesson is that when you invoke a function in VBA, be sure you know what you're calling for.

The following worksheet functions, shown by function category, are not members of the WorksheetFunction object. Where a direct equivalent VBA function is available, that function appears in italics following the name of the worksheet function. Where there is no VBA equivalent, your recourse is to provide code that returns the result, perhaps by way of entering the function in a worksheet cell and then picking up that cell's value.

Database
GETPIVOTDATA PivotTables(index).GetData

Date and Time
DATE *Date*
DATEVALUE *DateValue*
DAY
HOUR
MINUTE
MONTH
NOW
SECOND
TIME *Time*
TIMEVALUE *TimeValue*
TODAY
YEAR

Information
CELL
ERROR.TYPE
INFO
ISBLANK "" *(null string)*
ISREF
N
NA
TYPE

Logical
FALSE *False*
IF *If*

NOT *Not*
TRUE *True*

Lookup and Reference

ADDRESS *Address*
AREAS *Areas*
COLUMN *Column*
COLUMNS *Columns.Count*
HYPERLINK *Hyperlinks.Add*
INDIRECT
OFFSET *Offset*
ROW *Row*
ROWS *Rows.Count*

Math and Trig

ABS *Abs*
ATAN *Atn*
COS *Cos*
EXP *Exp*
INT *Int*
LOG(X) *Log(X) / Log(10)*
MOD *Mod operator*
RAND *Rnd*
SIGN *Sgn*
SIN *Sin*
SQRT *Sqr*
TAN *Tan*
TRUNC *Fix*

Statistical

AVERAGEA
MAXA
MINA
STDEVA
STDEVPA
VARA
VARPA

Text

CHAR *Chr*
CODE *Asc*
CONCATENATE *& operator*
EXACT

LEFT *Left*
LEN *Len*
LOWER *Lcase*
MID *Instr*
RIGHT *Right*
T
UPPER *Ucase*
VALUE

The Analysis ToolPak

The Analysis ToolPak, or ATP, is an add-in that accompanies Excel. It contains precoded statistical and engineering analysis capabilities, as well as 92 functions that you can use on the worksheet after installing the ATP add-in.

To install the add-in, you will have to have called for it during Office 2000 Setup. If you did not do so but want to use the ATP, choose Tools | Add-Ins and select the Analysis ToolPak. Excel installs the feature (you'll need the Office CD) and thereafter the following functions will be available:

Date and Time

EDATE
EOMONTH
NETWORKDAYS
WORKDAY
YEARFRAC

Financial

ACCRINT
ACCRINTM
AMORDEGRC
AMORLINC
COUPDAYBS
COUPDAYS
COUPDAYSNC
COUPNCD
COUPNUM
COUPPCD
CUMIPMT
CUMPRINC
DISC
DOLLARDE
DOLLARFR
DURATION
EFFECT
FVSCHEDULE

INTRATE
MDURATION
NOMINAL
ODDFPRICE
ODDFYIELD
ODDLPRICE
ODDLYIELD
PRICE
PRICEDISC
PRICEMAT
RECEIVED
TBILLEQ
TBILLPRICE
TBILLYIELD
XIRR
XNPV
YIELD
YIELDDISC
YIELDMAT

Information
ISEVEN
ISODD

Math and Trig
FACTDOUBLE
GCD
LCM
MROUND
MULTINOMIAL
QUOTIENT
RANDBETWEEN
SERIESSUM
SQRTPI

Engineering
BESSELI
BESSELJ
BESSELK
BESSELY
BIN2DEC
BIN2HEX
BIN2OCT

COMPLEX
CONVERT
DEC2BIN
DEC2HEX
DEC2OCT
DELTA
ERF
ERFC
GESTEP
HEX2BIN
HEX2DEC
HEX2OCT
IMABS
IMAGINARY
IMARGUMENT
IMCONJUGATE
IMCOS
IMDIV
IMEXP
IMLN
IMLOG10
IMLOG2
IMPOWER
IMPRODUCT
IMREAL
IMSIN
IMSQRT
IMSUB
IMSUM
OCT2BIN
OCT2DEC
OCT2HEX

These functions are not members of the WorksheetFunction object, and therefore code such as this would fail:

```
FoundRound = Application.WorksheetFunction.ISEVEN(Range("A1"))
```

If you need to use one of them in VBA, your best bet is to write the function and its arguments to a worksheet cell and then return the contents of that cell to a VBA variable. For example:

```
Range("C1").Formula = "=ISEVEN(A1)"FoundRound = Cells(1,3)
```

Appendix B

MOUS Core
Certification

This appendix explains how to obtain MOUS Core certification for Microsoft Excel. Here are the MOUS skills covered in this book for those of you who are planning to take the Core certification exam.

Skill Set	Skill	Chapters
Working with Cells and Cell Data	Insert, delete, and move cells	2
	Enter and edit cell data including text, numbers, and formulas	2
	Check spelling	2
	Find and replace cell data and formats	4
	Use automated tools to filter lists	7
Managing Workbooks	Manage workbook files and folders	3
	Create workbooks using templates	3
	Save workbooks using different names and file formats	3
Formatting and Printing Worksheets	Apply and modify cell formats	5
	Modify row and column settings	5
	Modify row and column formats	5
	Apply styles	2
	Use automated tools to format worksheets	5
	Modify Page Setup options for worksheets	5, 6
	Preview and print worksheets and workbooks	5, 6
Modifying Workbooks	Insert and delete worksheets	4
	Modify worksheet names and positions	4
	Use 3-D References	8

Creating and Revising Formulas	Create and revise formulas	8
	Use statistical, date and time, financial, and logical functions in formulas	8, 9
Creating and Modifying Graphics	Create, modify, position, and print charts	11
	Create, modify, and position graphics	12
Workgroup Collaboration	Convert worksheets into Web pages	3
	Create hyperlinks	17
	View and edit comments	2

The Microsoft Office User Specialist (MOUS) program is the best way for you to prove to yourself—and your employer—that you have mastered one or more of the programs included in the Microsoft Office suite. By providing a quantified benchmark, the MOUS program gives you a reliable way to measure your strengths and identify your weaknesses. In addition, by following the prescribed coursework and preparing for the exam, you are choosing the best way to improve your skills in either an individual Microsoft Office application or in the overall suite of Office software components.

Currently, there are two levels of MOUS Excel certification available:

■ Core

■ Expert

Core certification signifies that you can handle a wide range of everyday computing tasks. Expert certification signifies that you can handle more complex assignments.

Because the MOUS program is dynamic and changes frequently, for details on the most current MOUS certifications available, visit www.mous.net for additional information.

How to Get MOUS Certified[1]

The following information details the steps to follow to obtain the MOUS certification for Excel.

Step 1: Prepare for the Exam

As you begin to prepare for your MOUS certification, you should not only determine which Office product and level of proficiency you want to target, but also assess your

[1] Based on Excel 2000 MOUS certification.

current skill levels. The specific skill sets required for Core Excel certification are listed at the beginning of this appendix, along with the chapters that cover each skill.

The MOUS exams are scenario based and take place within the application itself. They are not multiple-choice or fill-in-the-blank tests; instead, you will be asked to perform specific real-world assignments. For example, in the Excel exam, you might be asked to modify the alignment of cell contents or to move between worksheets in a workbook or to use Excel's basic functions (AVERAGE, SUM, COUNT, MIN, MAX). Therefore, as you prepare for the exam, focus on how you will actually work; don't try to memorize information.

We have designed this book to be not only a comprehensive reference but also a complete study guide for Core Excel certification.

Step 2: Register for the Test

All exams are administered by an Authorized Testing Center. To find the testing center nearest to you, either call 1 (800) 933-4493 or check the Web site at www.mous.net. Many testing centers require advance registration, but others accept walk-in candidates as well.

Step 3: Take the Test

You will be judged on your ability to complete a task and on how long it takes you to do it. Using the program's Help system is permissible, but that will eat up your time.

Basic Guidelines for Taking a MOUS Exam

Microsoft provides the following guidelines for taking any of the MOUS exams:

General Tips

- Carefully read the instructions, which will be displayed at the bottom of the screen when you begin the test. Answer each question as if the end result must be shown to the test exam administrator. Do nothing extra; do only what is requested.

- Since all questions have equal value, try to answer all of them, including the more difficult ones.

- Pay close attention to how each question is worded. Responses must be precise, resolving the question exactly as asked.

- Scoring of answers is based on the end result, not on the route or time taken to complete the task. Errant keystrokes or mouse clicks will not count against your score as long as you achieve the correct end result. The result is what counts.

- Remember that the overall test is timed. While spending a lot of time on an individual answer will not adversely affect the scoring of that particular question, taking too long may not leave you with enough time to complete the entire test.

- Answers are either right or wrong. You do not get credit for partial answers. If the message "method is not available" displays on your computer screen, try solving the problem a different way.

- Important! Check to make sure you have entirely completed each question before clicking the Next button. Once you press the Next button, you will not be able to return to that question. A question will be scored as wrong if it is not properly completed before moving to the next question.

To ensure that a question is properly completed, do the following:

- Close all dialog boxes, toolbars, help windows, menus, and so on. Make sure all of a task's steps are completed. For example, when you select the Copy command, be sure to paste the item being copied rather than leave it on the clipboard.

- Make sure Office has completed the spreadsheet actions before clicking Next to move to the next task.

Don't do the following:

- Don't leave dialog boxes, toolbars, or menus open.

- Don't leave tables, boxes, or cells active or highlighted unless instructed to do so.

- Don't click the Next Task button until you have completely answered the question.

- Don't scroll in the question unless instructed to do so. Leave your answer visible.

Getting Your Test Results

Test results are displayed to each candidate as soon as the test is completed. They are completely confidential. If you pass, you will receive a certificate by mail within four to six weeks. If you fail, you will be informed where you need to focus more attention. You can take the test as many times as you want, but there are no refunds if you don't pass, and you must pay a new fee each time you take the test.

Once you have passed your test, you have proof for the world that you possess specific, relevant skills. Your certification can be invaluable if you are in the job market, as it will show your prospective employer that you have the skills to succeed. It will also show your current employer that he or she can rely on your knowledge with your demonstrated mastery of Microsoft Office skills.

Index

D

F

G

X

Y

Z

INTERNATIONAL CONTACT INFORMATION

AUSTRALIA
McGraw-Hill Book Company Australia Pty. Ltd.
TEL +61-2-9417-9899
FAX +61-2-9417-5687
http://www.mcgraw-hill.com.au
books-it_sydney@mcgraw-hill.com

CANADA
McGraw-Hill Ryerson Ltd.
TEL +905-430-5000
FAX +905-430-5020
http://www.mcgrawhill.ca

**GREECE, MIDDLE EAST,
NORTHERN AFRICA**
McGraw-Hill Hellas
TEL +30-1-656-0990-3-4
FAX +30-1-654-5525

MEXICO (Also serving Latin America)
McGraw-Hill Interamericana Editores S.A. de C.V.
TEL +525-117-1583
FAX +525-117-1589
http://www.mcgraw-hill.com.mx
fernando_castellanos@mcgraw-hill.com

SINGAPORE (Serving Asia)
McGraw-Hill Book Company
TEL +65-863-1580
FAX +65-862-3354
http://www.mcgraw-hill.com.sg
mghasia@mcgraw-hill.com

SOUTH AFRICA
McGraw-Hill South Africa
TEL +27-11-622-7512
FAX +27-11-622-9045
robyn_swanepoel@mcgraw-hill.com

**UNITED KINGDOM & EUROPE
(Excluding Southern Europe)**
McGraw-Hill Education Europe
TEL +44-1-628-502500
FAX +44-1-628-770224
http://www.mcgraw-hill.co.uk
computing_neurope@mcgraw-hill.com

ALL OTHER INQUIRIES Contact:
Osborne/McGraw-Hill
TEL +1-510-549-6600
FAX +1-510-883-7600
http://www.osborne.com
omg_international@mcgraw-hill.com